Forensic Anthropology

An Introduction

Forensic Anthropology

An Introduction

Edited by
MariaTeresa A. Tersigni-Tarrant
Natalie R. Shirley

CRC Press
Taylor & Francis Group
Boca Raton London New York

CRC Press is an imprint of the
Taylor & Francis Group, an **informa** business

CRC Press
Taylor & Francis Group
6000 Broken Sound Parkway NW, Suite 300
Boca Raton, FL 33487-2742

Printed in the United States of America on acid-free paper
Version Date: 20120801

International Standard Book Number: 978-1-4398-1646-2 (Hardback)

Visit the Taylor & Francis Web site at
http://www.taylorandfrancis.com

and the CRC Press Web site at
http://www.crcpress.com

I would like to dedicate this book to my parents, Dr. Anthony Tersigni and Flora Tersigni, as well as my mentor and friend, Dr. Norman J. Sauer. I am extremely grateful for your constant support and continued encouragement.

MariaTeresa A. Tersigni-Tarrant, PhD

I dedicate this book to my advisor, mentor, colleague, and friend, Richard Jantz. I learned more from him than I ever dreamed possible, and I continue to learn more every day.

Natalie R. Shirley, PhD

Contents

Foreword

In the late 1960s, I entered the developing field of forensic anthropology, but like many of my colleagues at that time, my primary interest was in the more general discipline of skeletal biology. Research results in forensic anthropology were presented frequently at the annual meetings of the American Association of Physical Anthropologists, but some had discovered an attentive audience at meetings of the American Academy of Forensic Sciences (AAFS). By the time I completed my graduate training in 1973, the center of academic gravity in forensic anthropology had begun to shift toward the AAFS with the formation of a physical anthropology section in 1972 and the later establishment of the certification/diplomate program of the American Board of Forensic Anthropology. In 1990–1991, one of my key advisors and professors at the University of Kansas, Ellis R. Kerley, became the first physical anthropologist to serve as AAFS president. These events helped catalyze academic momentum in forensic anthropology, leading to rapid growth, new research initiatives, and expanded applications.

Today, forensic anthropology represents a robust, dynamic, and international field that involves interdisciplinary research, continually improving methodology, and diverse applications. The discipline clearly has benefited from the development of forensic anthropology foci within key university departments, the attraction of gifted and dedicated students with strong research interests, and growing employment opportunities. International developments in the human rights and mass disaster arenas have led to new methodological applications, increased specialization, and globalization of training and research.

This edited volume addresses major issues in contemporary forensic anthropology. The authors represent an elite list of academic pioneers, accomplished practitioners, researchers, and educators who are among those who provide leadership in this field today. Writing on topics within their areas of accomplishment and expertise, these authors collectively provide the reader with an up-to-date look at both the fundamentals of forensic anthropology and cutting-edge research. The volume reveals the academic diversity within the field and the challenges that persist. As such, it provides a useful overview of the field of forensic anthropology from the perspective of authors who have helped shape it. The book reveals how far we have advanced since I first entered the field in the 1960s. It also reveals the dynamics of the research process and the growing applications that ensure forensic anthropology will continue to progress.

Douglas H. Ubelaker, PhD
Department of Anthropology
National Museum of Natural History
Smithsonian Institution
Washington, D.C.

Acknowledgments

I would like to thank my husband, Christopher Tarrant, for his unending patience and unwavering support of my every endeavor, and for being a stalwart of "Team Tarrant" as I completed this time-consuming text. I am extremely thankful to my coeditor, Natalie Shirley, for her tireless efforts to make this text a reality and for her unparalleled friendship. Her contributions to this text, which include editing, image preparation, and chapter contribution, were invaluable. Her contributions to my life have been immeasurable.

MariaTeresa A. Tersigni-Tarrant, PhD

The editors would like to thank the contributing authors for their efforts to make this text detailed and diverse. We would also like to thank Becky Masterman and Josie Banks-Kyle at Taylor & Francis Group for their endless patience during the preparation of this text.

I would like to acknowledge the University of Tennessee's Forensic Anthropology Center for their generous access to skeletal remains and photographs for this book. I would also like to acknowledge my employer, LMU DeBusk College of Osteopathic Medicine, for their cooperation during this time-consuming endeavor. I am endlessly thankful for the patience and support of my husband, George Shirley, during the many evenings and weekends that I spent working instead of socializing. Finally, special thanks to my coeditor, MariaTeresa Tersigni-Tarrant, for dreaming up this book, for sticking with me during its creation, and for being a brilliant colleague and wonderful friend.

Natalie R. Shirley, PhD

Editors

MariaTeresa A. Tersigni-Tarrant, PhD, serves as a forensic anthropologist at the Joint POW/MIA Accounting Command's Central Identification Laboratory and is a fellow of the American Academy of Forensic Sciences. She received her bachelor's degrees in microbiology and anthropology from Michigan State in 2000 as a student of Dr. Norman J. Sauer, PhD, D-ABFA. She received her MA (2002) and PhD (2005) in physical anthropology from the University of Tennessee in Knoxville as a student of Dr. Murray Marks, PhD, D-ABFA. Dr. Tersigni-Tarrant was awarded a postdoctoral fellowship in 2005 at the Joint POW/MIA Accounting Command's Central Identification Laboratory. During this fellowship, she was instrumental in establishing standard operating procedures for the histological analysis of human remains for the purpose of identifying missing armed-service members. Until June 2012, Dr. Tersigni-Tarrant was the consulting forensic anthropologist for the Georgia Bureau of Investigation. Her research interests include bone biology, human and nonhuman histology, child abuse—specifically, patterned fractures and timing of healing, human decomposition research, bone pathology, and developmental anatomy.

Natalie R. Shirley, PhD, is assistant professor of anatomy at LMU DeBusk College of Osteopathic Medicine and an adjunct faculty member at the University of Tennessee Anthropology Department. She received her BA (1998) and MA (2001) in anthropology from Louisiana State University and her PhD (2009) from the University of Tennessee in Knoxville as a student of Dr. Richard Jantz, Director Emeritus of the Forensic Anthropology Center. Her postdoctoral research was sponsored by the National Institute of Justice (Grant #2008-KN-BX-K182, *Improving Sex Estimation from Crania Using 3-Dimensional CT Scans*). Dr. Shirley's research interests include skeletal maturation in modern populations, age and sex estimation, secular change, and skeletal trauma. She is a member of the American Academy of Forensic Sciences, where she was awarded the Emerging Forensic Scientist Award (2007) for her research on secular change in skeletal maturation. Dr. Shirley also works as an instructor and researcher for the U.S. Department of Justice's International Criminal Investigative Training Assistance Program's initiative in Colombia.

Contributors Biographies

Bridget F. B. Algee-Hewitt, PhD, is a skeletal biologist whose research emphasizes the application of quantitative methods to questions of morphological variation and human identification in forensic contexts. She received her MA from Bryn Mawr College in classical and Near Eastern archaeology and her PhD in biological anthropology from the University of Tennessee. She is presently the Haslam Research Fellow in the Department of Anthropology at the University of Tennessee. In collaboration with the Forensic Anthropology Center and the Molecular Laboratories, she is investigating the relationship between genotype and phenotype for the estimation of biogeographic ancestry and biosocial race.

Bruce E. Anderson, PhD, is the forensic anthropologist for the Pima County Office of the Medical Examiner (PCOME) in Tucson, Arizona. Dr. Anderson received his PhD in 1998 from the University of Arizona, where he is an adjunct assistant professor of anthropology. Prior to his position with the PCOME, he served as a senior anthropologist for the U.S. Army's Central Identification Laboratory in Hawaii (CILHI), where his principal duties were the field recovery and laboratory analyses leading toward identification of human remains associated with past U.S. military conflicts. Dr. Anderson currently mentors anthropology students in the Forensic Anthropology Internship Program at the PCOME and works with predoctoral and postdoctoral fellows as part of a new PCOME Forensic Anthropology Fellowship. He is certified as a diplomate by the American Board of Forensic Anthropology (ABFA), is a fellow in the American Academy of Forensic Sciences (AAFS), is a founding member of the Scientific Working Group for Forensic Anthropology (SWGANTH), and serves as the western U.S. forensic anthropologist for the National Missing and Unidentified Persons System (NamUs) project.

Gregory E. Berg, PhD, is the forensic anthropology laboratory manager for the Joint POW/MIA Accounting Command's Central Identification Laboratory in Hawaii. In addition to laboratory work, he has conducted excavations in such countries as Laos, Vietnam, Cambodia, Germany, Palau, Papua New Guinea, and North and South Korea. His previous archeological field experience was concentrated in the southwestern United States. He has been involved in multiple forensic investigations in Hawaii. He has served as an expert witness in a murder trial in Honolulu, Hawaii, on research he conducted pertaining to prescription eyewear as a method of identification. He has also been involved with multiple mass disaster recoveries, identifications, and rescues. His research interests include mandibular metrics and morphology in regard to population affiliation, aging standards in physical anthropology, trauma analysis in human remains, prescription eyewear and identification, reliability standards for identification, and statistical applications in physical anthropology. Dr. Berg is a fellow of the American Academy of Forensic Sciences.

Hugh E. Berryman, PhD, D-ABFA, is a research professor in the Department of Sociology and Anthropology at Middle Tennessee State University and the director of the Forensic Institute for Research and Education (FIRE). He received his PhD in anthropology in 1981 from the University of Tennessee, Knoxville. In 2012, Dr. Berryman received the T. Dale Stewart Award for lifetime achievement in the physical anthropology section of the American Academy of Forensic Sciences (AAFS). He has also received the Ellis R. Kerley Award (2008) from AAFS for his research on detecting gunshot primer residue on bone. Dr. Berryman's interests include skeletal trauma, skeletal biology, and bioarcheology.

Angi M. Christensen, PhD, received her BA in anthropology from the University of Washington and her MA and PhD in anthropology from the University of Tennessee. She currently works as a forensic anthropologist for the Federal Bureau of Investigation (FBI) Laboratory in Quantico, Virginia. She assisted with the development of the FBI's Forensic Anthropology Program, whose mission is to provide casework services, operational assistance, consultation, research, training, and outreach to law enforcement at federal, state, and local levels. Her research interests have included methods and issues related to personal identification, error and error rates in forensic contexts, scientific admissibility issues, human remains in aquatic forensic contexts, and the interpretation of skeletal blast trauma. She also serves as an active member of the Scientific Working Group for Forensic Anthropology (SWGANTH), assisting to develop standards and best practices for the discipline of forensic anthropology.

Kate M. Crowley, DMD, D-ABFO, is a board certified forensic odontologist on staff with the Office of the Chief Medical Examiner's Office in Boston, Massachusetts. Dr. Crowley is also a periodontist working in private practice with offices located in Weymouth and Fall River, Massachusetts.

Joanne Bennett Devlin, PhD, received her BA in anthropology, with a specialization in archeology, from Hamilton College in New York. She received her MA and PhD in anthropology from the University of Tennessee in Knoxville, where she currently serves as a lecturer in the Department of Anthropology and staff member of the Forensic Anthropology Center. Her responsibilities at the Forensic Anthropology Center include casework, lecturing, and conducting training exercises. Dr. Devlin is a certified firefighter in Knox County, where she has served for over 10 years. She is also a consulting forensic anthropologist at the University of Tennessee Medical Center and an instructor for the National Forensic Academy. Her research interests include forensic anthropology, taphonomy, and archeology.

Alice E. Fazlollah, MS, is a doctoral student at the University of Tennessee, Knoxville. She received her MS from the University of Georgia (UGA) in 2011. Her research at UGA includes a comparison of age-at-death estimation methods on a modern sample and explores the application of these methods on cold cases from the Georgia Bureau of Investigation. In 2011, she also volunteered with the C.A. Pound Human Identification Laboratory at the University of Florida, where she worked closely with 3-D scanning technology in the production of digital bone images. She now works at the Forensic Anthropology Center at UT. Her current research projects include the use of preservation chemicals in the analysis of prehistoric bone.

Nicholas P. Herrmann, PhD, received his BA and MA from Washington University in St. Louis and his PhD from the University of Tennessee, Knoxville. As an assistant professor of anthropology at the Mississippi State University (MSU) with over 20 years of experience in field archeology and skeletal biology, Dr. Herrmann specializes in bioarcheology, forensic anthropology, computer applications in archeology, and GIS. He has taught at MSU since 2008, and his courses include introduction to physical anthropology, bioarcheology, mortuary archaeology field school, human identification, forensic anthropology, and human variation and origins. His forensic research focuses on burned human remains, stable isotopes, commingled remains, and stature estimation. He has served as a principal investigator or coprincipal investigator on four NIJ-funded projects.

Thomas D. Holland, PhD, D-ABFA, received his PhD in anthropology from the University of Missouri-Columbia in 1991 and was hired the following year by the Department of Defense Central Identification Laboratory in Hawaii. In 1994, he assumed the responsibilities as the scientific director for the entire organization. He has led recovery teams around the world, including sites in Iraq, China, Vietnam, Laos, Cambodia, Kuwait, South Korea, and North Korea. Dr. Holland is a diplomate of the American Board of Forensic Anthropology, as well as a fellow of the American Academy of Forensic Sciences, a member of the American Society of Crime Laboratory Directors, a member of the graduate faculty at the University of Hawaii, and a forensic consultant for the New York State Police. Dr. Holland has published widely in such journals as *American Antiquity*, *Current Anthropology*, the *Journal of Forensic Sciences*, and the *American Journal of Physical Anthropology*. In addition, he is the author of the mystery novels, *One Drop of Blood* and *KIA*.

Lee Meadows Jantz, PhD, received her BA, MA, and PhD in anthropology from the University of Tennessee. As coordinator of the Forensic Anthropology Center, Dr. Meadows Jantz is responsible for the body donation program and curation of the William M. Bass Donated and Forensic Skeletal Collections. She is an adjunct associate professor in the Department of Anthropology at university of Tennessee, Knoxville, and instructor at the National Forensic Academy for the outdoor recovery, taphonomy, and human identification courses offered through the Forensic Anthropology Center. Dr. Meadows Jantz is a founding member of the SWGANTH board and serves as a forensic anthropologist on the federal DMORT-WMD team. She consults with federal, state, and local law enforcement agencies on human identification cases. Her research interests include skeletal biology (past and recent populations), forensic anthropology, and human growth and development.

Richard L. Jantz, PhD, D-ABFA, was educated at the University of Kansas and has been a faculty member at the University of Tennessee since 1971. His research interests are mainly quantitative human variation with emphasis on American populations, both early and recent. In the mid-1980s, he established the forensic anthropology data bank, which serves as a resource to study skeletal variation among modern Americans. He, along with Steve Ousley, developed Fordisc, a software that automates estimation of sex, ancestry, and height from skeletal measurements. His primary research activity in forensic anthropology deals with improving estimates of sex, ancestry, and height and documenting the changes occurring in the American population during the twentieth century. He retired from his active faculty position in 2009 and as director of the Forensic Anthropology Center in

2011, a position he had held since 2000. He is now emeritus professor and is enjoying not going to meetings and working on research that has been put off for decades.

Erin H. Kimmerle, PhD, is an assistant professor of anthropology at the University of South Florida. She received her degrees in anthropology from the University of Tennessee (PhD), the University of Nebraska (MA), and Hamline University (BA). She previously served as chief forensic anthropologist for the United Nations, International Criminal Tribunal for the Former Yugoslavia (2001), and has worked on numerous missions in Nigeria, Peru, Kosova, Bosnia and Herzegovina, Croatia, and Bermuda since 2000. Dr. Kimmerle's research is in the areas of skeletal trauma, demography and aging, and human variation. Most recently, she was awarded funding from the National Institute of Justice for research in Nigeria on the estimation of biological parameters for identification in cases of missing persons, mass disasters, and human rights violations. She has authored numerous journal articles and book chapters and is coauthor of the book *Skeletal Trauma: Identification of Injuries in Human Rights Abuse and Armed Conflict* (CRC Press, 2008).

Alicja K. Lanfear, MS, is a doctoral candidate in the Department of Anthropology at the University of Tennessee, Knoxville, and an anatomy instructor at the DeBusk College of Osteopathic Medicine. Her research interests are varied but are centered in the field of human skeletal biology. They include human variation, secular change, aging techniques, fracture mechanics, skeletal trauma, taphonomy, and biomechanics. Lanfear's doctoral research investigates the anthropometric history of Poland using the records of the Institute für Deutsche Ostarbeit, an anthropometric dataset from World War II. Current research projects include hanging and its effect on decomposition, entomology and skeletal deposition of human cadavers, and primer-derived gunshot residue analysis on bone. Her research in collaboration with Dr. Hugh E. Berryman, PhD-D-ABFA, received the 2008 Ellis R. Kerley Award.

Stephen D. Ousley, PhD, attended the University of Tennessee, Knoxville. As a graduate research assistant, he worked as database administrator and data collector for the Forensic Data Bank, a repository of skeletal data from modern Americans. His master's thesis evaluated theories of the peopling of the New World using Native American anthropometrics, and his dissertation was a quantitative genetics analysis of fingerprints. For nine years, he was the director of the Repatriation Osteology Laboratory in the Repatriation Office of the National Museum of Natural History at the Smithsonian Institution. In 2007, he started teaching at Mercyhurst College. He is best known for coauthoring Fordisc, a computer program that aids in the identification of unknown human remains using various statistical methods. His research interests focus on forensic anthropology, human growth and development, human variation, geometric morphometrics, and dermatoglyphics.

James T. Pokines, PhD, D-ABFA, is an assistant professor in the Forensic Anthropology Program, Department of Anatomy and Neurobiology, Boston University, and is the forensic anthropologist for the Office of the Chief Medical Examiner, Commonwealth of Massachusetts, Boston. He served for over a decade as a forensic anthropologist and laboratory manager at the Joint POW/MIA Accounting Command, Central Identification Laboratory, Hawaii, after completing a postdoctoral fellowship there in forensic anthropology administered by the Oak Ridge Institute for Science and Education. Dr. Pokines received his BA in anthropology and archeology from Cornell University, his MA and PhD in anthropology from the University of Chicago, and his ABFA board certification in forensic anthropology. His research also includes comparative vertebrate osteology, zooarcheology, taphonomy, and paleoecology, and he has ongoing archeological projects in the Bolivian Andes (Tiwanaku and related sites), the Nile Delta (Egyptian through Byzantine phases of Tell Timai), and northern Jordan (sites including a natural faunal trap, Byzantine, Bronze Age, and Paleolithic). He has also conducted research in the Upper Paleolithic of Cantabrian Spain and modern predator behavior in Kenya.

Paul S. Sledzik, MS, is director of the National Transportation Safety Board's Transportation Disaster Assistance Division. Paul joined the board in 2004 after serving for six years as the team leader for the Region 3 Disaster Mortuary Operational Response Team, a division of the U.S. Department of Health and Human Services. During his career, he participated in the victim recovery and identification efforts in over 30 mass fatality events and transportation accidents. For 15 years, he served as a forensic anthropologist and museum curator at the National Museum of Health and Medicine of the Armed Forces Institute of Pathology. He has consulted for the Joint POW/MIA Accounting Command, Central Identification Laboratory, the National Center for Forensic Science, and the National Center for Missing and Exploited Children. He is a fellow of the American Academy of Forensic Sciences and serves on the Subcommittee on Forensic Science for the White House Office of Science and Technology Policy.

M. Katherine Spradley, PhD, received her PhD in anthropology from the University of Tennessee in 2006. She is currently an assistant professor in the Department of Anthropology at Texas State University–San Marcos, faculty for the Forensic Anthropology Center at Texas State (FACTS), and a consultant for the Smithsonian Institution. Dr. Spradley has collected data on more than 1500 skeletons from all over the world. Currently her research is focused on establishing a metric reference database of positively identified individuals considered Hispanic for use in generating accurate methods for sex and ancestry estimation. Dr. Spradley teaches a variety of graduate and undergraduate courses, including human biological variation, growth and development, laboratory methods in skeletal biology, and a biological anthropology seminar.

Denise To, PhD, RPA, is currently a forensic anthropologist in the Department of Defense's Central Identification Laboratory at the Joint POW/MIA Accounting Command, which seeks to recover and identify unaccounted U.S. military war-dead. Dr. To received her master's degree in anthropology with an emphasis in bioarcheology from the University of Arizona in 1999 and her PhD in physical anthropology from Arizona State University in 2008. She is a physical anthropologist with 16 years of experience as an archeologist, which includes excavation of the Pyramid of the Moon at Teotihuacan. In addition to numerous sites in the United States, she has worked in Belgium, France, Germany, Laos, Mexico, Papua New Guinea, South Africa, South Korea, Vietnam, and Wake Island. Dr. To has taught human remains recovery courses in Hawaii and Bogota, Colombia. She received the United States Joint Civilian Service Achievement Award in 2011 for her efforts in Kathmandu, Nepal, in response to the crash of Agni Air 101 and was also deployed to Louisiana in response to Hurricane Katrina as a member of the Disaster Mortuary Operational Response Team.

Katherine Weisensee, PhD, received her doctorate in anthropology from the University of Tennessee in 2008. She is currently an assistant professor in the Department of Sociology and Anthropology at Clemson University. Dr. Weisensee has performed research on human skeletal material from both prehistoric and modern contexts. Most recently, her research has focused on examining secular changes in craniofacial morphology using three-dimensional geometric morphometric methods in a documented skeletal collection from Lisbon, Portugal. Dr. Weisensee teaches a variety of undergraduate courses, including forensic anthropology, human variation, biological anthropology, and introduction to anthropology. She acts as a forensic anthropology consultant for several counties in upstate South Carolina. She has assisted the local medical examiners with the recovery and identification of several skeletons that have been discovered in the area since she arrived at Clemson.

Rebecca J. Wilson-Taylor, MA, is a doctoral candidate in physical anthropology in the Department of Anthropology at the University of Tennessee. She has been the assistant coordinator of the Forensic Anthropology Center for the last six years, where she helps facilitate research, maintain the body donation program, coordinate continuing education courses offered by the center, and conduct research at the Anthropological Research Facility. Taylor received her BS in biology and anthropology from Juniata College and her MA in anthropology from the University of Tennessee. She is also an adjunct instructor in anatomy and physiology with South College of Tennessee. Her research interests include paleopathology, taphonomy, and time since death.

Debra Prince Zinni, PhD, D-ABFA, is currently an assistant professor at Boston University School of Medicine, Department of Anatomy and Neurobiology, Forensic Anthropology Program, and the state forensic anthropologist for the Commonwealth of Massachusetts. She also serves as a DMORT Region 1 team member. She double majored in anthropology and psychology at James Madison University, where she received her BS in both subjects. She received her master's degree at The George Washington University, where she studied under Dr. Doug Ubelaker, and then received her PhD at the University of Tennessee. Dr. Prince Zinni received a postdoctoral fellowship at The Joint POW/MIA Accounting Command, Central Identification Laboratory, where she assisted in the recovery and identification of service members lost in previous conflicts. Dr. Prince Zinni is a fellow in the Physical Anthropology section of the American Academy of Forensic Sciences and a diplomate of the American Board of Forensic Anthropology.

Illustrator

Jennifer M. Stowe, MS, received her MS in medical illustration from Georgia Health Sciences University (GHSU) formerly the Medical College of Georgia. She also holds two bachelor's degrees in biology and scientific illustration from North Georgia College and State University. Upon graduating from GHSU, she formed Stowe Medical & Scientific Illustration, a freelance illustration business. Stowe is also the medical illustrator and animator for the GHSU/UGA Medical Partnership in Athens, Georgia. She is a member of the Association of Medical Illustrators and a Vesalius Trust Research Grant recipient.

Cover Artist

Amelia Sybenga, OMS-III, is a realism artist and native of Berkshire County, Massachusetts. She received an associate degree from Simon's Rock College of Bard and a bachelor of arts degree from the University of Dayton. With no formal training, she began exploring anatomical art during her first year of medical school at Lincoln Memorial University–DeBusk College of Osteopathic Medicine as a supplement to anatomical texts. The exploration of anatomical art developed into an appreciation of the human form, particularly skeletal, hand, and vascular sketches. *The Skull and Ribs in Leaves* is her first oil painting, consisting of shaved chalk pastels in olive and walnut oils, and resulted in the development of the company Art by ABS.

Brief History of Forensic Anthropology

1

MARIATERESA A. TERSIGNI-TARRANT
AND NATALIE R. SHIRLEY

Contents

Anthropology, as a discipline, seeks to understand the many intricate aspects of what it means to be human. Derived from the Greek word *anthropos* meaning "human" and *logia* referring to the "study of," anthropology seeks to shed light on human behavior, biology, language, and culture in past and present contexts. Anthropology is split into multiple subdisciplines, and the four most common are archaeology, socio-cultural anthropology, linguistic anthropology, and physical/biological anthropology. These subdisciplines are not mutually exclusive, and each seeks to define and interpret various aspects of the human condition. Archaeology reconstructs the history of past populations through contextual analysis of the artifacts and structures (i.e., material culture) that these populations have left behind. Socio-cultural anthropology uses participant observation and interviews to understand cultural groups or subcultures. Linguistic anthropology investigates the origins and use of language, as well as language changes over time. Physical/biological anthropology studies human biological origins, adaptation, and variation in an evolutionary context. Furthermore, each subdiscipline of anthropology is broken down further into smaller, more specialized subfields or applied areas of study that focus on specific aspects of what it means to be human. Figure 1.1 illustrates several common subfields of archaeology, cultural anthropology, linguistic anthropology, and physical/biological anthropology. Thus, anthropology is a holistic discipline in that it addresses all aspects of what it means to be human.

Note that forensic anthropology is an applied subdiscipline of physical/biological anthropology. Forensic anthropologists use their knowledge of modern human skeletal variation to help law enforcement identify unknown decedents and, if possible, provide information about the circumstances surrounding that person's death. The American Board of Forensic Anthropology defines forensic anthropology as "the application of the

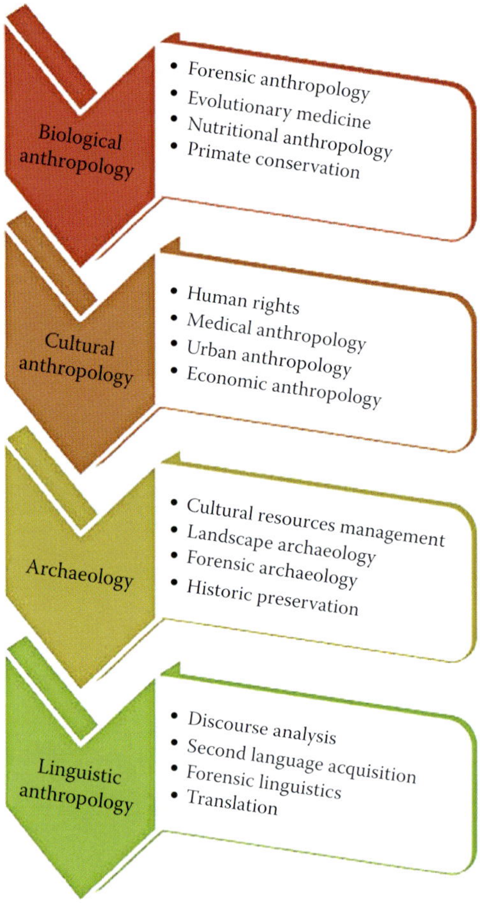

Figure 1.1 Subfields within the four major subdisciplines of anthropology.

science of physical or biological anthropology to the legal process," adding that "[p]hysical or biological anthropologists who specialize in forensics primarily focus their studies on the human skeleton" (www.theabfa.org). Forensic anthropology is a relatively young subfield within biological anthropology. The development of forensic anthropology is divided into three periods that are divided by events that arguably changed the path of the field: the formative period (early 1800s–1938), the consolidation period (1939–1971), and the modern period (1972–present).

Formative Period (Early 1800s–1938)

The origin of forensic anthropology is said to lie within the twisted tale of the Parkman murder in 1849. Dr. George Parkman was the physician that donated the land to Harvard upon which the medical school was built. It was in the medical school building that Dr. Parkman was murdered by Harvard Chemistry Professor John Webster who had purportedly borrowed money from Parkman and killed him to avoid paying back the debt. The local newspapers reported the salacious details of the case, suggesting that Webster mutilated Dr. Parkman's body, put parts of it in the anatomy laboratory and in a septic tank, and burned the head in the furnace. Harvard anatomy professors Oliver Wendell Holmes and Jeffries Wyman were asked to aid in the investigation of Dr. Parkman's death. Wyman and Holmes were able to put the pieces back together and to suggest that the skeleton belonged to a person whose description was consistent with George Parkman. Webster was eventually convicted of the murder when dentures found in the furnace were shown to match a mold of Parkman's teeth that his dentist had used to make the dentures.

The first avid practitioner of the applied study of forensic anthropology was Thomas Dwight (1843–1911). Dwight was considered the father of forensic anthropology in the United States (Stewart, 1979) because he was one of the first Americans to discuss identifying remains using information obtained from the human skeleton. In 1878, Dwight submitted an essay to the Massachusetts Medical Society entitled, "The Identification of the Human Skeleton. A Medico-Legal Study" (Dwight, 1878). Dwight succeeded Oliver Wendell Holmes in the Parkman Professorship of Anatomy position at Harvard. As a trained anatomist, Dwight recognized the need for research on methods to determine age, sex, and stature from the skeleton.

George Dorsey (1839–1931) learned from Dwight's research at Harvard. Dorsey received his doctorate from Harvard in anthropology in 1894, and became curator of the Field Museum of Natural History in Chicago. It was at this museum that Dorsey tested his theory that the articular surfaces of long bones could be used as an indicator of sex from the skeleton; he concluded that humeral head diameter was a better diagnostic tool for sex estimation than was the femoral head, a point later confirmed by Dwight (1905). Dorsey was asked to consult on the case of the Leutgert murder, where the Chicago sausage maker Adolph Leutgert was accused of killing his wife by placing her in a vat of potash, which effectively dissolved most of the body except for four small pieces of bone and the ring that she normally wore. Dorsey was able to say that the fragments came from a human rib, hand, and foot. Leutgert was later convicted, but Dorsey faced harsh criticism from other anatomists of the time for his testimony and conclusions in this case. This criticism is said to have caused Dorsey to abandon further pursuit of forensics, although Stewart believes that Dorsey's assertions about the skeletal remains were correct (Stewart, 1979). At the beginning of World War I, Dorsey removed himself from academe and joined the U.S. Navy.

Harris H. Wilder (1864–1928) was a contemporary of George Dorsey whose most notable contribution to forensic anthropology dealt with personal identification. Wilder was a European-trained zoologist who became interested in physical anthropology while teaching at Smith College late in his career. Wilder's physical anthropological focus was on dermatoglyphics (fingerprint analysis) and facial reconstruction using skulls. Wilder and Bert Wentworth published a book in 1918 entitled *Personal Identification: Methods for the Identification of Individuals, Living or Dead* (Wilder and Wentworth, 1918). However, Stewart (1979) points out that this text has no mention of Dwight's previous research on identification, suggesting that at that point Dwight's research may not have found its way to other scholars within and outside of the field.

Another American anatomist whose work had implications for forensic anthropology was Paul Stevenson (1890–1971). Stevenson spent a good deal of his career studying in China, and he contributed two important publications dealing with age determination based upon epiphyseal union (Stevenson, 1924) and stature estimation using long bones in a Chinese population (Stevenson, 1929). It is unclear, however, if Stevenson was aware of the impact of these contributions to forensic anthropology.

According to W.M. Krogman (1976), Aleš Hrdlička (1869–1943) was the "founding father of American Physical Anthropology." Hrdlička was born in Bohemia in 1869 and came to New York in 1882, at the age of 13, where he worked as a cigar maker and went to school at night. After a bout with typhoid at the age of 19, Hrdlička began studying medicine at the Eclectic Medical College of New York City, where he graduated in 1892. He went on to study at the New York Homeopathic College for 2 years, and he took an internship at the New York Homeopathic Hospital for the Insane, where he published on the somatometry of adult patients with various types of insanity. In 1896, Hrdlička received his training in physical anthropology in Paris under Manouvrier, where he learned how to quantitatively measure the skeleton. In 1897, Hrdlička began to study human skeletons at the College of Physicians and Surgeons in New York City. In 1899, Hrdlička embarked on a series of trips to study the American Indians of the southwestern United States and northern Mexico for the American Museum of Natural History. In 1903, he became a part of the Division of Physical Anthropology at the U.S. National Museum in Washington, DC (now known as the Smithsonian) and became curator in 1910. Hrdlicka was a giant in the field of physical anthropology, and the two contributions for which he is often remembered most are the beginning of the *American Journal of Physical Anthropology* (AJPA) in 1918 and the founding of the American Association of Physical Anthropologists (AAPA) in 1928. Hrdlicka was the editor of AJPA from 1918 until 1942.

Another physical anthropologist whose work on human variation shaped the theoretical foundations of biological and forensic anthropology was Earnest A. Hooton (1887–1954). Hooton received his doctorate in liberal arts at the University of Wisconsin in 1911. In 1912, he received his diploma in anthropology from Oxford University, and the following year he joined the anthropology department at Harvard. Hooton's research focused on human variation with respect to human origins and adaptation. Under his direction, Harvard was an important center for training physical anthropologists, and his students became prominent practitioners in the field.

T. Wingate Todd (1885–1938) was also a prolific researcher in anatomy and physical anthropology during the latter part of the formative period. Todd's work continues to influence forensic anthropology even today. Specifically, Todd was interested in skeletal aging methods and growth and development. He was trained in England as an anatomist and moved to the United States in 1912 to take Dr. Carl Hamann's vacated teaching position at Western Reserve University (Dr. Hamann had become Dean of the medical school). A recent change in Ohio state law permitted professors to retain cadavers that the medical students dissected, and Drs. Todd and Hamann had the foresight to begin an anatomical collection that would soon surpass any other in existence in terms of number of specimens and level of documentation (i.e., age, sex, ancestry, stature, weight, cause of death, and case history). In addition, Todd took anthropometric measurements and photographs of most of the cadavers. By the time of his death in 1938, Todd had managed to build a skeletal research collection containing over 3000 documented individuals. He used the specimens in the collection for numerous anatomical and anthropological studies, and the Hamann–Todd Collection continues to be an important resource for skeletal biology research today.

Todd's contributions to anthropology are numerous and include documenting differences in limb proportions between American Blacks and Whites, establishing the usefulness of endo- and ectocranial suture closure for age estimation, developing a method of age estimation based on age-related changes in the pubic symphysis, establishing principles of epiphyseal union, and extensively documenting various aspects of human postcranial and craniofacial growth, development, and maturation. During his career, Todd authored nearly 200 publications on various topics in anatomy and physical anthropology, many of which have significant implications for forensic anthropology. In addition, two of his students, Wilton Krogman and Montague Cobb, went on to make significant contributions to physical anthropology. We discuss Krogman in the following sections, but his legacy includes the landmark bulletin *Guide to the Identification of Human Skeletal Material* (1939) as well as the close mentoring of William M. Bass. Cobb was the first African-American to earn a Ph.D. in physical anthropology and left behind a legacy reminiscent of his mentor. The W. Montague Cobb Human Skeletal Collection at Howard University contains approximately 700 skeletons and serves many of the same research purposes as the Hamann–Todd Collection in Cleveland.

Robert J. Terry (1871–1966) was also an anatomist who had the foresight to curate a research collection of skeletal remains. Dr. Terry was an anatomy professor and department head at Washington University Medical School in St. Louis, Missouri. In the same manner as Todd, Terry began collecting skeletal remains from medical school cadavers during the 1920s. Terry Collection cadavers have associated morgue records with the individual's name, sex, age, ancestry, and date and cause of death. Terry also took photographs and anthropometric measurements of most of the cadavers, as well as skin and hair samples, although only the hair samples remain today. In addition, plaster death masks were made of 836 of the cadavers. Terry retired in 1941, and Dr. Mildred Trotter (1899–1991) assumed his anatomy teaching position and continued to build the collection until she retired 26 years later. Today, the nearly 2000 skeletons of the Terry Anatomical Collection are housed in the Smithsonian Institution in Washington, DC.

Consolidation Period (1939–1971)

It has long been posited that the end of the initial period of forensic anthropology (here termed the formative period) and beginning of the consolidation period was marked by the publishing of Wilton Marion Krogman's *Guide to the Identification of Human Skeletal Material* in the Federal Bureau of Investigation's (FBI's) Law Enforcement Bulletin in 1939. This publication was a summary of all that had been discovered about the identification of skeletal remains up until that time. The significance of this publication is that, for the first time, an article pertaining to forensic identification had been written by an anthropologist and was included in a journal focused on forensics, as opposed to anatomy or the broader discipline of physical anthropology.

Wilton Marion Krogman's prestigious career began in the spring of 1925 where he first lectured in physical anthropology at the University of Chicago. Krogman insists that it was this experience, coupled with a term paper assignment on the anthropology of teeth given by his professor Dr. Fay-Cooper Cole, which focused his entire professional career:

> That did it! Teeth lead to jaws, jaws to face, face to head, head to body: in other words a coordinated whole. But more than that, it led from statics to the dynamics of age progress. Thus launched my life-work in growth and development, comparative and human launched (Krogman, 1976).

The term paper introduced Krogman to paleontology, orthodontia, and the work of T. Wingate Todd. Krogman submitted a reworked version of this term paper to the First District Dental Society of New York City's Morris L. Chaim Prize, where T. Wingate Todd was one of the judges. Krogman won the prize, and Todd saw promise in the paper and in Krogman. On a stopover in Chicago, Todd sought out Krogman, who indicated he would like to do graduate work with Todd. In 1928, Krogman was awarded the Cleveland Foundation Fellowship in anatomy, thanks to Todd's arrangements. Krogman wrote his dissertation under Todd's direction. In 1929, Krogman instructed at the University of Chicago, and in 1930 he took a fellowship at the Hunterian Museum at the Royal College of Surgeons in London. In 1931, Krogman became an Associate Professor of Anatomy and Physical Anthropology at Western Reserve University. Krogman's appointment to his mentor's department put him in contact with the foremost physical anthropologists of the time. As Krogman (1976) explained, "Todd's department was a magnet for the physical anthropologists of the 1930s."

Krogman expanded upon his article in the FBI bulletin and produced the first textbook in Forensic Anthropology entitled *The Human Skeleton in Forensic Medicine* (Krogman, 1962). The textbook focused on the practical application of human osteology to forensics. Krogman's text became the primary reference for physical anthropologists doing forensic anthropology at that time; much like his 1939 article had been at the time of its publication. The overall theme of the book was human variation. Krogman emphasized that the methods identified within the text did not present hard and fast rules; instead, they were meant to be guidelines for assessing remains, with the understanding that humans represented a wide range of morphological variability. Krogman's dedication to research helped to push forensic anthropology forward. He imparted a great deal of his wisdom upon his graduate students. One of these students, William M. Bass, undoubtedly had the greatest impact on the modern era of forensic anthropology. We discuss the influence and legacy of Bass in greater detail in the following sections.

Modern Period (1972–Present)

The founding of the physical anthropology section of the American Academy of Forensic Sciences (AAFS) in 1972 is often referred to as the beginning of the modern period in forensic anthropology. It was at this time that the term "forensic anthropologist" first began to be used on a regular basis to refer to practitioners in the field. The section founding was thanks in a large part to Ellis R. Kerley (1924–1998). Kerley had joined AAFS in 1968 as part of the pathology/biology section. Through his encouragement, other physical anthropologists also joined the AAFS. By 1972, with 14 anthropologists as members of the academy, Kerley and colleagues had exceeded the minimum number of members required to establish a new section. Thus, the Physical Anthropology section of AAFS was born, and this formal organization of the field provided an appropriate stage for the presentation of new ideas. In addition, the academy's flagship journal, the *Journal of Forensic Sciences*, was well suited for research concerning new methods in identification of skeletal remains.

Ellis Kerley was also instrumental in establishing the American Board of Forensic Anthropologists (ABFA) in 1977. This board certifies forensic anthropologists in a similar manner to the certification of physicians by their various boards, using a rigorous application and examination process to ensure that each diplomate of the board is qualified and competent to undertake forensic anthropological casework. In 1987, Kerley became the Forensic Anthropology Consultant and Scientific Director of the United States Army Central Identification Laboratory in Hawaii, where he oversaw the identification of repatriated war remains. He also served as President of the AAFS from 1990 to 1991. In 2000, the Ellis R. Kerley Forensic Sciences Foundation was established in his memory. The foundation is dedicated to furthering the development of forensic anthropology by assisting students in the field of anthropology and continuing the research in forensic identification of the skeleton (http://www.kerleyfoundation.org/). Each year the foundation issues at least one scholarship to a graduate student who is enrolled in a physical or forensic anthropology program and who is involved with AAFS or the ABFA. In addition, the foundation hosts a reception at the AAFS annual meetings where it presents an award recognizing innovative efforts to continue research in human identification.

As mentioned earlier, William M. Bass was Kerley's student who went on to have the most significant impact on forensic anthropology. In the 1960s, Bass established a graduate program in physical anthropology at the University of Kansas and recruited Ellis Kerley and Thomas McKern to be a part of the department. This graduate program produced some of the foremost physical/forensic anthropologists, including Douglas Ubelaker, Walter Birkby, Judy Suchey, Linda Klepinger, and Richard Jantz.

In 1971, Dr. Bass moved from Kansas to Tennessee and in doing so began an anthropology program in the eastern United States that has produced more forensic anthropologists than any other program to date. By the time Dr. Bass retired in 1994, he had trained over 20 practitioners, including Bill Rodriguez, Anthony Falsetti, Hugh Berryman, Steve Symes, Murray Marks, Doug Owsley, Emily Craig, and Walter Birkby (Rhine, 1998). In fact, nearly 40% of practicing forensic anthropologists can trace some element of their academic lineage through Bass (Marks, 1995). Many of this new generation of graduates went on to change the face of forensic anthropology by taking it from a strictly academic discipline in which practitioners acted as consultants to an applied field that became incorporated into the medical examiner (ME) setting. Hugh Berryman was the first forensic anthropologist to be employed full-time outside of academia. In 1980, he was hired as Morgue Director of the Shelby County Medical Examiner and University of Tennessee Hospital Morgue in Memphis. During the past three decades, that single position has grown to over 20 full-time positions nationwide (Berryman, 2009) (Figure 1.2). While the majority of these positions are filled by PhD's, a little more than one-third of these employees have Master's degrees only. Several factors that contributed to the increase in full-time ME/Coroner positions over the last 30 years include a favorable economy, the realization that forensic anthropologists' skills include more than just skeletal analysis, and a number of mass disasters that required anthropological expertise (i.e., the Oklahoma City bombing, the 9/11 attacks on the Pentagon and World Trade Center, and the Tri-State Crematorium situation in Noble, Georgia) (Berryman, 2009).

Even though a number of forensic anthropologists attained full-time positions in coroner's and medical examiner's offices, many maintained academic appointments and continued to train new practitioners. For example, one of Bass' students, Richard Jantz, has mentored a number of forensic anthropologists, including Steve Ousley, with whom he created the Fordisc program. Fordisc stands for "forensic discrimination" and is currently in its third version. The Fordisc program has made it possible for forensic anthropologists to determine the sex, ancestry, and stature of unknown remains from cranial and/or postcranial measurements. We discuss this program in detail in Chapter 13.

1980s

• 1980 Hugh Berryman (pictured), PhD, D-ABFA	Shelby County ME & UT Chattanooga, Morgue Director
• 1981 Donna Fontana, MS	New Jersey State Police, Forensic Anthropologist
• 1982 David Wolf, PhD	Kentucky ME (first State Forensic Anthropologist)
• 1983 Craig Lahren, MA	Shelby County ME, Assistant Morgue Director
• 1984 William Rodriguez, PhD, D-ABFA	Caddo & Bossier Parish, LA, Deputy Chief Coroner
• 1986 William Rodriguez, PhD, D-ABFA	Onondaga, NY ME, Forensic Anthropologist & Chief of Operations
• 1986 Craig Lahren, MA	Hamilton County, TN ME, Coordinator of Forensic Services
• 1986 Robert Mann, PhD, D-AFBA	Shelby County ME, Assistant Morgue Director
• 1987 Steve Symes, PhD, D-AFBA	Shelby County ME, Assistant Morgue Director
• 1988 William Haglund, PhD	King County, WAME, Chief Medical Investigator
• 1989 William Rodriguez, PhD, D-ABFA	Office of the Armed Forces Medical Examiner, Chief Forensic Anthropologist and Deputy Chief ME

1990s

• 1994 Emily Craig (pictured), PhD, D-AFBA	Kentucky State Forensic Anthropologist
• 1994 Gwen Haugen, MA	St.Louis County MEO, Forensic Investigator/Forensic Anthropologist (1994-97; 2007-present)
• Deborah Gray	Riverside County, CA Sheriff's Department, Forensic Anthropologist/ Archaeologist/Coroner Sergeant
• 1995 Charles Cecil, PhD	San Francisco OCME, Medical Investigator II/Forensic Anthropologist
• 1995 Nici Vance, PhD	Oregon State Police Forensic Laboratory, Forensic Anthropologist; Osme, State Forensic Anthropologist (since 2006)
• 1996 Dana Austin, PhD, D-AFBA	Tarrant County, TX ME, Forensic Anthropologist
• 1996 Ann Marie mires, PhD	Massachusetts State OCME, Forensic Anthropologist
• 1997 Craig Lahren, MA	North Dakota State Forensic Examiner's Office, Administrator and Forensic Anthropologist
• 1997 Tom Bodkin, MA	Hamilton County, TN ME, Coordinator of Forensic Services
• 1997 Laura Fulginiti, PhD, D-ABFA	Maricopa County, AZ ME, Forensic Anthropologist
• 1997 Fran Wheatley, MA	Metropolitan Nashville/Davidson County ME, Death Investigator/Forensic Anthropologist
• 1998 Clyde Gibbs, BS, AS	North Carolina OCME, Chapel Hill, Medical Examiner Specialist
• 1999 Amy Mundorff, PhD	NewYork City OCME, Forensic Anthropologist

2000-Present

• 2001 Jennifer Love (pictured), PhD, D-ABFA	Regional Forensic Center, Memphis
• 2001 Alexis Gray, PhD	San Bernadino County Sheriff's Department, Coroner's Division, Forensic Anthropologist
• 2002 Robert Karinen, MA	Ada County Coroner's Office, Boise, ID, Forensic Supervisor
• 2002 Rick Snow, PhD	Georgia Bureau of Investigation, Forensic Anthropologist
• 2002 Gina Hart, MA	Newark Regional ME, Forensic Anthropologist/Death Investigator
• 2002 Brian Spatola, MA	Washington D.C. COME, Mortuary Supervisor and Anthropologist
• 2004 Katherine Taylor , PhD	King County, WA ME, Forensic Anthropologist
• 2004 Brad Adams, PhD, D-ABFA	NewYork City OCME, Director of Forensic Anthropology
• 2005 Jeanette Fridie, MA	NewYork City OCME, Forensic Anthropologist
• 2005 Pamela Steger, MS	Travis County Medical Examiner's Office, Medicolegal Death Investigator
• 2005 Daniel Jackson, MA	Travis County Medical Examiner's Office, Forensic Anthropologist/Death Investigator
• 2006 Christian Crowder, PhD, D-ABFA	NewYork City COME, Deputy Director of Forensic Anthropology
• 2006 Benjamin Figura, MA	NewYork City COME, Forensic Anthropologist/Director of Identification
• 2006 Fran Wheatley, MA	Shelby County ME, Administrator and Anthropologist
• 2006 Brian Spatola, MA	Central Virginia OCME, Morgue Su peMsor and Anthropologist
• 2006 Sharon Derrick, PhD	Harris County, TX ME, Agency Coordinator and Anthropologist
• 2006 Jennifer Love, PhD, D-ABFA	Harris County, TX ME, Forensic Anthropology Director
• 2006 Jason Wierserna, PhD	Harris County, TX ME, Mass Disaster Coordinator
• 2006 Bruce Anderson, PhD, D-ABFA	Tu scon, AZ Forensic Science Center, Forensic Anthropologist
• 2006 Laura Regan, PhD, Lt. Col.	Armed Forces Medical Examiner System, Director of Operations and Deputy Chief Forensic Anthropologist
• 2006 Lisa Leone, MA	Greenville Nonen Carolina Regional ME, Pathologist Assistant/Forensic Anthropologist/ Death Investigator
• 2007 Chris Rainwater, MS	NewYork City OCME, Forensic Anthropologist/Director of Photography
• 2007 Kristen Hartnett, PhD	NewYork City OCME, Forensic Anthropologist
• 2007 Dominique Semeraro, MS	Rhode Island OSME, Senior Medical Examiner Agent, RI State Forensic Anthropologist
• 2008 Murray Marks, PhD, D-ABFA	UT Regional Forensic Center, Forensic Anthropologist
• 2008 Lauren Zephro, PhD	Santa Cruz County Sheriff's Department, Latent Print Examiner, Forensic Anthropologist
• 2008 Hilary Sheaves, MA	North Carolina OCME, Chapel Hill, Autopsy Technician
• 2008 Olivia Alley, MA	Travis County Medical Examiner's Office, Forensic Anthropologist/Death Investigator
• 2009 Debra Prince Zinni, PhD, D-ABFA	Commonwealth of Massachusetts OCME, State Forensic Anthropologist

Figure 1.2 Forensic anthropologists working in the medical examiner's setting.

Anthropology Research Facility

Perhaps Bass' most notorious accomplishment is the establishment of the first outdoor research facility devoted to the study of human decomposition. The Anthropology Research Facility (ARF) was founded in 1980 in response to Dr. Bass' realization that the forensic community needed information about the postmortem interval that was based on controlled scientific research on human cadavers. The need for this type of research became evident to Dr. Bass in 1977 when he was asked to inspect decomposing remains that were discovered in a disturbed burial (Bass, 1984; Bass and Jefferson, 2003). Based on his field observations of the state of decomposition, Dr. Bass estimated that the remains had been in the grave approximately 1 year. However, after exhuming the remains and bringing them back to his laboratory for closer inspection, he noticed aspects of the clothing that indicated that they belonged to a Civil War colonel. To his dismay, Bass had underestimated the time since death by 113 years! To Bass' credit, Colonel Shy's remains had been uncharacteristically well preserved for that era due to embalming and a high quality iron casket. Nonetheless, a survey of the literature exposed a dearth of research on decomposition changes, so Dr. Bass resolved to remedy the situation. Fortunately, he had the full support of an open-minded UT administration and an available plot of land on which to establish the unconventional research facility.

The first ARF consisted of a 16 square-foot concrete slab enclosed on all sides and above by a chain link fence. The first donation arrived in 1981, and three more followed that year. Many of the early donations were unclaimed bodies from the State of Tennessee Medical Examiner, but as the donation program grew in popularity with increasing publicity, the donor population also grew in diversity. In 2009, the ARF received its 1000th donation. Furthermore, over 1700 individuals have filed paperwork to donate their bodies to the ARF for scientific research. The pre-registered donor paperwork requests information about donors such as birth date, sex, ancestry, height, weight, number of children, medical and dental history, occupation, habitual activities, handedness, shoe size, education level, childhood socioeconomic status, and photographs. In addition, hair and blood samples are taken as donations arrive, and fingerprints and laser scans are soon to be added to that protocol, as well. As a result of the increase in body donations, the ARF has expanded its initial 16 ft two plots to a 1.3 acre tract of land. Today the ARF is part of a larger establishment within the UT Anthropology Department—the Forensic Anthropology Center (FAC). The FAC oversees all activities at the ARF, including donor relations, law enforcement training and education, public outreach, and human identification services. The FAC offers hands-on training in forensic taphonomy, human identification, and human remains recovery to a variety of professionals, including the FBI's Emergency Response Teams, the National Forensic Academy, and to participants in the FAC's regular short courses.

Since its inception 30 years ago, the ARF has fulfilled Bass' initial goal. Anthropologists now understand the various stages of human decomposition and the variables affecting the rate at which the decomposition process occurs.* This understanding has enabled forensic anthropologists to give more accurate time since death (TSD) estimates. While much of the early research focused on general decomposition changes at the macroscopic level, some of the more recent projects have begun to explore decomposition at the microscopic level. For instance, Dr. Arpad Vass has isolated chemical signatures produced by volatile fatty acids during the decomposition process; he has used this information to predict TSD with a high degree of accuracy (Vass et al., 1992, 2002). Vass also developed a Decompositional Odor Analysis (DOA) Database for surface and buried remains that can be used for training cadaver dogs as well as in the development of portable analytical instruments to locate human remains in shallow burial sites (Vass et al., 2004, 2008). Other researchers have studied DNA recovery from various parts of decomposing remains (i.e., bone, hair,

* Chapter 18 provides a detailed discussion of the decomposition process and the variables affecting decomposition rates.

fingernails) in different environmental conditions (i.e., open ground, shaded ground, buried, aqueous) (Opel et al., 2006). In addition, projects have explored the effects of factors such as clothing and covers, indoor versus outdoor environments, insect and animal activity, and aqueous environments. One could say that for every question answered by research at the ARF, several more have surfaced. Many of these questions are related to the effects of different geographic locations and climates on the decomposition process (i.e., desert versus woodland). As a result, several new outdoor research facilities have been founded during the last several years, and these are discussed later in this chapter.

Documented Donated Skeletal Collections

After bodies are used for research at the ARF, the skeletal remains are collected carefully, cleaned, and curated in the William M. Bass Donated Skeletal Collection where they are used for teaching and research purposes. Since record keeping began in 1994, the Bass Collection has received over research visits ranging from universities to biomedical research companies to law enforcement agencies such as the FBI (Shirley et al. 2011). The Bass Collection is the largest collection of modern human skeletal remains in the country, and it has given researchers an unparalleled opportunity to gain an understanding of modern human skeletal variation. Researchers have documented differences between twentieth and twenty-first century Americans and their nineteenth century predecessors, including increases in stature and changes in cranial form (Jantz, 2001; Jantz and Jantz, 1999, 2000; Meadows and Jantz, 1995; Ousley and Jantz, 1997). These studies have demonstrated the importance of using modern skeletal samples to establish criteria for estimating age, sex, ancestry, and stature from skeletal remains. The Bass collection is predominantly American White males, but the demographic profile is increasing in diversity each year. Presently, the collection contains Americans of European, African, Hispanic, Native American, and Japanese ancestry. It is comprised of ~70% males and 30% females, with ages ranging from fetal to 101 years. To date, 600 of the skeletons have been scanned using computed tomography (CT) scanning, and these scans have been used in a variety of research projects in anthropology as well as biomedical engineering, including the development of a female knee implant design by Dr. Mohamed Mahfouz and colleagues in the UT Department of Mechanical, Aerospace, and Biomedical Engineering (Shirley et al., 2011).

Another important collection of modern human skeletal remains is the Maxwell Museum Documented Skeletal Collection at the University of New Mexico. This collection was established in 1984 and contains over 200 individuals with documented age, sex, ancestry, and cause of death. In addition, health and occupational data are available for donations dating 1995 and later. The Maxwell Donated Collection is housed in the Osteology Repository directly above the Maxwell Museum Laboratory of Human Osteology and serves as a resource for training, education, and research. During his tenure at UNM, Dr. Stan Rhine often consulted the collection to answer questions about forensic cases that he consulted on for the New Mexico Office of the Medical Investigator (Rhine, 1998). In addition, the collection has been used for instructional seminars in forensic anthropology and for research concerning bone response to repetitive motions, skeletal manifestations of disease, skeletal trauma, identification of handedness, and modern human variation.

Finally, a number of forensic anthropology laboratories curate remains from unsolved cases, as well as remains donated by the families of victims. The Louisiana State University FACES Laboratory is one such laboratory. Even though these collections do not have the extensive documentation that is associated with the donated collections at the University of Tennessee and the University of New Mexico, they serve as valuable research resources for a number of projects.

New Outdoor Decomposition Research Facilities

As mentioned earlier, there are many questions left to answer about the decomposition process, and many of these questions concern the effects of various climates and geographic locations on decomposition rates. The first of the new generation of decomposition research facilities was opened in 2006 at Western Carolina University in Cullowhee, North Carolina as part of the Western Carolina Human Identification Laboratory. The WCU facility is smaller than the ARF, but it allows for the study of decomposition in a mountain environment. In 2008, Dr. Jerry Melbye at Texas State University in San Marcos was able to obtain funding and land for the Forensic Anthropology Research Facility (FARF). The FARF is under the direction of Dr. Michelle Hamilton, a former student of Dr. Bass and Dr. Kate Spradley, a former student of Dr. Richard Jantz. The facility sits on 7 acre of the 4200 acre Freeman Ranch in Texas Hill Country and will have an adjoining laboratory to help with facility operations and processing. The ranch has already proven a valuable location to study vulture scavenging—a previously unaddressed topic in the literature (Reeves, 2009). Much like the ARF, the FARF will serve as a resource for forensic anthropology students as well as law enforcement agencies. Furthermore, the FARF will contribute much-needed data about decomposition in warm, arid climates. A nearby facility also opened recently at Sam Houston State University. The Southeast Texas Applied Forensic Science Facility (STAFS) is an outdoor research and training facility located on a 247 acre parcel of land near the Sam Houston National Forest. The research facility proper is a 1 acre plot surrounded by security fencing and an adjoining 8 acre of minimum security reserved for training activities. The STAFS has a variety of simulated environmental conditions, including a fluvial environment, and web cams are located to monitor the facility from computers. In addition, the STAFS has a morgue building with coolers, freezers, digital radiograph, and microscope capabilities (http://www.cjcenter.org/stafs/). Human decomposition outdoor research facilities have been proposed in Illinois, Nevada, and even India, and decomposition research on pigs has begun in Montana, as well.

Forensic Anthropology in the Public Eye

The rising popularity of the forensic sciences as a result of popular crime novels and television dramas such as CSI and Bones has led to a misconception of the true nature of forensic anthropology. Forensic cases are not solved in a day, and, unfortunately, many cases go unsolved for years or even decades. Furthermore, although DNA is an excellent way to identify unknown persons, it is expensive and time-consuming, often taking 6 months or more to get results. Whenever possible, a forensic anthropologist seeks out dental records or other radiographs to make a positive identification because these methods are quick and inexpensive.* This also helps alleviate DNA laboratories of excessive backlogs so that they can process other pertinent crime scene material. Nonetheless, there are some informative non-fiction texts and television shows that give an accurate depiction of forensic anthropology. For a list of some of these resources, please see the Additional Information section.

INTERVIEW WITH DR. BASS (PART I)—DECEMBER 17, 2009†

Question: Were you interested in forensic anthropology during your undergraduate education?

Dr. Bass: I graduated right out of high school right after the Second World War. I went to college the first year that the veterans got there and here were people 3–5 years ahead of me in experience and knowledge, so I didn't have a very good background to be honest with you. So, I had a tough time the first couple years in college. I … went to the University of Virginia and majored in psychology, because I didn't know what anthropology was; as a matter of fact, I was a junior in college before I knew what anthropology was. I had taken most or all of the required courses, and I was looking for an elective to take and anthropology was listed first, of course, if zoology had been listed first, I probably would have taken zoology. They only had one anthropologist at Virginia, a man named Clifford Evans, who had gotten his Ph.D. at Columbia, and he had just come back from Brazil and he was teaching in the sociology department.

So, I took anthropology classes and, looking back on it now, I was hooked then, I just didn't know it. I graduated and went into the service. I was in the Korean War in the army, and I was assigned to the Army Medical Research Laboratory. I worked for a year for the Army before I went to the University of Kentucky. I was stationed at Fort Knox where the Army Medical Research Laboratory was and still is, matter of fact. I wanted to be a college counselor, and then I met Charlie Snow, head of the department. He was a forensic anthropologist, and he was my professor in anthropology. I think two things happened: 1) I needed something in my education that was concrete, that if I knew it, I knew it, and I took Osteology from Charlie Snow. 2)

* Methods of positive identification are discussed in Chapter 20.

† The photograph of Dr. Bass is Courtesy of University of Tennessee Anthropology Department.

I went home and asked my wife if she would mind if I changed my major and my minor, just switch'em, and she said, "No," and that's the best move I ever made.

I graduated with my master's from Kentucky in 1956. On Clifford Evan's recommendation, I worked in the summer of 1956–57 and part of 1958 at the Smithsonian in Washington D.C. It was the first of 14 summers I spent working at the Smithsonian digging bones and so forth. Now, the best forensic anthropologist who existed at this time was Dr. Krogman at Pennsylvania. I wanted to go to Pennsylvania, so I started writing Krogman, and he gave me money to study at Pennsylvania, and it was the best move I could have made.

Because I had worked out in the plains every summer, I got to know the archeologists in the plains area. One night in the fall of '59, the phone rang and it was John Champ, who was the department head of the University of Nebraska, and he said, "I have a job for you if you'd like for a month, a semester, or a year." I accepted the job in Nebraska and stayed there a year. I was looking at some of the material that had been excavated in Nebraska… they dug up all this stuff, but there were no people to analyze it. Then I went to University of Kansas.

When the University of Tennessee decided that they wanted to go from an undergraduate program to a doctorate program, they hired me, I expect, because I had experience in what they wanted.

Question: When you were going to school, there were only a few practicing forensic anthropologists. Was it difficult for anthropologists to gain credibility when they first got into the AAFS?

Dr. Bass: Krogman was well known. He had worked with dentists and police and had been asked by the federal government to identify Hitler should we recover Hitler before the Russians did. Krogman and the guy with the FBI, J. Edgar Hoover, were friends. Krogman did some research for them. There were no forensic anthropologists at Michigan… W. W. Howell was at Harvard… but he wasn't really working as forensic anthropologist. Krogman only had one graduate student at time… my education with him was tutorial. He was more a father figure to me.

Question: What was the need at that time to build board certification [D-ABFA]? Were you being pushed by the forensic anthropologists or by the academy?

Dr. Bass: Ellis Kerley had been connected with the people. He was the one who knew more about the curriculum for the American Academy of Forensic Sciences. So… we started the physical anthropology program first, that was back in the days before we called it "forensic" anthropology. Then we saw a need for people who are dealing with forensics, dealing with the legal community (law enforcement & testifying), to be board certified, and that grew out of the founding of the physical anthropology section of American Academy of Forensic Sciences.

I'm not sure if all the branches of the American Academy of Forensic Sciences are board certified. I came along at a time where anthropology exploded in the 50s and 60s, and so we were putting out lots of students. Obviously, we flooded the market. It was obvious we weren't going to have jobs for students. I can't encourage students to come and spend two to four to six years and say "well I hope you find a job." So having known the pathologists pretty well through Krogman's connections, I began talking to the pathologists and telling them they need an anthropologist on their staff. My students not only began to get jobs in academics; what I tried to do was to find job openings—create openings—in areas that did not exist when I first started.

Question: What kind of reaction did you encounter when you brought up the idea of having a facility on U.T.'s campus—reactions from the university as well as the public.

Dr. Bass: When I came here, the medical examiner knew me and asked if I'd serve on the medical examiner staff. It wasn't long until bodies started coming in. The one that finally broke the camel's back… they brought in a body that smelled horrible, and I didn't have a place to put it, so I put it upstairs in the janitor's closet. (The janitor scolded Dr. Bass the next day.)

So, I went to see the dean of the college in Nov '71 and said, "Dean, I need some land to put dead bodies on." So, he (UT land controller) gave me a sow barn, and we started putting bodies out there. To run a body farm like we do now, you need graduate students. Well, we didn't have a master's program in the fall of '71. The master's program started in '73, PhD in '75 or '76. By 1980, we needed more land, so I went back to the university and asked for more land, and they gave us the two to three acres in back of the university hospital. A lady who was president of a group called "SICK," –Solutions of Issues for Concerned Knoxvillians, a blue-collar group sponsored by political science and what better way to get news coverage—started picketing the body farm. So I got a chain-linked fence put around the farm and a privacy wooden fence, too. This was the only real complaint that we had and it blew over.

My name was in the paper all the time and so people knew who I was. The major problem we had was a few years after that. We were getting our unclaimed bodies through the medical examiner's office (and we needed more bodies). (The unclaimed bodies cost the medical examiner's office $700 to dispose of, so they gave them to Dr. Bass for free.) We got a call one day from the state's Department of Veterans Affairs and they said,

> "We understand you have some veterans in your collection."

I don't know, how would I know if there are veterans or not if they come through the medical examiner?

> "Well, we know that there are,"

Well, if you can tell me who they are, I'll give them back to you. We're not trying to create problems. Okay, so we did this, but that didn't satisfy them, so they decided that…they would write up a bill to the legislature to put us out of business—They were going to close the body farm down. So, the university liaison to the legislature, he called me one day and said, "You know these people are building up some pressure. They had proposed a bill to put you out of business." And I called them once, but they were very political. I was thinking—what can I do? By this time, I had been in court about ten times a year for ten years, so I'd been in lots of courts and had helped lots of district attorneys. District attorneys are elected, but I don't care if they're democrats or republicans... I became friends with a lot of them, so I wrote six or eight of them, maybe even ten, all over the state saying, 'You know what I've done for you; you know you were able to solve this case and that case and these are the cases that I had done for them that were solved on the basis of the data we had done on the research at the body farm'... to make a long story short... we killed it (the bill) before it got there. Then Patricia Cornwell comes along in '95 and publishes "The Body Farm" and now everybody wants to go to the body farm now.

Question: What advice do you have for other schools that are attempting to get a facility up and running?

Dr. Bass: The major factor in the case is climate... we really need one in Florida and we need one in Wisconsin. Texas State has one... Boston University has just started one... and this is great: this is exactly what we wanted to do. I didn't set it up as a model for somebody else; we set it up so we could figure out what's going on – what happens in decay. [Sometimes the attitude of an administration is]—unless this makes money, we're not going to do it. Well, that's not education. They gave me two and a half to three acres of land over here [University of Tennessee] and no money. You don't need money. The graduate students and I poured the concrete slab and built the thing. You don't need 500,000 dollars to get it started.

References

Bass WM. 1984. Time interval since death. In: Rathbun TA and Buikstra JE, eds., *Case Studies in Forensic Anthropology*. Springfield, IL: Charles C. Thomas, pp. 136–147.

Bass WM and Jefferson J. 2003. *Death's Acre: Inside the Legendary Forensic Lab 'The Body Farm' Where the Dead Do Tell Tales*. New York: G.P. Putnam's Sons.

Berryman HE. 2009. Full time employment of forensic anthropologists in medical examiner's/coroner's offices in the United States—A history. *Proceedings of the American Academy of Forensic Sciences Annual Meeting*, Denver, CO, Vol. 15, p. 328.

Dwight T. 1878. The identification of the human skeleton: A medico-legal study. *Mass Med Soc* 12:165–218.

Dwight T. 1905. The size of the articular surfaces of long bones as characteristics of sex; an anthropological study. *Am J Anat* 4:19–32.

Jantz R. 2001. Cranial change in Americans. *J Forensic Sci* 46(4):784–787.

Jantz L and Jantz R. 1999. Secular change in long bone length and proportion in the United States, 1800–1970. *Am J Phys Anthropol* 110:57–67.

Jantz R and Jantz ML. 2000. Secular change in craniofacial morphology. *Am J Hum Biol* 12:327–338.

Krogman WM. 1962. *The Human Skeleton in Forensic Medicine*. Springfield, Thomas.

Krogman WM. 1976. Fifty years of physical anthropology: The men, the material, the concepts, the method. *Annu Rev Anthropol* 5:1–14.

Marks MK. 1995. William M. Bass and the development of forensic anthropology in Tennessee. *J Forensic Sci* 40(5):741–750.

Meadows L and Jantz R. 1995. Allometric secular change in the long bones from the 1800s to the present. *J Forensic Sci* 40(5):762–767.
Opel KL, Chung DT, Drabek J, Tatarek NE, Jantz LM, and McCord BR. 2006. The application of miniplex primer sets in the analysis of degraded DNA from human skeletal remains. *J Forensic Sci* 51(2):351–356.
Ousley SD and Jantz RL. 1997. The forensic data bank: Documenting skeletal trends in the United States. In: Reichs KJ, ed., *Forensic Osteology: Advances in the Identification of Human Remains.* Springfield, IL: Charles C. Thomas, pp. 442–458.
Reeves NM. 2009. Taphonomic effects of vulture scavenging. *J Forensic Sci* 54(3):523–528.
Rhine S. 1998. *Bone Voyage: A Journey in Forensic Anthropology.* Albuquerque, NM: University of New Mexico Press.
Shirley NR, Wilson RJ, and Jantz ML. 2011. Cadaver use at the University of Tennessee's Anthropological Research Facility. *Clin Anat Rev* 24(3):372–380.
Stevenson PH. 1924. Age order of epiphyseal union in man. *Am J Phys Anthropol* 7:53–93.
Stevenson PH. 1929. On racial differences in stature long bone regression formulae for the Chinese (with editorial note by Karl Pearson). *Biometrika* 21:303–318.
Stewart TD. 1979. *Essentials of Forensic Anthropology, Especially as Developed in the United States.* Springfield, IL: Thomas, Vol. 17, 300 pp.
Vass AA, Barshick SA, Sega G, Caton J, Skeen JT, Love JC, and Synstelien JA. 2002. Decomposition chemistry of human remains: A new methodology for determining the postmortem interval. *J Forensic Sci* 47(3):542–553.
Vass AA, Bass WM, Wolt JD, Foss JE, and Ammons JT. 1992. Time since death determinations of human cadavers using soil solution. *J Forensic Sci* 37(5):1236–1253.
Vass AA, Smith RR, Thompson CV, Burnett MN, Dulgerian N, and Eckenrode BA. 2008. Odor analysis of decomposing buried human remains. *J Forensic Sci* 53(2):384–391.
Vass AA, Smith RR, Thompson CV, Burnett MN, Wolf DA, Synstelien JA, Dulgerian N, and Eckenrode BA. 2004. Decompositional odor analysis database. *J Forensic Sci* 49(4):760–769.
Wilder HH and Wentworth B. 1918. *Personal Identification: Methods for the Identification of Indivduals, Living or Dead.* Boston, Gorham.

Additional Information

Useful Websites

American Academy of Forensic Sciences (www.aafs.org)
American Association of Physical Anthropologists (www.physanth.org)
American Board of Forensic Anthropology (www.theabfa.org)
Maxwell Museum of Anthropology Documented Skeletal Collection (http://www.unm.edu/~osteolab/coll_doc.html)
Scientific Working Group for Forensic Anthropology (www.swganth.org)
Skeletal Collections Database website—includes a list of collections from around the world (http://skeletal.highfantastical.com/)
Southeast Texas Applied Forensic Science Facility (http://www.cjcenter.org/stafs/)
Texas State University San Marcos Forensic Anthropology Center (http://www.txstate.edu/anthropology/facts/)
The Ellis Kerley Foundation (www.kerleyfoundation.org)
The Hamann-Todd Osteological Collection (http://www.cmnh.org/site/ResearchandCollections/PhysicalAnthropology/Collections/Hamann-ToddCollection.aspx)
The Robert J. Terry Anatomical Collection (http://anthropology.si.edu/cm/terry.htm)
The University of Tennessee Forensic Anthropology Center (http://web.utk.edu/~fac/)

Joint POW/MIA Accounting Command/Central Identification Laboratory (JPAC/CIL) History

2

THOMAS D. HOLLAND AND
MARIATERESA A. TERSIGNI-TARRANT

Contents

Perhaps more than any country the United States has always taken a great interest in the recovery and burial of its war dead. The extensive national cemetery system that was created largely in response to the carnage of the Civil War and is symbolized so iconically by the row-upon-row of white tombstones that populates Arlington National Cemetery is a tangible testament to that commitment. This, no doubt, is partially the result of the country's relative youth. Unlike the historical powers, such as Great Britain, which were fighting overseas wars decades or centuries before the advent of the logistical means of transporting remains home in an efficient manner (the return of Lord Nelson's remains from Trafalgar in a cask of brandy, notwithstanding), the United States did not begin fighting large-scale expeditionary wars until the twentieth century—a time that also witnessed the development of modern logistical methods and equipment. As a result, the United States from a very early time in its history, undertook the recovery and repatriation of its war dead. The first systematic repatriation of U.S. remains from an overseas theater occurred following the Spanish–American War in 1989. What was lacking, however, at least until the middle of the 1900s, was the ability to go one step further and actually identify the remains in a large-scale scientific manner.

Arguably, World War II saw the application of technology to the task of warfare on an unprecedented scale. Virtually every facet of the modern army was touched by science—from the creation of the atomic bomb to the dehydration of coffee. One aspect that goes largely unnoticed, however, was the enlistment of physical anthropologists in what was to become one of the largest biometric studies of a single population in the history of mankind. Early in the war the U.S. Quartermaster Corps, desiring to outfit a modern army with uniforms and equipment that fit and were efficient to use, hired physical anthropologists to compile anthropometric data on the American population. It is not surprising then that after the war, when the Quartermaster Corps was assigned the awesome task of identifying the remains of thousands of unaccounted-for U.S. soldiers, they turned to the same group of scientists for the solution. For this reason, much of the history of U.S. forensic anthropology as a scientific subdiscipline mirrors the history of the U.S. military's efforts to recover and identify its war dead. What follows, then is a brief history of that effort.

The responsibility for recovering and overseeing the identification of U.S. war dead fell to the U.S. Quartermaster's American Graves Registration Service (AGRS). The effort was concentrated—as was the war itself—in two geographic areas: Europe and the Pacific.

The European Theatre was much more organized. It benefitted from a relatively circumscribed geographic area (at least compared to the vast distances of the Pacific) and the existence of road and rail systems. To organize the recovery and identification effort in Europe, the army solicited the advice of Harry L. Shapiro, then Curator of Physical Anthropology at the American Museum of Natural History in New York. Shapiro provided guidance to the European teams as they conducted identifications of servicemen in that theater, though no anthropologists were working on these identifications.

It was not until the Pacific theater Central Identification Laboratory (CIL) was established at Schofield Barracks in [the Territory of] Hawaii that physical anthropologists became a permanent part of the identification process. In 1947, Charles Snow—then a physical anthropologist from the University of Kentucky (later to garner acclaim for his landmark bioarchaeology study of "The Adena People" published with William Webb) was selected to oversee the anthropology at the CIL.

Snow's tenure at the CIL was short-lived, but productive. Under his scientific leadership, the remains of over 1100 American servicemen were identified. With the war over, however, thousands of young veterans, eager to resume their lives began flooding college campuses, and Charles Snow found himself recalled to Kentucky after only a year. Recognizing the value of anthropologists in the identification process, however, the army began to cast about for a successor.

It was in this environment, in early 1948, that Francis E. Randall, a member of the Anthropology Unit of the Research and Development Branch of the Office of the Quartermaster General, organized a symposium on applied physical anthropology at the American Association of Physical Anthropology (AAPA) meetings. Among the speakers on the topic of medicolegal applications of physical anthropology were Wilton M. Krogman, Harry L. Shapiro, Charles E. Snow, and T. Dale Stewart (Curator of Physical Anthropology at the Smithsonian Institution). Snow and Shapiro, in particular, were able to draw upon their recent experiences working for the military to highlight how the field was evolving. Up to that point, physical anthropologists—including Snow and his staff at the CIL—relied heavily on Krogman's "Guide to the Identification of Human Skeletal Material" (1939) in their work, but the speakers at Randall's symposium realized that the immensity of the problem facing the military required a new suite of techniques—and that would require new research. In particular, Stewart noted that the stature estimation methods then being employed were developed from a small population of French cadavers measured by Rollet in 1888–1889 (see Chapter 11 for further details), and that modern populations required modern models. One attentive listener at the conference was Mildred Trotter—successor to Professor Terry's Anatomy position at Washington University in St. Louis. Stewart seized upon her interest and convinced Trotter that the CIL casework was an ideal research population on which to develop stature formulae applicable to a modern sample. Soon thereafter, Trotter accepted the offer to fill Snow's vacancy.

In late 1948, Mildred Trotter (Figure 2.1) arrived in Hawaii for what would become a 14 month stint as the CIL's Scientific Director. Despite some initial opposition on the army's part to her conducting research, Trotter was in fact able to gather the data that would later form the basis of her 1952 landmark work with Goldine Gleser on the "Estimation of Stature from Long Bones of American Whites and Negroes" published in the *American Journal of Physical Anthropology* (Trotter and Gleser 1952). But the job in Hawaii was never intended to be research-oriented. It was first and foremost an applied laboratory with an awesome mission—the identification of thousands of American servicemen lost in the

Figure 2.1 Dr. Mildred Trotter served as the CIL's Scientific Director in Hawaii from 1948–1949.

Pacific Theater. By the end of 1949, the Hawaii CIL had identified all of the skeletal remains that could be identified given the state of forensic science at the time—almost 7000—and the doors to the laboratory effectively closed. The remaining unidentified skeletal remains were interred as "unknowns" at the National Memorial Cemetery of the Pacific (NMCP)—known colloquially as the Punchbowl for its location within the basin-shaped caldera of an extinct volcano—in Hawaii.

Soon, however, the United States found itself embroiled in another overseas war—this time in Korea. To handle the identification of U.S. war dead retrieved from the battlefield the Army Quartermaster Corps established a Central Identification Unit (CIU) at Kokura, Japan. From 1951 until mid-1953, remains recovered from the battlefield were processed through the facility at Kokura. For the most part, however, these remains had been recovered from the battlefields after relatively short periods of time, and the services of physical anthropologists were not heavily relied upon. This changed dramatically after the Armistice brought an uneasy ceasefire to the peninsula in July 1953. At that time, negotiations between representatives of the United Nations Command and the Chinese and North Korean forces began for the purpose of arranging for an exchange of war dead. From August 31 to September 21, 1954, with smaller exchanges occurring as late as October and November, the North Korean government turned over to the United Nations the remains of over 4,000 allied personnel (by comparison, the remains of over 13,000 Chinese and North Korean soldiers were returned to the North). Many of these remains were unidentifiable without laboratory analysis. Accordingly, the Memorial Division of the Office of the U.S. Army Quartermaster General approached T. Dale Stewart (Figure 2.2) to ask for his suggestion regarding the direction of further research to help identify these war dead. He responded by pointing out that the methods currently in use to estimate skeletal age at death suffered from many of the sample problems that had plagued stature estimation before Trotter, and that analysis of war dead would be one means of correcting this problem. The army agreed, and the Army Quartermaster Corps's Memorial Division arranged with the Smithsonian Institution for Stewart to work at the laboratory from September 1954 to February 1955. During this time, Stewart and the laboratory staff conducted research on 450 skeletons to document age changes.

While Stewart was gathering the data for his research, the day-to-day mission of identifying U.S. soldiers killed in Korea fell to a team of physical anthropologists,

Figure 2.2 Dr. T. Dale Stewart, shown here at the Smithsonian Institution, worked at the CIU in Kokura, Japan, from 1954–1955.

including Ellis R. Kerley and Charles Warren. Technically, remains were not identified by the Kokura staff. Instead, the staff recommended identifications to a military review board that rendered the final decision. Several other physical anthropologists conducted research projects in Kokura, such as the estimation of body weight from bone (Baker and Newman 1957). Due to this work in Japan, a seminar was arranged in 1955 that dealt specifically with the forensic application of physical anthropology. The discussion included presentations about identification, specialist qualifications, identification of fragmentary remains, and age, sex, and stature estimation techniques, among other topics.

After this seminar, Thomas McKern and T. Dale Stewart published *Skeletal Age Changes in Young American Males* (1957), which included information gleaned from working with Ellis Kerley, Charles Warren, and a young Japanese anthropologist, Tadao Furue. This volume revolutionized the identification process of missing service members and provided a context for the development of further standards for identification within the field of forensic anthropology. The fact that the U.S. Army now accepted the idea of conducting research while pursuing the more pragmatic aspects of identifying war dead was in no small way the result of Dr. Trotter's groundbreaking work with the World War II dead and the professional manner in which she had conducted herself. At the Kokura laboratory, T. Dale Stewart also made the effort to compare the stature formulae derived by Trotter and Gleser with the recorded stature of American Korean War dead. His findings suggested that the formulae did not work for those of Asian or Hispanic origin, and it lead Trotter and Gleser to derive stature formulae for additional ancestries in their 1958 publication (Trotter and Gleser 1958).

Despite modest advances in forensic anthropology since the closing of the World War II CIL, the anthropologists at the Kokura laboratory soon encountered the limits of their science, and by 1955, the Kokura laboratory had identified all of the skeletal remains that could be resolved given the techniques available at the time. As a result, the laboratory was effectively closed, and over 840 skeletons were transferred to Hawaii and interred at the NMCP as "unknowns." In early 1956, some of the Kokura staff relocated to the U.S. military morgue at Yokohama and continued to provide identification expertise as required.

Within a decade, the U.S. again found itself in another Pacific war. Initial losses, in what would become known as the Vietnam War, were relatively few in number and did not require a large-scale identification operation in-country. From January 1961 through July 1965, individuals killed in Vietnam were airlifted to a small mortuary at Clark AFB in the Philippines where civilian morticians prepared the remains for funerals, and, if necessary, oversaw the identification of the remains. By 1965, however, the American death toll had risen to a point where an in-country facility for treating remains was required, and a mortuary function was created outside Saigon at the large U.S. Air Force base at Tan Son Nhut (TSN). In July 1966, the responsibility for staffing and operating the TSN facility was transferred to the U.S. Army's Graves Registration Command. As casualties continued to mount, a second mortuary was formed at Da Nang Air Base in June 1967.

Throughout most of the Vietnam War, the majority of casualties could be identified through traditional means such as visual recognition, dental records comparison, or fingerprint comparison. However, by late 1968, the U.S. Army recognized that as the casualty numbers grew, so did the number of remains that could not be readily identified, and thus new techniques and procedures were required. To this end, the army returned to a familiar source for help: T. Dale Stewart. From December 9 to December 11, 1968, the U.S. Army and the National Museum of Natural History cosponsored a seminar at the Smithsonian Institution for identification specialists. A number of the papers presented at this three-day event were given by physical anthropologists, and in 1970, T. Dale Stewart edited the report from this seminar entitled: Personal Identification in Mass Disasters (Stewart 1970). Nearly half of this volume was comprised of the papers given by anthropologists including D. Gentry Steele, Thomas McKern, Ellis Kerley, Mildred Trotter, and W.W. Howells. In reality, the 1968 conference probably had little impact on the day-to-day operations of the Vietnam mortuaries, but thanks to Stewart's foresight the seminar did begin to elevate the problem of human identification beyond the scope of war casualties to the broader issue of mass disasters—a role that forensic anthropology takes for granted today.

When the United States began troop reductions in Vietnam, both the need for and the ability to support the in-country mortuaries began to decline. The Da Nang Mortuary was closed in 1972, and the TSN facility was deactivated the following year. At that point, the responsibility for the identification of U.S. war dead shifted to the newly opened CIL at Camp Samae San, Thailand. Bearing the military acronym CIL-THAI, and employing Robert Pickering as a full-time anthropologist, the new laboratory remained in operation until May 1976 when pressure from the Thai government to reduce the U.S. footprint in that country caused the U.S. Army to relocate the laboratory to Honolulu, Hawaii. Here, it was rechristened the U.S. Army Central Identification Laboratory, Hawaii—or CILHI. With the change in name and location came an expanded mission: to recover and identify missing and unaccounted-for Americans lost in all past military conflicts (in practical terms this mandate extended to individuals lost in World War I, World War II, the Korean and Vietnam Wars, and the Cold War).

The early postwar years were difficult times for the CILHI. A general disinterest in all things Vietnam pervaded the American mindset, and a laboratory dedicated to the identification of the lingering reminders of the cost of the war proved to be particularly anathema. A shortage of money and resources severely crippled the laboratory's ability to function. The cumulative effects of governmental neglect continued to degrade the laboratory's effectiveness to a point where, in 1985 the army asked a panel of three noted forensic scientists—Ellis Kerley, William Maples (anthropologists), and Lowell Levine

Figure 2.3 Dr. Ellis Kerley worked at the CIU in Kokura, Japan, from 1954–1955 and served as the laboratory's Scientific Director in Hawaii from 1988–1991.

(odontologist)—to visit the CILHI and review its facilities, procedures, and staffing. In response to the panel's overall negative findings, the army instituted broad changes in how the laboratory was managed and operated, not the least of which was naming Ellis Kerley (Figure 2.3) as the CILHI Scientific Director. Despite this belated proaction on the army's part, in 1986 and 1987 the House Committee on Armed Services and the Senate Committee on Veteran's Affairs felt compelled to hold hearings into the operation of the CILHI, and even more restructuring was undertaken. This was followed in 1991 by further congressional hearings, this time as part of a broader investigation into the issue of Vietnam War Prisoners of War that was undertaken by the Senate Select Committee on Prisoner of War/Missing in Action Affairs. A resulting Government Accounting Office report on the operation of the CILHI found that the CILHI had made significant improvements [since the mid-1980s] to a point where its techniques and methodologies were "consistent with or even exceed[ed] those employed in other modern forensic laboratories" (GAO/NSIAD-93-7 POW/MIA Identifications 1992, p. 3).

Under Ellis Kerley's direction, the CILHI instituted a process of requiring peer reviews of all of the case reports that were completed in association with remains identification. This process was structured in such a way that each case report was reviewed by other CIL anthropologists prior to submission to the Scientific Director. The Scientific Director would then provide a final review of the case report. Kerley also began the process of bringing in outside consultants to review the finalized case reports. This began the process of surety and reliability among the anthropologists at the CIL.

Beginning in 1992, the CILHI began a period of sustained growth, reaching a full-time anthropology staff of 20 by 2004 and numbering almost 30 by 2010. With the increase in staffing came a concomitant increase in capacity and capability. In 1998, the CILHI identified the remains buried in the Vietnam Tomb of the Unknown Soldier at Arlington National Cemetery, and by 2000, the CILHI was identifying the remains of almost three missing Americans a week.

In October 2003, shortly after becoming the first skeletal identification laboratory to be certified by the American Society of Crime Laboratory Directors—Laboratory Accreditation Board (ASCLD-LAB), the then Deputy Secretary of Defense Paul Wolfowitz directed the de-establishment of the Army's CILHI and its simultaneous incorporation into a newly commissioned organization: the Joint POW/MIA Accounting Command (JPAC). In honor of its historic ancestry, the JPAC laboratory retained the title of CIL, and its overarching mission to recover and identify Americans lost in previous military conflicts remained the same. In 2008, the CIL co-sponsored with the FBI the creation of the Scientific Working Group for [Forensic] Anthropology (SWGANTH). The SWGANTH, drawing upon the collective knowledge of a wide range of physical and forensic anthropologists, has for the first time codified "Best Practices" for the discipline. This marks the beginning of a new era in the profession.

Today the CIL is the largest skeletal identification laboratory of its kind. It is a pioneer in the field, both in the development and refinement of laboratory techniques and methods, as well as in the areas of laboratory management and quality assurance. It remains a prominent force within the forensic anthropology discipline and is a source of employment, research, and training for many forensic anthropologists today.

References

Baker PT and RW Newman. 1957. The use of bone weights for human identification. *Am J Phys Anthropol* 15:601–618.

GAO/NSIAD-93-7. October 1992. POW/MIA Affairs: Issues related to the identification of human remains from the Vietnam conflict, Report to the Chairman and Vice Chairman, Select Committee on POW/MIA Affairs, U.S. Senate.

Krogman WM. 1939. A guide to the identification of human skeletal material. *FBI Law Enforcement Bulletin* 8(8):3–32.

McKern T and Stewart T. 1957. *Skeletal Age Changes in Young American Males Analysed from the Standpoint of Age Identification*. Natick, MA: Quartermaster Research and Development Center, Environmental Protection Research Division, pp. 89–97.

Stewart, TD. (Editor) 1970. *Personal Identification in Mass Disasters*. Washington, DC: National Museum of Natural History.

Trotter M and Gleser GC. 1952. Estimation of stature from long bones of American Whites and Negroes. *Am J Phys Anthropol* 10(4):463–514.

Trotter M and Gleser GC. 1958. A re-evaluation of estimation of stature based on measurements of stature taken during life and of long bones after death. *Am J Phys Anthropol* 16(1):79–124.

Forensic Anthropology Today

3

MARIATERESA A. TERSIGNI-TARRANT
AND NATALIE R. SHIRLEY

Contents

As discussed in Chapter 1, forensic anthropologists employ the principles of skeletal growth, development, degeneration, and variation to ascertain biological information about an individual, such as age, sex, ancestry, and stature. These four components are collectively referred to as the biological profile. If the remains are human, modern, and of forensic significance, a forensic anthropologist constructs a biological profile in order to assist law enforcement in identifying the unknown decedent. They may also use their understanding of bone biomechanics (i.e., the way that bone behaves under certain loads or forces) and/or bone healing to evaluate skeletal trauma (the interpretation of skeletal trauma is discussed in detail in Chapters 14 and 15). Furthermore, forensic anthropologists apply the principles of forensic taphonomy and bone weathering to determine what happened to the remains in a given depositional environment. Forensic taphonomy encompasses animal activity and bone weathering due to environmental factors such as sun, soil, plants, humidity, etc., and is discussed further in Chapter 17. Nationally, physical anthropology is recognized as one of the forensic sciences by the American Academy of Forensic Sciences (AAFS). The AAFS has 11 sections, each representing a different subdiscipline of forensic science. The AAFS has specific requirements for membership, as do each of the sections within the academy. Requirements have been developed for various levels of membership, from student and trainee affiliate members, to associate and full members and fellows. Promotion from one level of membership to the next is contingent on completing the necessary requirements for promotion, which vary by section. Figure 3.1 presents the membership of each AAFS section as a percentage of the total AAFS membership. Figure 3.2 imparts the notion that, although physical anthropology is not the largest section, it is the section with the highest percentage of student or trainee affiliates. This may represent a significant trend for the future membership of the Physical Anthropology section of the AAFS.

Of the AAFS recognized forensic science disciplines, physical anthropologists work most closely with forensic pathologists and forensic odontologists. Forensic pathologists are medical doctors with specialized training in pathology. Pathologists conduct forensic autopsies and determine cause of death. In the event that the forensic pathologist needs

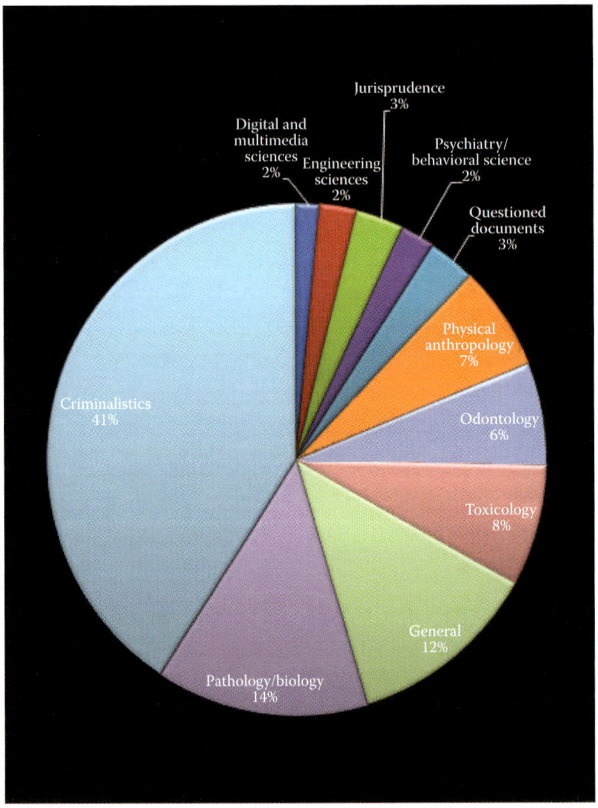

Figure 3.1 AAFS sections (by membership percentage, as of April 2011).

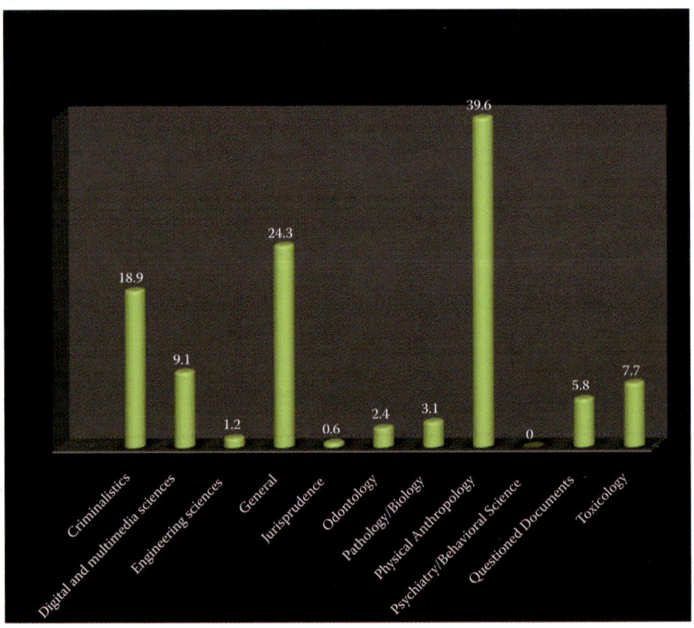

Figure 3.2 AAFS sections percentage of affiliate status membership (student or trainee).

an analysis of skeletal remains, he/she consults a forensic anthropologist to examine the remains and submit a case report. Forensic odontologists are also referred to as forensic dentists. Forensic anthropologists rely upon forensic odontologists to certify a positive identification of human remains using the dentition. In these instances, the odontologist compares antemortem records (typically radiographs) with postmortem radiographs to make the identification.

Most forensic anthropologists are affiliated with the AAFS, as well as with the International Association of Forensic Sciences. In addition, several regional forensic anthropology organizations exist throughout the United States: Mountain, Swamp and Beach Forensic Anthropologists (MS&B—Southeast United States); Mountain, Desert & Coastal Forensic Anthropologists (MD&C—Southwest United States); Northeast Forensic Anthropology Association (NEFAA—Northeast United States); Midwest Bioarcheology and Forensic Anthropology Association (BARFAA—Midwest United States). The annual meetings of these organizations, though often a slightly less formal affair than the AAFS annual meetings, allow for the presentation of anthropological research and symposium discussions that facilitate the dissemination of research and scholarship in burgeoning areas of physical and forensic anthropology.

What We Are "Not": Debunking Hollywood Myths

As mentioned in Chapter 1, a number of popular television dramas give inaccurate depictions of the forensic sciences. In most crime scenes, multidisciplinary collaborations between various branches of the forensic sciences are necessary to solve a crime. For example, criminalists process scene evidence such as fingerprints and blood spatter, toxicologists process evidence from bodily fluids, pathologists conduct a forensic autopsy on the body, and anthropologists may assist with skeletal trauma analysis. However, each of these tasks is accomplished by trained professionals within each discipline, and not by a single person with training in all areas of the forensic sciences. In other words, the forensic sciences are splintered into a number of highly specialized fields. This ensures that all aspects of a crime scene are analyzed by qualified experts and then assembled to give the most complete picture possible. Certainly, fictional television dramas use their artistic license in order to present a case in a one hour time slot using a limited number of actors. Nonetheless, a number of non-fiction programs give more accurate depictions of how forensic scientists work together to solve crimes (i.e., Forensic Files, The New Detectives, and FBI Files).

Another misconception about forensic anthropology involves the educational requirements to practice forensic anthropology. There is no formal degree in "forensic anthropology"; instead, forensic anthropologists pursue a degree in anthropology with a concentration in biological anthropology and further specialization in forensic anthropology. Forensic anthropologists are proficient in skeletal biology, anatomy, and modern human variation. In addition, many forensic anthropologists are knowledgeable in bone injury biomechanics, pathology, and taphonomy, as well as statistics and archaeological recovery methods. Recall from Chapter 1 that anthropologists emphasize a four-field approach and receive training in each subfield of anthropology. As a result of this multifaceted educational training, forensic anthropologists bring a unique perspective to understanding human variation in that they consider the biological and sociocultural determinants of human skeletal biology. For example, characteristic skeletal features indicate whether a skeleton is male or female, but other skeletal markers can reveal aspects of an individual's identity such as socioeconomic status, health history, and occupation. These clues give law enforcement a more complete picture of an unidentified person and assist greatly in the search for identity.

Unfortunately, with the increasing numbers of television (TV) dramas and movie plots based on the forensic sciences, the line between fiction and reality has been effectively blurred. This leads to a general public that is increasingly aware of the forensic sciences, but not necessarily well versed on what can actually be achieved through each type of analysis. Consequently, potential jurors and members of the public may have expectations of forensic analyses that are unattainable and unwarranted. Moreover, the fictionalization of forensic practitioners' ability to be able to analyze and report on multiple aspects of a crime (such as the fingerprint analysis, ballistics, and autopsy report) can cause confusion when the data is presented to families or in the courtroom. In sum, while these shows are intended to intrigue the audience and present a plausible (however unlikely) crime scene, it would behoove the curious viewer to perform a critical analysis of what is fact, what is fiction, and what is a stretch with regards to the forensic sciences, or for that matter, any discipline that is represented in a TV drama or Hollywood movie.

Educational and Employment Opportunities

In order to practice forensic anthropology, a master's or doctorate in physical anthropology with additional training and experience in forensic anthropology methods is recommended. Students interested in this career path should consult the American Board of Forensic Anthropology website for additional information (http://www.theabfa.org/). The Scientific Working Group for Forensic Anthropology website also offers a list of journal articles and publications concerning forensic anthropology practice and theory that was created by the Society of Forensic Anthropologists (SOFA); this resource can be found at http://www.swganth.org/news–resources.html. Although universities do not offer a formal "forensic anthropology" degree, a number of anthropology programs offer a focus in forensic anthropology. In addition to an anthropology curriculum, students may also benefit from coursework in genetics and biomechanics. According to a recent survey of the AAFS Physical Anthropology section members, nearly half of practicing forensic anthropologists (44.5%) are employed at an academic institution and do forensic casework on a consulting basis (Agostini and Gomez 2009). Within academia, forensic anthropologists are typically employed as physical anthropologists, anatomists, osteologists, and/or skeletal biologists. Other common employment agencies are medical examiner and coroner's offices (19.1%), federal agencies (12.7%), private consulting firms (i.e., self-employed consultants) (5.5%), museums (2.7%), and non-profit organizations (2.7%). The remaining 12.7% of the members surveyed were retired or students. The survey by Agostini and Gomez (2009) also revealed that the majority of forensic anthropologists report an annual income of $50,000–$100,000.

It is highly recommended that students interested in pursuing a career in forensic anthropology or any of the forensic sciences, whether applied or research-oriented, read the recent National Academy of Sciences Report entitled "Strengthening Forensic Science in the United States: A Path Forward" (2009), as this report will likely affect training, policy, and practice in the forensic sciences for years to come. The report is a final grant report published by the U.S. Department of Justice and contains recommendations for improving research, practice, and training in the forensic sciences. The report also proposes the creation of an independent federal entity, to be named the National Institute of Forensic Science, which would serve as an administrator and advisory board to enforce best practice in the forensic sciences. In effect, the NAS Report suggestions could potentially restructure the way in which many forensic anthropologists operate, particularly with respect to mandated laboratory accreditation and individual certification.

Ethics in Practice and Research

Unfortunately, when judged by today's ethical standards, physical anthropology has a tainted past when it comes to handling skeletal remains. Some of the existing skeletal collections (particularly collections of Native American remains) were obtained in an opportunistic manner that would be considered unethical today. However, at the time that the collections were amassed, there were no laws or regulations governing the collection and handling of human skeletal remains. Laws such as the Native American Graves Protection and Repatriation Act, or NAGPRA (1990), set a precedent for addressing ethical concerns that has spread beyond the handling of Native American skeletal material. Physical anthropologists have made great strides in correcting the misdoings of early practitioners and, in doing so, have created an environment in which research and education is conducted with the utmost respect and reverence. As researchers and curators of human skeletal material, physical anthropologists take their moral responsibility seriously. Indeed, a number of physical anthropologists have become involved in human rights organizations around the globe. Forensic anthropologist bring valuable skills to the table in dealing with human rights violations, including the ability to sort commingled remains in mass graves, establish a biological profile from unidentified skeletal remains, evaluate skeletal trauma, ascertain manner and/or cause of death, and handle the sociocultural factors affiliated with this type of work. Forensic anthropologists have done work in Bosnia, Kosovo, Rwanda, Argentina, Peru, and Iraq, to name a few countries. This type of work and the organizations under which it is performed are discussed in Chapter 21.

Scientific Working Group for Forensic Anthropology

Germane to the topics covered in this chapter is a review of the suggestions put forth by the Scientific Working Group for Forensic Anthropology (SWGANTH). Mirrored after similar scientific working groups in other disciplines, the SWGANTH was charged with identifying "best practices" within forensic anthropology. The SWGANTH was established by the Department of Defense Central Identification Laboratory (DoD CIL) and the Federal Bureau of Investigation (FBI) and consists of a 20-member board comprised of forensic anthropologists from various backgrounds and agencies. In an effort to remove the veil that often cloaks forensic anthropology methods and practice, the SWGANTH board established committees to review multiple aspects of forensic anthropology and to establish a "best practice model" for each of these areas. These committees drafted best practice suggestions in areas pertinent to the practice of forensic anthropology including proficiency testing, ethics, qualifications, laboratory management, age estimation, sex assessment, stature estimation, commingled remains, and many other aspects of case analyses (for a full listing of the guidelines established by the SWGANTH, go to www.swganth.org). Despite the thorough nature of the guidelines, the SWGANTH does not have the ability to enforce these guidelines within the field or regulate forensic anthropology practitioners. Instead, the onus is on the practitioners to be certain they are aware of these "best practices" and are striving to achieve these goals.

INTERVIEW WITH DR. BASS (PART II)—DECEMBER 17, 2009*

Question: Are you pleased with the direction that forensic anthropology is currently headed in terms of research, scholarship, and in the investigation and medicolegal side?

Dr. Bass: I would say to that—absolutely. I can see tremendous changes. An example: When I came here, I knew the medical examiner, Jerry Francisco. Jerry Francisco was a pathologist at the medical school in Memphis. Let me tell you how I know Jerry. In 1956, T.D. Stewart published, "Skeletal Changes in Young American Males." This was the result of the analysis of Korean War soldiers who died. Then the question came up, "Do women mature the same way as men do?" Nobody knew. I had a graduate student, Bob Gilbert who was interested. I knew enough of the pathologists that I decided to write them and say, "When you do an autopsy and get out the pubic bone—don't stop, take the pubic symphisis for my students to look at. I wrote about 6 to 8 letters … one of the people who helped me do that was Jerry Francisco. So I know Jerry, because Jerry got samples for Bob Gilbert to do his doctoral dissertation on skeletal changes in females. So Jerry asked if I'd serve as a forensic anthropologist for the medical examiner system and I said "sure!" So, that then got me into the medical examiner systems staff doing the cases … You need these cross fertilizations of fields.

Question: How do you feel about forensic anthropology on television shows, and in your opinion, does this help or hurt those who practice forensic anthropology?

* The photograph of Dr. Bass is Courtesy of University of Tennessee Anthropology Department.

Dr. Bass: You all are certainly aware of the "CSI effect." When I came along, nobody knew what I did … time goes by CSI comes along and explodes. Now I would say there are very few people in the United States who don't know who CSI, Bones, and what those programs are. Now, the other edge of that sword is that if you don't do it in court the way that people see it done on T.V., then there's something wrong with the police department. So you get that backlash, you see. They're entertaining—they're more Hollywood than science.

Question: So you feel that perhaps the TV programs create unrealistic expectations from juries?

Dr. Bass: Exactly, I couldn't have said it that well.

Question: And what about what they've done to the influx of students into the field. I've had students come up to me interested in forensics, but they really don't grasp what they're getting into, especially with forensic anthropology.

Dr. Bass: Let me give you an analogy there. Working with Krogman, I worked in the gross anatomy center and also occasionally taught anatomy in the medical school for him. We had 120 people in the medical school class. Four students to a cadaver, so bodies are everywhere. So the first week of medical school, you're going to lose four to five of those students. They're smart; make great physicians, except they haven't thought they've got to cut on someone to do that.

You take anthropology—you take ten students out to the body farm, and you get up there in the summer or fall. September is hotter than heck, and you show them a couple of those bodies and the next day there's only seven of them left. So, people see the exciting part of it, but they don't think about who's got to do the work to get it done.

Question: Where do you see forensic anthropology going in the future as far as research and number of programs and things like that? Do you think it's going to keep increasing or it will level out after a while?

Dr. Bass: Well, I think it will level out, I mean, we can't have everybody … the need is still there … the need is for body farms in various geographic or climatic zones, so the need is going to be there for a while before we get to that. One of these days there may be too many of them. But now they certainly need to increase, because we don't have enough now, and we really don't have an oversupply of students. There are still jobs out there.

Question: How does it make you feel to see your students practicing forensic anthropology all over the world?

Dr. Bass: Great—really great. As I said, I have two families: a biological family and an academic family, and it's great to see. It really is nice. The best move I made was when I was in Kentucky, and I went to my wife and said, "Do you mind if I switch from counseling to anthropology?"

References

Agostini GM and Gomez EJ. 2009. Forensic anthropology academic and employment trends. *Proceedings of the American Academy of Forensic Sciences Annual Meetings*, Denver, CO, February 16–21. Vol. 15, p. 346.

Committee on Identifying the Needs of the Forensic Sciences Community, National Research Council. 2009. Strengthening forensic science in the United States: A path forward, A Report. Document No. 228091. NIJ Award No. 2006-DN-BX-0001.

Native American Graves Protection and Repatriation Act (NAGPRA). 1990. PL 101–601, 104 Stat 3048, United States.

Additional Information

Helpful Websites

American Academy of Forensic Sciences (www.aafs.org)

Midwest Bioarchaeology and Forensic Anthropology Association (http://archlab.uindy.edu/barfaa/index.php)

Mountain, Desert, and Coastal Forensic Anthropologists (http://foil.ucsc.edu/mdc/)

SWGANTH (www.theswganth.org)

The NAS Report (http://www.ncjrs.gov/pdffiles1/nij/grants/228091.pdf)

Human Osteology

4

MARIATERESA A. TERSIGNI-TARRANT
AND NATALIE R. SHIRLEY

Contents

Human osteology is the study of the bones of the human skeleton ("osteo" means "bone" and "ology" means "the study of"). Forensic anthropologists receive extensive training in human osteology. A well-trained osteologist has a thorough understanding of microscopic and macroscopic bone anatomy, bone growth and development, normal and pathological variation, and comparative osteology. To develop skills in comparative osteology, many forensic anthropologists take courses in nonhuman osteology, or zooarchaeology. Proper knowledge of human and nonhuman osteology is necessary, because many forensic anthropology cases contain both human and nonhuman skeletal remains. This chapter provides a brief overview of human osteology and supplementary reading and reference materials for more detailed coverage.

Bone as a Connective Tissue

Bone is a calcified connective tissue that supports and protects the soft tissues of the body, provides attachment sites for muscles, produces blood cells, and stores calcium, nutrients, and lipids. Bone tissue is composed of an inorganic component that gives bone its rigidity and an organic component that provides flexibility. The inorganic constituent of bone is a carbonated hydroxyapatite crystalline matrix ($Ca_{10}(PO_4)_6(OH)_2$), and the organic component is primarily Type I collagen. Bone is laid down, maintained, and remodeled throughout life by several different types of bone maintenance cells. These cells include osteoprogenitor cells (which eventually give rise to osteoblasts), osteoclasts, osteocytes, and bone lining cells.

Osteoclasts are cells that dissolve (or resorb) bone. Osteoclasts are formed by the fusion of *monocytes* in the red marrow, which is found in spongy bone. This fusion is initiated by the release of parathyroid hormone when the serum calcium concentration in the blood is low. Fusion of the single nucleated monocytes forms a multinuclear and functionally polarized large cell (i.e., the osteoclast). Osteoclasts have a specialized ruffled acidic border that provides additional surface area for bone resorption. First, the acidic border demineralizes the bone tissue, and then enzymes dissolve the collagen. Osteoclasts can move

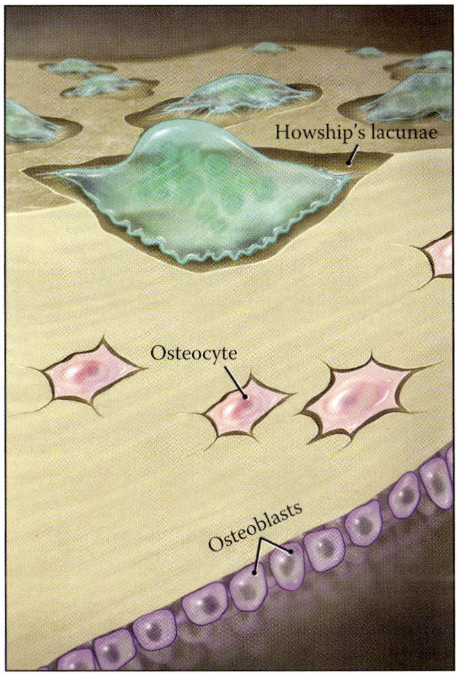

Figure 4.1 Multinucleated osteoclasts in Howship's lacunae. (Figure by Jennifer Stowe.)

quickly and erode as much as tens of micrometers of bone away per day. Osteoclasts live in resorptive bays, or spaces, called Howship's lacunae (Figure 4.1).

Osteoblasts are mononucleic bone building cells that are formed from differentiated mesenchymal osteoprogenitor cells. Mesenchymal cells are embryonic precursor cells, or stem cells, that are capable of differentiating into a variety of cell types, including bone cells, cartilage cells, and fat cells. The formation of osteoblasts is a 2–3 day process triggered by mechanical or metabolic stress (i.e., heightened serum calcium concentration triggers mesenchymal cells to differentiate into osteoblasts). Osteoblasts produce *osteoid*, which is the unmineralized organic portion of bone matrix, and are responsible for laying down new bone. Osteoid is comprised of collagen, noncollagenous proteins, proteoglycans, and water, making it a gel-like substance when deposited. The water is replaced by minerals (hydroxyapatite) as the osteoid mineralizes. Osteoblasts can lay down osteoid at a rate of 1 μm per day during skeletogenesis and fracture repair.

Osteocytes are actually osteoblasts that become surrounded by the bone matrix secreted by the osteoblasts. Once the osteoblasts are encased in the bone matrix, they become mature bone cells (osteocytes), and their function is converted from bone production to bone maintenance and communication. Osteocytes reside in pores, or spaces, called lacunae and communicate with other osteocytes through tentacle-like projections that are housed in canaliculi (little canals) (Figure 4.2). The projections communicate through ion transfer at gap junctions. That is, the tentacles come close enough to each other to pass ions and small nutrients to one another through and positive/negative flow. In this manner, the inside of the bone is connected to the outside of the bone, and the top of the bone is connected to the bottom of the bone, thereby allowing for communication (biochemical reciprocity) throughout the bone. Bone lining cells are also converted osteoblasts, although

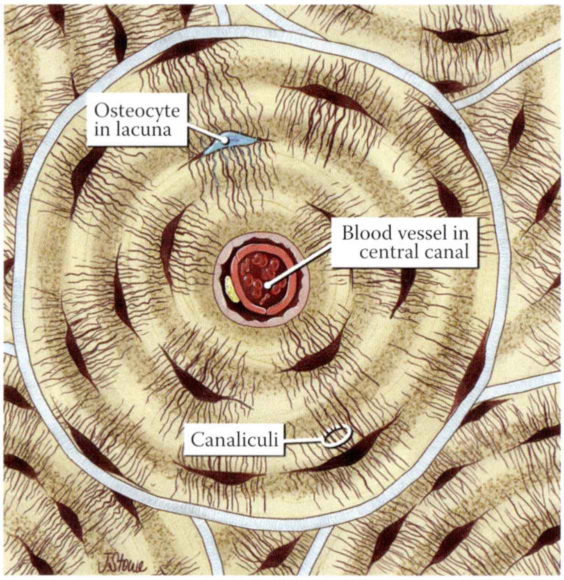

Figure 4.2 Haversian system (osteon). The dark- and light-colored bands in the osteon are the circumferential lamellae. (Figure by Jennifer Stowe.)

they live on the bone surface and do not become embedded in the osteoid. These are the cells that initiate bone remodeling (resorption and deposition) in response to mechanical stress such as fracturing.

Bone Structure

Two layers frame the microscopic structure of bone: periosteum and endosteum. The periosteum is an external fibrocellular sheath that contains collagen fibers and fibroblasts, which, in turn, forms an osteogenic/nourishing layer on the compact bone surface. The periosteum is connected to the underlying bone by bundles of collagen fibers (Sharpey's fibers) that protrude from the periosteum into the outer layers of bone tissue. The endosteum lines the surface of the inner marrow cavity as well as all Haversian and Volkmann's canals. Endosteum consists of osteogenic cells and thin reticular fibers.

Adult bone consists of two forms of bone: trabecular and compact bone (Figure 4.3). Trabecular bone, also known as cancellous or spongy bone, is the internal porous bone found in irregular bones, flat bones, and the articular ends of long bones. Trabecular bone is the latticework of bony spicules, or trabeculae, that are found within the shaft and the epiphyses (Ross et al., 1989). The bone matrix is laid down in the form of trabeculae that are usually <200 μm thick. In life, the pores within trabecular bone are connected and filled with red marrow. The arrangement of these trabeculae is irregular, although it is often in an orthogonal formation. Trabeculae can be visualized as beams of bone that form inner the scaffolding of bones.

Compact bone, also known as cortical bone, is the dense bone that forms the outer cortex covering the trabecular bone. Cortical bone is most abundant in the shafts of long bones, where its compact arrangement provides much-needed strength (Figure 4.3).

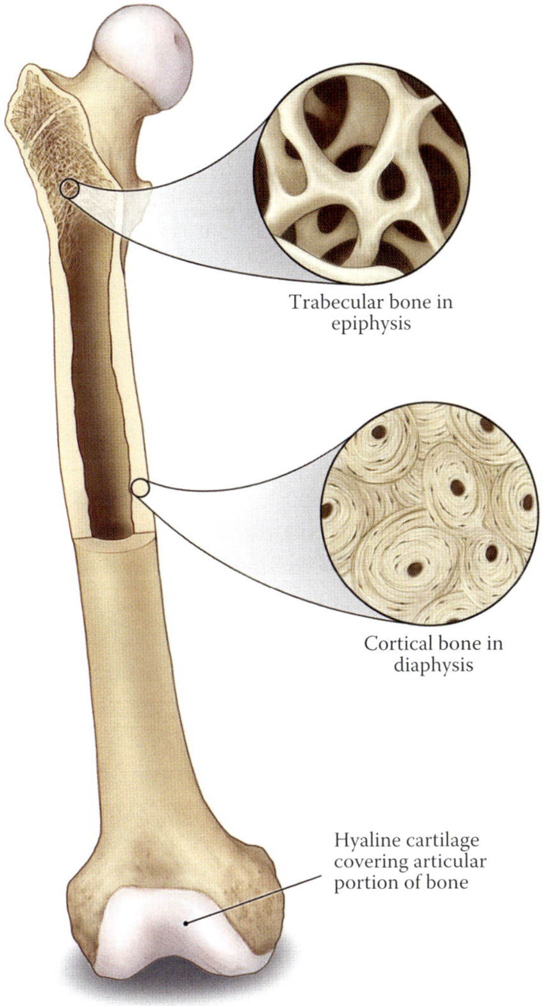

Figure 4.3 Locations of trabecular and cortical bone in a typical long bone. (Figure by Jennifer Stowe.)

The micro-organization of this bone consists of many small formations that allow the inside of the bone (endosteum) to communicate with the outside of the bone (periosteum). These formations include Haversian canals, Volkmann's canals, and resorptive bays (Howship's lacunae) (Figure 4.2). Haversian canals are narrow trenches aligned with the long axis of the bone that contain nerves and capillaries that allow nutrients to move throughout the entire bone matrix. Volkmann's canals are short transverse canals connecting Haversian canals to one another and allowing communication to the outer bone surface through blood vessels. Howship's lacunae are scoured out areas in which osteoclasts live during the initiation bone remodeling (discussed in the previous section). The density/porosity of both types of bone is dynamic and can be affected by pathologies or by mechanical or metabolic stimuli. Thus, trabecular bone can become more compact, and compact bone can become more porous depending on functional or metabolic demands. Any change in the original porosity of the bone can affect the mechanical/structural properties of the bone.

Compact bone can be further divided into primary and secondary bone. Primary bone is the first type of bone to be laid down during development and fracture repair. There are two types of primary bone found within different species: circumferential lamellae and plexiform bone. Circumferential lamellar bone (Haversian bone) has lamellae, or layers, that are laid down in a parallel orientation to the bone's surface. Blood vessels are encompassed by these circular lamellae, creating Haversian canals that run longitudinally throughout the bone. These blood vessels are used to move minerals, nutrients, and remodeling cells to the section of bone that needs attention. The entire unit of a circular set of lamellae surrounding a single Haversian canal is called a Haversian system, or osteon (see Figure 4.2). This type of primary bone is found in humans. Plexiform bone is a mixture of both woven and lamellar bone found in some animals. Plexiform bone is often described as having a brick wall pattern because the vascular structure is rectilinear, thus creating the image of individual bricks of bone separated by the vasculature as the brick's mortar. This type of bone is typical in large fast-growing animals, such as horses, cows, sheep, and goats.

Secondary bone is formed by the resorption of existing bone and the laying down of new lamellar bone in its place. This process is known as remodeling. Secondary osteons usually consist of a number of consecutive circumferential lamellae that have formed surrounding a Haversian canal that houses blood vessels and nerves. Secondary osteons are surrounded by a cement line, which demarcates where the osteoclasts (bone resorption cells) ended their resorption process. Most of the compact bone in adult humans consists of secondary bone, leaving a characteristic morphology of complete osteons and pieces of old osteons (interstitial lamellae) within a thin section of bone (see Chapter 19 for a more detailed discussion of bone microstructure).

Bone Types and Joints

The bones of the body are classified into four categories based upon their shape: long bones, short bones, flat bones, and irregular bones. Long bones are generally longer than they are wide and can be found in the arms and legs. Long bones have a diaphysis (shaft) and two epiphyses (articular portions), one at either end of the diaphysis (see Figure 4.3). The diaphysis is composed of dense compact bone covered by periosteum. The center of diaphysis is open and is called the medullary cavity, or intramedullary canal. The medullary cavity contains yellow bone marrow, which is primarily fat. The epiphyses are the ends of the bone and are composed of trabecular bone that contains red marrow. Articular cartilage, composed of hyaline cartilage, covers the external surface of each epiphysis and aids in decreasing joint friction. Long bones also have a nutrient foramen located on the diaphysis. The nutrient foramen serves as a site for the passage of blood vessels into the medullary canal. Frequently, the orientation of the nutrient foramen is useful in siding bone fragments. Short bones are composed of trabecular bone covered by a thin layer of compact bone. Short bones are found in the wrists and the ankles. Flat bones are composed of two layers of compact bone covering a thin trabecular bone layer (usually referred to as diploë). Examples of flat bones are the bones of the cranial vault and ribs. Irregular bones are bones of various sizes that do not fit into the other categories. They are composed of spongy bone with a thin compact bone covering. Examples of irregular bones include the vertebrae and the bones of the pelvic girdle.

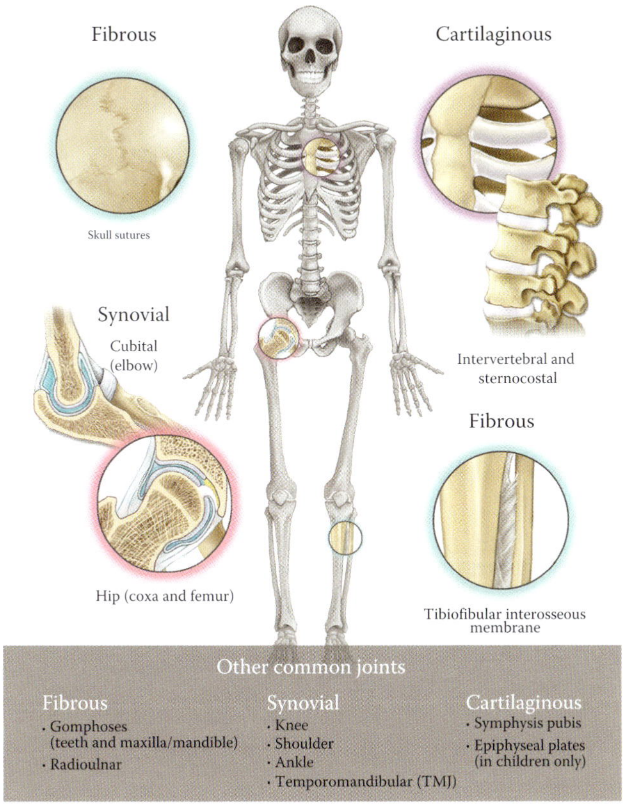

Figure 4.4 Fibrous, cartilaginous, and synovial joints. (Figure by Jennifer Stowe.)

Joints are the junction (i.e., articulation) points between two bones. Joints are classified on the basis of structure (primary tissue components) and function (range of movement). There are three different structural categories of joints within the skeleton: fibrous, cartilaginous, and synovial joints (Figure 4.4). Fibrous joints are joints where the bones are bound together by fibrous connective tissue. Fibrous joints have no joint cavity and usually do not allow for much movement. Examples of fibrous joints include the cranial sutures and the specialized syndesmosis joints between the shafts of the radius and ulna and the tibia and fibula. Cartilaginous joints are joints in which the bones are bound together with cartilage. Cartilaginous joints do not have a joint cavity. Cartilaginous joints can be divided into primary cartilaginous joints, or synchondroses, and secondary cartilaginous joints, or symphyses, based on the amount of movement permitted at the joint. The bones united by synchondroses are joined together with hyaline cartilage and allow for no movement, except for bone growth, at the site of the joint. Examples of synchondroses are the epiphyseal plates of the long bones (also known as growth plates) and the spheno-occipital synchondrosis in the base of the skull. The bones in a symphysis are united by fibrocartilage and allow for a small amount of movement at the joint surface. These include the intervertebral disks and the pubic symphysis. Synovial (diarthrodial) joints are joints that permit a great deal of movement. Synovial joint components include a joint cavity containing a membrane that secretes synovial fluid, and articular (hyaline) cartilage covering the bone surfaces invested in the joint.

The articular cartilage coupled with the synovial fluid allows for smooth movement of the bones within the joint. There are six different classifications of synovial joints based upon the type of articulation or type of movement produced at the articulation. The six classifications are plane, or gliding, joints; hinge joints; pivot joints; condylar joints; saddle joints; and ball-and-socket joints.

Bone Growth

The adult body has 206 bones, although occasionally an extra vertebra, rib, or additional sesamoid bones are present. However, the subadult skeleton has more than twice as many bony elements (around 450 ossification centers are present at birth). Growth is a term used to describe the changes in size and shape, or morphology, which occur as an organism develops and ages. Bones develop *in utero* from cartilage models (i.e., endochondral ossification) and/or vascular membranous templates (i.e., intramembranous ossification). During this developmental process, which is referred to as osteogenesis or ossification, the embryonic precursor tissues are replaced by bone at sites called primary ossification centers. In general, intramembranous ossification produces cortical and diploic bone, and endochondral ossification produces cancellous bone (Scheuer and Black, 2000). Secondary ossification centers or epiphyses appear after birth and are separated from the primary ossification centers by a layer of cartilage referred to as the epiphyseal plate. The epiphyseal plate attributes to the lengthening of the growing bone. Once bone growth is complete, the primary and secondary ossification centers fuse, the epiphyseal plate disappears, and the bone assumes its adult size and shape (Figure 4.5).

Body Orientations and Anatomical Terminology

Because the human body can assume a number of positions and change position relative to its environment, references to the body or parts of the body are made with respect to standard anatomical position. The human body is in standard anatomical position when standing erect with arms by the sides and palms facing forward (Figure 4.6). Standard anatomical position of the skull is referred to as Frankfurt horizontal. In this position, the lower margin of the orbit and the upper margin of the external acoustic meatus (ear hole) lie in the same horizontal plane, and that plane is parallel to the ground.

Now that we have established a standard position for the body, let us discuss basic anatomical orientation and directional terminology. Figure 4.6 illustrates three primary reference planes, which are imaginary planes used to divide the body into sections or halves. A coronal plane is any vertical plane that divides the body into anterior and posterior portions; the mid-coronal plane divides the body into equal front and back halves. A sagittal plane is any vertical plane that divides the body into left and right sections; the mid-sagittal plane divides the body into symmetrical left and right halves. A transverse plane is any horizontal plane that divides the body into superior and inferior sections and is perpendicular to the coronal and sagittal planes.

The terms anterior and posterior refer to front and back, respectively. Sometimes the terms ventral and dorsal are used to refer to front and back (or belly side and back side), as well. Superior and inferior mean "above/toward the head" and "below/away from the head" and are used to describe the trunk of the body. Similarly, the terms cranial and

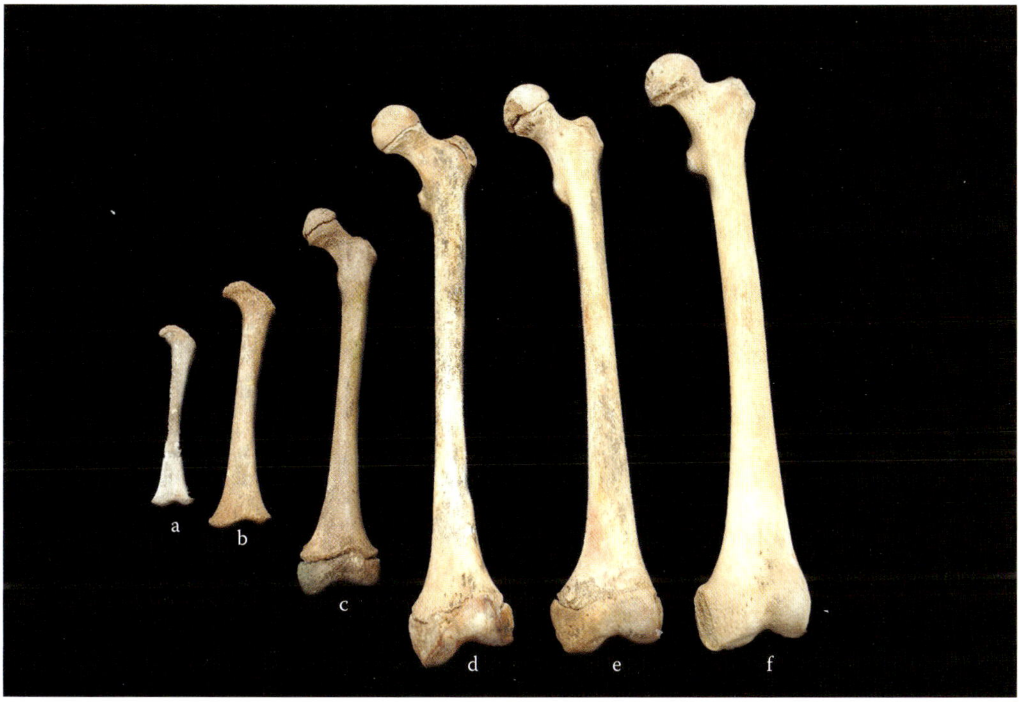

Figure 4.5 Growth and development of human femur. (a and b) Diaphysis without secondary ossification centers (epiphyses). (c) Secondary ossification centers for femoral head and distal end present. (d and e) Secondary ossification center for femoral head, distal end, and greater trochanter present. (f) All epiphyses completely united to diaphysis (growth is complete and bone has assumed adult morphology). (Courtesy of Sandra Cridlin.)

caudal mean "toward the head" and "toward the tail," but in human osteology the terms superior and inferior are used more frequently than cranial and caudal. When referring to limb bones, the terms distal and proximal are used preferentially. Distal means "farthest from the trunk" and proximal means "nearest the trunk." For example, the humerus is proximal to the radius and ulna, and the tibia is distal to the femur. Two additional terms frequently used in osteology are medial and lateral. Medial is toward the midline of the body, and lateral is away from the midline of the body.

Cranium and Mandible

The cranium and mandible are collectively referred to as the skull. Humans have always had a certain fascination with the skull, and perhaps for this reason it is the single skeletal element that has received the most attention in the research literature. Certainly, the skull is an important element in forensic anthropology, as it can be used to determine sex, ancestry, and age. However, many postcranial elements provide superior estimates of sex and age compared to those offered by the cranium. In addition, we have discovered that some postcranial elements are useful in determining ancestry (specifically the os coxa, femur, and tibia). Typically, the element(s) used to estimate the various parameters of the biological profile are determined simply by which bones are present and complete for analysis.

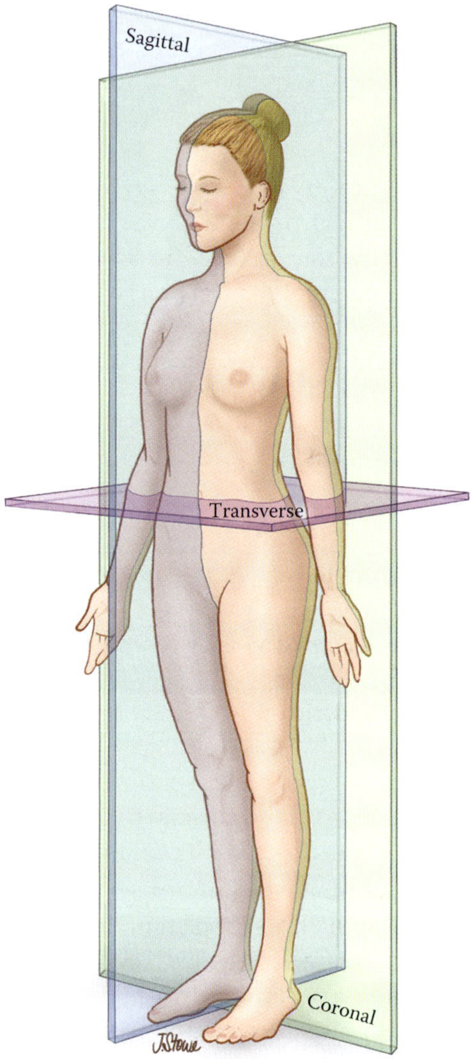

Figure 4.6 Anatomical position and planes. (Figure by Jennifer Stowe.)

As we begin to explore the bones of the skull, it is important to make certain that we understand the common terminology with which to discuss its main components. Therefore, the first part of this section will focus on some general terminology. Next, the bones of the skull will be discussed in brief detail. As this is not an osteology text, the discussion of each bone is limited to key anatomical landmarks, including the main sutures, metric, and nonmetric landmarks. Students interested in pursuing a degree in physical anthropology should take a human osteology course, which will cover in detail the various anatomical landmarks, as well as the growth and development of each bone of the skull.

Terminology

The skull refers to the complete osseous frame of the head including the mandible. The mandible, then, refers to the lower jaw. The portion of the skull that contains the brain is often referred to as the neurocranium, while the bony structure of the face is the splanchnocranium. The skull without the mandible is called the cranium. The cranium without the bones of the face is referred to as the calvaria (this refers to all of the bones that surround the brain). If the base is absent from the calvaria, the bony portion that remains is referred to as the calotte.

Cranial bones are unique in terms of their structure and composition. Particularly, the bones of the cranial vault, or neurocranium, are comprised of two layers of cortical bone and a layer of dense spongy bone referred to as diploe. The diploe is sandwiched between the endocranial and ectocranial cortical bone layers; its relative density compared to spongy bone in other areas of the skeleton is a result of the functional demands of the cranial vault (i.e., to provide a rigid, protective structure to house the brain). The neurocranial elements are flat bones, and the joints between these bones are unlike the joints in any other portion of the skeleton. Because of their jagged appearance, these joints are referred to as sutures. The major cranial vault sutures are the sagittal, coronal, lambdoidal, and squamosal sutures (Figure 4.9a):

- *Sagittal suture*: runs along the midsagittal plane; forms the articulation between the right and left parietal bones.
- *Coronal suture*: forms the articulation between the frontal bone and the parietal bones.
- *Lambdoidal suture*: forms the articulation between the occipital bone and the parietal bones.
- *Squamosal suture*: there are two squamosal sutures (right and left); they form the articulation between the temporal and parietal bones.

The remaining cranial bones are more structurally complex than the neurocranial elements and vary widely in terms of thickness and composition. These bones also articulate at suture sites, many of which derive their names from each of the two articulating elements (i.e., the zygomatico-maxillary suture). In the infant cranium, the gaps between the sutures are large in order to allow for cranial growth. Furthermore, sutural junction sites are comprised of cartilaginous membranes called fontanelles ("soft spots") that eventually ossify (Figure 4.7). As sutures represent naturally weak portions of the skull, they are frequently the site of fractures in cranial trauma cases; consequently, knowing the names and locations of these features is important for the forensic anthropology practitioner.

Another aspect of cranial terminology that is vital to the forensic anthropology practitioner is that of cranial landmarks. Cranial landmarks are points on the skeleton that are defined by the intersection of sutures, maximum or minimum curvature, or biological significance. These landmarks serve as the sites from which cranial measurements are taken. These measurements are used in conjunction with discriminant functions, regression equations, or with software packages such as the Fordisc program (see Chapter 13) to estimate sex and ancestry. Figure 4.8 shows some of the standard cranial landmarks used in forensic anthropology. Refer to the publications of Buikstra and Ubelaker (1994) and Moore-Jansen et al. (1994) in the Supplementary Reading and Reference Materials section for detailed descriptions of cranial landmarks and measurements.

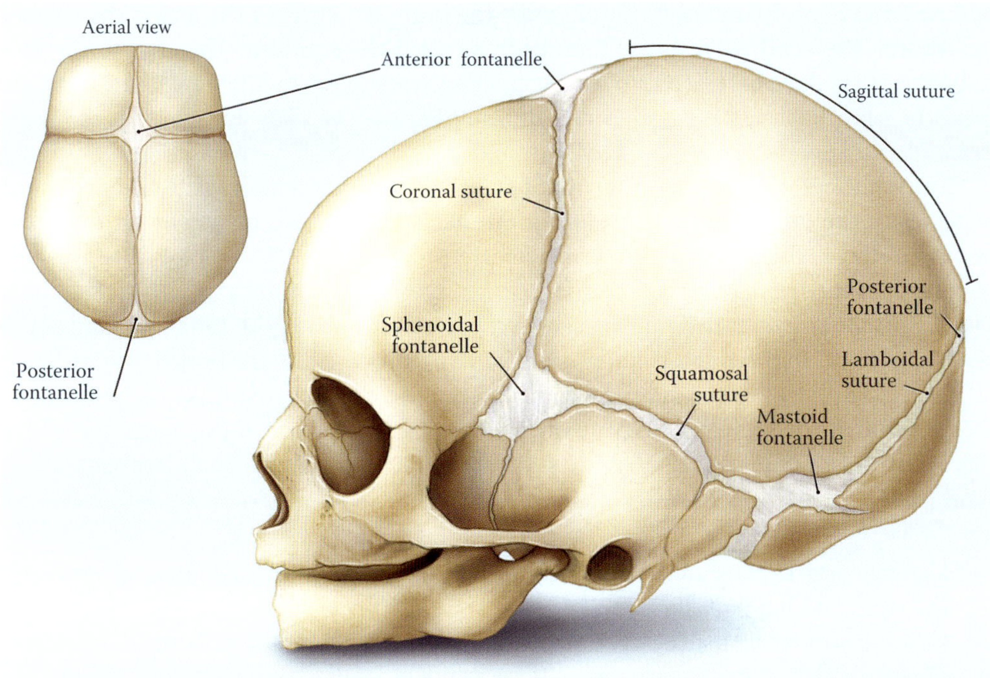

Figure 4.7 Fontanelles in infant cranium. (Figure by Jennifer Stowe.)

Bones of the Skull

This section provides a brief description of each of the bones of the skull, including the anatomical location of each bone, the cranial bones with which it articulates, key bony features, and pertinent metric landmarks that lie on the bone or at its borders. Chapter 13 provides an explanation of how cranial landmarks are used in forensic anthropology.

Frontal

The frontal bone comprises the anterior portion of the face, including the forehead and superior portion of the eye orbits (represented in pink in Figure 4.9b). The frontal bone articulates with the following bones:

- Right and left parietals (posteriorly) via the coronal suture
- Nasals (inferiorly) via the frontonasal suture
- Maxillae (inferiorly) via the frontomaxillary sutures
- Ethmoid (inferiorly) via the frontoethmoidal sutures
- Lacrimals (inferiorly) via the frontolacrimal sutures
- Zygomatic (inferio-laterally) via the zygomaticofrontal sutures
- Sphenoid (inferio-posteriorly)
- Right and left halves of the frontal fuse in the midline at the metopic suture (occasionally a visible remnant of this suture persists into adulthood)

Some key features of the frontal include the supraorbital margins, superciliary arches, temporal lines, and the frontal eminences or bosses.

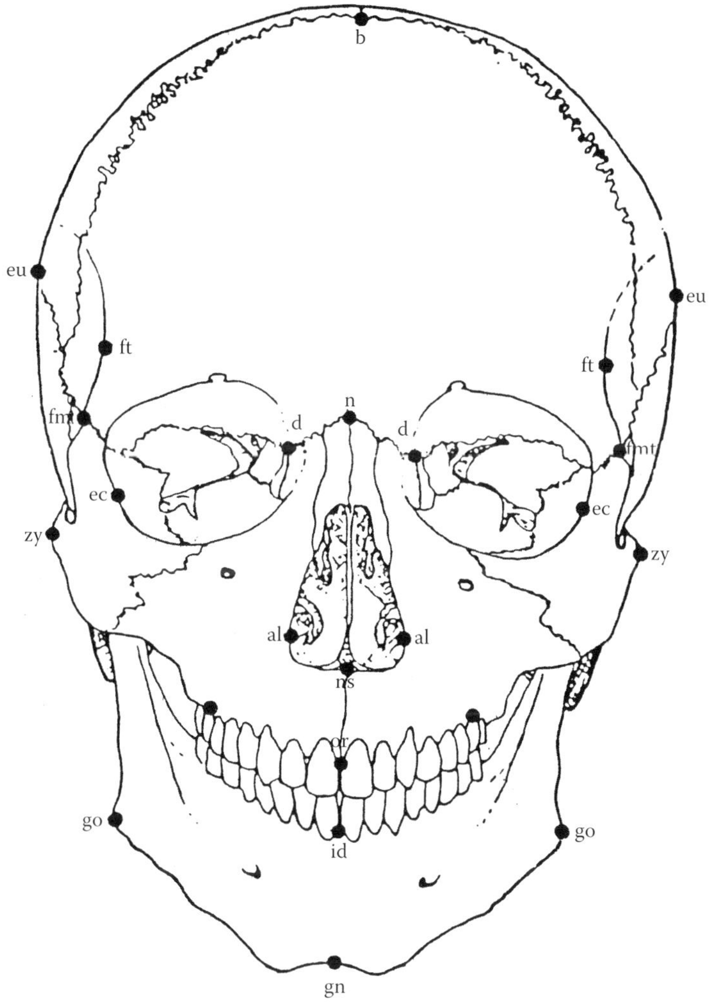

Figure 4.8 Cranial landmarks. B, bregma; eu, euryon; ft, frontotemporale; n, nasion; d, dacryon; fmt, frontomalare temporale; ec, ectoconchion; zy, zygion; al, alare; ns, nasospinale; go, gonion; gn, gnathion.

Cranial landmarks used for metric analysis that lie on the frontal or on its borders include Bregma, Dacryon, Frontomalare temporale, Frontotemporale, Glabella, and Nasion.

Parietals

The parietal bones are paired bones (right and left) that make up the sides and top of the skull (depicted purple in Figure 4.9b). The right and left parietal bones articulate with the following bones:

- Both articulate with the frontal bone (anteriorly) via the coronal suture.
- Both articulate with the occipital bone (posteriorly) via the lambdoidal suture.
- Right and left parietal articulate with each other in the midline of the skull at the sagittal suture.

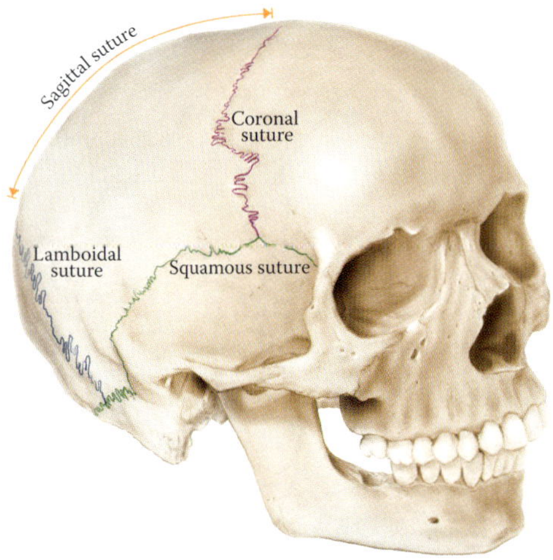

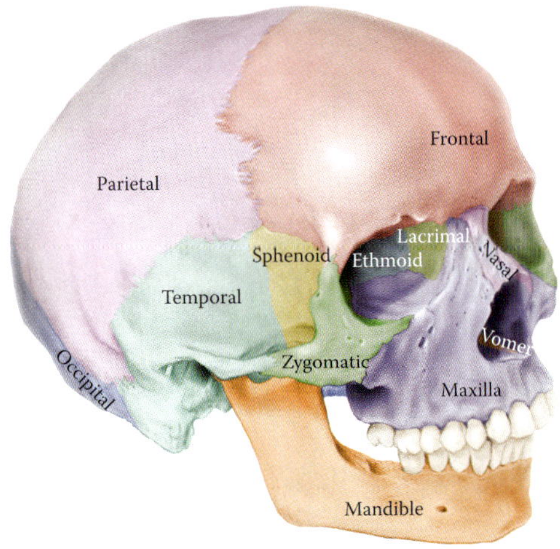

Figure 4.9 (a) Skull sutures and (b) bones. (Figure by Jennifer Stowe.)

- The right parietal articulates inferiorly with the right temporal via the squamosal suture and the right greater wing of the sphenoid at the sphenoidal angle.
- The left parietal articulates inferiorly with the left temporal via the squamosal suture and the left greater wing of the sphenoid at the sphenoidal angle.

Some key features of the parietal include the temporal lines, parietal foramina, meningeal grooves (endocranially), and parietal bosses. Cranial landmarks used for metric analysis that lie on the parietals or on the parietal borders include Bregma, Euryon, Asterion, and Lambda.

Temporals

The right and left temporal bones make up the most inferior-lateral portions of the cranial vault (depicted in light blue in Figure 4.9b). They are the lateral connection of the cranial vault to the cranial base. The right and left temporals each house the delicate bones of the inner ear, including the incus, malleus, stapes, and the vestibulocochlear complex. The right and left temporals articulate with the following bones of the skull:

- Both temporals articulate with the occipital (posteriorly) via the occipitomastoid sutures.
- The right temporal articulates with the right parietal (superiorly) via the squamosal suture and posterior-inferiorly via the parietomastoid suture, with the right zygomatic (anterior-laterally) via the zygomaticotemporal suture, and with the right greater wing of the sphenoid (anteriorly) via the sphenotemporal suture.
- The left temporal articulates with the left parietal (superiorly) via the squamosal suture and posterior-inferiorly via the parietomastoid suture, with the left zygomatic (anterior-laterally) via the zygomaticotemporal suture, and with the left greater wing of the sphenoid (anteriorly) via the sphenotemporal suture.
- The inferior surface of the right and left temporal bones articulate with the corresponding condyle of the mandible at the temporomandibular joint (TMJ).

Some key features of the temporals include the temporal squama, external acoustic/auditory meatus (EAM), suprameatal crest, supramastoid crest, zygomatic process, mastoid process, styloid process, temporomandibular articular surface, and petrous pyramid (endocranially).

Cranial landmarks used for metric analysis that lie on the temporals or on the temporal borders include Auriculare, Euryon, Mastoidale, and Porion.

Auditory Ossicles

The auditory ossicles are the three small bones found within the petrous portion of the right and left temporals. The auditory ossicles are the incus (anvil), malleus (hammer), and stapes (stirrup). The ossicles are the smallest bones in the body and typically are not recovered in a forensic context.

Occipital

The occipital is the most posterior bone of the skull. A portion of the occipital is visible posterior to the parietal in Figure 4.9b. The occipital articulates with the following bones:

- Right and left parietals (superior-anteriorly) via the lambdoidal suture
- Sphenoid (inferior-anteriorly) via the spheno-occipital synchondrosis (or basilar suture)
- Right and left temporals (anterolaterally) via the occipitomastoid sutures
- First cervical vertebra, or atlas, (inferiorly) via the occipital condyles

Some key features of the occipital include the foramen magnum, external occipital protuberance, superior and inferior nuchal lines, hypoglossal canals, cruciform eminence (endocranially), and the occipital condyles.

Cranial landmarks used for metric analysis that lie on the occipital or on its borders include Asterion, Basion, Inion, Lambda, Opisthocranion, and Opisthion.

Ethmoid

The majority of the ethmoid bone is hidden from view when looking at the external skull. The ethmoid is situated between the bony orbits, just inferior to the frontal in the midline of the skull. The ethmoid articulates with the following bones of the skull:

- Frontal (superiorly) via the frontoethmoidal suture
- Sphenoid (posteriorly) via the sphenoethmoidal suture
- Nasals, lacrimals, inferior nasal conchae and vomer (anteriorly)
- Maxilla and palatines (inferiorly)

Some of the key features of the ethmoid include the cribriform plate, crista galli, and perpendicular plate.

Sphenoid

The sphenoid spans the anterior width of the cranial base and makes up the posterior-inferior surface of the eye orbits (shown in yellow in Figure 4.9b). It is often referred to as the "bat-wing" or "butterfly" shaped bone. The sphenoid articulates with the following bones:

- Frontal (anterosuperiorly) via the sphenofrontal suture.
- Occipital (postero-inferiorly) via the spheno-occipital synchondrosis (basilar suture)
- Right and left parietals (posteriorly) at the sphenoidal angle
- Right and left temporals (posteriorly) at the greater wings of the sphenoid via the sphenotemporal suture
- Right and left zygomatics on the anterior surface of the right and left greater wings
- Vomer, ethmoid, palatines (anteriorly), and sometimes maxilla

Some key features of the sphenoid include the greater wings, lesser wings, medial and lateral pterygoid plates, and the sella turcica.

Lacrimals

The right and left lacrimals are extremely fragile, thin bones that surround the right and left lacrimal glands (the glands that produce tears), respectively, in the anteromedial portion of each eye orbit. The lacrimal articulates with the following bones:

- Frontal (superiorly)
- Ethmoid (posteriorly)
- Inferior nasal conchae (inferiorly)
- Maxilla (anteriorly)

Cranial landmarks used for metric analysis that lie on the lacrimals or the lacrimal borders include Dacryon.

Nasals

The right and left nasal bones are small, rectangular bones that meet in the midsagittal plane (depicted in purple in Figure 4.9b). The nasal bones form the nasal bridge, and the inferior border of the nasals make the roof of the bony nasal aperture. The right and left nasals articulate with the following bones:

- Frontal (superiorly) via the frontonasal suture
- Right and left nasals articulate with each other (medially)
- Maxillae (laterally) at the frontal processes of the maxilla

Cranial landmarks used for metric analysis that lie on the nasals or the nasal borders include Nasion.

Vomer

The vomer is a thin plate-like bone that articulates inferiorly with the maxillae, creating the postero-inferior portion of the nasal septum that divides the nasal cavity into two halves (visible in orange in the nasal opening; Figure 4.9b). The vomer articulates with the following bones of the skull:

- Sphenoid (superiorly)
- Ethmoid (anterosuperiorly)
- Maxillae and palatines (inferiorly)

Some key features of the vomer include the perpendicular plate and wings.

Inferior Nasal Conchae

The right and left inferior nasal conchae are thin-walled bones that lie along the lateral edge of the inferior nasal aperture. The inferior nasal conchae articulate with the following bones of the skull:

- Ethmoid and lacrimals (superiorly)
- Maxillae and palatines (inferiorly)

Palatines

The right and left palatines are thin, plate-like bones in the shape of an "L" that articulate with the posterior portion of the maxillae. The palatine bones articulate with the following bones of the skull:

- Vomer, inferior conchae and ethmoid (superiorly)
- Right and left palatines articulate with each other (medially)

Some key features of the palatines include the posterior nasal spine, horizontal and perpendicular plates.

Zygomatics

The right and left zygomatics make up the lateral portion of the anterior face and the inferior portion of the eye orbits (shown in green in Figure 4.9b). The zygomatics are often called the "cheek bones." The zygomatics articulate with the following bones:

- Both articulate with the frontal (supero-laterally) via the zygomaticofrontal sutures.
- Sphenoid (posteriorly).
- The right zygomatic articulates with the right temporal (posteriorly) via the zygomaticotemporal suture and the right maxilla (medially) via the zygomaticomaxillary suture.
- The left zygomatic articulates with the left temporal (posteriorly) via the zygomaticotemporal suture and the left maxilla (medially) via the zygomaticomaxillary suture.

Some key features of the zygomatics include the frontal, temporal, and maxillary processes.

Cranial landmarks used for metric analysis that lie on the zygomatics or on zygomatic borders include Ectoconchion, Frontomalare temporale, and Zygion.

Maxilla

The right and left maxillae are a set of paired bones that make up a large portion of the anterior face and hold the maxillary dentition (depicted in blue in Figure 4.9b). The maxilla makes up the medial portion of the eye orbits, the lateral and inferior portions of the nasal aperture, and the anterior part of the hard palate. The right and left maxillae articulate with the following bones:

- Both articulate with the frontal (superiorly) at the frontomaxillary sutures, with the sphenoid and ethmoid (posteriorly), and with the vomer (anteriorly).
- The right maxilla articulates with the right palatine (posteriorly), the right nasal bone (superomedially), the right lacrimal (superolaterally), the right inferior nasal concha (inferomedially), and the right zygomatic (laterally).
- The left maxilla articulates with the left palatine (posteriorly), the left nasal bone (superomedially), the left lacrimal (superolaterally), the left inferior nasal concha (inferomedially), and the left zygomatic (laterally).
- The right and left maxillae articulate with one another medially.

Some key features of the maxilla include the anterior nasal spine, infraorbital foramen, and the alveolar, zygomatic, frontal, and palatine process.

Cranial landmarks used for metric analysis that lie on the maxilla or on its borders include Alare, Alveolon, Dacryon, Ectomolare, Nasospinale, and Prosthion.

Mandible

The mandible is also known as the lower jaw and is shown in orange in Figure 4.9b. It articulates with the skull via the right and left temporal bones at the TMJs. The mandible serves as an attachment site for the muscles of mastication and houses the lower dentition. Like the frontal bone, the mandible develops as two separate halves and fuses in the midline (the symphysis).

Some key features of the mandible include the body (corpus), mental protuberance/eminence, ascending ramus, mandibular condyles, coronoid processes, gonial angles, and mental foramina.

Cranial landmarks used for metric analysis that lie on the mandible include Condylion, Gnathion, Gonion, and Infradentale.

Postcranial Skeleton

The postcranial skeleton is divided into axial and appendicular elements (Figure 4.10). The axial skeleton contains the bones of the trunk, including the ribs, sternum, vertebrae, sacrum, and hyoid. The appendicular skeleton consists of the bones of the limbs and limb girdles. Figure 4.11 illustrates the location and orientation of each postcranial element in the skeleton. More detailed descriptions and additional photographs of osteological features can be found in the reference texts suggested in "Supplementary Reading and Reference Materials."

Axial Skeletal Elements: Hyoid, Vertebrae, Sacrum, Sternum, and Ribs

Hyoid

The hyoid is a u-shaped bone found anterior to the cervical vertebrae in the neck. It is one of the few bones in the body that does not have a bony articulation with any other bone. The hyoid has three distinct parts: the body, greater horns, and lesser horns. The body of

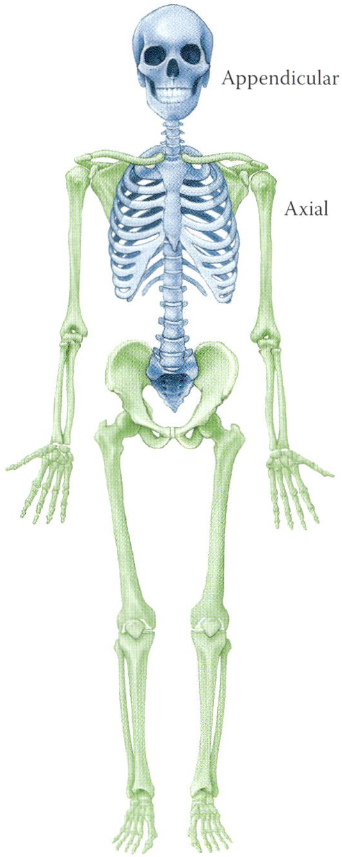

Figure 4.10 Axial and appendicular skeleton. (Figure by Jennifer Stowe.)

the hyoid is in the center of the bone. It has multiple sites for muscle attachments, many of which are used during speech. The greater horns project postero-laterally from the body. The lesser horns are found on the superior lateral aspect of the body. The fusion of the three parts of the hyoid is variable and not known to be age- or sex related (Scheuer and Black, 2000). The hyoid can be important in a forensic context, as it can show evidence of neck trauma such as that which occurs during strangulation.

Vertebrae

The vertebral column is the term typically used to identify the 33 bones that house the spinal cord, spanning from the base of the skull to the pelvic girdle. The vertebral column is important as it functions to support the body weight of an erect human. Additionally, its unique s-shape functions to align the trunk over our center of gravity (located at the pelvis). The vertebral column is composed of five different types of vertebrae: cervical, thoracic, lumbar, sacral, and coccygeal vertebrae. The cervical, thoracic, and lumbar vertebrae are found in the posterior midline of the body, and these vertebrae are normally moveable, although they may fuse in older or pathological individuals and become considerably less mobile (Figure 4.12). The sacral vertebrae are found within the pelvic girdle and are normally fused to one another in an adult, as are the coccygeal vertebrae.

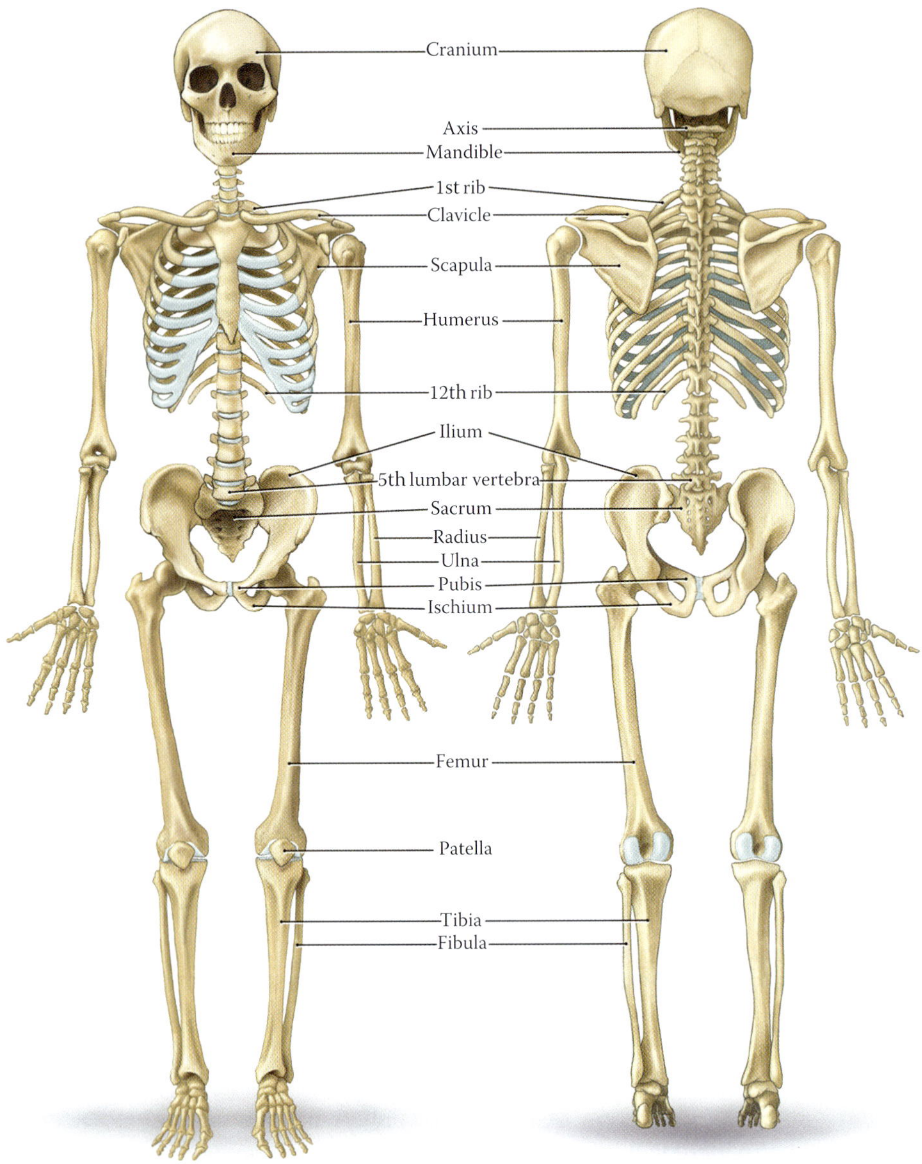

Figure 4.11 Major skeletal elements. (Figure by Jennifer Stowe.)

The cervical, thoracic, and lumbar vertebrae have several common features, including the fact that each of the 24 vertebrae that fall within these groups is separated by intervertebral disks. These fibrocartilage disks aid in shock absorption and allow for movement among the vertebrae. Other components shared by all vertebrae include the vertebral body, superior and inferior articular facets, spinous process, transverse processes, vertebral arch, vertebral foramen, lamina, and pedicle. The vertebral body is the ovoid-shaped portion of the vertebra that lies anterior to the pedicle and provides most of the weight-bearing support of the vertebral column. The vertebral bodies generally increase in size from superior to inferior, with the cervical bodies being the smallest and the lumbar bodies the largest. The lateral portion of the thoracic vertebral bodies contains articular facets for rib head

(a)

(b)

(c)

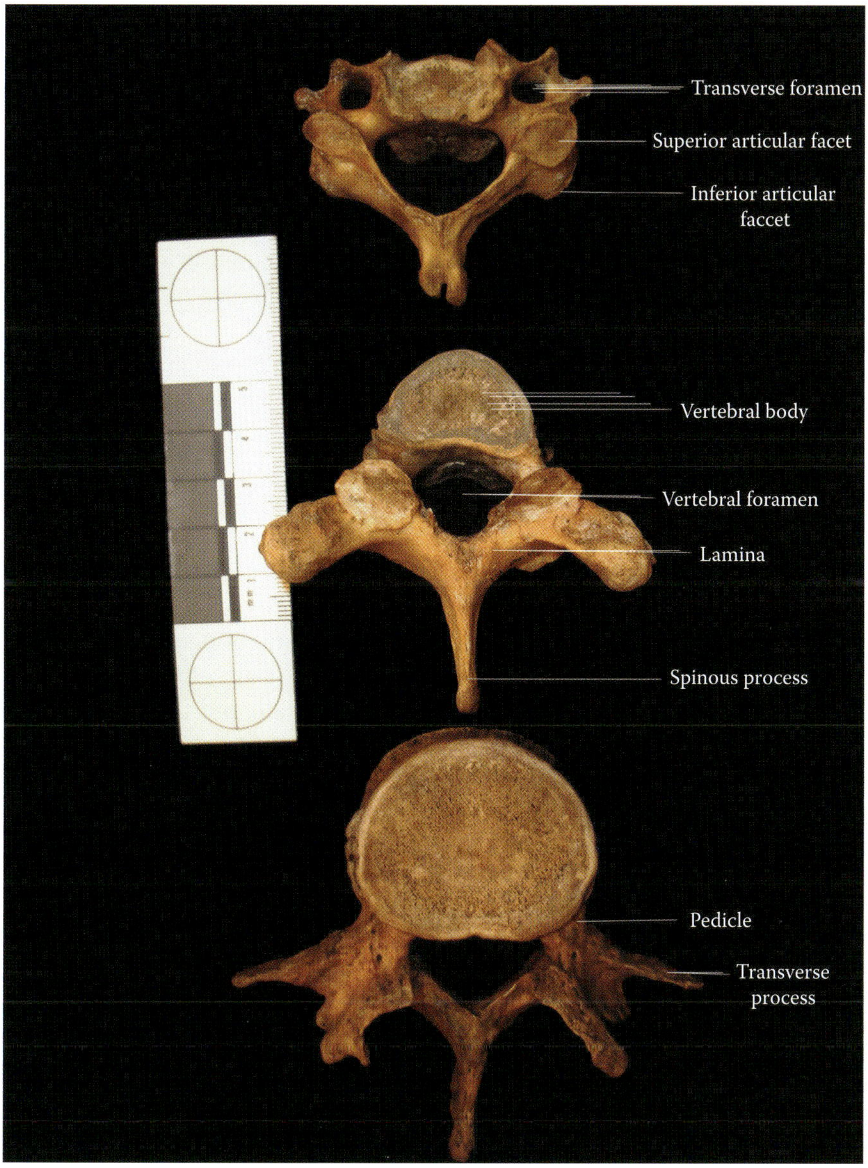

Figure 4.12 Vertebral elements: (a) Typical cervical, (b) thoracic, and (c) lumbar vertebra.

attachment. The superior articular facets are located on the superior surface of each vertebra and articulate with the inferior articular facets from the vertebra situated above. The spinous process is on the posterior surface of each vertebra in the midline of the bone. It serves as the site of ligamentous and muscular attachments and aids in movement of the vertebral column. The transverse processes are located on the lateral surfaces of each vertebra. The transverse processes are attachment sites for muscles and ligaments and aid in movement of the vertebral column. The transverse processes of the thoracic vertebrae have articular facets that serve as the sites of rib neck attachment. The vertebral arch is the ring of bone that surrounds the spinal cord. The vertebral arch is anterior to the spinous process and posterior to the vertebral body. The vertebral foramen is the space inside the vertebral arch through which the spinal cord passes. The lamina is a flattened portion of the vertebral arch that attaches the spinous process (posterior) to the pedicle (anterior). The pedicle is the portion of the vertebral arch which connects the vertebral body (anterior) to the lamina (posterior).

There are typically seven cervical vertebrae that sit directly below the skull in the posterior neck region. These cervical vertebrae are given the designation “C” (for cervical) followed by a number 1–7. They are numbered from superior to inferior, with the most superior cervical vertebra numbered as C1 and the most inferior cervical vertebra as C7. The first and second cervical vertebrae have a slightly different morphology than C3–C7. The atlas (C1) is the cervical vertebra that articulates with the inferior portion of the skull. It is named after the Greek Titan who was sentenced by Zeus to hold up the sky. The atlas has no body, spinous process, or intervertebral disks on the superior or inferior surfaces. The axis (C2) is the cervical vertebra that articulates inferior to the atlas and superior to C3. The axis does not have a vertebral body, yet its odontoid process (dens) projects superiorly and articulates with the atlas, creating a pivot point for the atlas. When nodding your head “yes” the cranial base pivots on the superior articular surfaces of the atlas. When shaking your head “no” the inferior articular surfaces of the atlas pivot on the superior articular surfaces of the axis. A unique feature of cervical vertebra is that each has transverse foramina located on vertebral arch lateral to the vertebral bodies. In life, these foramina are spaces in which the vertebral arteries travel into the base of the brain. Other distinctive properties are that the transverse processes are small, and the spinous processes are orientated horizontally and are frequently bifurcated at the tip.

Differentiating: C1 and C2 are easy to distinguish from the other cervical vertebrae based upon the characteristics mentioned previously. C7 can be distinguished because it is considered a transition vertebra (i.e., transitional in form between cervical and thoracic vertebrae, as it articulates with the first thoracic vertebra inferiorly). C7 has the largest body of all the cervical vertebrae and a spinous process similar to the thoracic vertebrae.

There are usually 12 thoracic vertebrae found in the posterior thorax, though some individuals may have 13. These vertebrae are given the distinction “T” (thoracic) followed by a number 1–12, with the most superior thoracic vertebra designated as T1 and the most inferior as T12. Thoracic vertebrae have characteristic costal facets or demifacets (half facets) located on the lateral surfaces of the vertebral bodies and the transverse processes. These allow for the articulation of the head of the rib and the neck of the rib, respectively. The spinous processes of the thoracic vertebrae are long and project inferiorly. When a thoracic vertebra is in proper anatomical position with the spinous process facing you, the overall morphology is often suggested to resemble a giraffe.

Differentiating: Several of the thoracic vertebrae can be distinguished from the others based upon their costal facet morphology. The first thoracic vertebra has a whole costal facet on the superior aspect of its body and a demifacet on the inferior aspect. T1 also has a spinous process and body similar to that of the cervical vertebrae. T10 has a single costal facet on the superior surface of both sides of the vertebral body and a facet on each transverse process. T11 has a single costal facet on the superior aspect of either side of the vertebral body but no articulation on the transverse processes. T12 resembles T11, but its inferior articular facets are oriented in an anterolateral position, much like the articular facets of the lumbar vertebrae. Since T12 is a transitional vertebra, it tends to look similar to a lumbar vertebra.

The lumbar vertebrae are the largest of the 24 trunk vertebrae. There are usually five lumbar vertebrae, though this can vary, with some people having six lumbar vertebrae, while others can have a sacralized fifth lumbar vertebra (L5 is fused to the sacrum). The lumbar vertebrae have large vertebral bodies and do not exhibit costal facets or transverse foramina. The spinous process is large and flat, while the transverse processes are smaller than the transverse processes on thoracic vertebrae. When the lumbar vertebra is in anatomical position with the spinous process facing you, the overall morphology is said to resemble a moose.

Differentiating: the first lumbar vertebra (L1) is the smallest of the lumbar vertebrae, while the fifth lumbar vertebra is the largest with widely flaring inferior articular facets for articulation with the sacrum.

Sacrum

The sacrum is composed of five sacral vertebrae that begin fusing together in early adolescence but do not complete fusion until postadolescence (S1–S2 are the last segments to complete fusion). The sacrum articulates superiorly with the inferior surface of the fifth lumbar vertebra, laterally with the iliac blades, and inferiorly with the coccyx. The major morphological characteristics of the sacrum include the alae, sacral auricular surfaces (sacroiliac joints), anterior sacral foramina, superior articular facets, and the median spine. The alae, or wings, project laterally and articulate with the iliac blades at the sacral auricular surfaces. The sacral nerves pass through the anterior sacral foramina on the anterior surface of the sacrum. The superior articular facets articulate with the inferior articular facets of the fifth lumbar vertebra. The median spine is a median projection on the posterior surface of the sacrum.

The most inferior portion of the vertebral column is called the coccyx. The coccyx is made up of three to five coccygeal segments that are variably fused. Often, portions of the coccyx are fused to the inferior surface of the sacrum. The most important bony landmark on the coccyx is the large tubercle on either side of the superior coccygeal body called the cornua.

Sternum

The sternum, or breast bone, is a midline structure located on the anterior portion of the thorax. It articulates superiorly with the clavicles and laterally with the ribs. The sternum is made up of three components: manubrium, sternal body, and xiphoid process. The manubrium is the thick and square-shaped superior portion of the sternum. The manubrium articulates with the clavicle via the clavicular notches on its superior surface. Between the clavicular notches, in the midline of the superior surface of the manubrium, is the suprasternal (jugular) notch. The sternal body (corpus sterni) is the middle portion of the sternum that is long and thin. The corpus sterni is formed by the fusion of several sternal segments, or sternebrae. The lateral portions of both the manubrium and the sternal body have structures called the costal notches, by which the ribs articulate with the sternum. The xiphoid process is the variably shaped structure at the inferior surface of the sternum. The three portions of the sternum fuse variably, and fusion (or lack thereof) is not known to be related to age or sex. In a small percentage of adults, the sternum has a midline foramen called a sternal foramen. To the untrained eye, this foramen can be mistaken for trauma (Figure 4.13).

Ribs

There are 24 ribs in the human skeleton—12 right ribs and 12 left ribs. Occasionally, there may be 11 or 13 ribs on a side, with the extra ribs typically occurring in the cervical or

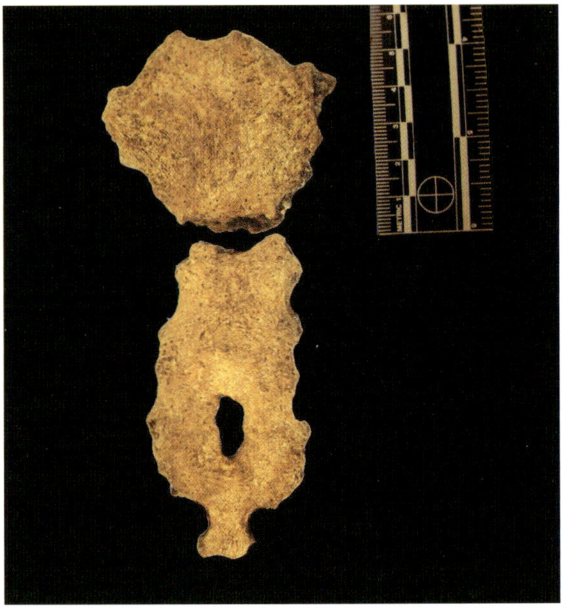

Figure 4.13 Sternum with sternal foramen.

lumbar area (Scheuer and Black, 2000). Ribs 1–10 articulate anteriorly with the sternum and posteriorly with the thoracic vertebrae, whereas ribs 11 and 12 articulate only with the vertebrae. Ribs 1–7 are referred to as true ribs because they articulate directly with the sternum via individual cartilaginous attachments. Ribs 8–10 are called false ribs because they articulate with the sternum via a common cartilaginous attachment. Ribs 11 and 12 are referred to as floating ribs because their medial ends do not articulate with the sternum.

Siding ribs 2–12: The sternal end of the rib is flat with a u-shaped excavation, and the vertebral end is rounded (this rounded feature is referred to as the rib head); the cranial or superior border of the rib is blunt, and the caudal or inferior surface is sharp. Rib 1 is flat and unusual compared to the rest of the ribs. To side the first rib, the head should point inferiorly when the sternal and vertebral ends are properly oriented. Ribs should be x-rayed and examined closely in forensic cases for evidence of sharp trauma and gunshot trauma. Furthermore, the subadult rib cage is frequently a site of healed fractures in child abuse cases.

Shoulder Girdle: Clavicle and Scapula

Clavicle

The clavicle is a tubular, s-shaped bone that is commonly called the "collar bone." The medial (sternal) end of the clavicle articulates with the sternum, and the lateral (acromial) end articulates with the acromion of the scapula. The clavicle is the first bone to ossify *in utero* and the last bone to fuse (the medial epiphysis completes fusion in the mid-20s). As such, the clavicle is important in a forensic context in that it provides accurate age estimates into the mid- to late 20s (Black and Scheuer, 1996; Langley-Shirley and Jantz, 2010; McKern and Stewart, 1957; Todd and D'Errico, 1928; Webb and Suchey, 1985).

Siding: The medial or sternal end is round, the lateral or acromial end is flat, the superior surface is smooth, and the inferior surface is irregular and rough; the medial half of the bone bows anteriorly, the lateral half bows posteriorly, and the acromial tip curves anteriorly.

Scapula

The scapula is a mostly flat, triangular-shaped bone that is located posterior to the rib cage and is commonly referred to as the shoulder blade. The scapula provides muscular attachment sites for the rotator cuff muscles, arm muscles, and many back muscles. The scapula articulates laterally with the head of the humerus and the acromial end of the clavicle. The glenoid cavity or glenoid fossa is the tear-drop shaped surface on the lateral aspect of the bone where the humeral head articulates. The scapular spine runs medio-laterally along the posterior surface of the bone and terminates at the lateral end into the enlarged process known as the acromion (the articulation site for the lateral aspect of the clavicle). The process protruding opposite of and anterior to the acromion is the coracoid process.

Siding: The smooth featureless surface of the scapula is anterior, the scapular spine is posterior, and the glenoid fossa is lateral. Much like the underlying ribs, the scapula should be inspected carefully for sharp force trauma. However, linear cracking of the thin bone can occur as the bone dries and weathers, and these taphonomic signatures should not be confused with sharp trauma.

Upper Limb: Humerus, Radius, Ulna, Carpals, Metacarpals, and Phalanges

Humerus

The humerus is the largest bone of the upper arm limb. It articulates proximally with the glenoid fossa of the scapula and distally with the radius and ulna. The humeral head is the rounded proximal feature of the bone that articulates with the glenoid fossa of the scapula in the gleno-humeral joint (a synovial joint). The rugose, roughened area on the lateral portion of the shaft is the deltoid tuberosity—an attachment site for the deltoid muscle of the shoulder. The distal end of the bone has an impression on the posterior surface called the olecranon fossa. The olecranon fossa accommodates the olecranon of the ulna during full extension of the arm and may be perforated, forming a foramen called a septal aperture. This foramen represents natural variation and should not be confused with perimortem trauma. The distal portion of the humeral shaft flares medially and laterally to form the medial and lateral epicondyles. The medial epicondyle is larger and more prominent than the lateral epicondyle; the epicondyles are attachment sites for many forearm muscles. The distal articular surface of the humerus is spool-shaped. The capitulum is the rounded lateral eminence of the spool that articulates with the head of the radius, and the trochlea is the medial grooved portion of the spool that articulates with the trochlear notch of the ulna.

Siding: The head is medial, the olecranon fossa is posterior, the deltoid tuberosity is lateral, and the nutrient foramen opens distally toward the elbow. The humerus is an important contributor to the biological profile because several measurements from humerus can be used to estimate sex with a high degree of accuracy (>90%) (Mall et al., 2001).

Radius

The radius is the lateral bone of the forearm. It articulates proximally with the capitulum of the humerus and the radial notch of the ulna and distally with the ulna, lunate, and scaphoid. The proximal end of the radius contains the rounded radial head. Immediately distal to the head is a rounded protuberance called the radial tuberosity or bicipital tuberosity where the biceps brachii muscle of the arm inserts. The ulnar notch is the concave hollow on the distal and medial surface where the radius articulates with the neighboring ulna. The styloid process is the pointed projection on the distal and lateral portion of the bone. The dorsal tubercle is the large tuberosity on the posterior aspect of the distal end. The interosseous crest is the sharp margin along the medial portion of the bone shaft where a tough fibrous membrane (a fibrous syndesmosis joint) attaches to the bone to divide the forearm into anterior and posterior compartments.

Siding: The head is proximal, the styloid process is distal and lateral, the ulnar notch is distal and medial, the interosseous crest and radial tuberosity are medial, the dorsal tubercle is posterior, and the nutrient foramen opens toward the elbow.

Ulna

The ulna is the medial bone of the forearm. It articulates proximally with the trochlea of the humerus and the head of the radius and distally with the ulnar notch of the radius. The proximal articular end of the ulna contains the u-shaped trochlear notch. The most proximal portion of the bone is the large, prominent olecranon process that serves as the insertion site of the triceps brachii muscle. You can feel the olecranon process as your bony elbow. The coronoid process is located opposite of and distal to the olecranon process. The radial notch is the small oval surface medial to the trochlear notch that receives the head of the radius. The interosseous crest is the sharp medial edge of the shaft. The styloid process is the sharp, most distal projection of the bone.

Siding: The olecranon process is proximal, the coronoid process is proximal and anterior, the styloid process is distal and posterior, the interosseous membrane and radial notch are lateral, and the nutrient foramen opens toward the elbow.

Carpals

The wrist is comprised of eight carpal bones. They are oriented in two rows, a proximal and distal row. When the bones are in anatomical position, the carpals in the proximal row (lateral to medial) are the scaphoid (navicular), lunate, triquetral, and pisiform. The carpals in the distal row (lateral to medial) are the trapezium (greater multangular), trapezoid (lesser multangular), capitate, and hamate (Figure 4.14).

- The scaphoid (navicular) articulates with the lunate and the distal radius as well as the capitate, trapezium, and trapezoid. The scaphoid has a *tubercle*, which is the blunt nonarticular portion of the bone. *Siding:* With the concave surface facing toward you, and the tubercle curving toward the ground, the tubercle will be on the side it is from.
- The lunate articulates with the distal radius, scaphoid, capitate, and triquetral, and indirectly with the ulna. *Siding:* If the crescent is facing down and the rounded facet points away from you, the flat facet facing you leans toward the side of origin.
- The triquetral articulates with the lunate, capitate, and pisiform. *Siding:* With the point of the triquetral facing up, the large facet is on the side of origin.
- The pisiform articulates with only the triquetral and forms within the flexor carpi ulnaris muscle. *Siding:* Place the bulging side of the pisiform away from you, with the round facet for the triquetral pointing down. The protrusion will point toward the side from which the bone comes.

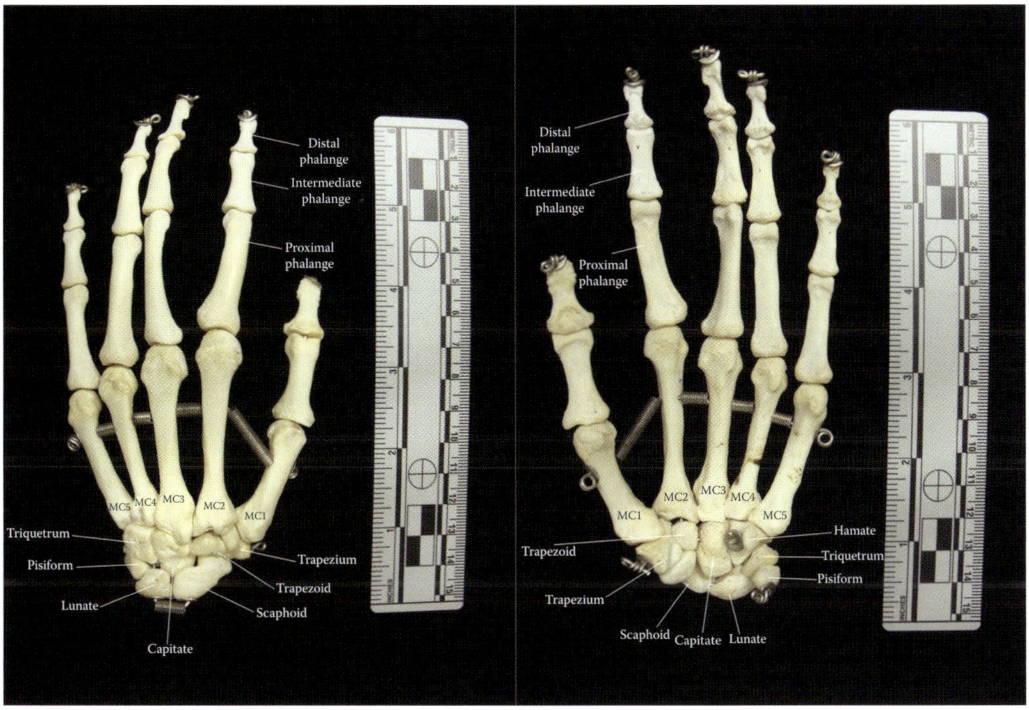

(a) (b)

Figure 4.14 (a) Dorsal view of the hand and (b) palmar view of the hand.

- The trapezium (greater multangular) articulates with the scaphoid, trapezoid (lesser multangular) and the first metacarpal. *Siding:* With the saddle facet facing upward, the ridge will pass down from the facet and point toward the side of origin.
- The trapezoid (lesser multangular) articulates with the trapezium (greater multangular), scaphoid, capitate, and second metacarpal. The trapezoid is shaped like a small boot. *Siding:* With the V-shaped ridge of the boot facing you and the sole of the boot on the table, the toe will point toward the side from which it comes.
- The capitate articulates with the trapezoid (lesser multangular), scaphoid, lunate, hamate, and the third metacarpal. The *head* of the capitate is the rounded end of the bone while the *base* is the squared portion of the bone. *Siding:* With the base pointed downward, the head up, and the narrow articular surface facing you, the articular surface is on the side of origin.
- The hamate articulates with the triquetral, capitates, and the fourth and fifth metacarpals. The *hamulus* of the hamate is the arch-shaped projection that does not articulate with any other bone. *Siding:* With the nonarticular flat surface pointing down, the large articular surface toward you, and the hamulus away from you, the hamulus leans toward the side the from which the bone comes.

Metacarpals

The palm of the hand is made up of five metacarpals. These metacarpals are designated MC 1 (thumb) through MC5 (the little finger), each corresponding with the developmental rays of the hand (Figure 4.14). The metacarpals are tube-shaped bones, each with a single distal articular surface that is rounded (head) and a proximal square base. It is this base that allows for differentiating and siding the metacarpals. Metacarpals 2–5 articulate with one another and with the distal row of carpals and the proximal row of phalanges.

- The first metacarpal does not articulate with any of the other metacarpals but does articulate proximally with the trapezium (greater multangular) at a rather large articular facet and distally with the first proximal phalange. *Siding:* With the dorsal surface facing you, the base of MC1 projects farther on the side from which the bone comes.
- The second metacarpal is usually the longest; MC2 articulates proximally with the trapezoid, capitate, and trapezium, medially with MC3, and distally with the second proximal phalange. The base has two processes, one pointed and the other more broad. *Siding:* With the dorsal (palmar) surface facing you, the longer process on the base of MC2 points toward MC3. The butterfly-shaped facet is medial and articulates with MC3.
- The third metacarpal has a single, sharp projection (styloid process) at the base. The base of MC3 articulates with the capitate; MC3 articulates laterally with MC2, medially with MC4, and distally with the third proximal phalange. *Siding:* With the dorsal side facing you, the styloid process points toward MC2, and the butterfly-shaped facet points toward and articulates medially with MC4.
- The fourth metacarpal is shorter than the second and third metacarpals. Its very square base articulates proximally with the hamate and sometimes the capitate. The base also articulates laterally and medially with MC3 and MC5, respectively. The head of MC4 articulates distally with the fourth proximal phalange. *Siding:* With the dorsal side facing you, the single, butterfly-shaped facet is medial and articulates with MC5, while the lateral surface has two small, rounded facets that articulate with MC3.
- The fifth metacarpal is the shortest of MC2–MC5. Its base articulates proximally with the hamate and laterally with MC4. The head of MC5 articulates distally with the fifth proximal phalange. *Siding:* The side of the base that does not have an articular surface is medial. The articular surface of the base points laterally toward MC4.

Phalanges

The hand has 14 phalanges: three phalanges on each of the second to fifth fingers and two phalanges on the thumb. Each finger has a proximal, middle, and distal phalange except for the thumb, which only has a proximal and distal phalange (Figure 4.14). Proximal phalanges have a single concave proximal articular facet for articulation with the head of the metacarpals. Intermediate phalanges have a double concave proximal articular facet. Distal phalanges have a double concave proximal articular facet and a flat nonarticular distal end. The finger phalanges are anteroposteriorly flattened and semicircular in cross section. The proximal and distal thumb phalanges are readily distinguishable from the other hand phalanges, as the proximal and distal thumb phalanges are shorter and thicker than the other proximal and distal phalanges of the hand. Siding phalanges is nearly impossible unless the whole hand is present or antemortem radiographs are obtained. Therefore, they are inventoried as the number of proximal, intermediate, and distal phalanges that are present.

Pelvic Girdle

Os Coxae (Innominates)

The hip bones are referred to as the right and left os coxae (plural), meaning "bone of the tail region." They are irregularly shaped and, as such, are also called the innominates, meaning "bones with no name." Each os coxa (singular) articulates posteriorly and medially with the sacrum, laterally with the head of the femur, and anteriorly with its counterpart at the pubic symphysis. The os coxa consists of three separate elements in subadults: the ilium, ischium, and pubis. These elements fuse to form a single bone in the adult skeleton. The ilium is the large, laterally situated, blade-like portion of the os coxa. The postero-inferior portion of the ilium contains the u-shaped greater sciatic notch. The posterior portion contains the ear-shaped auricular surface where the ilium articulates with the sacrum. The ischium is the blunt inferior portion of the os coxa known as the "sit bones." The hamstring muscles attach to the rugose ischial tuberosity. The pubis is the anterior portion of the os coxa. The pubic symphysis is the oval-shaped joint surface located medially. The superior pubic ramus is the strut of bone that connects the pubis to the ilium, and the ischiopubic ramus is the strut of bone connecting the pubis to the ischium. The obturator foramen is the large foramen formed by the superior pubic ramus and ischiopubic ramus. The acetabulum is the round socket on the lateral surface of the os coxa where the head of the femur articulates with the pelvis. The acetabulum is formed from portions of the ilium, ischium, and pubis.

Siding: The acetabulum is lateral, the ilium is lateral and superior, the auricular surface is posterior, the pubic symphysis is anterior, and the ischial tuberosity is inferior. Forensically, the os coxa is one of the most important skeletal elements for constructing a biological profile. Many pelvic features are used to determine sex, including the greater sciatic notch, ischiopubic ramus, and obturator foramen, as well as the overall shape of the bone (see Chapter 8). In addition, the pubic symphysis and auricular surface are important features for age estimation (see Chapters 9 and 10).

Lower Limb: Femur, Patella, Tibia, Fibula, Tarsals, Metatarsals, and Phalanges

Femur

The femur is typically the longest and heaviest bone in the body. It is commonly referred to as the "thigh bone," and it articulates proximally with the os coxa at the acetabulum and distally with the tibia and patella. The head of the femur lies at the proximal end of the bone and is the rounded portion of the bone that articulates with the acetabulum of the os coxa via a ball and socket joint (a synovial diarthrotic joint). The head of the femur can be distinguished easily from the head of the humerus, as the head of the femur is more sphere-shaped, while the humeral head is typically hemispheric. The fovea capitis is the small notch found on the medial surface of the femoral head where the ligamentum teres attaches the femoral head firmly to the acetabulum of the os coxa. The neck of the femur is the strut of bone that attaches the head to the shaft of the femur. The greater trochanter is the large prominence on the lateral surface of the proximal femur. It is the insertion site for multiple muscles of the hip and thigh that aid in bipedal locomotion. The lesser trochanter is a smaller prominence on the postero-medial surface of the proximal femur near the femoral neck; it is the site of hip flexor muscle attachments. The femoral shaft is the term used to refer to the long tube of bone that extends from the proximal to distal ends of the femur. The linea aspera is an elevated ridge running most of the length of the posterior femoral shaft that serves as a site of muscle attachment for multiple muscles of the thigh and hip, including the powerful adductor muscle group. The nutrient foramen is found on the posterior surface of the midshaft near the linea aspera. The distal end of the bone has both condyles and epicondyles. The medial condyle is the large articular surface on the medial side of the distal femur. The medial condyle typically projects more distally than the lateral condyle. The lateral condyle, then, is the articular surface on the lateral side of the distal femur. The medial epicondyle is the projection on the medial surface of the medial condyle and is the site of ligamentous attachment. The lateral epicondyle is a projection on the lateral surface of the lateral condyle, and is the site of a ligamentous and muscle attachments. The patellar articular surface is a smooth articular surface on the anterior portion of the distal femur that allows for the movement of the patella over the distal femur during flexion and extension. The lateral portion of this articular surface is raised and projects more anteriorly than the medial aspect to guard against lateral dislocation of the patella during extension.

Siding: The head is proximal and medial, and the condyles are distal. The greater trochanter is lateral. The nutrient foramen opens distally, or away from the knee ("flees the knee"). The patellar articular surface is anterior, and the lesser trochanter and linea aspera are posterior. The femur contributes important metric information to help determine the sex, ancestry, and stature components of the biological profile.

Patella

The patella is a large sesamoid bone (i.e., a bone that develops and is encased in a tendon) that articulates with the distal femur and is often called the knee cap. The patella lies within the quadriceps tendon and glides smoothly over the knee joint. The patella has three major components: the apex, the medial articular facet, and the lateral articular facet. The apex of the patella is the pointy nonarticular portion of the patella that points distally. The medial articular facet is on the posterior surface and is smaller than the lateral articular facet. The lateral articular facet is on the posterior surface of the patella and is the larger of the two facets.

Siding: Place the patella on a flat surface with the articular processes touching the surface and with the apex pointed away from you; the patella will fall to the side from which it comes (since the larger articular surface is lateral).

Tibia

The tibia, or shin bone, is the largest bone in the lower leg and supports the majority of the weight placed upon the leg. It lies in the medial position. It articulates superiorly with the femur, laterally with the fibula (at the proximal and distal ends) and distally with the talus. The following is a description of some of the major features of the tibia. The tibial plateau is the proximal surface with which the distal femur articulates. The tibial plateau is divided into the medial condyle and the lateral condyle. The medial condyle is the medial portion of the tibial plateau, while the lateral condyle is the lateral portion of the tibial plateau. The superior fibular articular facet is on the postero-inferior portion of the lateral condyle. The tibial tuberosity is on the anterior surface of the proximal tibia just inferior to the tibial plateau. It is the site of a ligamentous attachment. The nutrient foramen is on the posterior surface of the bone, proximal to the midshaft. The anterior crest is the sharp portion of the anterior shaft that is commonly referred to as the shin. The interosseous crest is on the lateral portion of the shaft and serves to attach the interosseous membrane that binds the shafts of the tibia and fibula. The medial malleolus is a bulbous projection on the disto-medial surface of the tibia. It forms the medial bulge of the ankle and articulates with the talus. The fibular notch is the most disto-lateral edge of the tibia. This is the site of the ligamentous attachment creating the distal tibio-fibular syndesmosis. This syndesmosis binds the distal ends of both bones in a tight u-shaped attachment that surrounds the trochlea of the talus. The inferior fibular articular surface is the articular surface of the distal tibia that lies on the inferior portion of the fibular notch.

Siding: The tibial plateau is proximal. The medial malleolus is distal and medial. The fibular notch is distal and lateral. The tibial tuberosity and anterior crest are anterior. The nutrient foramen opens away from the knee ("flees the knee"). The tibia can provide metric information important for the estimating stature and sex.

Fibula

The fibula is the lateral bone in the leg. It is a long and skinny bone that is easily broken with laterally applied force. The fibula articulates proximally with the tibia and distally with the tibia and talus. The head, styloid process, shaft, interosseous crest, malleolar articular surface, malleolar fossa, and the nutrient foramen are important features of the fibula. The head is the bulbous proximal end of the fibula. It is larger and more rounded than the distal end of the fibula. The head also has a proximal projection on the posterior surface called the styloid process. The shaft of the fibula is thin tube of bone attaching the proximal and distal ends of the fibula. The interosseous crest is a raised crest of bone that runs the medial length of the shaft. It is the site of the interosseous ligament attachment that binds the shafts of the tibia and fibula together. The malleolar articular surface is the distal articular surface of the fibula. It is a flattened triangular surface that points medially and articulates with the talus. The malleolar fossa lies posterior to the malleolar articular surface and is the site of ligamentous attachments for the ankle joint. The nutrient foramen is found on the posterior surface of the fibula near midshaft.

Siding: The head is proximal, the malleolar fossa is distal and posterior. The nutrient foramen opens away from the knee ("flees the knee"). If you position the head superiorly, turn the malleolar fossa toward you and place your thumb in the fossa, you thumb nail will point in the direction from which the bone comes. The fibula can provide accurate stature estimates.

Tarsals

The tarsals form the posterior portion of the foot and the anterior portion of the longitudinal arch. The foot has seven tarsals: calcaneus, talus, navicular, cuboid, medial (first) cuneiform, intermediate (second) cuneiform, and lateral (third) cuneiform (Figure 4.15).

- The calcaneus is the largest tarsal and forms the heel of the foot. The calcaneal or Achilles tendon inserts on the most posterior portion of the calcaneus (the *calcaneal tuber*). The calcaneus articulates superiorly with the talus and anteriorly (distally) with the cuboid. The medial shelf-like projection that supports the head of the talus is referred to the *sustentaculum tali*. *Siding:* The calcaneal tuber is posterior, the largest articular facet is superior, and the *sustentaculum tali* is medial; when held in anatomical position, the larger superior facet is on the side from which the bone comes.

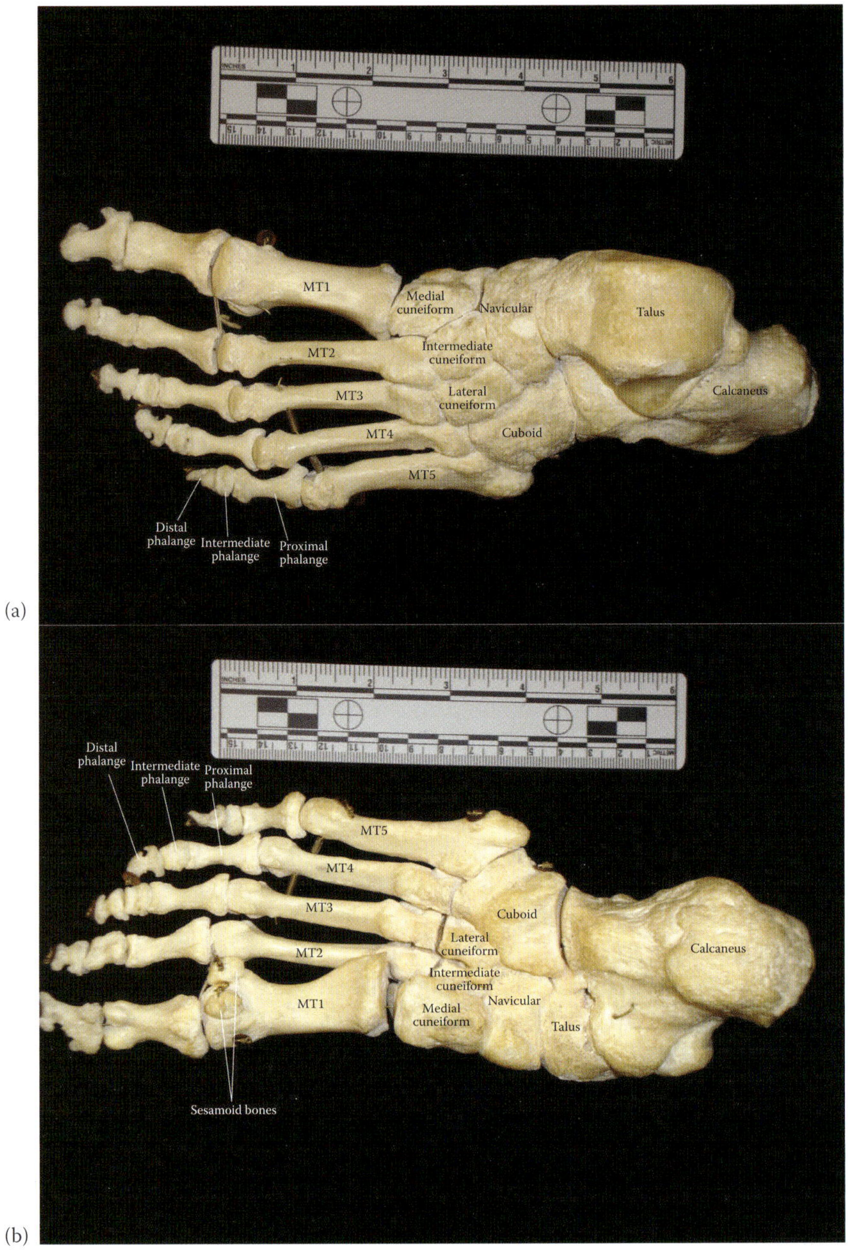

Figure 4.15 (a) Dorsal view of the foot and (b) plantar view of the foot.

- The talus is the second largest tarsal bone. It articulates superiorly and medially with the tibia, laterally with the fibula, inferiorly with the calcaneus, and anteriorly with the navicular. The most obvious features of the talus are the saddle-shaped *trochlea* that articulates with the tibia and fibula and the round *head* that articulates with the navicular. *Siding:* The trochlea is superior, the head is anterior; when viewed from above, the head is on the medial side of the bone, and the articular surface for the fibula is on the side from which the bone comes.

- The navicular is a bowl-shaped bone because of the concave proximal surface where it articulates with the head of the talus. Distally, the navicular articulates with the medial, intermediate, and lateral cuneiforms via a three-part articular surface. *Siding:* The concave surface is proximal, the three-part surface is distal, and the projecting tubercle is medial.
- The cuboid is located on the lateral side of the foot; it articulates proximally with the calcaneus, medially with the navicular and lateral cuneiform, and distally with the fourth and fifth metatarsals. The cuboid has a large tuberosity on the infero-lateral surface of the bone called the *cuboid tuberosity. Siding:* Look at the flat nonarticular surface of the bone with the cuboid tuberosity facing you; the bone will resemble a ballerina's foot, and the toe (the pointed tip) is on the side from which the bone comes.
- The medial (first) cuneiform is the largest cuneiform. It articulates proximally with the navicular, distally with the first metatarsal, and laterally with the intermediate (second) cuneiform. *Siding:* Hold the bone with the point up and the L-shaped articular facet facing you (the L will be upside-down); the tip points to the side from which the bone comes.
- The intermediate (second) cuneiform is the smallest cuneiform. It articulates proximally with the navicular, distally with the second metatarsal, medially with the medial cuneiform, and laterally with the lateral cuneiform. *Siding:* Hold the bone with the pistol-shaped facet facing you; the barrel of the gun points to the side from which the bone comes.
- The lateral (third) cuneiform articulates proximally with the navicular, distally with the third metatarsal, medially with the intermediate cuneiform, and laterally with the cuboid. *Siding:* Hold the bone with the double facet facing you (this facet resembles a butterfly's wing); the narrower side of the bone points to the side from which the bone comes.

Metatarsals

The five metatarsals form the anterior portion of the longitudinal arch and are situated between the tarsals proximally and the phalanges distally (Figure 4.15). Metatarsals have a rounded head distally and a concave or flat base proximally.

- The first metatarsal is the shortest and most robust metatarsal; it articulates distally with the first proximal phalange, proximally with the medial (first) cuneiform, and laterally with the second metatarsal. *Siding:* The concave base is proximal, the round head is distal, the single round portion of the head is superior, the grooved portion of the head is inferior, the flat nonarticular surface is medial, and the convex lateral side with an articular facet for the second metatarsal is latcral.
- The second metatarsal is usually the longest metatarsal; it articulates distally with the second proximal phalange, proximally with the intermediate cuneiform, medially with the first metatarsal, and laterally with the third metatarsal. The base of the second metatarsal is triangular in shape, and the distal shaft has a single medial facet for articulation with the first metatarsal and a double lateral facet for articulation with the third metatarsal.

- The third metatarsal articulates proximally with the lateral cuneiform, distally with the third proximal phalange, medially with the second metatarsal, and laterally with the fourth metatarsal. The base is triangular in shape, and the distal shaft has a double medial facet for articulation with the second metatarsal and a rather large, single lateral facet for articulation with the fourth metatarsal.
- The fourth metatarsal articulates proximally with the cuboid, distally with the fourth proximal phalange, medially with the third metatarsal, and laterally with the fifth metatarsal. The base of the fourth metatarsal is distinctly square and resembles a slice of bread. The distal shaft has single medial and lateral articular facets for the adjacent third and fifth metatarsals.
- The fifth metatarsal articulates proximally with the cuboid, distally with the fifth proximal phalange, and medially with the fourth metatarsal. The distal shaft has a single large medial articular facet for the adjacent fourth metatarsal and a long pointed nonarticular lateral surface. *Siding metatarsals 2–5*: The base is proximal, the round head is distal, the single rounded portion of the head is dorsal (superior), and the double rounded portion of the head is plantar (inferior); held in anatomical position, the base of the metatarsal leans to the side from which the bone comes.

Phalanges

As with the hand, the foot has 14 phalanges: three phalanges on each of the second to fifth toes and two phalanges on the great toe. Each toe consists of a proximal, middle, and distal phalange except for the great toe, which only has a proximal and distal phalange (Figure 4.15). Proximal phalanges have a single concave proximal articular facet and a head with two rounded protrusions. Intermediate phalanges have a double concave proximal articular facet and a head with two rounded protrusions. Distal phalanges have a double concave articular facet and a flat nonarticular distal end. Proximal toe phalanges can be distinguished from proximal finger phalanges by examining the shape of the shaft: finger phalanges are anteroposteriorly flattened and ovoid in cross section, whereas toe phalanges are narrower in the medio-lateral dimension and rounder in cross section. Intermediate and distal toe phalanges are not likely to be confused with their finger counterparts because toe phalanges are much smaller. Siding phalanges is a nearly impossible task unless the entire foot is present, and even then it can be extremely challenging. Consequently, phalanges are usually inventoried only as proximal, intermediate, and distal when writing up a forensic case report. Interestingly, foot bones can tell a lot about a person, including preferred shoe type, athletic activities, habitual activities and postures, and health information (i.e., gout or congenital defects).

References

Black S and Scheuer L. 1996. Age changes in the clavicle from the early neonatal period to skeletal maturity. *Int J Osteoarchaeol* 6:425–434.

Langley-Shirley NR and Jantz RL. 2010. A Bayesian approach to age estimation in modern Americans from the clavicle. *J Forensic Sci* 55(3):571–583.

Mall G, Hubig M, Buttner A, Kuznik J, Penning R, and Graw M. 2001. Sex determination and estimation of stature from the longbones of the arm. *Forensic Sci Int* 117(1–2):23–30.

McKern T and Stewart T. 1957. *Skeletal Age Changes in Young American Males Analysed from the Standpoint of Age Identification.* Natick, MA: Quartermaster Research and Development Center, Environmental Protection Research Division. pp. 89–97.

Ross MH, Romrell LJ, and Gordon IK. 1989. Bone In *Histology A Text and Atlas*, 3rd ed., pp. 150–187, Williams and Wilkins, Baltimore, MD.

Scheuer L and Black S. 2000. *Developmental Juvenile Osteology.* New York: Academic Press.

Todd T and D'Errico J. 1928. The clavicular epiphyses. *Am J Anat* 41:25–50.

Webb P and Suchey J. 1985. Epiphyseal union of the anterior iliac crest and medial clavicle in a modern multiracial sample of American males and females. *Am J Phys Anthropol* 68(4):457–466.

Supplementary Reading and Reference Materials

Bass WM. 2005. *Human Osteology: A Laboratory and Field Manual*, 5th edn. Missouri Archaeological Society, Colombia, MO.

Buikstra JE and Ubelaker DH. 1994. *Standards for Data Collection from Human Skeletal Remains.* Arkansas Archeological Survey, Fayetteville, AR.

Moore-Jansen PM, Ousley SD, and Jantz RL. 1994. *Data Collection Procedures for Forensic Skeletal Material.* University of Tennessee Anthropology Department, Knoxville, TN.

Scheuer L and Black S. 2000. *Developmental Juvenile Osteology.* New York: Academic Press.

Scheuer L, Black S, and Schaefer MC. 2008. *Juvenile Osteology: A Laboratory and Field Manual.* New York: Academic Press.

White TD and Folkens PA. 2005. *The Human Bone Manual.* New York: Academic Press.

Human Odontology and Dentition in Forensic Anthropology

5

DEBRA PRINCE ZINNI AND KATE M. CROWLEY

Contents

Estimating the biological profile for an unknown individual is a crucial part of forensic anthropology, bioarchaeology, and paleodemography. Teeth are often recovered in forensic cases, mass disasters, armed conflicts, and mass graves associated with human rights violations, all of which may result in mass casualties or commingled remains. Due to its vast postmortem longevity, dentition is an important tool in determining the biological profile and identity of an individual.

Dentition offers immense information in the forensic setting, providing important clues about the identity of an unknown individual. Due to their highly mineralized composition, teeth are highly resistant to physical and chemical influences and therefore have a vast postmortem longevity. Teeth are the most durable structures in the human body; they are more resilient than bone and thus are often the only human remains recovered from forensic scenes and archaeological sites (Maples 1978, Marcsik et al. 1992, Ohtani 1995, Prince 2004, Prince and Konigsberg 2008).

Physical anthropologists utilize dental features in three main areas: paleontology, skeletal biology, and forensic anthropology. Within paleontology, dental morphology is often utilized to reconstruct phylogenetic relationships (i.e., evolutionary relationships among organisms). Skeletal biologists use dental characteristics to surmise population adaptations to environmental factors, as well as to assess an individual's ability to survive in particular environments. Forensic anthropologists use dentition as a means of positive identification of unknown skeletal remains. This chapter will focus on the latter use of dental information and will provide an overview of dental morphology and how dentition is utilized in the identification process.

Forensic anthropologists work very closely with forensic odontologists, who are licensed dentists applying their knowledge of dentition, dental appliances, and dental work to medicolegal matters, particularly in the realm of positive identification and bite-mark analysis. Forensic odontology is the scientific discipline that utilizes the principles of dentistry to aid in the positive identification of human remains. The assistance of forensic odontologists is often requested when human remains are decomposed, burned, skeletonized, or beyond the point of clear facial recognition due to severe facial disfigurement. The successful use of the human dentition, as a means to identify unknown individuals, is correlated to three basic facts about teeth: the survivability of dental evidence, infinite points of dental comparison, and dynamic and accessible patient-dental databases (Kessler 1997).

Teeth have an outer enamel layer, making them one of the hardest substances in the human body. They are not easily destroyed by high temperatures, decomposition, desiccation, or long-term submersion in water, which is particularly beneficial in incidences of mass disasters or fragmentation (Kessler 1997). In addition, the materials dentists typically use during the restorative phase of treatment, including amalgam, porcelain, gold, and resins, are very resilient to exposure to extreme environments (Kessler 1997). Specifically, gold alloys, fused porcelain, synthetic porcelain, and porcelain denture teeth can withstand temperatures greater than 1600°F (Kessler 1997). Consequently, dental evidence has a high survivability and is sometimes the only evidence remaining at a scene.

Another aspect of dentition that makes it useful in a forensic setting is that, much like fingerprints, each person's dentition is unique. The human permanent dentition is typically composed of 32 teeth. Each tooth can be virgin, restored, rotated, fractured, and/or missing. When restored or fractured, any of five different tooth surfaces may be involved for each of the 32 teeth. In addition to surfaces restored and fractured, forensic odontologists can analyze the size, depth, and anatomy of altered tooth surface(s) providing infinite points of dental comparison between antemortem and postmortem dental radiographs (Kessler 1997).

A high percentage of the general population seeks dental care on a regular basis, therefore providing criteria for positive identification in the form of patient databases for many individuals. Dentists commonly update dental radiographs every 12–16 months, providing a dynamic database of individuals' unique and changing dental features (Kessler 1997). These radiographs not only depict the unique pattern of virgin, restored, or damaged teeth, but also document the roots of each tooth, thereby providing an additional data set with which to compare antemortem and postmortem radiographs (Kessler 1997).

Tooth Anatomy and Dental Morphology

The dental-facial complex, often referred to as the splanchnocranium, is not a static entity as it changes with the development of the mandible, face, and dentition. Therefore, a dynamic relationship exists between the hard and soft palate of the oral cavity. Several factors affect the dental-facial complex: genetic composition, environmental factors (such as nutrition and healthcare), and functional factors (such as muscle movements).

The main function of the dental-facial complex is mastication (chewing); secondary functions include breathing, speech, vision, olfaction, and hearing.

Tooth Anatomy

Three groups of tissues comprise the dental-facial complex: skeletal tissues, soft tissues, and dental tissues. Skeletal tissues in the splanchnocranium include bone and cartilage, while soft tissue refers to muscles, glands, nervous, and vascular structures. The five dental tissues found in the dental-facial complex are enamel, dentin, cementum, pulp, and gingiva (Figure 5.1). Teeth are highly mineralized, with the majority of the tooth being composed of hydroxyapatite (Ca_{10} $[PO_4]_6[OH])_2$. Enamel is the hardest element in the human body and composed of approximately 97% hydroxyapatite and approximately 3% water and organic material (Schroeder 1991). Dentin is less mineralized, composed of approximately 70% hydroxyapatite, calcium, and phosphate, approximately 20% organic materials (primary proteins), and approximately 10% water (Schroeder 1991). Cementum is composed of approximately 45% hydroxyapatite, approximately 33% proteins (mainly collagen), and approximately 22% water (Schroeder 1991).

The crown and root comprise the gross anatomy of the tooth. The crown is covered by enamel and is the portion of the tooth that is exposed in the oral cavity. The root is covered by cementum and is the portion of the tooth anchored to the alveolar bone in a special joint called a gomphosis. Within the gomphosis, the periodontal ligament anchors the tooth to the alveolar bone of the maxilla and mandible. The alveolar bone between two teeth is called the interdental septum, while the alveolar bone between two roots of a single tooth

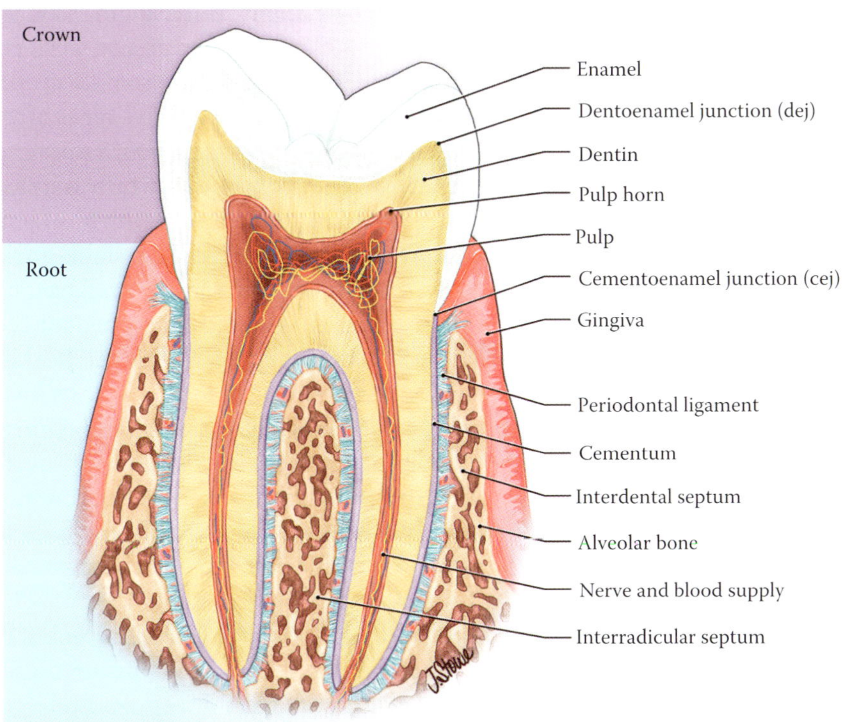

Figure 5.1 Diagram of tooth cross-sectional anatomy.

is called the interradicular septum. The neck of the tooth refers to the region of the root immediately adjacent to the crown, while the cemento–enamel junction (CEJ) is the point of junction of the crown and root. The apical foramen is located at the apex of the tooth root and is the opening through which the nerve, blood, and lymph supply each tooth.

Enamel is the hardest, most mineralized, and most brittle (i.e., least pliable or ductile) material in the human body and is composed mainly of calcium and phosphorus (Schroeder 1991). Enamel is an acellular material that covers the crown of the tooth (Schroeder 1991), and, as such, it does not have any capacity to remodel.

Dentin forms the bulk of the tooth and is not normally exposed in the oral cavity. In the crown, enamel covers the coronal dentin, and, in the root, a hard substance called cementum covers the root dentin. Attrition, carious lesions, age, and fracture can expose dentin. Microscopically, dentin is composed of intertubular dentin, which is formed during odonotogenesis, and of dentin tubules, which contain specialized odontoblastic processes that secrete dentin during tooth formation (Schroeder 1991). Peritubular dentin, which lines the inner walls of the dentin tubules, is deposited gradually throughout life (Schroeder 1991). Peritubular dentin has a higher mineralized content than intertubular dentin due to differences in the organic matrices of these compounds, the former composed of mucopolysaccharides, while the latter is composed of collagen (Schroeder 1991). Since peritubular dentin is gradually deposited throughout life, the pulp cavity is gradually reduced, in addition to the diameter of the dentin tubules. Primary dentin consists of all dentin that is formed until completion of the root, while dentin deposited after the completion of the root is termed secondary dentin (Schroeder 1991).

Cementum is a mineralized, avascular connective tissue that coats the tooth root between the dentin and periodontal ligament (Schroeder 1991). The primary function of cementum is to anchor the collagen fibers of the periodontal ligament to the tooth, thus anchoring the tooth firmly to the alveolar bone (Schroeder 1991). Cementum also performs adaptive and reparative processes to orthopedic forces and trauma to the root (Schroeder 1991). Cementum is laid down in two forms, acellular and cellular, of which, five types of cementum can be distinguished in human teeth: acellular, afibrillar cementum, which does not contain cementocytes or collagen fibers; acellular extrinsic fiber cementum, which is almost exclusively composed of Sharpey's fibers; cellular mixed fiber cementum, which is composed of cementocytes, Sharpey's fibers and intrinsic bundles of collagen fibers; cellular intrinsic fiber cementum, which is composed of cementocytes and intrinsic bundles of collagen fibers; and Intermediate cementum (Schroeder 1991, Kagerer and Grupe 2001). Intermediate cementum, which is acellular, lines the entire root in a very thin sheath. An additional, thicker layer of acellular cementum is located at the cervical (neck) region of the tooth, while cellular cementum is laid down on the remaining one-half to two-thirds of the tooth root (Schroeder 1991).

The pulp, or pulp organ, is the nerve center of the tooth and is centrally located in the pulp chamber of the tooth (Schroeder 1991). The pulp has sensory, reparative, and nutritive properties (Schroeder 1991). Odontoblasts, which are specialized cells that secrete dentin, line the inside edge of the pulp chamber. As a result, the pulp chamber changes shape with age, becoming smaller as secondary dentin forms and is laid down in the pulp chamber.

The gingiva (gums) is part of the oral mucosa and mirrors the alveolar bone and cemento–enamel junction. The function of the gingiva is to help anchor the teeth and secure them in the alveolar bone (Schroeder 1991). In addition, the gingiva offers a peripheral defense against infection since it has a high turnover rate of epithelial and connective tissue components (Schroeder 1991). Typical dental nomenclature can be found in Box 5.1

BOX 5.1 DIAGRAM OF DENTAL NOMENCLATURE; COMMON TERMINOLOGY USED TO REFER TO THE TOOTH SURFACES AND AS DIRECTIONAL TERMS

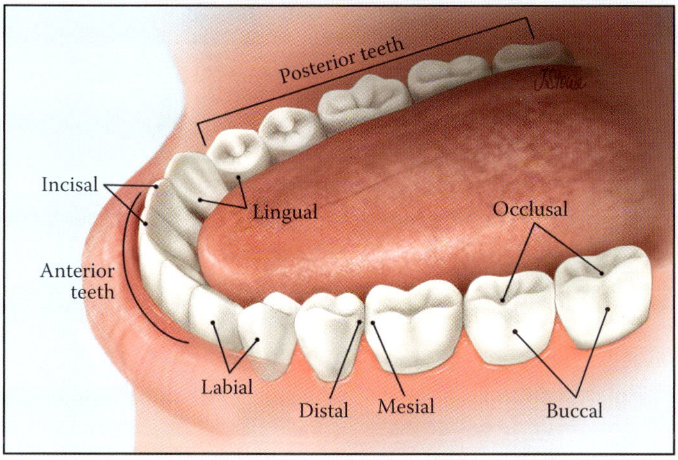

and include directional terms, such as mesial, meaning towards the midline, distal referring to away from the midline, lingual referring to the tooth surface that is tongue-side, labial, referring to the surface lip-side, and buccal, referring to the surface check-side.

Dental Numbering Systems

Several notational methods for dental charting have been devised as a shorthand method of notation to quickly identify a tooth without writing the entire cumbersome anatomic description (Sopher 1976, Hillson 1996, Alt and Türp 1998). Today, there are over 30 different systems for charting teeth (Clark 1991); however, this chapter presents the two most widely used systems: the Universal Numbering System and the FDI (Fédération Dentaire Internationale) system* (Fédération Dentaire Internationale).

In 1882, Gustav Julius Parreidt, a German dentist, proposed the Universal Numbering System (UNS), which is used frequently today throughout the United States (Figure 5.2). For the permanent (adult) dentition, the UNS assigns a unique number (1–32) to each tooth, starting with the maxillary right third molar (#1) and continuing medially across the maxillary dentition to the right central incisor (#8), then distally from the left central incisor (#9) to the maxillary left third molar (#16). This numbering system continues with the mandibular left third molar (#17) and continues mesially across the mandibular dentition to the left central incisor (#24), then distally from the right central incisor (#25) and ends with the mandibular right third molar (#32). The deciduous (baby) dentition (Figure 5.3) is labeled similarly, using the letters A–T, beginning with the maxillary right second deciduous molar (A) continuing across the maxillary arcade to the maxillary left second deciduous molar (J), dropping down to the mandibular left second deciduous molar (K), and ending with the mandibular right second deciduous molar (T). Notation

* For a discussion of other dental notation systems, please see Hillson (1996) or Alt and Türp (1998).

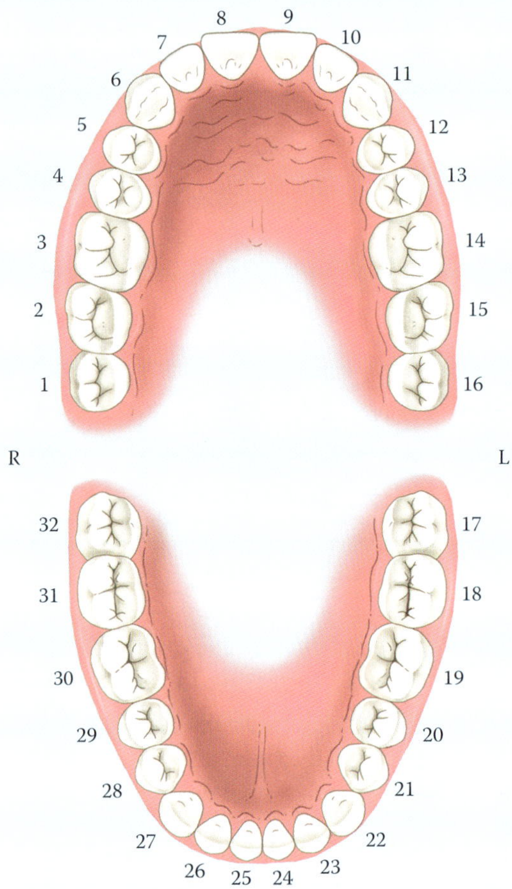

Figure 5.2 Diagram of the UNS for permanent dentition.

for supernumerary teeth (additional teeth other than the 32 found in the normal permanent dentition or the 20 found in the deciduous dentition) varies; however, one of the most common is to note where the extra tooth is located (e.g., "a supernumerary tooth is located between #8 and #9").

In 1971, the FDI devised a system that is used throughout the world by organizations such as Interpol, the World Health Organization, and the International Association of Dental Research (Figure 5.4). This system provides a unique two-digit number for each tooth. The first number in the pair represents the quadrant of the mouth, and the second number delineates the tooth, numbered from mesial to distal per quadrant. Any number beginning with "1" represents the permanent maxillary right quadrant, "2" represents the permanent maxillary left quadrant, "3" permanent mandibular left quadrant, and "4" permanent mandibular right quadrant. All central incisors have a second digit of 1, while all third molars have a second digit of 8. Deciduous quadrants are delineated with the first numbers 5–8 in the same fashion (Figure 5.5). These notation systems allow for quick entry into a computer database with a unique number representing each tooth.

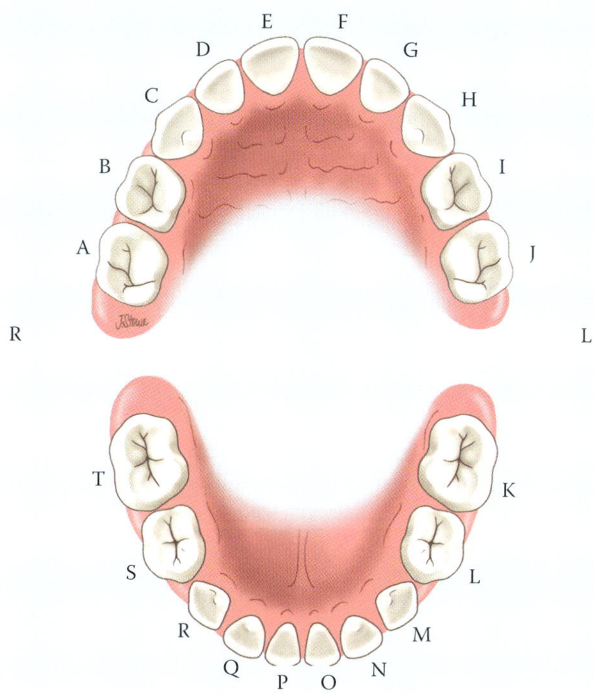

Figure 5.3 Diagram of the UNS for deciduous dentition.

Dental Morphology

Humans are heterodontic, meaning that we have different types of teeth with different forms and functions. Homodonts, on the other hand, have the same types of teeth that all form the same function; many reptiles and bony fish are homodonts. The human permanent dentition is composed of 32 teeth, with eight teeth per quadrant. There are four tooth types in the adult dentition: incisors, canines, premolars, and molars. The dental code, then, for each quadrant of the normal adult dentition is 2:1:2:3, that is, two incisors, one canine, two premolars, and three molars (Figure 5.6). The maxillary dentition decreases in size from the anterior-to-posterior teeth, such that the central incisor is larger than the lateral incisor, the first premolar is large than the second premolar, and the first molar is larger than the second, which is in turn larger than the third. The mandibular dentition exhibits the opposite form, in that the central incisor is smaller than the lateral, and the first premolar is smaller than the second; however, the molars follow the same sizing parameters of the maxillary dentition (the first molar is larger than the second, which is larger than the third).

The incisors are categorized as central and lateral incisors, according to their location in the dental arcade. Incisors are spatulate-shaped teeth, and their main functions are cutting, tearing, and ripping. The permanent maxillary central incisors (teeth #8 and #9) are the longest and widest anterior teeth. The crown of the maxillary central incisor is wider mesiodistally than labiolingually. To side the maxillary central incisors, the mesioincisal

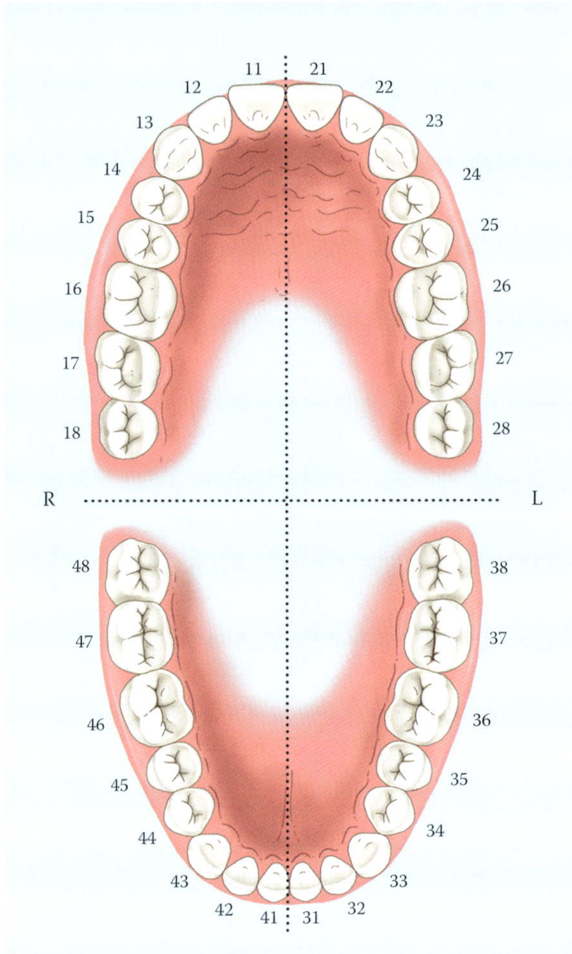

Figure 5.4 Diagram of the FDI dental notation system for permanent dentition.

edge exhibits a straight edge, while the distoincisal aspect is rounded. The lingual surface exhibits a concavity, called the lingual fossa, and a convex aspect, which is the cingulum. The maxillary lateral incisors (teeth #7 and #10) resemble the maxillary central incisor, but the crowns are smaller in all dimensions. The crown of the maxillary lateral incisor is wider mesiodistally than labiolingually. Siding of the maxillary lateral incisors is similar to the maxillary central incisors, in that the mesioincisal edge is straighter than the distoincisal edge.

The mandibular central incisors (teeth #24 and #25) are the smallest teeth in the dental arcade. Each mandibular central incisor is wider labiolingually than mesiodistally and has a very symmetric crown. Due to the symmetry of the crown, siding the mandibular central incisors is often difficult; however, the cingulum is slightly offset to the distal aspect of the tooth. The mandibular lateral incisors (teeth #23 and #26) are slightly larger than the mandibular central incisors and slightly less symmetric. Therefore, the distoincisal edge is often more rounded than the mesioincisal edge. The cingulum of the mandibular lateral incisor is also offset slightly to the distal aspect of the tooth.

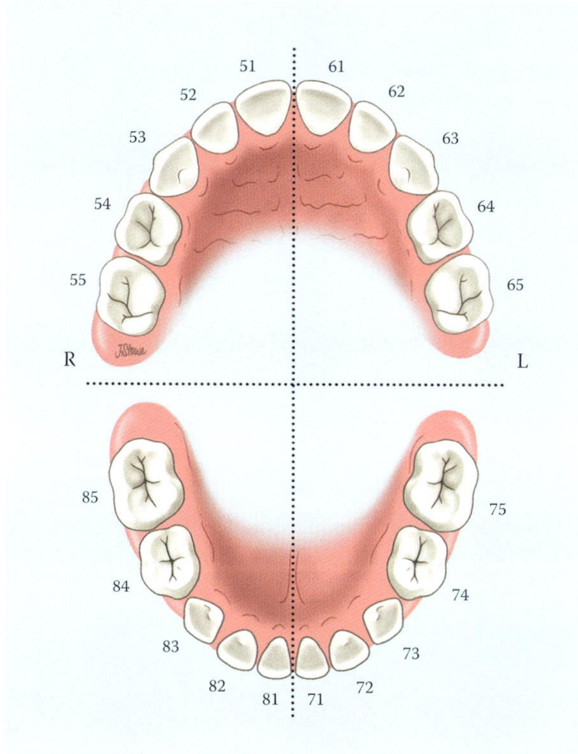

Figure 5.5 Diagram of the FDI dental notation system for deciduous dentition.

Canines exhibit a somewhat pointed shape that is transitional from the incisors to the premolars. Their main functions are cutting, tearing, and ripping. The maxillary canines (teeth #6 and #11) have a large and centered cingulum and are wider labiolingually than mesiodistally. Typically, the maxillary canines have the longest roots of all dentition. The distal aspect of the maxillary canine is more rounded than the mesial aspect, which aids in siding. In addition, the root often deviates distally. The mandibular canines (teeth #22 and #27) have a longer crown than the maxillary canines; however, the root is typically shorter than the maxillary canines, and the tooth is smaller mesiodistally and labiolingually. Similar to the maxillary canine, the mandibular canine is rounder distally, and the root often deviates to the distal aspect.

Premolars are transitional in form and function between the canines and molars. The main functions of the premolars are tearing and grinding. The maxillary first premolars (teeth #5 and #12) have a buccal cusp and a lingual cusp, with the former being the larger of the two. Due to the buccal and lingual cusps, this tooth is larger buccolingually than it is mesiodistally. The root of the maxillary first permanent premolar is often bifurcated. The maxillary first premolar also has a very prominent mesial marginal groove (Figure 5.7), which is a groove that extends onto the mesial aspect of the tooth. In addition, the buccal cusp is offset toward the distal surface. The maxillary second premolars (#4 and #13) are slightly smaller than the maxillary first premolars. The maxillary second premolars also have a buccal and lingual cusp; however, the cusps are more symmetric in size. As with the maxillary first premolar, the maxillary second premolar is also larger buccolingually versus mesiodistally.

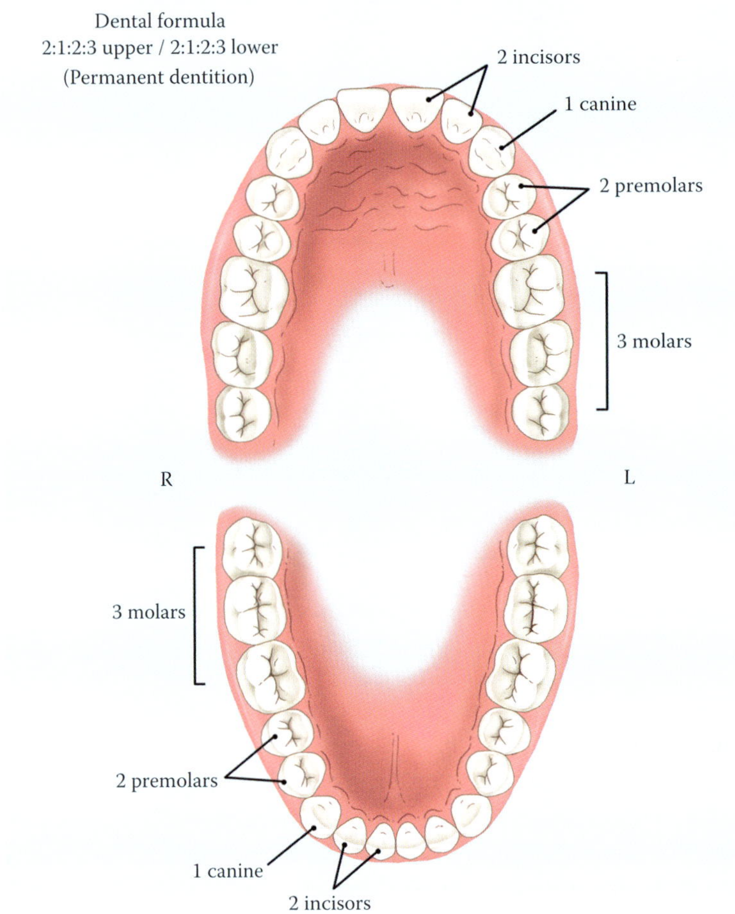

Figure 5.6 Diagram of the human dental formula (by quadrant) for the permanent dentition.

The mandibular first premolars (#21 and #28) resemble the canine more so than the molars in form and function. The buccal cusp is much larger than the lingual cusp in the mandibular first premolar. The buccal and lingual cusps are both offset to the mesial aspect of the tooth. The mandibular second premolars (#20 and #29) are larger than the mandibular first premolars, and the cusps are more symmetric in size. The mandibular second premolar has one buccal cusp and either one or two lingual cusps. In cases where there are two lingual cusps, the mesiolingual cusp is typically larger; therefore, the lingual groove is offset to the distal aspect. In cases of one lingual cusp, the buccal cusp will be larger than the lingual (see Box 5.2).

The main function of the molars is grinding. The typical crown and root morphology of the molars will be presented; however, additional cusps and roots are exhibited in some specimens. The maxillary molars have three roots, two of which are set buccally (one mesial, one distal) and the third is lingual. The lingual root is typically the longest root, followed by the mesiobuccal root. The crowns of the molars are wider buccolingually than mesiodistally. The maxillary first molars (#3 and #14) are typically the largest teeth in

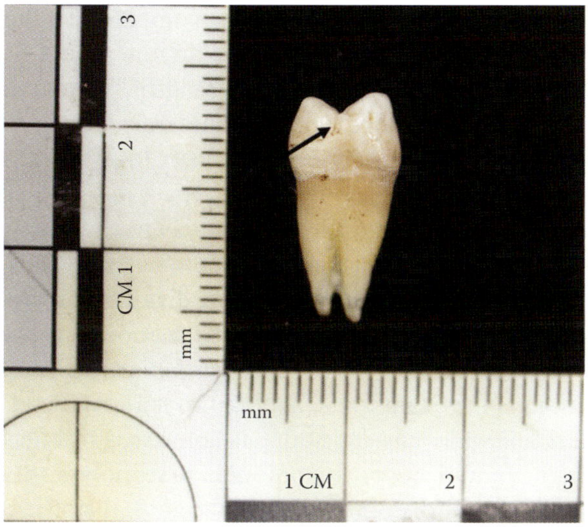

Figure 5.7 Mesial surface of tooth #5 depicting the mesial marginal groove and bifurcated root.

the dental arcade. The maxillary first molar typically consists of four cusps: mesiobuccal, distobuccal, mesiolingual, and distolingual. The mesiolingual cusp is typically the largest cusp, with the mesiobuccal cusp the next largest, and the distolingual cusp the smallest. Although the maxillary first molar is the most static, an accessory cusp may be located on the mesiolingual cusp, known as the cusp of Carabelli. Typically, a mesial marginal groove will also be exhibited on the maxillary first molar.

The maxillary second molars (#2 and #15) are similar to the maxillary first molars, except that the crowns are smaller. The distobuccal cusp is smaller in all dimensions in the maxillary second molar as compared to the first molar, and, therefore, the distolingual cusp may be observed from the buccal aspect. Similarly, the distolingual cusp is smaller

BOX 5.2 DIAGRAM OF MANDIBULAR RIGHT SECOND PREMOLAR VIEWED FROM EACH OF THE FIVE DENTAL SURFACES

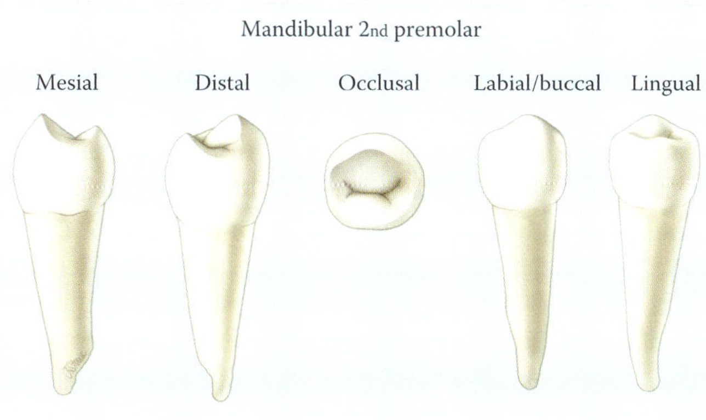

in all dimensions in the maxillary second molar as compared to the first, and therefore the distobuccal cusp can often be observed from the lingual aspect. Typically, the roots of the first and second maxillary molars are similar in length. The buccal roots of the second maxillary molar are typically closer together and equal in length as compared to the roots of the maxillary first molar. Due to the roots being closer together, it is not uncommon for the roots to be fused.

The maxillary third molars (#1 and #16) are similar to the maxillary second molars, except that they are smaller in all dimensions. The roots are shorter than those of the maxillary second molar and are often fused together. The distolingual cusp is small and often missing in the maxillary third molar. Maxillary and mandibular third molars are often congenitally missing or impacted and are the most variable of all teeth.

The mandibular molars have two roots, a mesial root and a distal root. On the crown, the mandibular molars are wider mesiodistally as compared to buccolingually. Whereas maxillary first molars have four cusps, mandibular first molars (#19 and #30) typically exhibit five cusps: mesiobuccal, distobuccal, mesiolingual, distolingual, and distal cusp. The mesiobuccal is the largest of the cusps, while the distal is the smallest. The mesiolingual and distolingual cusps are similar in size, with the former exhibiting slightly larger proportions. The distobuccal cusp is the second smallest cusp. The roots of the mandibular first molar typically derivate to the distal aspect.

The mandibular second molars (#18 and #31) are the most symmetric of all the molars and typically have four cusps arranged in a "+" pattern: mesiobuccal, distobuccal, mesiolingual, and distolingual. The cusps of the mandibular second molar are more equal in size as compared to the mandibular first molar; however, the mesiobuccal cusp is typically the largest while the distolingual cusp is typically the smallest. The roots of the mandibular molar angle to the distal aspect and are sometimes fused.

The mandibular third molars (#17 and #32) can have five cusps, such as in the mandibular first molars or four, such as the second. The roots of the mandibular third molars are typically shorter than the mandibular first and second molars and are often fused.

Humans have two separate sets of dentitions and are therefore diphyodonts. There are 20 deciduous teeth in the human dentition, with five teeth per quadrant: two incisors, one canine, and two molars. Therefore, the dental code for each quadrant of deciduous teeth is 2:1:0:2, as there are no premolars in the deciduous dentition (Figure 5.8). The deciduous dentition is smaller in all respects in comparison to their permanent counterparts. Since the deciduous dentition is replaced by the permanent dentition by approximately age 13, less developmental emphasis is placed on building highly mineralized deciduous teeth. In such, the deciduous dentition is not as strong as the permanent dentition, and the enamel is neither as mineralized nor as thick due to differences in diet and facial musculature. Due to mineralization differences, the deciduous dentition is typically exhibit a grayish hue. The mixed dentition period (the stage in which deciduous and permanent teeth are present in the oral cavity at the same time) is approximately aged 6/7 through 13/15 years. The permanent incisors replace the deciduous incisors, the permanent canines replace the deciduous canines, and the deciduous molars are replaced by the permanent premolars. The permanent molars erupt distal to the deciduous second molar. The first permanent molar erupts at approximately age 6, the second molar erupts at approximately age 12, and the third molar erupts at approximately age 18.

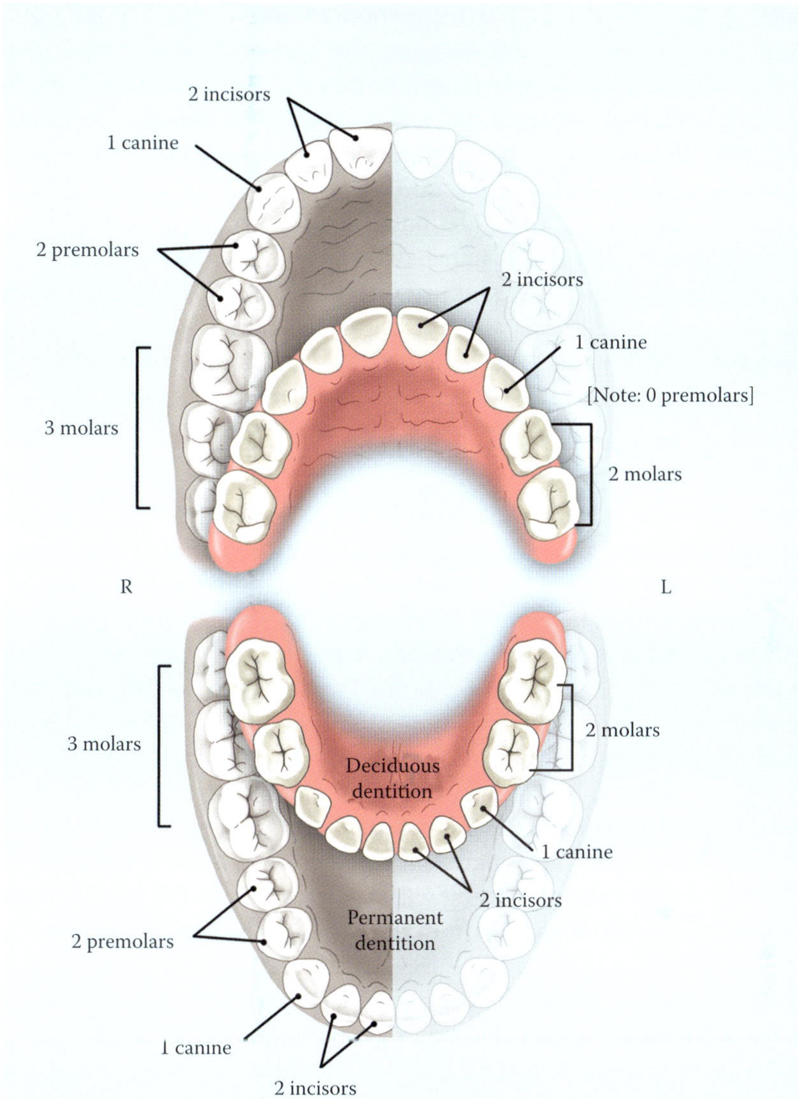

Figure 5.8 Diagram of the human dental formula (by quadrant) of deciduous dentition overlayed on the permanent dentition.

Employing Dentition in Forensic Anthropology

Dentition is highly important in the identification of unknown remains, as their postmortem longevity often surpasses that of bone, especially when remains are highly fragmentary. Teeth can aid in developing the biological profile in cases of comingled remains, such as those resulting from mass disasters or mass graves. Physical anthropologists use information from dentition to aid in the assessment of age, sex, and ancestry of unidentified individuals even in cases where the osseous remains yield little information for the biological profile.

Variation in development and deterioration of the skeletal system differ among individuals, across populations, and between the sexes (Hanihara 1952, Brooks 1955, Biggerstaff 1977, Zhang 1982, Moore-Jansen and Jantz 1986, Ubelaker 1989, Konigsberg and Frankenberg 1992, Molleson et al. 1993, Plato et al. 1994, Kemkes-Grottenthaler 1996, 2002, Jackes 2000, Boldsen et al. 2002, Hoppa and Vaupel 2002, Prince and Ubelaker 2002, Ross and Konigsberg 2002, Komar 2003, Šlaus et al. 2003, Prince 2004, Prince and Konigsberg 2008). Differences can be attributed to socioeconomic status, cultural differences, genetic differences, differences in behavior, environmental factors, diet, and disease (Buckberry and Chamberlain 2002, Kemkes-Grottenthaler 2002). This variation is apparent in the skeleton and in dentition, and, therefore, appropriate reference samples must be employed, when determining the biological profile for unknown remains.

Subadult Age-at-Death Estimation from Dentition

Dentition offers the most reliable age estimates for subadults. Both eruption into the oral cavity (Ubelaker 1989) and tooth mineralization (Moorrees et al. 1963, Demirjian et al. 1973, Mincer et al. 1993) have been utilized for the estimation of age-at-death, with the latter providing the most reliable method (Moorrees et al. 1963). It must be noted, however, that mineralization and eruption patterns are sex and ancestry dependant, and therefore, the appropriate reference sample must be utilized when employing any method.

There are three periods in the development and maturation of the human dentition: Primary dentition period, mixed dentition period, and permanent dentition period. The primary emergence sequence of deciduous dentition is central incisors (approximately 6–10 months of age), lateral incisors, first molars, canines, and second molars (approximately 24–30 months of age). The mixed dentition period extends approximately from 6/7 to 13/15 years of age, typically beginning with the eruption of the first permanent molar at approximately age 6. Although the timing is variable, the typical eruption sequence of the permanent dentition occurs in three waves with resting periods between each wave: first molar, central incisor, lateral incisor at approximately 6/7 years of age; canine, first premolar, second premolar, and second molar at approximately 10–12/13 years of age; and the third molar at approximately 16/17–21/25 years of age. The resting periods allow for the growth of the dental-facial complex and provide room for the next eruption phase.

One of the most widely used methods of subadult age estimation is that of Moorrees et al. (1963). Their method incorporates radiographs from a longitudinal study of middle-class White children from Ohio (110 females and 136 males) and Boston (51 females and 48 males). Dental formation is accessed via radiographs and is assigned a stage of development starting with initial cusp formation to closure of the apex of the root (see Moorrees et al. 1963). The amount of mineralization is assessed and placed into the most appropriate phase of mineralization. Age is then determined by referencing tables, which equate the mineralization phase with the mean age of attainment for males and females. The age range is reported as two standard deviations from the mean.

Adult Age-at-Death

Estimation of adult skeletal age-at-death is one of the most important identifying features for an unknown individual but also one of the most difficult to achieve (Prince and

Konigsberg 2008). Repeatability, high accuracy, and high correlation with age are traits of a good age indicator. These features are critical when developing a biological profile, whether for forensic or paleodemographic purposes. Aging methods developed on indicators that are less susceptible to individual lifestyle aid in increasing the precision of age ranges, especially for older individuals.

Several researchers have developed techniques to determine age-at-death for adults by employing dentition and dental morphology. Most methods involve assessing age-related changes in dental attrition/wear (Zuhrt 1955, Miles 1962, 1963, 1978, Brothwell 1963, 1989, Lavelle 1970, Molnar 1971, Ito 1972, Lunt 1978, Scott 1979, Smith 1984, Lovejoy 1985, Li and Ji 1995), secondary dentin deposits (Morse et al. 1993, Kvaal et al. 1994), cementum apposition (Stott et al. 1982, Charles et al. 1986, Condon et al. 1986, Groβkopf 1989, Wittwer-Backofen 2000, Kagerer and Grupe 2001, Wittwer-Backofen and Buba 2002, Wittwer-Backofen et al. 2004), apical translucency (Bang and Ramm 1970, Prince 2004, Prince and Konigsberg 2008), periodontal recession (Solheim 1992, Borrman et al. 1995), root resorption (Borrman et al. 1995), aspartic acid racemization (Helfman and Bada 1975, 1976, Shimoyama and Harada 1984, Ogino et al. 1985, Masters 1986, Ritz et al. 1990, 1993, Ohtani and Yamamoto 1991, 1992, Mörnstad et al. 1994, Ohtani 1994, 1995, Ohtani et al. 1995, Carolan et al. 1997), color change of the root (Ten Cate et al. 1977, Solheim 1988, Borrman et al. 1995), or a combination of several of these indicators (Gustafson 1950, Johanson 1971, Maples 1978, Maples and Rice 1979, Lamendin and Cambray 1980, Matsikidis and Schultz 1982, Kashyap and Koteswara Rao 1990, Lamendin et al. 1992, Solheim 1993, Kvaal et al. 1995, Russell 1996, Prince and Ubelaker 2002, González-Colmenares et al. 2007, Ubelaker and Parra 2008). Several researchers have analyzed these features individually and multifactorially (Baccino and Zerilli 1997, Baccino et al. 1999). The most reliable methods for assessing adult age-at-death from dental remains are those that analyze translucency of the root, cementum annuli, aspartic acid racemization on the enamel, dentin, or cementum, and secondary dentin deposits.

Gösta Gustafson, a Swedish stomatologist, was a pioneer in assessing age-related changes to dentition and laid the foundation for utilizing dental microstructure to estimate age-at-death (Gustafson 1950). He assessed age-related changes in six features of the human dentition: attrition, secondary dentin deposits, translucency of the root, periodontal recession, cementum annulation apposition (thickness), and root resorption. He assigned a numeric score (0–3 points) to account for the degree of the dental change in each feature and assessed the amount of change by making longitudinal sections of the tooth. In the point system, increased score was equated with increased age. A correlation coefficient of 0.98 was produced from his analysis, and he concluded that root translucency and secondary dentin deposits were the best indicators of age.

The advantage of this method is that it considers a number of different dental features and, when possible, uses information from several teeth. Poor oral heath was found to influence the scoring and age estimates. Individuals with poor oral health produced higher age estimates than their actual age. Disadvantages of this method are that it is a destructive method, the observer must have a thorough knowledge of dental histology to interpret the features, and the original statistical application was applied improperly. Although the importance of Gustafson's research was evident, many authors noted problems with his analysis, in particular, the statistical methodology, and offered improvements to his method (Dalitz 1962, Saunders 1965, Bang and Ramm 1970, Johanson 1971, Burns and Maples 1976, Maples 1978, Maples and Rice 1979, Metzger et al. 1980, Solheim and

Sundnes 1980, Haertig et al. 1985, Nkhumeleni et al. 1989, Kashyap and Koteswara Rao 1990, Lamendin et al. 1992, Marcsik et al. 1992, Solheim 1993, Borrman et al. 1995, Lucy and Pollard 1995, Lucy et al. 1996, Aykroyd et al.1997, Ubelaker et al. 1998, Baccino et al. 1999, Monzavi et al. 2003).

A direct relationship exists between chronological age and apical transparency; as age increases, the amount of transparency in the tooth root also increases (Gustafson 1950, Marcsik et al. 1992, Hillison 1996). This physiological feature typically does not appear before age 18 and is the "result of gradual mineralization of the peritubular dentine, which leads eventually to obliteration of the dentine tubules" (López-Nicolás et al. 1993, p. 2). Translucency of the root should not be confused with sclerotic dentin found in the crown, which is a result of pathological conditions (Pindborg 1970, Mendis and Darling 1979). Vasiliadis et al. (1983) compared apical translucency in pathological and nonpathological teeth and concluded that the development of root translucency is independent of pathological conditions.

Several authors have reported that translucency of the root is the best dental indicator of age and is most closely correlated to chronological age (Gustafson 1950, Miles 1963, Bang and Ramm 1970, Johanson 1971, Maples 1978, Metzger 1980, Solheim and Sundnes 1980, Kósa et al. 1983, Vasiliadis et al. 1983, Sognnaes et al. 1985, Lorensten and Solheim 1989, Solheim 1989, López-Nicolás et al. 1990, 1993, 1996, Schroeder 1991, Sengupta et al. 1998, 1999, Ajmal et al. 2001); however, translucency apposition may be influenced by genetic, environmental, and cultural factors (López-Nicolás et al. 1996, Prince 2004). Acquisition of apical translucency may be related to a myriad of individual lifestyle variables. Mastication and heavy-loading forces may increase the amount of translucency associated with an individual or a population. This may be one of the factors associated with the variation in translucency acquisition between samples.

Translucency of the root can been analyzed in longitudinal thin sections (see Gustafson 1950, Dechaume et al. 1960, Nalbandian et al. 1960, Johanson 1971, Solheim and Sundnes 1980, Vasiliadis et al. 1983, Whittaker and Bakri 1996, Sengupta et al. 1998, 1999) or on intact teeth (see Bang and Ramm 1970, Colonna et al. 1984, Solheim 1989, Drusini et al. 1991, Lamendin et al. 1992, Prince and Ubelaker 2002, Sarajlić et al. 2003, Prince and Konigsberg 2008). Translucency of the root can be seen macroscopically, but is enhanced with the aid of a light box, such as those used to view radiographs. There are several advantages of taking measurements directly from intact teeth: it is nondestructive, less expensive, and less time consuming than other methods, and it is not necessary to have a complete knowledge of dental histology.

Quantifications of apical translucency have been suggested in several different formats: subject indices (Gustafson 1950, Johanson 1971), direct measurement from the apex toward the CEJ (Miles 1963, Bang and Ramm 1970, Sengupta et al. 1998, 1999), area of translucency (Lorentsen and Solheim 1989, Sengupta et al. 1998, 1999), length expressed as a proportion of the total root (Lamendin and Cambray 1980, Drusini et al. 1991, Lamendin et al. 1992, Thomas et al. 1994, Sengupta et al. 1998, 1999, Prince and Ubelaker 2002, Sarajlić et al. 2003, Prince and Konigsberg 2008), area expressed as a proportion of the total root area (Johnson 1968, Vasiliadis et al. 1983, Drusini et al. 1991, Sengupta et al. 1998, 1999), computer-assisted image analysis (López-Nicolás et al.1990, 1993, 1996, Drusini et al. 1991, Sengupta et al. 1998, 1999), and by total volume (Manly and Hodge 1939, Rathod et al. 1993).

Several researchers have found a significant difference in translucency between the sexes (Lorentsen and Solheim 1989, Prince and Ubelaker 2002), while others have not (Drusini et al. 1991, Lamendin et al. 1992). Lorentsen and Solheim (1989) suggested that sexual dimorphism in translucency may be attributed to differences in masticatory forces. Similarly, ancestry variation has been noted by several authors (Whittaker and Bakri 1996, Prince and Ubelaker 2002, González-Colmenares et al. 2007, Prince and Konigsberg 2008, Ubelaker and Parra 2008). As with any aging indicator, taphonomic processes may affect the properties and visual assessment of apical translucency. These processes include water insults, soil conditions, temperature and humidity, and faunal, fungal, or bacterial scavenger activity (Sengupta et al. 1999, Prince 2004).

Lamendin et al. (1992) proposed a quick and nondestructive method of adult age-at-death estimation by assessing apical translucency and periodontal regression. To estimate age-at-death, three measurements are taken from the labial surface of each tooth and recorded in millimeters: root height (RH), maximum distance from the apex of the root to the CEJ, periodontal regression, maximum distance from the CEJ to the line of soft tissue attachment, and translucency of the root, which is measured from the apex of the root toward the CEJ with the aid of a light box. From multiple regression analysis, Lamendin et al. (1992) established the following equation to estimate age at death: $A = (0.18 * P) + (0.42 * T) + 25.53$, where A represents age in years, P represents the periodontal measurement * 100/RH, and T represents the translucency of the root measurement * 100/RH. These researchers produced a mean error of +10 years on their working sample and +8.4 years on their forensic control sample.

Although apical translucency has been reported to be a reliable indicator of age, periodontal recession has serious limitations. Several intrinsic and extrinsic factors can influence periodontal recession other than age, such as inflammation of the periodontium (van der Velden 1984), poor dental hygiene (Foti et al. 2001, Prince and Ubelaker 2002, Prince 2004), extrinsic irritation (physical, chemical, or mechanical; Foti et al. 2001), systemic diseases (Foti et al. 2001), and drug treatments (Foti et al. 2001). In addition, Foti et al. (2001) yielded no correlation between periodontal recession and chronological age and concluded that Lamendin's technique cannot be used on teeth with periodontal disease (Foti et al. 2001). Supporting the conclusions made by Foti et al. (2001), Solheim (1992) and Prince (2004) also conclude that periodontal recession as a single indicator for estimation of age-at-death is not possible.

Modeled after the method of Lamendin et al. (1992), Prince and Ubelaker (2002) offer a similar method for application in the United States based on a sample of 100 Black males, 100 Black females, 100 White males, and 100 White females. The authors created new formulae separating individuals by sex and ancestry and included root height, which significantly lowered the mean errors, in order to make the age-at-death estimates more applicable to skeletal remains recovered in the United States.

Analysis of cementum annulations has proved extremely useful in estimating age-at-death, with some reports of mean errors as low as ±2.5 years (Wittwer-Backofen et al. 2004). Broomell (1898) was the first to note that the correlation between cementum thickness and chronological age was independent of functional stresses. The first age-at-death estimates utilizing cementum apposition measured the thickness of the band of cementum in longitudinal thin sections after Gustafson's methodology (Gustafson 1950, Johanson 1971, Azaz et al. 1974, Maples 1978, Nitzan et al. 1986, Kashyap and

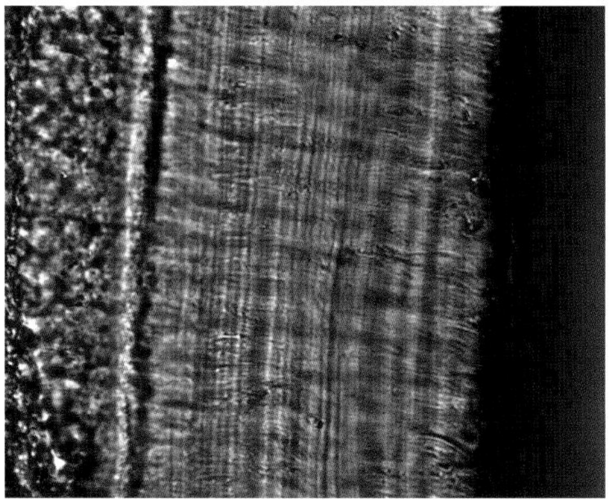

Figure 5.9 Transverse thin section depicting cementum annuli.

Koteswara Rao 1990, Solheim 1993). In mammalian aging studies, incremental cementum annuli were counted from transverse thin sections. Incremental bands of cementum are laid down in alternating light and dark bands (Figure 5.9). Each pair of light and dark bands is considered to equate to 1 year of life (Stott et al. 1982, Kagerer and Grupe 2001). Age-at-death is estimated by adding the number of incremental bands to the age of eruption for the particular tooth. The counting of cementum annuli has provided reliable and accurate estimates of age for seasonal animals; however, differences have been noted between human cementum annuli and other mammals in that human incremental bands are closer together and are more numerous (Kvaal and Solheim 1995). Several factors have been cited as the cause of this "annual" apposition, such as seasonal changes, "UV-radiation dose, climatic parameters, differential food quality, and hormonal status" (Kagerer and Grupe 2001, p. 75).

Several researchers followed the procedure of counting cementum annuli in humans to estimate age-at-death, instead of measuring the thickness of the band (Stott et al. 1982, Naylor et al. 1985, Charles et al. 1986, Condon et al. 1986, Lipsinic et al. 1986, Miller et al. 1988, Groβkopf 1989, Solheim 1990, Stein and Corcoran 1994, Kvaal and Solheim 1995, Renz et al. 1997, Geuser et al. 1999, Wittwer-Backofen 2000, Jankauskas et al. 2001, Kagerer and Grupe 2001, Wittwer-Backofen and Buba 2002, Wittwer-Backofen et al. 2004). Conflicting results on the reliability and accuracy of counting cementum annuli have been reported. Several researchers reported problems with this technique and concluded that it is an unreliable technique to estimate age-at-death (Lipsinic et al. 1986, Lucas and Loh 1986, Miller et al. 1988), while others state that it is a moderately reliable technique (Charles et al. 1986, Condon et al. 1986, Stein and Corcoran 1994), and others claim that it is a highly reliable method and that poor results are produced by incorrect procedures, rather than inherent flaws with the method itself (Stott et al. 1982, Groβkopf 1989, Wittwer-Backofen 2000, Kagerer and Grupe 2001, Wittwer-Backofen and Buba 2002, Wittwer-Backofen et al. 2004).

Conflicting results have also been reported on the effects of periodontal disease and cementum annulations. Several authors report that periodontal disease increases the error rate of this method (Condon et al. 1986, Kvaal and Solheim 1995), and others report that cementum annuli production is halted by periodontal disease (Kagerer and Grupe 2001); however, other authors report that periodontal disease has no effect on cementum annuli (Groβkopf et al. 1996, Wittwer-Backofen 2000, Wittwer-Backofen and Buba

2002, Wittwer-Backofen et al. 2004). Doubling cases, which refers to observing twice as many incremental lines as predicted, have been reported by several authors (Condon et al. 1986, Stein and Corcoran 1994, Wittwer-Backofen 2000), and therefore all methods available for age estimation should be utilized in order to detect doubling cases (Kagerer and Grupe 2001).

Enamel (Helfman and Bada 1975, Ohtani and Yamamoto 1992), dentin (Helfman and Bada 1976, Shimoyama and Harada 1984, Masters 1986, Ritz et al. 1990, Ohtani and Yamamoto 1991, 1992, Ritz et al. 1993, Mörnstad et al. 1994, Carolan et al. 1997), and cementum (Ohtani 1995, Ohtani et al. 1995) have been evaluated for their usefulness of aspartic acid racemization (i.e., changes in amino acid molecules that occur after death) in estimating age-at-death. This process assesses the changes in living tissue over time:

> The racemization of amino acids is a reversible first-order reaction, which is relatively rapid in living tissues that have a slow metabolic rate. The amino acids composing proteins are L-enantiomers. However, over the course of time, amino acids undergo racemization with an increased ratio of D-enantiomers, metamorphosing into a racemate (King and Bada 1979). Aspartic acid shows a high racemization reaction rate and is considered to provide useful information on changes occurring in living tissues over time (Ohtani 1995, p. 805).

Ohtani (1995) evaluated the correlation of the D- and L-aspartic acids in cementum with chronological age, documented the rate of the racemizing reaction, and compared the results with those obtained from similar analyses with enamel and dentin. Cementum yielded the fastest reaction, followed by dentin, and then enamel. Overall, dentin had the highest correlation with age, followed by cementum, and then enamel, $r = 0.992$, $r = 0.988$, and $r = 0.961$, respectively. The authors concluded that aspartic acid racemization is a precise and useful method to estimate age-at-death. Master (1986) evaluated the effects of postmortem changes to aspartic acid racemization. She concludes that aspartic acid racemization is a more accurate method of estimating age-at-death than other skeletal methods, especially in older individuals, but notes that postmortem conditions may affect the racemization rate. She suggests that further studies be conducted with a larger sample to test for such effects.

Radiographs are an excellent source for assessing age-related changes in dentition and have been used to assess Gustafson's method (Matsikidis and Schultz 1982), secondary dentin deposits (Morse et al. 1993, Kvaal and Solheim 1994), and proportions of the tooth (Kvaal et al. 1995). Techniques that utilize dental radiographs are completely nondestructive, offer simple procedures, and can be used on forensic and archaeological material as well as living individuals (Kvaal et al. 1995). In addition, taking dental radiographs is common practice in dental clinics, which offers a large resource.

Deposition of secondary dentin was thought to be influenced by attrition, where dentin would be deposited in the lining of the pulp chamber to combat the loss of the crown, but several authors have reported a weak correlation between attrition and secondary dentin deposits (Philippas 1961, Solheim 1993, Kvaal et al. 1995). Other extrinsic factors have also been attributed to influencing secondary dentin deposits, such as changes in osmotic pressure throughout the tooth (Philippas 1961). The amount of secondary dentin deposition has been used to estimate age at-death with relatively high correlations with age (Philippas 1961, Moore 1970, Ito 1975, Lantelme et al. 1976, Feng 1985, Nitzan et al. 1986, Solheim 1992, Kvaal et al. 1994). Solheim (1992) tested three secondary dentin deposit scoring methods—Gustafson's (1947), Dalitz's (1962), and Johanson's (1971)—and concluded that there was no significant difference between tooth age and chronological age. Although all three methods yielded strong correlations with chronological age, Johanson's (1971) method produced the highest correlation between secondary dentin deposits and chronological age.

Age-at-Death Summary

Most dental aging methods are derived from Gustafson's (1950) features of dental attrition, secondary dentin deposits, cementum annulation apposition, and translucency of the root. Many authors suggest that measurement of apical translucency is the best univariate age indicator, although some concern has been noted regarding its utility with archaeological material. Two destructive methods, aspartic acid racemization and counting tooth cementum annuli, have both produced exceptionally high correlations with age by several different authors. Both of these dental methods have produced high correlations with age, accurate age estimates, and precise age ranges. Although these methods are destructive, they offer extremely valuable demographic information. Again, as with apical translucency, both methods are prone to increased error with increased antiquity of the dental material, in addition to other taphonomic factors. Taphonomic processes affect all aging methods, whether they are skeletal phase-oriented methods or measurements of continuous variables. Such processes can lead to missing and/or misinterpreted data. Previous research illustrates the need for continued research and development of techniques to counter problems pertaining to taphonomic processes.

All available skeletal and dental age indicators should be assessed when possible. There are several important advantages to multiple-trait age estimates. A more robust age estimate can be derived when multiple indicators corroborate an age range. In addition, interpersonal variation can be better understood when multiple indicators are analyzed. Focusing on only one or two age indicators will offer only a minimum understanding of the actual aging process and may be subject to significant error if one of those age indicators is pathological. As technological, methodological, and statistical advances add to the resources physical anthropologists employ to estimate age-at-death from skeletal indicators, we will continually refine and improve techniques to more accurately establish a biological profile from skeletal remains.

Ancestry Determination from Dentition

Although there have been numerous studies on age assessment from dentition, far fewer methods are available to assess ancestry. Most methods that assess ancestry affinity from dentition analyze nonmetric dental traits and cusp morphology (Lasker and Lee 1957, Hinkes 1990, Hsu et al. 1997, Harris 2007). Nonmetric dental traits include shovel-shaped incisors (Figure 5.10), which occur more frequently with Asian ancestries, Carabelli's cusp (Figure 5.11), which occurs more frequently with European ancestries, and crenulated molars (Figure 5.12), which are more common in African ancestries. Scott and Turner (1997) offer a plethora of information on dental trait frequencies across populations, and Turner et al. (1991) provide scoring procedures for nonmetric traits. The Arizona State University (ASU) Dental Anthropology System (Turner et al. 1991) provides dental casts that exhibit variation in expression of over 20 nonmetric dental traits.

Edgar (2005) offers a method to discriminate nonmetric dental traits with the use of Bayesian probabilities and logistic regression probabilities. Her method assesses eight nonmetric dental traits: maxillary canine tuberculum dentale (UCTD), mandibular

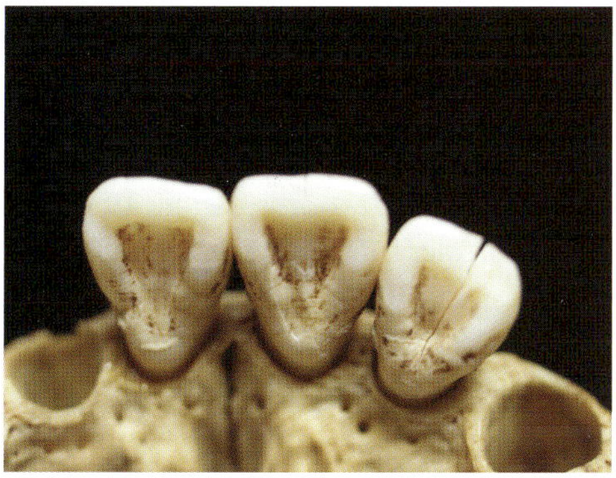

Figure 5.10 Shovel-shaped incisors (teeth #8, #9, and #10).

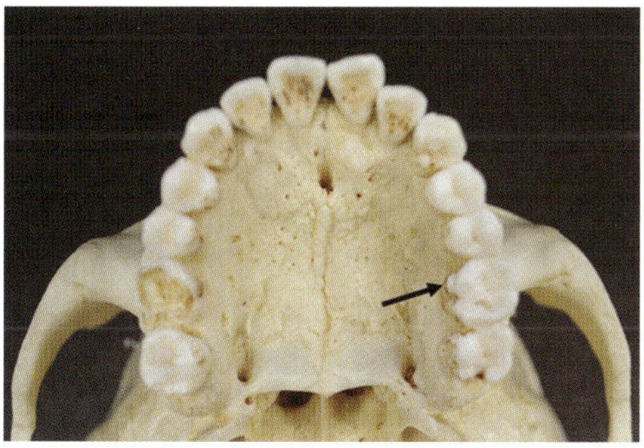

Figure 5.11 Carabelli's cusp located on the mesial–lingual surface on tooth #14.

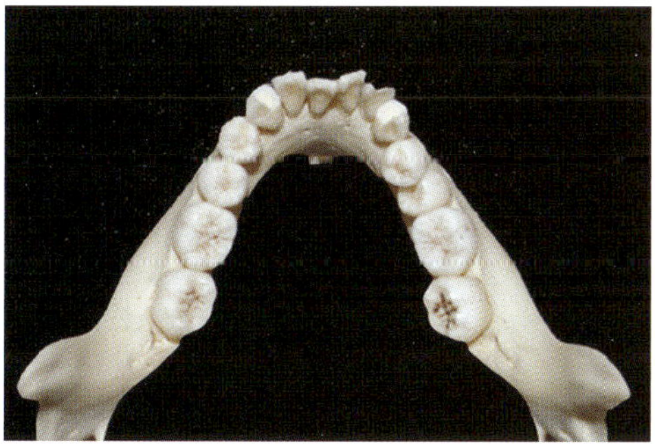

Figure 5.12 Crenulated molars depicted on teeth #18, #19, #30, and #31.

anterior premolar cusp variation (LaPCV), mandibular posterior premolar cusp variation (LpPCV), first mandibular molar deflecting wrinkle (LM1DW), first mandibular molar trigonid crest (LM1TC), second mandibular molar cusp 5 (LM2C5), third mandibular molar cusp 5 (LM3C5), and first mandibular molar cusp 7 (LM1C7). These eight traits are assessed and scored according to the ASU Dental Anthropology System (see Turner et al. 1991). Edgar's method provides Bayesian and logistic regression probabilities that distinguish European American and African American ancestries.

Sex Estimation from Dentition

Sex estimation from dentition is limited primarily to sexual dimorphism in odontometrics. Most studies analyze differences between the sexes in mesiodistal and buccolingual tooth dimensions (Moorrees 1957, 1959, Moorrees et al. 1957, Garn et al. 1964, 1966, 1977, Maudrich 1977, De Vito and Saunders 1990, Teschler-Nicola and Prossinger 1998); however, some classification rates are only slightly greater than chance. Another consideration is that dental dimensions are extremely variable across populations, thus decreasing the usefulness of dental dimensions in a forensic setting. However, determining the sex of an unknown individual is not only important for identification purposes, but also because the correct estimation of other parameters, such as age, is dependent on an accurate estimate of sex. In general, females are precocious to males in epiphyseal union, dental calcification, and dental eruption.

Common Dental Anomalies and Pathologies

Dental anomalies are craniofacial abnormalities of facial form, function, position of teeth, and tissues of the jaw and mouth. Anomalies can range from congenitally missing teeth to stained teeth, arch malocclusions, and cleft palate. The etiology of dental anomalies can be caused by inherited genetic defects or from genetic mutations. Dental deformities are also related to trauma, environmental, and nutritional factors.

Genetic Dental Anomalies

The most common craniofacial genetic defect is clefting of the lip or palate. Clefting is more prevalent in families with histories of the defect, therefore suggesting it is a hereditary disorder. Clefting is more common in males than females and is typically unilateral. Dentinogenisis imperfecta is another common genetic defect involving the dentin tubules and odontoblasts, which results in severely discolored teeth, poorly attached enamel, and teeth that easily fracture and exhibit extreme attrition, with the crown becoming completely worn down to the gum line. Amelogenesis imperfecta is a disorder that is correlated with thin enamel layers on the teeth as a result of defective proteins in the enamel, resulting in a translucency of the crown that allows the dentin to show through. Teeth often appear yellow and are weak and cavity-prone.

A less debilitating genetic anomaly is misaligned arches of the jaw, known as malocclusion. Most malocclusions are inherited; however, they can also be caused by accidents (i.e., traumatic loss of teeth) and individual habits, such as prolonged thumb sucking. Malocclusion and tooth crowding are increasing due to evolutionary factors affecting the modern human dentition. Teeth are not downsizing as fast as the soft tissues; therefore, rates of malocclusion and crowding are increasing. Malocclusions can be corrected by orthodontia. Other dental defects include microdontia, an inherited condition that causes smaller than normal teeth, and andodontia, a dental condition in which one or more permanent teeth fail to develop and are consequently missing in the adult dentition.

Environmental Dental Anomalies

Although teeth are very durable after death, they are susceptible to environmental factors during life. Environmental anomalies are often caused by diet/nutrition and agents such as fluoride and antibiotics, which can be related to dental anomalies. For example, a lack of vitamin C can cause scurvy that affects the periodontal and connective tissues of the individual, resulting in red, inflamed, and bleeding gums. A lack of iron, such as in anemia, can cause fiery red gums, whereas fluorosis, defined as an overabundance of fluorine in the diet, creates white or "mottled" spots on teeth. Caries (i.e., cavities), the most common dental pathology, are the result of bacterial plaque coming in contact with the tooth surface. Acid production from the bacteria attacks the surface of the tooth and penetrates the enamel or dentin, causing destruction to the tooth and, in severe cases, infection of the alveolar bone in the form of an abscess.

Dentition offers immense information that can be utilized by forensic anthropologists and odontologists when presented with unknown remains. Parameters of the biological profile such as age, sex, and ancestry can be obtained through analysis of dentition as well as information pertaining to the individual's life history, such as diet, disease, and nutrition. Most importantly, forensic odontologists use dentition to positively identify unknown individuals through comparison of antemortem and postmortem dental records. Due to the survivability of dental evidence, the infinite number of dental comparisons, and dynamic and assessable patient dental databases, the human dentition offers a wealth of information and is an integral tool forensic specialists utilize in the medicolegal setting.

References

Ajmal M, Mody B, Kumar G. 2001. Age estimation using three established methods. A study on Indian population. *Forensic Science International*, 122:150–154.

Alt KW, Türp JC. 1998. Roll Call: Thirty-two white horses on a red field. The advantages of the FDI two-digit system of designating teeth, In Alt KW, Rösing FW, Teschler-Nicola M (eds.), *Dental Anthropology: Fundamentals, Limits, and Prospects*, pp. 41–55, Springer, Wien, New York.

Aykroyd RG, Lucy D, Pollard AM, Solheim T. 1997. Regression analysis in adult age estimation. *American Journal of Physical Anthropology*, 104:259–265.

Azaz B, Ulmansky M, Moshev R, Sela J. 1974. Correlation between age and thickness of cementum in impacted teeth. *Oral Surgery*, 38:691–694.

Baccino E, Ubelaker DH, Hayek LA, Zerilli A. 1999. Evaluation of seven methods of estimating age at death from mature human skeletal remains. *Journal of Forensic Sciences*, 44:931–936.

Baccino E, Zerilli A. 1997. The two step strategy (TSS) or the right way to combine a dental (Lamendin) and an anthropological (Suchey-Brooks System) method for age determination (abstract). *Proceedings of the American Academy of Forensic Sciences*, 3:150.

Bang G, Ramm E. 1970. Determination of age in humans from root dentin transparency. *Acta Odontologica Scandinavica*, 28:3–35.

Bass WM. 1987. *Human Osteology: A Laboratory and Field Manual*, 3rd edn. Missouri Archaeological Society, Columbia, MO.

Biggerstaff RH. 1977. Craniofacial characteristics as determinants of age, sex and race in forensic dentistry. *Dental Clinics of North America*, 21:85–97.

Boldsen JL, Milner GR, Konigsberg LW, Wood JW. 2002. Transition analysis: A new method for estimating age from skeletons, In Hoppa RD, Vaupel JW (eds.), *Paleodemography: Age Distributions from Skeletal Samples*, pp. 73–106, Cambridge University Press, Cambridge, NY.

Borrman H, Solheim T, Magnusson B, Kvaal SI, Stene-Johansen W. 1995. Inter-examiner variation in the assessment of age-related factors in teeth. *International Journal of Legal Medicine*, 107:183–186.

Broomell IN. 1898. The histology of cementum. *Dental Cosmos*, 51:697–722.

Brooks ST. 1955. Skeletal age at death: The reliability of cranial and pubic age indicators. *American Journal of Physical Anthropology*, 13:567–597.

Brothwell D. 1963. *Digging up Bones: The Excavation, Treatment and Study of Human Skeletal Remains*. British Museum (Natural History), London, U.K.

Brothwell D. 1989. The relationship of tooth wear to aging. In İşcan MY (ed.), *Age Markers in the Human Skeleton*, pp. 303–316, Charles C. Thomas, Springfield, IL.

Buckberry JL, Chamberlain AT. 2002. Age estimation from the auricular surface of the ilium: A revised method. *American Journal of Physical Anthropology*, 119:231–239.

Burns KR, Maples WR. 1976. Estimation of age from individual adult teeth. *Journal of Forensic Sciences*, 21:343–356.

Carolan VA, Gardner ML, Lucy D, Pollard AM. 1997. Some considerations regarding the use of amino acid racemization in human dentine as an indicator of age at death. *Journal of Forensic Sciences*, 42:10–16.

Charles DK, Condon K, Cheverud JM, Buikstra JE. 1986. Cementum annulation and age determination in Homo sapiens: I. Tooth variability and observer error. *American Journal of Physical Anthropology*, 71:311–320.

Colonna M, Introna F, Favia G, Pesce-Delfino V. 1984. Valutazione della transparenza della dentina per la determinazione dell'eta: Revisione metodologica e analisi di un campione. In deFazio F, Vernole B (eds.), *La Laurea in Odontoiatria e Protesti dentaria. I Problemi Medico-legali in Odontostomatologia*. CIC Edizioni Internazionali, Rome, Italy, pp. 357–368.

Condon K, Charles DK, Cheverud JM, Buikstra JE. 1986. Cementum annulation and age determination in *Homo sapiens*: II. Estimates and accuracy. *American Journal of Physical Anthropology*, 71:321–330.

Dalitz GD. 1962. Age determination of adult human remains by teeth examination. *Journal of the Forensic Science Society*, 3:11–21.

Dechaume M, Derobert L, Payen J. 1960. De la valeur de la determination de l'age par examen des dentes en coupes minces. *Annales de Medicine Legale (Paris)*, 40:165–167.

Demirijian A, Goldstein H, Tanner JM. 1973. A new system of dental age assessment. *Human Biology*, 45(2):211–27.

De Vito C, Saunders S. 1990. A discriminant function analysis of deciduous teeth to determine sex. *Journal of Forensic Sciences*, 35:845–858.

Drusini A, Callieari I, Volpe A. 1991. Root dentine transparency: Age determination of human teeth using computerized densitometric analysis. *American Journal of Physical Anthropology*, 85:25–30.

Edgar, HJH. 2005. Prediction of race using characteristics of dental morphology. *Journal of Forensic Sciences*, 50:269–273.

Fédération Dentaire Internationale (FDI). 1971. Two-digit system of designating teeth. *International Dental Journal*, 21:104–106.

Feng J. 1985. Age determination from structure of teeth. *Acta Anthropologica Sinica*, 4:380–384.

Foti B, Adalain P, Signoli M, Ardagna Y, Dutour O, Leonetti, G. 2001. Limits of the Lamendin method in age determination. *Forensic Science International*, 122:101–106.

Garn SM, Cole PE, Wainwright RL. 1977. Sex discriminatory effectiveness using combinations of permanent teeth. *Journal of Dental Research*, 56:697.

Garn SM, Lewis AB, Kerewsky RS. 1964. Sex differences in tooth size. *Journal of Dental Research*, 43:306.

Garn SM, Lewis AB, Kerewsky RS. 1966. Sexual dimorphism in the buccolingual tooth dimension. *Journal of Dental Research*, 45:1819.

Geuser G, Bondioli L, Capucci E, Cipriano A, Grupe G, Savorè C, Macchiarelli R. 1999. Dental cementum annulations and age at death estimates. Osteodental biology of people of Portus Romae (Necropolis of Isola Sacra, 2nd–3rd cent. AD). In Bondioli L, Macchiarelli R (eds.), *Digital Archives of Human Paleobiology*, Vol. 2. Museo Nazionale Preistorico Etnografico "L. Pigorini," Rome, Italy.

González-Colmenares G, Moreno-Rueda G, Fernández-Cardenete JR. 2007. Age estimation by a dental method: A comparison of Lamendin's and Prince and Ubelaker's technique. *Journal of Forensic Sciences*, 52(2):1156–1160.

Groβkopf B. 1989. Incremental lines in prehistoric cremated teeth. A technical note. *Zeitschrift für Morphologie und Anthropologie*, 77:309–311.

Groβkopf B, Dender JM, Krüger W. 1996. Untersuchengen zur Zementapposition bei Paradontitis marginalis profunda. *Deutsche Zahnärztliche Zeitschrift*, 25:1763–1768.

Gustafson G. 1947. Åldersbestämnigar på tänder. *Odontologisk Tidskrift*, 54:556–568.

Gustafson G. 1950. Age determination on teeth. *Journal of the American Dental Association*, 41:45–54.

Haertig A, Crainic K, Durigon M. 1985. Medicolegal identification by the dental system. *Presse Medical*, 14:543–545.

Hanihara K. 1952. Age changes in the male Japanese pubic bone. *Journal of the Anthropological Society of Nippon*, 62:245–260.

Harris EF. 2007. Carabelli's trait and tooth size of human maxillary first molars. *American Journal of Physical Anthropology*, 132(2):238–246.

Helfman PM, Bada J. 1975. Aspartic acid racemization in enamel from living humans. *Proceedings of the National Academy of Sciences USA*, 72:2891–2894.

Helfman PM, Bada J. 1976. Aspartic acid racemization in dentine as a measure of ageing. *Nature*, 262:279–281.

Hillson S. 1996. *Dental Anthropology*, Cambridge University Press, Cambridge, UK.

Hinkes MJ. 1990. Shovel-shaped incisors in human identification. In Gill GW, Rhine JS (eds.), *Skeletal Attribution of Race*, pp. 21–26, Anthropology Papers4, Maxwell Museum of Anthropology, Albuquerque, NM.

Hoppa RD, Vaupel JW. 2002. *Paleodemography: Age Distributions from Skeletal Samples*. Cambridge University Press, Cambridge, NY.

Hsu JW, Tsai P, Liu K, Ferguson D. 1997. Logistic analysis of shovel and Carabelli's tooth traits in a Caucasoid population. *Forensic Science International*, 89(1-2):65–74.

Ito S. 1972. Research on age estimation based on teeth. *Japanese Journal of Legal Medicine*, 26:31–41.

Ito S. 1975. Age estimation based on tooth crowns. *International Journal of Forensic Dentistry*, 3:9–14.

Jackes M. 2000. Building the basis for paleodemographic analysis: Adult age Determination. In Katzenberg AM, Saunders SR (eds.), *Biological Anthropology of the Human Skeleton*, pp. 417–466, Wiley-Liss, Inc., New York.

Jankauskas R, Barakauskas S, Bojarun R. 2001. Incremental lines of dental cementum in biological age estimation. *Homo*, 52:59–71.

Johanson G. 1971. Age determination from human teeth. *Odontologisk Revy*, 22:1–126.

Johnson CC. 1968. Transparent dentine in age estimation. *Oral Surgery*, 25:834–838.

Kagerer P, Grupe G. 2001. Age-at-death diagnosis and determination of life-history parameters by incremental lines in human dental cementum as an identification aid. *Forensic Science International*, 118:75–82.

Kashyap VK, Koteswara Rao NR. 1990. A modified Gustafson method of age estimation from teeth. *Forensic Science International*, 47:237–247.

Kemkes-Grottenthaler A. 1996. Critical evaluation of osteomorphognostic methods to estimate adult age at death: A test of the "complex method." *Homo*, 46:280–292.

Kemkes-Grottenthaler A. 2002. Aging through the ages: Historical perspectives on age indicator methods. In Hoppa RD, Vaupel JW (eds.), *Paleodemography: Age Distributions from Skeletal Samples*, pp. 48–72, Cambridge University Press, Cambridge, NY.

Kessler HP. 1997. An overview of forensic dentistry. In Kessler HP, Pemble CW (eds.), *33rd Annual Course Forensic Dentistry*, Bethesda, MD, March 3–8.

King K, Bada JL. 1979. Effect of in situ leaching on aminoacid racemisation rates in fossil bone. *Nature*, 281(13):135–137.

Komar DK. 2003. Twenty-seven years of forensic anthropology casework in New Mexico. *Journal of Forensic Science*, 48:521–524.

Konigsberg LW, Frankenberg SR. 1992. Estimation of age structure in anthropological demography. *American Journal of Physical Anthropology*, 89:235–256.

Kósa F, Szendrenyi J, Toth V. 1983. Afogak transzparenciajanak vizsgalata az eletkor megallapitasara. *Morphologiai es Igazsagugyi Orvosi Szemle*, 23:286–291.

Kvaal SI, Kolltveit KM, Thomsen IO, Solheim T. 1995. Age estimation of adults from dental radiographs. *Forensic Science International*, 74:175–185.

Kvaal SI, Koppang HS, Solheim T. 1994. Relationship between age and deposit of peritubular dentine. *Gerondontology*, 11:93–98.

Kvaal SI, Solheim T. 1995. Incremental lines in human dental cementum in relation to age. *European Journal of Oral Science*, 103:225–230.

Lamendin H, Baccino E, Humbert JF, Tavernier JC, Nossintchouk RM, Zerilli A. 1992. A simple technique for age estimation in adult corpses: The two criteria dental method. *Journal of Forensic Sciences*, 37:1373–1379.

Lamendin H, Cambray JC. 1980. Etude de la translucidite et des canalicules dentinaires pour appreciation de l'age. *Societe de Medecine Legale*, 9:489–499.

Lantelme RL, Handelman SL, Herbison RJ. 1976. Dentin formation in periodontally diseased teeth. *Journal of Dental Research*, 55:48–51.

Lasker GW, Lee MMC. 1957. Racial traits in human teeth. *Journal of Forensic Sciences*, 2:401–419.

Lavelle CLB. 1970. Analysis of attrition in adult human molars. *Journal of Dental Research*, 49:822–828.

Li C, Ji G. 1995. Age estimation from the permanent molar in northeast China by the method of average stage of attrition. *Forensic Science International*, 75:189–196.

Lipsinic FE, Paunovich E, Houston GD, Robison SF. 1986. Correlation of age and incremental lines in the cementum of human teeth. *Journal of Forensic Sciences*, 31:982–989.

López-Nicolás M, Canteras M, Luna A. 1990. Age estimation by IBAS image analysis of teeth. *Forensic Science International*, 45:143–150.

López-Nicolás M, Morales A, Luna A. 1993. Morphometric study of teeth in age calculation. *Journal of Forensic Odontostomatology*, 11:1–8.

López-Nicolás M, Morales A, Luna A. 1996. Application of dimorphism in teeth to age calculation. *Journal of Forensic Odontostomatology*, 14:9–12.

Lorensten H, Solheim T. 1989. Age assessment based on translucent dentine. *Journal of Forensic Odontostomatology*, 7:3–9.

Lovejoy CO. 1985. Dental wear in the Libben population: Its functional pattern and role in the determination of adult skeletal age at death. *American Journal of Physical Anthropology*, 68:47–56.

Lucas PW, Loh HS. 1986. Are the incremental lines in human cementum laid down annually? *Annual Academy of Medicine*, 15:384–386.

Lucy D, Aykroyd RG, Pollard AM, Solheim T. 1996. A Bayesian approach to adult human age estimation from dental observations by Johanson's age changes. *Journal of Forensic Science*, 41:189–194.

Lucy D, Pollard AM. 1995. Further comments on the estimation of error associated with the Gustafson dental age estimation method. *Journal of Forensic Sciences*, 40:222–227.

Lunt DA. 1978. Analysis of attrition in adult human molars. In Butler PB, Joysey J (eds.), *Development, Function, and Evolution of Teeth*, pp. 465–482, Academic Press, London, U.K.

Manly RS, Hodge HC. 1939. Dentistry and refractive index studies of dental hard tissues I. *Journal of Dental Research*, 18:133–141.

Maples WR. 1978. An improved technique using dental histology for estimation of adult age. *Journal of Forensic Sciences*, 23:764–770.

Maples WR, Rice PM. 1979. Some difficulties in the Gustafson dental age estimations. *Journal of Forensic Sciences*, 24:168–172.

Marcsik A, Kósa F, Kocsis G. 1992. The possibility of age determination on the basis of dental transparency in historical anthropology. In Smith P, Tchernov E (eds.), *Structure, Function and Evolution of Teeth*, pp. 527–538, Freud Publishing House Ltd., London, U.K.

Masters PM. 1986. Age at death determinations for autopsied remains based on aspartic acid racemization in tooth dentin: Importance of post-mortem conditions. *Forensic Science International*, 32:179–184.

Matsikidis G, Schultz P. 1982. Altersbestimmung nach dem Gebiss mit Hilfe des Zahnfilms. *Zahnaerztliche Mitteilungen*, 72:2527–2528.

Mendis BR, Darling AI. 1979. Distribution with age and attrition of peritubular dentine in the crowns of human teeth. *Archives of Oral Biology*, 24:131–139.

Metzger Z, Buchner A, Gorsky M. 1980. Gustafson's method for age determination from teeth—A modification for the use of dentists in identification teams. *Journal of Forensic Science*, 25:742–749.

Miles AEW. 1962. Assessment of the ages of a population of Anglo-Saxons from their dentitions. *Proceedings of the Royal Society of Medicine*, 55:881–886.

Miles AEW. 1963. Dentition and the estimation of age. *Journal of Dental Research*, 42:255–263.

Miles AEW. 1978. Teeth as an indicator of age in man. In Butler PM, Joysey KA (eds.), *Development, Function and the Evolution of Teeth*, Academic Press, London, U.K., pp. 455–462.

Miller CS, Dove, SB, Cottone JA. 1988. Failure of use of cemental annulations in teeth to determine the age of humans. *Journal of Forensic Sciences*, 33:137–143.

Mincer HH, Harris EF, Berryman HE. 1993. The A.B.F.O. study of third molar development and its use as an estimator of chronological age. *Journal of Forensic Sciences*, 38:379–390.

Molleson T, Cox M, Waldron AH, Whittaker DK. 1993. The Spitalfields Project. Vol.2, The middling sort: CBA Research Report no. 86. Council for British Archaeology, York, U.K.

Molnar S. 1971. Human tooth wear, tooth function and cultural variability. *American Journal of Physical Anthropology*, 34:175–190.

Monzavi BF, Ghodoosi A, Savabi O, Hasanzadeh A. 2003. Model of age estimation based on dental factors of unknown cadavers among Iranians. *Journal of Forensic Sciences*, 48:1–3.

Mörnstad H, Pfeiffer H, Teivens A. 1994. Estimation of dental age using HPLC-technique to determine the degree of aspartic acid racemization. *Journal of Forensic Sciences*, 39:1425–1431.

Morse DR, Esposito JV, Schoor RS. 1993. A radiographic study of aging changes of the dental pulp and dentin in normal teeth. *Quintessence International*, 24:329–333.

Moore GE. 1970. Age changes occurring in the teeth. *Journal of the Forensic Sciences Society*, 10:179–180.

Moore-Jansen PH, Jantz RL. 1986. A computerized skeletal data bank for forensic anthropology. Department of Anthropology, University of Tennessee: Knoxville, TN.

Moorrees CFA. 1957. The Aleut Dentition: *A Correlative Study of Dental Characteristics in an Eskimoid People*. Harvard University Press, Cambridge, MA.

Moorrees CFA. 1959. *The Dentition in the Growing Child*. Harvard University Press, Cambridge, MA.

Moorrees CFA, Fanning EA, Hunt EE. 1963. Age variation of formation stages for ten permanent teeth. *Journal of Dental Research*, 42:1490–1502.

Moorrees CFA, Thomsen SO, Jenson E, Yen PKJ. 1957. Mesiodistal crown diameters of deciduous and permanent teeth. *Journal of Dental Research*, 36:39–47.

Nalbandian J, Gonzales F, Sognnaes F. 1960. Sclerotic age changes in root dentin of human teeth as observed by optical, electron, and x-ray microscopy. *Journal of Dental Research*, 39:598–607.
Naylor JW, Miller WG, Stokes GN, Stott GG. 1985. Cementum annulation enhancement: A technique for age determination in man. *American Journal of Physical Anthropology*, 68:197–201.
Nitzan DW, Michaeli Y, Weinreb M, Azaz B. 1986. The effect of aging on tooth morphology: A study on impacted teeth. *Oral Surgery*, 61:54–60.
Nkhumeleni FS, Raubenheimer EJ, Monteith BD. 1989. Gustafson's method for age determination revised. *Journal of Forensic Odonto-Stamatology*, 7:13–16.
Ogino T, Ogino N, Nagy B. 1985. Application of aspartic acid racemization to forensic odontology: Postmortem designation of age at death. *Forensic Science International*, 29:259–267.
Ohtani S. 1994. Age estimation by aspartic acid racemization in dentin of deciduous teeth. *Journal of Forensic Sciences*, 68:77–82.
Ohtani S. 1995. Studies on age estimation using racemization of aspartic acid in cementum. *Journal of Forensic Sciences*, 40:805–807.
Ohtani S, Sugimoto H, Sugeno H, Yamamoto S, Yamamoto K. 1995. Racemization of aspartic acid in human cementum with age. *Archives of Oral Biology*, 40:91–95.
Ohtani S, Yamamoto K. 1991. Age estimation using the racemization of amino acid in human dentin. *Journal of Forensic Sciences*, 36:792–800.
Ohtani S, Yamamoto K. 1992. Estimation of age from a tooth by means of racemization of an amino acid, especially aspartic acid—Comparison of enamel and dentin. *Journal of Forensic Sciences*, 37:1061–1067.
Philippas GG. 1961. Influence of occlusal wear and age on formation of dentin and size of pulp chamber. *Journal of Dental Research*, 40:1186–1198.
Pindborg JJ. 1970. *Pathology of the Dental Hard Tissues*. WB Saunders, Philadelphia, PA.
Plato CC, Fox KM, Tobin JD. 1994. Skeletal changes in human aging. In Crews DE, Garruto RM (eds.), *Biological Anthropology and Human Aging. Perspectives on human Variation Over the Life Span*, pp. 272–300, Oxford University Press, Oxford, U.K.
Prince DA. 2004. Estimation of adult skeletal age-at-death from dental root translucency. PhD dissertation, The University of Tennessee, Knoxville, TN.
Prince DA, Konigsberg LW. 2008. New formulae for estimating age-at-death in the Balkans utilizing Lamendin's dental technique and Bayesian analysis. *Journal of Forensic Sciences*, 53(3):578–587.
Prince DA, Ubelaker DH. 2002. Application of Lamendin's adult dental aging technique to a diverse skeletal sample. *Journal of Forensic Sciences*, 47:107–116.
Rathod H, Roberts D, Gray C, Jones SJ, Boyde A. 1993. Autofluorescence mode confocal microscopy of dental tissues. *Proceedings of Bone and Tooth Society*, 1:39.
Renz H, Schaefer V, Duschner H, Radlanski RJ. 1997. Incremental lines in root cementum of human teeth: An approach to their ultrastructural nature by microscopy. *Advances in Dental Research*, 11:472–477.
Ritz S, Schütz H-W, Peper C. 1993. Postmortem estimation of age at death based on aspartic acid racemization in dentin: its applicability for root dentin. *International Journal of Legal Medicine*, 105:289–293.
Ritz S, Schütz H-W, Schwatzer B. 1990. The extent of aspartic acid racemization in dentin: A possible method for a more accurate determination of age at death? *Zeitschrift für Rechtsmedizin*, 103:457–462.
Ross AH, Konigsberg LW. 2002. New formulae for estimating stature in the Balkans. *Journal of Forensic Science*, 47:165–167.
Russell KF. 1996. Determination of age-at-death from dental remains. PhD dissertation, Kent State University, Kent, OH.
Sarajlić N, Klonowski EE, Drukier P, Harrington R. 2003. Lamendin's and Prince's dental aging methods applied to a Bosnian population. *Proceedings of the Fifty-fourth Annual American Academy of Forensic Sciences*, 6:239–240 (abstract).

Saunders M. 1965. Dental factors in age determination. *Medicine, Science and the Law*, 5:34–37

Schroeder HE. 1991. *Oral Structural Biology: Embryology, Structure, and Function of Normal Hard and Soft Tissues of the Oral Cavity and Temporomandibular Joints*, Georg Thieme Verlag, Stuttgart, Germany.

Scott EC, 1979. Dental wear scoring technique. *American Journal of Physical Anthropology*, 51:213–218.

Scott GR, Turner CG, II. 1997. *The Anthropology of Modern Human Teeth: Dental Morphology and Its Variation in Recent Human Populations*. Cambridge University Press, Cambridge, NY.

Sengupta A, Shellis RP, Whittaker DK. 1998. Measuring root dentine translucency in human teeth of varying antiquity. *Journal of Archaeological Science*, 25:1221–1229.

Sengupta A, Whittaker DK, Shellis RP. 1999. Difficulties in estimating age using root dentine translucency in human teeth of varying antiquity. *Archives of Oral Biology*, 44:889–899.

Shimoyama A, Harada K. 1984. An age determination of an ancient burial mound man by apparent racemization reaction of aspartic acid in tooth dentin. *Chemistry Letters*, 1984:1661–1664.

Šlaus M, Strinović D, Škavić J, Petrovečki V. 2003. Discriminate function sexing of fragmentary and complete femora: Standards for contemporary Croatia. *Journal of Forensic Science*, 48:509–512.

Smith BH. 1984. Rate of molar wear: Implications for developmental timing and demography in human evolution. *American Journal of Physical Anthropology*, 63:220.

Sognnaes RF, Gratt BM, Papin PJ. 1985. Biomedical image processing for age measurements of intact teeth. *Journal of Forensic Sciences*, 30:1082–1089.

Solheim T. 1984. Dental age estimation. An alternative technique for tooth sectioning. *American Journal of Forensic Medicine and Pathology*, 5:181–184.

Solheim T. 1988. Dental attrition as an indicator of age. *Gerodontics*, 4:299–304.

Solhiem T. 1989. Dental root translucency as an indicator of age. *Scandinavian Journal of Dental Research*, 97:189–197.

Solhiem T. 1990. Dental cementum apposition as an indicator of age. *Scandinavian Journal of Dental Research*, 98:510–519.

Solheim T. 1992. Recession of periodontal ligament as an indicator of age. *Journal of Forensic Odontostomatology*, 19:32–42.

Solheim T. 1993. A new method for dental age estimation in adults. *Forensic Science International*, 59:137–147.

Solheim T, Sundnes PK. 1980. Dental age estimation of Norwegian adults—A comparison of different methods. *Forensic Science International*, 16:7–17.

Sopher IM. 1976. *Forensic Dentistry*, Charles C. Thomas, Springfield, IL.

Stein TJ, Corcoran JF. 1994. Pararadicular cementum deposition as a criterion for age estimation in human beings. *Oral Surgery, Oral Medicine, Oral Pathology, Oral Radiology and Endodontics* 77:266–270.

Stott GG, Sis RF, Levy BM. 1982. Cemental annulation as an age criterion in forensic dentistry. *Journal of Dental Research*, 61:814–817.

Ten Cate AR, Thompson GW, Dickinson JB, Hunter HA. 1977. The estimation of age of skeletal remains from colour of roots of teeth. *Journal of the Canadian Dental Association*, 43:83–86.

Teschler-Nicola M, Prossinger H. 1998. Sex determination using dental tooth dimensions. In Alt KW, Rösing FW, Teschler-Nicola (eds.), *Dental Anthropology: Fundamentals, Limits, and Prospects*, pp. 479–500, SpringerWien, New York, NY.

Thomas GJ, Whittaker DK, Embery G. 1994. A comparative study of translucent apical dentine in vital and non-vital human teeth. *Archives of Oral Biology*, 39:29–34.

Turner CG, II, Nichol CR, Scott GR. 1991. Scoring procedures for key morphological traits of the permanent dentition: The Arizona State University Dental Anthropology System. In Kelley MA, Larsen CS (eds.), *Advances in Dental Anthropology*, pp. 13–31, Wiley-Liss, New York.

Ubelaker DH. 1989. *Human Skeletal Remains, Analysis, Interpretation*, revised edition. Taraxacum, Washington, DC.

Ubelaker DH, Baccino E, Zerilli A, Oger E. 1998. Comparison of methods for assessing adult age at death on French autopsy samples (abstract). *Proceedings of American Academy of Forensic Sciences IV*, 174–175.

Ubelaker DH, Parra RC. 2008. Application of three dental methods of adult age estimation from intact single rooted teeth to a Peruvian sample. *Journal of Forensic Sciences*, 53(3):608–611.

Vasiliadis L, Darling AI, Levers BGH. 1983. The amount and distribution of sclerotic human root dentine. *Archives of Oral Biology*, 28:645–649.

van der Velden U. 1984. Effects of age on the periodontium. *Journal of Clinical Periodontology*, 11:281–294.

Whittaker DK, Bakri MM. 1996. Racial variations in the extent of tooth root translucency in ageing individuals. *Archives of Oral Biology*, 41:15–19.

Wittwer-Backofen. 2000. Tooth cementum annulation: A validation study for individual age at death estimates. Report for the Max-Planck-Institut für Demografische Forschung, Rostock, Germany.

Wittwer-Backofen U, Buba H. 2002. Age estimation by tooth cementum annulation: Perspectives of a new validation study. In Hoppa RD, Vaupel JW (eds.), *Paleodemography: Age Distributions from Skeletal Samples*, Cambridge University Press, Cambridge, NY, pp. 107–128.

Wittwer-Backofen U, Gampe J, Vaupel JW. 2004. Tooth cementum annulation for age Estimation: Results from a large known-age validation study. *American Journal of Physical Anthropology*, 123:119–129.

Zhang Z. 1982. A preliminary study of estimation of age by morphological changes in the symphysis pubis. *Acta Anthropologica Sinica*, 1:132–136.

Zuhrt R. 1955. Stomatologische Üntersuchungen an Spätmittelalterlichen Funden von Reckkahn (12–14 Jh.): I. Die Zahnkaries und ihre Folgen. *Deutsche Zahn-Mund und Kieferheilkunde*, 25:1–15.

Suggested Readings

Bowers CM. 2004. *Forensic Dental Evidence: An Investigators Handbook*. Elsevier Academic Press, San Diego, CA.

Bowers CM, Bell GL (eds.) 1997. *Manual of Forensic Odontology*, 3rd edn. Manticore Publishers, Ontario, Canada.

Cawson RA, Eveson JW. 1987. *Oral Pathology and Diagnosis*. W.B. Saunders Company, Philadelphia, PA.

Clark DH (ed.) 1992. *Practical Forensic Odontology*. Butterworth-Heinemann Ltd., Oxford, U.K.

Fuller JL, Denehy GE. 1999. *Concise Dental Anatomy and Morphology*, 3rd edn. Year Book Medical Publishers, Inc., Chicago, IL.

Hillson S. 1996. *Dental Anthropology*. Cambridge University Press, Cambridge, U.K.

Luntz LL, Luntz P. 1973. *Handbook for Dental Identification: Techniques in Forensic Dentistry*, J.B. Lippincott Co., Philadelphia, PA.

Sopher IM. 1976. *Forensic Dentistry*. American Lecture Series No. 990. Charles C. Thomas, Springfield, IL.

Whittaker DK, MacDonald DG. 1989. *Color Atlas of Forensic Dentistry*. Wolfe Medical, London, U.K.

Crime Scene Methodology

6

DENISE TO

Contents

Introduction: General Principles

The majority of skeletal cases that pass through the laboratory for a forensic anthropologist to analyze are usually recovered from a field context. That is, the remains were discovered in a location outside the laboratory. This is in contrast to skeletal material that may occasionally be mailed to the medical examiner's office or, even, dropped off at the doorstep of the laboratory. In these situations, *where* the bones came from may never be truly known. But in the majority of cases, skeletal analysis begins "in the field." Remains are sometimes discovered by citizens who inadvertently stumble upon them—while hiking in mountains, while doing construction, etc. Sometimes, law enforcement personnel discover remains while investigating an area for other reasons. And sometimes, even, they are led to a location by an informant who specifically points out a location where a decedent is buried. The actual location, or *site*, where skeletal remains are discovered may contain a wealth of information regarding how they originally got there. This contextual information is critical to ascertain, especially if a crime was committed. Therefore, the proper recovery of skeletal material in the field is of paramount importance to the forensic anthropologist.

While numerous law enforcement personnel and crime scene investigators are trained in processing crime scenes, a forensic anthropologist is most needed when skeletonized (or partially skeletonized) human remains are discovered—and they are especially useful when skeletal remains and evidence are *incorporated into the natural environment.* In these situations, the term *forensic archaeology* is oftentimes used. For many of these crime scenes, skeletal remains and associated material evidence get "buried" by the natural environment, such as under soil, shrubs, grasses, and leaves. In some cases, this occurs naturally (e.g., if a lone hiker dies in the woods and is not discovered until many years later). In other cases, the remains and evidence are covered up on purpose (e.g., where a perpetrator is attempting to conceal a crime). In all cases, however, the incorporation of skeletal remains and material evidence into the natural environment constitutes the *archaeological record*. That record of natural and cultural events, captured above and below ground in a single location, can be very dynamic because, as the years pass, the record can be transformed by the addition and subtraction of information. Thus, the archaeological record is fragile and, when data need to be extracted from the archaeological record, a forensic archaeologist is best suited for the task. There are fundamental differences between traditional archaeology and forensic archaeology in that traditional archaeology examines the archaeological record of a site (such as an ancient village) for research-driven motives, whereas in forensic archaeology, the anthropologist is focused on collecting data from the archaeological record for medicolegal reasons. However, to collect such data correctly, the forensic anthropologist must employ some of the same methods and techniques used in traditional archaeology. Forensic archaeology simply refers to the application of traditional research-oriented excavation techniques and methods to modern forensic sites and crime scenes.

But crime scenes come in all shapes and sizes. A crime scene can be in a homeowner's backyard, inside the trunk of a car, on the top of a snowy mountain, in the middle of a corn field, or even in a cemetery. A crime scene can be as small as a shoe box or bigger than a football field. Every crime scene is unique, and some sites where remains are discovered turn out not to be crime scenes at all. A crime scene is any location where a crime has potentially been committed. If a forensic anthropologist is called to a potential crime scene, it usually means that skeletal remains were discovered at that site. But not all sites to which a forensic anthropologist is called turn out to be crime scenes because it is possible that no *crime* was actually committed. For example, it is not uncommon for skeletons to be found in the woods. But was a crime committed here? Is this a victim of a homicide? Was this murder? Or was this an accident? Did a lone hiker get attacked by a wild animal? Or did this lone hiker have a heart attack after a particularly difficult hike? Perhaps a forensic anthropologist is called to a scene where a box of bones is found in a private garage. Again, was a crime committed here? Is this a homicide from long ago that someone has tried to cover up? Or, perhaps, are these legally acquired bones used for teaching anatomy classes at the local community college? In some places, it was commonplace for a family to bury loved ones on their own property, rather than in a local cemetery. And for many locations throughout the world, ancient skeletons that have long slumbered within the ground are rediscovered by intrusion and development of ever-expanding urbanism. Forensic anthropologists are frequently called out to investigate these types of burials.

Ancient archaeological sites and other sanctioned burials that are deemed by the forensic anthropologist as having little "forensic value" can be simply catalogued and photographed; however, the majority of sites with skeletal remains require processing as potential crime scenes. In actuality, it is not necessarily the job of the forensic anthropologist to determine whether or not a crime has actually taken place. That determination is made by the detectives only *after* the scene has been processed and the skeletal remains have been analyzed in the laboratory. Therefore, a good forensic anthropologist will respond to all sites with the same amount of professionalism and scientific integrity. The best practice is to process a site as if a crime has been committed until otherwise determined.

In the Past

Finding human remains and processing a crime scene require an organized, systematic approach. But crime scenes have not always been treated with the same meticulous attention that they are today. Imagine a standard Easter Egg Hunt at a park (a grassy field, some shrubs, and a few trees). A dozen children happily and hastily run off to look for colorful plastic eggs to claim the candy reward inside them. What direction do the children run off in? The answer: they run in all directions. And when one child finds an egg in the tall grass, the children who were searching the nearby shrubs abandon their search there, run to the tall grass, and begin searching there instead. In the end, some children find many eggs, while others are not so lucky. Some locations get searched over and over again by the children, hoping that more plastic eggs turn up, while other locations are never searched. The final result is that some eggs are never found. This method of searching describes an *unsystematic* approach. The children worked independently. Their goals were based on personal gain—trying to find and claim the candy reward for themselves before other children could do so. No coordinated search pattern was established, and the locations searched were random. And the search ended—not when the area was thoroughly investigated, but surely when a parent decided it should.

While an Easter Egg Hunt may never reach the same level of significance as searching for human remains at a crime scene, the distinction in the methodology is paramount. If a plastic egg is left behind at an Easter Egg Hunt, lives will hardly be affected. But if an investigator misses a crucial fragment of human remains or evidence at a crime scene, that error may be the difference between a mysterious victim being positively identified or forever left unknown. It may even mean the difference between solving a homicide and finding the victim's killer or allowing the perpetrator to escape justice.

Unfortunately, the Easter Egg Hunt method is not too dissimilar from how many crimes scenes used to be processed. In the past, untrained personnel and unsystematic methods were used. Crime scenes were crowded with media reporters, political officials, and curious on-lookers. Evidence was found by looking in random places rather than through a thorough and methodical search from one end of the crime scene to the other. Wearing gloves was oftentimes an ignored practice. Evidence was contaminated and sometimes even ignored. Photographs of the crime scene were scarce and/or poor. Documentation of the methods used was rare. Occasionally, a victim's body was repositioned, and evidence was discarded (sometimes by law enforcement personnel themselves) for "the sake of decency"—that is, to avoid potentially corrupting the victim's image or shocking survivors, family members, or even the public. The result was poor scientific integrity. While this may seem appalling by today's standards, these deficiencies were simply due to a lack of regulations or standardized practices regarding crime scene processing.

Today, more attention is paid to the science of crime scene investigation, especially in developed nations where the criminal justice system relies heavily on the validity of solid empirical evidence. And with the growing trend of publicizing criminal trials, greater scrutiny is placed on all aspects of a criminal case, including crime scene methods. Scientific evidence is increasingly used in court trials to convict a criminal or to absolve an accused. Over the years, the result has been a significant improvement in the way crime scenes are processed.

The difference, then, between the Easter Egg Hunt and modern crime scene methodology is to process a site in a *systematic* fashion that stands up to the highest level of scrutiny. The Department of Defense's Central Identification Laboratory defines scientific integrity as a "strict adherence to the scientific method with transparency and accountability for all actions. Scientific integrity requires sound and accepted methods and high ethical standards regardless of the nature of the work (JPAC Laboratory Manual 2011)." It means everyone works together with the common and unbiased goal of processing the crime scene according to a set plan of methods and techniques considered to be the best practices, used to ensure maximum recovery of humans and evidence and minimal alteration of the context of the crime scene (see Box 6.1). If you deviate from using a systematic search, it means you have no system, and if you have no system, you might as well be searching for Easter Eggs.

Controlled Deconstruction

One of the most fundamental concepts in crime scene methodology is understanding that to process a crime scene is to tamper with it—even possibly destroy it. Examining the archaeological record through excavation cannot be accomplished without *excavating* the site. The systematic excavation of a site is one of the most intrusive and destructive methods used to examine the archaeological record. In the most basic sense, determining what happened at the crime scene *requires* altering it. For example, because investigators must physically walk through the crime scene, their footsteps may alter the floor. Because an investigator needs to move a body to the morgue, the position of the victim's arms and legs will change. Because an investigator needs to pick up a weapon and transport it to the laboratory, the weapon will have to be moved from its original position. Even small actions, such as turning on a light or opening a window, can alter the crime scene.

Because of this, it is crucial for an investigator to understand that to process a crime scene means to alter the original *context* of everything at the crime scene. To complete the job, you *have* to alter it—you *have* to walk through it with your footsteps, you *have* to move the body eventually, and you *have* to put the weapon in a bag and take it to the laboratory. The key is to alter the crime scene *correctly*. This is known as controlled destruction or, rather, *controlled deconstruction*. Crime scene methodology is based on a series of steps used to *deconstruct* the crime scene in order to maximize evidence collection, while at the same time minimizing contamination and alteration of the crime scene and preserving the context of the evidence. It is possible that the investigation team that processes the crime scene may be the only people to ever see it; therefore, the team has an ethical obligation to process the site to a high level of scientific integrity, or else justice may not be served. A forensic anthropologist only gets one chance to process a crime scene or excavate a site. Consequently, a skeleton must be excavated correctly because, if it is not, it cannot be put back in the ground for a second try.

Scene Documentation: Protecting the Scene Integrity

Because forensic archaeology is a destructive science—and because it is possible that the investigation team that processes the crime scene may be the only people to ever see it—it

BOX 6.1 CSI EFFECT: SCIENCE IN ACTION (BACKWARD AND WRONG)

The recent popularity of laboratory crime dramas and "whodunits" that focus on the collection and application of evidence, such as *CSI*, *NCIS*, and *Bones*, have exposed viewers to the detail-oriented world of forensic evidence collection and scientific analysis. An entire generation of viewers has became fascinated with and influenced by the dramatized careers of crime scene investigators, forensic anthropologists, and pathologists who are fictionalized on these shows, sometimes as gun-toting, slightly nerdy professionals with model-good looks who interrogate suspects, serve arrest warrants, and carry out laboratory analysis—all after processing the entire crime scene in the first place. While most viewers ignore the inaccurate portrayal of crime scene investigators and forensic anthropologists in favor of good entertainment, some viewers actually believe the many Hollywood embellishments as fact. Small inaccuracies (such as the telephone fingerprint analyzer or the standard laboratory holographic skeleton imaging device) are comical when real forensic anthropologists get asked about them by the public. But more serious fictionalizations, such as outrageously and inaccurately portrayed timelines to process and analyze evidence (e.g., DNA analysis), can have a detrimental effect on public citizens who may become a victim of a real-life crime—their expectations of the investigation are unrealistic and can be emotionally devastating. In addition, the opinions and expectations that many lay viewers develop about forensic science and how evidence is collected and processed can have detrimental effects on genuine cases, should they be called into court for jury duty.

But the biggest crime of which these television shows are guilty is the presentation of science conducted backward. In these shows, the investigators visit a crime scene, and, after just moments of examining the scene, they immediately formulate and verbalize their opinions as to *what* crime was committed, *how* it was committed, and even *why* it was committed. A twist half-way through the episode when a laboratory technician discovers something shocking about a piece of evidence causes a dramatic and sudden change of opinion.

But good forensic science does not work this way, and depicting it as such in these television shows is a gross disservice for those who actually work these jobs. In reality, a good forensic scientist *never* develops a hypothesis about what happened at a crime scene until after *all* the data have been collected—until after *all* the facts are presented on the table. Waiting for all the facts to surface can take days, weeks, even months. It is only *after* all the data has been collected and analyzed that a good forensic scientist even *begins* to create a theory. What is depicted on these television shows is actually backward. If you develop a theory before all the facts are in, you will bias yourself and the inevitable will occur—you will begin to twist the facts to suit your theory—and that makes for poor science.

BOX 6.2 PHOTOGRAPHY

Because crime scene processing is a destructive science, proper and thorough documentation of the crime scene is crucial. Photography is paramount in good documentation because it provides a visual accompaniment for all written descriptions and actions. Context can be much better understood with photographs, and no amount of written description can substitute. Photographs of the actions conducted by the investigation team are important to document the methods used by the team. Actions such as walking a pedestrian survey, clearing vegetation, excavating a burial, screening sediments, and removing and bagging evidence are some of the many actions performed by the team that should be documented photographically. Photographs of evidence and human remains discovered at a scene are vital and should always start with wide shots in order to capture an item in relation to its surroundings. Progressively closer photographs of the evidence help to capture the complexity of a busy site. Finally, detailed, close-up photographs of the evidence while still *in situ* are a must. Good photographs always include a scale (and direction-of-view for the wider shots—cardinal directions work best).

is crucial for the team to document everything that is seen and done at the crime scene. *Documentation* of a crime scene investigation is the collection of data through written field notes and photography (see Box 6.2). The goal of crime scene documentation is to create a permanent record of what was discovered, how it was discovered, in what condition it was discovered, and the steps taken by the investigators to process the site. This permanent record can be used later by other people, such as law enforcement personnel, laboratory analysts, attorneys, and other forensic anthropologists to understand the context of everything at the crime scene. Good documentation is crucial because these other investigators must be able to theoretically (even physically) recreate the crime scene as accurately as possible weeks, months, even years after it was initially processed.

Good documentation protects not only the integrity of the investigation, but that of the investigator. For cases that result in courtroom testimony, an investigator may be questioned by an attorney years after the initial incident. The time differential can make it difficult for an investigator to remember the details of the case, including questions such as, "Who was with you at the crime scene? What did you do with the evidence once you found it?" Even if an investigator was able to remember these kinds of details, he or she may not be able to provide evidence supporting the answers if required in court. Relying on memory for these kinds of details is hardly an efficient technique. Instead, proper documentation of the crime scene allows an investigator to refer back to the moment of scene processing in order to answer these types of questions with confidence.

As a baseline, scene documentation begins with the basics of "who-what-where-when-and-how," but ultimately, the documentation should be much more in depth. For example:

- Who called you for help in the first place? (A detective?)
- What time of day did you arrive at the location?
- Where exactly is the crime scene? (What is the address?)

- If it is an outdoor crime scene, what was the weather like when you arrived? (Was it raining?)
- Who was there when you showed up? (Who might potentially contaminate the scene?)
- Who was part of your investigation team?
- What does the crime scene look like? (Describe this in as much detail as possible)
- Where were the remains found? (Under a bed, in a tree, in a grave?)
- What methods did you use to search for more evidence?
- What kind of evidence did you find? (Human remains, weapons, clothing?)
- Where did you find the items? (Were evidentiary items touching each other? Were the items far apart?)
- What did you do with the evidence? (How did you contain the items and where and when were they taken?)
- If you had to excavate, how did you go about doing this?
- How much did you excavate?
- Did you draw a sketch map of the excavated area?

These are only a handful of questions that a good investigator must be sure to answer when documenting a crime scene. It is important to remember that the documentation must be good enough for another person to recreate the crime scene in the future (see Box 6.3). Poor documentation can result in the loss of information—and even the loss of crucial evidence.

- *In-text quiz:* You process a crime scene in the woods that has no street address. How would you document that location so that another investigator can find that exact spot in the future?
- *Answer:* For most crime scenes that are *off the beaten path*, be sure to document the location with a global positioning system (GPS) grid coordinate. A future investigator can input the grid coordinates into another GPS device to lead them to it. Document the distance and bearing of the closest road and town and be sure to document all landmarks in the area in as much detail as possible so the crime scene can be relocated. Detailed topographic maps are available for most locations in the United States. In addition, commercial services available online, such as Google Maps®, can provide relatively accurate aerial photography of an area. Be sure to mark the crime scene location on one of these types of maps and include it in your documentation.

Processing the Crime Scene

Some sites are easy—they are small with simple topography and little vegetation, have very few items to document, and are thus relatively straightforward. Processing these kinds of sites requires few personnel, minimal resources, and little time. Other sites are not simple—they are large, complicated, and filled with many items to map and photograph. The site may also be in a heavily wooded area that requires a long, arduous hike. These sites can take many hours to process—even days (see Box 6.4). But regardless of how simple or complex the site, an investigator must follow the same set of principals and methods at all sites.

BOX 6.3 DOCUMENTATION EXERCISE: TEST YOUR ABILITY TO DOCUMENT A CRIME SCENE WITH THIS SIMPLE EXERCISE

You will need two additional helpers and numerous building blocks of different colors and shapes (Figure 6.1), available at your local toy store or craft store. Have one helper build up a tower with the blocks in a random pattern. Once complete, your job is to *deconstruct* the tower, but you must document the process. To test your documentation ability, have the other helper reconstruct the tower *based entirely on your notes*. If your documentation is adequate, the reconstructed tower should be identical to the first.

Figure 6.1 Building blocks of different colors and shapes. (Courtesy of Denise To.)

BOX 6.4 TEAMWORK

Small sites can be processed quickly with a small number of personnel (sometimes the team consists of just one person—the forensic anthropologist—and that person does all the work). But when faced with a large site, the forensic anthropologist may need the help of other people. The kind of help other people can provide will depend on who is available and the experience they have. But one must be conservative when choosing help. Community residents, for example, may have good intentions, but their lack of training can sometimes lead to accidentally contaminating and disturbing the crime scene. Worse yet, they may unknowingly damage and destroy a crucial piece of evidence. Available law enforcement personnel can be useful when large searches need to be conducted, but for actual handling and processing of data and evidence, stick to professional crime scene investigators only.

All investigations begin with a *preliminary assessment*—an initial step where the forensic anthropologist must determine exactly what needs to happen at the site. During this initial step, the anthropologist determines if the skeletal remains are human (to the untrained eye animal remains are often mistaken for human remains). If the remains are indeed human, the anthropologist determines if they have forensic value. If so, then the anthropologist makes a logistical assessment of what needs to be done to process the site. Do additional personnel and resources need to be mobilized to assist? Has the medical examiner's office been notified of the discovery of human remains? Does special equipment need to be brought in? How much time will the investigation take? Is there enough daylight to complete the task or will lights be needed? At this point, processing of the crime scene has begun, and the anthropologist must begin documentation and photography.

The first major step in processing a crime scene is to determine its boundaries. One effective method to determine site boundaries is with a *visual pedestrian survey* of the area. This is a systematic and controlled search of the area wherein a team of people walks across the crime scene—lined up in a row side-by-side, approximately one arm's length apart from each other—and visually search as much of the crime scene as possible (Figure 6.2). Investigators walk a *transect* (straight line) across the crime scene, wherein each person visually inspects the area within arm's reach until the team collectively takes the next step. As possible evidence is discovered, it is marked with a pinflag, numbered, photographed, and left in place until it can be mapped and documented. The goal of the pedestrian survey is to cover as much of the crime scene as possible so that no evidence is missed. During the pedestrian survey, the team looks for human remains and items that may be related to the case (weapons, clothing, wallets, etc.), but they also look for other clues that may not be so obvious, such as changes in the soil and vegetation (depressions, mounds, odors, stains) as well as areas with differential insect or animal activity that may indicate decaying organic matter. The number of people needed for a pedestrian survey depends on the size of the area. Figures 6.3 and 6.4 illustrate a typical walking path followed during a pedestrian survey. The survey is conducted first in one direction, followed by another pedestrian survey conducted in the perpendicular direction. This method doubles the area covered and decreases the likelihood that possible evidence is overlooked.

Figure 6.2 Line of investigators conducting a pedestrian survey. (Courtesy of M. Morrow.)

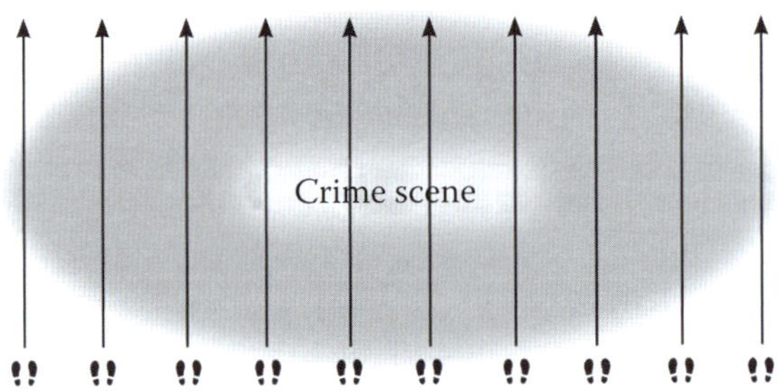

Figure 6.3 Diagram of the first phase of a typical walking path used in a pedestrian survey.

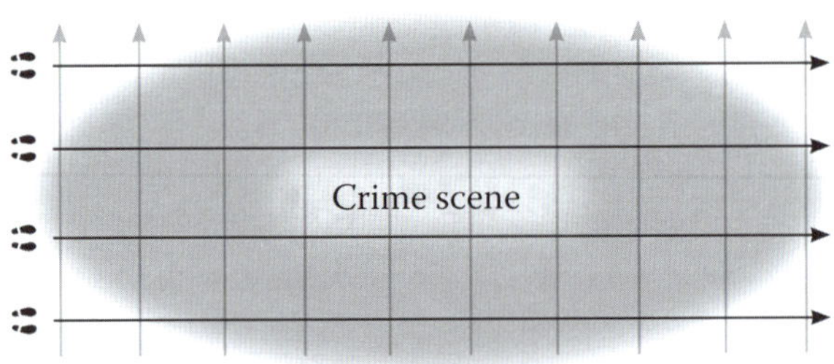

Figure 6.4 Diagram of the second phase of a typical walking path used in a pedestrian survey. The same area is resurveyed from the perpendicular direction to decrease the likelihood of overlooking possible evidence.

Understanding Site Formation

As mentioned earlier, every site is unique, and the distinctive nature of each site will dictate which techniques will be used by the investigator. Some sites may require a mechanical excavator to remove a cement slab overburden, while others may require rappelling equipment to gain access to a remote location. A water hose may be needed at one site to screen muddy sediments, while another site may require machetes to clear tall shrubbery. In general, however, the forensic anthropologist will face two major types of sites—*surface sites*, where the majority of human remains are on top of the ground surface (or relatively near it), and *subsurface sites*, where remains are buried below the ground surface. At surface sites, the human remains are easier to find, but they are often disturbed from the original context because they are more easily moved and affected by other processes. Worse yet, they can disappear from the site, either taken away by animals and/or by natural processes such as erosion and flooding. As a result, preservation of the remains and the integrity of the site get worse the longer they remain on the surface.

Subsurface sites are those where the majority of human remains are found below the ground surface, such as those buried in a grave or covered by a landslide. These remains can be either shallow or deep and can be very hard to find. These sites can be more time-consuming, as they require more work to recover since excavation may be required. However, the remains are usually in a better state of preservation, as is the context and integrity of the archaeological record at the site. The general principals of crime scene processing (in terms of documentation, evidence collection, and scientific integrity) are the same regardless of whether remains are on the surface or below it.

However, subsurface sites pose a new set of challenges for the forensic anthropologist. In some situations, the presence of subsurface skeletal remains is confirmed by the actual discovery of remains from that assemblage. In other cases, the presence of subsurface remains is only hearsay (e.g., when an informant believes a body was buried in a specific area). It is up to the forensic anthropologist to confirm or refute the possibility. The techniques used to investigate the subsurface environment range from minimally invasive and variably effective (such as remote sensing devices) to highly invasive and very effective (excavation). The unique nature of each site will dictate which technique is most appropriate. For example, the use of a cadaver dog, or a dog specially trained to identify the scent of decaying human tissue, can be very useful, especially when remains are believed to be shallow and relatively fresh (i.e., recently deceased). However, the efficacy of cadaver dogs can decline when the remains have been buried for a significant period of time. Certain *remote sensing and geophysical devices* can be useful to anthropologist, but these machines do not actually detect skeletal material—they only provide a snapshot of information about the subsurface that may or may not be the result of human remains. For example, metal detectors and magnetometers use a magnetic field that penetrates into the ground surface to detect the presence of anomalies caused by metal items such as firearms, ammunitions, and nails. Ground penetrating radar, a method by which radar pulses are used to image the subsurface, can be useful in detecting anomalies and voids in the soil, such as those similar to ones produced by graves. Resistivity and conductivity devices use electricity to view the subsurface, the former by measuring the soil's ability to resist an electrical current and the latter by measuring the soil's ability to conduct an electrical current. Because remote-sensing devices do not actually detect the presence of skeletal material, these techniques can only be used as a proxy to determine if human remains are present; the "images" of the subsurface produced by these machines may not have any relation to human remains. A skeleton with no associated metal items will have little effect on a metal detector. A decaying tree stump can produce an anomaly detected with ground penetrating radar similar to that of a grave. And electrical geophysical devices can fluctuate due to soil changes in water and temperature.

Therefore, remote-sensing devices can be useful in determining where human remains *might* be present, rather than actually detecting human remains. In other words, once a specific location is determined to potentially contain human remains, the only way to confirm that possibility is with more intrusive techniques. Simple, small-scale tools, such as soil probes and augers, may provide preliminary samples of what is below ground. In the end, large-scale techniques, such as excavation of test pits and trenches, as well as block excavation can be the only way to confirm or refute the presence of a burial. Sometimes, *looking* for human remains can take a lot longer than actually excavating them.

Mapping

One of the most effective ways of documenting the crime scene is to take spatial control of all items in the area—not just evidence, such as weapons and human remains, but also mundane items like a desk and chair or a tree and shrub. Maintaining *spatial control* is the understanding and documenting of the three-dimensional location of all the items at a crime scene relative to other items. An item's three-dimensional location at a crime scene is known as its *provenience*. Determining an item's provenience can be accomplished by superimposing, both theoretically and physically, a grid system onto the crime scene. Sometimes, this is done in real life using tape measures, string, wooden stakes, etc. Traditionally, graph paper is used to recreate and document the grid system at the crime scene, and all the items are drawn on the graph paper. This constitutes the heart of *mapping* a crime scene. The tools used to create a sketch map can be simple (graph paper, pencil, tape measure, and compass) or complex (laser-assisted computer-modeling theodolite systems). The end product should be the same: a highly detailed sketch map of the crime scene illustrating the locations of all the items within the boundaries of the scene (Figure 6.5). If the height of important items, or topography, is deemed a significant influence on the site, more complex maps should be generated (Figure 6.6).

Large-scale maps (such as a state map) and medium-scale maps (such as a city map) may already exist and would simply require an X placed on the map to represent the crime scene. The sketch map drawn by the investigator would encompass the entire crime scene, and additional detailed sketch maps zoom in on a particular feature. The sketch map also helps guide recovery strategies, as it is drawn concurrently while the crime scene is being processed. As an area is searched, it can be documented on the map—as an area is excavated, it can be delineated as such. Smaller areas, such as burials, may require a more detailed map (Figure 6.7).

A sketch map is usually to scale (the horizontal and vertical distances on the graph paper are equal and the items drawn within the map are of accurate distances relative to each other, as well as with the scale of paper) and includes written information such as the site designations, direction of North, and descriptions of items. Were the remains found in a box under a bed or buried several feet underground? Were they found at the back of a cave inside a burlap sack or on the ground surface within the grass? This type of information is both drawn on the sketch map and written in the field notes.

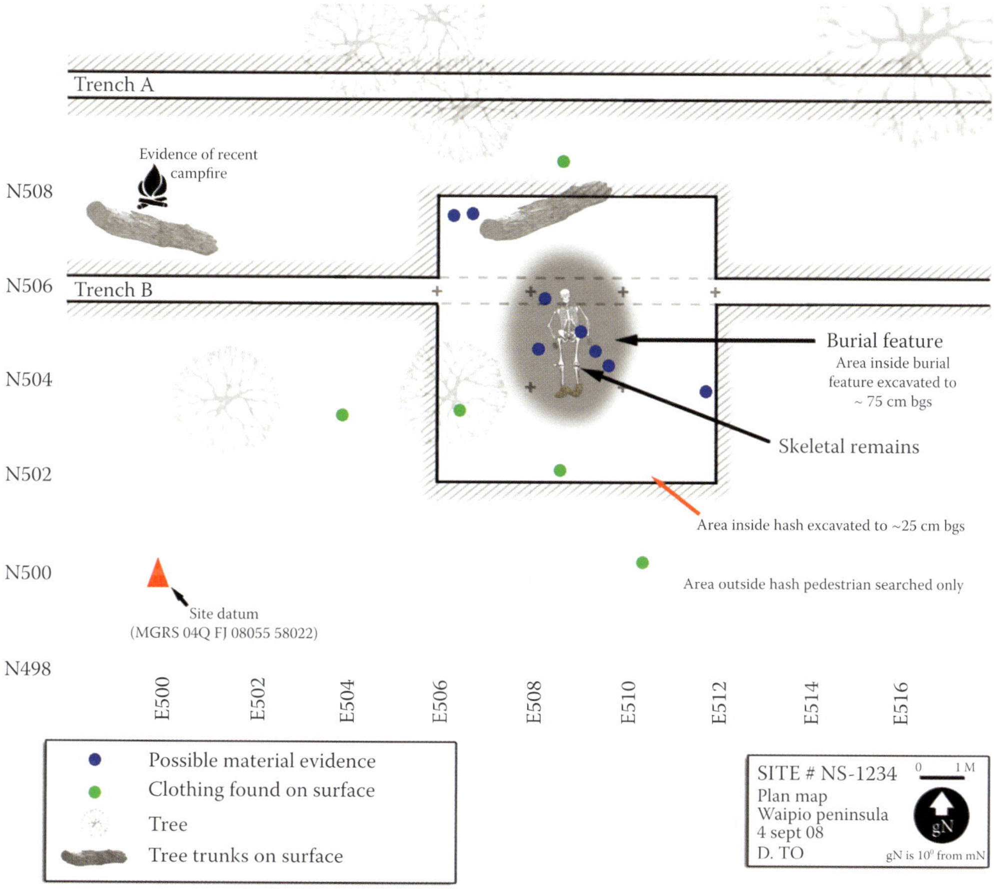

Figure 6.5 Sample sketch of a crime scene.

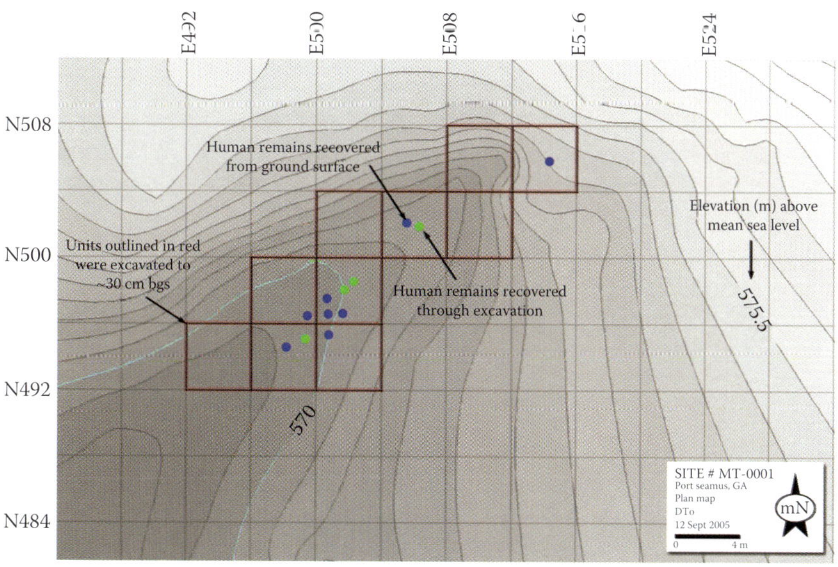

Figure 6.6 Sample sketch of a crime scene illustrating topographic variation.

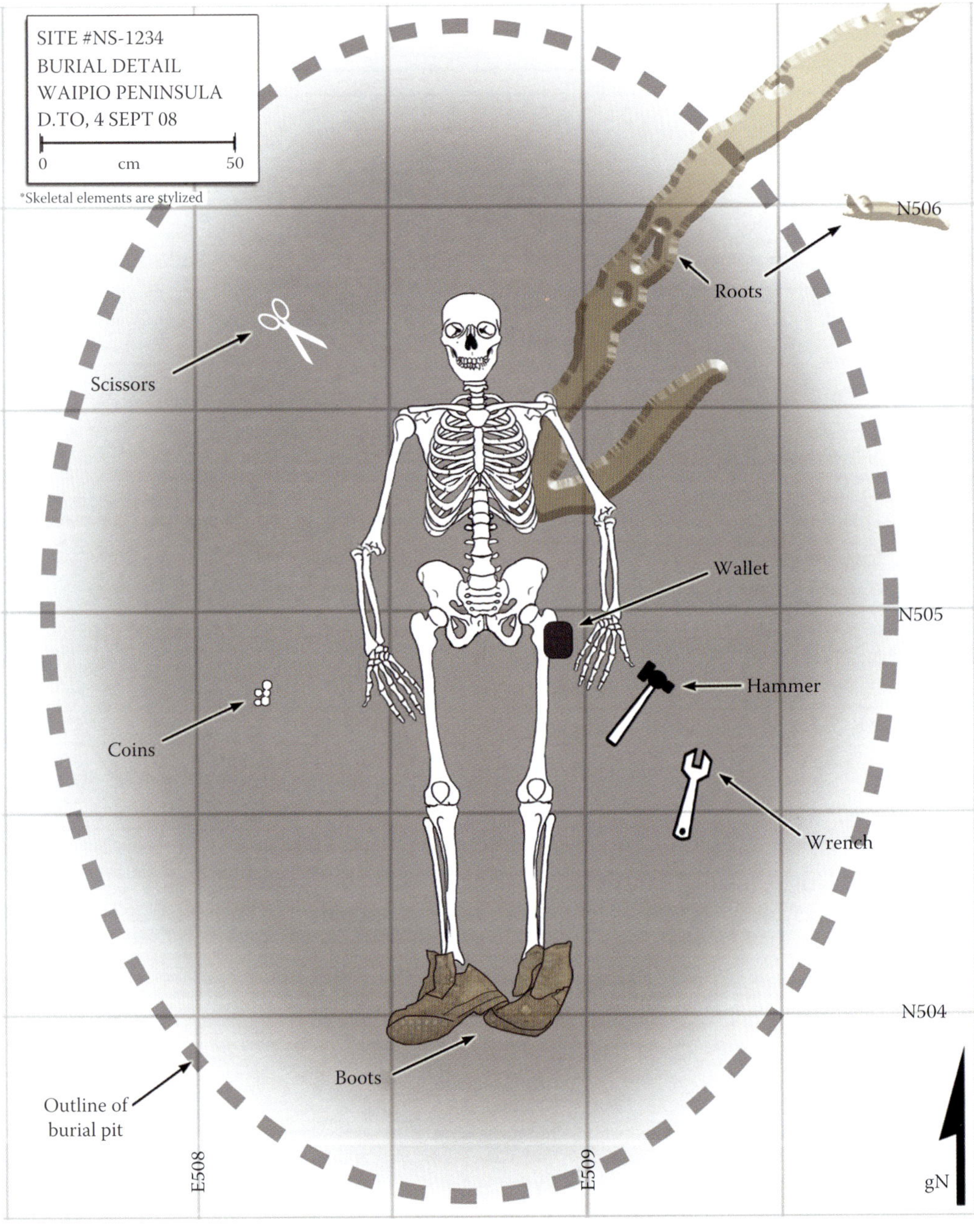

Figure 6.7 Sample detail sketch of a burial.

Between the sketch map, field notes, and photography, a good investigator can then obtain two necessary pieces of information in order to fully understand the crime scene: *provenience* and *context*. *Provenience* refers to an item's origin or source; that is, its three-dimensional location at a crime scene. *Context* refers to the abstract relationship that an item has with that of other items at the crime scene (in reference to its provenience). By weaving together contextual information at the crime scene, a forensic anthropologist is able to piece together the archaeological record and better understand the event that occurred in the past and all the subsequent processes that have affected it since then.

Excavation and Recovery

As the subject matter expert, the forensic anthropologist's main responsibility is the proper recovery of human skeletal remains. Regardless if they are on the ground surface or below it, accuracy and care in the steps taken to recover human remains at a crime scene are crucial in order to maximize data collection and minimize potential damage to the remains. Oftentimes, when human remains are discovered at the crime scene, they are referred to as a "burial." This term specifically refers to a human body placed under the ground surface, but the term *burial* is used occasionally in a general sense to describe all human remains (even if not entirely accurate). For example, skeletal material found scattered on the surface has been referred to as a *burial* by law enforcement personnel—despite the fact that the remains were not buried. In another example, a single bone was found underground—does a single bone constitute a *burial*? In a generic sense, yes.

When remains are discovered at a crime scene, it is important to determine the *type of deposition*. Is this an entire skeleton? Or just a few elements? Is this a single person or a multiple-individual burial? Or possibly even a mass burial? To answer these questions, detailed data collection must be done concomitantly with all recovery of skeletal remains. As much information as possible should be documented prior to anyone touching the remains. Where are they located (in the context of the crime scene)? Who discovered them? Have they been altered since discovery? In what condition are they? Extensive photographic documentation is crucial at this step.

A detailed description of the remains is vital as much data can be collected by this description. Does it appear as though an entire skeleton is present? Are the remains buried under soil? Are they articulated? Can you determine the position of the skeleton? This type of information can be very useful in determining the context of the burial (see Box 6.5; Figure 6.8). Think of a standard American cemetery. The typical way a person is buried in our society is *extended* (stretched out) and *supine* (face up). If a skeleton is found in this position in a residential backyard, one might believe the homeowners if they claimed it was an ancestor who died of natural causes. Especially if there was corroborating evidence near it, such as a grave marker. While a residential backyard may not be the standard way to bury the dead in today's American society, the context here might suggest that no major crime was committed. But take, for example, a similar situation, where a skeleton is found in someone's backyard, and the remains are *prone* (face down) in a *semiflexed* position. Does this look like a considerate burial of an ancestor? Or was there some foul play involved? And what if this skeleton was found in the backyard under a concrete slab? How would that change things? A description of skeletal position, therefore, is vital to understanding context at a crime scene.

The documentation should also include a detailed description of the *condition* of the remains. How is the preservation? Do the bones fall apart at the slightest touch? What color are they? Is each element whole or are they crushed and in pieces? Is there an odor? Is clothing present? Are there insects in close association to the remains? Documenting these details at the moment of recovery is essential because many of these variables can change once the remains are removed from the archaeological record and transported to

BOX 6.5 SKELETAL POSITIONING

One type of data that can be very useful to forensic anthropologists is the description of the skeletal positioning—that is, the position of the skeletal elements. A skeleton that is *articulated* has all the elements in correct anatomical position. This means that the body was whole when it was buried. An articulated skeleton that is *extended* is stretched out to its full height. One that is *semiflexed* is a skeleton whose limbs are gently bent (see Figure 6.8). One that is *flexed* is the one that was curled up tightly. When it is *disarticulated*, it means that the elements were not in their correct anatomical position, and the body had likely become skeletonized while it was still above ground.

Knowing the position of a skeleton can help determine the context of the burial. Is the positioning of the skeleton as found at the crime scene the original position of the body shortly after death? If so, this is called a *primary* deposition. In other words, it has been relatively untouched and undisturbed since the time the body was placed (regardless if it was deliberate or accidental). A *secondary* deposit refers to an assemblage of human remains that has been disturbed (either deliberately or naturally). The location and position of the remains at the crime scene, therefore, represent a secondary location after its original primary context.

- *In-text quiz:* What might a scattered, partially articulated skeleton represent?
- *Answer:* Partially articulated skeletal remains may indicate that there was soft tissue on the body at the time of deposition. But the fact that they are scattered may indicate that the skeleton was disturbed prior to complete skeletonization. Check for tooth gnawing that may suggest that an animal has moved the remains or look for rain erosion channels that may indicate that the body was washed down from someplace else.

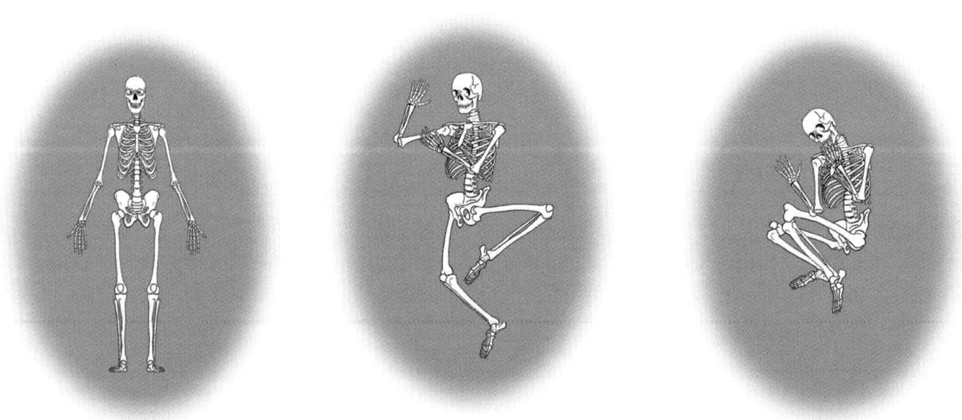

(a) (b) (c)

Figure 6.8 Documentation of the position of skeletal remains can assist in understanding the context with which they were buried. The standard positions include extended (a), semiflexed (b), and flexed (c).

the laboratory. The physical movement of the remains can have a strong effect on the condition of the remains, as can the environmental conditions.

In addition to a description of the remains, good documentation includes a description of the immediate area surrounding the remains. If they are buried, this documentation includes details on the kinds of soil or substrate that surrounds the remains (whether it is sand, silt, clay, or a combination of all three). Is it muddy? What color is the soil, and what sort of inclusions are in the layer? Each layer of material in the ground is called a *stratum*, and burials can be found between and below many different strata, creating a stratification of the sediments. Interpreting the strata is called *stratigraphy*. Understanding some basic concepts of geology can be crucial in interpreting the stratigraphy of a crime scene. Many of the basic concepts, such as the laws of superposition and association, are born out of the idea of *uniformitarianism*. Adams and Valdez Jr. (1997) describe the concept of uniformitarianism as the assumption that there is continuity in the physical processes that form strata on earth. In other words, processes that act on the earth (such as gravity and water erosion) work the same way today as they did in the past. This concept may seem simple and obvious, but it functions as the basis to understanding stratigraphy at crime scenes. For example, skeletal remains found within a streambed likely washed *downstream* rather than *upstream*.

Another important principle in understanding stratification is the *law of superposition*, which Adams and Valdez Jr. (1997) describe as the concept wherein in most situations, "the oldest layers are on the bottom and the youngest layers are on the top" (p. 236). The stratification of the layers is thus a snapshot of many events (both physical and cultural), with the most recent layer/event represented as the material found on the ground surface. In excavating a burial, this concept is important for the forensic archaeologist because excavating the sediments is done from the top-down; therefore, the youngest stratum is excavated first. This law functions in most cases, but specific environments can disrupt it, such as stratigraphy in caves. Sites that have significant animal disturbance (e.g., rodent burrows) can result in mixture of sediments. Likewise, burials can disturb layers because the burial fill is put back into the grave in a random manner.

Another simple, yet significant concept is the *law of association*. This concept states that the distance of items within a deposit *and* the integrity of the stratum determine the reliability of any observed spatial and chronological relationship between the two objects. For example, if a weapon and body are found within the same stratum of a sealed grave, those two items can be associated with each other by (1) context (i.e., they were found within the same layer) and (2) integrity (i.e., the grave was sealed so one can assume little disturbance). In fact, if the weapon was found within clothing that was surrounding the skeletal remains, then the spatial proximity of the weapon strengthens the proposed association. However, it is important to remember that "sealed graves" are hardly the norm in forensic archaeology. Crime scenes can be heavily disturbed, and items that may be spatially associated in the same deposit may, in fact, be chronologically separated by a great deal of time. A vertical sketch of the burial stratigraphy can greatly aid in the understanding and documentation of the crime scene. This sketch, called a *section drawing*, is drawn much the same way a two-dimensional plan map of the site is made, except the two dimensions in a section drawing represent depth of the deposits and horizontal distance spanning one specific cross-section (Figure 6.9).

Finally, any details regarding how the remains got there and any *disturbance processes* should be noted. This includes cultural (human-caused) disturbances, such as rubbish or construction material found in association with the remains; natural disturbances, such

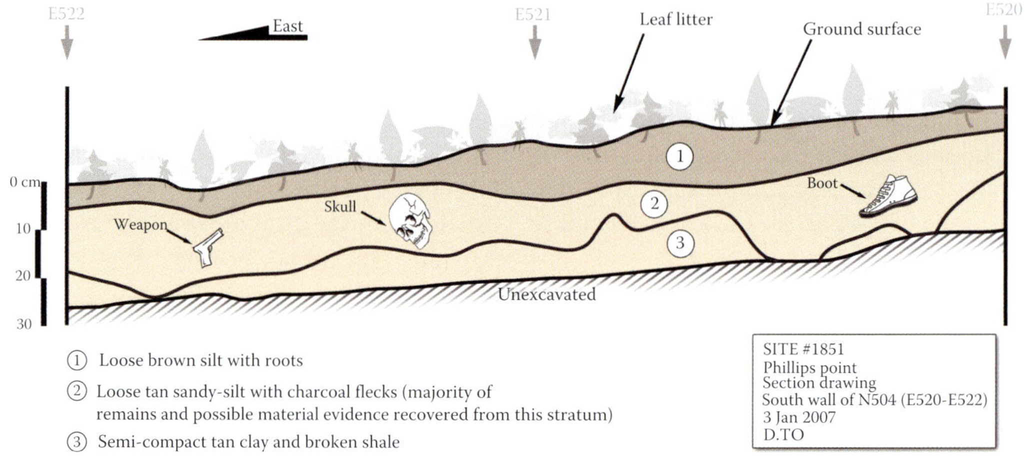

Figure 6.9 Sample section drawing of the soil stratigraphy at a crime scene.

as processes like a brush fire or rock fall; mechanical disturbances (when remains appear to have been moved by processes such as gravity or water); biological activity, such as that from animals, tree roots, or anything organic; and, finally, chemical disturbances, such as rust or oil stains. All these details are fundamental to understanding the context of skeletal remains.

For skeletal material that is underground, traditional archaeological excavation techniques are necessary to remove them from the ground. This process can be very laborious and time-consuming, depending on the depth of the burial, its complexity and preservation, and the density and inclusions of the soil around it. Excavation of a burial is usually accomplished with trowels, brushes, and other small hand tools. Occasionally, larger tools, such as a shovel, can be used to remove overburden. Excavation of a burial should be conducted only by experienced personnel and is accomplished in three stages: *defining the burial*, *exposing the remains*, and *lifting the remains*.

During the first stage, *defining the burial*, an anthropologist determines how much of the skeleton is present and in what position it is laying. Gentle removal of small amounts of soil with a trowel and brush will expose small amounts of skeletal material for the anthropologist to identify. Eventually, and without exposing too much bone, the anthropologist can determine where all the skeletal elements are laying and in what direction. Removing too much soil too soon will expose the bone prematurely. If the remains are exposed to the environment and surroundings longer than they need to be, they can be damaged, and data can be lost (see Box 6.6). The second stage, *exposing the remains*, can take the longest as this is the stage in which the majority of the soil is removed from the burial and the skeletal elements are exposed. An experienced anthropologist should direct and closely monitor all work during every stage, but the second stage, particularly, should be conducted only by the most experienced personnel. The third stage, *lifting the remains*, comes only after all the data have been collected, all sketch maps have been drawn, and all photographs have been taken. The remains can then be lifted by hand, one-by-one. Elements (such as the hand phalanges and ribs) that can be difficult to side in the laboratory and/or elements that are heavily fragmented should be isolated by side or seriation when possible. The remains are placed immediately in a padded container or bags, secured, and prepared for immediate transportation to the laboratory.

BOX 6.6 AVOID BONE FEVER

A crucial facet in proper crime scene technique is processing a site in a careful and methodical way. But a common mistake is when one contracts “bone fever.” This is when skeletal remains are discovered on-site (usually found underground), and a person at the crime scene gets excited and rushed with the false idea that the remains need to be removed from the ground as fast as possible. When bone fever strikes, a person can get tunnel vision and can get so obsessed with cleaning off and digging out the remains that they forget all the other important steps in processing the crime scene, such as photography, documentation, and observation of other important clues. Bone fever most often affects the inexperienced and the nonanthropologists, but anyone can get it. It can be avoided by taking the necessary steps to process the site in a careful manner. A good forensic anthropologist will plan several steps ahead, but will never go to the next step until it is time.

A final step in excavation is to screen the soil in the burial in order to maximize the likelihood of recovering small bones and associated evidence. Screening is a process wherein the soil within a burial fill is placed through a metal mesh to separate significant items from the soil matrix. The size of the mesh varies, but a good standard for burial fill is a 1/4 in. mesh. The soil will pass through the mesh, but skeletal elements and other items larger than 1/4 in. will stay in the screen, thus allowing for it to be collected. Screening is an important step to catch many of the smaller bones in the body that may not be seen during excavation, such as hand and foot bones. In addition, screening is helpful to find small pieces of evidence that may have been missed as well, such as buttons and jewelry—even bullets. It is important not to confuse screening with *sifting*—which is a process wherein the soil that falls through the mesh is the material that is kept, like when a bread baker sifts flour. In archaeology, screening can oftentimes reveal items that are of great significance. All burial fill should be screened, including any disturbed soil located under the remains. In the end, after the remains and evidence have been removed, the floor of the excavated burial pit should be an undisturbed soil layer.

Evidence Management

Everything found at a crime scene can potentially be related to the incident. But should all items be considered evidence? Is everything photographed, placed into a container, and taken to the laboratory? Usually not. Only the items deemed important are treated as potential evidence—items that are believed to be related to the incident, items that may have come in direct or indirect contact with perpetrators and victims, and items that may contain clues to help solve the riddle of what happened at the crime scene. But who decides what is evidentiary and what is not? In most situations, the forensic anthropologist works together with crime scene investigators, death investigators, and local detectives to determine that. In many situations, the forensic anthropologist is responsible for the skeletal remains, while fingerprints, weapons, clothing, personal effects, and other types of material items that are considered evidence are handled by the crime scene personnel. But in reality, the anthropologist who processes the crime scene also shares in this responsibility. Therefore, it is crucial to handle all evidence properly. The consequences of mishandling evidence can be significant, including a prosecution that is dismissed in court. It can even lead to an innocent person being wrongly convicted of a crime. Therefore, a forensic anthropologist must be vigilant about handling evidence properly.

One of the biggest mistakes in evidence handling is the *contamination* of evidence. That is, their original integrity from the site is compromised. Contamination of evidence is a serious problem, and a good forensic anthropologist takes all the necessary steps to prevent it. The first step to prevent contamination is to minimize the number of people that come in contact with the evidence (see Box 6.7; Figure 6.10). Only those people who absolutely need to touch something at the crime scene should be allowed to touch it. The second step is for investigators to minimize personal contact with the evidence by wearing

BOX 6.7 ACCESS CONTROL

One of the most critical steps in processing a crime scene is controlling who has access to the site. Some people (such as the forensic anthropologists) need to have access to everything at the scene. But everyone—even law enforcement personnel—get curious about the crime scene and, without controlling access from the beginning, too many people in the area may clutter the area. At worst, having too many people mingling around a crime scene may lead to destruction or contamination of evidence.

There are generally three zones of access for a crime scene. As the lead investigator, it is up to the forensic anthropologist to decide where these zones actually exist. Marking these areas with "police tape" or "crime scene tape" is sometimes necessary.

- The inner zone (Zone 1) consists of the entire crime scene. This area should be accessed only by the forensic anthropologist and the team processing the scene. Zone 1 should not include governmental or law enforcement onlookers, some of whom think that their presence is acceptable because they are "allowed to be there." However, be strict and conservative with who is allowed in Zone 1 as anyone in this area runs a high risk of coming in contact with evidence. In addition, Zone 1 should not include family members related to the crime scene incident when the area is being processed. Some crime scenes are gruesome, and emotional family members can potentially disturb evidence.
- Zone 2 is the area where supporting law enforcement personnel can stage. This zone is where equipment can be staged and where work vehicles that will transport evidence are controlled and protected. Local government representatives and additional law enforcement personnel should stage in this zone. Immediate family members related to the crime scene incident may stage here, but they should be kept far away from evidence.
- Beyond the perimeter of Zone 2 is Zone 3—or the rest of the world. Law enforcement activity sometimes attracts curious bystanders, news and media outlets, or local residents. For best crime scene management and for their safety, it is crucial that these persons be kept at a reasonable distance.

Figure 6.10 Access control of the crime scene should be established early and done so with at least three areas of control.

gloves, shoe covers, and even personal protective equipment, if necessary. The third step is to minimize the amount of handling of an item. Ideally, an item should be picked up only once and then immediately placed in an evidence container. It does not need to be passed around from person to person for examination. When possible, items should only be handled by their edges. Be mindful to handle them in such a way that the fingerprints are not rubbed off. Even an investigator's own skin cells can potentially contaminate evidence. Skin cells can float in the atmosphere and transfer to an item—if that item is subsequently sampled for DNA analysis, the investigator's skin cell may be included in that sample. If excavation is needed to expose skeletal remains, sloppy excavation can result in scrapes and damage to the bone surfaces. It is important for all investigators to remember that crime scenes are complicated enough on their own—they do not need to be further complicated through evidence contamination.

Collecting the evidence is critical, but evidence can lose much of its value if it is placed in a container with no associated information. Accurate and detailed labeling is crucial, because, once an item is recovered and taken to the laboratory, it is important that the item just collected is not confused with other pieces of evidence from the same case—or even combined with evidence from other cases. Some cases can contain hundreds—even thousands—of individual items. Without the proper associating information, an item loses all of its potential evidentiary value. At minimum, the following information should be included in or on each and every container of evidence:

- Unique case number
- Item description

- Provenience
- Date recovered
- Unique evidence/bag number
- Initials of person(s) who collected the item

The final step in collecting evidence is creating a paper trail that permanently follows an item once it is collected at the crime scene that keeps a record of all the people who have had control of the item. This paper trail is called the *chain of custody*. A chain of custody is a simple piece of documentation that contains all the same information that is on the label of the evidence container. When a person hands control of the evidence over to another person, both people sign it until, eventually, it makes its way back to the laboratory where the evidence manager takes care of it for good.

Review Questions

6.1 What is forensic archaeology?
6.2 In your own words, describe the difference between doing something systematically and unsystematically.
6.3 What is meant by "controlled deconstruction"?
6.4 How are human remains found on the surface different from those found below ground?
6.5 What is documentation and why is it so important?
6.6 What does a forensic anthropologist do during a preliminary survey of a crime scene?
6.7 What is a visual pedestrian survey?
6.8 What is a cadaver dog?
6.9 Why is it important to know the position of a body within a burial?
6.10 Name several processes that can disturb remains.
6.11 Describe the three stages of excavating remains.
6.12 Why is it important to prevent contamination of evidence?

References

Adams REW and Valdez F Jr. 1997. Stratigraphy. In *Field Methods in Archaeology*, 7th edn., Hester TR, Shafer HJ, and Feder KL (Eds.), Mayfield Publishing Company, Mountain View, CA, pp. 235–252.

JPAC Laboratory Manual: Part I, SOP 1.1, Section 7.1, revised August 11, 2011.

Processing and Inventory of Remains

7

LEE MEADOWS JANTZ

Contents

> In order to make skeletal material and features more accessible for forensic anthropological analyses, and in order to procure material that may be have additional investigative value, it is sometimes necessary to sample and/or process skeletal material or other tissues associated with skeletal material. The condition of the remains at arrival and throughout the process of preparation and sampling should be documented. Any alterations caused by the process of sampling and preparation should also be documented.
>
> **--Scientific Working Group for Forensic Anthropology, 2011**

Skeletal Preparation

This chapter emphasizes the methods and techniques useful for the preparation of remains in order to enable the anthropological examination. The ideal is to minimize any contamination or unnecessary destruction during the preparation of the skeletal material. Ultimately the goal of skeletal preparation is to remove any adhering soft tissue or soil in order to better examine the bone morphology or surface features, while being mindful of the potential evidentiary nature of all of the material recovered. The condition of recovered remains may range from relatively fresh material taken at autopsy or from an explosion to decomposing soft tissue remains or dry skeletal remains. Each of these conditions and the requisite processing techniques are discussed.

Prior to any preparation, a case number or identification number should be assigned and maintained. This allows for the tracking of the remains throughout cleaning and analysis. It is important to obtain radiographic images of the recovered materials prior to any cleaning or maceration in order to identify any potential nonbone evidence such as bullets or bullet fragments, as well as to identify any possible accessory bones such as sesamoids in the hands or feet. If this step is omitted, this vital evidence may be lost or washed down the drain. Examination of the radiographs will not only allow the examiner to identify nonosseous items, it will also identify the approximate location of these materials (Appendix 7.B: example from Scott county case). The recovery of this type of evidence prior to cleaning may prevent loss or further damage or destruction of the evidence. Proper handling and bagging of this evidence is necessary, as well as notification of the investigating agency. In addition, all remains and associated evidence should be thoroughly photographed prior to cleaning.

Soft Tissue Removal

In situations where remains are presented or recovered with any soft tissue adhering to the bone, the goal is to remove all of this soft tissue in order to facilitate closer osteological examination. Using tools that permit grasping such as forceps, pick-ups, or hemostats, will pull most of the tissue away from the bone. If necessary, scissors may be used to cut portions away from the bone. Only if a large amount of tissue removal is required should a scalpel or knife be used. These instruments, known as *sharps*, not only require special handling protocols, but also may cause small cuts in the bone during the removal process. Special handling of sharps is necessary in order to prevent a cut or puncture by a potentially contaminated tool. Most laboratories have protocols in place regarding the use of these tools as well as the safe disposal of sharps in designated containers (see Figures 7.1 and 7.2).

If any tool marks are made on the bone, such as scratches or nicks, these must be carefully recorded. If not, then these marks made during the cleaning of the bones may be misinterpreted as trauma relating to the individual's death. Once the majority of the soft tissue has been removed, then it is typically necessary to heat the bone with water. A slow cooker, pot, or steam-jacketed kettle may be used. It is important to put the bones in the water prior to the water reaching a hot temperature in order to prevent cracking of the bones or teeth. The bones may soak in a very warm to simmering water bath for a period of 1–2 hours. It is important to not let the water boil as this may destroy the integrity of the bone or, at the very least, damage the DNA in the bone. Circumstances may indicate that

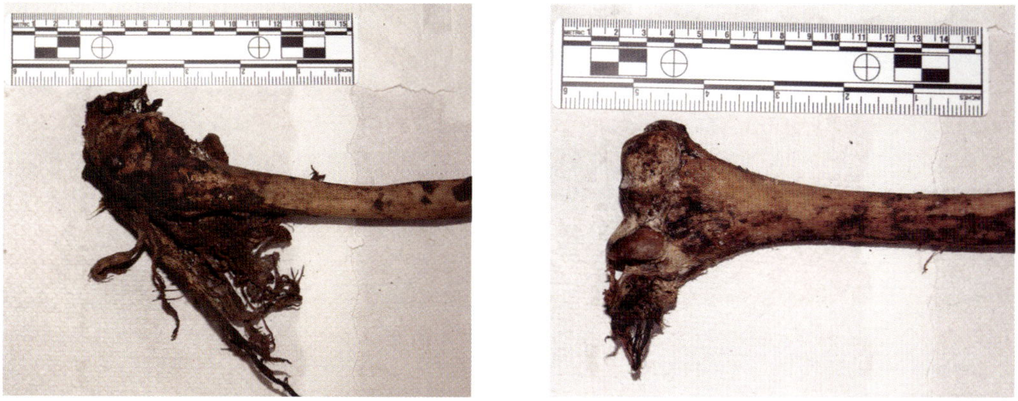

(a) (b)

Figure 7.1 (a) Posterior view of a distal left radius with adhering mummified tissue. (b) Anterior view of distal right humerus with adhering tissue.

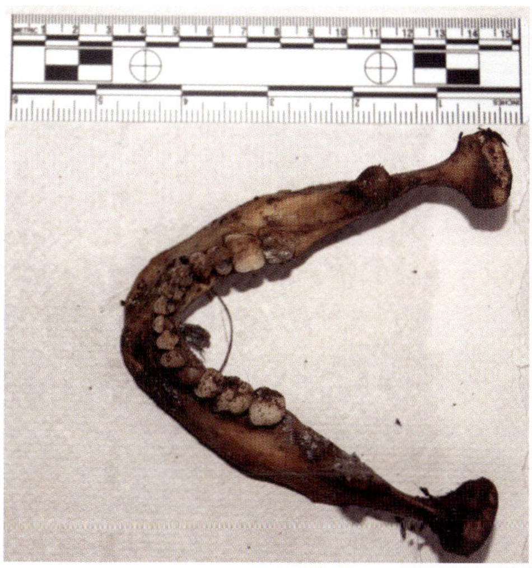

Figure 7.2 Occlusal view of mandible with adhering soil debris.

the use of a mild soap or detergent is warranted, but it is not usually necessary. The current best practice is to alter the bone as little as possible during cleaning. Once the bones have "cooked" for a period, they should be removed from the water and allowed to reach room temperature naturally. Do not immediately place the bones in cool or cold water as the risk of cracking increases with any rapid change in temperature. Once cool enough to handle, the bones may then be rinsed with water and brushed with a soft-to-medium-bristle brush in order to remove any remaining adhering tissue. Metal brushes should be avoided as they can be fairly destructive. Again, forceps or other grasping or scraping tools may be used to further remove tissue. The bones should then be allowed to dry at room temperature. This may be repeated as many times as necessary in order to remove the soft tissue and degrease the bone as long as the bone surface remains in good condition. If the bone is already compromised due to bone thinning or disease, it is recommended to simply allow some of the tissue to dry and remain. If adipocere or other tissue is very difficult to remove, then the bones should be allowed to dry followed by brushing with a firmer brush while dry. This will often successfully remove this stubborn material.

Finally, during the process of cleaning the remains, it is important to take care when cleaning the areas of the skeleton that are examined for the biological profile evaluation. For example, the areas of the pubic symphysis, auricular surface, sternal rib ends, or any epiphyses, should be treated very carefully. It is possible to scrub these areas too hard and remove some of the bony surface. This is to be avoided.

Dry Bone

If skeletal material has been recovered in a relatively dry or skeletal condition, it is still essential to radiograph it prior to any brushing of dirt or leaf litter as there may be adhering evidence. Upon completion of the imaging, the bone may then be brushed with a soft-to-medium-bristled brush to remove any loose material. If the bone is covered in dried mud, water may be used to rinse this away from the bone surface.

Postprocessing Care and Handling

Once the remains are clean and ready for analysis, they should be placed either on trays or on a table. Care should be taken that the case number or identification number is associated with the remains either by tags or labels on the trays or table. The bones should be placed in anatomical position in order to determine if any elements are missing, repeated or duplicated. A careful and detailed inventory should be recorded of the remains in order to identify if all the skeletal elements are present, as well as to identify if there are duplicated elements that may represent multiple individuals. The inventory may be in the form of a diagram or list (Figure 7.3). A diagram allows a layman or investigator to see straightforwardly what elements may be missing.

During this inventory, skeletal elements that may not be human are identified as nonhuman and sorted separately from the human remains. Any nonhuman bones should be identified to species if possible and examined for any evidence of association with the human remains. It is common to have nonhuman skeletal remains gathered at the same time as the human, particularly if nonexperts are involved. This is to be commended and recommended. Because many of the investigators who search and recover the skeletal remains have little or no training in human osteology, they should be encouraged to collect any and all bones they discover. Ultimately, the amount of detail provided on any nonhuman remains in the final report should be based on potential involvement in the case. It may be that a simple species list is sufficient, or it may be determined that an inventory for each species and detailed description is necessary. This is something that is decided between the anthropologist and the investigators.

If the human skeletal remains are to be curated or retained for further analysis, each element should be labeled with the identifying case number. A fine-tipped permanent ink pen is recommended. The location of the label may be determined by the anthropologist. Figure 7.4 illustrates the locations used for labeling by the Smithsonian Institution Natural History Museum (personal communication, David Hunt) and the Forensic Anthropology Center, University of Tennessee. Because the cortex of the bone is porous, it will often absorb the ink along fine cracks in the bone surface. Do not put the label on

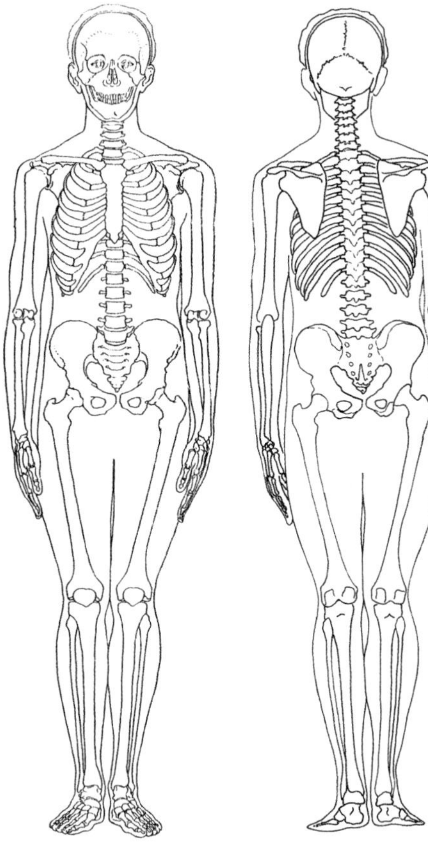

Figure 7.3 Inventory diagram.

or near an area of the bone examined for biological profile evaluations or observations of trauma or disease. The labels should be small but legible. Loose teeth, small bones, and fragments may be difficult to label; however, it is necessary that these elements be treated carefully in the event that they become disassociated with the other material. If material is too small or greasy, this may be put into separate cloth or paper bags with a paper label marked in pencil. Pencil will not fade with light or contact with the grease, whereas ink may fade.

At this stage, consideration of using the Forensic Data Bank (FDB) forms is necessary. These forms are available as downloads within FORDISC 3.0 (Jantz and Ousley 2005). The FDB inventory page allows for a quick and easy documentation of the inventory as well. Circumstances of the case, biological profile parameters, metrics, and dental information are also easily recorded on the FDB forms. Once the forensic case is complete, these forms can be copied easily and then sent to the curators of the FDB or uploaded for inclusion in this important database.

Preparing a Case Report

A number of factors may be included in a forensic anthropology case report. The contents of the report should be directed at the intended audience (i.e., medical examiner or

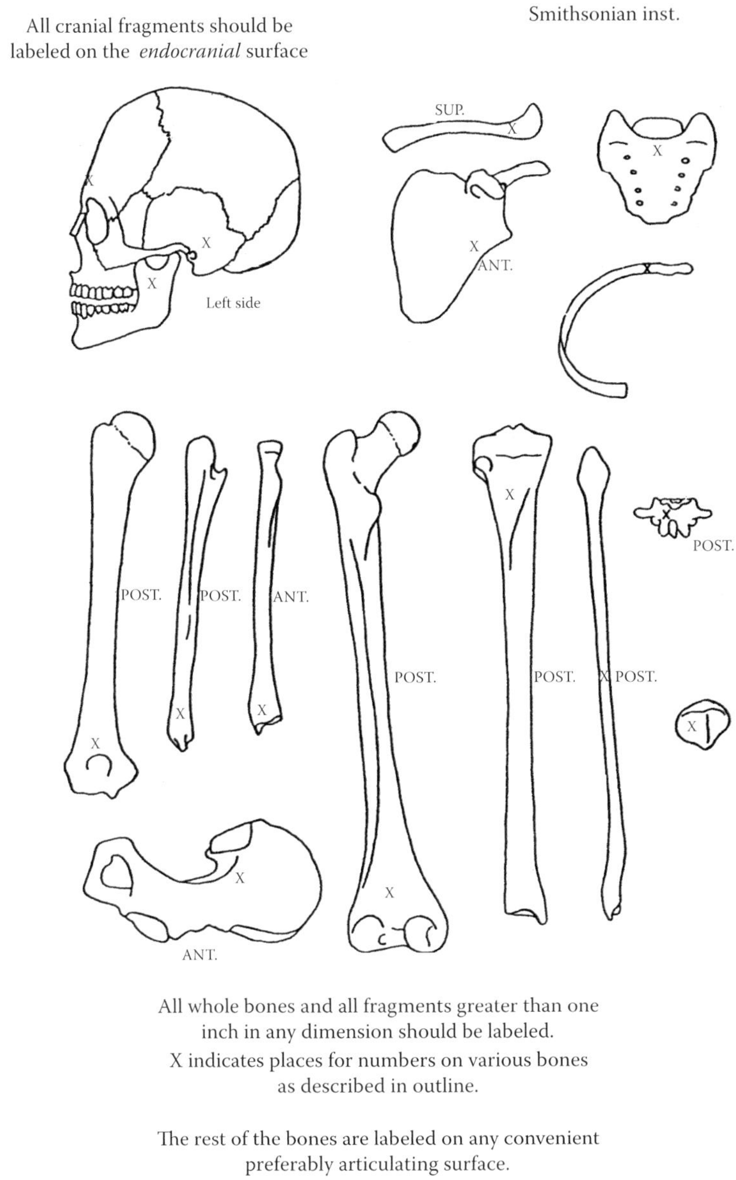

Figure 7.4 Bone-labeling diagram.

coroner, law enforcement agency, etc.). Regardless, *every* report should be written with the idea that it may ultimately be presented in a court of law. If the primary audience is a law enforcement officer or agency, then excessive technical jargon should be avoided. However, this does not mean that proper terminology should be avoided. If the forensic anthropology report is for a forensic pathologist, the same recommendation holds. Why? Because it is possible for your report to become used at trial and thus read by a jury of laypeople. Furthermore, some medical examiners may prefer that you do not make a statement about cause or manner of death, as this is the primary task of the pathologist's report and having an additional statement about this may unnecessarily complicate things in a court of law.

Formats for forensic reports may be dictated by the agency employer such as the Federal Bureau of Investigation, the Joint POW-MIA Accounting Command Central Identification Laboratory (JPAC CIL), or a large medical examiner office. It may also be the case that, as an independent practitioner or consultant, the format is determined by you. Formats may range from a single page fill-in the blank form to extensive prose. Regardless of the format, the same general content needs to be conveyed, including

- The inventory and condition of elements present for examination
- The factors in a biological profile (age, sex, ancestry, stature, disease)
- Trauma analysis, if applicable
- Estimation of time since death (if necessary)
- A dental assessment (this may be provided by a forensic odontologist)
- Supporting diagrams and/or photographs of these elements

If possible and applicable, a discussion of the recovery of the elements, including a map of the location of the remains, may be warranted. A description of how you received the case (e.g., recovered at the scene or received from a law enforcement or medical examiner's office) is useful. A summary of the findings is also helpful. All of these topics may play a role in a forensic anthropology analysis. Because these are all parts of an analysis, you will want to keep detailed bench notes on these, which are considered supporting documents. If the format of the final report is the brief one page style, the bench notes provide the information to support your findings and may be subject to examination. These notes serve as the references for your conclusions. Currently, the American Board of Forensic Anthropology and the SWGANTH both recommend/require supporting documents for case reports.

Traditionally, Forensic Anthropology Center (FAC) reports are sent to the investigator(s), the county medical examiner, and the state medical examiner. The state medical examiner serves as the representative for the state Department of Health. Local prosecutors may also require a copy of the report. The case number, date of report, and subject are included at the beginning of the report (see Appendices 7.A and 7.B for case report examples). The body of the report begins with a brief introduction essentially explaining how the case began and proceeded. This is followed by the biological profile discussions, as well as descriptions of trauma or disease. If the investigators are interested in an estimation of the time since death, the report should include your analysis and interpretations as well. Photographs are an excellent means to illustrate points made in a report. Figure 7.5

Figure 7.5 Photograph of a skeleton *in situ* in a burial showing the position of the body as it was placed in the burial. Note the arm extended above the head.

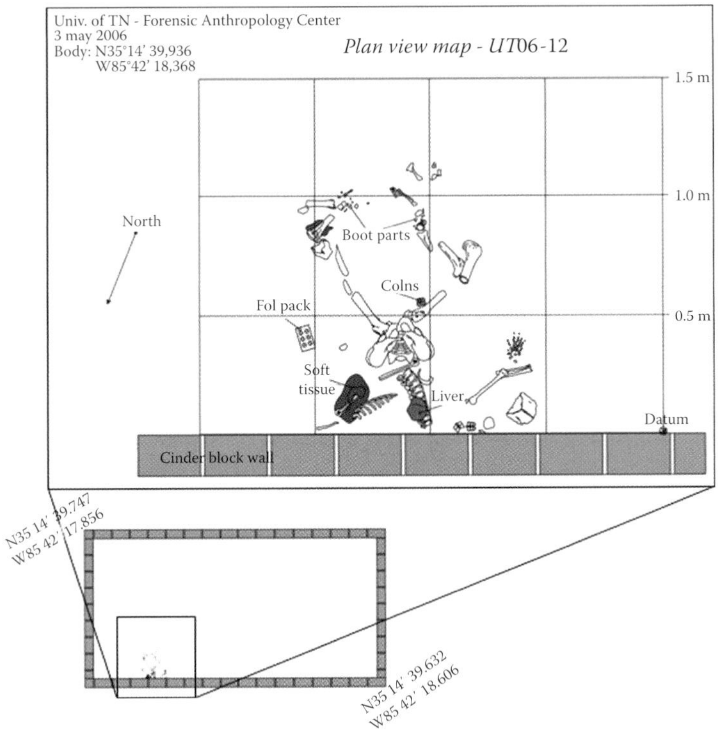

Figure 7.6 Map of skeletal remains prior to recovery.

shows the *in situ* position of the victim's arms in the burial. A map or drawing can also be employed (Figure 7.6); however, the photograph has the stronger impression. If you are new to writing case reports, it is a good idea to have a peer review your report and make suggestions prior to submitting the official report.

Appendix 7.A

To: Larry B. Davis, Special Agent, Tennessee Bureau of Investigation
William Barker, Bomb and Arson Section, State Fire Marshall's Office
Byron Harbolt, D.O., Grundy County Medical Examiner
Tennessee Department of Health

From: Lee Meadows Jantz, PhD, Coordinator, Forensic Anthropology Center
Joseph T. Hefner, MA, Asst. Coordinator, Forensic Anthropology Center
Joanne Devlin, PhD, Forensic Anthropology Center, University of Tennessee

Re.: Recovery and analysis of burned human remains from fatal house fire in Grundy County, Tennessee

Case No.: UT06-12F

Date: March 27, 2012

On Tuesday, May 2, 2006, TBI Special Agent Davis contacted the Forensic Anthropology Center (FAC) requesting assistance in the recovery and analysis of burned human

Figure 7.7 Grundy County, Tennessee, and the approximate location of the structure fire.

remains discovered in the burned remnants of a small residential structure located on White City Circle in Tracy City, Tennessee, a small community located within Grundy County (Figure 7.7). According to investigators, the structure had burned on April 27th, 6 days prior to the arrival of the FAC recovery team. The human remains were discovered on May 2nd at which time the area was secured and our laboratory was contacted. The Forensic Anthropology Center Recovery Team, composed of Lee Meadows Jantz, Joseph Hefner, Rebecca Wilson, Donna McCarthy, and Kevin Hufnagl, responded to the scene on Wednesday, May 3, 2006 to assist investigators with the recovery of all associated skeletal material.

Description of Scene and Field Methods

An initial search of the secured area by the forensic recovery team revealed human skeletal elements within an isolated area in the northeast quadrant of the remaining block foundation. Though partially obscured by debris from the fire, the remains of a single individual were visible. The skull was located next to the block foundation with the postcranial elements extending in the general direction of the center of the structure (Figure 7.8). The position, condition, and associated fire debris indicates the remains were burned during the fire that occurred at the structure.

A 2 m × 1.5 m grid was established over the area to control for spatial distribution and facilitate a thorough excavation and recovery. The grid was divided into 50 cm size units, which were processed using standard archaeological procedures. Using hand trowels, the top 2–3 cm of ash and debris were removed to expose skeletal elements. At this stage of excavation, a plan view map was produced (Figure 7.8) which suggests that all of the skeletal elements are in approximate anatomical position. A photographic record was produced using a Nikon D70 digital camera. Photographs were taken before, during, and after processing. Field notes were collected throughout the process.

Skeletal elements were identified and collected. Following recovery of all bones and fragments, any remaining debris was screened through wire mesh to enable identification of small osseous or evidentiary material.

All recovered elements were transported to the Forensic Anthropology Center at the University of Tennessee for analysis.

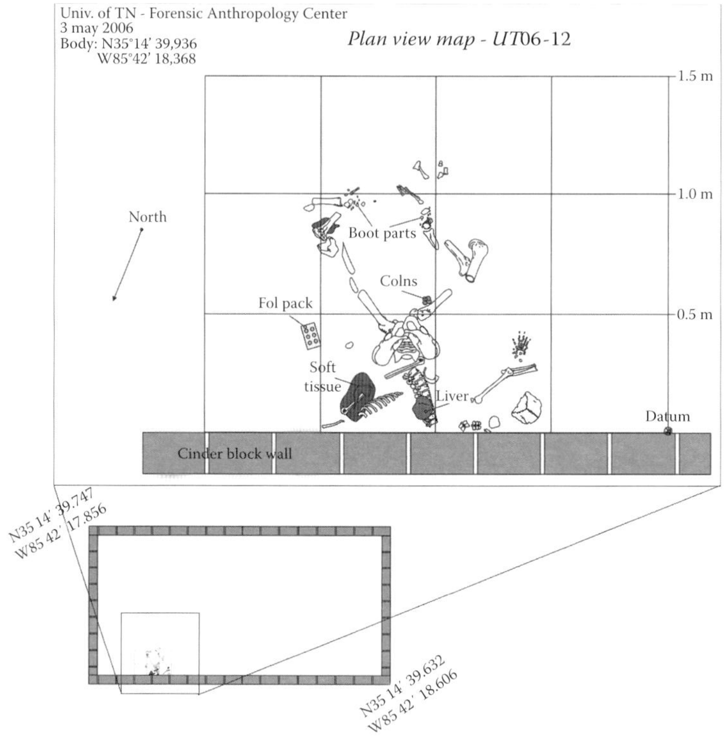

Figure 7.8 Plan-view map showing position of body, grid, and spatial distribution of skeletal elements.

Biological Profile and Skeletal Analysis

A nearly complete skeleton was recovered from the scene. There is no irregular duplication of elements and all skeletal elements are consistent in morphology, age, and taphonomy. All elements display evidence of exposure to fire. Minimal soft tissues remained, all of which exhibit charring and heat damage. Exposure to heat dehydrates and subsequently can destroy the organic component of bone resulting in fragile and distorted material. Heat-affected bone also demonstrates differential coloration, fragmentation, and shrinkage. The skeletal elements recovered from Grundy County exhibit characteristics consistent with thermal alteration.

Sex: Male

Although heat-induced shrinkage occurred, the robust condition of the remains is consistent with male morphology. A visual inspection of several regions of the skeleton confirms this assessment. A prominent external occipital protuberance and blunted orbital margins are present on the skull. Pelvic elements display a moderately narrow sciatic notch, absence of a ventral arc, and a narrow subpubic concavity.

Age: 20–30 Years

Age at death was determined using multiple indicators of the postcranial skeleton. The pubic symphyseal morphology is consistent with Phase III of the Suchey–Brooks method, suggesting an estimated age of 30 years (±10 years). The sternal ends of the ribs are between Phases 3 and Phases 5 (range of 20–30 years) using the Iscan and Loth technique for age estimation for males. The anterior border of the first sacral vertebra is in the process of fusing, but has not yet completely fused to S2, indicating an age <30 years. The superior aspect of the S1 centrum shows marked lipping; however, spondylolisthesis present on L5 may have resulted in increased mechanical loading and osteophytosis on the first sacral vertebra. Slight osteophytic activity is present on the vertebral elements. The presence of osteophytosis to this degree is generally indicative of early middle age 20s to the 30s.

Ancestry: White

Although the skeletal material is extremely fragmented, several nonmetric traits indicative of European ancestry (e.g., white) are noted. These include the following: the presence of a nasal sill, a marked anterior nasal spine, a jagged transverse palatine suture, and a "curved" zygomaticomaxillary suture.

Stature

The degree of shrinkage observed in the postcranial skeleton of UT06-12 may result in error for stature estimation; therefore, living stature was not calculated.

Trauma

Although gross, radiographic, and macroscopic analyses did not reveal evidence of perimortem trauma, the degree of thermal alteration exhibited may obscure or destroy such signatures.

Pathology

Skeletal pathology includes slight osteoarthritis and osteophytosis on several vertebrae in the form of arthritic lipping. While arthritic lipping is often associated with age-related changes, it may also be the result of stress-related activity. A *pars defect*, or spondylolisthesis, is noted on the lamina of the fifth lumbar vertebra. The etiology and significance of this pathological condition is uncertain in the clinical literature, although it is noted in approximately 6%–12% of the population.

Taphonomy

Coloration and preservation is grossly visualized and appears to be resultant from thermal destruction.

Summary

The skeletal remains presented to this laboratory for analysis represent a single individual. Analysis indicates the remains are those of a 20–30 year old White male. All remains show evidence of burning and concomitant thermal damage. Coloration, fragmentation, and distortion of the bone are consistent with exposure to high temperatures (in excess of 800°F).

If we can be of further assistance in this or any other matter, please do not hesitate to contact us.

Lee Meadows Jantz, PhD
Coordinator Forensic Anthropology Center

Joseph T. Hefner, MA
Forensic Anthropology Center

Joanne Devlin, PhD
Forensic Anthropology Center

Appendix 7.B

To: Steve Vinsant, Special Agent, Tennessee Bureau of Investigation
Bobby Ellis, Sheriff, Scott County Sheriff's Office
Maxwell Huff, MD, Scott County Medical Examiner
Tennessee Department of Health

From: Joanne B. Devlin, PhD, Forensic Anthropology Center
Lee Meadows Jantz, PhD, Coordinator, Forensic Anthropology Center

Re: Recovery, analysis, and positive identification of human remains recovered from burial in Scott County, Tennessee

Case No: UT10-06

Date: July 6, 2010

Introduction

On May 11, 2010, Meadows Jantz received a call requesting assistance in the excavation and recovery of a burial identified by an informant. Arrangements were made for Meadows Jantz, Devlin, and graduate assistant Sandra Cridlin to travel to the Chitwood Mountain area of Scott County that afternoon. Once at the suspected burial site, examination revealed an area of relatively large flat rocks arranged in a semicircle near the edge of the creek bank. Following minimal probing, this area was cleared of leaf litter and overburden revealing a small zone of discoloration; more yellow brown than the surrounding soil. Preliminary trowel scraping revealed loose soil and a continuation of the brown-yellow-colored soil. While no grave boundary was apparent at this time, a trench was placed in N-S direction and excavated to a depth of approximately 2 ft below the surface, bone was encountered. At this time, the excavation was expanded in an E-W direction to reveal the full extent of the burial. Ultimately, a full set of skeletal remains was exposed with the individual in a supine position with the arms extended over the head and flexed at the elbow. These remains were recovered and taken back to Knoxville for further analysis.

Immediately after recovery, the anthropologists traveled to the Scott County Sheriffs Office to collect dental records of *Jean Johnson*, a woman reported missing in February 2007. In addition, TBI SA Vinsant provided several radiographs of Jean Johnson.

The remains were predominantly skeletonized although residual soft tissues maintained the posterior portion of the torso in articulation. Several elements were in a fragmentary form at the time of recovery. Prior to submitting the remains for a radiographic analysis, a metallic object was discovered within the cranial vault. This artifact was released to SA Vinsant. All of the skeletal elements were radiographed, which were all negative for radiopacities; however, the brain matter did exhibit tiny radioopacities.

Biological Profile

Sex: Female

Based on nonmetric skeletal traits exhibited by the os coxae including wide pubic bones, presence of a ventral arc, subpubic concavity, pronounced pre-auricular sulcus, and a ridge on the medial aspect, the remains are estimated to represent a female (Phenice 1969). The skull exhibits prominent frontal bossing, reduced mastoid processes, and moderately sharp supraorbital margins. These attributes in conjunction with the quality of the mental eminence indicate the remains are those of a female.

Age: 50+ years

The skeletal remains are those of an adult as evidenced by closed epiphyses and the condition of the medial clavical. Standard techniques for estimating the degree of degenerative change to the os coxa and the right fourth rib were used to estimate the age. The pubic symphysis is characterized by erosion along the ventral margin, with irregular ossification and crenulations across the depressed surface; late phase 5/early phase 6 on the Suchey–Brooks scale, mean ages of 48.1 (95% range: 25–83 years) and 60 (95% range: 42–87 years), respectively (Suchey and Katz 1998). Following the Lovejoy approach, the auricular surfaces are irregular; slight microporosity and dense patches are visible. Though there is some residual transverse organization, the apex and superior demiface exhibit some lipping, osteophytes are visible in the retroauricular area and the inferior face extends beyond the body of the innominate. These characteristics are consistent with age ranges 50–60 years (Lovejoy et al. 1985). Assessment of the rib following the approach of Iscan et al. (1985) reveals a slightly irregular U-shaped rim, a prominent plaque-like deposit, and small windows suggestive of phase 6 mean age 50.7 years (95% confidence interval of 43.3–58.1 years). The synthesis of these techniques indicates that the remains represent those of an individual >50 years of age.

Ancestry: European American or White

Ancestry of this individual is estimated as White or European. Morphological features of the cranium include angled orbits, pinched nasals, and a relatively narrow nasal aperture. All of these features support the estimate as White (Bass 2005). Metric analysis of the skull was not performed due to trauma.

Stature: 5′2″–5′6″

FORDISC 3.0 (Jantz and Ousley 2005) was used to estimate stature using the maximum lengths of the clavicle (132 mm), femur (437 mm), and fibula (350 mm); all elements are from the right side of the body. Estimated stature with a 90% prediction interval is 61.8–66 in.

Trauma

The skeletal remains of this individual exhibit evidence of perimortem trauma. The cranium shows evidence of ballistic trauma while the humeri exhibit characteristics consistent with blunt force trauma. The skeleton also exhibits evidence of injuries that occurred during the antemortem period. The left femur demonstrates evidence of surgical repair by the presence of bone growth around an orthopedic rod and associated screws. The left shoulder also indicates bone growth around the humeral head and the glenoid fossa of the scapula; evidence of an antemortem injury that affected the bones of this joint. Further, healed fractures are visible on the left ribs (4–8) at the midpoint of each shaft.

The cranial trauma consists of a network of fractures across the craniofacial skeleton and vault, with a projectile traveling anterior to posterior. The entrance is located just left of midline impacting the left nasal and maxilla, producing separation of the palatine process, fragmentation of the sphenoid and separation of both zygomatics. The mandible is fractured vertically through the left mental foramen separating the ramus and resulting in two mandibular fragments. A corresponding fracture is visible across the mandibular dental plate (Figure 7.9). The projectile impacted the endocranial surface of the occipital squama approximately 1 cm left of midline resulting in radiating and concentric fractures which displaced three fragments of bone (Figure 7.10). These fragments were maintained in anatomical position in the vault given the presence of soft tissues. Removal of these three fragments revealed external beveling commonly associated with exit wounds.

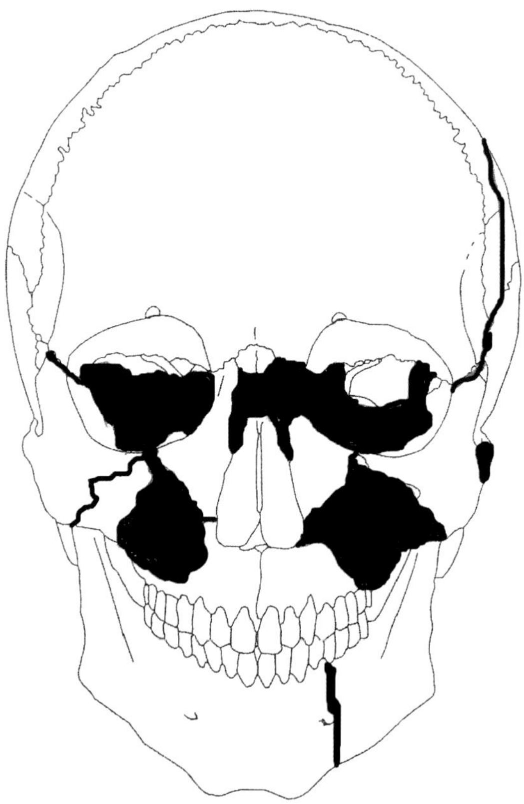

Figure 7.9 Anterior view with highly fragmented and unreconstructable portions colored black.

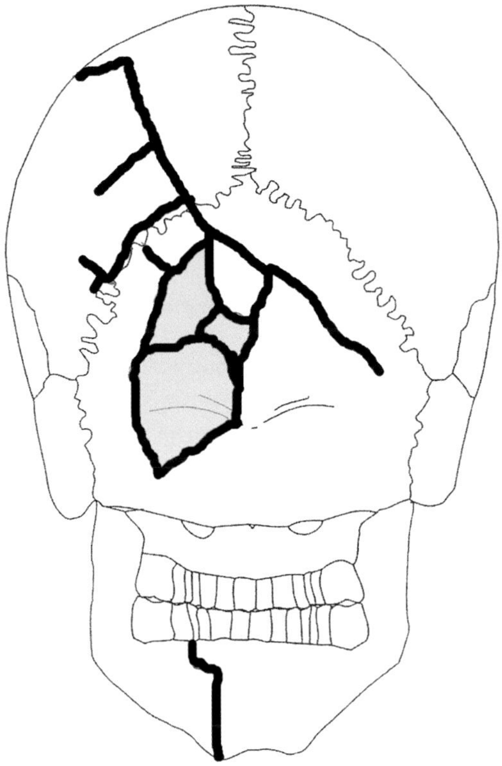

Figure 7.10 Posterior view. Fracture lines noted and displaced fragments shaded.

As noted, a metallic object was recovered from within the cranial vault. The skull was reconstructed to facilitate radiographic comparison against antemortem records.

Perimortem trauma, specifically blunt force trauma, is present in both the left- and right humeri. The left humeral diaphysis exhibits a butterfly fracture slightly distal of mid-shaft. The position of the wedge segment indicates the force was applied to the anterior-medial aspect of the shaft superior to the medial edge of the trochlea. The right humeral diaphysis exhibits two fractures; a butterfly fracture slightly proximal to midshaft and a transverse fracture approximately 15 mm inferior to the surgical neck. The nature of these intersecting fractures is such that the transverse fracture occurred prior to the butterfly fracture. The latter consists of a large wedge of bone, which indicates a force impacted the lateroanterior aspect of the shaft.

Identification

The identity of the remains was established via several complimentary sources. Radiographs of the skull and lower torso, written dental records, and notations of injuries and treatment were provided to the FAC by SA Vinsant.

Antemortem radiographs of Jean Johnson were available for evaluation and comparison. Specifically, an anteroposterior view of the frontal sinus patterns of the skull and the frontal sinus pattern as reflected in the antemortem radiograph of Johnson (dated September 30, 2006) were compared. While the most superior portion of the frontal sinus was not captured in the antemortem film, the inferior patterns of the sinus margins corresponded with those exhibited in the postmortem radiograph. No inconsistencies were identified and the following specific regions of correspondence were noted: (1) Left lateral aspect of the frontal sinus from the supraorbital notch extending across the orbital margin and continuing in a superiorly arcing path, (2) the shape of the frontal sinus as observed within the superiomedial area of the right orbit, (3) the frontal sinus shape as observed within the superiomedial area of the left orbit, (4) the undulating inferior margin of the sinuses across the interorbital region, and (5) the shape and location of two centrally located sinus pouches extending from the anatomical landmarks nasion to glabella.

Additional radiographs dated September 30, 2006, further supported the identity of the remains. The proximal portion of the left humerus showing what appears to be an old, healed injury resulting in an unusual morphology is recorded. This is also noted in the medical records provided to the FAC. The left humerus recovered from the burial site also exhibits the same unusual morphology involving the head, neck, and tubercle.

Another area of consistency concerns the dentition and the written dental record with a last entry of June 10, 1991. The written dental record of Johnson notes the presence of only six mandibular teeth; all incisors and the both canines. The record notes that Johnson was edentulous in the maxillae. The dental record further notes the presence of a partial mandibular plate. The recovered remains consist of an edentulous maxilla and a mandible with the crowns of five single-rooted teeth (the incisors and the right canine) with only the root present for the left canine. A partial dental plate for the mandible was recovered. The teeth represented in the dental arcade of the remains (and the presence of the plate) are consistent with the written dental record of Johnson.

A final point of correspondence is the documentation of a well-healed fracture of the left femur that was reportedly treated with an orthopedic rod insertion into the bone. The left femur recovered from the burial site exhibits a well-healed fracture of the distal third of the shaft with an orthopedic rod inserted into the medullary cavity of the bone.

In conjunction, these points of correspondence are such that the remains represent Jean Johnson.

Summary

The remains recovered from a burial in the Chitwood Mountain area of Scott County represent a white female >50 years of age. The individual reported to have been in this location is Jean Johnson, a white female 69 years of age. Perimortem trauma is evident by means of a gunshot to the head and blunt force to both upper arms. Comparison of the antemortem radiographs to the skeletal remains resulted in no inconsistencies, and the reported dental condition and old femur trauma and orthopedic treatment are consistent. Based on all of these points, we believe that the recovered skeletal remains are of Jean Johnson.

These remains were returned to the family for burial on June 3, 2010. If we can be of further assistance, please feel free to contact us.

Joanne B. Devlin, PhD
Forensic Anthropology Center

Lee Meadows Jantz, PhD
Coordinator, Forensic Anthropology Center

References

Bass, W.M. (2005) *Human Osteology: A Laboratory and Field Manual*, 5th edn. Columbia, MO: Missouri Archaeological Society.

Iscan, M.Y., Loth, S.R., and Wright, R.K. (1985) Age estimation from the rib by phase analysis: White females. *Journal of Forensic Sciences* 30:853–863.

Jantz, R.L. and Ousley, S.D. (2005) *FORDISC 3: Computerized Forensic Discriminant Functions. Version 3.0*. Knoxville, TN: The University of Tennessee.

Lovejoy, C.O., R.S. Meindl, T.R. Pryzbeck, and Mensforth, R.P. (1985) Chronological metamorphosis of the auricular surface of the ilium: A new method for the determination of adult skeletal age at death. *American Journal of Physical Anthropology* 68: 15–28.

Phenice, T.W. (1969) A newly developed visual method of sexing the os pubis. *American Journal of Physical Anthropology* 30: 297–301.

Scientific Working Group for Forensic Anthropology (SWGANTH) (2011) Skeletal sampling and preparation. Issue Date: 05/25/2011.

Suchey, J.M. and Katz, D. (1998) Applications of pubic age determination in a forensic setting. In Reichs, K. J. (Ed.), *Forensic Osteology: Advances in the Identification of Human Remains*, 2nd edn. Springfield, MA: Charles C. Thomas, pp. 204–236.

Determining the Sex of Unknown Human Skeletal Remains

8

GREGORY E. BERG

Contents

Introduction

This chapter explores the approaches and methods used to determine sex from the human skeleton. Skeletal sex determination from either medicolegal or archaeological contexts is a key component of personal identification and of the remainder of the biological profile. Sexing methods typically are divided into two categories: morphological (shape) and metric (size). Morphological aspects of the human skeleton that are sex specific are found primarily in the pelvis, and less so in the other bones of the body. Metric differences between the sexes are found in the skull, but also in the postcranial skeleton. Both categories have varying accuracy rates, with the pelvis being the best indicator, although some metric methods are accurate >90% of the time. This chapter details several morphological techniques and provides a discussion of the statistical aspects to metric sex determination. As with any rigorous science, a solid foundation in basic techniques is necessary, and that foundation is the goal of this chapter.

Sex vs. Gender

Two specific terms frequently are confused in common usage: sex and gender. This is a major issue in science because the difference between these words is a distinction between a biological reality and a social category. For scientists, sex is a biological fact, whereas gender is a socially ascribed and perceived identity. The confusion may stem from several sources: it could be because the general public lacks awareness of the distinction between the two terms and perhaps from the common usage of "gender" on governmental and business forms when in fact "sex" is meant. Overall, the confusion likely lies in the fact that most people believe these words to be synonyms when they are not. As anthropologists, we can only determine the biological sex of an individual from skeletal remains, not that individual's gender character or role. In some cases, gender might be implied from examining the material culture found in conjunction with skeletal remains such as clothing, jewelry, weaponry, and class symbols, but this determination can be very difficult and is fraught with uncertainty. We must remember that when a police investigator asks for the "gender" of an unknown decedent, it is not a question of how that individual dressed, acted, or performed various roles in society, but rather a very simple question of biologically "male or female." We should be mindful of how we apply these terms in everyday professional discussions, casework, or publications, so we do not perpetuate this misconception.

Sexual Dimorphism

When an anthropologist is asked to determine the sex of an individual, he/she always starts with 50/50 odds of being correct, as there are only two biological states: male and female. In order to increase the odds of accuracy, the anthropologist needs to understand sexual dimorphism. Sexual dimorphism generally refers to size and shape differences between males and females of a given species, although other differences in anatomy, function, behavior, and psychology are present. In many ways, this statement oversimplifies the definition, although for purposes of this chapter, it functions as a basis for the discussion on sexing skeletal remains. Easily seen soft tissue differences between the sexes are not the only physical manifestation of sexual dimorphism; the hard tissues of the skeleton also are affected. In some species, the differences are extremely marked, but in others, only subtle differences exist. For the skeletal system, size is often the most dramatic and easily observed disparity between males and females. For instance, given a selection of 25 male and 25 female gorilla skulls mixed together, an untrained observer could place the skulls into a contiguous line, from males to females solely based on size, and likely would be 100% correct. Given the same scenario for human skulls, the untrained observer may achieve a 60% correct classification based on size, if lucky, and where the males and females meet in the middle of the chain would be very hard to determine. This is because humans are not nearly as sexually dimorphic as gorillas—we do have differences but they are more subtle, less pronounced, and often are population specific.

Skeletally, sexual dimorphism develops with the onset of the production of sexual hormones around the time of puberty; these hormones control and regulate the production of the secondary sexual characters. As would be expected in most human populations, these changes are better defined nearing the age of 17, although they can be present much earlier in developmentally precocious individuals. Therefore, estimating sex from the skeleton is easier in adults and late adolescents, and much harder in subadults. Most anthropologists would argue that sexing individuals younger than 15 years of age results in an educated guess, although there are techniques that can be applied. How those techniques fare depends on the preservation of the skeletal elements, the population from which they originated, and whether known sex comparative specimens from that same population are available. The Scientific Working Group for Forensic Anthropology (SWGANTH) has specifically weighed in on this topic. (The SWGANTH is a joint venture between the Federal Bureau of Investigation and the Department of Defense Central Identification Laboratory that is developing consensus best-practice forensic anthropology guidelines and is establishing minimum standards; in addition, the committee is disseminating the guidelines, studies, and findings from these meetings that can benefit the forensic community. These guidelines are available at http://www.swganth.org/index.html). For subadult sex determination, the SWGANTH states that sexing individuals under 12 years of age is an unacceptable practice, although results may be achieved if the pelvis is fusing and methods for adults are applied to the remains (that are greater than 14 years of age) (SWGANTH 2010, p. 3). Other good reviews of the challenges, techniques, and pitfalls for subadult sex estimation can be found in Komar and Buikstra (2007) and Scheuer and Black (2000).

For the most part, sexual dimorphism in the human skeleton can be stated as "males are larger and more robust than females, or females are smaller and more gracile than males." A favorite saying is that males are usually bigger than females. Males can be upwards of 20%–30% larger than females in certain skeletal dimensions (for example, the size of the femur and humerus heads). However, individual variation can make this general rule hard to follow—as with any good bell curve, some individuals are much larger or small than the average. Given two even, 20% overlapping bell curves, the area where the curves overlap is where misidentification happens (Figure 8.1). Said differently, small, gracile males can be easily confused with large, robust females. Complicating the picture, human populations vary across time and geographic space. As a simple example, populations with life-ways focused on hunting and gathering frequently tend to produce large and rugose individuals, whereas sedentary populations are often less rugose and potentially smaller due to less stress placed on the skeletal tissue. If a hunter/gatherer female is compared to a sedentary male, it is quite possible to confuse the sexes of these two individuals based on size and rugosity, and vice versa. This example is not meant to factor in all of the biological complexities that surround this issue; rather it is a simple explanation of a very difficult problem. For these reasons, the anthropologist always must examine as much skeletal data as possible before assigning sex to an unknown individual, and population- and period-specific standards should be used for each case examined. Becoming extremely knowledgeable of the individual variation within a population can alleviate some problems, and seriating the

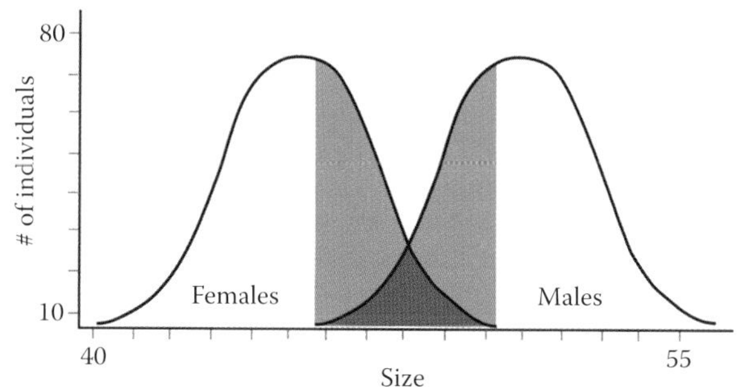

Figure 8.1 Two even 20% overlapping bell curves. The gray-shaded area where the curves overlap is an ambiguous zone in which misidentifications occur. (Illustration by J. Hefner.)

population (creating a series from largest to smallest) can become a good practical exercise for establishing familiarity with a given population's variation.

DNA

Advances in science someday will make the determination of sex easier for the anthropologist. The state of molecular technology (DNA testing) is such that a simple test for the presence or absence of a Y-chromosome can determine sex from skeletal remains. This is particularly helpful in cases involving juvenile remains. Unfortunately (or fortunately, depending on your view), DNA testing is not cheap, and for large skeletal assemblages, it is cost prohibitive. The time required for DNA tests is frequently several weeks to several months, vs. a determination by the anthropologist that can be made in a matter of minutes. Furthermore, DNA analysis requires destruction of bone, and acquiring the necessary permissions for testing in archaeological contexts can be very difficult. These limiting factors will dictate the need for anthropologists to determine sex of most unidentified individuals for the foreseeable future. That stated, it behooves the cautious anthropologist to seek out DNA testing in medicolegal cases involving juvenile remains where this is a feasible option.

Documentation

Perhaps the most important aspect to an anthropologist's work is the documentation of the procedures, methods, and interpretations made in the course of skeletal analysis. Proper scientific documentation is the backbone of any good analysis. Each SWGANTH document expressly indicates that relevant tests, observations, exemplars, and decision-making processes are documented as part of a case file. A standardized notes packet is helpful in these regards. For sex determination, good documentation includes a comprehensive skeletal inventory, notes on the condition of the remains, the age of the remains (both skeletally and temporally), details of any pathological conditions or deleterious processes that have affected the remains, and any contrary or disparate sex indicators. The notes should state the observations complied, measurements taken, methods used, and the results of these analyses. An overall sex assignment is annotated, and the reasons for the assignment are explicitly stated. Any departures from normal methods or processes used should be clearly and effectively communicated. When a case is approached in this manner, the anthropologist can be confident of a positive outcome for their portion of the case. It is always a best practice to consistently and completely document the entirety of an analysis than to cut corners, risking a negative professional outcome.

There are two main approaches to sex determination for the human skeleton, morphological and metric. Each approach has its own advantages and detractors, and each technique has error rates associated with it. Understanding the limitations to each method is crucial to the correct diagnosis of sex. In addition, the approach employed will depend on the elements present for analysis. Archaeological preservation, taphonomic change, scavenger activity, intentional destruction, and other factors play a huge role in which skeletal elements may be present for analysis. The competent anthropologist evaluates each case and uses the best approach possible given the remains present, and frequently employs both morphological and metric methods together. Techniques used in both approaches will be examined in detail later, focusing on various regions of the skeleton.

Morphological Approaches to Sex Determination

Traditional morphological approaches for sex determination from the human skeleton focus on the pelvis and the skull. As one would expect, based on human reproductive differences, the pelvis is highly sexually dimorphic, and even on gross observation, females are usually quite easy to separate from males. Similarly, multiple morphological traits on the human skull are sexually dimorphic, although the accuracy rates tend to be lower than the pelvis. Anthropologists can expect a sexing accuracy rate of 70% to high 80% from the cranium, and 90%–95% accuracy from the pelvis. The most common morphological traits for both areas are defined and given scoring systems in *Standards for Data Collection from Human Skeletal Remains* (Buikstra and Ubelaker 1994). The scoring systems are widely employed across the biological anthropology field and have been improved and quantified by later research (e.g., Walker 2005, 2008). The pelvis should be used as the primary indicator of sex, when present.

Pelvis

There are several very distinguishable traits of the pelvis that can be used for sex determination. In gross appearance, the female pelvis (to include the sacrum) is much broader and with a round pelvic inlet compared to the narrower male counterpart, with its heart-shaped inlet. The pelvic outlet is also narrower and more constricted in males than in females. The pelvic blades are broader and more flared in females, and smaller and narrower in males. The male sacrum is narrower and more anteriorly curved than the female sacrum. Frequently in females, the sacroiliac joint forms a low plateau above the surrounding bone, while in males the normal form is an even contour forming a smooth surface. As is generally true with the rest of the skeleton, the male pelvis tends to be larger and more muscle marked than the female pelvis. Figure 8.2 shows a male and female pelvis for comparison.

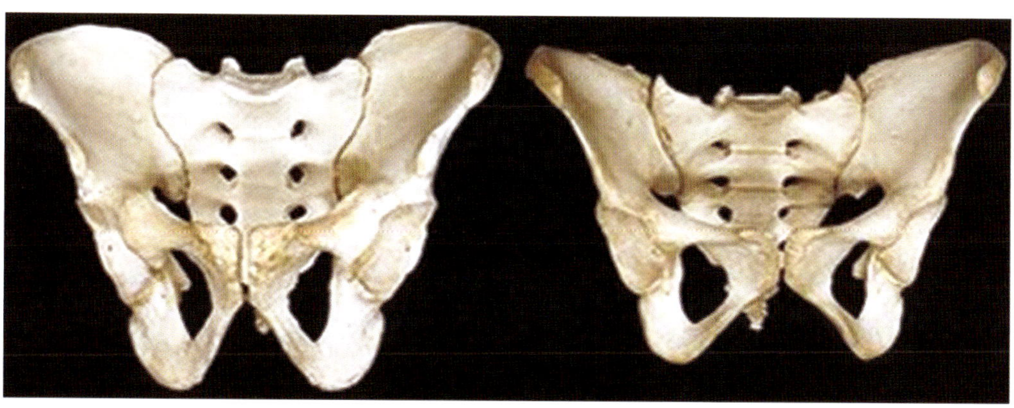

(a) (b)

Figure 8.2 Male pelvis (a) vs. female pelvis (b).

Arguably the most accurate morphological sexing method was developed in the late 1960s by Phenice (1969). In his study of 275 males and females from the Terry collection, he developed a visual method of sexing the pelvis that has an accuracy rate of 95% or greater. He examined three principal traits of the subpubic region: the ventral arc, the degree of subpubic concavity, and the shape of the medial aspect of the ischiopubic ramus. The pubis bones and the subpubic region are where the two narrow halves of the pelvis meet anteriorly in the midline of the body. The ventral arc is a slightly elevated ridge of bone that runs inferiorly and laterally across the ventral surface of the pubis, merging with the medial border of the ischiopubic ramus (Figure 8.3a and b). In females, this ridge of bone is nearly always present; in males, it is nearly always absent. The subpubic concavity is observed inferior to the pubic symphysis and is the shape of the ischiopubic ramus when examined in an antero-posterior orientation. In females, the ischiopubic ramus exhibits a large concavity in this location, whereas in males, there is little to no concavity (Figure 8.4a and b). For the final trait, the pelvis is oriented such that the pubic symphysis is directly facing the observer. Females exhibit a sharply ridged region of bone directly inferior to the pubic symphysis, while males exhibit a wide and flat medial aspect to the ischiopubic ramus in

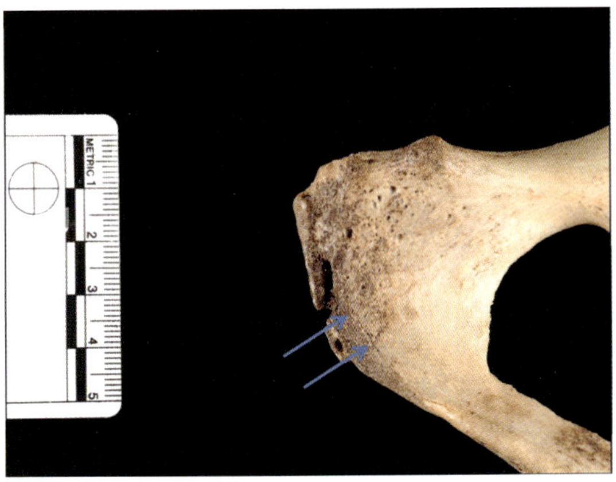

(a)

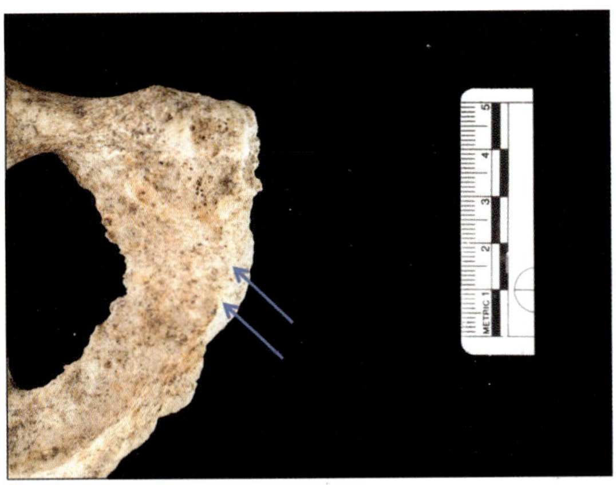

(b)

Figure 8.3 (a) Female pubis (ventral aspect): arrows indicate the ventral arc. (b) Male pubis (ventral): arrows show location where ventral arc would be located; this feature is absent in males.

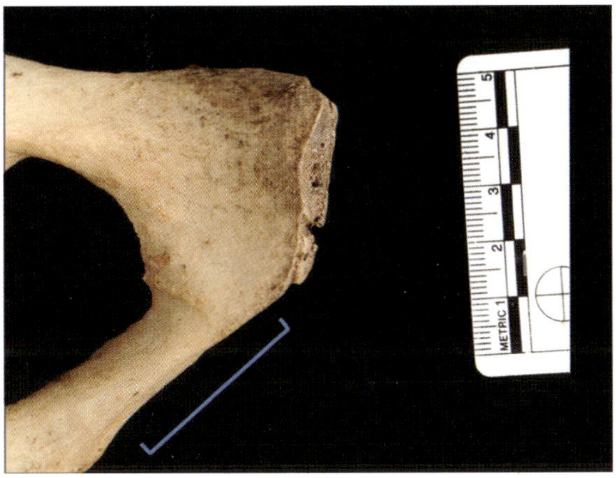

(a)

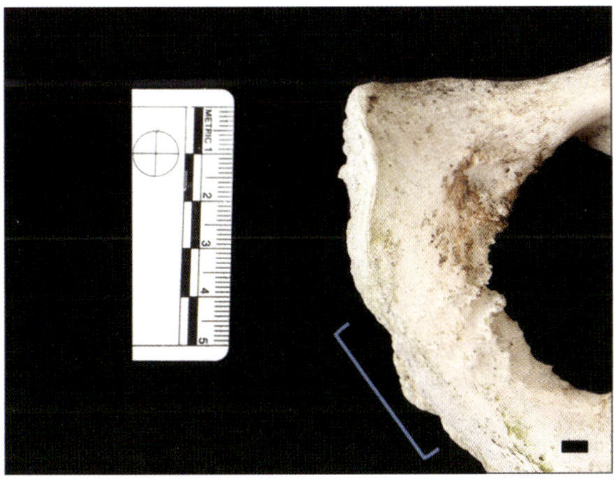

(b)

Figure 8.4 (a) Female pubis (dorsal view): bracket showing area of ischiopubic concavity. (b) Male pubis (dorsal): bracket indicating absence of concavity.

this location (Figure 8.5a and b). Collectively, these three traits are now referred to as the "traits of Phenice." If there is no ventral arc or subpubic concavity, and the medial aspect of the ischiopubic ramus is wide and flat, the pelvis is a male, and this determination is 96% accurate. Conversely, pelvises that exhibit a ventral arc, subpubic concavity, and a sharp medial aspect of the ischiopubic ramus are female. The traits also can be used singly, or in different combinations, but the accuracy rates decline (Phenice 1969).

Two other traits, the sciatic notch and the preauricular sulcus, are examined using a standardized scoring system (Buikstra and Ubelaker 1994). The most important of these, the sciatic notch is usually a wide, open notch in its female form, and a narrow, U-shaped notch in the male expression. The notch is scored on an ordinal scale from 1 (female) to 5 (male) (Figure 8.6a through e). A study by Walker (2005) using an American/British white sample and an American black sample ($n = 296$) found that sciatic notch scores of 3 or greater were 91% likely to be from males, and those with a score of 1 were 88% likely to be female. The indeterminate category, a score of 2, was still more likely to be from a male (66% chance) than from a female. The preauricular sulcus is scored as 0 (absent) or 1–4

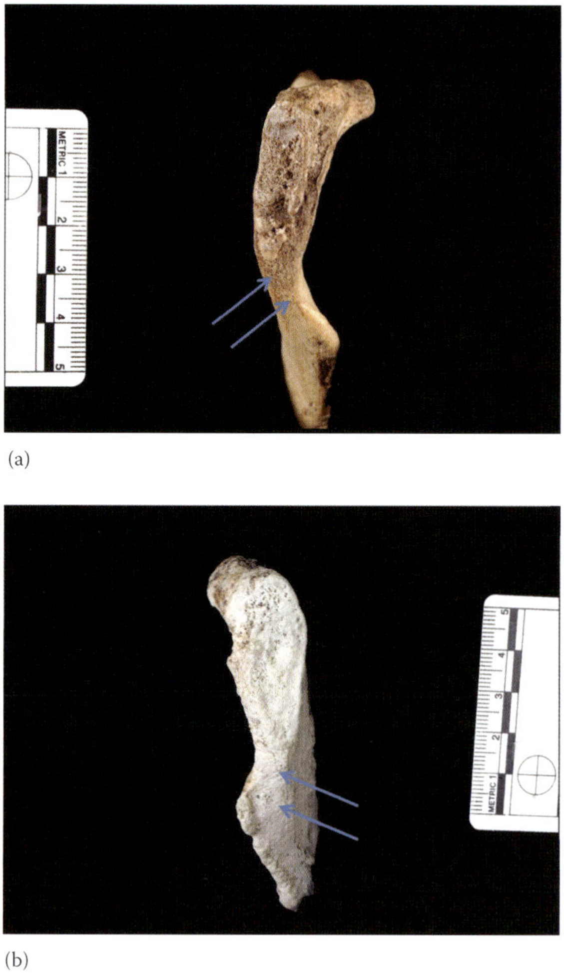

Figure 8.5 (a) Female pubis (medial view): arrows pointing to narrow ischiopubic ramus with a ridge on the medial aspect. (b) Males pubis (medial view): arrows indicating wide, flat ischiopubic ramus.

(depending on the characters of sulcus). This sulcus is much more variable; a female expression tends to be large, wide sulcus with deep pits, whereas the male expression tends to be absent, or a small, narrow, and shallow groove (Figure 8.7a and b). This trait is not nearly as powerful as others, as both males and females frequently exhibit contrary morphology.

Skull

Unlike the pelvis, which has sexually dimorphic features due to the necessary reproductive differences, the cranium has shape differences that are primarily due to size. These differences manifest with the onset of puberty. Many experienced anthropologists would argue that this is the second best area in the body to use for morphological sex estimation. Relative to male crania, female crania are smaller and more gracile. Several tendencies are present: male crania tend to have narrower and less bossed parietal and frontal bones; the posterior root of the zygomatic process typically extends as a crest beyond the external

(a)

(b)

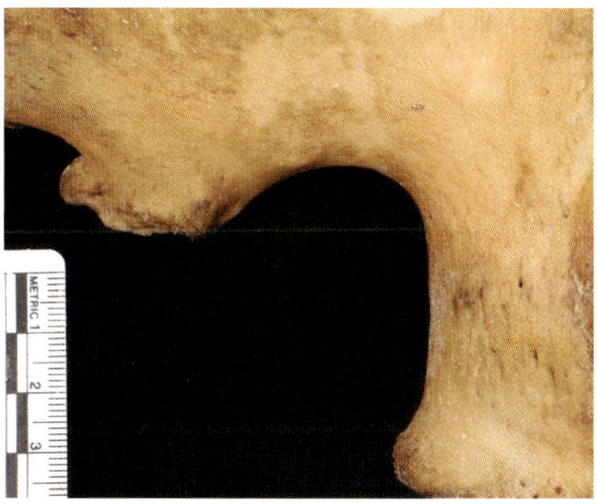

(c)

(d)

(e)

Figure 8.6 (a) Wide sciatic notch (score = 1; female). (b) Relatively wide sciatic notch (score = 2; probably female). (c) Score = 3 (ambiguous). (d) Relatively narrow sciatic notch (score = 4; probable male). (e) Narrow sciatic notch (score = 5; male).

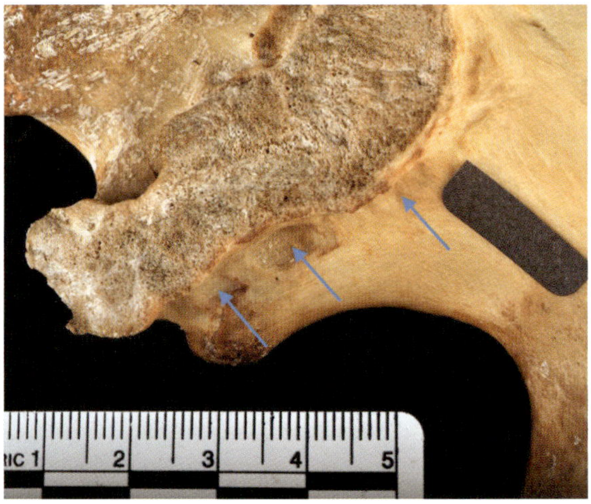

(a)

(b)

Figure 8.7 (a) Female sacroauricular joint with pre-auricular sulcus. Arrows showing pits in the sulcus. (b) Male sacroauricular joint. Bracketed area demonstrating absence of pre-auricular sulcus (score = 0).

auditory meatus; and the frontal sinuses are larger. Most authors recommend not sexing the skull without other individuals from the population it was drawn from as comparatives, as morphological traits are not without intermediate forms, and absolute differences seldom exist (Bass 2005; Braz 2009; White and Folkens 2005). Overall, accuracy rates for sexing skulls range from 70% to the high 80%, but much of the higher accuracy rates are attributable to the experience of the anthropologist conducting the analysis (Stewart 1979).

Scoring systems for skull morphology have been codified for several important features and are found in Buikstra and Ubelaker (1994). Five features are typically scored: the size and rugosity of the nuchal crest, the size and shape of the mastoid process, the size and shape of the supraorbital margin and ridge (glabella), and the size of the mental eminence (chin). Scores range from 1 (female) to 5 (male). On the posterior aspect of the skull, a large nuchal crest, to include having an inion hook, is a very male character state, whereas a

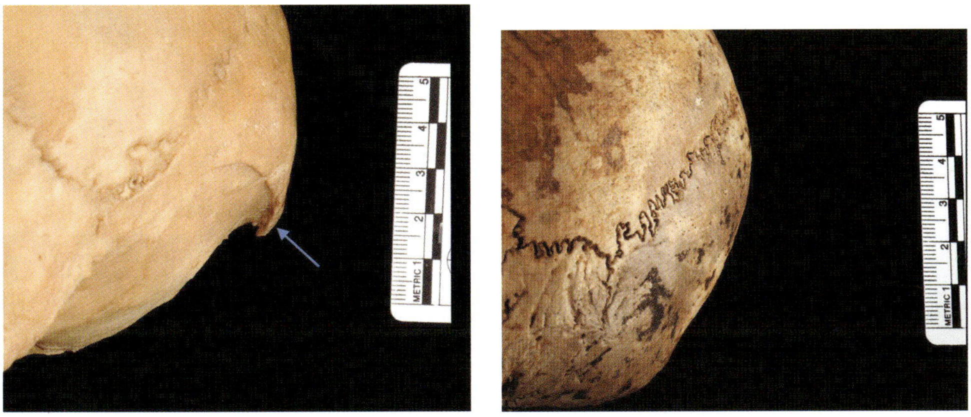

(a) (b)

Figure 8.8 (a) Male nuchal crest with an inion hook (score = 5). (b) Female nuchal region—note the absence of rugosity (score = 1).

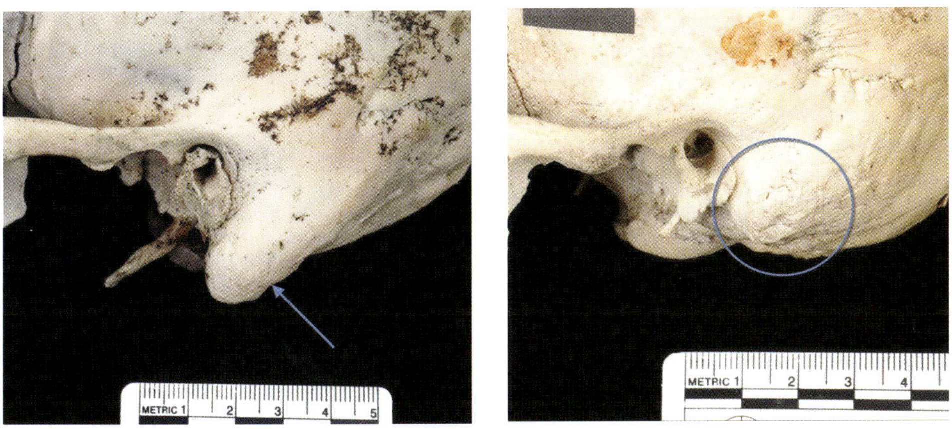

(a) (b)

Figure 8.9 (a) Male mastoid (score = 5). (b) Female mastoid (score = 1).

very female expression is a smooth nuchal region without prominent ridging (Figure 8.8a and b). The mastoid process in males is wider and longer in relation to the external auditory meatus, as compared to a smaller and shorter process in females (Figure 8.9a and b). The supraorbital margin in males is rounder and blunt, and in females it is more superiorly angled, creating a sharp contour (Figure 8.10a and b). The glabellar region in males is much more pronounced, showing a heavy ridge of bone (frequently called the brow ridge), and in females, this area tends to be relatively flat (Figure 8.11a and b). The mental eminence in males has a massive bony expression, and by contrast, in females this area tends to be smooth and much less prominent (Figure 8.12a and b).

Similar to the morphological traits of the pelvis, Walker (2008) examined the likelihood of correct sex determination using these features. His study sample was composed of 304 modern American and English white individuals and a Native American test sample. Using a statistical approach, he provided empirical probabilities of being male for a given score for each cranial trait; if multiple traits are considered logistic discriminant equations

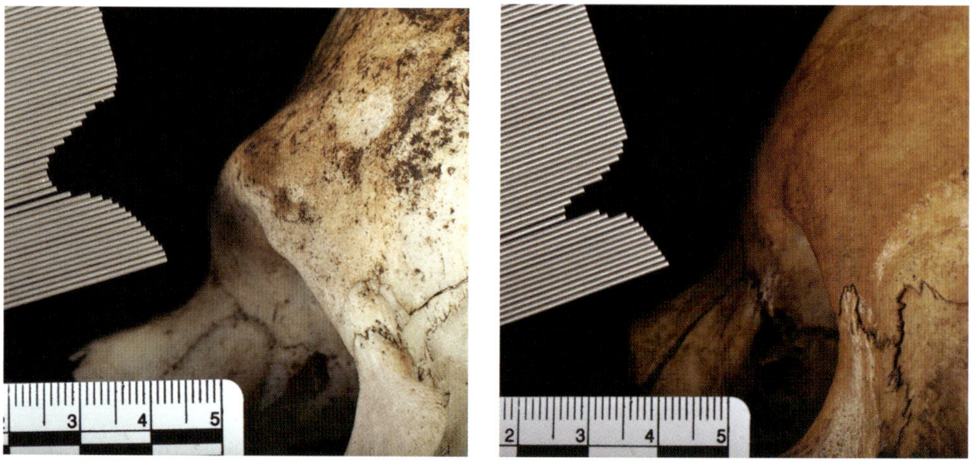

(a) (b)

Figure 8.10 (a) Male supraorbital margin (score = 5). (b) Female supraorbital margin (score = 1). The contour gauge in upper left corner is showing the profile of the supraorbital margin. This instrument was pressed onto the supraorbital margin in order to obtain a profile view of the sharpness/thickness of the margin.

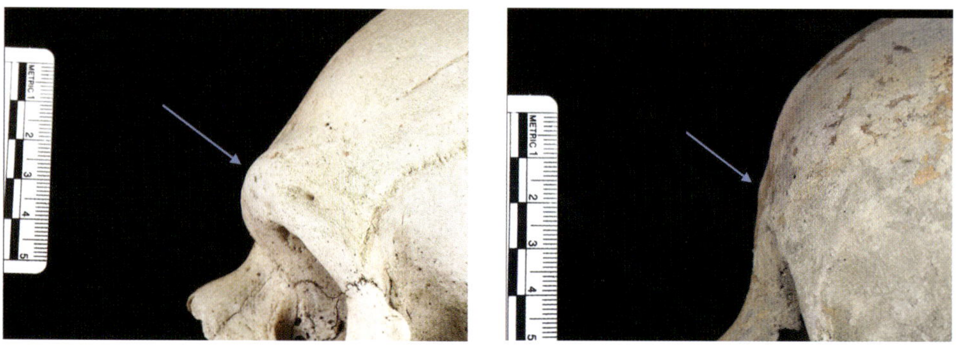

(a) (b)

Figure 8.11 (a) Male glabellar region (score = 5). Note the prominent glabellar protuberance indicated by the arrow and the sloping frontal bone. (b) Female glabellar region. Note the absence of a glabellar ridge and the vertical frontal bone.

can be used. For example, if a single trait is present, the probability of the individual being male can be determined; if the mastoid process is scored as 4, the probability of being male is 0.9, or 90%. On the other hand, if the observer can score glabella, the mental eminence, and the mastoid process, a provided discriminant function will predict sex with an approximate 87% accuracy. His work provides the anthropologist with an estimate of the error rate for cranial sex estimation.

Sex determination from the mandible has been explored by multiple authors with varied results. Loth and Henneberg (1996) produced a method using the posterior border of the mandible and reported a sexing accuracy rate of over 90%. Blind tests of this method by Donnelly et al. (1998) and Haun (2000) showed much lower accuracy rates, between 62% and 68%. Berg (2008) explored seven mandibular morphological traits for sex

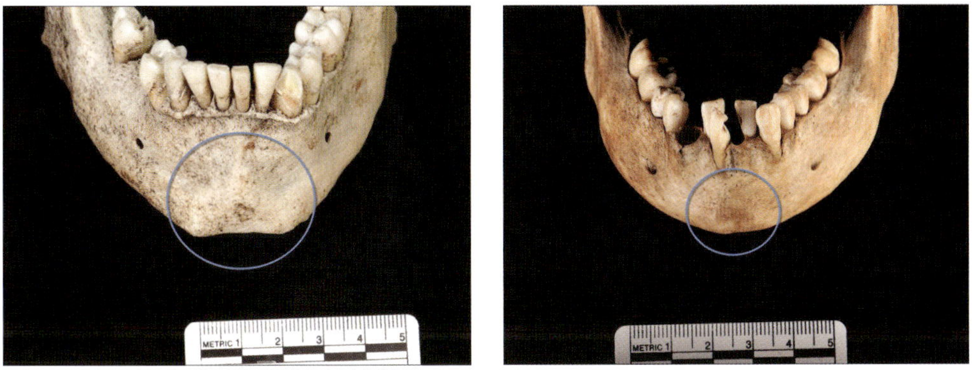

(a) (b)

Figure 8.12 (a) Male mandible showing prominent mental eminence (score = 5). The male mental region is square compared to females. (b) Female mandible (score = 1/2) with small mental eminence and a more v-shaped mental region.

determination; nearly all of the traits showed some amount of sexual dimorphism, but they were population dependent. Discriminant functions based on up to five traits achieved cross-validated accuracy rates between 63% and 80%. Unfortunately, the magnitude and direction of the misclassification rates were such that he did not recommend using these traits to determine sex without mandibular metric variables. Taking all of these studies together, it appears that while the mandible does offer some utility for sex determination (using morphological traits), the accuracy provided does not appear to warrant sole reliance on this portion of the skull.

Other Postcranial Bones

Other morphological methods for the postcranium focus on the distal humerus and the medial clavicle. Rogers (1999) devised a system for scoring sexually dimorphic characters of the distal humerus using a predominantly American white skeletal sample from various collections. She examined the shape of the olecranon fossa, the angle of the medial epicondyle, the degree of trochlear constriction, and the amount of trochlear asymmetry. Females have a more oval olecranon fossa, an angled medial epicondyle, a symmetrical and more constricted trochlea than males. When all four characters are present and able to be scored, her system has an accuracy rate of over 90%. A blind test of this method by Falys et al. (2005) found that indeed, the distal humerus is sexually dimorphic and is recommended for use. For the medial clavicle, Rogers et al. (2000) determined that the presence or absence of a rhomboid fossa can be used to determine sex. This study used 344 clavicle pairs from the William F. McCormick collection, representing 231 males and 113 females. A deeply pitted rhomboid fossa (an excavation on the inferior medial clavicle at the insertion of the costoclavicular ligament) is typically associated with male individuals. Using their grading scale that employs alpha designators for the various states of expression, a rhomboid fossa scoring at least a "C" on the left side of the body indicates a male individual 92.2% of the time, and if present on the right side, 81.7% of the time. For morphological sex determination, best practice stipulates that the published comparison photographs and/or line drawings be consulted in the original publications to classify the traits.

Metric Approaches to Sex Determination

Metric analysis of human remains for sex determination seems like a relatively straightforward task, but can be very complex. Metric evaluations have been used in anthropology since the inception of the discipline and, before this time, when anthropology was principally incorporated into the field of anatomy. There are a huge number of publications on metric sex determination on nearly every bone in the human body using a wide variety of statistical approaches. These methods typically use some of the 34 skull and 43 postcranial measurements that are standard for human skeletal documentation (Buikstra and Ubelaker 1994; Moore-Jansen et al. 1994). Commonly, cranial measurements are employed, followed by various diameters and lengths of the postcranial skeleton, although other measurements have been used. This section primarily is dedicated to providing the reader with an understanding of the principles of several commonly encountered statistical methods (section points and discriminant functions) used in metric sex determination, so that the reader can use any number of published sources easily and effectively. In addition, a brief overview of the computer program, FORDISC 3.0 (Jantz and Ousley 2005) is highlighted (for a more detailed description of this program, see Chapter 13). While other major statistical methods are used in anthropology, such as simple and multiple linear regression analysis and principal component analysis, they are beyond the scope of this chapter.

Examples of sex determination using quantitative measures are extremely proliferative in the anthropological literature, and because of their abundance, only a few examples are discussed in this introductory text. Cranial measurements, initially explored by Giles and Elliot (1963) in the infancy of multivariate metric sex determination, yield relatively high accuracy rates (typically 80%–90%). Their work was built upon by other researchers who have surveyed sexual dimorphism from world populations (cf Giles 1970; Howells 1973, 1989). When a complete skull is not present, fragments from the cranial base can be used to determine sex (Holland 1986) or from complete or partial mandibles (Berg 2008). The postcranial elements work quite effectively for sex determination, as well. Frequently, measurements from the humerus, femur, or tibia yield correct sex determinations with 80%–95% accuracy rates (Dittrick and Suchey 1986; France 1998; Holland 1991; Holman and Bennett 1991; Iscan and Miller-Shaivitz 1984; King et al. 1998; Spradley and Jantz 2011; Stewart 1979). Even the metacarpals and metatarsals produce similarly high accuracy rates (Case and Ross 2007; Lazenby 1994; Robling and Ubelaker 1997). These are just a few of the studies anthropologists have to choose from when determining sex from human remains. But how do most of these studies work?

A sectioning point is a simple statistical approach to metric sexing of the skeleton. A section point for a data set is the mathematical point that maximizes the differences between two groups, for example, males and females, in one dimension. It is a univariate analysis method (an analysis using one variable instead of many variables) and is common in older publications, although it still does appear in more recent research articles (Berrizbeitia 1989; MacLaughlin and Bruce 1985; McCormick et al. 1991). A sectioning point can be thought of as the point where two data distributions, frequently expressed as curves, overlap (Figure 8.13). This approach generally uses one variable, such as femur head diameter, although multiple variables expressed as a ratio (which creates only one variable) can be incorporated. The accuracy of a generated sectioning point depends on the amount

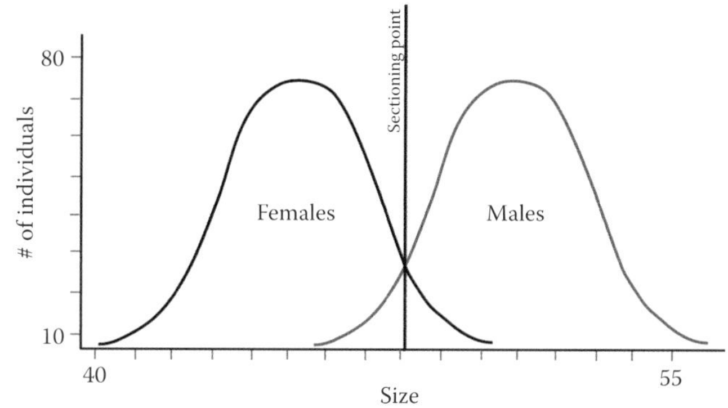

Figure 8.13 The sectioning point for a single variable from two data distributions (male and female). (Illustration by J. Hefner.)

of sexual dimorphism present in the data spread of two populations. The data spread is the total value range for a given measurement regardless of population in an analysis. For example, the femur head diameter might have a data spread for White males and females from 34 (extremely female) to 57 mm (extremely male). Highly sexually dimorphic measurements have a large data spread with little overlap between males and females, and therefore will produce excellent prediction accuracy rates. Conversely, a narrow data range with a large amount of data overlap between the sexes will produce lower accuracy rates. While this sounds simple, complex sectioning points can be created that minimize error in one direction while maximizing it in another. For example, a sectioning point can be created that is 90% accurate for male sex determination, but at the same time, the measurement will misclassify females 30% of the time. This occurs when the sectioning point is moved along the data curve until 90% of one group is to the right of the point (Figure 8.14). Such accuracy trade-offs can be very valuable, but need to be used judiciously.

In the anthropological literature, section point methods are expressed as a single value, with males having higher values than females—remember males are typically bigger than

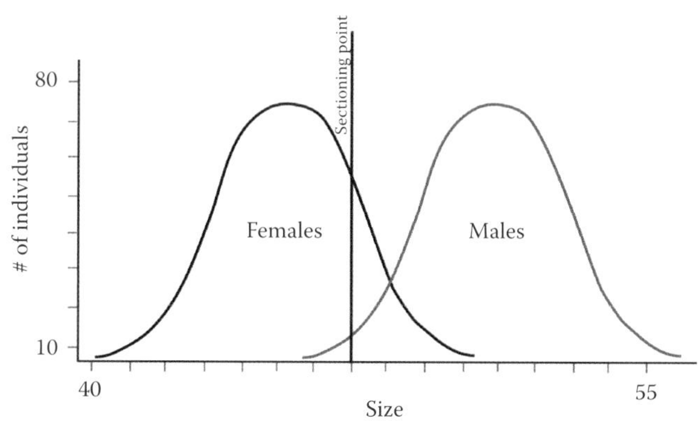

Figure 8.14 An adjusted sectioning point for a single variable from two data distributions (male and female). As this sectioning point has been shifted toward the male distribution, it will classify males correctly at the expense of misclassifying females. (Illustration by J. Hefner.)

females. For example, a sectioning point for the maximum diameter of the femur head might be expressed in a publication as

$$\text{Female} = \langle 45.0\ \text{mm} \rangle = \text{Male}$$

Interpreting this equation is straightforward: all measurements <45.0 mm are classified as female, and all measurements >45.0 mm are classified as male. Section point methods can have an indeterminate category built into the equation as well. An example of a sectioning point with an indeterminate category can be found in Stewart's (1979) sex determination method for the maximum diameter of the femur head. His analysis of 100 white and black males and females in the Terry collection generated the following sectioning system:

$$\text{Female} = < 43.0\ \text{mm},\ 44.0\text{–}46.0\ \text{mm} = \text{Indeterminate},\ > 45.0\ \text{mm} = \text{Male}$$

For this study, all individuals with femur head measurements of 44.0–46.0 mm cannot be sexed accurately, while those with measurements of 43.0 mm and below are females, and those of 47.0 mm and above are males. In applications such as the previous example, an accuracy level could be established for a predetermined value, perhaps 90%. Therefore, the high and low section points would be 90% accurate and the values in between would be classified as indeterminate for sex. Since there are so many different ways of generating a sectioning point, it is imperative to know how each was created in order to avoid misapplication of the research.

Sexing the human skeleton using metric measurements greatly moved forward with the adoption of the discriminant function statistic, which was developed by Fischer in the 1940s. For many years, discriminant function analysis was unpractical and unwieldy, utilizing many hand calculations and long formulae to develop each classification function. The personal computer changed that situation; today calculations are automated, and the time needed to generate a discriminant function has become minutes or seconds instead of days and weeks. The application of these computer-generated functions easily is conducted with a hand calculator in a matter of minutes. In today's anthropology, discriminant function analysis is relied upon heavily for sex assignments.

The discriminant function has allowed anthropologists to move away from univariate and simpler statistical approaches into complex multidimensional space. The objective of a discriminant function is to maximize the differences between two or more groups. The function accomplishes this objective by weighting and combining two or more discriminating variables in a linear manner so that the intercorrelations of the variables are considered and the ratio of between-group variance to within-group variance is maximized (Pietrusewsky 2000). These transformed variables are used to place or assign individuals or groups into multidimensional space. The distances between these groups then can be visualized or measured. Each individual in the analysis is classified into one of the original groups based on its discriminant scores, and the probability of group membership can be mathematically calculated. In this manner, unknown individuals can be placed into the analysis, and their probability of group membership to one of the reference populations can be computed (a detailed explanation is found in Pietrusewsky [2000]). Leave-one-out analyses (also called cross-validating analyses) or boot-strapping analyses of the function are useful tools to determine the overall classification accuracy of a discriminant function. These analyses are typically computed within the computer program generating the function, which often will supply the cross-validated or boot-strapped accuracy rates as part of the results and output. A good discriminant function will have a cross-validated accuracy rate between 85% and 95%.

In a much more simplified explanation, the discriminant procedure takes the analytical variables and rank-orders them based on the amount of information they contain about differences between the reference populations. A centroid is computed for each reference population (the centroid is the average value of all variables entering the analysis for a population in multidimensional space). Once these positions are determined, an unknown individual can be mathematically mapped into the same multidimensional space, and the distance from each reference population centroid measured. These distances are used to classify the unknown; the smaller the distance, the higher the classification score. A large assumption made when using discriminant function analysis is that the unknown individual actually is *from* one of the reference populations. If the unknown does not originate from any one of the reference populations, the individual might still classify, but the probability of group membership likely will be extremely low.

A discriminant function often is presented as a formula containing the variables, each multiplied by a function weight, added or subtracted together, and added to a constant. The constant is a special number that is computed for the function and does not vary (hence the name). The resulting value is compared to a section point (frequently set to 0), and the groups, in this case, the sexes, are on either side of zero. A three variable cranial measurement sex function can look like this:

$$X = \text{ZYB}(0.245) + \text{BPL}(0.123) - \text{WFB}(0.754) + 0.232$$

In this example, ZYB (bizygomatic breadth) is multiplied by 0.245, added to the product of BPL (basion-prosthion length) and 0.123, the resulting value has the product of WFB (minimum frontal breadth) and 0.754 subtracted from it, and finally 0.232 is added to the total. If X is greater than 0, the skull is male, if less than 0, then it is female. Functions typically compare two groups at a time; for more than two groups, the variables have to be added into a second, third, or fourth function, and those results will determine the final classification. If more than two groups are in the analysis, for example, Black and White males and females (a four-way discriminant function analysis), the function will likely be computed in a computer and not completed by hand, as the analysis is far too complex.

Discriminant function analysis for the classification of sex of unknown human remains has become fairly commonplace, particularly due to the introduction of the computer program FORDISC, developed at the University of Tennessee by Richard Jantz and Steve Ousley. As of 2011, the program is in its third version (FORDISC 3.0). This program is widely used in forensic anthropology for the construction and use of custom discriminant functions to classify unknown remains into populations. In its most simplistic use, the program allows the user to enter the standard cranial and postcranial measurements of an unknown skeleton into a worksheet. The user selects either cranial or postcranial measurements, as well as the reference populations to compare the unknown against, such as White males and females. Due to limitations of the program, cranial and postcranial measurements cannot be analyzed simultaneously, and the program in its present version cannot be used to determine the sex of unknown remains solely; instead, sex determination must be made in the context of ancestry. Therefore, prior knowledge of the unknown's ancestry is helpful, but not necessary—large analyses that include multiple ancestral reference populations can be undertaken easily. After the data are entered, FORDISC creates a series of custom discriminant functions that classifies the unknown remains into one of the chosen reference populations. The classification accuracy (cross-validated) for the overall model is provided in the final output. In addition, the program calculates posterior and typicality probabilities (additional analyses that inform the user on the likelihood of a correct assignment to a given population, and how typical the unknown is for that population). Therefore, the practitioner can formulate a detailed and informed opinion based on the output generated from the program.

In FORDISC, the provided reference data vary depending on the region of the skeleton. There are more cranial reference populations than there are for the postcranial bones. Standard cranial reference populations include White, Black, Native American, and Japanese males and females, as well as male samples of Hispanic, Vietnamese, Guatemalan, and Chinese populations. For the postcranial measurements, only Black and White males and females have representative populations. A separate module in the program contains additional cranial data sets, including Howell's sample of worldwide populations and the University of Tennessee data sets of nineteenth and twentieth century Black and White groups. This module has additional, nonstandard measurements that can be used in the analyses. In more advanced applications of the program, the user can import their own data, create discriminant functions, and classify unknown remains using the constructed functions. Additionally, the program allows the user to select specific statistical procedures to be used in the function generation, and permits the use of shape transformations for cranial analyses. Since this program can conduct analyses containing only a few to a large number of variables, it is extremely flexible, and is usually a principal and valuable component in the anthropologist's toolbox for estimating sex and ancestry from unknown human remains.

With any metric analysis, the user must understand the limitations of the method. In the case of FORDISC, the user must be aware that the program will classify the unknown remains into one of the provided reference populations, *regardless* of whether the unknown is actually from *any* of the reference populations (see the discussion on discriminant analysis provided earlier). The anthropologist must interpret the data and determine if the statistical probabilities support classifying the unknown remains into one of those groups. Often this issue is more complicated in the assignment of ancestry and less so for the determination of sex. If the output statistics indicate only male classifications with high accuracy rates, then in all probability, the unknown remains are male (and vice versa). Having stated this point, if the analyzed remains are *not* from the reference populations provided in the program, the probability of a sex misclassification will increase, and the user should fully be aware of this possibility.

When Methods Disagree

One of the trickiest problems in sex determination is when conflicting results are obtained from the same skeleton. Each anthropologist has his/her own way of dealing with this particular problem, and its solution is based on experience, the amount and types of analyses conducted, and familiarity and confidence in the methods used; all of these solidify to form a sort of "gestalt" in the mind of the anthropologist. A gestalt is the unwritten criteria needed to assign a sex category or other determination to a set of unknown remains. For example, a novice anthropologist may not be willing to commit to a sex assignment for a particular set of remains based solely on midrange cranial morphology, whereas the more experienced individual may definitively state sex for the same remains due to trust in the methods and their own experiences. Regardless, what is absolutely necessary for sex determination is the proper documentation of the tests and observations that form the basis of the opinion. Without the documentation, the anthropologist's opinion quickly can be challenged, potentially jeopardizing the outcome of an analysis.

In this chapter, sex determination from the pelvis is emphasized; the pelvic girdle should be consulted first and foremost due to the distinct *biological* reasons for differences between males and females. According to the guidelines produced by the SWGANTH (2010, p. 2), "Methods based on the shape and size, and the presence or absence of features of the pelvis are preferred." However, if the markers are missing, or the pelvis is incomplete, then what methods does the anthropologist place the most emphasis on for sex assignment, particularly if the results disagree?

Until recently, there were few statistical methods to determine error with morphological traits of the skull and pelvis. Using the older research (Phenice 1969) and newer studies (Walker 2005, 2008), we can quantify the amount of error associated with morphological sex determination from the pelvis and skull. In addition, morphological sex determination from other body elements has calculable error rates; therefore, it is possible to quantify the chances of being wrong when using these studies. Metric assessments of skeletal remains using discriminant functions or sectioning points also have known error rates for each analysis. Therefore, it is a matter of weighing the error and determining which method(s) present the least chance of a misclassification.

A final set of options for sex determination is available to the anthropologist, which is to use qualifying language to describe the results of a particularly troublesome analysis. Since there are only two biological states, male and female, there can then be up to *three* additional qualified states: probable male, probable female, and indeterminate. A *possible* sex estimate cannot exist, because if it is *possibly* female, then it could be *possibly* male as well. The indeterminate state is used in those cases that have a poor representation of skeletal elements in which no sound scientific opinion can be rendered. The probable categories are used in situations where the majority of the evidence indicates one sex, but the associated method error rates do not inspire high confidence in a definitive sex assignment. It is up to each individual to decide how much error is allowed before placing a set of remains into a probable category. Conversely, a probable category can be used to "upgrade" an assignment from the indeterminate category, if there is enough evidence to justify it. As familiarity with different methods grows and more cases are examined, the judicious use of the probable category will come into the anthropologist's toolkit.

Conclusion

Sex determination of human skeletal remains is a primary anthropological undertaking, whether in cases of medicolegal interest or in research on ancient populations. It serves as a foundational key for developing the rest of the biological profile. An accurate determination is necessary, even if the most accurate assignment is "indeterminate." Morphological sex determination from the pelvis is the best indicator for a complete set of remains; in cases of partial remains, the skeletal elements available will dictate the approaches available to the anthropologist. Frequently, both morphological and metric methods will be utilized to assess sex, and accuracy rates for both are available. Proper documentation of the testing and findings is absolutely necessary. With increasing practice and familiarity with the metric and morphological methods, the task of sexing a set of unknown remains becomes more accurate and straightforward.

Acknowledgments

The author and editors would like to thank the C.A. Pound Human Identification Laboratory at the University of Florida and the University of Tennessee Department of Anthropology for use of the skeletal elements pictured in Figures 8.2–8.12.

References

Bass WM. 2005. *Human Osteology: A Laboratory and Field Manual*, 5th edn., Special Publication No. 2 of the Missouri Archaeological Society, Columbia, MO.

Berg GE. 2008. Biological affinity and sex determination using morphometric and morphoscopic variables from the human mandible. PhD dissertation, University of Tennessee, Knoxville, TN.

Berrizbeitia EL. 1989. Sex determination with the head of the radius. *J Forensic Sci* 34:1206–1213.

Buikstra JE and DH Ubelaker (eds.). 1994. *Standards for Data Collection from Human Skeletal Remains*. Arkansas Archeological Survey Research Series No. 44, Fayetteville, AR.

Braz VS. 2009. Anthropological estimation of sex. In: *Handbook of Forensic anthropology and Archaeology*, Blau S and DH Ubelaker (eds.), Left Coast Press, Walnut Creek, CA.

Case DT and AH Ross. 2007. Sex determination from hand and foot bone lengths. *J Forensic Sci* 52:264–270.

Dittrick J and JM Suchey. 1986. Sex determination of prehistoric Central California skeletal remains using discriminant analysis of the femur and humerus. *Am J Phys Anthropol* 70:3–9.

Donnelly SM, Hens SM, Rogers NL, and KL Schneider. 1998. Technical note: A blind test of mandibular ramus flexure as a morphologic indicator of sexual dimorphism in the human skeleton. *Am J Phys Anthropol* 107:363–366.

Falys CG, Schutkowski H, and DA Weston. 2005. The distal humerus—A blind test of Rogers' sexing technique using a documented skeletal collection. *J Forensic Sci* 50:1–5.

France DL. 1998. Observational and metric analysis of sex in the skeleton. In: *Forensic Osteology: Advances in the Identification of Human Remains*, 2nd edn., Reichs KJ (ed.), Charles C Thomas, Springfield IL, pp. 163–186.

Giles E. 1970. Discriminant function sexing of the human skeleton. In: *Personal Identification in Mass Disasters*, Stewart TD (ed.), National Museum of Natural History, Smithsonian Institution, Washington DC, pp. 99–109.

Giles E and O Elliot. 1963. Sex determination by discriminant function analysis of crania. *Am J Phys Anthropol* 21:53–68.

Haun SJ. 2000. Brief communication: A study of the predictive accuracy of mandibular ramus flexure as a single morphologic indicator of sex in an archaeological sample. *Am J Phys Anthropol* 111:429–432.

Holland TD. 1986. Sex determination of fragmentary crania by analysis of the cranial base. *Am J Phys Anthropol* 70:203–208.

Holland TD. 1991. Sex assessment using the proximal tibia. *Am J Phys Anthropol* 85:221–227.

Holman DJ and KA Bennett. 1991. Determination of sex from arm bone measurements. *Am J Phys Anthropol* 84:421–426.

Howells WW. 1973. *Cranial Variation in Man. A study by Multivariate Analysis of Patterns of Difference Among Recent Human Populations*, Papers of the Peabody Museum of Archaeology and Ethnology, Harvard University Press, Cambridge, MA, Vol. 67.

Howells WW. 1989. *Skull Shapes and the Map. Craniometric Analyses in the Dispersion of Modern Homo*, Papers of the Peabody Museum of Archaeology and Ethnology, Harvard University Press, Cambridge, MA, Vol. 79.

Iscan MY and P Miller-Shaivitz. 1984. Discriminant function sexing of the tibia. *J Forensic Sci* 29:1087–1093.

Jantz RL and SD Ousley. 2005. *FORDISC 3.0*, University of Tennessee, Knoxville, TN.

King CA, Iscan MY, and SR Loth. 1998. Metric and comparative analysis of sexual dimorphism in the Thai femur. *J Forensic Sci* 43:954–958.

Komar DA and JE Buikstra. 2007. *Forensic Anthropology. Contemporary Theory and Practice*, Oxford University Press, Oxford, U.K.

Lazenby RA. 1994. Identification of sex from metacarpals: Effect of side asymmetry. *J Forensic Sci* 39:1188–1194.

Loth SR and M Henneberg. 1996. Mandibular ramus flexure: A new morphologic indicator of sexual dimorphism in the human skeleton. *Am J Phys Anthropol* 99:473–485.

MacLaughlin SM and MF Bruce. 1985. A simple univariate technique for determining sex from fragmentary femora: Its application to a Scottish Short Cist population. *Am J Phys Anthropol* 67:413–417.

McCormick WF, Stewart JH, and H Greene. 1991. Sexing of human clavicles using length and circumference measurements. *Am J Forensic Med Pathol* 12:175–181.

Moore-Jansen PM, Ousley SD, and RL Jantz. 1994. Data collection procedures for forensic skeletal material. Report of Investigations No. 48, The University of Tennessee, Knoxville, TN.

Pietrusewsky M. 2000. Metric analysis of skeletal remains: Methods and applications. In: *Biological Anthropology of the Human Skeleton*, Katzenberg MA and SR Saunders (eds.), Wiley-Liss, New York, pp. 375–416.

Phenice TW. 1969. A newly developed visual method of sexing the os pubis. *Am J Phys Anthropol* 30:297–301.

Robling AG and DH Ubelaker. 1997. Sex estimation from the metatarsals. *J Forensic Sci* 42:1062–1069.

Rogers NL. 1999. A visual method of determining the sex of skeletal remains using the distal humerus. *J Forensic Sci* 44:57–60.

Rogers NL, Flournoy LE, and WF McCormick. 2000. The rhomboid fossa of the clavicle as a sex and age estimator. *J Forensic Sci* 45:61–67.

Scheuer L and S Black. 2000. *Developmental Juvenile Osteology*, Academic Press, San Diego, CA.

Spradley MK and RL Jantz. 2011. Sex estimation in forensic anthropology: Skull versus postcranial elements. *J Forensic Sci* 56:289–296.

Stewart TD. 1979. *Essentials of Forensic Anthropology*, Charles C Thomas, Springfield, IL.

SWGANTH (Scientific Working Group for Forensic Anthropology). 2010. Sex assessment. Issue date 06/03/2010. Electronic document available at http://swganth.startlogic.com/Sex%20Rev0.pdf

Walker PL. 2005. Greater sciatic notch morphology: Sex, age, and population differences. *Am J Phys Anthropol* 127:385–391.

Walker PL. 2008. Sexing skulls using discriminant function analysis of visually assessed traits. *Am J Phys Anthropol* 136:39–50.

White TD and PA Folkens. 2005. *The Human Bone Manual*. Elsevier/Academic Press, San Diego, CA.

Age Estimation Methods

9

NATALIE R. SHIRLEY, ALICE E. FAZLOLLAH, AND MARIATERESA A. TERSIGNI-TARRANT

Contents

Forensic anthropologists use a number of methods to estimate the age at death for skeletal remains. In general, the methods are based largely upon the morphology of the skeletal elements, that is, the presence of non-metric traits or specific morphological features on each of the bones of the skeleton. These characteristics include the fusion of the proximal and distal epiphyses, fusion of the cranial sutures, dental eruption patterns, and morphological changes to portions of the os coxae and the ribs.

Subadult Age-at-Death Estimation

Although the discussion of aging in this chapter will focus mainly on adult skeletal aging methodologies, it is important to have an understanding of the methods used to age subadult remains. For our purposes, *subadult* refers to any individual whose skeleton has not completed skeletal or dental development, that is, a skeleton that is skeletally or dentally immature. A state of skeletal maturity is reached when all of the epiphyses in the skeleton have fused to their respective diaphyses. Similarly, a state of dental maturity is reached when all of the permanent dentition has completed development, calcification and/or has erupted into the oral cavity, and no further dental development is seen within the alveolar bone. Although these two maturation events can occur at different times within a single skeleton and are variable throughout populations of skeletons, the term *subadult* usually refers to an individual of 18 years of age or younger.

The processes of skeletal and dental development and maturation occur at known rates in humans. By looking at three main areas of growth and development, we can derive a fairly accurate age-at-death estimate for immature remains. What follows is a summary of the three most commonly used methods of subadult aging: dental development, calcification, and eruption; long bone length; and the appearance and union of epiphyses. Although there is some suggestion that particular populations reach skeletal and dental maturity at a more precocious rate than others, most methods for aging immature remains can be used for all ancestral groups as well as for both sexes. It is important to note that adult methods of age estimation are not applicable to subadult remains, as most of the adult aging methods do not include subadults in their original sample populations. Additionally, most of the methods used for adult age-at-death estimation assess the degradation of skeletal morphology over time, a process that does not begin until development is complete.

Dental Development, Calcification, and Eruption

The development, calcification, and eruption of human dentition occur at a regular and predictable rate. This is true for both the permanent and deciduous human dentition (for a review of human dentition, refer to Chapter 5). This predictability, then, allows for the construction of a clear methodology for the identification of age at death based upon the presence or absence of particular parts of each tooth (i.e., crown, root, etc.) of the deciduous and permanent dentition, as well as their eruption into the oral cavity.

The most widely used standards for the aging of immature remains based on the development, calcification, and eruption of the dentition are those described by Moorees et al. (1963a,b). These methods use an alphanumeric scoring system that describes the level of formation of the crown, root, and apex of particular deciduous and permanent teeth. As much of this method requires the assessment of dental development occurring within the alveolar bone (crown development, root length, and apical closure), postmortem radiographs of the skull and mandible are necessary to assess age accurately. This methodology can be used to assess age in remains from 4 months gestation to ~35 years of age. Buikstra and Ubelaker (1994) attempted to simply this scoring system by creating a 14-stage coding system that can be used to score teeth with single or multiple roots, as well as deciduous or permanent dentition. The scores for each tooth are then associated with an age range. Additionally, Ubelaker (1989) published a sequence diagram for the formation and eruption of the dentition detailing the deciduous and permanent dentition at various ages. This diagram, although based on data for American Indians, clearly depicts the periods of deciduous eruption, mixed dentition, and full permanent dentition eruption linked with suggested age ranges.

Growth and Development of Long Bones

Another method for the assessment of immature remains focuses on the metric analysis of long bones. Just as dental development begins during fetal development, long bone diaphyses, like much of the rest of the skeleton, begin forming before birth and grow at a predictable rate until the proximal and distal epiphyses of each bone fuse to the diaphyses, preventing further growth (Figure 9.1). Accordingly, measurements of these diaphyseal regions can be correlated to particular age ranges. Fazekas and Kosa (1978) detailed the methodology for the metric analysis of long bones in immature remains to determine

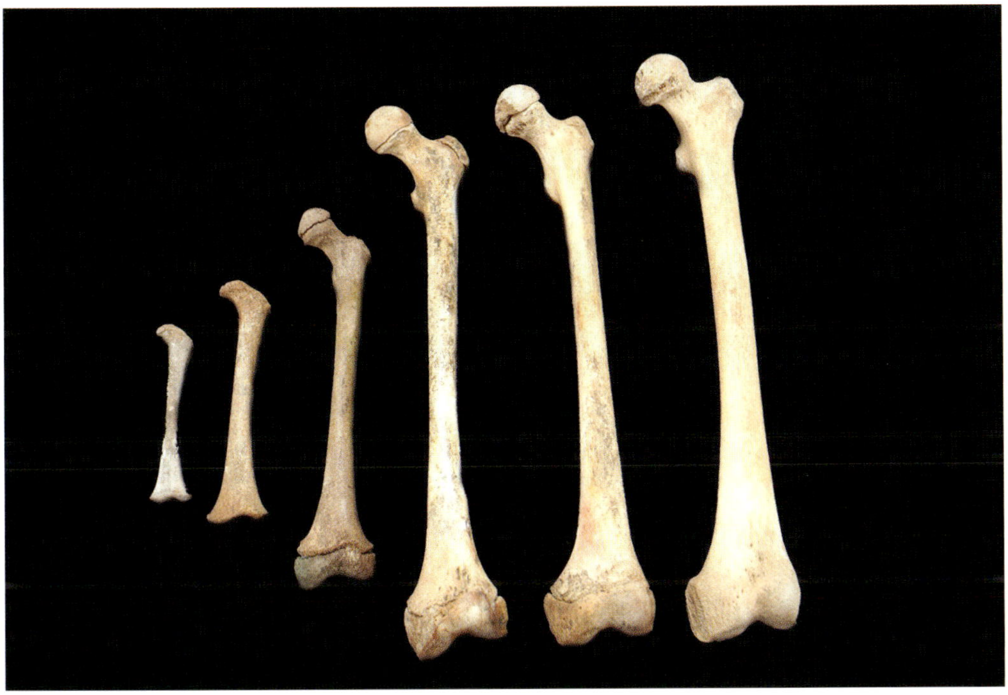

Figure 9.1 This series of photographs of the human femur shows the process of growth and maturation from infancy (far left) to adulthood (far right). (Courtesy of Sandra Cridlin.)

skeletal age at death. This text details the formation and appearance of the bones of the skeleton and associates the length of long bone diaphyses with age ranges. Buikstra and Ubelaker (1994) summarize these measurements and provide a concise diagram of each pertinent measurement, as well as a recording form to aid in the assessment of age at death based upon long bone metrics. Scheuer and Black (2000) also incorporated the Fazekas and Kosa (1978) standards into their text *Developmental Juvenile Osteology*.

Appearance and Union of Epiphyses

A third method for the estimation of age at death of subadult remains is the morphological assessment of skeletal epiphyses. As described previously, the epiphyses of the human appendicular skeleton begin forming very early in life. Once fully formed, the proximal and distal epiphyses fuse to their respective diaphyses at known age intervals. Likewise, axial skeletal epiphyses such as those of the vertebrae and ribs develop in a similar manner. By assessing which epiphyses are present, as well as which epiphyses are fused or partially fused, one can develop an age-at-death estimate for subadult remains, regardless of whether dentition is available for analysis (Figure 9.2).

Based upon the earlier work of Fazekas and Kosa (1978), as well as recent research on the development of the human skeleton, Scheuer and Black (2000) developed a text detailing the development of the immature skeleton. This text describes the formation, development, and epiphyseal fusion of each bone of the skeleton from the appearance of the primary ossification center to completion of bone formation/growth. This detailed description is coupled with a developmental chronology for each bone. This text, coupled

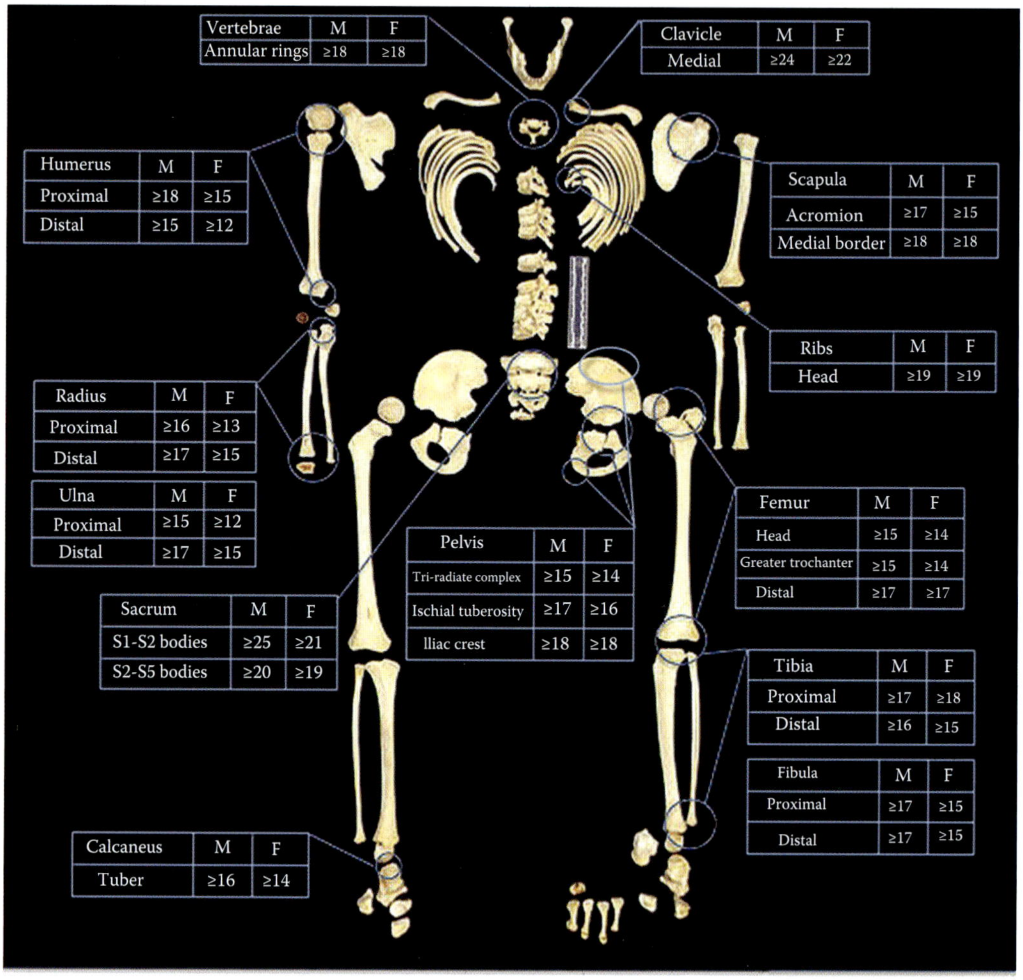

Figure 9.2 Epiphyseal union timing of some of the major skeletal epiphyses.

with an inventory of the skeletal remains that includes a detailed documentation of the present epiphyses and a description of the state of formation and degree of fusion of each epiphysis (i.e., no union, partial fusion, and complete fusion), is customarily used to arrive at an age estimate for immature remains. It is important to note that when inventorying a subadult skeleton, all epiphyses should to be well documented, as their mere presence will aid with the age estimation of a particular skeleton.

In 2009, Schaefer et al. published a condensed laboratory manual version of the 2000 text that provides a concise reference complete with tables that give age ranges for males and females based on the degree of epiphyseal union of each skeletal element. Each table is segregated by sex and provides developmental age ranges for immature remains derived from a plethora of sources using various ancestral populations.

This brief overview of age-at-death estimation methods for immature skeletal remains should not been confused as adequate preparation for the assessment of age at death of immature remains. Prior to determining the age of any immature remains, it is imperative to have a strong working knowledge of skeletal growth and development, including normal and abnormal variations. As such, the authors suggest hands-on work with fetal and immature skeletons in addition to coursework in human growth and development and/or developmental human osteology to prepare students interested in undertaking forensic casework involving immature skeletal remains.

Adult Age-at-Death Estimation

Whereas age estimation of subadult remains is based on skeletal development and maturation, adult skeletal age estimation is based on degenerative changes at various joint surfaces (i.e., the breakdown or wear and tear of the skeleton). While degenerative changes take place at a relatively predictable rate, these changes are not similar in everyone because of individual and/or population variation in activity levels, lifestyles, and personal habits. As a result, wide age ranges are necessary to encompass this variation, and adult age estimates are not as precise as subadult age estimates. In other words, precision (a narrow age range) is sacrificed for accuracy (a correct estimate). The remainder of this chapter briefly describes the most frequently used methods to estimate adult skeletal age at death. Chapter 10 explains the problems with some of these methods and gives an advanced overview of the ways in which the forensic anthropology community is striving to address present shortcomings.

The most commonly employed methods for aging adult remains focus on the gross morphological changes of the pubic symphysis, the auricular surface, and the sternal end of the fourth rib. It is precisely because of their frequency of use that these methods should be subjected to continued validation and accuracy of use assessments. In addition, cranial and maxillary palate suture closure may be used for age estimation, although these methods are less favored, largely on account of their imprecision. The following sections provide a description of the gross morphology of each skeletal element used by these methods and a brief literature review of several of the most common methods of age estimation.

Medial Clavicular Epiphysis and First Sacral Segment (S1–S2)

The epiphysis at the sternal end of the clavicle is the last to fuse. The epiphysis unites to the shaft of the clavicle during the second decade of life, thus making this epiphysis particularly informative of age in young adults. When examining a skeleton with fused epiphyses, one should examine the medial clavicle (if present) to ascertain whether or not the individual is likely older than 25–30 years of age.

Medial epiphyseal ossification begins at the onset of puberty, but the epiphysis does not fuse to the shaft completely until some 10 years after its initial appearance (Kreitner et al. 1998, Scheuer and Black 2000). The epiphysis appears initially as a small speck of bone in the central area of the sternal end and spreads until it nearly covers the entire medial surface. Scheuer and Black (2000) offer the following timeline for clavicular maturation: a well-defined medial flake appears between 16 and 21 years; the flake covers the majority of the medial surface between 24 and 29 years; and complete fusion occurs between 22 and 30 years. Figure 9.3 shows the various stages of epiphyseal union of the medial clavicle. Fusion ages of the medial clavicle have been documented in a number of sources from skeletal collections ranging from historic European populations to modern Americans (Todd and D-Errico 1928, McKern and Stewart 1957, Webb and Suchey 1985, Black and Scheuer 1996, Langley-Shirley and Jantz 2010). Many of these researchers used different scoring systems

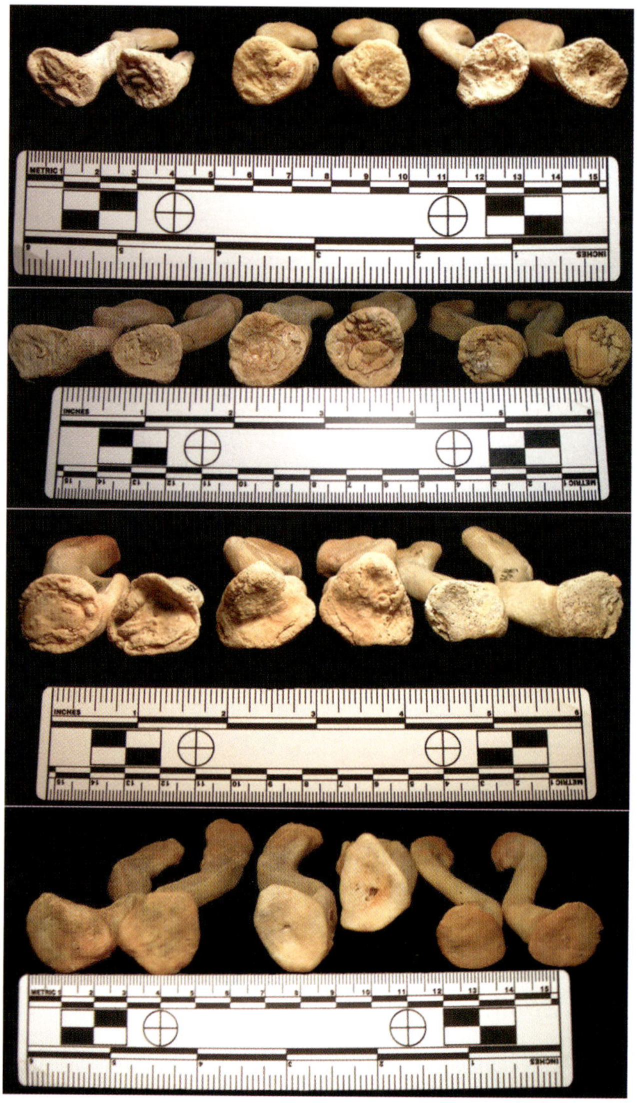

(a)
(b)
(c)
(d)

Figure 9.3 Epiphyseal union of the medial clavicle. (a) no fusion (no epiphysis present; medial end of the clavicle is vascular and coral-like in appearance). (b and c) fusing (epiphysis is in the process of uniting to the diaphyses, ranging from a small speck of bone to near complete coverage of the medial end). (d) complete fusion (medial end appears quiescent with no remnants of the fusion event).

to record the stage of epiphyseal union. Langley-Shirley and Jantz (2010) found that a simple three-phase system (not fused, fusing, and fused) provides accurate age estimates and lower observer error rates than more complicated scoring methodologies.

Another late-fusing maturation site is the first two sacral vertebral bodies (S1–S2). The sacral segments fuse in a caudal to cranial direction, with S4–S5 and S3–S4 fusing around 12 years, S2–S3 fusing around puberty, and S1–S2 fusing during early adulthood (25+ years) (Scheuer and Black 2000). The sacrum in Figure 9.4 illustrates the caudo-cranial fusion of the sacrum. Note that S1–S2 is unfused, S2–S3 is not completely fused, and S3–S4 and S4–S5 are in the process of fusing. One might infer from the information

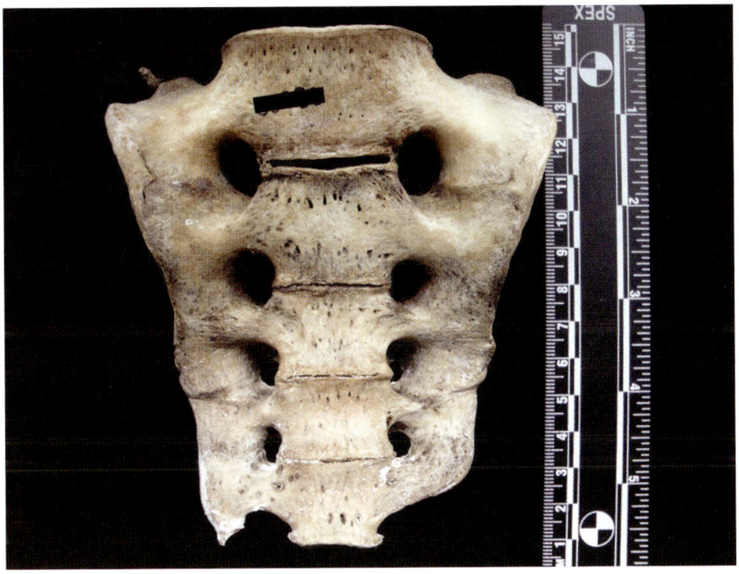

Figure 9.4 Caudocranial fusion of the sacral vertebral bodies.

that this individual could be around the age of puberty, and probably younger than 20 years of age.

Cranial and Palate Sutures

In the 1920s, Todd and Lyon (1924) identified specific points on the cranium to assess the degree of suture closure. Later, using research from Baker (1984) and Mann et al. (1987), Meindl and Lovejoy (1985) suggested a revised method in which 17 landmarks of the cranium and palate are scored. The degree of closure of a suture at a particular point is scored as one of four categories: open, minimal closure, significant closure, and complete obliteration. Figure 9.5 illustrates each of the four categories. A composite score is then compared to an associated age range derived from Meindl and Lovejoy's original sample populations. Today, practitioners debate the relationship between age and the physiological process of suture ossification. Generally, it is now considered an unreliable, or, at best, an imprecise predictor of age at death. The age ranges associated with the composite scores are so broad (sometimes >30 year intervals) that they are not particularly useful in a forensic context. Nonetheless, some forensic anthropology cases consist of only a skull without dentition, and, in these instances, suture closure may be the only option for aging. However, the practitioner should be familiar with pathological conditions that cause premature suture closure before blindly applying this method. Current research focuses on the microanalysis and histological investigation of the sutures in order to better understand the varying timetables of suture union (2011).

Gross Morphology of the Auricular Surface

There are three key areas of the posterior ilium that are illustrative of age-related changes. These are the overall morphological appearance of the auricular surface, the bony changes at the apex, and the bony buildup or activity of the retroauricular area (Figure 9.6).

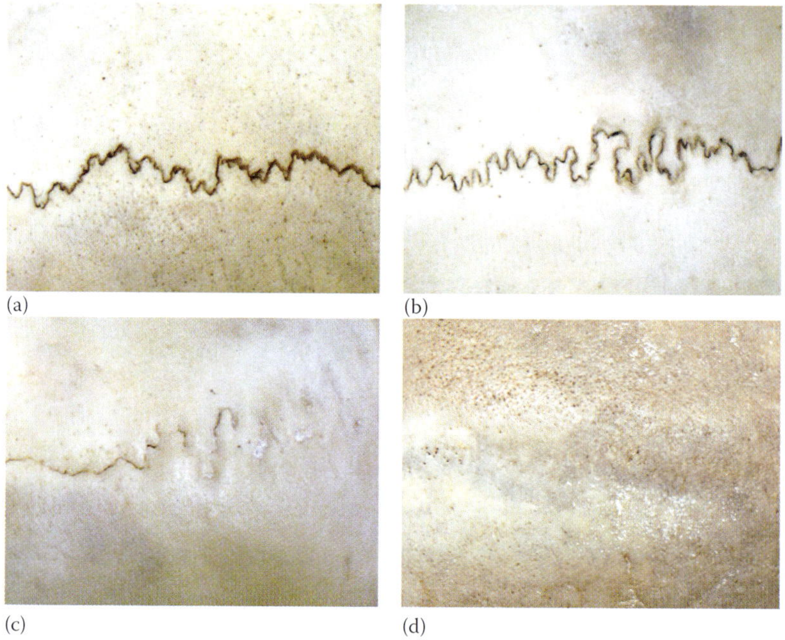

Figure 9.5 Fusion states of cranial sutures. (a) open, (b) beginning fusion (some bridging beginning to occur), (c) significant fusion (>50% bridging), and (d) obliteration.

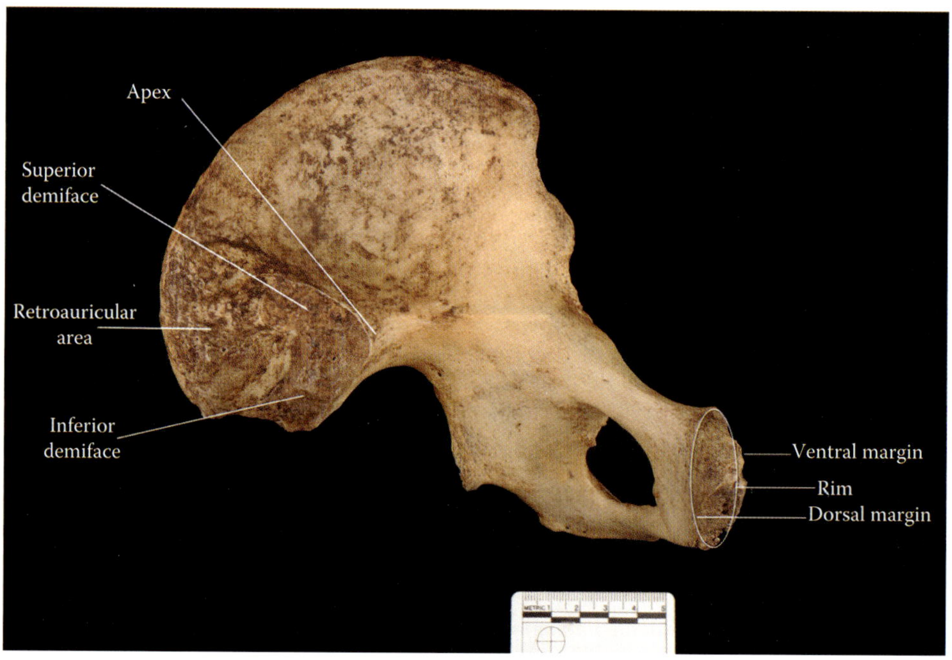

Figure 9.6 Key areas of morphological change on the auricular surface (left side of image) and pubic symphysis (right side).

The first characteristic identified is the morphology of the auricular surface, specifically the transverse organization of that surface. As a subadult, bony billows of low relief suggest horizontal, or transverse, organization of the joint surface. With time, the billows become replaced by tiny striae in the bone, traces of which may remain throughout life. Eventually the surface loses most evidence of transverse organization and changes texture. With age, the texture transitions from fine-grained to coarse-grained sand paper and then densifies further. The surface can display signs of microporosity early on, and later, the larger holes of macroporosity may become evident (Lovejoy et al. 1985). In the latter phases of auricular surface aging techniques, the surface begins to erode from below the outer table of bone, and the resulting subchondral destruction can be visible (Lovejoy et al. 1985, Osborne et al. 2004).

The next region on the posterior ilium used for age estimation is the apex of the auricular surface. In young individuals, the apex is often a sloping angle with a smooth margin. Over time, the margins of the auricular surface become irregular, resulting in bony buildup and lipping at the apex. This process can make the apex appear more prominent and sharp (Lovejoy et al. 1985). Apical changes in advanced age groups can be mild to moderate and can have considerable variation throughout the phases of age estimation (Lovejoy et al. 1985, Osborne et al. 2004). Similar to the apex, the bone of the retroauricular area can show distinct signs of morphological change over time. In subadults and younger adults, the area is generally smooth. It then transitions to a coarse texture and develops an uneven and irregular surface. Later in life, prolific osteophytic growths can occur at either a high or low relief. At this stage, the entire posterior portion of the ilium can appear disorganized and irregular due to both erosion of the bone and extra bony growth (Lovejoy et al. 1985). See Figure 9.7a–f for illustrations of the degenerative changes described here.

Gross Morphology of the Pubic Symphysis

Age-at-death estimation methods utilizing the pubic symphysis also speak to morphological changes that occur throughout life. These include the appearance of the pubic face and changes in the boney rim and texture of the face (Figure 9.6). Like the auricular surface, the morphology and texture of the most prominent feature, the pubic face, changes significantly in appearance over time. In subadults, the face often is covered by a deep ridge and furrow system that runs transversely across the face. As life progresses, the ridges and furrows begin to fill in and become worn down, ultimately leading to a flattened joint surface. The smooth texture of the bone of the face can then become granular and, in the final phases, can display signs of pitting and depression in the center. This later process is generally accompanied by overall erosion of the surface of the symphyseal face (Todd 1920).

The second feature paramount to the age assessment of the pubic symphysis is the formation and deterioration of the rim. The rim of the pubic face generally begins forming as the ridge and furrow system of the symphyseal face flattens and as the ventral and dorsal margins are built up with bone. The dorsal margin is the first to become delineated, as the ridge and furrow system flattens first dorsally and then proceeds ventrally. The ventral margin is the last portion of the rim to form, although in some cases, it may never reach completion. Typically, a ventral bevel forms as an ossific nodule on the superior portion of the face begins to become incorporated into the superior portion of the face, contributing to a ventral bevel on the superior ventral margin. This bevel meets the inferior lip of the ventral margin, completing the symphyseal rim, except in cases in which a hiatus remains.

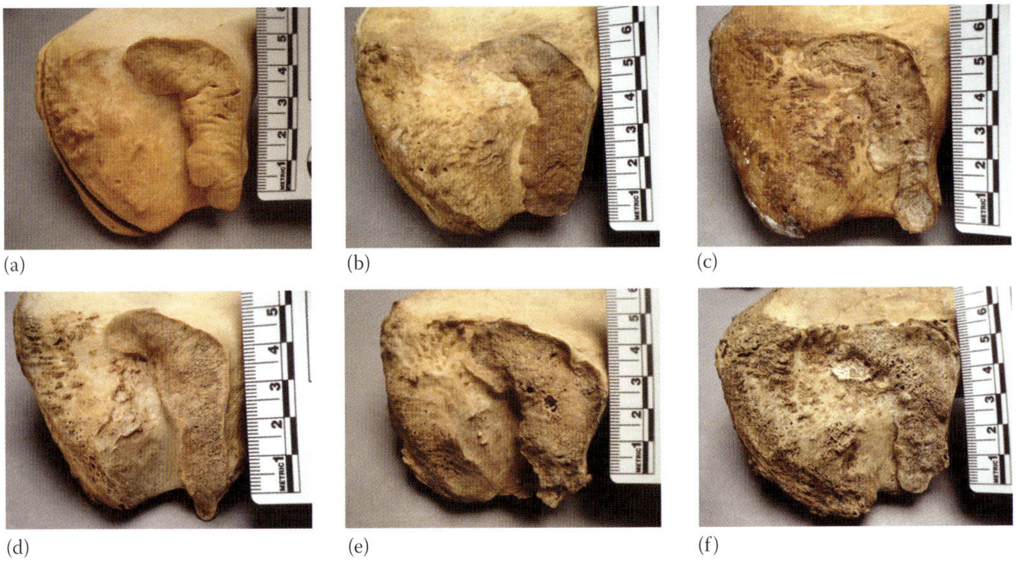

Figure 9.7 (a) Fine-grained, billowed surface with no apical or retroauricular changes; (b) Fine-grained surface with billows and striae; (c) striae, slight apical changes, and retroauricular activity; (d) coarse-grained, striae around apex and on inferior demiface, microporosity, moderate retroauricular activity; (e) loss of transverse organization, some densification, course granularity, microporosity, moderate apical, and retroauricular activity; and (f) microporosity, macroporosity, severe apical and retroauricular activity, course granularity, and no transverse organization. (Courtesy of Forensic Anthropology Center, University of Tennessee, Knoxville, TN.)

As individuals age, the distinct rim that has formed begins to lip, then deteriorate, and erode. Erosion of the rim can distort the symphyseal face, and it often loses its oval shape. In later phases, the rim can completely disintegrate, leaving only an irregularly shaped and surfaced face along with various bony outgrowths on the anterolateral portions of the pubic bone (Todd 1920).

A final key change in the pubic symphysis is the change in texture of the pubic face. As with the auricular surface, the texture of the pubic symphysis changes from finely granular to coarsely granular. In addition, porosity begins to appear on the symphyseal face with advancing age, contributing to the change in texture and to the pitting and irregularity of the joint surface. Figures 9.8 and 9.9 depict the morphological changes of the male and female pubic symphysis, respectively.

Gross Morphology of the Fourth Sternal Rib End

As with other cartilaginous joints in the body, the ribs can show morphological signs indicative of age-related change. The articular surface of the sternal end displays the greatest change in two key areas—the rim and the pit (Figure 9.10). In younger individuals, the rim is smooth, uniform, and rounded. The edges show signs of distinct and uniform scalloping (Figure 9.11a), and the pit is shallow and, in very young individuals, billowed. In adulthood, the scallop pattern initially becomes smooth and takes on an arc shape (Figure 9.11b), and then gradually becomes increasingly irregular and the pit deepens. From the slender youthful shape, the rim can begin to flare into a U-shape with age. This

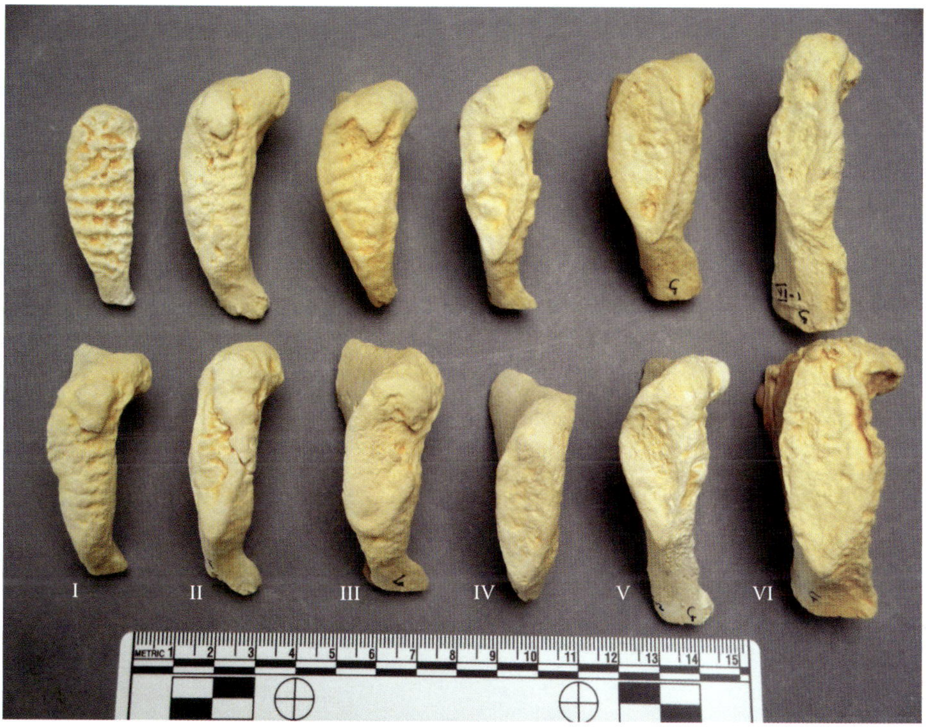

Figure 9.8 Photograph of casts of the Suchey–Brooks pubic symphyseal changes in males (casts by France casting). Phases 1–6 are represented. The top row depicts early stages of a phase, and the bottom row depicts later stages, such that each "column" of casts represents the variation within a given phase.

irregular rim can then exhibit bony projections, especially on the superior and inferior borders (Figure 9.11c). Each projection can grow long enough to join another, forming a "window" created by the ossified cartilage (Figure 9.11d). At this later phase, the pit is generally very deep and pitted and shows signs of erosion (Işcan et al. 1984a,b, 1985). Recent research (Hartnett 2010) emphasizes that a loss in weight of the ribs can accompany deformation of the rim and pit as an individual ages. Porosity in the pit is visual evidence of this loss of bone density over time.

Age-at-Death Estimation Methods

As an element for age estimation, the auricular surface has proved to be problematic for researchers. Lovejoy et al. (1985) first noticed, despite little movement throughout life, the iliac portion of the sacroiliac joint showed signs of change over time. Lovejoy and colleagues collected data from 750 individuals from the Hamann-Todd collection and archaeological specimens. A majority of the individuals in the sample were of unknown age, sex, and ancestry, and as a result, the age was estimated using other methods of the time (Lovejoy et al. 1985, Komar and Buikstra 2008). Using the estimated ages as well as the sacroiliac morphology, the researchers developed the auricular surface age estimation method that is still in use today. The eight phases of the method are comprised of descriptions of the subtle changes to the particular auricular surface components described earlier. Each phase is representative of a 5-year-age range, and there is no overlap in the ranges. Additionally,

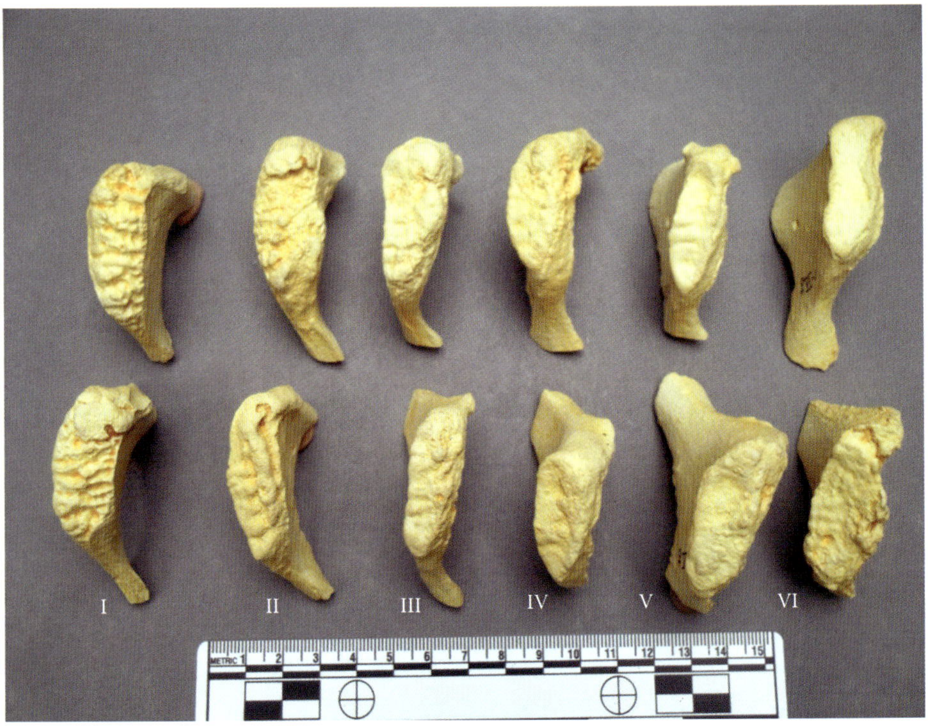

Figure 9.9 Photograph of casts of the Suchey–Brooks pubic symphyseal changes in females (made by France casting). Phases 1–6 are represented. The top row depicts early stages of a phase, and the bottom row depicts later stages, such that each "column" of casts represents the variation within a given phase.

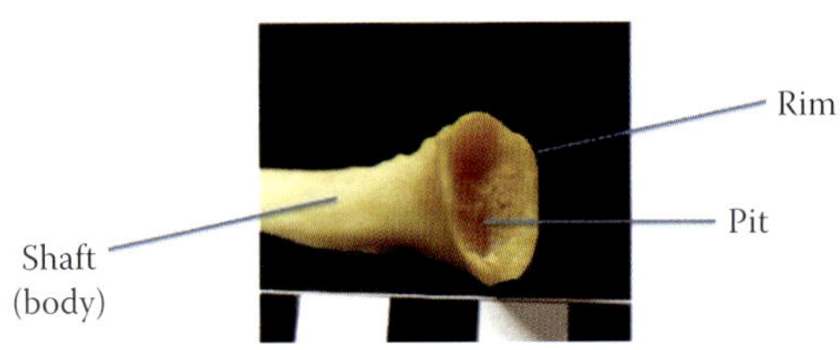

Figure 9.10 Key areas of morphological change on the sternal end of the right fourth rib.

no mean ages from the sample were published with the phases (Lovejoy et al. 1985). The narrow age ranges of each phase, as well as the morphological changes that are challenging to detect, particularly for less experienced practitioners, have created considerable debate within the field about the applicability and reliability of this method.

Subsequent testing of the Lovejoy et al. method proved it was applicable to both sexes and across various ancestral backgrounds. A study by Murray and Murray (1991) confirmed the method was applicable for use with both sexes, while also demonstrating that is was useful on both Blacks and Whites. Buckberry and Chamberlain (2002) developed a revised method for aging the auricular surface using a sample from several archaeological collections. The resulting method utilized all but one of the characteristic changes originally identified by Lovejoy and colleagues. This method was based upon a set of scores for each morphological component. The scores were then combined to form a composite score,

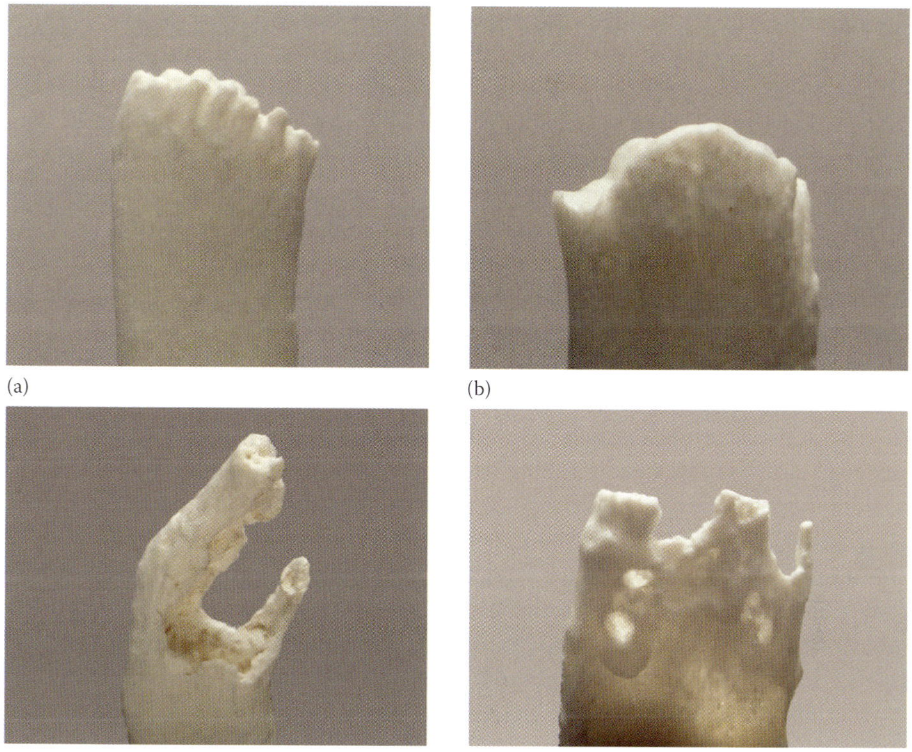

(a) (b) (c) (d)

Figure 9.11 Photographs of Işcan rib end casts (casts by France casting). (a) Scalloped rim. (b) Central arc forms as scallops wear down. (c) Bony projections on the superior and inferior borders. (d) Windows formed by the union of ossified cartilage projections.

which correlates to an associated age range. These ranges were much wider than those of Lovejoy and colleagues. Additional studies by Falys et al. (2006) and Mulhern and Jones (2005) demonstrated that Buckberry and Chamberlain's composite scoring method was similarly accurate to the Lovejoy et al. phase method.

Recently Osborne et al. (2004) returned to the phase system structure and created an alternate six-phase method for aging based on the auricular surface using Terry and Bass collection data. Each phase is associated with a larger predicted age range than the narrow 5-year ranges of Lovejoy and colleagues' method. The Osborne et al. (2004) method ranges significantly overlap one another, suggesting there is more variation in the aging process of the auricular surface than previously thought. Moreover, this new method is applicable to both sexes and across ancestral groups.

The methodology for analyzing the surface of the pubic symphysis has been revisited many times over since the original Todd method for pubic symphyseal age estimation was developed in 1920. In his article, Todd (1920) described 10 stages of grossly observable changes to the pubic symphysis that occur throughout life. Although the Todd method utilized a limited sample, it provided the first research proving the importance of the pubic symphysis as a useful morphological element for age estimation. In an attempt to consolidate the age ranges produced by Todd's method, Brooks (1995) found that Todd's age ranges could be narrowed by several years for each phase. In 1957, McKern and Stewart developed a component method for estimating age from morphological changes of the pubic symphysis. McKern and Stewart derived their data from a sample of American soldiers between the ages of 18 and 35 who died in the Korean War. This sample was relatively limited by age and sex, and as a result, Gilbert and McKern (1973) developed a similar method to address the issue of age estimation in females using the pubic symphysis. Meindl et al. (1985) showed that the morphological changes of the pubic symphysis related to age as identified by Todd demonstrate the most accurate estimations of age.

The most popular method used today was developed by Brooks and Suchey (1990) and is based on Todd's original system (Garvin and Passalaqua 2012). Suchey and Brooks used data from a large sample of 1225 known individuals from the Los Angeles Medical Examiner's Office. The sample incorporated individuals of both sexes and a larger spectrum of ages and ancestries than previous methods. In contrast to the 10 phase Todd method, the Suchey–Brooks approach uses only six morphological phases with significantly expanded age ranges associated with each phase. The phase descriptions and age ranges are specific to males and females, and there is significant overlap between phases. One of the main critiques of the Suchey–Brooks method is the extremely large age ranges associated with the phases. This problem was most recently addressed by Hartnett (2010b) using a modern and diverse sample from the Forensic Science Center in Arizona to identify a concise set of characteristics that define each stage of typical symphyseal aging. A number of these characteristics are similar to those originally detailed by Todd and highlighted in the Suchey–Brooks method. These include face shape, rim formation, and marginal lipping. In addition to these characteristics, the Hartnett method also emphasizes tactile characteristics of the bone, such as the weight and feel of the bone, especially in the later phases. The method is comprised of seven phases, with a description of the morphological characteristics of each phase. Although there are notes within a number of these phase descriptions identifying characteristics specific to either males or females, the phase descriptions are generally not differentiated by sex. However, individual phase descriptions are associated with age ranges specific to each sex. These age ranges are significantly narrower than the age ranges given for each of the Suchey–Brooks phases and overlap one another to a lesser degree.

The fourth rib also has proved to be extremely important to age-at-death estimation. Işcan et al. (1984a,b, 1985) identified significant morphological change throughout life in the sternal end of the right fourth rib. Işcan and colleagues used an American sample to develop a phase-based method with nine distinct phases of morphological change, eight of which have a narrow associated age range. The phase descriptions and ages for this method are applicable across Black and White ancestral populations but are separated by sex. Their research also suggests that rib numbers 3 and 5 show similar change over time and can be used in the event that the fourth rib is not available. Yoder et al. (2001) tested the Işcan method and ultimately suggested that a composite score be used instead of the phase approach, arguing that scoring morphological changes across multiple ribs is a more accurate predictor of age than the traditional phase method. Hartnett (2010a) also reassessed the Işcan method of rib aging using the Arizona Forensic Science Center sample and developed a more concise method. Similar to her previous research with pubic symphyseal aging, the revised method utilizes a number of the characteristics emphasized by Işcan and colleagues with the additional emphasis of overall weight of the rib. The Hartnett method is comprised of seven phases with specific age ranges for each sex. These ranges are narrower than those originally published by Işcan and colleagues, but broader than those suggested by the casts created for use with the Işcan method.

The application of many of these methods is enhanced by the use of drawings and/or casts that illustrate the morphological change for each phase or component (casts available through France Casting, Fort Collins, Colorado).

New Methods

In addition to conducting extensive validation tests on existing methods, during the past decade researchers have begun to investigate new skeletal age indicators. DiGangi et al. (2009) developed a method for age estimation from the first rib based on an earlier paper by Kunos et al. (1999). They evaluated 11 traits and found that two of the traits were most appropriate: geometric shape of the costal face and surface texture of the tubercle facet. As the sample consisted of positively identified individuals who were victims of human rights violations in Kosovo, the analysis was done solely on males. However, the authors are optimistic that the method can be used to estimate the age of female remains, as well, but suggest extensive testing before drawing these conclusions. Their analysis of the data was statistically sophisticated and robust, and this aging method shows promise both as a stand-alone method and for use in conjunction with other aging methods. For more accurate estimates, the authors advocate a multifactorial approach toward age-at-death estimation. In addition, the publication contains excellent descriptions and photographs for ease of scoring (DiGangi et al. 2009).

In that morphological age-related changes have been documented in the pelvic auricular surface, we would expect to see changes in the adjacent sacral auricular surface. Passalacqua (2009) developed a method for age estimation from the human sacrum that considers changes in the sacral auricular surface as well as fusion of the sacral vertebral bodies and fusion of the superior vertebral ring of the first sacral body. Passalacqua's method encompasses changes in the sacrum that occur across an individuals' lifespan; in other words, he considers both developmental and degenerative changes in the sacrum. Using Todd and Bass collection sacra, he scored six traits as present or absent (S1/S2 fusion, S2/S3 fusion, microporosity, macroporosity, surface relief changes of the auricular surface, and apical changes), and one trait as *incomplete fusion*, *fused*, or *absorbed* (S1 ring fusion). The scores for these traits are recorded and compared to a table that is used to assign a phase that corresponds to an age range. The system is highly accurate and can be applied equally to males and females. Additional discussion of the method can be found in Passalacqua (2009).

Another area of the pelvis that has received recent attention as a reliable age indicator is the acetabulum (Rougé-Maillart et al. 2004, Rissech et al. 2006a,b, Calce and Rogers 2011). Rissech et al. (2006a) identified seven morphological traits that correlate closely with age (acetabular groove, rim shape, rim porosity, apex activity, activity on outer edge of acetabular fossa, activity of fossa, and porosity of fossa) using a sample of 242 males from the Coimbra collection in Portugal. This study was an expansion of earlier work by Rougé-Maillart et al. (2004) on a small Spanish and French sample. The seven variables and their morphological states are described thoroughly and accompanying photographs are included in the article by Rissech et al. (2006a). They reported 89% accuracy using 10-year intervals and 67% accuracy using 5-year intervals. Furthermore, unlike many aging methods that perform better in young age groups than in older age groups, the method does equally well across age categories. Rissech et al. (2006b) conducted a test of their method on four documented Western European collections (the Lisbon and Coimbra collections in

Portugal, University Autonòma Barcelona collection, and St. Bride collection in London). They achieved accuracy rates between 83% and 100%, with the lowest accuracy rates coming from the most geographically distant reference collection. A similar validation study was conducted on a Canadian collection, the Grant collection at the University of Toronto (Calce and Rogers 2011). The authors suggested revising some of the trait descriptions and reducing the number of variable states per trait, as they found that some descriptions needed clarification and reported difficulties in deciding between variable states on account of morphological overlap. Like the previous validation study (Rissech et al. 2006b), Calce and Rogers (2011) found that the geographic distance of the reference population affects the method's accuracy and maintain that the chosen reference population must be geographically close to the test specimen if the method is to perform reliably. However, they did find the method effective in older age groups and recommend additional testing on other geographic populations. Calce (2012) recently published a revision of the Rissech et al. (2006a) method. The revised method uses only three variables and collapses the ages into three broad ranges that correspond to young, middle, and old adults. She also extended the method's application to include females. Calce (2012) reported 81% accuracy with substantial observer agreement in scoring.

Other Age Indicators

Most experienced forensic anthropologists use a combination of the methods described in this chapter and gather more subjective information from the skeleton that ultimately informs their age estimate. This type of information gathering is a natural product of years of experience in handling skeletal material and making age assessments from the skeleton. Degenerative changes that experienced osteologists look at include vertebral osteophytes, bony lipping around joint peripheries, eburnation on joint surfaces, dental attrition, bone density changes, and costal cartilage ossification. Several studies have developed scoring systems with variable states and associated age ranges for some of these morphological changes.

Dental attrition has been studied and quantified by a number of researchers (far more than can be mentioned in the scope of this chapter). Perhaps one of the earliest systems was devised by Gustafson (1950), and since then many researchers have conducted similar analyses and validation studies (Murphy 1959, Miles 1962, Brothwell 1963, Scott 1979, Smith 1984, Li and Ji 1995, Kim et al. 1999, Ajmal et al. 2001, Yun et al. 2007, Prince et al. 2008). Prince et al. (2008) used a Bayesian approach based on Smith's (1984) system, which was adapted from Murphy's (1959) method. They concluded that dental wear may be more appropriate for grouping individuals into large cohorts than for accurately estimating age at death. The reason for this is that substantial variation in dental wear patterns exist among individuals and populations because of differences in diet, enamel thickness, dental care and hygiene, chewing, and habitual activities (i.e., tooth grinding). Nonetheless, dental wear can supplement age estimates from other skeletal indicators. Furthermore, because of the durable nature and survivability of teeth, these methods can be useful, particularly in mass disasters.

Costal and thyroid cartilage ossification can also provide supplementary information about age at death, and several studies have developed scoring systems and accompanying age ranges for evaluating these cartilage changes (Michelson 1934, Cerny 1983, McCormick and Stewart 1988, De la Grandmaison 2003, Dang-Tran et al. 2010, Garamendi et al. 2011). In addition, degenerative changes associated with the vertebral column can be useful for estimating age. In general, vertebral osteophytes do not appear prior to age 35 in normal, healthy individuals. Experienced osteologists examine the condition of the vertebrae and frequently incorporate this impression into their overall age estimate. Watanabe and Terazawa (2006) developed a scoring system for osteophyte formation and devised regression equations for estimating age from osteophyte formation in males and females.

While anthropologists vary in terms of favored aging methods, practitioners should be familiar with all methods and be able to apply them with equal skill, as the condition and number of elements present in a particular forensic case will dictate which method is most appropriate. Likewise, forensic anthropologists should understand the limitations of each method and know the sample(s) from which it was developed, as these factors may have consequences for the final age estimate. For a review of current practices in age estimation by forensic anthropologists see Garvin and Passalaqua (2012). Chapter 10 discusses in detail some of the limitations and problems associated with estimating age at death from skeletal remains.

References

Ajmal M, Mody B, and Kumar G. 2001. Age estimation using three established methods. A study on Indian population. *Forensic Sci Int* 3:150–154.

Baker RK. 1984. The relationship of cranial suture closure and age analyzed in a modern multi-racial sample of males and females. A Master's Thesis. California State University, Fullerton, CA.

Black S and Scheuer L. 1996. Age changes in the clavicle from the early neonatal period to skeletal maturity. *Int J Osteoarch* 6:425–434.

Brooks ST. 1995. Skeletal age at death: The reliability of cranial and pubic age indicators. *Am J Phys Anthropol* 13:567–597.

Brooks S and Suchey JM. 1990. Skeletal age determination based on the os pubis: A comparison of the Acsádi-Nemeskéri and Suchey-Brooks Methods. *Hum Evol* 3(5):227–238.

Brothwell D. 1963. *Digging up Bones*. London, U.K.: British Museum of Natural History.

Buckberry JL and Chamberlain AT. 2002. Age estimation from the auricular surface of the ilium: A revised method. *Am J Phys Anthropol* 119: 231–239.

Buikstra JE and Ubelaker DH. 1994. Standards for the data collection from human skeletal remains. *Proceedings of a Seminar at the Field Museum of Natural History*. Arkansas Archaeological Survey Research Series No. 44, Fayetteville, AR.

Calce SE. 2012. A new method to estimate adult age-at-death using the acetabulum. *Am J Phys Anthropol* 148(1):11–23.

Calce CE and Rogers TL. 2011. Evaluation of age estimation technique: Testing traits of the acetabulum to estimate age at death in adult males. *J Forensic Sci* 56(2):302–311.

Cerny M. 1983. Our experience with estimation of an individual's age from skeletal remains of the degree of thyroid cartilage ossification. *Acta Univ Palacki Olomuc Fac Med* 3:121–144.

Dang-Tran K, Dedouit F, Joffre F, Rougé D, Rousseau H, and Telmon N. 2010. Thyroid cartilage ossification and multislice computed tomography examination: A useful tool for age assessment? *J Forensic Sci* 55(3):677–683.

De la Grandmaison GL, Bansar A, and Durigon M. 2003. Age estimation using radiographic analysis of laryngeal cartilage. *Am J Forensic Med Pathol* 24(1):96–99.

DiGangi EA, Bethard JD, Kimmerle EH, and Konigsberg LW. 2009. A new method for estimating age-at-death from the first rib. *Am J Phys Anthropol* 138:165–176.

Falys CG, Schutkowski H, and Weston D. 2006. Auricular surface aging: Worse than expected? A test of the revised method on a documented historic skeletal assemblage. *Am J Phys Anthropol* 130:508–513.

Fazekas IG and Kosa F. 1978. *Forensic Fetal Osteology*. Budapest, Hungary: Aksdémiai Kiadó.

Garamendi PM, Landa MI, Botella MC, and Alemán I. 2011. Forensic age estimation on digital x-ray images: Medial epiphyses of the clavicle and first rib ossification in relation to chronological age. *J Forensic Sci* 56(S1):S3–S12.

Garvin HM and Passalacqua NV. 2012. Current practices by forensic anthropologists in adult skeletal age estimation. *J Forensic Sci* 57(2):427–433.

Gilbert BM and McKern TW. 1973. A method of aging the female os pubis. *Am J Phys Anthropol* 38:31–38.

Gustafson G.1950. Age determination on teeth. *J Am Dent Assoc* 41:45–54.

Harntett KM. 2010a. Analysis of age-at-death estimation using data from a new, modern autopsy sample- part II: Sternal end of fourth rib. *J Forensic Sci* 55:1152–1156.

Harntett KM. 2010b. Analysis of age-at-death estimation using data from a new, modern autopsy sample- part I: Pubic bone. *J Forensic Sci* 55:1145–1151.

Işcan MY, Loth SR, and Wright RK. 1984a. Metamorphosis at the sternal rib end: A new method to estimate age at death in White Males. *Am J Phys Anthropol* 65:147–156.

Işcan MY, Loth SR, and Wright RK. 1984b. Age determination from sternal ends of ribs. *J Forensic Sci* 29:1094–1104.

Işcan MY, Loth SR, and Wright RK. 1985. Age estimation from the rib by phase analysis: White females. *J Forensic Sci* 30(3):853–863.

Kim YK, Kho HS, and Lee KH. 1999. Age estimation by occlusal tooth wear. *J Forensic Sci* 45(2):303–309.

Komar DA and Buikstra JE. 2008. *Forensic Anthropology: Contemporary Theory and Practice*. New York: Oxford University Press.

Kreitner K, Schweden F, Riepert T, Nafe B, and Thelen M. 1998. Bone age determination based on the study of the medial extremity of the clavicle. *Eur Radiol* 8:1116–1122.

Kunos C, Simpson S, Russell K, and Hershkovitz I. 1999. First rib metamorphosis: Its possible utility for human age-at-death estimation. *Am J Phys Anthropol* 110:303–323.

Langley-Shirley N and Jantz RL. 2010. A Bayesian approach to age estimation in modern Americans from the clavicle. *J Forensic Sci* 55(3):571–583.

Li C and Ji G. 1995. Age estimation from the permanent molar in northeast China by the method of average stage of attrition. *Forensic Sci Int* 3:189–196.

Lovejoy CO, Meindl RS, Pryzbeck TR, and Mensforth RP. 1985. Chronological metamorphosis of the auricular surface of the ilium: A new method for the determination of adult skeletal age at death. *Am J Phys Anthropol* 68:15–28.

Mann RW, Symes SA, and Bass WM. 1987. Maxillary suture obliteration: Aging the human skeleton based on intact or fragmentary maxilla. *J Forensic Sci* 32:148–157.

McCormick WF and Stewart JH. 1988. Age related changes in the human plastron: A roentgenographic and morphologic study. *J Forensic Sci* 33(1):100–120.

McKern T and Stewart T. 1957. Skeletal age changes in young American males. Analysed from the standpoint of age identification. Natick, MA: Quartermaster Research and Development Center, Environmental Protection Research Division.

Meindl RS and Lovejoy CO. 1985. Ectocranial suture closure: A revised method for the determination of skeletal age at death based on the lateral-anterior sutures. *Am J Phys Anthropol* 68:57–66.

Meindl RS, Lovejoy CO, Mensforth RP, and Walker RA. 1985. A revised method of age determination using the os pubis, with a review and tests of accuracy of other current methods of pubic symphyseal aging. *Am J Phys Anthropol* 68:29–45.

Michelson N. 1934. The calcification of the first costal cartilage among Whites and Negroes. *Hum Biol* 6:543–557.

Miles AEW. 1962. Assessment of the ages of a population of Anglo-Saxons from their dentitions. *Proc R Soc Med* 55:881–886.

Moorees CFA, Fanning EA, and Hunt EE. 1963a. Formation and resorption of three deciduous teeth in children. *Am J Phys Anthropol* 21:205–213.

Moorees CFA, Fanning EA, and Hunt EE. 1963b. Age formation by stages for ten permanent teeth. *J Dental Res* 42:1490–1502.

Mulhern DM and Jones EB. 2005. Test of revised method of age estimation from the auricular surface of the ilium. *Am J Phys Anthropol* 126:61–65.

Murphy T. 1959. Gradients of dental exposure in human molar tooth attrition. *Am J Phys Anthropol* 17:179–186.

Murray KA and Murray T. 1991. A test of the auricular surface aging technique. *J Forensic Sci* 6(4): 1162–1169.

Osborne D, Simmons T, and Nawrocki SP. 2004. Reconsidering the auricular surface as an indicator of age at death. *J Forensic Sci* 49(5):1–7.

Passalacqua NV. 2009. Forensic age-at-death estimation from the human sacrum. *J Forensic Sci* 54(2):252–262.

Prince DA, Kimmerle EH, and Konigsberg LW. 2008. A Bayesian approach to estimate skeletal age-at-death utilizing dental wear. *J Forensic Sci* 53(3):588–593.

Rissech C, Estabrook GF, Cunha E, and Malgosa A. 2006a. Using the acetabulum to estimate age at death of adult males. *J Forensic Sci* 51(2):214–229.

Rissech C, Estabrook GF, Cunha E, and Malgosa A. 2006b. Estimation of age-at death for adult males using the acetabulum, applied to four Western European populations. *J Forensic Sci* 52(4):774–778.

Rouge-Maillart CL, Telmon N, Rissech C, Malgosa A, and Rouge D. 2004. The determination of male adult age by central and posterior coxal analysis. A preliminary study. *J Forensic Sci* 49:1–7.

Schaefer M, Black S, and Scheuer L. 2009. *Juvenile Osteology: A Laboratory and Field Manual*. London, U.K.: Elsevier, Inc.

Scheuer L and Black S. 2000. *Developmental Juvenile Osteology*. London, U.K.: Academic Press.

Scott EC. 1979. Dental wear scoring technique. *Am J Phys Anthropol* 51:213–218.

Smith BH. 1984. Patterns of molar wear in hunter-gatherers and agriculturalists. *Am J Phys Anthropol* 63(1):39–56.

Todd TW. 1920. Age changes in the pubic bone: I, The male White pubis. *Am J Phys Anthropol* 3:286–334.

Todd T and D'Errico J. 1928. The clavicular epiphyses. *Am J Anat* 41:25–50.

Todd TW and Lyon DW Jr. 1924. Endocranial suture closure, its progress and age relationship. Part I. Adult males of White stock. *Am J Phys Anthropol* 7:325–384.

Ubelaker DH. 1989. *Human Skeletal Remains: Excavation, Analysis, Interpretation*, 2nd edn. Washington, DC: Taraxacum.

Watanabe S and Terazawa K. 2006. Age estimation from the degree of osteophyte formation of vertebral columns in Japanese. *Leg Med* (Tokyo) 8(3):156–160.

Webb P and Suchey J. 1985. Epiphyseal union of the anterior iliac crest and medial clavicle in a modern multiracial sample of American males and females. *Am J Phys Anthropol* 68(4):457–466.

Yoder C, Ubelaker DH, and Powell JF. 2001. Examination of variation in sternal rib end morphology relevant to age assessment. *J Forensic Sci* 46:223–227.

Yun J, Lee JY, Chung J, Kho H, and Kim Y. 2007. Age estimation of Korean adults by occlusal tooth wear. *J Forensic Sci* 52(3):678–683.

Age Estimation in Modern Forensic Anthropology

10

BRIDGET F. B. ALGEE-HEWITT

Contents

Forensic anthropology is an applied, case-driven, goal-oriented subfield within skeletal biology (Ubelaker 2008). In keeping with the complexity of our negotiations among theory, method, and application, and in response to the demands of new casework and the diversity of legal systems both home and abroad, Blau and Ubelaker (2009a) encourage a dynamic understanding of forensic anthropology. As practitioners, forensic anthropologists seek to aid the medicolegal community in making identifications for unknown, mostly skeletal, and often fragmentary human remains by first developing a biological profile (ABFA 2010). Using a combination of grossly observable and measurable morphological features on the available skeletal elements, we rely upon our technical expertise to estimate demographic parameters as they relate to the population-at-large, and isolate unique traits that characterize *an* individual as *the* individual (such as sex, ancestry, age at death, stature, pathology). We also look to identify those taphonomic variables that help to explain the circumstances surrounding the unknown individual's death, deposition, and decomposition (including markers of peri- and postmortem trauma and approximations of time since death). We estimate these features with some degree of statistical certainty based upon our application of standard criteria, casework experience, and advanced techniques supported by interdisciplinary collaboration.

Practicalities of Aging: The Significance of Age at Death in Anthropology

Sex and ancestry are often the first two parameters that a forensic anthropologist must establish given the fact that many other methods of identification are sex and population specific. While the estimation of sex removes 50% of the possible candidates from further consideration (assuming an equal male–female ratio), ancestry may have limited evidentiary value when we consider geographical context and the population demographics (Konigsberg et al. 2009). Age at death, however, is arguably the most significant variable for narrowing potential "positive" identities using a missing person's list or other medicolegal documents. As an example of modern U.S. trends, consider the current missing persons cases for the state of Tennessee, obtained from the Missing Persons Database and made available through the National Missing and Unidentified Persons System (NamUs 2010). Figures 10.1 and 10.2 graphically display the frequency of missing individuals in each age cohort, subdivided by sex and race, relative to the total number of cases ($n=72$). These data represent open cases with assigned National Crime Information Center (NCIC) numbers, include juveniles and adults with reported sex and race, and have last known alive (LKA)

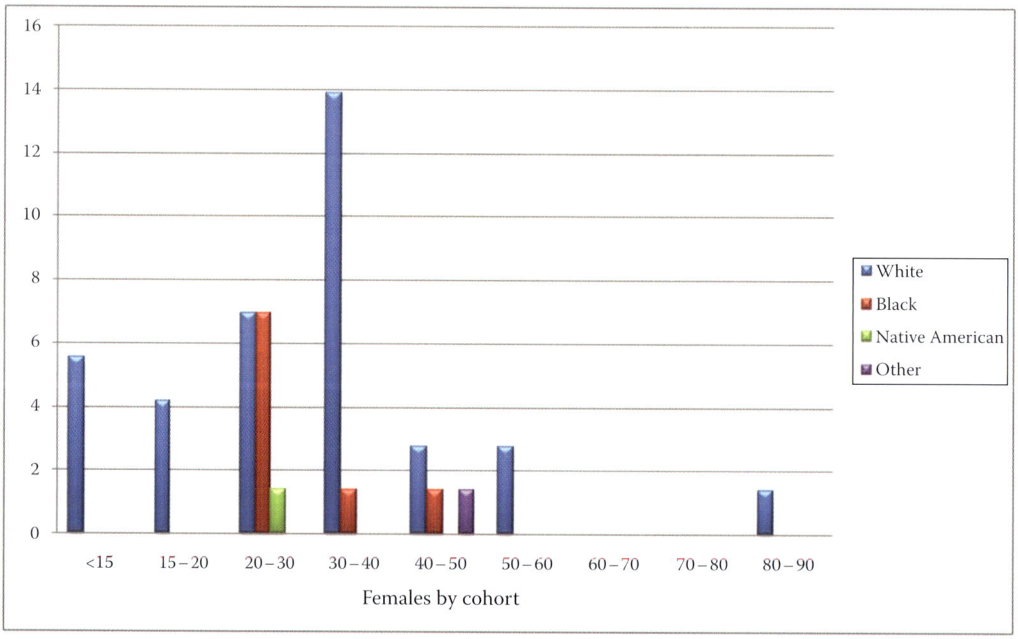

Figure 10.1 Frequency of females ($n=36$) in each age cohort, subdivided by race, and relative to the total number of individuals reported missing in Tennessee ($n=72$), after data obtained from NamUS. Cohorts are based on the age of the individual when she/he was last known to be alive. The >15 year cohort includes all juveniles, the 15–20 year cohort is a 5 year interval, and all other age cohorts are 10 year intervals.

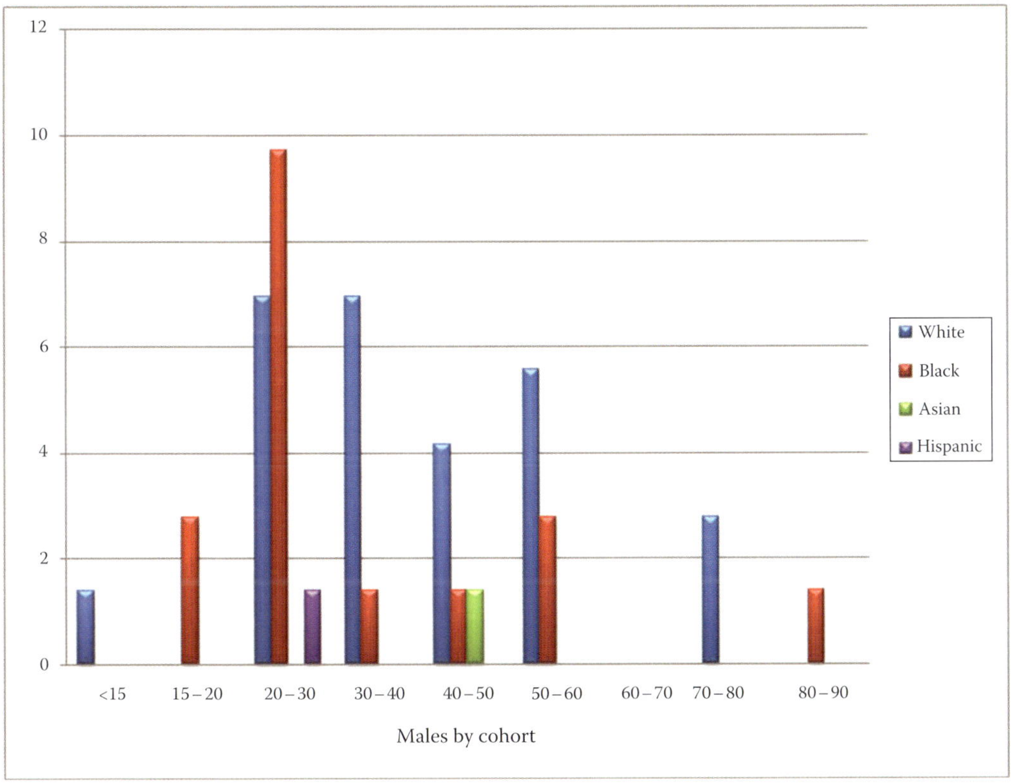

Figure 10.2 Frequency of males in each age cohort (n=36), subdivided by race, and relative to the total number of individuals reported missing in Tennessee (n=72), after data obtained from NamUS. Cohorts are based on the age of the individual when she/he was last known to be alive. The >15 year cohort includes all juveniles, the 15–20 year cohort is a 5 year interval, and all other age cohorts are 10 year intervals.

dates spanning 30 years, from 1969 to 2009. As of May 2010, there are 72 persons reported missing in Tennessee: 36 (50%) are female; of those females, 6 (17%) are between the ages 40 and 60, and 2 (33%) are identified as non-White. In this example, an assignment of any remains in question to this broad "middle age" range (ages 40–60) would reduce possible female matches from 36 active case files to only 6 probable identities. This number has potential for even further reduction when ancestry (or reported race) is considered.

In theory, the narrower the estimated age interval, the more useful the skeletal analysis may be for medicolegal investigators in excluding cases, finding a presumptive match among open cases, and eventually establishing a positive identification. Reporting a restricted age range, however, is not always realistic and is often unwise on account of the acknowledged variability in patterns of skeletal aging (attributable to genetics, environment, health, and lifestyle). As illustrated by the TN data, the estimated age interval of 20 years (ages 40–60) offers a considerable reduction in the number of possible matches. Even such a broad interval can help law enforcement intelligently refocus their investigation into the unknown's identity; here, dropping the total 72 missing persons registered by almost 95% when only sex is "known" for the remains. A wider age range also better accounts for individual variation in age-progressive traits and is more likely to capture the unknown individual's chronological age; thus, reducing the risk of excluding the unknown's true identity from the missing persons files considered and thereby failing to make a correct match for the remains under evaluation.

Considering the importance of age at death in contributing a chapter to the individual's (or skeletal population's) osteobiography, it should not be surprising that age estimation is among the most critical and yet the most problematic of endeavors when establishing a biological profile. Within the publication history of skeletal biology, few topics have generated as much heated debate as the issue of assigning age at death. This discussion extends beyond questioning the accuracy of the ages themselves (i.e., the point estimates or intervals) to unseating assumptions surrounding the very practice of *estimation* and its relevance. These debates take into account the imperfect correlation between skeletal maturation stages (biological age) and chronological age (calendar years since birth). The skeletal indicators, procedures, analytical techniques and statistical methods, the applicability of standard criteria to diverse groups (both modern and archaeological), and even the validity of continuing this type of research are all called into question by experts heavily influenced by their philosophical views, anatomical and statistical experience, and research agendas.

A simple search for the topic "age" or "aging" in the Web of Science (2010) citation database across all years of publication for the *American Journal of Physical Anthropology* (*AJPA*) and the *Journal of Forensic Sciences* (*JFS*) shows the sustained and increasing interest in the topic of age estimation by anthropologists and our colleagues writing over the last century. The recent explosion in technologies (e.g., multi-core processors and advances in computational statistics, high-resolution imaging and virtual modeling devices, and improved techniques for biochemical and molecular analyses) has forever altered our approach to all aspects of human skeletal biology, past and present. The field of physical anthropology is experiencing a fragmentation into subspecializations, a significant shift toward interdisciplinary concerns, a burgeoning of new research directions, and the introduction of a theoretical complexity previously unattainable in the absence of our current enhanced exploratory tools. Despite this broadening of research topics, Figure 10.3 shows that in the last two decades at least 10% of all *AJPA* and *JFS* publications have been concerned with age-at-death estimation and that this interest has continued to grow—exceeding 20% of all publications in the last year. The publication patterns illustrated in Figure 10.3 are also useful as a guide for tracking the historical trends in research on age-at-death estimation, whose complex scholarly foundation rests heavily upon the collective knowledge and experience of many contributors (human anatomists, [paleo] demographers, [bio]archaeologists, and forensic anthropologists alike) and whose developmental trajectory follows in similar suit with the evolution of [physical] anthropological theory and thought.

Aging Takes Time: A Historical Overview

Early publications concerned with skeletal morphology were firmly rooted in a descriptive, typological tradition that characterized the turn of the century's approach to decoding, organizing, and explaining our human cultural and biological history. Science was used to reinforce ideas tied to Linnaean taxonomy so that "evolutionism became cast in traditional descriptive historicism" (Armelagos et al. 1982; Armelagos and Van Gerven 2003, p. 55). Owing much to the research methods of human anatomists, the training of many

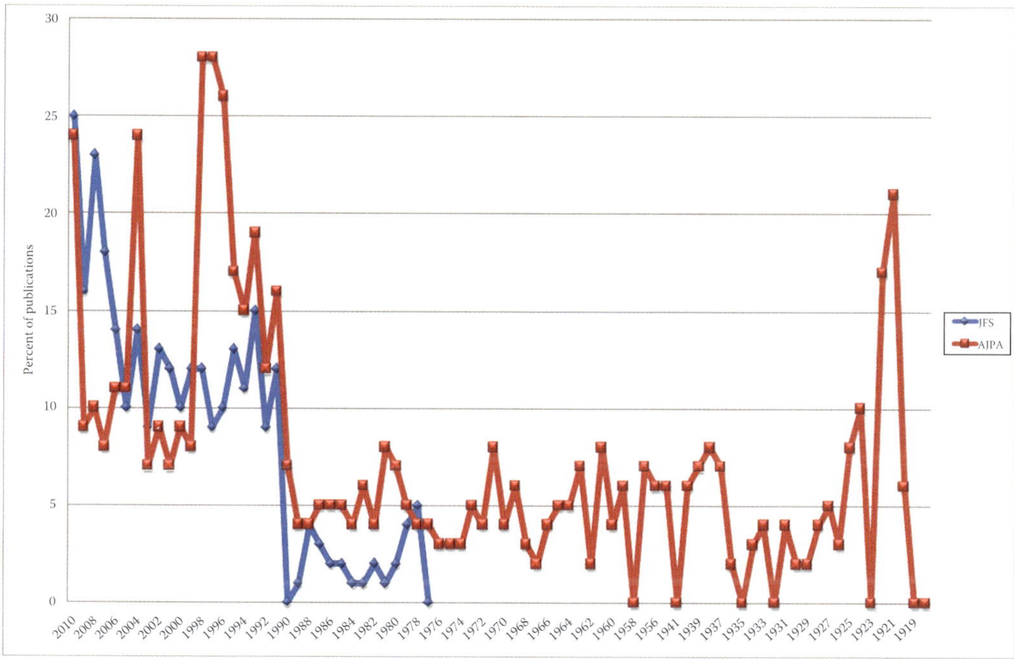

Figure 10.3 Annual percent of publications addressing, in some part, age-at-death estimation for the *AJPA* and the *JFS* calculated using counts obtained from a Web of Science search. Query parameters: Databases = SCI-EXPANDED, SSCI, A&HCI, CPCI-S, CPCI-SSH; Topic = "age" or "aging"; Time Span = All Years. AJPA record count = 1617 of 21,219; JFS record count = 687 of 7068.

founding forensic anthropologists (from Dwight and Dorsey, to Hrdlička and Hooton) as practitioners within medical schools and in pathology departments, and the continued interdisciplinary concern for classification through the identification of difference (be it in race, belief, behavior) focused on studies documenting variation between sexes, among populations, and through time (Stewart 1979, Lovejoy et al. 1982, Armelagos and Van Gerven 2003, Ubelaker 2009).

The anatomist T. Wingate Todd is often credited for laying the foundation for the first systematic and analytical approach to age estimation using skeletal indicators (Iscan and Loth 1989). Underlying his seminal analysis of the pubic symphysis (1920) and his work with Lyon (1924) on the relationship between age and cranial suture closure is a concern for both the descriptive and the analytical. By isolating differences in pubic symphyseal morphology, linking progressive bony change to increasing age, and sorting out the observed metamorphosis into phases, Todd (1921a–c, 1923, 1930) developed a model system of age-at-death estimation, using but a single part of the pubic bone, that was applicable to the classic White male and relevant for use in both anatomical studies and legal medicine. His consideration of the pubic bone as a unit within the larger context of growth and development (i.e., by treating the symphysis as an epiphysis that undergoes buildup and breakdown throughout the lifetime), and his treatment of the cranial sutures as part of a complex within the context of functional morphology (i.e., by addressing suture closure as it relates to the shape of the braincase), and his recognition of biological variation (interpreting differences within and among tested skeletal series) cleared the way for a broadened direction in future analyses. Nonetheless, Todd's research remained constrained by his more traditional concern for documenting skeletal norms, providing static descriptions and, from these, establishing a corpus of classic criteria.

It was not until the mid-century paradigm shift toward Washburn's (1951, 1953a,b) "New Anthropology," with its interest in explaining evolutionary mechanisms and adaptation through hypothesis testing, that scholarship in age-at-death estimation took up the more "dynamic approach now introduced into anthropometrical analyses" (Brooks 1955, p. 567). This new approach to understanding biological processes was problem-oriented. The concern for formulating research questions and testing hypotheses, coupled with the identification of unexpected and unexplained trends in age distributions for past populations, fostered an environment in which researchers undertook studies on age estimation that questioned past procedures and their built-in assumptions. These new projects were directed toward testing, redeveloping, and validating methods that appreciated all degrees of variation and served a practical purpose in the field. Brooks (1955), for example, tested Todd's methods for the pubic symphysis and cranial sutures on both the original and a new sample produced error rates for use and suggested modifications to the general framework for the pubic symphysis. Following this work, McKern and Stewart (1957) were the first to abandon Todd's original phase-aging system and introduced a new component scoring approach that incorporated greater within-group skeletal variation and reduced error. Although the widespread use of the McKern and Stewart method is limited by the narrow distribution of their reference sample of young, White American, male soldiers who had died in the Korean War (few of whom surpassed young adulthood), their component approach has contributed considerably to questions of methodology and forms the basis for the newly developed and very promising transition analysis (TA) coding method that is swiftly growing in popularity today (Boldsen et al. 2002, Milner and Buikstra 2006).

An interest in adopting a functional approach to understanding the skeletal "form," emerging ideas about the adaptive process in the subfield of bioarchaeology, and the contributions of multivariate statistics to the social sciences further refined the direction of research into age-at-death estimation (Moss and Young 1960, Moss 1968, Buikstra 1977, Enlow 1996, Armelagos 2003, 2008). By the 1970s questions, although still problem-oriented, were backed by a wealth of raw data and analyses were being driven by greater accessibility to quantitative methods (Armelagos and Van Gerven 2003). This shift from qualitative descriptions to quantitative statistical analyses encouraged efforts in data synthesis and method validation. At this same time, the term *bioarchaeology* (after Clark 1972) was introduced to physical anthropology for population studies using human remains (Buikstra 1977). Bioarchaeology brought with it a more holistic, population-oriented, and statistically grounded approach to age estimation. The emergence of multi-indicator or summary methods for age estimation reflect this emphasis on conducting broader-based anthropological analyses by redirecting the practitioner's focus from an individual skeletal marker and to the skeletal whole. Although new to method refinement and rigorous evaluation, the multi-indicator approach had been a topic of discussion in earlier work. Todd (1920) and later Brooks (1955) had recommended the use of more than one indicator and posited improved age assessment despite initial findings to the contrary (specifically, Brooks found that the cranial sutures deviated unreliably from the ages estimates using the pubic symphysis). This shift toward multiple age markers was also foreshadowed in application by McKern (1957) who pooled observations from the pubic symphysis, skeletal epiphyses, and cranial sutures. These methods grew in popularity because they promised a more complete picture of the aging process by considering all possible morphological variation as it is dispersed throughout the skeleton. For example, the multifactorial summary age (MSA) method of Lovejoy et al. (1985a) derives age estimates statistically, makes use of age-progressive information obtained from many markers (both classic, including the pubic symphysis and cranial sutures, and newer introductions, such as the auricular surface and sternal rib ends), and provides assessments of observer error. Studies such as these ultimately brought about change in what was considered acceptable or conventional methodology through the reevaluation and, at times, rejection of presumed levels of accuracy and precision, reliability and repeatability, and applicability and significance for the age estimation methods in use. To this point, Kemkes-Grottenthaler (2002) has declared that the rapid expansion of the field of forensic anthropology "undisputedly elevated classical individualization techniques to a new level of scientific inquiry" (p. 49). The establishment of the Physical Anthropology section of the American Academy of Forensic Sciences (AAFS) in 1972, the first publication of the *Journal of Forensic Sciences*, that same year, and the founding of the American Board of Forensic Anthropology (ABFA) in 1977 are testaments to a directed attention toward innovation, quality control, and consensus (Kerley 1978, Snow 1982, Iscan 1988, Weinker and Rhine 1989, Reichs 1995, 1998).

As Hoppa (2002) recalls, "the 1980s marked a pivotal point for paleodemography" (p. 15). In 1982, hefty criticism was first levied against age-at-death estimation in the context of past population studies and, in response, an intensive debate followed on the validity of the methods used for constructing age-at-death distributions. Bocquet-Appel and Masset (1982) argued that, since "the information conveyed by the age indicators is so poor," the estimation of vital rates for past skeletal populations is simply a product of "random fluctuations and errors of method" (p. 329). They advocated for the complete abandonment of age-related research and asserted that the estimation of adult skeletal age at death is a wholly unreliable endeavor because (1) target age-at-death distributions are heavily influenced by the distribution of the reference sample, (2) age-at-death estimates are biased, and (3) the correlation between skeletal age indicators and chronological age is unacceptably low (Bocquet-Appel and Masset 1982, 1985, Bocquet-Appel 1986). However, the accurate estimation of skeletal age at death is the key source of information for the reconstructions of mortality and fertility schedules; morbidity patterns; and the density, distribution, and age composition of skeletal populations. Approximations of age, as point estimates or, preferably, as ranges for forensic cases are an essential part of the biological profile and play an important role in assigning identity to unknown skeletal remains. For these reasons, a concentrated effort began for better explaining and improving the method and theory of age-at-death estimation (Konigsberg and Frankenberg 1992, 1994, 2002, Konigsberg et al. 1997, Hoppa and Vaupel 2002a). As Iscan (1989) remarks, "The 1980s has seen an unquestionable increase in interest in forensic anthropology as well as the introduction of the first aging methods from new sites in over 60 years" (p. 7). Using a large modern sample and multivariate statistics, Suchey et al. presented a revised method for age-at-death estimation from the pubic symphysis that simplified Todd's 10-phase method (1920) and produced the 6-phase system now commonly known as the Suchey–Brooks method (Katz and Suchey 1986, 1989, Suchey et al. 1986, Brooks and Suchey 1990, Suchey and Katz 1998). Lovejoy et al. (1985b) proposed an additional pelvic, phase-aging method using the auricular surface and incorporated cranial suture closure into their multi-indicator (MSA) method (1985a). Cranial vault sutures were also reevaluated by both Meindl and Lovejoy (1985) and Masset (1989), while Mann et al. (1987, 1991) presented the utility of maxillary sutures for aging intact and fragmentary remains. Finally, Iscan et al. (1984, 1985) introduced a new method for estimating age from gross morphological changes observed at the sternal end of the fourth rib (Loth and Iscan 1989). The combined instances of conflict, recovery, and growth in opinions on "age" alongside these new efforts in revision, innovation, and refinement for "aging" have resulted in a continued movement toward codifying sound age estimation theory and its methodological application, the identification of best practices in the field, lab, and in publication, and the dissemination of the correct, consistent use, and interpretation of these ideas for both skeletal assemblages and the individual skeleton in archaeological and forensic contexts.

Aging Today: Current Trends in Estimation

While skeletal biologists today are still interested in the identification of new indicators and new estimation formulae (Rissech et al. 2006, Algee-Hewitt et al. 2008, Prince and Konigsberg 2008), refining the approach to, or redefining the best combination of, known age-informative markers (Boldsen et al. 2002, Osborne et al. 2004, Shirley-Langley and Jantz 2010) and the mechanics of their practical application in the classroom, lab or field (Buikstra and Ubelaker 1994, Moore-Jansen et al. 1994), the research focus of current forensic anthropologists is often guided by casework. We seek answers to new problems introduced by the contexts of the remains under study, we attempt to better define population- or group-specific characteristics that may aid in the identification of future unknowns, and we revisit those issues not yet, or adequately, resolved because of limitations imposed by reference samples, technology, and political or medicolegal circumstances. The estimation of age at death in forensic anthropology is following a course that is responding organically to the advances in technology (especially in computational statistics and imaging) and the demands of the ever-changing medicolegal and academic environments in which, we, as its practitioners, work. As a result, age-at-death estimation has reached subdisciplinary maturity. The questions posed are no longer framed by concerns for its basic utility but reflect the need for refinement in two areas relevant to the role of the forensic anthropologist in the larger identification process: (1) diagnostics and (2) estimation and evidence.

First, how can we improve access to and increase availability of reference samples for method development and testing or specimen comparison, simplify access to the skeletal indicators required for analysis, and make use of new technologies for information retention and sharing? The contributions of "virtual anthropology" to age-at-death estimation are showing promise as viable solutions. Significant improvements in computerized modeling techniques, for example, are providing us with high-quality two- and three-dimensional reconstructions of bones, indicators, and the macroscopic features relevant to age estimation procedures (Zollikofer and Ponce de Leon 2005). Age information for each skeleton can be archived as a virtual reference collection in a convenient format that allows for economical and perpetual storage, repeated access to the "indicators" for reevaluation or new testing, and easy data sharing among researchers. Indeed, relationships have been found between individual chronological age and the stage of the indicators obtained from virtual reconstructions produced using multi-slice computed tomography (CT) and laser scans: Dedouit et al. (2008) applied the Iscan method to CT scans of right fourth ribs, Barrier et al. (2009) used the Lovejoy method on CT scans of the auricular surface, Ferrant et al. (2009) tested new CT scan-based criteria on multiple pelvic indicators, and Shirley et al.

(2010) recently evaluated the utility of laser scans as surrogates for the actual boney indicators (pubic symphyses and auricular surfaces). Although there is an acknowledged loss of some detailed information and questionable difficulties in navigating equipment and software, additional testing of virtual samples is warranted given the potential benefits to virtual autopsy, digital archiving, and data sharing of full specimens.

Second, after using known scoring systems to evaluate the macroscopic features that define a phase or stage, how do we extract the most accurate estimates given the complications of sex and population variability and limited reference samples? Moreover, what evidentiary contributions do our age-at-death estimates make to putative identifications when we consider the many new and changing requirements for expert testimony and the rules for the admissibility of evidence in courts, both at home and abroad? As the legal guidelines established by the judiciary body must be met for each method used, the value of an estimate will always be dependent upon the expectations of the system in which the testimony or admitted evidence of age at death is given. Although the rules of evidence vary by legal context (across systems, populations, and geography), the Daubert guidelines (following from the 1993 landmark case, Daubert v. Merrell Dow Pharmaceuticals, Inc.) support conservative admissibility criteria that should complement the level of expectations of most systems, including international humanitarian courts (Sapir 2002, Christensen 2004, Grivas and Komar 2008, Kimmerle et al. 2008a, Wiersema et al. 2009). Kimmerle et al. (2008b), Konigsberg et al. (2008), and Berg (2008), for example, address these issues in an international forensic context by testing the applicability of age-at-death estimation from the pubic symphysis using American, Asian, and Eastern European skeletal populations. These publications demonstrate how the choice of appropriate statistical methods and making informed decisions regarding reference samples and population parameters can provide well-founded estimates that meet current standards of evidence, identify areas of variability, and offer practical answers to the questions of age estimation in individual identification.

A combination of innovative statistical treatments, such as TA, Bayesian methods, and hazard analysis, allows for the estimation of the complete age-at-death distribution and individual ages at death that are grounded in robust objective methods and supported by probabilities. In forensic applications, we can obtain convincing statistics that can be used as support of our contribution to the personal identification of the "unknown" remains (Steadman et al. 2006). Boldsen et al. (2002) have contributed significantly to the ease with which the anthropological community can apply the new TA method* to both individual cases of forensic significance and archeological samples by providing a robust multi-indicator, component-based scoring method for which Milner and Boldsen (2008) have composed a detailed manual. The concomitant development of free-access, user-friendly software (e.g., the ADBOU Age Estimation Software by Milner and Boldsen and NPHASES program by Konigsberg) simplifies the execution of the statistical procedures required for estimating age using TA, including logistic regression (Boldsen et al. 2002) and the probit model (Konigsberg and Herrmann 2002). The open-source statistical software, R, can also be used to call to the "polr" (proportional odds logistic regression) function (included in the MASS package), with which we can conveniently fit a logistic or probit regression model to an ordered factor response. These programs

* The Transition Analysis method is discussed in more detail later in this chapter.

are increasing both the accessibility of the method to the anthropological community and the use of this approach among forensic practitioners for routine casework. Wilson and Algee-Hewitt (2009) and Shirley et al. (2010) have demonstrated the accuracy of the estimates obtained and low degrees of inter- and intraobserver error; these researchers and practitioners attest to the ease of producing results using the TA coding manual and the ADBOU computer program. Using NPHASES, Kimmerle et al. (2008b), Berg (2008), and DiGangi et al. (2009) have also shown the applicability of this approach to human rights cases, questions of population-specific standards, and to testing new methods. The success of the current directions in age-at-death estimation suggests that future studies will continue to refine the research well underway using robust statistical methods (including Bayesian statistics, hazard models, TA procedures, and component coding systems), advanced digital techniques (virtual anthropology and biomedical imaging), and computational technologies (age estimation software), all of which promise for forensic casework (1) an increased accessibility to robust methods, (2) further ease in obtaining improved results, and (3) a greater degree of confidence in the conclusions that are drawn.

Problems with Aging: Difficulties in Estimating Age at Death

Chronological and Biological Age

In their study on the history of the human lifespan, Acsádi and Nemeskéri (1970) argued that, while both sex and age are the "two fundamental biological characteristics of man" (p. 100), the estimation of adult age at death from skeletal remains is more important to the reconstruction of population dynamics than the determination of sex. Despite the fact that accurate age estimation is a precondition for forensic identifications and paleodemographic reconstructions, they contended that "there are not many investigators who would treat age determination with a thoroughness that can withstand scientific criticism" (p. 100). We see this same sentiment later reiterated by Mays (1998), who claimed that "at present the lack of a wholly satisfactory technique for estimating age at death in adult skeletons from archaeological sites is one of the thorniest problems facing human osteoarchaeology" (p. 50). Therefore, age-at-death estimation is just as Howell (1976) has aptly characterized it: "a subject which is simultaneously intensely interesting and devilishly difficult" (p. 25). Comments such as these are rooted in the very crux of the problem of determining skeletal age in any context: biological age and chronological age are not equivalent, "aging" is highly variable, and this variation is the significant source of method error.

Skeletally derived ages at death represent subjective assessments of the physiological state of the individual; these age estimates are inferred from an imperfect correlation between skeletal maturation stages (biological age) and calendar years since birth (chronological age). Variation in the timing of developmental and degenerative changes produces individual and population differences through time and across groups that confounds age estimation when "classic" phase-to-age criteria are applied to any case, without question (Kemkes-Grottenthaler 2002). Although Acsádi and Nemeskéri (1970) note that the regressive senescent processes (i.e., those changes that characterize what we call "aging" in the adult) begin at the transitional point between juvenile development and post-maturity heterostasis (when, e.g., the union of all epiphyses is complete), the qualification and quantification of all subsequent degenerative age-related morphological changes is not as straightforward. There is no question that senescence, or "aging," is universal: all populations undergo age-related and age-progressive changes from birth to death regardless of sex, ancestry, temporal distribution, or geographical location. The human lifespan is, however, "an environmentally and genetically labile characteristic, and there are no species-specific lifespans … [U]nder different environmental conditions, different samples of the same species may have very different average and minimum lifespans" (Harper and Crews 2000, pp. 495–496). The magnitude, rate, and proximal causes of senescent changes are not constants, and this plasticity permits differences across and within species (Finch 1994). There are, therefore, several notable sources of variation in morphology of importance to us as skeletal biologists: (1) vertical differences through time (e.g., evolutionary change between [sub]species and secular change within groups), (2) horizontal differences within and between populations (by sex and ancestry), and (3) within-subject variability in the timing of age-progressive changes observed throughout a single skeleton (asymmetry in bilateral indicators, disagreement between indicators from different regions).

While chronological age is independent of natural factors (i.e., the number of chronological age years increases systematically in accordance with the passing of calendar years in the individual's numerical "age" progression from birth to death), biological "aging" is an individual experience (Bryant and Pearson 1994). Factors that affect the timing of bone remodeling and degeneration and bring about the morphological changes upon which most methods for determining age are based can include genetic differences, diet, disease, endocrine status, climate, cultural practices, socio-economic status, and individual or group behaviors. Consequently, an individual's living conditions greatly affect the condition of the individual's skeleton at death. Buckberry and Chamberlain (2002) extend this argument further by positing that two individuals living under the same or similar environmental conditions will age at varying rates. These emerging views on the interpersonal and within-subject plasticity of the senescent process improve our understanding of the biology of aging on the one hand (a concern expressed by Lovejoy et al. [1997]) but, on the other hand, call into question the requisite uniformitarian assumption held for any estimation of demographic parameters: that the patterns of age-progressive changes observed in one population/individual are not significantly different from what one would expect to observe in another population/individual regardless of time and space (Howell 1976). Arguments that bones and teeth do experience age-related morphological changes over the course of the human lifespan and, moreover, that each individual element of the skeleton undergoes degeneration at different rates and magnitudes that are dependent upon structure, function, location, and the unique stresses on the element under study challenge the validity of the uniformitarian position that "observable biological markers of maturity [always] correspond to certain chronological ages" (Howell 1976, p. 27). Chronological (i.e., calendar) age and biological (i.e., physiological) age are never quite equal, and so age estimates are approximations based on observed similarity and concordance. This inherent variability in the biological process of human aging is often considered to be the "fundamental source of error for present osteological aging criteria" (Hoppa 2000, p. 185). Despite this problem of unresolved "error," the physical anthropologist remains interested in obtaining data on age to better understand population structure, and the forensic anthropologist is specifically charged with providing a useful age estimate to the medicolegal community for human identification purposes. The challenge for age-at-death estimation is, therefore, to develop tools that tease out biological information from the skeleton that is most closely related to chronological age. Several phase-based aging methods are available, that, despite the overarching issues of variation and error, are regularly used to estimate chronological age because their approach captures the general progression, the senescent phases or stages, of biological change through time.

Phase-Aging

Even in the early years of studies on skeletal age at death, it was recognized that the post-developmental remodeling of osseous tissue, usually in the form of bony breakdown, was informative of age. Sashin (1930), for example, explained that the changes useful to age estimation from the auricular surface of the ilium are "progressive, and increase in extent and intensity with the age of the individual" (p. 909). It was determined early on that the age of the adult skeleton could be most profitably estimated by locating specific age-informative areas (i.e., sites that are invariant to environment or activity and undergo progressive, regular morphological change over time), by assessing these for the degree and pattern of macroscopic bony breakdown expressed over the lifetime and by assigning this observed degeneration to a phase that is linked to chronological age. Techniques that make use of age-informative traits in this way require practitioners to properly apply the method's predefined criteria. We are expected to (1) correctly identify the indicator/age-informative location on the bone, (2) correctly interpret the description of the bony changes of interest and the definition of the phases (i.e., what type of change characterizes each phase), (3) correctly follow the scoring procedures and employ them with consistency (i.e., with low inter- and intraobserver error), and (4) to correctly translate our categorical data on phase assignment into a chronological age estimate using published standards and, when appropriate, execute the statistical procedures necessary to calculate point estimates, age ranges, and measures of variation. Most conventional methods rely upon this phase-to-age theory for adult age-at-death estimation. Popular examples include the following: estimating age from the pubic symphysis of the os pubis (e.g., Todd 1920, 1921a,b; Brooks 1955; McKern and Stewart 1957; Gilbert and McKern 1973; Suchey and Katz 1986; Brooks and Suchey 1990), the auricular surface of the os coxae (Lovejoy et al. 1985b, Meindl and Lovejoy 1989, Buckberry and Chamberlain 2002, Osborne et al. 2004), the sternal ends of the ribs (Loth and Iscan 1989, Yoder et al. 2001), craniofacial suture closure (Todd and Lyon 1924, Singer 1953, Brooks 1955, Meindl and Lovejoy 1985, Mann et al. 1987, 1991, Masset 1989, Key et al. 1994), ossification of the medial clavicle (Stevenson 1924, Todd and D'Errico 1928, McKern and Stewart 1957, Webb and Suchey 1985, Black and Scheuer 1996), and from patterns of dental wear (Gustafson 1950, Miles 1963, Molnar 1971, Brothwell 1989). Although many improvements have been made to these adult phase-aging methods over time (e.g., Suchey and Brooks' refinements to Todd's pubic aging standards, reducing the original scheme from 10 to 6 phases), difficulties unavoidably remain for any method that requires the observer to subjectively assess a skeletal element for "wear and tear" and then assign it to an ordinal phase category for which age ranges have been previously determined from reference samples of "known" chronological ages (Schmitt et al. 2002). Problems with adult phase-aging methods are widely recognized among paleodemographers (Hoppa and Vaupel 2002a), but also have significant implication for forensic anthropologists:

1. Necessary indicators are often absent (due to taphonomic filters).
2. Morphological changes are not regular across and within all groups for the available indicators, and population-specific standards are not always available.

3. Methods are interpreted variably and subjectively applied, thereby producing inter- and intraobserver error.
4. Age intervals are broad (e.g., a 95% age range of 25–83 years for Suchey–Brooks females Phase V), and often the last phase is defined as an open-ended terminal interval such that the "old" are lumped together and assigned a collective age of, for example, 50+ years for Todd's pubic symphyseal Phase X and 60+ for Lovejoy's auricular surface Phase 8.
5. Phases often overlap (consider Suchey–Brooks female Phase IV, 26–70 years, vs. Phase V, 25–83 years).
6. Estimates are frequently biased, so ages for younger individuals are overestimated and ages for older individuals are underestimated (this tendency is referred to as "attraction to the middle").
7. Ages estimated for the target sample reflect the ages of the reference sample when improper priors are used (this phenomenon is called "age mimicry," whereby the age estimate of the target sample mimics or is shaped by the age distribution of the reference sample upon which the method was developed).
8. Poor theoretical and statistical choices produce inaccurate age estimates, as well as misleading age-at-death distributions.

Choice of Indicators

As Iscan (1989) reflects on the history of skeletal aging techniques, remarking that "from the 1920s on, most skeletal biologists have relied almost solely on the cranial sutures and pubic symphysis for age estimation in the adult" (p. 7), it can be argued that the parts of the skeleton selected as preferred age-informative indicators were not always chosen first for their accuracy in providing age estimates, but instead for practical and historical reasons. Crania are typically more resistant to taphonomic processes than are more fragile elements (e.g., sternal rib ends), exhibit obvious age changes (i.e., open vs. obliterated sutures), and have long been a subject of fascination among anthropologists for a variety of research questions (Kemkes-Grottenthaler 2002, Boldsen et al. 2002, Waldron 1987). This preferential treatment given to individual traits as a result of availability, logic, and tradition may result in choices that compromise biological reality. When the skeletal system is treated as a collection of isolated age indicators, we take up a view that denies the fact that developmental and degenerative patterns in the aging skeleton are influenced by many interrelated factors, and we tacitly accept a low or limited yield of age information from the isolated indicator. From assessing trends in publication, we can safely assume that it is common knowledge among skeletal biologists that age information can be obtained from many different parts of the skeleton, that these age-informative regions offer different types and levels of information, and that they contribute differently to making the final age estimate (i.e., some work better than others). For these reasons, it is often held as true that individual age indictors and methods can be combined and that comprehensive approaches should produce superior results (Workshop of European Anthropologists 1980, Saunders et al. 1992, Baccino et al. 1999, Boldsen et al. 2002).

There are sound arguments for the use of multiple traits methods such as the MSA and TA methods because they can provide a more holistic picture of the aging process by including all possible morphological variation in the assessment of the individual's age (Acsádi and Nemeskéri 1970, Lovejoy et al. 1985a, Boldsen et al. 2002). The combination of several stand-alone age estimation methods in research* and in practice† has also been encouraged as a means of correcting for bias in any one method, accounting for population variability in one method, and evaluating if or how the senescent process varies throughout the single skeleton or skeletal assemblage (Aykroyd et al. 1999). These additive approaches have not, however, always yielded the best estimates. For some, research continues profitably using only a single, robust, skeletal, or dental age indicator (Buckberry and Chamberlain 2002, Prince and Konigsberg 2008, Prince et al. 2008). Nonetheless, method tests, assessments of bias, and tests of the assumption of conditional independence continue to produce conflicting results (Kemkes-Grottenthaler 1996, Holman et al. 2002). The use of multiple indicators does not effectively remove the issue of reference sample bias "by cancelling each other out" (Milner et al. 2008), combined traits do not contribute information on age at death in equal amounts, and conditional independence is probably not a fair assumption for all traits.‡ Given the complex architecture of the skeleton, age indicators are correlated with each other so that the information provided by one is not independent of another, and so age estimates are biased and intervals are too narrow (Boldsen et al. 2002, Milner et al. 2008). However, the good results recently obtained using, for example, the TA method, suggest that the inconsistencies observed in the quality of multi-trait estimates may be attributable to the specifics of individual research design, methodological choices, and statistical assumptions and not to the underlying "theory" that supports a combined approach (Usher et al. 2000, Boldsen et al. 2002, Buikstra et al. 2006, Wilson and Algee-Hewitt 2009).

Choice of Methods

The modal, phase-based design common among most age estimation methods is often criticized for failing to consider biological reality. Modal phase methods dictate that changes in skeletal morphology are assigned to discrete, ordered stages, that progress through chronological time from young to old. Methods that use phases require the practitioner to subjectively assign the indicator to one of several artificially constructed categories that may bear little relationship to their actual distributions in any living or extinct population. This reliance on ordinal age-phase strategies results in additional problems that inhibit the accurate estimation of age at death. Accuracy and reliability is dependent on both the overall experience of the observer in recognizing the subtleties and variation in age-related morphological changes and on the observer's specific familiarity with the age-phase technique at hand. Assigning skeletal elements to subjectively determined categories leaves a study open to the possibility of introducing inter- and intraobserver error (Lynnerup et al. 1998). The morphological assessment of age change requires the categorization of three-dimensional skeletal features by following often ambiguous written descriptions or by comparisons to limited "exemplary" photographs or casts. For example, any observer interested in evaluating the sternal end of the fourth rib for the purpose of making classification into a predefined age cohort by assigning the rib to a phase must take into account a host of morphological changes using only reference photographs or

* See McKern and Stewart (1957) for testing many separate age-informative regions on the Korean War sample.

† See Houck et al. (1996) for the analysis of the Branch Dravidian compound victims.

‡ See Boldsen et al. (2002) or Lucy and Pollard (1995) for more information.

casts representing "classic" ribs by stages accompanied by descriptions of the features to be observed. Consider the Loth and Iscan (1989) description of Phase 4 (ages 24–32):

> There is noticeable increase in the depth of the pit, which now has a wide V-or narrow U-shape with, at times, flared edges. The walls are thinner, but the rim remains rounded. Some scalloping is still present, along with the central arc; however the scallops are not as well defined and the edges look somewhat worn down. The quality of the bone is fairly good, but there is some decrease in density and firmness (p. 112).

As the descriptive language used here is not universal among the publications of age estimation methods using other indicators, and the authors do not provide pictures or casts that account for every possible variation, observer interpretations are necessarily best guesses—what Paine and Boldsen (2002) call "investigator-specific, weightings of categorical observations" (p. 170). A significant portion of inter- and intraobserver error can be explained by the fact that the observations derived from these traditional methods cannot be quantified. Consider again Loth and Iscan's description of a Phase 4 rib end. Observers evaluate a suite of morphological characteristics (including the contour and depth of the pit, thickness of the walls, the shape of the wall edges, the regularity of the rim, the presence of bony outgrowths, and the condition of the entire bone), which in their multiplicity increase the potential for error. In addition, these characteristics are scored following the ambiguous qualitative language used in the Phase 4 description (e.g., "more irregular," "some decrease," "still good"), which, in the absence of immediate comparative materials, does not facilitate quantification. This inherent subjectivity in age-phase assignment complicates age-at-death estimations by affecting repeatability. Even a reasonably experienced practitioner may not consistently choose the same age-phase assignment for a case scored at different times, and any two equally experienced observers may not interpret the method's criteria identically and, in turn, produce comparable estimates. Findings of considerable intra- and interobserver error discredit the reliability of the method and the accuracy of the conclusions drawn from the analysis (Schmitt et al. 2002). This issue is not unique to Loth and Iscan's (1989) method nor is it limited to aging techniques using the thoracic region, but it is a problem that burdens all phase-based procedures for all skeletal elements.

As studies of the pubic symphysis by Todd (1920, 1921a–c, 1923), Brooks (1955), Meindl et al. (1985), and Brooks and Suchey (1990) represent the seminal work that relies upon this traditional "age-phase" theory, let us also review the classification criteria in a phase from the Suchey–Brooks method. The description of Phase III (ages 21–53 for females and 21–46 for males) follows:

> Symphyseal face shows lower extremity and ventral rampart in process of completion. There can be a continuation of fusing ossific nodules forming the upper extremity and along the ventral border. Symphyseal face is smooth or can continue to show distinct ridges. Dorsal plateau is complete. Absence of lipping of symphyseal dorsal margin; no bony ligamentous outgrowths.

A quick read of this definition reveals problems similar to those noted for the rib, in Phase 4; but, what is of particular importance here is the risk confusion between morphological states of buildup and breakdown when we consider the characteristics of subsequent phases (Kimmerle et al. 2008c). Suchey and Katz (1998) even remark themselves that

> Phase III is somewhat problematic; it peaks in the mid to late twenties, but there are outlying cases trailing into the sixties. These outlying cases are probably interpretative errors on the part of Suchey and Brooks who may have confused buildup of the ventral rampart with breakdown of the ventral rampart (p. 221).

While this intramethod ambiguity substantiates serious concerns for observer error, and reliability, it also serves to highlight the problem of forcing traits that are continually undergoing progressive change over time into discrete categories. Saunders et al. (1992) assert that weaknesses in language interpretation and picture correlation for the Lovejoy et al. (1985b) auricular surface method contributed to the high observer error obtained (19.3%). They attribute this inaccuracy to difficulties in assessing the characteristics examined (especially grain and density), and to the limited photographs, which do not sufficiently reflect the potential range of variation and provide only a modal surface appearance for each phase. They also report that 50% of the means differed between two identical analyses conducted by the same observer for the lateral anterior system of Meindl and Lovejoy's (1985) ectocranial cranial suture method. Kemkes-Grottenthaler (1996) posits that problems in the reliability of this method, and possibly for others not yet investigated, may be a direct result of the failure to take into account the sex-specific patterns of suture closure and the differential rates of obliteration (what Todd and Lyon had already noted in 1924 as "lapsed union"). Here, then, the importance of both recognizing and taking into account the observed variation within and between individuals is paramount.

This problem of application is also compounded by the weakness often seen in the final age estimate. Phase-based aging methods typically generate wide age intervals that have little practical use, especially when the intention is to arrive at age ranges with sufficient informational value for comparison with missing persons lists and for practical use in other medicolegal or research contexts. Consider, for instance, the "most frequently used" (Meindl et al. 1985, p. 29) and "most reliable" (Buikstra and Ubelaker 1994, p. 21) method for the pubic symphysis. Suchey–Brooks Phase V for females includes all ages from 25 to 83 years, for which the mean is 54 years (Brooks and Suchey 1990). This wide range tells us very little about the real age distribution of the population and similarly provides little help in assigning an age to an unknown individual for the purpose of forensic identification. The age ranges are so broad that only the very young (<25 years) and very old (>83 years) are mutually exclusive. Furthermore, since the relationship between the phase and chronological age is nonlinear, phases tend to overlap and vary in length, such that an age range associated with a particular phase is not exclusively tied to that phase but may be attached to multiple phases. Suchey–Brooks Phases IV (26–70 years) and V (25–83 years) both describe the symphyseal morphology expected for females between the ages of 26 and 70. As a result, logical confusion may arise over assigning ambiguous skeletal elements to the "best" of the overlapping categories. Any such uncertainty increases the potential for interobserver error due to misclassifications, and valuable information on the individual is lost when overlapping age phases are employed (Love and Müller 2002). The issue of overlap is equally a problem for methods that use significantly smaller age ranges per phase and, consequently, more age categories (i.e., Todd's 10-phase compared to Suchey–Brooks collapsed 6-phase system). As Buckberry and Chamberlain (2002) observe, Lovejoy et al. (1985b) auricular surface method "oversimplifies the changes seen" (p. 232) by failing to recognize that the features of interest (e.g., porosity, surface texture, and marginal changes) develop and degenerate independently. The 5 year intervals in this system are "optimistically narrow" as they fail to capture the range of the variation in these features, and considerable overlap exists between different phases. This problem was restated recently by Osborne et al. (2004) who used the auricular surface for age estimation in forensic contexts. They show that only 33% of their target sample was accurately aged when using the 5 year intervals. They attribute this error in estimation to the fact that the mean ages of several of the intervals are not significantly different. Further, the use of these intervals with the constant width of 5 years presupposes that all individual age estimates have the same degree of error. This assumption is clearly problematic in light of the fact that every skeleton has its own degree of error, which is dependent upon the individual's suite of indicators and state of preservation (Boldsen et al. 2002, p. 75). A decrease in the number of phases, a reduction in the size of age ranges, and/or the standardization of these intervals do not appear to adequately lessen observer confusion and diminish the error associated with the larger theoretical problem of "quantification," that is, assigning the biological age indicator to its actual chronological age stage (Paine and Boldsen 2002, p. 170).

The task of estimating age for older individuals is also shown to be problematic when using modal, phase methods. Individuals who have lived to old age have skeletons that have experienced the greatest amount and diversity of age-related remodeling and degeneration.* As these skeletons show the most bony breakdown, irregularity, and complex deterioration, their indicators are less easily assigned to age phases that are typically defined by a limited set of age-informative characteristics. This problem of ambiguity is often resolved by making the terminal age-phase an open-ended interval to which all skeletons over a method-specific age are assigned.† This fix is not only unsatisfying to those anthropologists interested in working with skeletons of older individuals, but it is also wasteful of potentially important age information for personal identification. The inability to capture the individuals who are representative of the most extreme right-tail of the age-at-death distribution results in a skewed mortality schedule for paleodemographic research and an overly broad estimation of age for forensic casework. If the method makes use of an age indicator that is not sufficiently sensitive to the senescent changes that are particular to the target sample under analysis, then it is not helpful to studies that are concerned with evaluating the full variation of age at death within the population or in determining the age of an obviously older individual.

While formulating criteria for the best choice of indicator and method is wise in theory, it is also important to consider the practical problem of preservation or recovery bias, which may confound attempts at upholding guidelines for best practice. Any skeletal sample is a small percentage of the population at large and may be a poor representation of the once-living population. Sample composition is shaped by both human and natural factors that influence the condition in which the remains are retained and recovered (Haglund and Sorg 1997, 2001, Larsen 1997). Standards for successful age estimation methods rely upon indicators that are simultaneously the most informative of age and also subject to

* See Wood et al. (1992) for an explanation of the *osteological paradox*.

† See, for example, Todd's (1920, 1921a–c) method for the pubic symphysis, which lumps all individuals >50 into the terminal category, Phase X, or Lovejoy et al.'s (1985b) method for the auricular surface, which offers only a slight 10-year improvement by assigning all individuals over age 60 into the final Phase 8.

poor preservation: consider the more fragile, yet reliable pelvic indicators versus the more resistant, yet less effective, cranial sutures (Buikstra and Ubelaker 1994). The sample may be inherently biased by the singular or combined actions of poor preservation due to taphonomic processes, differential burial, and incomplete recovery (Walker et al. 1988, Wood et al. 1992, Waldron 1994). These taphonomic factors can compound method-based sources of error by placing limitations upon the selection of the most robust age indicator, the use of multi-indicator methods, the estimation of the target age-at-death distribution, and, in turn, the quality of the estimates produced and the value of the information obtained from these results.

Error, Bias, and Statistics

Closely tied to these concerns of method and indicator choice, are the reports of bias in age estimates for the "target" sample resulting from the use of inappropriate "reference" samples or "priors." This issue is what Meindl and Russell (1998) define as "Bias = Σ (estimated age − real age)/number of individuals; that is, sign is considered" (p. 383). We can better reach, and appreciate the source of this aging bias and detangle the knotty statistical relationship between the estimated ages for the target sample of "unknowns" and the documented ages of the reference sample of "knowns" by considering the following:

1. "The calibration problem"
   a. The decision of when it is appropriate to use inverse or classical calibration for the estimation of age at death for unknown individuals or skeletal populations using regression techniques (Konigsberg et al. 1997, 1998)
2. "Attraction to the middle"
   a. The "cause of systematic error tending to accumulate in the middle-aged categories uncompensated errors committed in the outer age categories" Masset (1989, 1982)
3. "Age mimicry"
   a. The tendency for the estimated age-at-death distribution of the target sample to mimic the age-at-death distribution of the reference sample (Bocquet-Appel and Masset 1982)

When we conduct an analysis using inverse calibration, we regress the dependent variable (typically denoted as x) on the independent variable (represented by y). For age estimation contexts, we accordingly regress the fixed variable of age on the age indicator and estimate age of an individual by ordinary least squares (OLS). For classical calibration, the reverse is true (OLS regression of y on x, followed by solving for x), so that instead we regress the indicator on age, and then solve for age. As inverse calibration involves regression toward the mean, any age-at-death estimate generated will naturally be skewed or "biased" in the direction of the mean age. This is what Masset (1989, 1982) has called the "attraction to the middle" and what can be more simply defined in practice as the chronic tendency to underage older individuals and to overage younger individuals so that, in many cases, the estimated ages more closely reflect the mean age than the chronological ages of the individuals for whom the estimates were made. As inverse calibration is a Bayesian method, we are framing our estimates of age for our unknown sample in terms of probabilities that are informed by what we know about ages at death from a documented reference collection; our analysis is said to be conditional upon prior information. Regression of age on the indicator requires us to assume correctly that the "target sample" (i.e., our unknown sample or case, comprised of the individual[s] for whom estimate[s] of age at death are desired) comes from the "same" (similar, comparable) age-at-death distribution as the "reference sample" (a documented collection of skeletons of known ages, used for method testing, and often referred to as a "prior"). Inverse calibration should only be employed in casework when a suitable reference sample or prior can be obtained for target skeleton(s); if an inappropriate prior is used, aging biases will result.

Although "age mimicry" was first discussed among paleodemographers working with skeletal populations from archaeological settings (Bocquet-Appel and Masset 1982), it also has significant implications for case analysis in forensic contexts. Age mimicry occurs when the age distribution obtained for the target, unknown skeletal sample is said to reflect the age distribution of the known reference sample (the skeletal series used to develop the estimation method). Although the distribution for the reference sample will not actually be duplicated, estimates will be nevertheless biased in the direction of the reference sample (Konigsberg and Frankenberg 1992). This "mimicry" is especially problematic if a reference sample with a badly skewed age distribution has been used in the development of the method, as is the case for McKern and Stewart's (1957) method using the pubic symphysis. We know that this method used a reference population of American soldiers killed in the Korean War and, so, it has a rather unique, restricted age, sex, and race distribution: mostly young White American males, few of whom survived beyond age 30. On account of this skewed distribution with an "oversampling" of young ages, any observed morphological changes in the pubic symphysis will appear characteristic of younger aged White males. The traits or components identified will in turn be mistakenly associated with aging in early adulthood even if in the population at large the observed age characteristic is associated with individuals of middle or older age: age features will appear common in young men simply because more young men comprise reference sample. When this method is applied to other cases, like random "unknowns" selected from the distribution of current U.S. forensic cases, the ages estimated for these target skeletons will not be representative of their "true" chronological ages but will be biased toward the skewed age-at-death distribution of the young soldiers making up the Korean War reference sample. The result is mimicry and age-at-death reconstructions that bear less, little, or no resemblance to the actual mortality profiles of the original populations regardless of how well the practitioner applies the method. The trouble with mimicry is related to the method itself; the age distributions produced are merely artifacts of errors in method, as Bocquet-Appel and Masset (1982) have argued.

Maples' (1989) statement that "age determination is ultimately an art, not a precise science" (p. 323) is what Aykroyd et al. (1999) call a "cautionary tale for biological anthropologists when determining age in an adult skeleton" (p. 87). Although the importance of the "art" of *knowing* the skeleton, its system and elements, its variations and adaptations, and its patterns of senescence based on experience, should not be undervalued, Hoppa and Vaupel (2002b) remind us that "the concept of age estimation has, despite a variety of possible techniques, followed the same series of short steps" (p. 5): (1) assess skeletal morphology, (2) link skeletal morphology to chronological age through a reference collection, and (3) estimate age. Step "1" may well belong to the realm of art and experience, and so is subject to issues of error involving the observer(s) and the degrees of error associated with the skeletal elements themselves. Steps "2" and "3" bring to the fore the last and perhaps most difficult problem to consider how to ground age estimation techniques in the most robust theoretical foundation and in the best statistical practices. The considerable number of publications focused on testing, tweaking, and introducing new and improved osteological methods suggests that skeletal biologists recognize the inconsistency in estimation performance and know that there is no single method or best combination of estimation techniques that can produce ages at death for casework or paleodemographic reconstructions of age structures with 100% accuracy. The assignments of indicators to phases are best guesses, and the calculated ages from phase information and reference samples are best estimates. Results may be improved at two levels: (1) at the level of the observer, who can reduce bias or error by choosing and using methods thoughtfully, by acquiring more "aging" experience, and by replacing point estimates with age ranges that are sufficiently broad to capture true age but narrow enough to aid in identification, and (2) at the level of analysis by avoiding various statistical pitfalls (including compounding error using additive methods, using inappropriate reference samples, and ignoring issues of conditional independence).

Still, the nagging issue of the imperfect correlation between biological and chronological age promises a reality in which the variability or error in age estimates can never be fully fixed. Consequently, the question of determining age at death should be framed in the context of probabilities (e.g., Lucy et al. 1996, Gowland and Chamberlain 1999, Schmitt and Broqua 2000). Despite the slight variation in indictors and methods, the practical application of a typical phase-based age estimation method to a reference population for method development yields a set of osteological data that demonstrate how skeletal morphology relates to known chronological age. The data tell what skeletons of which ages should fall into what phases and forms the basis for morphological aging criteria (i.e., the rules and expectations for an age-phase method). This same osteological data can then be used to estimate the probability of observing a suite of skeletal characteristics conditional upon a known age. This is noted mathematically as $Pr(c|a)$, or the probability of c given a, where c represents the skeletal characteristic (as it is related to the morphological age-indicator phase, stage, or category), and a represents chronological age at death. Konigsberg and Frankenberg (1992, 1994, 2002) have clearly explained, however, that the estimate of real interest is the age of an individual or group of individuals within a skeletal sample. To obtain the age-at-death estimates expected for forensic reports and for modeling the mortality schedule of a population, we need instead to estimate $Pr(a|c)$: the probability that the unknown individual died at a particular age a given evidence that her/his skeleton displays particular age-informative characteristics c. Although both probabilities, $Pr(c|a)$ and $Pr(a|c)$, appear at first glance to deal with the same things (ages, a, and aging characteristics, c), it is key to further calculations that we understand that they are not equal. $Pr(c|a)$ can be obtained from a thoughtfully chosen reference sample, while Bayes theorem must be used to calculate $Pr(a|c)$ *from* $Pr(c|a)$. While many of us would argue that Bayesian statistics are familiar to most anthropologists and may even "consider forensic anthropologists as being implicit Bayesians because they often do bring prior information to their cases" (Konigsberg et al. 2009, p. 84), solving for $Pr(a|c)$ is a complicated matter as the calculations require information about the age-at-death distribution of the target population (finding $f(a)$), and a method to link the observed frequencies of age-related traits in the target population to the underlying probability distribution of these characteristics (defining the probability of these characteristics, $Pr(c)$). With these computational rules defined, we can see that $f(a)$, the probability distribution of ages at death of the skeletal under analysis, must be estimated before $Pr(a|c)$ can be calculated.* In Bayesian discussions, $f(a)$ is considered the prior distribution of ages at death, because it must be obtained before, or *prior to*, the estimation of $Pr(a|c)$. The consequence of this Bayesian approach is that, as Boldsen et al. (2002) explain, "Any individual age estimate is, in effect, a secondary by-product of the aggregate-analysis" (p. 77). Konigsberg and Frankenberg (1994) have identified this issue of order in estimation as *the* paradoxical problem in the implementation of the statistical methods necessary to obtain the desired age(s)-at-death estimates. Restating the guidelines for age-at-death estimation in a complex statistical framework begs a theoretical question for practical application: if $f(a)$, the target age-at-death distribution, is required to generate the individual target ages, and these individual estimates can only be calculated for the target sample after obtaining $f(a)$, how can we produce the age-at-death distribution for the target population without the individual age estimates?

These statistical problems, however thorny, are not impassible and do not signal an end to profitable age estimation research, but instead call for change in focus—with attention being paid to the consequences of a poor theoretical and methodological framework. Solutions can be found in laying down improved statistical foundations and developing disciplinary protocol from these foundations that guides practitioners away from making poor choices given conditions particular to the composition and context of forensic casework and individual research programs.

New Solutions to Some Aging Problems: Improving Age Estimation

In 1982, "farewell" was first bid to quantitative pursuits in age estimation in the face of what seemed to be insurmountable statistical hurdles: attraction to the middle, age mimicry, biased estimates, errors in method design and observer application, and poor theoretical foundations for age estimation methodology (Bocquet-Appel and Masset 1982). Since then skeletal biology has profited from a steady vested interest in age-at-death research that seeks to simultaneously isolate and remedy these aging problems in theory, method, and practice. The last three decades have been punctuated by significant high points in improved osteological and mathematical approaches that have been turning points in the shift from what was arguably an uncoordinated use of "standard" but unsatisfactorily defined age estimation techniques (Jackes 2000), toward a concerted effort in defining the best practices in the field (Rosing et al. 2007, Ritz-Timme et al. 2000). As senescent changes form the basis for adult age-at-death estimates, and the biology of aging is highly variable across populations, within [sub]groups and subjects, and through time and space, skeletally derived ages are always infected with some degree of error that can be improved but not removed. So, for discussions of age estimation based on the degenerative changes with maturity, we can collate the many problems (i.e., the eight points previously identified) associated with conventional adult aging methods, into the "four basic analytical

* See the *Rostock Manifesto* in Hoppa and Vaupel 2002b.

difficulties in adult age estimation, all of which become more critical in older skeletons" (Boldsen et al. 2002, p. 75).

1. How can we best tease out the most and optimal age-related information from the skeleton—by choosing one robust indicator or by combining many indicators distributed throughout the skeleton?
2. How can we most advantageously score areas informative of age to account for the complex architecture of the skeletal and capture the most age-informative morphological variation in the indicators—using phase or component methods?
3. How can we obtain unbiased estimates of ages given the potential obfuscatory effect of the reference sample on obtaining estimates that best reflect the true chronological ages of the target individuals, as well as the acknowledged problems of "attraction to the middle" and "age mimicry"?
4. How can we account for the uncertainty implicit within the estimation of adult ages at death?

The first two questions can be addressed by a discussion of the choice of indicator and method, while the last two can be resolved by the appropriate use of statistics.

Indicators and Methods

The suitability of our approach to the estimation of age at death has both significant social and legal ramifications. Although in the last 30 years much has been written on the ways aging methods and indicators affect our understanding of the lifespan and life history of past peoples through the reconstruction of mortality schedules for ancient (i.e., archaeological, cemetery) populations in paleodemography (Lovejoy et al. 1977, Ruff 1981, Howell 1982, Molleson and Cox 1993), the more recent contributions of age-at-death estimates toward resolving issues of identification in medicolegal contexts are influenced by many of these same concerns, as well as by a set of disciplinary problems unique to forensic anthropology. No skeletal biologist would deny that the choice of both method and indicator influences how well we can produce age-at-death distributions for modern assemblages of many skeletal remains and how much high-quality information we can bring to efforts in personal identification for unknown individuals in the aid of the medicolegal community. In response to these demands of forensic practice, we must strive for age estimation methods that fulfill a set of standardized criteria that uphold good science (Ritz-Timme et al. 2000). The *Daubert* ruling (Daubert v. Merrell Dow Pharmaceuticals 92–102, 509 U.S. 579, 1993) and its four requirements of admissibility serve as a general guide for standards in testing, publication, peer review, known error rate, and acceptance. According to Daubert, methods should be

1. Rigorously tested, and data on accuracy and precision should be made available
2. Known among the scientific community through peer review and publication
3. Proven sufficiently successful to warrant acceptance as a best practice given by case conditions of use

In order to better meet these standards, we first need to address the unique problems identified for the traditional methods for age-at-death estimation and respond specifically to the choice of indicator and to the conventional use of phase-based approaches.

Choosing an Appropriate Indicator

Not all skeletal indicators of age perform equally well given the biological attributes of the samples (including sex, ancestry, pathology, life history, and modern versus ancient skeletons), particulars of the recovery conditions (forensic or archaeological, taphonomy, and degree of preservation, fragmentation, or commingling), and the tenets of aging methods to which they are subjected (macro or microscopic, gross or metric, phase, or component based). The first step in choosing an appropriate indicator is to evaluate its applicability to two broad age cohorts—subadults and adults—and, sometimes, to two additional subdivisions—young adults and very old adults. The next step is to select from the available indicators those that have proven successful for use on skeletons that match that broad age class.

Methods applicable to juvenile remains trace the developmental events associated with the formation and eruption of dentition and the growth of the skeleton in utero, from birth through youth, and up to the point of maturity. On the other hand, adult aging methods capture the post-developmental degenerative changes that characterize individuals progressing, or "senescing," from adulthood, to old age, to death. With the exception of the few sites of "late" epiphyseal union that begin their growth-related changes in youth but do not complete their union prior to the second decade of life (e.g., some segments of sacrum and the sternal end of the clavicle) or the highly variable eruption of the third molars (e.g., anytime between teenage and early adult years, if at all), there is limited overlap between indicators that are helpful for estimating age in skeletons of "the growing" and "the grown-up." This lack of overlap is attributable to the fundamental differences in the aging processes at work in subadults versus adults: development versus degeneration, growth versus senescence, and buildup versus breakdown, respectively (McKern and Stewart 1957, Webb and Suchey 1985, Hillson 1998, Scheuer and Black 2000, Shirley-Langley and Jantz 2010). Because there is not the same regularity in age-related changes in adulthood as in the synchronized development of youth, *and* because this irregularity in bony morphology increases with age, the selection of an appropriate indicator is most difficult for skeletons of postmaturity.

As many highly variable senescent changes occur throughout the adult skeleton, researchers have amassed many indicators to choose from and continue to seek out new markers or refine scoring techniques for traditional indicators that allow for better quantification of the subtleties of aging. Each of these markers has their own weaknesses, such that choosing a good or "the best" indicator is as difficult as it is essential. For example, recall that few macroscopic, phase-based methods can estimate age accurately for individuals over 45–50 years because of the irregularity in degenerative change, apparent cessation in quantifiable activity in the indicator, or lack of the necessary sensitivity in the scoring systems to capture the subtleties in age-related change that may characterize skeletons of older years. Also remember that chronological and biological age cannot be linked without some degree of uncertainty, that biological aging is highly variable, that evidence suggests that patterns of skeletal aging are not consistent among or within groups, and that different standards are required for males and females and for individuals of different populations and life history.* Furthermore, many age estimation methods have been developed using reference populations (e.g., autopsy, donated, and museum collections)

* For more information, see Schmitt et al. (2002), Konigsberg et al. (2008), Berg (2008), and Hoppa (2000).

that have been sampled for a host of reasons, including their representation of the trait(s) of interest, but forensic casework and population-based research is to some degree always dependent upon materials that have undergone taphonomic alteration and are subject to preservation error and directional biases related to the effects of factors such as deposition, decomposition, and destruction (Meindl et al. 1990, Usher 2002, Wilson et al. 2007, 2008, Komar and Grivas 2008). From these few examples, we can see how important it is that the skeletal biologist makes use of a robust indicator for age estimation (Aykroyd et al. 1999). An appropriate age indicator should

1. Be highly correlated with chronological age.
   a. This relationship should be validated by statistical means.*
2. Be invariant, so that the rate of change is consistent across all samples (Müller et al. 2002).
   a. It is neither easily subject to environmental alterations nor significantly affected by metabolic and nutritional changes.
3. Exhibit age monotonicity (Milner et al. 2008).
   a. The indicator exhibits a clearly identifiable sequence of morphological change with age, and these changes occur within intervals and not throughout the entire lifespan.
4. Be widely applicable across populations and between the sexes.
   a. If variation is found to exist, per-group corrective criteria should be developed and thoughtfully applied given what is reasonably known about the individual, for example, sex, ancestry, "race," or ethnic affiliation.†
5. Be reasonably resistant to the effects of natural filters.
   a. Taphonomic processes may cause preservation bias and oversampling of certain age cohorts or social groups (Walker et al. 1988, Wood et al. 1992, Konigsberg and Frankenberg 1994, Waldron 1994).

The choice of the indicator and method may be seen as steps in the age estimation process that are inextricably joined: if the state of the remains dictates what indicator(s) can be most reliably evaluated, then the approach to age estimation is tied to the methods developed for the available indicator(s). We are often faced with the conundrum of working with what we have. Klepinger (2006) has offered her view on "best" practice: "I am inclined to disregard cranial suture closure when other markers can be used. There are, however, occasions when the cranial sutures are all there is, and then the best option is to employ one of Nawrocki's (1998) regression formulae for various combinations of endocranial, ectocranial, and palatine suture closure" (p. 58). The obvious question is if a poor estimate is better than no estimate; the answer is most profitably framed in terms of observer experience and specifics of the case—so the decision to estimate is largely philosophical, situational, and variable. If many good indicators are available, then we are fortunate to have the option of being selective. In these instances, it is best to select robust indicators and methods that

* See Kemkes-Grottenthaler (2002, p. 56) for a summary table of coefficients of correlations between common age indicators and ages at death.

† See Ubelaker (2008), for a collection of studies that addresses the applicability of methods developed in the United States to individuals in the Balkan area and considers females separately. See Usher (2002) for available reference collections.

are free of the phase-aging problems and to combine these in such a way that captures the greatest amount of variation in the skeleton and, in turn, provides the strongest and most biologically informed estimates.

Choosing an Appropriate Method

To increase accuracy in age-phase techniques and broaden their applicability to diverse groups and situations, most methods have been rigorously tested and improvements have been made accordingly. It is important that, as practitioners, we are not only educated in "the standards" but that we are also active participants in the theoretical and technical conversations on the new directions in age estimation research. We should keep abreast of the advances in the method and theory of age estimation so that we do not necessarily choose the most common or most conventionally applied method when other approaches may be more successful or appropriate given the constraints of the unknown remains recovered. Let us again take the pubic symphysis as an example of a standard indicator that is subject to both conventional and new methods. Although many forensic anthropology textbooks and lab manuals still provide instructions for Todd's system (Bass 2005, White and Folkens 2005), and it remains a part of the scoring procedure for casework (Buikstra and Ubelaker 1994; Forensic Databank data forms*), over five decades of testing have shown that that the revised, six-phase, Suchey–Brooks method produces more accurate results (after Suchey and Katz [1986] or Brooks and Suchey [1990]). For forensic casework in particular, Klepinger et al. (1992) have reported supportive findings from a test of the McKern–Stewart, Gilbert–McKern, and Suchey–Brooks methods on a large, diverse, contemporary autopsy sample: "The results suggest that the Suchey–Brooks methods are superior in forensic applications and that racially specific refinements for males should be used" (p. 763). Recent tests that include the pubic symphysis as part of the TA method have shown potential for greater improvement in results: Wilson and Algee-Hewitt (2008) scored known forensic cases from the WM Bass collection and obtained highly repeatable estimates that corresponded closely to known ages and yielded small interobserver error, regardless of sex or ancestry; Buikstra et al. (2006) also found that the TA scoring procedures are "replicable and are effective in resolving historical issues" (p. 59). These data would suggest that there is merit in turning to traditional indicators as many have held fast for good reason, but that stepping outside of the traditional applications and looking toward more methodologically rigorous and holistic techniques may yield improved results. The success of TA (as defined by Boldsen et al. [2002]) is in part attributable to the fundamental design of its scoring scheme, which does not make use of the typical age-phase approach but instead is component based (Milner and Boldsen 2008). Before we can move forward and fully appreciate the contributions of new methods, we need first to revisit the weaknesses in using any phase-aging approach and consider specifically the problem of "fixing" the "phase" itself.

The phase-based approach assumes that the complex morphological changes observed in a single indicator, and representative of a single phase, are synchronized in their occurrence: they are progressive, unidirectional, and metamorphosing in unison. This is, however,

* These forms are available at http://web.utk.edu/~fac/databank.shtml

rarely the case for our complex biological reality. Indeed, the range of morphology varies considerably at any given age because different parts of a single bone, region, or indicator change at different rates and in different ways. As phase-based methods require that all of the bony characteristics (i.e., the complex senescent changes) used to define a particular phase are fully observable in order to obtain an unambiguous classification of the indicator, there is (1) a loss of clarity in the indicator-to-phase assignment when the observed patterns shows variation away from the fixed definition of the phase, (2) a disregard for any age-informative changes that may occur as the bony features transition through stages of change *between* the phases, and (3) a failure to deal with the complications in scoring resulting from cases that span several phases by retaining some features of young age or showing early progression in features indicative of older age (a problem noted for Suchey–Brooks phase III by Suchey and Katz [1998] and again by Kimmerle et al. [2008c]). To mitigate the problems of "phase" aging, we may choose to redefine our methods so that they use broad morphological categories. This can be done by reducing the number phases, relaxing the criteria to include more variation, and widening the estimated age intervals. Unfortunately, widening the intervals and accepting more variation simply introduces different obstacles to obtaining the best possible age estimates. In creating phases that cover large areas of the lifespan, like Suchey–Brooks phases IV (26–70 years) and V (25–83 years), we lose information on age, encounter the problem of overlapping phases, and reduce the method's utility in instances when, for example, estimated age ranges are to be used for trimming down missing persons' lists to only possible matches. A more effective approach may be to make use of methods that do not require the classification of the skeletal indicator into a phase. Methods using dental metric features, such as tooth root translucency and periodontal recession, do not rely on adult phase-aging techniques and have the added benefits of narrower age ranges and of capturing age-informative information for older individuals (Prince and Konigsberg 2008). Teeth are also durable, more resistant to taphonomic degradation than other bony indicators, and sometimes the only remains recovered at forensic case sites. Unfortunately, recent tests of interobserver error using dental metrics have shown significant differences in root height, periodontal recession, and translucency of the root taken by similarly trained observers (Kimmerle et al. 2008c). Consequently, the utility of the well-known and widely used Lamendin technique has been questioned given findings on interobserver error (Prince and Ubelaker 2002, Klepinger 2006). In addition, dental methods, like single indicator phase-methods, are limited regionally; when used alone, potential age information from the rest of the skeleton is disregarded. We are wise, therefore, to look forward to approaches that use a phase-free system, allow for flexibility in the areas analyzed, capture considerable variation when scoring, and allow for easy combination.

One such approach is the previously mentioned method of TA. TA is a robust alternative to phase-aging methods that permits the inclusion of multiple indicators when estimating age. Although TA is a new method (Boldsen et al. 2002), the basis for its scoring system can be traced back to McKern and Stewart's (1957) and Gilbert and McKern's (1973) component approaches for the pubic symphysis, which are in keeping with the common practice of scoring cranial sutures in segments and obtaining a composite score (see Meindl and Lovejoy 1985). Unlike phase-aging methods (e.g., the Todd or Suchey–Brooks pubic symphysis methods, Lovejoy's method for the auricular surface, and Iscan's sternal rib end method) that rely on the classification of a single indicator in its entirety into one of several predefined categories, component scoring treats the skeletal marker as a complex of features. These features, the "components," are scored individually, and each component is coded based on a series of stages. The estimation procedure underlying TA is a parametric method that provides information on the timing of the "transition" from one stage to the next, that is, the probability that an individual has attained a certain phase given age and the mean age of transition. The general statistical procedure can be applied to any indicator, assuming that (1) phases do not overlap, (2) phases cannot be skipped, and (3) progression through phases is unidirectional (i.e., indicator states move from one phase to the next and never backward).

Milner and Boldsen (2008) have chosen three known age-informative markers (cranial sutures, pubic symphysis, and auricular surface) to include as part of the coding criteria for the TA method and have devised a component-based scoring system for each of these markers. For the pubic symphysis, for example, they identified five components: symphyseal relief, symphyseal texture, superior apex, ventral symphyseal margin, and dorsal symphyseal margin. Each of these components is coded separately given predefined characteristics, so that the first component of the pubic symphysis, symphyseal texture, is evaluated on the following four unidirectional stages: (1) smooth/fine grained, (2) coarse grained, (3) microporosity, and (4) macroporosity. Counting all the TA scoring criteria for left, right, and midline indicators, the skeleton is evaluated on 171 characteristics, spread out over 19 components. As such, a multicomponent method better captures the complex biological changes and large degree of variation in the human skeleton, and, in turn, provides a more holistic understanding of skeletal aging patterns. As the TA method is designed to incorporate all or some of the components and additional indicators may also be added, it provides a flexible scoring framework that may prove particularly useful in situations with fragmentary remains. Validation work by Boldsen et al. (2002) and independent analyses by Wilson and Algee-Hewitt (2009) have shown that the quality of the age estimates can be improved by simply increasing the number of indicators included in the analysis. Moreover, they found that the effect of knowing or changing sex and ancestry on the age estimates was reduced as more indicators were included in the analysis. Boldsen et al. (2002) have also demonstrated that TA makes it possible for the user to code for "old age" traits and to obtain age ranges for individuals comprising the right extreme tail of the age-at-death distribution (i.e., those cases that would otherwise have been lumped in an open-ended terminal phase such as "50+"). Being able to better address the skeletons of older cohorts is a critical step forward in our methodological progress and in our ability respond to changing demands in casework, as the elderly are the fastest growing subgroup of the U.S. population, and similar increase is noted for the very old (i.e., age 85+) in many other countries (Harper and Crews 2000). Adopting the TA component scoring, phase-free, multi-indicator method allows us for the first time to combat at once several of the key issues with adult age-at-death estimation. We can deal more effectively with the entire mortality distribution, diverse samples, and remains of varying degrees of preservation in both forensic and archaeological contexts, in an easily applied and methodologically sound way.

Statistics

Quantitative methods in anthropology have always been hotly debated for their contributions to understanding skeletal characteristics and their relationship to worldwide, population, subgroup and individual levels of variation in modern, archaeological, and evolutionary contexts. Yet, never before have sound statistical approaches to understanding patterns of human variation and methods for detecting the unique biological attributes that identify each of us as individuals been more important or more profitable, particularly in the forensic sciences. The modern technological revolution not only enables computationally intensive quantitative approaches but, in doing so, also demands more precise tools, accurate methods, reliable applications, and greater accountability in scholarly output. The importance of science to the biological profile and for the estimation of age at death is apparent when we consider the increasing contributions of the community of forensic anthropologists and skeletal biologists to research in areas of medicolegal concern, the criteria of the three rules of law in the United States (the Federal Rule of Evidence 702, the *Frye* test, and the *Daubert* ruling), and the increasing role of forensic practice and testimony in singular cases, mass disasters, and international humanitarian work (Klepinger 2006, Komar and Buikstra 2008, Blau and Ubelaker 2009, Steadman 2009). Ubelaker (2008) has aptly commented on our motivation for case-oriented research in response to forensic anthropological work in the former Yugoslavia: "stimulus consists of penetrating questions directed toward the forensic anthropologist expert witness in a legal proceeding. Such questioning of applied methodology in discussion of case testimony can represent a powerful incentive to address key issues that seem vulnerable" (p. 606). For these reasons, anthropologists have been working to refine probability-based techniques that are applicable to standard skeletal methods of personal identification and provide verifiable estimates and evidence (Christensen 2004, 2005, Rodgers and Allard 2004, Konigsberg et al. 2006, 2008, 2009). The most gainful solutions to the issues affecting the estimation procedure and the quality of the estimates are found in improved statistical methods that address issues associated with regression analysis, reference populations, and the estimation of ages at death using a robust Bayesian approach.

Prior Distribution Problems

Although regression in the form of inverse calibration is a common approach used in anthropology research, it is also among the most problematic and prone to misuse given that an appropriate prior distribution is required for unbiased age estimation. A good "reference sample" or "prior" should have an age-at-death distribution similar to the distribution of ages expected for the "target sample" (i.e., the unknown remains for whom the forensic anthropologist must develop an age estimate). Usher (2002) provides a detailed discussion of available skeletal collections, with known-age and sex that may be appropriate for use as informative priors given the different conditions and contexts of the unknown skeletons and the goals of our individual research on age-at-death estimation.* Advances in collection development in the area of modern forensic cases through the growth of donated skeletal collections representing the diversity of the modern American population lessens this concern by providing comparative skeletal materials for use in U.S. contexts (e.g., the WM Bass Donated and Forensic Skeletal collections housed at the University of Tennessee and the Maxwell Museum's Documented Skeletal collection housed at the University of New Mexico). Age-at-death information from the University of Tennessee's

* See also the web-based "Reference Collection Database" at http://www2.potsdam.edu/usherbm/reference

Forensic Anthropology Data Bank (FDB) may also serve as an appropriate forensic prior as it stores a large sample of demographic and skeletal records for recent (since 1986) documented cases submitted by practicing forensic anthropologists from across the United States (Ousley and Jantz 1998; http://web.utk.edu/~fac/databank.shtml). Although we may accept these reference samples as reasonable representations of contemporary American casework, their applicability to future casework or to analyses conducted outside of the United States is unknown. As a cautionary example, Wilson and Algee-Hewitt (2009) tested the suitability of using U.S. national homicide data as an informative prior for the cases documented in the FDB and found that, although homicides do contribute to the average forensic anthropologist's case load and both samples are similar in time and space, the age-at-death distributions of the two groups were not sufficiently similar for unbiased use. This suggests that making what may seem to be logical assumptions on sample similarity in the absence of appropriate testing and choosing "best fit" reference collections can have compromising effects on our age-at-death results. We have to agree with Usher (2002) that marrying populations with priors is "one of the most overlooked, but basic, sources of error in skeletal age estimation" (p. 29).

Calibrated Approaches

A more forward-thinking approach to this problem of reference samples is to devise statistical ways to circumvent the required external age-at-death distribution. Classical calibration can be used in place of inverse calibration when no suitable prior is available for the target sample, when age estimation is applied to an untested population for which differences in senescent patterns may be a concern or are unknown, or when determining the structure of the age-at-death distribution of the target sample is not possible. Classical calibration assumes an uninformative prior for age at death and produces maximum likelihood estimates (MLE) of age by regressing the dependent variable (x, the age indicator) on the independent variable (y, the age), and then solving for age (Konigsberg et al. 1998). The prediction interval for classical calibration is larger than that from inverse calibration, so the estimated age ranges are wider, but the real age value is more likely to be captured within the expanded confidence interval and, importantly, the results are unbiased. In the context of applying TA, this is what Boldsen et al. (2002) consider a uniform prior distribution. This solution is not, however, without problems as this "uniform," "flat," and "uninformative" prior is not reflective of real mortality distributions: we must make the assumption that each skeleton in the target sample has an equal probability of being all ages (Hoppa and Vaupel 2002b). The uniform prior has been variably criticized for putting heavy weight on very old, and, so, less likely ages at death (Di Bacco et al. 1999); it was shown to overestimate old ages when compared to an informative prior (Boldsen et al. 2002); and it has been considered wasteful for disregarding all of the information on the age structure of the target sample (Konigsberg and Frankenberg, 1992). In instances when a prior is in question, the most satisfying solution is to incorporate models of mortality (also known as "hazard models") into our approach to the estimation of the probability distribution of the ages at death in the target population.* In practical applications, when

* See Hermann and Konigsberg (2002), Holman et al. (2002), and Love and Müller (2002) for more information about hazard modeling.

applying TA, age at death can be calculated from the age-at-death distribution estimated using hazard analysis and the ages of transition; the estimate for an individual skeleton can be then obtained by generating the highest posterior density for each stage. A series of publications by Konigsberg (2008) and colleagues (see Kimmerle et al. 2008b, Prince and Konigsberg 2008, Prince et al. 2008, DiGangi et al. 2009) have demonstrated the promise of this unbiased approach by obtaining reliable individual age-at-death estimates for international forensic casework, using a variety of scored indicators, including the pubic symphysis, first rib, and dental roots and wear.

Getting Better with Age: Best Practices in Age Estimation

Returning to Maples' (1989) assertion that "age determination is ultimately an art" (p. 323), it is remarkable that the most productive approaches to our acknowledged troubles with aging are those that recognize the importance of precise science to concerns of skeletal biology and actively engage its theoretical and biostatistical principles. A significant turning point in this paradigm shift from "art" to "science" came in 1999 and 2000, when the Laboratory of Survival and Longevity at the Max Planck Institute for Demographic Research in Rostock, Germany, held a workshop on mathematical modeling in paleodemography, whose goal was to reach a consensus on how best to tackle the unresolved issues in age-at-death estimation. A theoretical framework for the estimation of age distributions from skeletal populations emerged out of these meetings and its synthesized form became what is now called the *Rostock Manifesto*. The publication of this guide for age estimation in paleodemography marked not only the first collective effort to offer clear, codified, and statistically rooted solutions to many of the problems of estimating age at death from skeletal samples, but was also the first step in defining a sound theoretical framework for answering age-at-death questions relevant to forensic anthropologists working in diverse, modern contexts (Hoppa and Vaupel 2002a,b). The influence of the *Manifesto*'s guidelines is palpable in the response of the anthropological community to medicolegal questions of identification methodology. The organization of the 2004 American Academy of Forensic Sciences symposium entitled "Estimation and Identification in American and International Populations" (Dallas, Texas) and the subsequent papers published in *Journal of Forensic Sciences* in 2008 clearly demonstrate the applicability of the *Manifesto*'s theory to contemporary concerns of significant humanitarian consequence. In response to the rapidly changing demands in forensic anthropological practice and output, we are witness to examples of "good practice" and recommendations for "best practice" in the application of laboratory methods for assessing age of skeletal remains, cadavers, and living humans (Houck et al. 1996, Ritz-Timme et al. 2000, Schmitt et al. 2006, Rosing et al. 2007, Steadman 2009). As Ritz-Timme et al. (2000) have explained, there is an immediate need "to find common standardization, calibration, and evaluation or to develop means of quality assurance for methods of age estimation … [e]fforts in these directions are necessary to guarantee quality standards and adequate answers to the important legal and social issue of age estimation in forensic medicine" (p. 129). For the United States, these concerns for principles of forensic practice are in the process of being addressed through the efforts of the newly formed "Scientific Working Group for Forensic Anthropology," or SWGANTH (www.swganth.org; see also Adams and Lothridge 2000). The SWGANTH is a board of forensic professionals that "aims to develop consensus guidelines, that is, 'best practices', for the discipline of Forensic Anthropology, and to disseminate those guidelines to the broader forensic community … to identify and codify existing standards, or, where clear standards don't exist, to formulate and establish them … to examine targeted issues for the purpose of identifying what is best practice today and what paths should be followed in the future" (www.swganth.org).

As with any scientific study, our (age-at-death) results are only a good as our (skeletal) data. It is, therefore, essential that we are knowledgeable in the options available for the collection of age information from skeleton and are wise to the practices that may yield the most accurate and helpful data, and, in turn, the most reliable estimates that will ultimately contribute "age" to the case of individual identification. There are no adequate substitutions for the original method reports when learning how to properly identify indicators and areas of interest, how to apply the system of evaluation, and how to obtain the ages and associated ranges following the method's protocol. Nonetheless, when we also consider that our assessment may be communicated in the courtroom, it is essential that we understand the types and degrees of error associated with each technique and can provide documented statistics on method accuracy and reliability. We may instead choose in the final "estimation" stage to employ alternative computational techniques (i.e., the TA method) that we know to be more statistically robust based on validation tests.

While forensic anthropology is undergoing a paradigm shift toward rigorous scientific studies, we should embrace this [r]evolution and "direct the field's development into the most professional, efficient, and profitable pathway" (SWGANTH 2010). We must appreciate that methods once held as "gold standards" may be improved (given the introduction of new technologies, advances in statistics, or greater understanding of the proximate causes of aging or the patterns of skeletal variation) or altered in response to the changing demands of forensic casework (accounting for secular change, population differences, and the expectations of the medicolegal community). We must also understand that these modifications may require the relearning of evaluation procedures in order to obtain more accurate, reliable, and applicable results. Observer experience is a crucial factor in accurate age-at-death estimation; this is also true for any "applied" skeletal method that relies upon gross visual assessment (i.e., sex and ancestry estimation, assessment of trauma, and pathologies). As forensic *practitioners*, we must *practice* in the osteology lab and make use of reference skeletons with known demographic data to measure our own proficiency across the full spectrum of available age estimation methods and assemble a reliable toolkit for case evaluation.

Regardless of age cohort (i.e., 0–3, 20–35, 50+ years) or general classification (young to old, juvenile or adult), the theory for age-at-death estimation is founded upon our knowledge that the skeleton undergoes changes throughout the lifetime, from our first days into our last years. These changes for the young skeleton are uniquely related to growth. The processes of bone formation and development occur along a unidirectional trajectory until homeostasis, or the cessation of growth, is achieved. This moment of stability (i.e., the theoretical point-in-time without skeletal change) marks the pivotal transition between the progress in the juvenile and the regress in the adult skeleton. Growth, therefore, is immediately followed by the lengthy period of remodeling and degeneration that characterizes the majority of our lifetime and continues throughout our post-adolescent years from maturity until death. As the two broad age stages of our lifespan, subadulthood and adulthood, undergo oppositional bony activities in the form of skeletal buildup for the former and breakdown for the latter, the techniques that we use to assess individual age must consider the difference in these processes. Consequently, estimation methods for age at death are tailored to capture the types of morphological change that are distinctive of each stage.

Age Estimation for the Juvenile

As metamorphosis in the juvenile skeleton is inextricably tied to growth, biological age is inferred from the degree of maturation observed for bone (i.e., appearance and fusion of epiphyses, morphology of ossification centers, skeletal dimensions), teeth (i.e., formation, eruption, wear), or both tissue systems combined. The resulting physiological age estimate is translated into chronological age following published standards obtained mostly from modern clinical growth studies of living children.

As the growing skeleton undergoes regular changes, indicator events for age estimation occur sequentially and are relatively consistent in timing and duration. Because of this regular progression and the short time period in which human growth occurs relative to the complete lifespan, more accurate age-at-death estimates may be produced for immature skeletal remains than for adult lifespan. That is not to say, however, that age-at-death estimation methods for immature remains are without their own set of problems. The limited size and composition of reference samples, the frequent application of radiographic standards directly to skeletal and dental remains, the increased variability in the rate of aging with the increase in the age of the cohort, the inaccuracy in sex and ancestry estimation in prepubescent skeletons, the known sex and geographic variation in the rate of maturity, and recent secular changes in skeletal maturation in some populations all represent sources of error in estimation and potential weaknesses in our current methods.

The most common and easily implemented approaches to age-at-death estimation for the juvenile skeleton involve the assessment of the epiphyses (e.g., appearance and/or timing of fusion), the development of dentition, and the use of skeletal dimensions.* Ossification centers, epiphyses, teeth, and osteometrics are convenient macroscopic indicators of age that can be easily accessed either by gross inspection of dry remains or observed radiographically. For example, age estimate ranges can be obtained by comparing the pattern of epiphyseal fusion throughout the skeleton.†

In the post-cranial skeleton, fusion occurs at the growth plate between a primary and secondary ossification center, called an epiphysis. This type of fusion follows a set of forward steps that facilitates interval-based estimation: the excretion of the growth hormone ceases, the growth plate ossifies, and the epiphysis (secondary ossification center) is united with the metaphysic (primary ossification center), and longitudinal growth stops. We can obtain the age information necessary for constructing an estimated age range by (1) observing the suite of the potential points of union in the entire remains, (2) locating the most recent or "last" union, and (3) identifying the "next" union expected to occur. An age interval can be formed by taking the age standards associated with both the "last" and "next" sites and assigning the lower age limit to the former and the upper age limit to the latter. It is important to be aware that evaluations may vary based on the method

* Thorough explanations of these and other methods, as well as the comparative age standards are available in Ubelaker (1987, 1989a,b), Smith (1991), Buikstra and Ubelaker (1994), Hillson (1998), Saunders (2000), Scheuer and Black (2000, 2004), Lewis and Flavel (2006), Warren (1999) speak specifically to forensic contexts.

† For detailed charts, see Scheuer and Black (2000) or Buikstra and Ubelaker (1994).

of inspection (i.e., dry bones versus x-rays). When using radiographs, for example, Cope (1946) observed persistent fusion lines on the distal femur and proximal tibia in an individual over age 71; while Hillson (1998) noted that the developing dentition will appear later on film than in direct inspection of dissected tissues, as enamel and dentine are first deposited as a poorly mineralized matrix. White and Folkens (2005) also caution us that "regular" events do not mean "constant" events, and, thus, it is important to make use of the most applicable standards in order to reduce the confounding effects of inconsistencies related to secular change, sex, and population differences.

Let us consider, for example, the case of sex and rates of fusion. Female skeletons are known to mature faster than males, so that epiphyseal fusion typically occurs at a younger chronological age in girls. As the expected ages per bone region or by epiphysis are known to vary between the sexes, any estimate that relies upon pooled sex standards will be less informative of true age. In other words, combining males and females increases the amount of variation, which in turn necessitates broader intervals. If we take age data for fusion of the humerus, as reported by Scheuer and Black (2000), we see that the distal epiphysis fuses for females at 11–15 and 12–17 years for males. A simply combined sex interval would estimate age at 11–17 years; although this range should capture the true age, regardless of sex, it encompasses a considerable portion of the juvenile lifespan and, in its breadth, may be unhelpful to making a personal identification. The opposite problem is of equal concern. Although these sex-specific standards are available from documented clinical studies, as yet, we are not able to estimate sex (or ancestry) from the subadult skeleton with any statistical certainty, at least for the pre-pubescent years. Even when sexually dimorphic features are recognized (i.e., those features that differ significantly between males and females), the degree of overlap between males and females is often too great to recommend their use for consistent sex identification (e.g., Holcomb and Konigsberg 1995, for the sciatic notch). An incorrect assignment of sex would erroneously truncate the age interval estimated from the sex-specific epiphyseal information, thereby making the interval too low for a "true" female or too high for a "true" male. Reporting such a narrow interval may result in the exclusion of the correct individual from the list of possible matches.

Recent studies have also demonstrated that different epiphyses provide different levels of accuracy and precision for different individuals. This information attests to considerable variation in developmental timing across ancestry groups and secular trends in maturation (Crowder and Austin 2005, Schaefer and Black 2005, Shirley-Langley and Jantz 2010). Any of our estimates (wide or narrow) may be compromised further by these population-specific patterns and maturation trends (Klepinger 2001) without the appropriate choice of reference standards and improvements in our ability to estimate sex and ancestry for juvenile remains (Buck and Strand Vidarsdóttir 2004, Cardoso 2008, Cardoso and Saunders 2008). As skeletal development is ultimately an individual process, factors affecting the single skeleton may also result in unexpected patterns: for some individuals complete fusion may lag, extend into adulthood, or never be fully achieved. For this reason, the extent of closure is evaluated using a progressive scoring system: unfused/nonunion, fusing/uniting, fully fused/complete union. Despite this variation in union, the assessment of epiphyseal fusion is preferable to epiphyseal appearance for practical purposes. For example, the common clinical method of assessing hand and foot maturation based on the appearance of secondary ossification centers are not advisable for recovered skeletal remains (e.g., Greulich and Pyle 1959; Tanner Whitehouse

System, TW-2 1975, or TW-3 2001). As separate, partially formed epiphyses are small and irregular, they may be damaged easily or overlooked in the field and are often difficult to reassociate with a particular bone in the lab.

Methods estimating age from dentition follow a similar process to the evaluation of epiphyseal union. Two popular dental methods proposed by Demirjian (1978, 1990) and Moorees et al. (1963a,b) require (1) the identification of the physiological state or the tooth development stage by direct visual assessment or from radiographs and (2) the association of the observed state or a calculated "maturity score" (Smith 1991), with known age standards obtained from reference samples. Most skeletal biologists recognize, however, that dental development more closely reflects chronological age than skeletal maturation. This is likely due to the fact that markers of skeletal maturity are more easily influenced by external factors such as activity, social and physiological stress, and nutrition, while tooth formation is under greater genetic control (Saunders 2000, Cardoso and Padez 2008). Although sex and population variability in teeth is known (Demirjian and Levesque 1980, Tomkins 1996, Chaillet et al. 2005), dental development is typically accepted to be quite regular regardless of subgroup (i.e., females are, on average, only 1–6 months more advanced in development than males) and published dental charts have been shown to be reliable, easily interpreted, and simply applied.* Ubelaker's (1987, 1989a,b) revision of Schour and Massler's (1941) original dental development diagram, although originally designed for use on native Americans materials, is now a recognized worldwide standard (Buikstra and Ubelaker 1994, Hillson 1998). Age estimates from tooth development are preferred to those derived from the assessment of alveolar emergence or gingival eruption as they consider the whole development of the dentition and, so, avoid potential estimation errors related to variation in the timing and sequence of singular tooth eruption or sex and population differences (Hillson 1998).

Subadult age may also be calculated using osteometrics, including individual bone (diaphyseal) lengths and total skeletal size (Fasekas and Kosa 1978, Scheuer and Black 2000). This method proves less reliable as bone size increases, and there is considerable metric variation among populations (Ubelaker 1989a,b, Saunders 2000). Its utility is therefore limited to skeletons of young ages (<10 years) and is best and most widely used for fetal, infant, and early post-natal skeletons and in cases for which population-specific reference data is not available (Byers 2005).

Age Estimation for the Adult

The identification of "adult" in biological or osteological terms is often tricky because there exists a brief window during which the young adult may be subject simultaneously to the progressive and regressive changes that characterize skeletal immaturity and maturity, respectively. Evaluation of the "adult" skeleton may include, therefore, the examination of the degree of union at sites whose fusion is known to extend into post-adolescent years and the assessment of late-stage dental development. Recent work on the utility of these markers of young adulthood (e.g., clavicle, vertebrae, ribs, sacrum, anterior iliac crest, and third molar) in forensic casework has yielded mixed results (Webb and Suchey 1985, Mincer et al. 1993, Albert 1998, Kunos et al. 1999, Rois et al. 2008, Shirley-Langley and Jantz 2010).

* For a list of population-specific dental studies see Lewis and Flavel (2006, p. 246).

Shirley-Langley and Jantz's (2010) reanalysis of the age-related change in the medial epiphysis (sternal end) of the clavicle shows promising results for quantifying this change using a robust statistical approach and simplifying the scoring system considerably. They also provide convincing evidence for secular change in the maturation of the clavicle, as well as sexual dimorphism in the onset of fusion (with females maturing earlier). Their results demonstrate the importance of using appropriate, modern skeletal standards for the reliable use of the sites of late-stage development for age estimation in forensic cases. Patterns of age-related fusion in the sacrum reported by Rios et al. (2008) also demonstrate the same sex difference in fusion. This accumulating evidence suggest that the accelerated maturation observed in young females in ontogeny holds true for the developmental changes occurring in the early adult years, and so should encourage careful study of sex differences in other maturation indicators, as well as inspire further research in sex estimation from the growing skeleton. Rios et al. (2008) do not obtain, however, the same level of precision in age estimates as those offered by other adult maturation methods, and, thus, they advise that sacral fusion is best used for the initial assignment of skeletons to broad age groups. These results may be attributed to the later ages at which final fusion was observed in this and other studies (into the third decade by Rios et al. [2008]; but even as late as 54 years by Belcastro et al. [2008]), as we have observed that skeletal variation increases with the increase in the age at which the event occurs.

Like the late-fusing bone markers, the development of third molar (M_3) has also been used to provide estimates of age that span the transitional young adult period, from approximately 15 years into the second decade. However, M_3 has been long recognized to be the most variable tooth in size and shape, in timing of formation and eruption, and even in its presence or absence. For these reasons, the third molar has been tested for use in modern forensic odontology casework. Results show that M_3 has little (if any) sexual dimorphism in its timing, that the degree of associated variation is in keeping with the amount expected given the positive, direct relationship between variation in dental development and increasing age, and that distinct root development stages exist for White Americans and can be identified using diverse samples and independent examiners (Garn et al. 1962, Mincer et al. 1993, Hillson 1998). Despite these findings, the considerable variation in the third molar does not recommend its use as s sole age indicator. More accurate dental estimation methods are available that provide coverage for this same period of early adulthood, offer flexibility in tooth choice, and have been shown to be successful in forensic cases with target ages spanning the adult lifetime. These include age estimation from dental wear patterns (Miles 1962, 1963, 1978, Smith 1984a,b, Prince et al. 2008), and dental metric features for single-rooted teeth, including root translucency and periodontal recession (Lamendin et al. 1992, Prince and Ubelaker 2002, Prince and Konigsberg 2008).

Although Shirley-Langley and Jantz (2010) note that "young adults constitute a large portion of forensic casework" (p. 571), most conventional adult age-at-death estimation methods are less concerned with patterns of late development. Instead, they focus on tracing the progressive, degenerative changes in skeleton that characterize senescence throughout the entire post-maturation period of adulthood, which constitutes the largest segment of our total lifespan and the most variable in age-related morphology. Standard osteological methods for obtaining adult age estimates involve the macroscopic, visual assessment of bony features using predefined criteria. When the goal is identification, as in the forensic case, the typical protocol may include the following steps: (1) score all available elements using either phase and/or component methods to obtain individual or combined indicator results, (2) supplement the indicator-based assessment with an overall evaluation of "age" using generalized degenerative changes distributed throughout the skeleton (which may include scoring for degrees of joint wear, macro- and microporosity, and/or osteophytic development), and (3) come to a consensus age based on multiple points of evidence, preferably using robust Bayesian methods and obtaining probability-based estimates of the individual's age at death (see the recommendations by Buikstra and Ubelaker [1994], Ritz-Timme et al. [2000], Baccino and Schmitt [2006], Rosing et al. [2007], or Komar and Buikstra [2008]). We may choose to reverse the order of steps 1 and 2 and first evaluate the overall appearance of the skeleton to obtain a broad age classification (young adult, middle age, old age), which can then be used to select the most appropriate indicator and method (Aiello and Molleson 1993). More specialized techniques are also available and sometimes necessary, but often they are more expensive, invasive, and destructive (e.g., histological or molecular methods). An expert in these advanced laboratory methods should be consulted when the condition of the remains (e.g., highly fragmented, burned) or the circumstances of the forensic case warrants additional methods or secondary confirmation (Robling and Stout 2008, Stout 2009, Marks et al. 2009).

For method development, testing, and validation, and when the focus of the analysis is not identification at the level of the individual, we should restructure our protocol to incorporate blind scoring, multiple observers, and repeated measures. We should also pay careful attention to our choice of reference collection (modern, forensic, archaeological, multiethnic), sampling methods (randomly chosen, or a subset), data collection decisions (lefts, rights, or both sides for bilateral indicators) approaches to missing data (elimination by case or by variable), and treatment of pathological cases (inclusion as normal variation or exclusion as an outlier). Thorough evaluation and careful documentation is also essential to any skeletal analysis as reassessment may not be possible, be it on account of reburial under the Native American Graves Protection and Repatriation Act (NAGPRA) or the release of remains to the next-of-kin following a positive identification or the closing of the case. In all circumstances, we should initially score the indicators or features individually without reference to other age-informative areas or to the partner indicator (in the case of bilateral traits) and collect as much raw data as available during the preliminary, and often only, skeletal assessment. *Post-hoc* manipulation of the information collected (e.g., data cleaning, sample partitioning, and variable selection) and the choice of statistical methods allow us to refocus the final analysis toward questions of particular interest and to obtain unbiased estimates.

In order to best capture only the age-related information contained in the adult skeleton, we rely on age markers that have been identified, tested, and validated for (1) their progressive, unidirectional, and regular changes, (2) their coverage of the entire adult lifespan, and (3) their invariance to the effects of individual environment and life-ways (such as activity, weight, muscularity, and stress). Some assumptions regarding these indicators may at times be relaxed when certain other conditions are met or when corrections have been made, as long as this is acknowledged properly. Conventional, phase-aging methods typically make use of one or some combination of the following skeletal indicators: pubic symphyses, auricular surface, sterna rib ends, and cranial sutures. New areas of interest (e.g., for the acetabulum, see Rouge-Maillart et al. 2007, Rissech et al. 2006, 2007) and combinations of many low-information "subjective" traits are also are being continually proposed and tested (Algee-Hewitt et al. 2008).

As Meindl et al. (1985) have argued that "the anatomical feature most frequently used for determination of age at death in both demographic and forensic osteology is the pubic symphyseal face … it is frequently the only source of information used for age estimation, even when used in conjunction with other criteria it is universally considered to be the most reliable" (p. 29), it is not surprising then that estimation methods that make use of the pubic symphysis are often the anthropologist's first choice. Buikstra and Ubelaker (1994) explain that "morphological changes in the pubic symphyseal face are considered to be among the most reliable criteria for estimating age at death in human remains" (p. 21). This confidence in the pubic symphysis is likely based in part on (1) the many studies that demonstrate the relatively consistent and recognizable morphological developments in the pubic symphysis as it progresses through a series of irreversible age-related changes (e.g., Todd 1920, Brooks and Suchey 1990, Suchey and Katz 1998), (2) continued interest in making refinements to its use (Brooks 1955, McKern and Stewart 1957, Hanihara and Suzuki 1978, Zhang 1982, Snow 1983, Meindl et al. 1985, Garmus 1990, Boldsen et al. 2002, Konigsberg et al. 2008), and (3) the considerable amount of data now accumulated for assessing its use in both well-documented and emerging methods, for example, the Todd, McKern, and Stewart, Suchey–Brooks, Complex MSA, and, only recently, the TA method (Suchey et al. 1986, Klepinger et al. 1992, Kemkes-Grottenthaler 1996, Wilson and Algee-Hewitt 2009).

Few skeletal biologists concerned with age estimation would disagree that the contribution of greatest effect is the scoring system defined by Suchey, Katz and Brooks in the mid-1980s. Validation tests of the Todd (1920), McKern and Stewart (1957), and Gilbert and McKern (1973) methods lead Katz and Suchey (1986) to revise Todd's 10-phase system using a large ($n = 1225$), modern, and diverse sample of documented remains from the Los Angeles Medical Examiner's Office. They simplified Todd's scoring method by collapsing phases I through III and phases IV, V, VII, and VIII into two categories, made changes to select features of interest in each stage, and expanded the estimated age range for each phase. These modifications produced the six-phase system now commonly known as the Suchey–Brooks method (Suchey et al. 1986, Brooks and Suchey 1990, Suchey and Katz 1998).The widespread use of this method is facilitated by the availability of casts that provide examples of the range of variation observable in each phase. These three-dimensional models offer the practitioner tangible comparative material that aids in reducing subjectivity in phase assignment (Klepinger et al. 1992). It is important to note, however, that this method often fails to capture the variability that characterizes certain groups (Klepinger 1996)—a conclusion recently supported by Schmitt's (2004) test of the Suchey–Brooks method on an identified Asian sample. Here, both bias and inaccuracy increased with age, and true age was underestimated. Nevertheless, the Suchey–Brooks method remains "the symphyseal technique of preference for U.S. anthropologists today" (Komar and Buisktra 2008, p. 142), and has emerged "throughout the world as the standard for estimating age from the pubic symphysis" (Kimmerle et al. 2008b, p. 558).

Lovejoy et al. (1985b) proposed an alternative method for the estimation of age from the pelvis using the gross morphology of the auricular surface. As the auricular surface method was developed using archaeological materials and anatomical specimens from the Hamann–Todd collection, it has received attention in both bioarchaeological and forensic research. Although it is often considered the more difficult of the two pelvic methods in interpretation and correct application, it remains popular for its use of a region of the skeleton that is more resistant to taphonomic damage. In their original study, Lovejoy et al. (1985b) described eight phases of age-informative changes defined by characteristics related to the progressive breakdown of the surface, including billowing, granularity, density, and porosity. The method's scheme assumes that changes first occur at 5 year intervals between ages 20 and 49 years and then broaden to 10 year intervals from ages 50 to 59 years before terminating with an open-ended category for individuals older than age 60 (i.e., 60+). Although this later terminal phase allows for slightly better estimates of old age than the 50+ phase of the Suchey–Brooks method, the eight stages and their narrow age ranges also fail to account sufficiently for variability in morphology. Osborne et al. (2004) recently proposed a revision of this original configuration, in a similar spirit to Brooks, Katz, and Suchey treatment of Todd's 10-phase system, by reducing the number of phases from 8 to 6 and widening the prediction intervals for each phase. Osborne and colleague's modified method shows great promise for forensic applications as it was validated, in part, using the modern and well-documented WM Bass Skeletal collection, returned acceptable levels of interobserver error, and found that sex and ancestry had little effect on the age estimates.

Iscan et al. (1984, 1985) have extended this same phase-based approach to the thoracic region by proposing age estimation criteria for use with the medial (sternal) surface of the fourth rib. The original method involved the classification of the right fourth rib into one of eight modal phases, with sex-specific standards defined individually for White and Black Americans. Loth and Iscan (1989) have subsequently reported that ribs 3 and 5 follow the same age progression through phases 1–8 and may be treated using the same "fourth rib" criteria; more recently, however, Yoder et al. (2001) have proposed the use of a composite rib score instead of relying upon a single rib. The increased flexibility in rib choice offers improved potential for use in settings in which the "ideal" rib end may not be preserved. However, additional large samples studies are necessary for continued improvement in the rib scoring criteria and in the accuracy of the estimates produced.

Without question, the most problematic of all adult aging methods in the estimation of reliable and reasonably focused ages at death is the degree of closure of the cranial and maxillary sutures. Although this topic has generated consistent publications throughout the last century since Todd and Lyon's (1924) initial studies, none of these tests and revisions have offered convincing methods or solutions that correct for the significant problems of accuracy, precision, and the confounding effects of secular change (Singer 1953, Meindl and Lovejoy 1985, Mann et al. 1987, 1991, Masset 1989, Nawrocki 1989, Milner and Boldsen 2008). Buikstra and Ubelaker (1994) propose that individuals should be assigned to broad age classes based upon an overall assessment (young adult, 20–34 years; middle adult, 35–49 years; old adult, 50+ years) and that weight should be given to age estimates from post-cranial features over cranial suture scores. Repeated attempts have been made to improve methodology by obtaining composite scores for vault and laterals anterior sites (Meindl and Lovejoy 1985, Lovejoy et al. 1985a), by scoring only the sutures from regions with good prediction rates (Milner and Boldsen 2008), or by choosing sutures that represent closure patterns for many areas of the skull, including endocranial, ectocranial, and palatine sutures (for the standard on combined scoring sites, see Buikstra and Ubelaker 1994) and by subjecting these to proper statistical analyses (e.g., for regression equations, see Nawrocki 1998; for TA, see Boldsen et al. 2002). Nevertheless, they all have made but weak improvements and have yielded very mixed results. The best decision regarding the evaluation of cranial sutures may ultimately rest in the context of the case: the preservation of other age indicators, the need for external validation of other methods, the contribution of the cranial suture scores to the final age estimate, and the evidentiary standards required for the age estimate should all be weighed carefully.

Adding up the Years: Chapter Summary of Age-at-Death Estimation

The estimation of age at death in forensic anthropology is an essential step in (1) the formulation of a biological profile and (2) the contribution of evidence toward making the identification for unknown skeletal remains of medicolegal significance. The theory for the estimation of age at death is predicated upon our knowledge that our skeleton undergoes changes throughout our lifetime that reflect "maturation" in the young (bone growth and development) and "senescence" in the old (bone breakdown and degeneration). Current age estimation methods are tailored to capture the variations in skeletal morphology that are unique to each of these two broad age classes. Choice of indicator and method is guided by both the context of the materials under study (including the maturity of the skeleton, its state of preservation, the available indicators, and information about sex and population affinity), as well as the ultimate goal of the analysis (evidence for legal testimony regarding the individual or a series of remains, method development, or method testing). There is, therefore, no single and consistent "best choice" for the age-related indicator or method; nevertheless, we can identify criteria for "best practice." We should choose techniques for their accuracy and precision; we must be cognizant of the acknowledged problems with age estimation methods and well-informed about the implementation of possible solutions; we should be experienced in osteological practices, knowledgeable of our own weaknesses, and proactive in maintaining high professional standards of proficiency; we should meet current medicolegal expectations for our estimation technique and promote the use of rigorous science in the production of our results; we must embrace interdisciplinary collaboration and seek aid from experts when the conditions of our casework call for assistive studies or confirmatory analyses. Finally, we are wise to remember that age-at-death estimation, like any other gross morphological assessment of the skeleton, produces estimates, and estimates can always be improved through future research and enhanced methodologies.

Questions

10.1 How is age at death important to the forensic casework? Is the goal of the estimation process different for the skeletal biologist as forensic anthropologist than as paleodemographer?

10.2 Why should we say that we "estimate" age at death instead of "determine" it?

10.3 Provide a brief explanation of the major problems with age-at-death estimation? Discuss the ways in which these difficulties have been/can be overcome. What smart choices can be made?

10.4 What difficulties still lie ahead and what future improvements can be made to the method and theory of age estimation?

10.5 What defines a "good" reference sample? Why do we need a "prior"? What can we do in its absence?

10.6 How does our approach to "aging" differ between subadult and adult skeletons?

10.7 What is unique about estimating age in young adults? What is the problem with very old adult skeletons?

10.8 What defines a "good" indicator and a "good" method?

10.9 Discuss the difference between phase and component scoring procedures. Is one approach better than the other? If so, under what conditions? Why?

10.10 What is TA? How can it contribute to improved age-at-death estimation?

10.11 What do we mean by "group variation"? Does sex or population affect the way we estimate age at death or the results produced?

10.12 How do biological and chronological age differ? Which of these ages do we estimate? Which is most useful in medicolegal contexts?

10.13 Do our genes or our environment affect our biological age? If so, which or both? In what way?

10.14 Why are standards important for age-at-death estimation? Have legal expectations affected the way we obtain and report ages? If so, which rulings? How?

10.15 Provide a brief outline of the history of age estimation. How have philosophic and temporal trends in anthropology and biology affected this scholarship?

10.16 What is the *Rostock Manifesto*? Explain its guidelines.

10.17 What are $Pr(a|c)$, $Pr(c|a)$, $f(a)$? What do we need practically and statistically to obtain an age estimate?

10.18 When estimating age for the individual skeleton, should we provide law enforcement with a point estimate or an age range? How are these different in terms of the information that they provide? What effect can our choice have on making an identification? In the courtroom?

10.19 What new technologies are contributing the ways in which we collect age-informative data, how we use this data to estimate age, and our confidence in the results produced?

10.20 Is estimating age at death an "art" or a "science" or both? Why?

References

Acsádi, G. and J. Nemeskéri. 1970. *History of Human Life Span and Mortality*. Budapest, Hungary: Akadémiai Kiadó.

Adams, D. E. and K. L. Lothridge. 2000. Scientific Working Groups. Forensic science communications 2: www.fbi.gov/hq/lab/fsc/backissu/july2000/swgroups.htm

Aiello, L. and T. Molleson. 1993. Are microscopic ageing techniques more accurate than macroscopic ageing techniques. *Journal of Archaeological Science* 20:689–704.

Albert, M. A. 1998. The use of vertebral ring epiphyseal union for age estimation in two cases of unknown identity. *Forensic Science International* 97:11–20.

Algee-Hewitt, B. F. B., K. E. Weisensee, and G. R. Milner. 2008. Age is subjective: A non-traditional method of age estimation for the adult skeleton. Paper presented at the *Annual Meeting of the American Academy of Physical Anthropologists*, Columbus, OH.

American Board of Forensic Anthropology, 2010. ABFA home page: www.theabfa.org

Armelagos, G. J. 2003. Bioarchaeology as anthropology. In *Archaeology Is Anthropology*, S. D. Gillespie and D. Nichols (Eds.). Archaeological Papers of the American Anthropological Association Series, No. 13. Arlington, VA: American Anthropological Association, pp. 27–41.

Armelagos, G. J. 2008. Biocultural Anthropology at its origins: Transformation of the new physical anthropology in the 1950s. In *The Tao of Anthropology*, A. J. Kelso (Ed.). Gainesville, FL: University of Florida Press, pp. 269–288.

Armelagos, G. J., D. S. Carlson, and D. P. Van Gerven. 1982. The theoretical foundations and development of skeletal biology. In *A History of American Physical Anthropology*, F. Spencer (Ed.). New York: Academic Press, pp. 305–328.

Armelagos, G. J. and D. P. Van Gerven. 2003. A century of skeletal biology and paleopathology: Contrast, contradictions, and conflict. *American Anthropologist* 105:51–62.

Aykroyd, R. G., D. Lucy, A. M. Pollard, and C. A. Roberts. 1999. Nasty, brutish, but not necessarily short: A reconsideration of the statistical methods used to calculate age at death from adult human skeletal and dental age indicators. *American Antiquity* 64:55–70.

Baccino, E. D. and A. Schmitt. 2006. Determination of adult age at death in forensic context. In *Forensic Anthropology and Medicine: Complementary Sciences from Recovery to Cause of Death*, A. Schmitt, E. Cunha, and J. Pinheiro (Eds.). Totowa, NJ: Humana Press, pp. 259–280.

Baccino, E., D. H. Ubelaker, L. A. Hayek, and A. Zerilli. 1999. Evaluation of seven methods of estimating age at death from mature human skeletal remains. *Journal of Forensic Sciences* 44:931–936.

Barrier, P. F., F. Dedouit, J. Braga et al. 2009. Age at death estimation using multislice computed tomography reconstructions of the posterior pelvis. *Journal of Forensic Sciences* 54:773–778.

Bass, W. M. 2005. *Human Osteology*, 5th edn. Columbia, MO: Missouri Archaeological Society.

Belcastro, M. G., E. Rastelli, and V. Mariotti. 2008. Variation of the degree of sacral vertebral body fusion in adulthood in two European modern skeletal collections. *American Journal of Physical Anthropology* 135:149–160.

Berg, G. E. 2008. Pubic bone age estimation in adult women. *Journal of Forensic Sciences* 53:569–577.

Black, S. and L. Scheuer. 1996. Age changes in the clavicle from the early neonatal period to skeletal maturity. *International Journal of Osteoarchaeology* 6:425–434.

Blau, B. and D. H. Ubelaker. 2009a. Forensic anthropology and archaeology: Introduction to a broader view. In *Handbook of Forensic Anthropology and Archaeology*, D. H. Ubelaker and S. Blau (Eds.). Walnut Creek, CA: Left Coast Press, pp. 21–25.

Blau, S. and D. H. Ubelaker. 2009b. *Handbook of Forensic Anthropology and Archaeology*. World Archaeology Congress Research Handbooks in Archaeology. Walnut Creek, CA: Left Coast Press.

Bocquet-Appel, J.-P. 1986. Once upon a time: Paleodemography. *Mitteilungen der Berliner Gesellschaft für Anthropologie, Ethnologie und Urgeschichte* 7:127–133.

Bocquet-Appel J.-P. and C. Masset. 1982. Farewell to paleodemography. *Journal of Human Evolution* 11:321–333.

Bocquet-Appel J.-P. and C. Masset. 1985. Paleodemography: Resurrection or ghost? *Journal of Human Evolution* 14:107–111.

Boldsen, J. L., G. R. Milner, L. W. Konigsberg, and J. W. Wood. 2002. Transition analyses: A new method for estimating age from skeletons. In *Paleodemography: Age Distributions from Skeletal Samples*, R. D. Hoppa and J. W. Vaupel (Eds.). Cambridge, NY: Cambridge University Press, pp. 73–106.

Brooks, S. T. 1955. Skeletal age at death: The reliability of cranial and pubic age indicators. *American Journal of Physical Anthropology* 13:567–597.

Brooks, S. and J. M. Suchey. 1990. Skeletal age determination based on the os pubis: A comparison of the Acsádi-Nemeskéri and Suchey-Brooks methods. *Human Evolution* 5:227–238.

Brothwell, D. 1989. The relationship of tooth wear to aging. In *Age Markers in the Human Skeleton*, M. Y. Iscan (Ed.). Springfield, MA: Charles C. Thomas, pp. 303–316.

Bryant, L. J. and J. D. Pearson. 1994. Modeling the variability in longitudinal patterns of aging. In *Biological Anthropology and Aging. Perspectives on Human Variation over the Lifespan*, D.E. Crews and R.M. Garruto (Eds.). Oxford, NY: Oxford University Press, pp. 373–393.

Buck, T. J. and U. Strand Vidarsdóttir. 2004. A proposed method for the identification of race in sub-adult skeletons: A geometric morphometric analysis of mandibular morphology. *Journal of Forensic Sciences* 49:1159–1164.

Buckberry, J. L. and A. T. Chamberlain. 2002. Age estimation from the auricular surface of the ilium: A revised method. *American Journal of Physical Anthropology* 119:231–239.

Buikstra, J. E. 1977. Biocultural Dimensions of Archaeological Study: A Regional Perspective. In *Biocultural Adaptation in Prehistoric America*, R. L. Blakely (Ed.). Athens, Greece: University of Georgia Press, pp. 67–84.

Buikstra, J. E, G. R. Milner, and J. L. Boldsen. 2006. Janaab' Pakal: The age-at-death controversy re-revisited. In *Janaab' Pakal of Palenque: Reconstructing the Life and Death of a Maya Ruler*, V. Tiesler and A. Cucina (Eds.). Tucson, AZ: University of Arizona Press, pp. 48–59.

Buikstra, J. E. and D. H. Ubelaker. 1994. *Standards for the Data Collection from Human Skeletal Remains*. Research Series 44. Fayetteville, NC: Arkansas Archeological Survey.

Byers, S. 2005. *Introduction to Forensic Anthropology: A Textbook*. Boston, MA: Allyn & Bacon Publishers.

Cardoso, H. F. V. 2008. Sample-specific (universal) approaches for determining the sex of immature human skeletal remains using permanent tooth dimensions. *Journal of Archaeological Science* 35:158–168.

Cardoso, H. F. V. and C. Padez. 2008. Changes in height, weight, BMI and in the prevalence of obesity among 9 to 11 year-old affluent Portuguese schoolboys, between 1960 and 2000. *Annals of Human Biology* 35:624–638.

Cardoso, H. F. V. and S. R. Saunders. 2008. Two arch criteria of the ilium for sex determination of immature skeletal remains: A test of their accuracy and an assessment of intra- and inter-observer error. *Forensic Science International* 178:24–29.

Chaillet, N., M. Nystrom, and A. Demirjian. 2005. Comparison of dental maturity in children of different ethnic origins: International maturity curves for clinicians. *Journal of Forensic Sciences* 50:1164–1172.

Christensen, A. M. 2004. The impact of Daubert: Implications for testimony and research in forensic anthropology (and the use of frontal sinuses in personal identification). *Journal of Forensic Sciences* 49:427–430.

Christensen, A. M. 2005. Testing the reliability of frontal sinuses in positive identification. *Journal of Forensic Sciences* 50:18–22.

Clark, J. D. G. 1972. *Star Carr: A Case Study in Bioarchaeology*. Reading, MA: Addison Wesley.

Cope, Z. 1946. Fusion lines of bones. *Journal of Anatomy* 25:280–281.

Crowder, C. and D. Austin. 2005. Age ranges of epiphyseal fusion in the distal tibia and fibula of contemporary males and females. *Journal of Forensic Sciences* 50:1001–1007.

Daubert v. Merrell Dow Pharmaceuticals, 113 S.Ct. 2786; 1993 U.S. LEXIS 4408.

Dedouit, F., S. Bindel, D. Gainza et al. 2008. Application of the Iscan method to two- and three-dimensional imaging of the sternal end of the right fourth rib. *Journal of Forensic Sciences* 53:288–295.

Demirjian, A. 1978. Dentition. In *Human Growth*, Vol. 2, F. Falkner and J. Tanner (Eds.). New York: Plenum Press, pp. 413–44.

Demirjian, A. 1990. Dentition. In *Human Growth: A Comprehensive Treatise*, Vol. 2, F. Falkner and J. M. Tanner (Eds.). New York: Plenum, pp. 269–297.

Demirjian, A. and G. Y. Levesque. 1980. Sexual differences in dental development and prediction of emergence. *Journal of Dental Research* 59:1110–1122.

Di Bacco, M., V. Ardito, and E. Pacciani. 1999. Age-at-death diagnosis and age-at-death distribution estimate: Two different problems with many aspects in common. *International Journal of Anthropology* 14:161–169.

Digangi, E. A., J. D. Bethard, E. H. Kimmerle, and L. W. Konigsberg. 2009. A new method for estimating age-at-death from the first rib. *American Journal of Physical Anthropology* 138:164–176.

Enlow, D. H. 1996. *Essentials of Facial Growth*. Philadelphia, PA: W.B. Saunders Company.

Fazekas, I. and K. Kosa. 1978. *Forensic Fetal Osteology*, 1st edn. Budapest, Hungary: Akademiai Kiado Publishers.

Ferrant, O., C. Rougé-Maillart, L. Guittet et al. 2009. Age at death estimation of adult males using coxal bone and CT scan: A preliminary study. *Forensic Science International* 186:14–21.

Finch, C. E. 1994. *Longevity, Senescence, and the Genome*. Chicago, IL: University of Chicago Press.

Garmus, A. K. 1990. The determination of the age of an individual by the morphological signs of the *pubic* symphysis. *Sudebno-Meditsinskaia Ekspertiza* 33:22–24.

Garn, S. M., A. B. Lewis, and J. H. Vicinus. 1962. Third molar agenesis and reduction in the number of other teeth. *Journal of Dental Research* 41:717.

Gilbert, B. M. and T. W. McKern. 1973. A method for aging the female Os pubis. *American Journal of Physical Anthropology* 38:31–38.

Gowland, R. and A. Chamberlain. 1999. The use of prior probabilities in aging perinatal skeletal remains: Implications for the evidence of infanticide in Roman Britain. *American Journal of Physical Anthropology Supplement* 28:138–139.

Greulich, W. W. and S. I. Pyle. 1959. *Radiographic Atlas of Skeletal Development of the Hand and Wrist.* Stanford, CA: Stanford University Press.

Grivas, C. R. and D. A. Komar. 2008. Kumho, Daubert, and the nature of scientific inquiry: Implications for forensic anthropology. *Journal of Forensic Sciences* 53:771–776.

Gustafson, G. 1950. Age determination on teeth. *Journal of the American Dental Association* 41:45–54.

Haglund, W. D. and M. H. Sorg. 1997. *Forensic Taphonomy: The Postmortem Fate of Human Remains.* Boca Raton, FL: CRC Press.

Haglund, W. D. and M. H. Sorg. 2001. *Advances in Forensic Taphonomy: Method, Theory, and Archaeological Perspectives.* Boca Raton, FL: CRC Press.

Hanihara, K. and T. Suzuki. 1978. Estimation of age from the pubic symphysis by means of multiple regression analysis. *American Journal of Physical Anthropology* 48:233–240.

Harper, G. J. and D. E. Crews. 2000. Aging, senescence, and human variation. In *Human Biology: An Evolutionary and Biocultural Perspective*, S. Stinson, B. Borgan, R. Huss-Ashmore, and D. O'Rourke (Eds.). New York: Wiley-Liss, pp. 465–506.

Herrmann, N. P. and L. W. Konigsberg. 2002. A re-examination of the age-at-death distribution of Indian Knoll. In *Paleodemography: Age Distributions from Skeletal Samples*, R. D. Hoppa and J. Vaupel (Eds.). Cambridge, NY: Cambridge University Press, pp. 243–257.

Hillson S. 1998. *Dental Anthropology.* Cambridge, NY: Cambridge University Press.

Holcomb, S. M. C. and L. W. Konigsberg. 1995. A statistical study of sexual dimorphism in the human fetal sciatic notch. *American Journal of Physical Anthropology* 97:113–125.

Holman, D. J., J. W. Wood, and K. A. O'Connor. 2002. Estimating age-at-death distributions from skeletal samples: Multivariate latent-trait approach. In *Paleodemography: Age Distributions from Skeletal Samples*, R. D. Hoppa and J. W. Vaupel (Eds.). Cambridge, NY: Cambridge University Press, pp. 193–221.

Hoppa, R. D. 2000. Population variation in osteological aging criteria: An example from the pubic symphysis. *American Journal of Physical Anthropology* 111:185–191.

Hoppa, R. D. 2002. Paleodemography: Looking back and thinking ahead. In *Paleodemography: Age Distributions from Skeletal Samples*, R. D. Hoppa and J. W. Vaupel (Eds.). Cambridge, NY: Cambridge University Press, pp. 9–28.

Hoppa, R.D. and J. W. Vaupel. 2002a. *Paleodemography: Age Distributions from Skeletal Samples.* Cambridge, NY: Cambridge University Press.

Hoppa, R. D. and J. W. Vaupel. 2002b. The Rostock Manifesto for paleodemography: The way from stage to age. In *Paleodemography: Age Distributions from Skeletal Samples*, R. D. Hoppa and J. W. Vaupel (Eds.). Cambridge, NY: Cambridge University Press, pp. 1–8.

Houck, M. M., D. H. Ubelaker, D. W. Owsley et al. 1996.The role of forensic anthropology in the recovery and analysis of Branch Davidian compound victims: Assessing the accuracy of age estimations. *Journal of Forensic Sciences* 41:796–801.

Howell, N. 1976. Toward a uniformitarian theory of human paleodemography. In *The Demographic Evolution of Human Populations*, R. H. Ward and K. M. Weiss (Eds.). NewYork: Academic Press, pp. 25–40.

Howell, N. 1982. Village composition implied by a paleodemographic life table: The Libben site. *American Journal of Physical Anthropology* 59:263–269.

Iscan, M.Y. 1988. Rise of forensic anthropology. *Yearbook of Physical Anthropology* 31:203–230.

Iscan, M. Y. 1989. Assessment of age at death in the human skeleton. In *Age Markers in the Human Skeleton*, M. Y. Iscan (Ed.). Springfield, MA: Charles C. Thomas, pp. 5–18.

Iscan, M. Y. and S. R. Loth. 1989. Osteological manifestations of age in the adult. In *Reconstruction of Life from the Skeleton*, M. Y. Iscan and K. A. R. Kennedy (Eds.). New York: Alan R. Liss, pp. 23–40.

Iscan, M. Y., S. R. Loth, and R. K. Wright. 1984. Age estimation from the rib by phase analysis: White males. *Journal of Forensic Sciences* 29:1094–1104.

Iscan, M. Y., S. R. Loth, and R. K. Wright. 1985. Age estimation from the rib by phase analysis: White females. *Journal of Forensic Sciences* 30:853–863.

Jackes, M. 2000. Building the bases for paleodemographic analysis: Adult age determination. In *Biological Anthropology of the Human Skeleton*, A. M. Katzenberg and S.R. Saunders (Eds.). New York: Wiley-Liss, pp. 417–466.

Katz, D. and J. M. Suchey. 1986. Age determination of the male os pubis. *American Journal of Physical Anthropology* 69:427–435.

Katz, D. and J. M. Suchey. 1989. Race differences in pubic symphyseal aging patterns in the male. *American Journal of Physical Anthropology* 80:167–172.

Kemkes-Grottenthaler, A. 1996. Critical evaluation of osteomorphognostic methods to estimate adult age at death: A test of the "complex method." *Homo* 46:280–292.

Kemkes-Grottenthaler, A. 2002. Aging through the ages: Historical perspectives on age indicator methods. *Paleodemography: Age Distributions from Skeletal Samples*, R. D. Hoppa and J. W. Vaupel (Eds.). Cambridge, NY: Cambridge University Press, pp. 48–72.

Kerley, E. R. 1978. Recent developments in forensic anthropology. *Yearbook of Physical Anthropology* 20:160–173.

Key, C. A., L. C. Aiello, and T. Molleson. 1994. Cranial suture closure and its implications for age estimation. *International Journal of Osteoarchaeology* 4:193–207.

Kimmerle, E. H., R. L. Jantz, L. W. Konigsberg, and J. P. Baraybar. 2008a. Skeletal estimation and identification in American and East European populations. *Journal of Forensic Sciences* 53:524–532.

Kimmerle, E. H., L.W. Konigsberg, R. L. Jantz, and J. P. Baraybar. 2008b. Analysis of Age-at-death estimation through the use of pubic symphyseal data. *Journal of Forensic Sciences* 53:558–568.

Kimmerle, E. H., D. A. Prince, and G. E. Berg. 2008c. Inter-observer variation in methodologies involving the pubic symphysis, sternal ribs, and teeth. *Journal of Forensic Sciences* 53:594–600.

Klepinger, L. L. 2001. Stature, maturation, variation and secular trends in forensic anthropology. *Journal of Forensic Sciences* 46:788–790.

Klepinger, L. L. 2006. *Fundamentals of Forensic Anthropology*. Hoboken, NJ: Wiley-Liss.

Klepinger, L. L., D. Katz, M. S. Micozzi, and L. Carroll. 1992. Evaluation of cast methods for estimating age from the os pubis. *Journal of Forensic Sciences* 37:763–770.

Komar, D. and J. Buikstra. 2008. *Forensic Anthropology Contemporary Theory and Practice*. Oxford, NY: Oxford University Press.

Komar, D. and C. Grivas. 2008. Manufactured populations: What do contemporary reference skeletal collections represent? A comparative study using the Maxwell Museum Documented Collection. *American Journal of Physical Anthropology* 137:224–233.

Kongisberg, L. W., B. F. B. Algee-Hewitt, D. W. Steadman. 2009. Estimation and evidence in forensic anthropology. *Sex and Race* 139:77–90.

Konigsberg, L. W. and S. R. Frankenberg. 1992. Estimation of age structure in anthropological demography. *American Journal of Physical Anthropology* 89:235–256.

Konigsberg, L. W. and S. R. Frankenberg. 1994. Paleodemography: "Not quite dead." *Evolutionary Anthropology* 3:92–105.

Konigsberg, L. W. and S. R. Frankenberg. 2002. Deconstructing death in paleodemography. *American Journal of Physical Anthropology* 117:297–309.

Konigsberg, L. W., S. R. Frankenberg, and R. B. Walker. 1997. Regress what on what? Paleodemographic age estimation as a calibration problem. In *Integrating Archaeological Demography: Multidisciplinary Approaches to Prehistoric Population*, R. R. Paine (Ed.). Carbondale, IL: Southern Illinois University Press, pp. 64–88.

Konigsberg, L. W., S. M. Hens, L. M. Jantz, and W. L. Jungers. 1998. Stature estimation and calibration: Bayesian and maximum likelihood perspectives in physical anthropology. *Yearbook of Physical Anthropology* 41:65–92.

Konigsberg, L. W. and N. P. Herrmann. 2002. Markov chain Monte Carlo estimation of hazard model parameters in paleodemography. In *Paleodemography: Age Distributions from Skeletal Samples*, R. D. Hoppa and J. W. Vaupel (Eds.). Cambridge, NY: Cambridge University Press, pp. 222–242.

Konigsberg, L. W., N. P. Herrmann, D. J. Wescott, and E. H. Kimmerle. 2008. Estimation and evidence in forensic anthropology: Age-at-death. *Journal of Forensic Sciences* 53:541–557.

Kunos, C. A., S. W. Simpson, K. F. Russell, and I. Hershkovitz, 1999. First rib metamorphosis: Its possible utility for human age-at-death estimation. *American Journal of Physical Anthropology* 110:303–323.

Lamendin, H., E. Baccino, J. F. Humbert, J. C. Tavernier, R. M. Nossintchouk, and A. Zerilli. 1992. A simple technique for age estimation in adult corpses: The two criteria dental method. *Journal of Forensic Sciences* 37:1373–1379.

Larsen, C. S. 1997. *Bioarchaeology: Interpreting Behavior from the Human Skeleton*. Cambridge Studies in Biological Anthropology 21. Cambridge, NY: Cambridge University Press.

Lewis, M. and A. Flavel. 2006. Age assessment of child skeletal remains in forensic contexts. In *Forensic Anthropology and Medicine: Complementary Sciences from Recovery to Cause of Death*, A. Schmitt, E. Cunha, and J. Pinheiro (Eds.). Totowa, NJ: Humana Press, pp. 243–257.

Loth, S. R. and M. Y. Iscan. 1989. Morphological assessment of age in the adult: The thoracic region. In *Age Markers in the Human Skeleton*, M. Y. Iscan (Ed.). Springfield, MA: Charles C. Thomas, pp. 105–136.

Love B. and H.-G. Müller. 2002. A solution to the problem of obtaining a mortality schedule for paleodemographic data. In *Paleodemography: Age Distributions from Skeletal Samples*, R. D. Hoppa and J. Vaupel (Eds.). Cambridge, NY: Cambridge University Press, pp. 73–106.

Lovejoy, C. O., R. S. Meindl, R. P. Mensforth, and T. J. Barton. 1985a. Multifactorial determination of skeletal age at death: A method and blind test of its accuracy. *American Journal of Physical Anthropology* 68:1–14.

Lovejoy, C. O., R. S. Meindl, T. R. Pryzbeck, and R. P. Mensforth. 1985b. Chronological metamorphosis of the auricular surface of the ilium: A new method for the determination of adult skeletal age at death. *American Journal of Physical Anthropology* 68:15–28.

Lovejoy, C. O., R. S. Meindl, T. R. Pryzbeck, R. P. Mensforth, T. J. Barton, K. G. Heiple, and D. Kotting. 1977. Paleodemography of the Libben site, Ottawa County, Ohio. *Science* 198:291–293.

Lovejoy, C. O., R. S. Meindl, R. G. Tague, and B. Latimer. 1997. The comparative senescent biology of the human pelvis and its implications for the use of age-at-death indicators in the human skeleton. In *Integrating Anthropological Demography: Multidisciplinary Approaches to Prehistoric Population*, R. Paine (Ed.). Carbondale, IL: Center for Archaeological Investigations, pp. 43–63.

Lovejoy, C., C. Owen, R. P. Mensforth, and G. J. Armelagos. 1982. Five decades of skeletal biology as reflected in the American journal of physical anthropology. In *A History of American Physical Anthropology* 1930–1980, F. Spencer (Ed.). New York: Academic Press, pp. 329–336.

Lucy, D., R. G. Aykroyd, A. M. Pollard, and T. Solheim. 1996. A Bayesian approach to adult human age estimation from dental observations by Johanson's age changes. *Journal of Forensic Sciences* 41:189–194.

Lucy, D. and A. M. Pollard. 1995. Further comments on the estimation of error associated with the Gustafson dental age estimation method. *Journal of Forensic Sciences* 40:222–227.

Lynnerup, N., J. L. Thomsen, and B. Frohlich. 1998. Intra- and inter-observer variation in histological criteria used in age at death determination based on femoral cortical bone. *Forensic Science International* 91:219–230.

Mann, R. W., R. L. Jantz, W. M. Bass, and P. S. Willey. 1991. Maxillary suture obliteration: A visual method for estimating skeletal age. *Journal of Forensic Sciences* 36:781–791.

Mann, R. W., S. A. Symes, and W. M. Bass. 1987. Maxillary suture obliteration: Aging the human skeleton based on intact or fragmentary maxilla. *Journal of Forensic Sciences* 32:148–157.

Maples, W. R. 1989. The practical application of age estimation techniques. In *Age Markers in the Human Skeleton*, M. Y. Iscan (Ed.). Springfield, MA: Charles C. Thomas, pp. 319–324.

Marks, M. K., K. Marden, and D. Mileusnic-Polchan. 2009. Forensic osteology of child abuse. In *Hard Evidence: Case Studies in Physical Anthropology,* 2nd edn. D. W. Steadman (Ed.). Upper Saddle River, NJ: Prentice Hall, pp. 205–220.

Masset, C. 1989. Age estimation on the basis of cranial sutures. In *Age Markers in the Human Skeleton*, M. Y. Iscan (Ed.). Springfield, MA: Charles C. Thomas, pp. 71–103.

Mays, S. 1998. *The Archaeology of Human Bones*. New York: Routledge.

McKern, T. W. 1957. Estimation of skeletal age from combined maturational activity. *American Journal of Physical Anthropology* 15:399–408.

McKern, T. and T. Stewart. 1957. Skeletal age changes in young American males. Technical Report EP-45. Natick, MA: Headquarters, Quartermaster Research and Development Center, Environment Protection Research Division.

Meindl, R. S. and C. O. Lovejoy. 1985. Ectocranial suture closure. A revised method for the determination of skeletal age at death based on the lateral-anterior sutures. *American Journal of Physical Anthropology* 68:57–66.

Meindl, R. S. and C. O. Lovejoy. 1989. Age changes in the pelvis: Implications for paleodemography. In *Age Markers in the Human Skeleton*, M. Y. Iscan (Ed.). Springfield, MA: Charles C. Thomas, pp. 137–168.

Meindl, R. S., C. O. Lovejoy, R. P. Mensforth, and R. A. Walker. 1985. Revised method of age determination using the os pubis, with a review and tests of other current methods of pubic symphyseal aging. *American Journal of Physical Anthropology* 68:29–45.

Meindl, R. S. and K. F. Russell. 1998. Recent advances in method and theory in paleodemography. *Annual Review of Anthropology* 27:375–399.

Meindl R. S., K. F. Russell, and C. O. Lovejoy. 1990. Reliability of age at death in the Hamann Todd Collection: Validity of subselection procedures used in blind tests of the summary age technique. *American Journal of Physical Anthropology* 83:349–357.

Miles, A. E. W. 1962. Assessment of the ages of a population of Anglo-Saxons from their dentitions. *Proceedings of the Royal Society of Medicine* 55:881–886.

Miles, A. E. W. 1963. Dentition and the estimation of age. *Journal of Dental Research* 42:255–263.

Miles, A. E. W. 1978. Teeth as an indicator of age in man. In *Development, Function and the Evolution of Teeth*, P. M. Butler and K. A. Joysey (Eds.). London, U.K.: Academic Press, pp. 455–462.

Milner, G. R. and J. L. Boldsen. 2008. *Transition Analysis Age Estimation Skeletal Scoring Procedure*, 7.v.07.

Milner, G. R. and J. E. Buikstra. 2006. Skeletal biology: Northeast. In *Handbook of North American Indians: Environment, Origins, and Population,* Vol. 3, D. H. Ubelaker (Ed.). Washington, DC: Smithsonian Institution Press, pp. 630–639.

Milner, G. R., J. W. Wood, and J. L. Boldsen. 2008. Advances in paleodemography. In *Biological Anthropology of the Human Skeleton*, 2nd edn. M. A. Katzenberg and S. R. Saunders (Eds.). New York: Wiley-Liss, pp. 561–600.

Mincer, H. H., E. F. Harris, and H. E. Berryman. 1993. A.B.F.O. study of third molar development and its use as an estimator of chronological age. *Journal of Forensic Sciences* 38:379–390.

Molleson, T. and M. Cox. 1993. The spitalfields project, Vol. 2. In *The Middling Sort*. York, U.K.: Council for British Archaeology.

Molnar, S. 1971. Human tooth wear, tooth function and cultural variability. *American Journal of Physical Anthropology* 34:175–190.

Moore-Jansen, P. M., S. D. Ousley, and R. L. Jantz. 1994. Data Collection Procedures for Forensic Skeletal Material. Report of Investigations 48. Knoxville, TN: Department of Anthropology, University of Tennessee.

Moorrees, C. F. A., E. A. Fanning, and E. E. Hunt. 1963a. Formation and resorption of three deciduous teeth in children. *American Journal of Physical Anthropology* 21:205–213.

Moorrees, C. F. A., E. A. Fanning, and E. E. Hunt. 1963b. Age variation of formation stages for ten permanent teeth. *Journal of Dental Research* 42:1490–1502.

Moss, M. L. 1968. A theoretical analysis of the functional matrix. *Acta Biotheoretica* 18:1–4.

Moss, M. L. and R. W. Young. 1960. A functional approach to craniology. *American Journal of Physical Anthropology* 18:281–292.

Müller, H. G., B. Love, and R. D. Hoppa. 2002. A semiparametric method for estimating demographic profiles from age indicator data. *American Journal of Physical Anthropology* 117:1–14.

NamUS (National Missing and Unidentified Persons System). 2010. U.S. Department of Justice. www.namus.gov

Nawrocki, S. P. 1998. Regression formulae for estimating age at death from cranial suture closure. In *Forensic Osteology: Advances in the Identification of Human Remains,* 2nd edn., K. J. Reichs (Ed.). Springfield, MA: Charles C. Thomas, pp. 276–292.

Osborne, D. L., T. L. Simmons, and S. Nawrocki. 2004. Reconsidering the auricular surface as an indicator of age at death. *Journal of Forensic Sciences* 49:1–7.

Ousley, S. D. and R. L. Jantz. 1998. The forensic data bank: Documenting skeletal trends in the United States. In *Forensic Osteology,* 2nd edn., K. J, Reichs (Ed.). Springfield, MA: Charles C. Thomas, pp. 441–458.

Paine, R. R. and J. L. Boldsen. 2002. Linking age-at-death distributions and ancient population dynamics: A case study. In *Paleodemography: Age Distributions from Skeletal Samples*, R. D. Hoppa and J. W. Vaupel (Eds.). Cambridge, NY: Cambridge University Press, pp. 169–180.

Prince, D. A., E. H. Kimmerle, and L. W. Kongisberg. 2008. A Bayesian approach to estimate skeletal age-at-death utilizing dental wear. *Journal of Forensic Sciences* 53:588–593.

Prince, D. A. and L. W. Konigsberg. 2008. New formulae for estimating age-at-death in the Balkans utilizing Lamendin's dental technique and Bayesian analysis. *Journal of Forensic Science* 53:578–587.

Prince D. A. and D. H. Ubelaker. 2002. Application of Lamendin's adult dental aging technique to a diverse skeletal sample. *Journal of Forensic Sciences* 47:107–116.

Reichs, K. J. 1995. A professional profile of diplomates of the American board of forensic anthropology: 1984–1992. *Journal of Forensic Sciences* 40:176–182.

Reichs, K. J. 1998. Forensic anthropology: A decade of progress. In *Forensic Osteology: Advances in the Identification of Human Remains*, K. J. Reichs (Ed.). Springfield, MA: Charles C. Thomas, pp. 13–38.

Rissech, C., G. F. Estabrook, E. Cunha, and A. Malgosa. 2006. Using the acetabulum to estimate age at death of adult males. *Journal of Forensic Sciences* 51:213–229.

Rissech, C., G. F. Estabrook, E. Cunha, and A. Malgosa. 2007. Estimation of age at death for adult males using the acetabulum, applied to four Western European populations. *Journal Forensic Sciences* 52:774–779.

Ritz-Timme, S., C. Cattaneo, and M. J. Collins. 2000. Age estimation: The state of the art in relation to the specific demands of forensic practice. *International Journal of Legal Medicine* 113:129–136.

Robling, A. G. and S. D. Stout. 2008. Methods of determining age at death using bone microstructure. In *Biological Anthropology of the Human Skeleton,* 2nd edn., M. A. Katzenberg and S. R. Saunders (Eds.). New York: Wiley-Liss, pp. 149–171.

Rodgers T. and T. Allard. 2004. Expert testimony and positive identification of human remains through cranial suture patterns. *Journal of Forensic Sciences* 49:203–207.

Rois, L., K. E. Weisensee, and C. Rissech. 2008. Sacral fusion as an aid in age estimation. *Forensic Science International* 180:111–117.

Rösing, F. W., M. Graw, B. Marré et al. 2007. Recommendations for the forensic diagnosis of sex and age from skeletons. *Homo* 58:75–89.

Rouge-Maillart, C., N. Jousset, B. Vielle, A. Gaudin, and N. Telmon. 2007. Contribution of the study of acetabulum for the estimation of adult subjects. *Forensic Science International* 171:103–110.

Ruff, C. B. 1981. A reassessment of demographic estimates for Pecos Pueblo. *American Journal of Physical Anthropology* 54:147–151.

Sapir, G. I. 2002. Legal aspects of forensic science. In *Forensic Science Handbook*, Vol. I, 2nd edn., R. Saferstein (Ed.). Upper Saddle River, NJ: Prentice Hall, pp. 2–24.

Sashin, D. 1930. A critical analysis of the anatomy and the pathological changes of the sacro-iliac joints. *Journal of Bone and Joint Surgery* 28:891–910.

Saunders, S. R. 2000. Subadult skeletons and growth related studies. In *Biological Anthropology of the Human Skeleton,* M. A. Katzenberg and S. R. Saunders (Eds.). New York: Wiley, pp. 135–161.

Saunders, S. R., C. Fitzgerald, T. Rogers, J. C. Dudar, and H. McKillop. 1992. A test of several methods of skeletal age estimation using a documented archaeological sample. *Canadian Society of Forensic Science Journal* 25:97–118.

Schaefer, M. C. and S. M. Black. 2005. Comparison of ages of epiphyseal union in North American and Bosnian skeletal material. *Journal of Forensic Sciences* 50:777–784.

Scheuer, L. and S. Black. 2000. *Developmental Juvenile Osteology*. London, U.K.: Academic Press.

Scheuer, L. and S. Black. 2004. *The Juvenile Skeleton*. London, U.K.: Elsevier.

Schmitt, A. 2004. Age-at-death assessment using the os pubis and the auricular surface of the ilium: A test on an identified Asian sample. *International Journal of Osteoarchaeology* 14:1–6.

Schmitt, A. and C. Broqua. 2000. Application pratique de la méthode d'estimation de l'âge au décès de *Schmitt* et *Broqua. Bulletin Memoires Society Anthropology* 16:115–120.

Schmitt, A., E. Cunha, and J. Pinheiro (Eds.). 2006. *Forensic Anthropology and Medicine: Complementary Sciences from Recovery to Cause of Death*. Totowa, NJ: Humana.

Schmitt, A., P. Murail, E. Cunha, and D. Rougé. 2002. Variability of the pattern of aging on the human skeleton: Evidence from bone indicators and implications on age at death estimation. *Journal of Forensic Sciences* 47:1–7.

Schour, I. and M. Massler. 1941. The development of the human dentition. *Journal of the American Dental Association* 28:1153–1160.

Scientific Working Group for Forensic Anthropology (SWGANTH). 2010. Homepage: www.swganth.org

Shirley, N. R., B. F. B. Algee-Hewitt, and R. J. Wilson. 2010. The reality of aging virtually: A test of transition analysis on pelvic laser scans. Paper presented at the *Annual Meeting of the American Academy of Physical Anthropologists*, Albuquerque, NM.

Shirley-Langley, N. and R. L. Jantz. 2010. A Bayesian approach to age estimation in modern Americans from the clavicle. *Journal of Forensic Sciences* 55:571–583.

Singer, R. 1953. Estimation of age from cranial suture closure. *Journal of Forensic Medicine* 1:52–59.

Smith, B. H. 1984a. Patterns of molar wear in hunter-gatherers and agriculturalists. *American Journal of Physical Anthropology* 63:39–56.

Smith, B. H. 1984b. Rate of molar wear: Implications for developmental timing and demography in human evolution. *American Journal of Physical Anthropology* 63:220.

Smith, B. H. 1991. Standards of human tooth formation and dental age assessment. In *Advances in Dental Anthropology*, M. Kelly and C. Larsen (Eds.). New York: Wiley-Liss, pp. 143–168.

Snow C. C. 1982. Forensic anthropology. *Annual Review of Anthropology* 11:97–131.

Snow C. C. 1983. Equations for estimating age at death from the pubic symphysis: A modification of the McKern-Stewart method. *Journal of Forensic Sciences* 28:864–870.

Steadman, D. W. (Ed.). 2009. *Hard Evidence: Case Studies in Forensic Anthropology*, 2nd edn. Upper Saddle River, NJ: Prentice Hall.

Steadman, D. W., B. Adams, and L. Konigsberg. 2006. The statistical basis for positive identifications in forensic anthropology. *American Journal of Physical Anthropology* 131:15–26.

Stevenson, P. 1924. Age order of epiphyseal union in man. *American Journal of Physical Anthropology* 7:53–93.

Stewart, T. D. 1979. *Essentials of Forensic Anthropology: Especially as Developed in the United States.* Springfield, MA: Charles C. Thomas.

Stout, S. D. 2009. Small bones of contention. In *Hard Evidence: Case Studies in Physical Anthropology,* 2nd edn. D. W. Steadman (Ed.). Upper Saddle River, NJ: Prentice Hall, pp. 239–247.

Suchey, J. M. and D. Katz. 1986. Skeletal age standards derived from an extensive multiracial sample of modern Americans. Paper presented at the *Fifty-Fifth Annual Meeting of the American Association of Physical Anthropologists*, Albuquerque, NM.

Suchey, J. M. and D. Katz. 1998. Applications of pubic age determination in a forensic setting. In *Forensic Osteology: Advances in the Identification of Human Remains,* 2nd edn., K. J. Reichs (Ed.), Springfield, MA: Charles C. Thomas, pp. 204–236.

Suchey, J. M., D. V. Wiseley, and D. Katz. 1986. Evaluation of the Todd and McKern-Stewart methods for aging the male os pubis. In *Forensic Osteology: Advances in the Identification of Human Remains*, K. J. Reichs (Ed.). Springfield, MA: Charles C. Thomas, pp. 33–67.

Tanner, J., R. M. Healy, H. Goldstein, and N. Cameron. 2001. *Assessment of Skeletal Maturity and Prediction of Adult Height (TW3 Method).* London, U.K.: W. B. Saunders.

Tanner, J., R. Whitehouse, N. Cameron, W. Marshall, M. Healy, and H. Goldstein. 1975. *Assessment of Skeletal Maturity and Prediction of Adult Height (TW2 Method)*, 2nd edn. London, U.K.: Academic Press.

Todd, T. W. 1920. Age changes in the pubic bones. I. The male white pubis. *American Journal of Physical Anthropology* 3:285–334.

Todd, T. W. 1921a. Age changes in the pubic bones. II. The pubis of the male Negro-white hybrid. II. The pubis of the white female IV. The pubis of the female Negro-white hybrid. *American Journal of Physical Anthropology* 4:4–70.

Todd, T. W. 1921b. Age changes in the pubic bones. V. Mammalian pubic bone metamorphosis. *American Journal of Physical Anthropology* 4:333–406.

Todd, T. W. 1921c. Age changes in the pubic bones. V. The interpretation of variations in the symphyseal area. *American Journal of Physical Anthropology* 4:407–424.

Todd, T. W. 1923. Age changes in the pubic bones. VII. The anthropoid strain in human pubic symphysis of the third decade. *Journal of Anatomy* 57:274–294.

Todd, T. W. 1930. Age changes in the pubic bones. VII. Roentgenographic differentiation. *American Journal of Physical Anthropology* 14:255–271.

Todd, T. and J. D'Errico. 1928. The clavicular epiphyses. *American Journal of Anatomy* 41:25–50.

Todd, T. W. and D. W. Lyon. 1924. Endocranial suture closure: Part I. Adult males of white stock. *American Journal of Physical Anthropology* 7:325–384.

Tomkins, R. L. 1996. Human population variability in relative dental development. *American Journal of Physical Anthropology* 99:79–102.

Ubelaker, D. H. 1987. Estimating age at death from immature human skeletons: An overview. *Journal of Forensic Sciences* 23:1254–1263.

Ubelaker, D. H. 1989a. *Human Skeletal Remains: Excavation, Analysis, Interpretation,* 2nd edn. Washington, DC: Taraxacum.

Ubelaker, D. H. 1989b. The estimation of age at death from immature human bone. In *Age Markers in the Human Skeleton*, M. Y. Iscan (Ed.). Springfield, MA: Charles C. Thomas, pp. 55–69.

Ubelaker, D. H. 2008. Issues in the global applications in methodology of forensic anthropology. *Journal of Forensic Sciences* 53:606–607.

Ubelaker, D. H. 2009. Historical development of forensic anthropology: Perspective from the United States. In *Handbook of Forensic Anthropology and Archaeology*, D. Ubelaker and S. Blau (Eds.). Walnut Creek, CA: Left Coast Press, pp. 76–86.

Usher, B. 2002. Reference samples: The first step in linking biology and age in the human skeleton. In *Paleodemography: Age Distributions from Skeletal Samples*, R. Hoppa and J. Vaupel (Eds.). London, U.K.: Cambridge University Press, pp. 29–47.

Usher, B. M., J. L. Boldsen, and D. Holman. 2000. Age estimation at Tirup cemetery: An application of the transition analysis method. *American Journal of Physical Anthropology Supplement* 30:307.

Waldron, T. 1987. The relative survival of the human skeleton: Implications for paleodemography. In *Death, Decay, and Reconstruction: Approaches to Archaeology and Forensic Science*, A. Boddington, A. N. Garland, and R. C. Janeway (Eds.). Manchester, U.K.: Manchester University Press, pp. 55–64.

Waldron T. 1994. *Counting the Dead: The Epidemiology of Skeletal Populations*. New York: John Wiley & Sons.

Walker, P. L., J. Johnson, and P. Lambert. 1988. Age and sex biases in the preservation of human skeletal remains. *American Journal of Physical Anthropology* 76:183–188.

Warren, M. W. 1999. Radiographic determination of developmental age in fetuses and stillborns. *Journal of Forensic Sciences* 44:708–712.

Washburn, S. L. 1951. The new physical anthropology. *Transactions of the New York Academy of Science, Series II* 13:298–304.

Washburn, S. L. 1953a. The new physical anthropology. *Yearbook of Physical Anthropology* 7:124–130.

Washburn, S. L. 1953b. The strategy of physical anthropology. In *Anthropology Today*, A. L. Kroeber (Ed.). Chicago, IL: University of Chicago Press, pp. 714–727.

Web of Science. 2010. *ISI Web of Knowledge*. Thomson Reuters: apps.isiknowledge.com

Webb, P. and J. Suchey. 1985. Epiphyseal union of the anterior iliac crest and medial clavicle in a modern multiracial sample of American males and females. *American Journal of Physical Anthropology* 68:457–466.

Weinker, C. and S. Rhine. 1989. A professional profile of the physical anthropology section membership. American Academy of Forensic Sciences. *Journal of Forensic Sciences* 34:12.

White, T. and P. Folkens. 2005. *The Human Bone Manual*. New York: Elsevier.

Wiersema, J., J. C. Love, and L. G. Naul. 2009. The influence of the Daubert guidelines of anthropological methods of scientific identification in the medical examiner setting. In *Hard Evidence: Case Studies in Forensic Anthropology*, 2nd edn., D. W. Steadman (Ed.). Upper Saddle River, NJ: Prentice Hall, pp. 80–90.

Wilson, R. J. and B. F. B. Algee-Hewitt. 2009. [Inter]facing age: A test of the ADBOU age estimation software in a forensic context. Paper presented at the *Annual Meeting of the American Academy of Physical Anthropologists*, Chicago, IL.

Wilson, R. J., B. F. B. Algee-Hewitt, and L. M. Jantz. 2007. Demographic trends within the Forensic Anthropology Center's body donation program. Paper presented at the *Annual Meeting of the American Academy of Physical Anthropologists*, Philadelphia, PA.

Wilson, R. J., B. F. B. Algee-Hewitt, and L. M. Jantz. 2008. Age-at-death distributions in the W.M. Bass Donated Skeletal Collection, Part II: Modeling mortality in a Body Donation Program. Paper presented at the *Annual Meeting of the American Academy of Physical Anthropologists*, Columbus, OH.

Wood, J. W., G. R. Milner, H. C. Harpending, and K. M. Weiss. 1992. The osteological paradox: Problems of inferring prehistoric health from skeletal samples. *Current Anthropology* 33:343–370.

Workshop of European Anthropologists. 1980. Recommendations for age and sex diagnoses of skeletons. *Journal of Human Evolution* 9:517–549.

Yoder, C., D. H. Ubelaker, and J. F. Powell. 2001. Examination of variation in sternal rib end morphology relevant to age assessment. *Journal of Forensic Sciences* 46:223–227.

Zhang, Z. 1982. A preliminary study of estimation of age by morphological changes in the symphysis pubis. *Acta Anthropologica Sinica* 1:132–136.

Zollikofer, C. P. E. and M. S. Ponce de León. 2005. *Virtual Reconstruction: A Primer in Computer-Assisted Paleontology and Biomedicine*. New York: Wiley.

Why Do Forensic Anthropologists Estimate Ancestry, and Why Is It So Controversial?

11

M. KATHERINE SPRADLEY AND KATHERINE WEISENSEE

Contents

Introduction

Forensic anthropology is a young discipline that has its roots in biological anthropology. The establishment of forensic anthropology in the United States can be traced back to Ales Hrdlicka working at the Smithsonian Institution's National Museum of Natural History (NMNH) (Ubelaker 1999). At the time Hrdlicka worked at the NMNH, the FBI headquarters was located across the street, and Hrdlicka consulted on a variety of medicolegal cases (Ubelaker 1999). Forensic anthropology has changed considerably since its beginnings in Washington D.C. Dirkmaat et al. (2008) suggested that the incorporation of forensic archaeology, forensic taphonomy, forensic trauma analysis, and the widespread use of quantitative methods has created a paradigm shift within the field. Early practitioners drew from their general knowledge of human skeletal variation in past and present populations to provide law enforcement with information about the biological profile. Today, however, forensic anthropologists generate original research geared toward a forensic application. Forensic anthropologists may focus their research efforts and expertise in any number of areas within the field (i.e., biological profile, human decomposition, and skeletal trauma). Even with this paradigm shift, the biological profile (estimation of ancestry, sex, age, and stature) is still a key element of the forensic anthropological assessment of remains and usually the one of the first topics learned by students in a forensic anthropology course (Box 11.1).

Of all the components of the biological profile, ancestry estimation is the most controversial. Some critics suggest that because biological races do not exist, estimating race

BOX 11.1 FORENSIC ANTHROPOLOGY DATA BANK

FDB demographics*

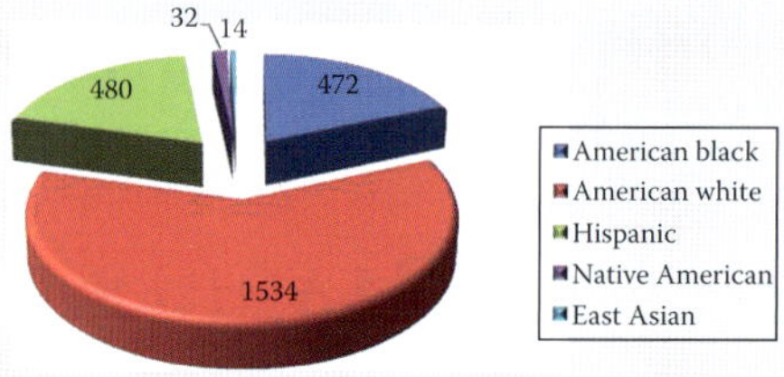

The Forensic Anthropology Data Bank (FDB) was started in 1986 by Dr. Richard L. Jantz with a grant from the National Institute of Justice. The concept for the FDB was discussed in a meeting among members of the physical anthropology section of the American Academy of Forensic Sciences. In attendance was Dr. Clyde Snow who discussed the fact that when forensic anthropologists positively identify an individual, the remains are given back to the family. Dr. Snow and others suggested that a system should be in place for forensic anthropologists to collect and submit data to a central repository so that information could be archived and used for research.

It was Dr. Richard L. Jantz that applied for and received funding from the National Institute of Justice to start the FDB. In the early years of the FDB, Dr. Jantz and his graduate students traveled to skeletal collections in the United States to collect data for the FDB. Dr. Lawrence Angel's forensic case reports were also obtained and input into the FDB. Currently, over 100 laboratories submit data to the FDB. However, the University of Tennessee still remains the largest contributor due to the efforts of Dr. Jantz training his students and sending them out to collect data. Additionally, data obtained from the William M. Bass donated skeletal collection, curated at The University of Tennessee, now numbering over 800 individuals, were also entered into the FDB.

The importance of the FDB cannot be overstated. It is an archive of the cases seen around the country by forensic anthropologists. It also generates reference samples for methods of sex, age, ancestry, and stature estimation. It serves as the forensic reference sample in the program FORDISC 3.1. The FDB is unique because the majority of cases in it are derived from forensic anthropology cases and then it is applied to forensic cases (e.g., analyzing skeletal remains in FORDISC 3.1). Further, the FDB is reflective of the U.S. population demographics. According to the U.S. Census Bureau, the three largest population groups in the United States are White, Hispanic, and Black, the three largest population groups in the FDB.

The FDB depends on submissions from forensic anthropologists around the country in order to continue growth. According to Dr. Jantz, "the population is a moving target, and like daily weather reporting requires continued updating" (2007 personal communication). Fortunately, submissions to the FDB allow forensic anthropologists access to data from recent skeletal remains.

To download a copy of the FDB, visit the Inter University Consortium for Political and Social Research (ICPSR) http://www.icpsr.umich.edu/icpsrweb/ICPSR/ and search for forensic anthropology.

For more information on the FDB, visit http://web.utk.edu/~fac/databank.html

*Data are from positively identified individuals only, with the exception of the Hispanic category.

The Hispanic individuals are largely contextually identified from U.S./Mexico border-crossing fatalities.

is not useful and is a practice that reverts back to nineteenth-century typology, thus reinforcing racial typology (Armelagos and van Gerven 2003; Armelagos and Goodman 1998; Smay and Armelagos 2000). In order to address these criticisms, this chapter will focus on three key questions:

1. Why do forensic anthropologists estimate ancestry?
2. How are they able to estimate ancestry?
3. Why is this topic controversial?

Why Do Forensic Anthropologists Estimate Ancestry?

Searching for Missing Individuals

When unknown human remains are found, the forensic anthropologist creates a biological profile that includes information on ancestry, sex, age, and stature, the same categories in a missing persons report. It is this information that is used to search through missing person's databases to find a potential match. The biological profile is important because it helps narrow the search of an unidentified individual. For example, when a forensic anthropologist examines a case for law enforcement, a biological profile along with any individualizing characteristics (e.g., description of dental restorations, healed antemortem trauma, surgical appliances) is provided to begin a search through missing person's records. When an individual goes missing, a family will usually fill out a missing person's report that includes information regarding age, sex, weight, height, and race. The more accurate the biological profile, the more likely a match will be found in a timely manner, which may ultimately lead to a positive identification.

A practical application of using the biological profile to narrow the search for missing individuals is the use of this information in conjunction with automated databases such as CODIS (Combined DNA Index System, www.fbi.gov/about-us/lab/codis/codis). The University of North Texas Center for Human Identification received funding for processing DNA samples from unknown skeletal remains and uploading the information directly into CODIS maintained by the FBI. CODIS contains DNA profiles of missing persons (if available), profiles of unidentified human remains, and profiles from family members. The CODIS system can compare the unidentified profiles to family reference profiles or the missing person's profile to assist with an identification. However, CODIS operates by first filtering through metadata (age, sex, race, date last missing, etc.) in order to narrow down a list of DNA profiles for comparison. Thus, the more accurate the parameters of the biological profile, especially ancestry, for unidentified skeletal remains, the better the chance for by sex identification. For example, if you search for a missing male, this narrows your search but if you include age and race, your initial search will be with fewer people.

Population-Specific Data

Ancestry estimation is also important because different population groups express sexual dimorphism differently. Sexual dimorphism refers to differences in size and shape between males and females. Males, on average, are larger than females in skeletal elements. The pelvis in males and females also differs in shape due to the fact that women give birth.

Sex estimation from pelvic gross morphology provides accurate results (Phenice 1969; Volk and Ubelaker 2002). If, however, the pelvis is missing due to an incomplete recovery in the field or from taphonomic processes such as scavenging, postcranial metric sex estimation is the next best method of sex estimation and provides estimates superior to metric and nonmetric analysis of the skull (France 1998; Konigsberg and Hens 1998; Spradley 2011). Postcranial methods of sex estimation provided in most osteology or forensic anthropology textbooks are population-specific and represent individuals born prior to the twentieth century and therefore may not be appropriate to use on a recent forensic case (Bass 2005; Byers 2002; Krogman and Iscan 1986; Schwartz 2007). Thus, when estimating sex from postcranial remains, it is important to use a method derived from an appropriate reference population that is similar to the skeletal remains you are attempting to analyze. For example, there are no postcranial sex estimation methods for individuals considered Hispanic. As a result, methods derived from American Whites are typically applied to this group, resulting in considerably greater error than would be attained with a Hispanic reference sample. When trying to use American White criteria for humeral head diameter on Hispanic individuals, 100% of females classified as female, although only 47% of males were correctly classified for an overall classification rate of 73.5% (Spradley et al. 2008). When a population-specific method was developed for a Hispanic sample derived from U.S./Mexico border crossers using humeral head diameter, the overall classification rate (using humeral head diameter) increased to 85% (Tise and Spradley 2010). It is important to estimate the ancestry of an unknown skeleton prior to estimation of sex. If the sex estimate is incorrect in a forensic anthropologist's report to law enforcement, then the individual will likely remain unidentified.

How Are Forensic Anthropologists Able to Estimate Ancestry?

The chapter on FORDISC 3.1 (Jantz and Ousley 2005) of this text (Chapter 13) will instruct the reader on the specific applications of estimating ancestry using metric data. This section addresses the underlying theory of ancestry estimation with an emphasis on osteometric data from the cranium. *Osteometric data* refers to measurements that archive the overall morphology (i.e., size and shape) of the skeleton. Osteometric data, particularly *craniometric data*, are the most widely used data source for the estimation of ancestry (Dirkmaat et al. 2008; Jantz and Ousley 2005). When the skull is not recovered, select postcranial remains may provide an accurate estimate of ancestry (Holliday and

Falsetti 1999; Jantz and Ousley 2005; Wescott 2005). Holliday and Falsetti (1999) found that long bone lengths, trunk height, and biliac breadth provide good results for ancestry estimation for American Whites and Blacks. Wescott (2005) found the platymeric index ([subtrochanteric anterior – posterior diameter/subtrochanteric mediolateral diameter] * 100) a useful indicator for distinguishing between Native Americans and American Blacks and Whites. However, postcranial studies of ancestry have not been as abundant as studies using the cranium. Currently, FORDISC 3.1 provides postcranial discriminant function analysis for American Blacks and Whites using standard postcranial measurements.

Why Are Craniometric Data Reflective of Ancestry?

Craniometric data are considered complex or quantitative traits (polygenic), meaning that they are influenced by a number genes as well as the environment and provide an archive of overall craniofacial morphology, i.e. phenotype. Narrow sense heritability (h^2), also referred to as "heritability," "measures the degree to which, in a given population, the offspring phenotype is explained by the parental phenotypes" (Abney et al. 2000, p. 629). Thus, pedigreed data sets are utilized to estimate heritability. Heritability is typically estimated for each linear measurement; then the heritabilities for all measurements are averaged. Heritability estimates of craniometric data suggest that, on average, craniofacial morphology is moderate to highly heritable with an average h^2 of 0.55 (Devor 1987).

As with any quantitative trait, there is a genetic component and an environmental component. Secular changes (i.e., short-term generational changes or microevolutionary changes) have been documented in the cranium. These changes are thought to be the result of an improvement or decline in environmental conditions and can be either positive or negative (Cameron et al. 1990). Secular changes impact the generation born during these dramatic shifts in environmental conditions. For example, studies of craniofacial secular change in the United States in both American Whites and Blacks by Jantz (2001), Jantz and Meadows Jantz (2000), and Wescott and Jantz (2005) found that the most significant secular changes are in the cranial vault. They also suggested that the cranial vault is positively and significantly correlated with birth-year (Jantz 2001; Jantz and Meadows Jantz 2000; Wescott and Jantz 2005). Although the observed changes are moving in the same direction, significant morphological differences in these two population groups still remain. In other words, even though vault height is increasing in the American population as a whole, it is still possible to distinguish between ancestral groups for purposes of ancestry estimation (Box 11.2).

These studies suggest that secular changes are likely due to a combination of factors including gene flow (admixture), selection, and environmental factors, rather than solely environmental factors. Further, in a study of world-wide craniometric variation, Relethford (2004) suggested that short-term secular changes in the cranium resulting from the environment, selection, and/or gene flow do not alter the long-term population structure reflected in overall craniofacial morphology. Population structure refers to factors that affect mate choice and genetic distance between population groups (Mielke et al. 2011).

BOX 11.2 SECULAR CHANGE

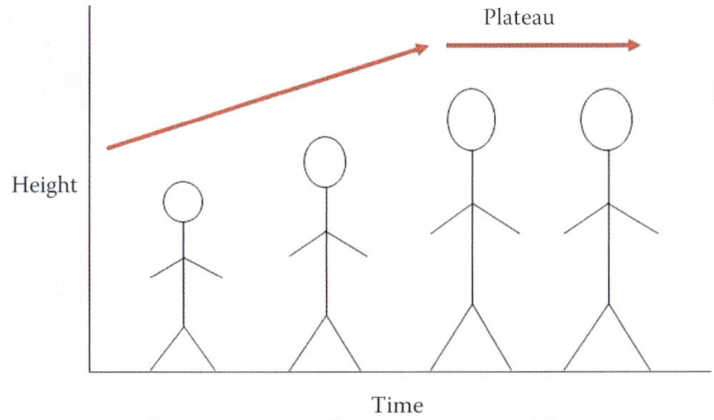

The National Health and Nutrition Examination Survey (NHANES) has been documenting trends in stature in the U.S. population. According to the NHANES data, the American population has experienced a positive secular trend since 1910 with a plateau in stature beginning around 1950. This means that stature (the standing height of an individual) has increased in the American population for individuals born during or after 1910. However, for individuals born after 1950, stature has hit a plateau (Americans are not getting taller). The exact nature of the causes of this secular change in stature is unknown. However, it is thought that population increases in stature such as these are due to improvement in economic conditions that directly influence nutritional factors (Komlos 1994). Because stature is a quantitative trait, it is influenced by both genes and the environment. Thus, there is a genetic limit to how tall a person can grow.

Estimation of Ancestry

In the United States, ancestry estimation is possible because there is a concordance (agreement) between the social race categories "White" and "Black" and the population structure and population history of these two groups (Ousley et al. 2009; Sauer 1992). Sauer (1992) posed the seminal question "if races don't exist, why are forensic anthropologists so good at identifying them?" (p. 107). As Ousley et al. (2009) point out, Sauer suggested that forensic anthropologists are good at ancestry estimation because there is a concordance between social race and skeletal biology. Ousely et al. (2009) further suggest that this concordance is due to population history and assortative mating practices. The majority of Black individuals in the United States have ancestors from West Africa while the majority of White individuals have ancestors from Europe. When enslaved West Africans were brought to the American colonies, there was limited gene flow between these two groups. Today, assortative mating practices still maintain differences in population structure between these two groups (Ousley 2009).

In sum, ancestry estimation is possible in the United States because of population history and assortative mating practices. There are multiple population groups living in the United States, including American Black, American White, and Hispanic. Although there are more population groups in the United States, these groups are the three largest, and, consequently, the groups for which forensic anthropologists have the most data. Each group has different ancestral origins. For example, American Blacks derive a large number of genes from Africa, particularly West Africa, with some European admixture (Parra et al. 1995, 1998). American Whites derive most of their genes from Europe. The population group considered Hispanic derives their genes from multiple sources depending on the nationality (geographic origin) of the individuals that make up this group. According to the U.S. Census Bureau American Community Survey (Dockterman 2011) of the individuals who report their ethnicity as Hispanic, 64% report Mexican origin. Individuals from Mexico have varying amounts of Native American and European and, in some areas, African-derived genes (Bonilla et al. 2005; Cerda-Flores et al. 2002; Lisker et al. 1986, 1990, 1996; Rangel-Villalobos 2008; Rubi-Castellanos et al. 2009). These groups all have different population histories that have influenced their genetic structure. Because of their different population histories and population structure it is possible for forensic anthropologists to use multivariate statistical methods to reliably estimate ancestry from osteometric data (Ross et al. 2004; Spradley et al. 2008) (Box 11.3).

Why Is This Topic Controversial? What Are the Main Criticisms of Ancestry Estimation in Forensic Anthropology?

The topic of ancestry remains under close scrutiny largely due to the typological approach of the nineteenth century. The typological approach refers to taking measurements of crania from multiple groups and ranking each group from superior to inferior based upon these measurements. Because Europeans were the ones making these observations and because many of these observations were made during colonization, Europeans were usually found to be "superior" over all other groups. Nott and Gliddon's (1854) depiction of an African adjacent to a chimpanzee was meant to suggest that Africans did not rank close to Europeans, rather suggesting that Africans are subhuman. The scientists that fostered the typological approach were not trained as anthropologists, rather most were medical doctors. Their work had a profound effect on anthropology by generating data on skull shapes or brain weights and classifying and ranking different groups, with European populations on the top of the chain and African populations on the bottom of the chain (Gould 1981).

In the twentieth century, there was a shift away from the typological studies, focusing instead on the variation in human populations in the context of evolutionary explanations to account for biological variation. Yet, when a student interested in forensic anthropology sits down with a textbook, usually only three groups are portrayed: African, Asian, and European (Bass 2005; Burns 2006; Byers 2002, 2008; Klepinger 2006) often referred to as Negroid, Mongoloid, and Caucasoid (see Brace [1996] for a discussion of the origin of these terms). Forensic anthropology texts that use the three group model fail to present discussions on human variation and do not acknowledge that ancestry estimations can be accomplished using geographic origin (within a continent or between continental regions), tribal affinity, and/or temporal groups (Jantz 1977, 2001; Jantz and Meadows Jantz 2000; Jantz and Willey 1983; Ousley et al. 2005, 2009; Relethford 1994, 2004, 2001; Roseman 2004; Ross et al. 2004, 2008; Spradley et al. 2008). It should be made clear that these texts are not advocating nineteenth-century typology and are in no way ranking groups of people. However, these texts typically instruct a student how to "determine" race without

BOX 11.3 OFFICE OF MANAGEMENT AND BUDGET STATISTICAL DIRECTIVE NUMBER 15

The Office of Management and Budget (OMB) is a component of the Executive Office of the President of the United States and helps to implement policies set by the President. Such policies include affirmative action plans, desegregation plans, and access to the Equal Credit Opportunity Act (http://www.whitehouse.gov/omb/fedreg_notice_15). In order to monitor these policies, racial and ethnic categories were created in order to statistically analyze data. These categories are also used by the U.S. Census Bureau to keep track of our constantly changing population. The OMB recognizes that these categories are not scientific or anthropological in nature (http://www.whitehouse.gov/omb/fedreg_notice_15); rather, they are used to track trends in population growth and monitor Presidential policies.

The OMB Statistical Directive No. 15 includes the following racial and ethnic categories:

Ethnicity: Spanish, Hispanic, or Latino (Mexican, Mexican American, Puerto Rican, Cuban, or other). If a person is Hispanic, they must check "yes" and then choose a race.

Race: White, Black, American Indian, or Alaska native. Other categories include Asian Indian, Chinese, Filipino, Japanese, Korean, Vietnamese, Native Hawaiian, Guamanian, Samoan, or other Pacific Islander (write in), or some other race (write in).

Forensic Anthropology and the OMB Statistical Directive Number 15

Forensic Anthropologists are not bound by the OMB definitions of race and ethnicity. However, a missing person's report is usually reported with OMB terminology, and this terminology is widely used in our society. Forensic anthropologists cannot estimate ethnicity from skeletal remains; rather, they can estimate ancestry or the most likely geographic origin of an individual. Thus, in an analysis using FORDISC 3.1, an individual may exhibit craniofacial morphology most similar to the Hispanic group. The Hispanic reference group is largely composed of individuals who died crossing the U.S./Mexico border and predominantly from Mexico (Anderson 2008). Therefore, the forensic anthropologist would tell law enforcement that the skeletal remains represent someone who is Hispanic. In this sense, Hispanic is viewed as a population group of people who share common geographic origin rather than an ethnicity.

For more information on the OMB, visit http://www.whitehouse.gov/omb/fedreg_notice_15

For more information on the racial and ethnic categories used by the U.S. Census Bureau, visit http://www.census.gov/prod/2001pubs/c2kbr01-1.pdf

providing the background on human variation that is necessary to understanding why and how forensic anthropologists estimate race. Further, lists of nonmetric or morphoscopic traits (e.g., orbit shape, postbregmatic depression) are usually provided to help the student estimate ancestry.

These trait lists can be traced to Earnest Hooten (1887–1954) (Hefner 2009). As presented, these lists serve to reinforce descriptive typological analysis and lack statistical rigor (Hefner 2009). Ousley and Hefner (2005) and Hefner and Ousley (2006) have derived a method of analyzing morphoscopic (nonmetric) traits with well-known statistical concepts. Like craniometric analysis, this approach takes into consideration the distribution of each trait rather than forcing the trait into one of three racial categories (i.e., African, Asian, European) (Hefner 2009). However, many anthropologists still use observational data and personal expertise by observing the overall cranial Gestalt (overall craniofacial morphology) (Hefner 2009; Hefner and Ousley 2006). In this case, an estimation by observation is only as good as the experience of the observer. Wheat (2009) found that forensic anthropology practitioners in the Western United States were better at estimating ancestry for individuals considered Hispanic, while practitioners from the Southeastern United States were better at estimating American Black individuals. Wheat's findings are in agreement with the population demographics of the United States and suggest that a forensic anthropologist's familiarity with their caseload influences their ability to accurately estimate ancestry from nonmetric traits. Individuals considered Hispanic have higher population densities in the western United States, and American Black individuals have higher population densities in the southern United States (www.census.gov). However, if a Polynesian skull is brought to the lab of any forensic anthropologist in the continental United States, an observation of the Gestalt only will likely perplex the observer.

Critics often cite Boas' (1911) immigrant study as proof that craniofacial morphology can change dramatically in a single generation due to a new environment and dietary changes, as evidence that craniofacial morphology is not fixed and cannot be used for ancestry estimation (Armelagos and van Gerven 2003; Smay and Armelagos 2000; Thomas 2000; Williams et al. 2005). Boas' study was important, as the major philosophical implication was that human potential is not fixed (Mielke et al. 2011). Boas found that cephalic index* changed for American-born children when compared to European-born children, indicating that if the cephalic index can change, racial types are not fixed, and therefore social rank is mobile/not fixed. Recent reanalysis of these data suggests that there was change in the cephalic index between foreign-born and American-born children (Gravlee et al. 2003a,b; Sparks and Jantz 2002, 2003). However, Sparks and Jantz (2002, 2003) point out that this difference in the cephalic index is negligible and that the majority of variation is found *among* ethnic groups used in the study rather than *between* American-born and foreign-born individuals. This would suggest that the majority of variation in Boas' original samples is due to genetic variation rather than environmental influence (Sparks and Jantz 2002, 2003).

Recently, Jantz and Logan (2010) found that it was the abandonment of cradle boarding that caused the biggest difference in the cephalic index of Hebrews, the group with the most change in cephalic index. So rather than a new geographic environment, it was the abandonment of cradle boarding, a common cultural practice, that caused the dramatic change. The changes observed in the immigrant study can be referred to as secular changes, however, as previously mentioned; these secular changes do no obscure the underlying genetic structure of the population groups meaning that the American-born children are most similar (in terms of cranial morphology) to the foreign-born children despite the change in the cephalic index (Sparks and Jantz 2003).

Another criticism of ancestry estimation is that most studies of human biological variation indicate that 85%–90% of variation is found within groups, while the remaining

* Cephalic index = (Maximum cranial breadth/maximum cranial length) × 100

15%–10% is found between groups. For example, if you take multiple quantitative traits and derive an Fst estimate (measure of subpopulation variation relative to total population variation, Mielke et al. [2011]) for 20 population groups, the majority of variation is found within all 20 groups, while only 10%–15% of the variation is found among the 20 population groups (for more information on Fst, see Edwards [2003]). Some interpret this data as suggesting that so little variation between groups makes it difficult to morphologically distinguish between population groups at a level smaller than geographically separated continents (Williams et al. 2005). However, despite the fact that there is only 10%–15% of variation found among groups using various types of quantitative traits, this variation is structured in a way that is informative to geographic ancestry (Bamshad et al. 2004).

Summary

This chapter provides a review of why forensic anthropologists estimate ancestry, how they are able to estimate ancestry, and why this topic is controversial. Ancestry and sex estimation provide key information when searching for missing individuals, especially when filtering through missing person's automated databases and websites, such as CODIS and NamUs. Because sex estimation is population-specific, ancestry estimation is needed for accurate sex estimation in the absence of the pelvis (Spradley et al. 2008). Furthermore, even though many identifications are made through the use of DNA, it is the components of the biological profile that help forensic practitioners arrive at a potential match for DNA comparison.

In order to estimate ancestry, osteometric data are utilized, particularly craniometric data. Because craniometric data are considered quantitative and heritable phenotypic traits, they are particularly useful for ancestry estimation. Although secular changes have been documented in the American population, and demographic population structures are changing, the population history of the United States, along with assortative mating practices, enables forensic practitioners to reliably estimate ancestry. While critics claim that ancestry estimation reverts back to nineteenth-century typology, forensic anthropologists do not, in practice or in publications, rank populations from superior to inferior.

References

Abney M, McPeek MS, and Ober C. 2000. Estimation of variance components of quantitative traits in inbred populations. *The American Journal of Human Genetics* 66:629–650.

Armelagos GJ and Goodman AH. 1998. Race, racism, and anthropology. In: Goodman AH and Leatherman TL (Eds.). *Building a New Biocultural Synthesis*. Ann Arbor, MI: University of Michigan Press, pp. 359–377.

Armelagos G and van Gerven DP. 2003. A century of skeletal biology and paleopathology: Contrasts, contradictions, and conflicts. *American Anthropologist* 105(1):51–62.

Bamshad M, Wooding S, Salisbury BA, and Stephens JC. 2004. Deconstructing the relationship between genetics and race. *Nature Reviews Genetics* 5:598–609.

Bass WM. 2005. *Human Osteology: A Laboratory and Field Manual*. Columbia, MO: Missouri Archaeological Society.

Bonilla C, Gutiérrez G, Parra EJ, Kline C, and Shriver MD. 2005. Admixture analysis of a rural population of the state of Guerrero, Mexico. *American Journal of Physical Anthropology* 128(4):861–869.

Brace C. 1996. A four-letter word called "Race." In: Lieberman LTRaL (Ed.). *Race and Other Misadventures: Essays in Honor of Ashley Montagu in his Ninetieth Year*. Dix Hills, NY: General Hall, Inc., pp. 106–141.

Burns KR. 2006. *Forensic Anthropology Training Manual*. Upper Saddle River, NJ: Prentice Hall.

Byers SN. 2002. *Introduction to Forensic Anthropology: A Textbook*. New York: Allyn and Bacon.

Byers SN. 2008. *Forensic Anthropology Laboratory Manual*. Boston, MA: Pearson.

Cameron N, Tobias PV, Fraser WJ, and Nagdee M. 1990. Search for secular trends in calvarial diameters, cranial base height, indices and capacity in South African Negro crania. *American Journal of Human Biology* 2:53–61.

Cerda-Flores RM, Budowle B, Jin L, Barton SA, Deka R, and Chakraborty R. 2002. Maximum likelihood estimates of admixture in northeastern Mexico using 13 short tandem repeat loci. *American Journal of Human Biology* 14(4):429–439.

Devor EJ. 1987. Transmission of human craniofacial dimensions. *Journal of Craniofacial Genetics and Developmental Biology* 7:95–106.

Dirkmaat DC, Cabo LL, Ousley SD, and Symes SA. 2008. New perspectives in forensic anthropology. *American Journal of Physical Anthropology* 137(S47):33–52.

Dockterman D. 2011. Hispanics of Mexican Origin in the United States, 2009 statistical profile. Washington, D.C., Pew Hispanic Research Center.

Edwards AW. 2003. Human genetic diversity: lewontin's fallacy. *Bioessays* 25(8): 798–801.

France DL. 1998. Observational and metric analysis of sex in the skeleton. In: Reichs KJ (Ed.). *Forensic Osteology: Advances in the Identification of Human Remains*, 2nd edn. Springfield, IL: Charles C. Thomas.

Gould SJ. 1981. *The Mismeasure of Man*. New York: W.W. Norton & Company.

Gravlee CC, Bernard HR, and Leonard WR. 2003a. Heredity, environment and cranial form: A reanalysis of boas' immigrant data. *American Anthropologist* 105(1):125–138.

Gravlee CC, Bernard HR, and Leonard WR. 2003b. Boas' changes in bodily form: The immigrant study, cranial plasticity, and boas' physical anthropology. *American Anthropologist* 105(2):326–332.

Hefner JT. 2009. Cranial nonmetric variation and estimating ancestry. *Journal of Forensic Sciences* 54(5):985–995.

Hefner JT and Ousley SD. 2006. *The Statistical Determination of Ancestry Using Cranial Non-Metric Traits*. Seattle, WA: American Academy of Forensic Sciences.

Holliday TW and Falsetti AB. 1999. A new method for discriminating African-American from European-American skeletons using postcranial osteometrics reflective of body shape. *Journal of Forensic Sciences* 44(5):926–930.

Jantz RL. 1977. Craniometric relationships of Plains populations: historical and evolutionary implications. *Plains Anthropologist* 114:146–155.

Jantz RL. 2001. Cranial change in Americans: 1850–1975. *Journal of Forensic Sciences* 46(4):784–787.

Jantz RL and Logan MH. 2010. Why does head form change in children of immigrants? A reappraisal. *American Journal of Human Biology* 22(5):702–707.

Jantz RL and Meadows Jantz L. 2000. Secular change in craniofacial morphology. *American Journal of Human Biology* 12:327–338.

Jantz RL and Ousley SD. 2005. *FORDISC 3.1: Personal Computer Forensic Discriminant Functions*. Knoxville, TN: The University of Tennessee.

Jantz RL and Willey P. 1983. Temporal and geographic patterning of relative head height in the central plains and middle Missouri areas. *Plains Anthropologist* 28:59–67.

Klepinger LL. 2006. *Fundamental of Forensic Anthropology*. In: Cartmill M and Brown K (Eds.). Hoboken, NJ: John Wiley & Sons, Inc.

Komlos J. 1994. *Stature, Living Standards, and Economic Development: Essays in Anthropometric History*. In: Komlos J (Ed.). Chicago, IL: University of Chicago Press.

Konigsberg LW and Hens SM. 1998. Use of ordinal categorical variables in skeletal assessment of sex from the cranium. *American Journal of Physical Anthropology* 107:97–112.

Krogman WM and Iscan MY. 1986. *The Human Skeleton in Forensic Medicine*. Springfield, IL: Charles C. Thomas.

Lisker R, Perez-Briceno R, Granados J, Babinsky V, de Rubens J, Armendares S, and Buentello L. 1986. Gene frequencies and admixture estimates in a Mexico City population. *American Journal of Physical Anthropology* 71(2):203–207.

Lisker R, Ramirez E, and Babinsky V. 1996. Genetic structure of autochthonous populations of Meso-America: Mexico. *Human Biology* 68(3):395–404.

Lisker R, Ramirez E, Briceno RP, Granados J, and Babinsky V. 1990. Gene frequencies and admixture estimates in four Mexican urban centers. *Human Biology* 62(6):791–801.

Mielke JH, Konigsberg LW, and Relethford JH. 2011. *Human Biological Variation*. New York: Oxford University Press.

Nott JC and Gliddon GR. 1854. *Types of Mankind*. Philadelphia, PA: Lippincott, Grambo, & Co.

Ousley SD, Billeck WT, and Hollinger RE. 2005. Federal repatriation legislation and the role of physical anthropology in repatriation. *American Journal of Physical Anthropology* 128(S41):2–32.

Ousley SD and Hefner JT. 2005. *The Statistical Determination of Ancestry*. New Orleans, LA: American Academy of Forensic Sciences.

Ousley S, Jantz R, and Freid D. 2009. Understanding race and human variation: Why forensic anthropologists are good at identifying race. *American Journal of Physical Anthropology* 139(1):68–76.

Parra EJ, Marcini A, Akey J, Martinson J, Batzer MA, Cooper R, Allison DB, Deka R, Ferrell RE, and Shriver MD. 1998. Estimating African American admixture proportions by use of population-specific alleles. *American Journal of Human Genetics* 63:1839–1851.

Parra EJ, Teixeira Ribeiro JC, Caeiro JLB, and Riveiro A. 1995. Genetic structure of the populations of Cabo Verde (West Africa): Evidence of substantial European admixture. *American Journal of Physical Anthropology* 91:381–389.

Phenice T. 1969. A newly developed visual method of sexing the os pubis. *American Journal of Physical Anthropology* 30(2):297–301.

Rangel-Villalobos H, Munoz-Valle JF, Gonzalez-Martin A, Gorostiza A, Magana MT, Paez-Riberos LA. 2008. Genetic admixture, relatedness, and structure patterns among Mexican populations revealed by the Y-chromosome. *American Journal of Physical Anthropology* 135(4):448–461.

Relethford JH. 1994. Craniometric variation among modern human populations. *American Journal of Physical Anthropology* 95:53–62.

Relethford JH. 2001. Global analysis of regional differences in craniometric diversity and population substructure. *Human Biology* 73(5):629–636.

Relethford JH. 2004. Boas and beyond: Migration and craniometric variation. *American Journal of Human Biology* 16:379–386.

Roseman CC. 2004. Detecting interregionally diversifying natural selection on modern human cranial form by using matched molecular and morphometric data. *Proceedings of the National Academy of Sciences* 101:12824–12829.

Ross AH, Slice DE, Ubelaker DH, and Falsetti AB. 2004. Population affinities of 19th century Cuban crania: Implications for identification criteria in south Florida Cuban Americans. *Journal of Forensic Sciences* 49:1–6.

Ross AH, Ubelaker DH, and Guillen S. 2008. Craniometric patterning within ancient Peru. *Latin American Antiquity* 19(2):158–166.

Rubi-Castellanos R, Martínez-Cortés G, Muñoz-Valle JF, González-Martín A, Cerda-Flores RM, Anaya-Palafox M, and Rangel-Villalobos H. 2009. Pre-Hispanic Mesoamerican demography approximates the present-day ancestry of Mestizos throughout the territory of Mexico. *American Journal of Physical Anthropology* 139(3):284–294.

Sauer NJ. 1992. Forensic anthropology and the concept of race: If races don't exist, why are forensic anthropologists so good at identifying them? *Social Science and Medicine* 34:107–111.

Schwartz JH. 2007. *Skeleton Keys*. New York: Oxford University Press.

Smay D and Armelagos GJ. 2000. Galileo wept: A critical assessment of the use of race in forensic anthropology. *Transforming Anthropology* 9(2):19–29.

Sparks CS and Jantz RL. 2002. A reassessment of human cranial plasticity: Boas revisited. *Proceedings of the National Academic of Sciences USA* 99(23):14636–14639.

Sparks CS and Jantz RL. 2003. Changing times, changing faces: Franz Boas's immigrant study in modern perspective. *American Anthropologist* 105:333–337.

Spradley MK and Jantz RL. 2011. Sex estimation in forensic anthropology: Skull vs. postcranial elements. *Journal of Forensic Sciences* 56(2):289–296.

Spradley MK, Jantz RL, Robinson A, and Peccerelli F. 2008. Demographic change and forensic identification: Problems in metric identification of Hispanic skeletons. *Journal of Forensic Sciences* 53(1):21–28.

Tise ML and Spradley MK. 2010. *A Metric Analysis of the Postcranial Skeleton of Hispanic Individuals to Improve the Estimation of Sex*. Seattle, WA: American Academy of Forensic Sciences.

Thomas DH. 2000. *Skull Wars: Kennewick Man, Archaeology, and the Battle for Native American Identity*. New York: Basic Books.

Ubelaker DH. 1999. Ales Hrdlicka's role in the history of forensic anthropology. *Journal of Forensic Sciences* 44(4):724–730.

Volk C and Ubelaker DH. 2002. A test of the Phenice method for the estimation of sex. *Journal of Forensic Sciences* 47(1):19–24.

Wescott DJ. 2005. Population variation in femur subtrochanteric shape. *Journal of Forensic Sciences* 50(2):286–293.

Wescott DJ and Jantz RL. 2005. Assessing craniofacial secular change in American Blacks and Whites using geometric morphometry. In: Slice DE (Ed.). *Modern Morphometrics in Physical Anthropology*. New York: Kluwer Academic/Plenum Publishers, pp. 231–245.

Wheat AD. 2009. Assessing ancestry through nonmetric traits of the skull: A test of education and experience. Theses and dissertations-Anthropology. Paper 17. http://ecommons.txstate.edu/anthroptad/17

Williams FL, Belcher RL, and Armelagos GJ. 2005. Forensic misclassification of ancient Nubian crania: Implications for assumptions about human variation. *Current Anthropology* 46(2):340–346.

Stature Estimation

12

NATALIE R. SHIRLEY

Contents

History

The theoretical underpinnings of estimating living stature from skeletal measurements date back over two centuries. Jean Joseph Sue (1710–1792) was a French anatomist who published data on maximum length of long bones and several body measurements, including stature, from 14 cadavers ranging from 6 weeks *in utero* to 25 years old (Sue 1755). The intended purpose of Sue's publication was to provide artists with information about body proportions (Stewart 1979). Sue's measurements were introduced to the medicolegal community by Matthieu Joseph Bonaventure Orfila (1787–1853), a professor of legal medicine who published two textbooks on the subject (Orfila 1821–1823; Orfila and Lesueur 1831). Orfila also added measurements from 51 cadavers and 20 skeletons to Sue's original dataset. In order to estimate stature using the Sue–Orfila skeletal measurements, the user simply looked up the bone measurement and corresponding cadaver length in a table. As cadaver length can vary from living stature by as much as 2 inches, a certain amount of error was automatically built into the Sue–Orfila stature estimates.

In the late nineteenth century, Paul Broca (1824–1880), a medical anthropologist better known for his work in neuroanatomy, introduced the osteometric board for taking accurate long bone measurements (Figure 12.1). One of Broca's students, Paul Topinard (1830–1911) devised a series of ratios of long bone lengths to stature; Topinard's ratios provided more accurate stature estimates than Orfila's rather simplistic tables (Topinard 1885). Étienne Rollet (1862–1937) followed Topinard's work closely and published a doctoral thesis relating the average lengths of long bones from cadavers of the same length. Rollet's data were quickly snatched up and reorganized by Topinard's successor, Léonce Manouvrier (1850–1927). Manouvrier's tables relate the average lengths of cadavers with the same long bone lengths. He also included a correction factor for dry bone measurements since Rollet's data were derived from measurements taken on fresh bone (Manouvrier 1893). Nonetheless, not long after Manouvrier's publication, the English biometric school released a statistical technique that would change the face of stature estimation permanently. In 1899, Karl Pearson (1857–1936) published a monograph detailing his regression theory, which used the correlation between long bone length and stature to derive a linear equation that would predict stature from long bone length (Pearson 1899). Although Pearson's equations were intended primarily for evolutionary studies, his work had a profound influence on forensic anthropology. Paul Stevenson (1890–1971)

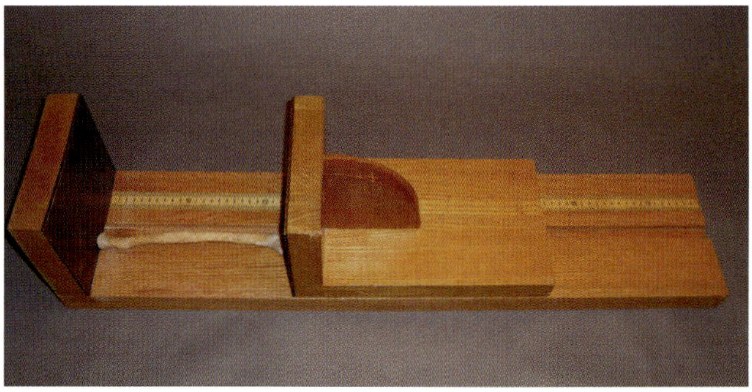

Figure 12.1 A standard osteometric board used to measure long bones.

was the first to test Pearson's equations, but the equations did not perform well because Stevenson tested them on a Chinese population, and Pearson's equations were based on Rollet's European data (Stevenson 1929). Likewise, the Chinese regression equations that Stevenson developed were not successful for estimating European stature. This initial test called attention to human variation in long bone length and proportions and pointed to the need for population-specific standards. During the 1950s, Trotter and Gleser (1952, 1958) published regression equations for the modern American population based on a living stature data from a large sample of males and females from a variety of ethnic backgrounds. These equations remained the most appropriate for forensic use in the United States until the release of Fordisc 2.0 (Jantz and Ousley 1996).

Several years before the publication of Pearson's regression manuscript, Thomas Dwight (1843–1911), an American anatomist from Harvard upon whom T. Dale Stewart suitably conferred the title "Father of American Forensic Anthropology," distinguished between two methods of stature estimation: mathematical versus anatomical (Dwight 1894). Dwight explained that mathematical methods rely on the proportion of specific bones to height, and anatomical methods consist of assembling the skeleton in anatomical position, applying a correction factor for soft tissue, and measuring height. The mathematical method is more susceptible to error resulting from population differences in body proportions and/or age-related decreases in stature. Consequently, Dwight seemed to prefer the anatomical method.

Stature Estimation Methods

What emerges from this brief historical synopsis is that stature estimation can be accomplished using more than one method; the nature of the forensic case usually dictates which method is most appropriate. The Scientific Working Group for Forensic Anthropology (SWGANTH) recommends incorporating information about the population, sex, and time period in selecting the most appropriate stature estimation method. Ideally, the method with the smallest error should be selected above other methods, and that method should be applied reliably and objectively. The SWGANTH guidelines for stature estimation clarify the difference between anatomical and mathematical techniques and give recommendations for best practice (http://swganth.startlogic.com/stature.pdf).

Anatomical methods of stature estimation are suitable only when the skeleton is mostly complete. Dwight (1894) was the first to suggest an anatomical method for estimating stature. His technique was modified by Fully (1956) and Fully and Pineau (1960), and Fully's technique was later revised by Raxter et al. (2006). These methods require that the cranium, all vertebrae (except the atlas), sacrum, femur, tibia, talus, and calcaneus are present. The method involves measuring all of the elements and using a correction factor for soft tissues. Occasionally, supernumery vertebrae are present and require an additional correction factor (Lundy 1988; Raxter and Ruff 2010). One advantage of anatomical methods of stature estimation is that they are robust to population and/or individual variation in body proportions and age-related changes in stature (Maijanen 2009). In addition, they can be employed regardless of the sex or ancestry of the individual and provide a more accurate stature estimation than approaches that use only one or a limited number of skeletal elements. However, anatomical methods are not feasible if any of the required elements are missing, as is frequently the situation with forensic anthropology casework. In this instance, the forensic anthropologist must resort to another technique.

Because many forensic anthropology cases involve incomplete skeletal remains, the most frequently used technique for stature estimation in a forensic setting is the mathematical or regression approach. This approach requires measuring bone length(s) and selecting the most appropriate formula according to sex, ancestry, and time period. Typically, measurements from the lower limb are favored over those of the upper limb, but in the absence of a femur, tibia, or fibula, upper limb bones give adequate stature estimates. When present, the femur, tibia, and fibula maximum length should be used preferentially, as these measurements outperform those from the upper limb (Wilson et al. 2010). After the bone(s) are measured, the measurement(s) are plugged into the appropriate regression formula. The linear regression equation for stature estimation from a single skeletal measurement is

$$\text{Stature} = a + bx + SE$$

where

a is the y-intercept of the line
b is the slope
x is the bone measurement
SE is the standard error

Additionally, multiple regression formulae are available for use with multiple measurements. Calculations may be done manually or automatically using a computer program such as Fordisc (Jantz and Ousley 2005).* The Fordisc computer program gives the user the option of using the Trotter and Gleser (1952, 1958) equations or "forensic" equations based on the Forensic Data Bank, a collection of skeletal measurements and biological data from modern individuals. However, when using Trotter and Gleser's formulae with tibial length, the user should note that this measurement was reported incorrectly in the original publications (1952, 1958). Jantz et al. (1995) discovered that Trotter's measurement excluded the medial malleolus, although she reported that she had included it. Consequently, one should omit the medial malleolus from tibial length when using Trotter's formulae or simply use another bone. Because many populations have experienced significant increases in adult height during the course of the last century, the forensic equations are more appropriate

* Refer to Chapter 13 for a detailed discussion of the Fordisc program.

than the Trotter and Gleser equations for the majority of forensic casework (Jantz and Jantz 1999; Meadows and Jantz 1995). The Trotter and Gleser equations were developed using the Smithsonian Institution's Terry Collection, which consists primarily of individuals born between 1850 and 1900. During this time period, the American population was significantly shorter than it is presently, so these equations may underestimate stature in modern individuals.

Fordisc gives the option of using a 90% or 95% prediction interval for stature estimation. When using multiple measurements, the program outputs several stature estimates and the associated error terms and R^2 value; the user should select the estimate with the lowest standard error, highest R^2 value, and smallest prediction interval. Note that stature is reported as an interval and not a range. A range is simply the difference between the maximum and minimum values in a dataset of observations. Instead, stature is reported in terms of a confidence interval or a prediction interval. A confidence interval is a way of expressing the uncertainty that a given regression line represents the true best-fit linear regression line. A prediction interval demarcates the area in which a specified percentage of the data surrounding the fitted regression line falls. For example, with a 95% confidence interval, we can be 95% confident that the upper and lower confidence limits contain the true best-fit regression line for estimating stature. With a 95% prediction interval, we expect 95% of all data points surrounding the regression line used to estimate stature to fall within those bounds. A prediction interval is wider than a confidence interval and is the preferred and more useful parameter for reporting a stature estimate.

Another option for estimating stature involves using a ratio between stature and bone length, such as the femur/stature ratio (Feldesman et al. 1990). This method is not as mathematically complex as the regression approach, and the authors report that sex and ancestry differences are negligible with the ratio approach. However, several criticisms of the ratio method are that it overestimates stature (particularly in taller individuals), yields a larger prediction interval than regression estimates, and is consequently less accurate and that the regression approach performs better overall (Jantz et al. 1995; Konigsberg et al. 1998).

Additional Considerations

Although this chapter focuses on stature estimation in a forensic context, biological anthropologists use stature estimates to approach a variety of questions. For example, paleoanthropologists estimate the stature of hominid fossils to compare modern human morphology with the physical form of our distant relatives. Bioarchaeologists use stature as an indicator of overall health in past populations. Indeed, while there is undoubtedly a genetic component to height, this aspect of a person's physical make-up is affected greatly by the environment, especially the conditions surrounding growth and development (Ulijaszek 2006). In fact, stature increases have been documented for entire populations as nutrition, sanitary conditions, and medical care have improved in many countries around the world (Alberman et al. 1991; Buretic-Tomljanovic et al. 2004; Fredriks et al. 2000; Hoppa and Garlie 1998; Leung et al. 1996; Meredith 1976; Ulijaszek 1993; Vercauteren and Susanne 1985). Changes in long bone lengths as a result of stature increases have also been documented in modern Americans (Jantz and Jantz 1999; Meadows and Jantz 1995). For this reason, it is imperative to use regression formulae from the appropriate time period to estimate stature.

In the event that no complete limb bones are available to measure, two options exist to arrive at a stature estimate. The first option is to use the fragmentary element to estimate total bone length and then to apply this measurement to a regression formula. The second option is to use a bone other than a limb bone, such as the cranium, vertebrae, sacrum, sternum, scapula, tarsals, metatarsals, metacarpals, or phalanges. Both of these solutions will result in wider prediction intervals than limb bones, but the latter solution is preferable to the former because estimating a measurement from a bone fragment introduces additional error into the stature estimate.

Another variable that can affect the accuracy of stature estimates is age-related stature decrease in middle-aged and older adults. Studies indicate that stature begins to decrease by age 45 (Galloway 1988) and perhaps as young as age 30 (Trotter and Gleser 1951). Trotter and Gleser (1951) found that stature decreases at a linear rate by about 0.6 mm a year, but Galloway (1988) reported a larger decrease of 1.6 mm per year, and Giles (1991) found that the rate of decrease was variable and not linear. Although several of these studies investigated sex and ancestry differences in stature decrease, they reached variable conclusions, and, consequently, this topic warrants further investigation. Whether or not the stature estimate warrants adjustment for age depends largely on the antemortem records available for comparison.

Nevertheless, the reliability of antemortem stature records is often questionable, particularly with self-reported stature. For example, Willey and Falsetti (1991) found that college students' driver's licenses tend to overreport stature by nearly 1 cm, and male driver's licenses overreport stature to a greater degree than females. Furthermore, taller individuals report their stature more accurately than shorter individuals, and older individuals tend to overreport stature, although perhaps this phenomenon is confounded by age-related stature decreases (Giles and Hutchinson 1991). However, even official measurements have been found to vary considerably. Stature records for a single individual who was measured 19 times during a 20-year period by various medical and legal personnel ranged between 62 and 67 inches (Snow and Williams 1971). This variation could have been a result of age, time of day, instrument calibration, or observer error, but it is illustrative of the considerable variation in antemortem stature records.

Antemortem stature records can come from a variety of sources, including medical or military records (i.e., measured stature) or self-reported statures such as those on driver's licenses (i.e., forensic stature), and regression equations vary in terms of the antemortem stature source used to derive the equations (Ousley 1995; Wilson et al. 2010). Indeed, some equations were derived using cadaver length instead of antemortem records. Discrepancies in antemortem stature estimates or measures attribute additional error to postmortem stature estimates based on long bone length(s). Consequently, Willey (2009) recommends carefully considering the measuring context and the source of antemortem stature record when making comparisons between skeletal-based stature estimates and antemortem records. Ousley (1995) recommends using a wide estimation interval (i.e., a 90% prediction interval) in forensic casework to compensate for discrepancies in reported stature as well as for the inherent error in stature estimates. Finally, the SWGANTH guidelines warn that the dearth of research on subadult stature estimation makes these estimates suspect. In particular, because of the uniqueness of subadult body proportions and allometric changes throughout growth and development, adult regression formulae should not be used to estimate subadult stature. Indeed, subadult stature estimation is one area where the forensic community would benefit greatly from further research.

References

Alberman E, Filakti H, William S, Evans S, and Emanuel I. 1991. Early influences on the secular change in the adult height between the parents and children of the 1958 birth cohort. *Ann Hum Biol* 18:127–136.

Buretic-Tomljanovic A, Ristic S, and Brajenovic-Milic B. 2004. Secular change in body height and cephalic index of Croatian medical students (University of Rijeka). *Am J Phys Anthropol* 123:91–96.

Dwight T. 1894. Methods of estimating the height from parts of the skeleton. *Med Rec* 46:293–296.

Feldesman MR, Kleckner JG, and Lundy JK. 1990. Femur/stature ratio and estimates of stature in mid and late Pleistocene fossil hominids. *Am J Phys Anthropol* 83:359–372.

Fredriks A, Van Burren S, and Burgmeijer R. 2000. Continuing positive secular growth change in the Netherlands 1955–1997. *Pediatr Res* 47(3):316–323.

Fully G. 1956. Une nouvelle me´thode de de´termination de la taille. *Ann Med Legale* 35:266–273.

Fully G and Pineau H. 1960. Determination de la stature au moyen de squelette. *Annales de Medicine Legale* 40:145–154.

Galloway A. 1988. Estimating actual height in the older individual. *J Forensic Sci* 33:126–136.

Giles E. 1991. Corrections for age in estimating older adults' stature from long bones. *J Forensic Sci* 36:898–901.

Giles E and Hutchinson DL. 1991. Stature and age-related bias in self-reported stature. *J Forensic Sci* 36:765–780.

Hoppa RD and Garlie TN. 1998. Secular changes in the growth of Toronto children during the last century. *Ann Hum Biol* 25(6):553–561.

Jantz RL, Hunt DR, and Meadows L. 1995. The measure and mismeasure of the tibia: implications for stature estimation. *J Forensic Sci* 40(5):758–761.

Jantz L and Jantz R. 1999. Secular change in long bone length and proportion in the United States, 1800–1970. *Am J Phys Anthropol* 110:57–67.

Jantz RL and Ousley SD. 1996. *FORDISC 2.0: Computerized Forensic Discriminant Functions*. Knoxville, TN: University of Tennessee.

Jantz R and Ousley S. 2005. *FORDISC 3.0: Computerized Forensic Discriminant Functions*. Knoxville, TN: University of Tennessee.

Konigsberg L, Hens SM, Jantz LM, and Jungers WL. 1998. Stature estimation and calibration: Bayesian and maximum likelihood perspectives in physical anthropology. *Yearbk Phys Anthropol* 41:65–92.

Leung S, Lau J, Xu Y, and Tse L. 1996. Secular changes in standing height, sitting height and sexual maturation of Chinese—the Hong Kong growth study, 1993. *Ann Hum Biol* 23(4):297–306.

Lundy JK. 1988. Sacralization of a sixth lumbar vertebra and its effect upon the estimation of living stature. *J Forensic Sci* 33(4):1045–1049.

Maijanen H. 2009. Testing anatomical methods for stature estimation on individuals from the W. M. Bass donated skeletal collection. *J Forensic Sci* 54(4):746–752.

Manouvrier L. 1893. Le determination de la taille d'apres les grande os des membres. *Mem de la Soc d'Anthropologie de Paris* 4:347–402.

Meadows L and Jantz R. 1995. Allometric secular change in the long bones from the 1800s to the present. *J Forensic Sci* 40(5):762–767.

Meredith H. 1976. Findings from Asia, Australia, Europe and North America on secular change in mean height of children, youths and young adults. *Am J Phys Anthropol* 44(2):315–326.

Orfila MJB. 1821–1823. *Leaons de Medicine Legale*, Vols 1–2. Paris, France: Bechet Jeune.

Orfila MJB and Lesueur O. 1831. *Traite des exhumations juridiques, et considerations sur les changements physiques que les cadavres eprouvent en se pourrissant dan la terres, dan l'eau, dans les fosses d'aisance et dans le fumier*, Vols 1–2. Paris, France: Bechet Jeune.

Ousley S. 1995. Should we estimate biological or forensic stature? *J Forensic Sci* 40:768–773.

Pearson K. 1899. Mathematical contributions to the theory of evolution: On the reconstruction of the stature of prehistoric races. *Philos Trans R Soc Lond* 192:169–244.
Raxter MH, Auerbach BM, and Ruff CB. 2006. Revision of the fully technique for estimating statures. *Am J Phys Anthropol* 130:374–384.
Raxter MH and Ruff CB. 2010. The effect of vertebral numerical variation on anatomical stature estimates. *J Forensic Sci* 55(2):464–466.
Snow CC and Williams J. 1971. Variation in pre-mortem stature estimates of skeletal remains. *J Forensic Sci* 16:455–464.
Stevenson PH. 1929. On racial differences in stature long bone regression formulae, with special reference to stature reconstruction formulae for the Chinese. *Biometrika* 21:303–321.
Stewart TD. 1979. *Essentials of Forensic Anthropology: Especially as Developed in the United States.* Springfield, IL: C.C. Thomas.
Sue JJ. 1755. Sur les proportions des squelette de homme, examine depuis l'age du plus tendre, jusqu' B celui de vingt cinq, soixante ans, and audel. *Acad Sci Paris Mem Mathemat Phys Present Divers Savants* 2:572–285.
Topinard P. 1885. *Elements d'anthropologie generale.* Paris, France: Delahaye and Lecrosnier.
Trotter M and Gleser GC. 1951. The effect of aging on stature. *Am J Phys Anthropol* 9:311–324.
Trotter M and Gleser GC. 1952. Estimation of stature from long bones of American Whites and Negroes. *Am J Phys Anthropol* 10(4):463–514.
Trotter M and Gleser GC. 1958. A re-evaluation of estimation of stature based on measurements of stature taken during life and of long bones after death. *Am J Phys Anthropol* 16:79–124.
Ulijaszek S. 1993. Evidence for a secular trend in heights and weights of adults in Papua New Guinea. *Ann Hum Biol* 20(4):349–355.
Ulijaszek S. 2006. The international growth standard for children and adolescents project: Environmental influences on preadolescent and adolescent growth in weight and height. *Food Nutr Bull* 27(4 Suppl Growth Standard):S279–S294.
Vercauteren M and Susanne C. 1985. The secular trend of height and menarche in Belgium: Are there any signs of a future stop. *Eur J Pediatr* 144(4):306–309.
Willey P. 2009. Stature estimation. In: Blau S and Ubelaker DH, eds., *Handbook of Forensic Anthropology and Archaeology.* Walnut Creek, CA: Left Coast Press Inc.
Willey P and Falsetti T. 1991. Inaccuracy of height information on driver's licenses. *J Forensic Sci* 36:813–819.
Wilson RJ, Herrmann NP, and Jantz LM. 2010. Evaluation of stature estimation from the database for forensic anthropology. *J Forensic Sci* 55(3):684–689.

Introduction to Fordisc 3

13

RICHARD L. JANTZ AND
STEPHEN D. OUSLEY

Contents

Fordisc 3 (FD3) is computer software that automates metric estimation of sex, ancestry, and stature techniques described in Chapters 8, 11, and 12. It uses a technique known as linear discriminant function analysis to compare measurements from an unknown skeleton to reference samples in order to estimate the ancestry or sex to which the person would likely have belonged in life, and linear regression to estimate how tall the person would have been in life. Most of the statistical procedures Fordisc uses have been around for a long time; Fordisc simply makes them available in flexible form for analysis of a single case. We present a brief review of the historical background of these statistics and how they led to development of the software.

Historical Background

Linear discriminant functions were developed by Fisher and apparently first used by Barnard (1935) and formally published by Fisher (1936). A related statistic, also important in Fordisc, is the Generalized Distance, developed by Mahalanobis (1936). Although the statistical methods were in place by early to mid-twentieth century, they were little used because they were computationally burdensome with the hand calculators of the time.

The computational burden involved in computing linear discriminants and Mahalanobis distances led to some innovative attempts to reduce computation while remaining faithful to the central elements of the more complex statistics. Rao (1952) suggested some short cuts, which replicated the Mahalanobis distance, but still involved considerable computation. A strategy suggested by Penrose (1954) involved decomposing distance into size and shape components and incorporating an average correlation to replace the covariance matrix required by the Mahalanobis distance. This reduced the computational burden considerably, resulting in widespread use of Penrose's distances.

Linear discriminant functions were introduced to forensic anthropology in the late 1950s (Thieme 1957; Thieme and Schull 1957) and the early 1960s (Giles and Elliot 1962, 1963). These works were on the leading edge of use of electronic computers to overcome the computational burden mentioned earlier. The two works by Giles and Elliot became classics and were used extensively by forensic anthropologists until the early 1990s when Fordisc 1.0 became available. Giles and Elliot enabled forensic anthropologists to use precomputed discriminant coefficients by multiplying coefficients times measurements to get a score, something easily accomplished with desk calculators. As computers became more widely used, many discriminant functions were devised for sex and ancestry estimation, a process that continues to the present.

Linear regression is the technique Fordisc uses to estimate height. Like linear discriminant functions, it was developed around the turn of the century. The term "regression" was coined by Francis Galton (Smith 1980) from his observation that offspring tend to be closer to the population mean than their parents, hence regression to the mean. Karl Pearson developed the statistical basis for regression, as well as the related correlation coefficient, derived from the more descriptive term "co-relation."

Forensic Anthropology Data Bank

Development of Fordisc depended first and foremost on the existence of an appropriate database. The idea of developing a database of modern forensic cases belongs to Clyde Snow, using the reasoning that only forensic anthropologists have the opportunity to examine skeletal remains of modern Americans. A grant from the National Institute of Justice launched the formal beginning of the Forensic Anthropology Data Bank (FDB) (Jantz and Moore-Jansen 1988). The FDB now serves as a repository of data collected from skeletons of Americans with twentieth and twenty-first century birth years. Skeletal data consist of cranial and postcranial measurements, aging criteria such as pubic symphysis phases and rib end phases, and dental and epiphyseal development stages. Since most of the skeletal remains are eventually identified, we are also able to obtain premortem and perimortem information, the most important being age, sex, race/ancestry, height, weight, and manner of death. The data bank now contains skeletal information on over 3000 individuals, many of which are no longer available for study, having been returned to their families once they have been positively identified. Box 13.1 summarizes the most common way information gets into the FDB.

One of the observations often made about the FDB is that the sampling framework is biased, depending as it does on mostly nonnatural manners of death such as homicide or suicide. Figure 13.1 demonstrates the extent of that bias; over half the individuals in the data bank are homicides or suicides. What at first may seem like a problem is actually an advantage because the unknown forensic cases to be identified are drawn from the same population as the reference sample. Another advantage of the forensic sampling

BOX 13.1 SEQUENCE OF EVENTS REQUIRED FOR DATA FROM A FORENSIC CASE TO GET INTO FDB

1. Homicide, suicide, or some other unattended death
2. Extended postmortem interval
3. Remains discovered, authorities notified, and forensic anthropologist consulted
4. Forensic anthropologist works up case
5. Remains positively identified
6. Family claims remains
7. Forensic anthropologist provides data to FDB

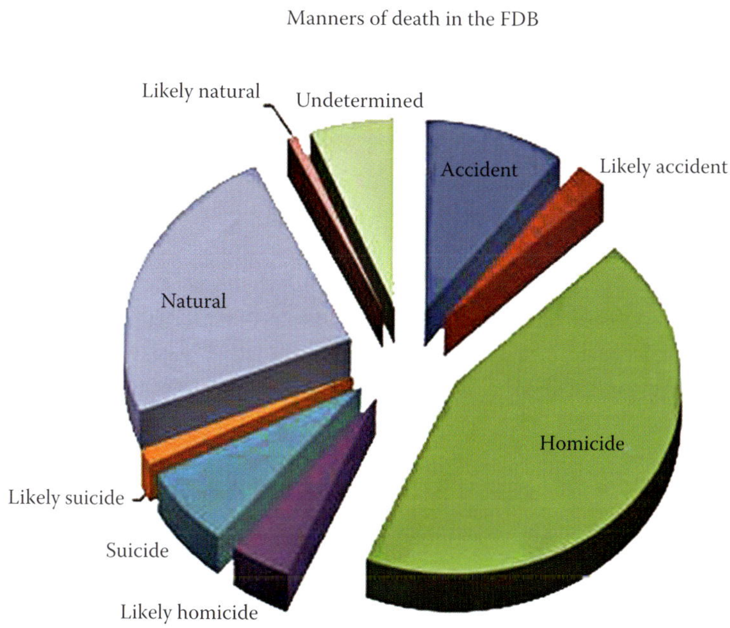

Figure 13.1 Distribution of manners of death in the FDB, showing the large number due to Homicide and Suicide.

framework, unfortunate as it is, is that young adults and children are often victims and hence are represented in the data bank, whereas they are seldom found in anatomical and donated collections. Consequently, the forensic sampling framework provides an ideal database for the basic job Fordisc is asked to perform.

Introduction to Fordisc

In order to use Fordisc effectively, one must have a basic understanding of cranial and postcranial measurements and how to take them accurately. The measurements, techniques, and instruments required are described in Moore-Jansen et al. (1994). Fordisc help files also provide definitions, and in the case of cranial measurements, illustrations. One must also have a basic understanding of the statistical procedures Fordisc uses and how to interpret its output. It is sometimes assumed that Fordisc absolves the user of any responsibility and simply provides the desired answer concerning sex, ancestry, or stature. Like everything about analyzing a forensic case, the ultimate interpretation is up to you. In what follows, we will attempt to guide you through what Fordisc does and how best to interpret it.

Basic Fordisc

Launching FD3 presents an opening screen like the one shown in Figure 13.2. The basic options provided by Fordisc are given on this opening screen. They include blanks where measurements from the skull to be analyzed can either be entered from the keyboard or loaded from a previously saved file and a check box beside each measurement that allows it to be included or excluded from the analysis. Variable names in blue have missing data that will reduce sample size, and those in red will seriously reduce sample size. Population samples of groups to which the unknown skull is to be compared have check boxes for the user to select. Of the available reference groups, Whites and Blacks are predominantly forensic cases, although the samples also include donated individuals from the University of Tennessee and the University of New Mexico donated collections. The Hispanic sample consists of forensic cases, many of which were border crossers in the Southwest, and none of which come from the Caribbean area. The American Indian sample is a combination of forensic cases and known historical individuals. The Asian samples are from anatomical collections in the countries from which they come. All individuals in Fordisc's database are positively identified as to sex and ancestry from premortem information, and all have twentieth century birth years except some of the American Indians.

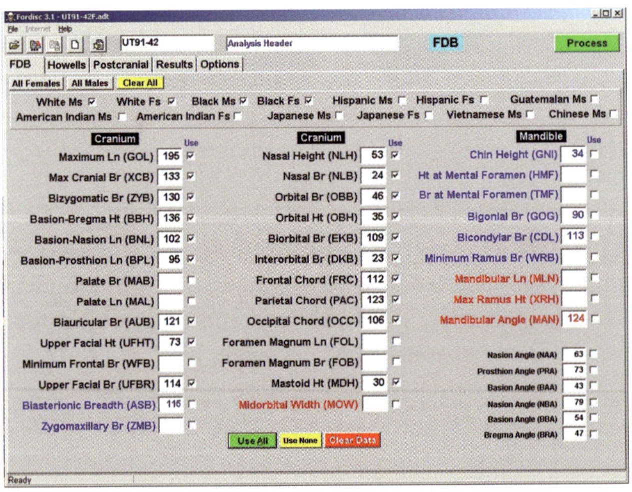

Figure 13.2 Basic Fordisc entry screen showing measurement entry blanks for the unknown case, reference samples against which it can be compared, and check boxes to include or exclude measurements and groups.

Sex and Ancestry from Cranial Measurements

We begin with an illustration of a forensic case (case UT 91-42) examined by University of Tennessee forensic anthropologists. The authors of Fordisc have a certain emotional attachment to this case, since it is the first forensic case analyzed using Fordisc. It was recovered from a creek near Oak Ridge, Tennessee, and the original visual assessment suggested it was a White male. Here we compare it to White and Black males and females, as indicated by the groups checked in Figure 13.2, allowing a simultaneous assessment of ancestry and sex. Once the user has selected the measurements and groups, processing is initiated by pushing the "Process" button at the upper right of the screen. Basic FD3 output is shown in Table 13.1. It consists of three parts, which will be explained in turn:

1. Fordisc first gives the case identification number, the variables utilized and a classification matrix of the reference samples selected. This classification matrix indicates how well Fordisc classified the individuals in its own reference samples. In this example, its overall correct classification rate is 81.3%, given at the bottom of the classification table. The individual rows and columns give results for specific groups. For example, of the 125 White males, 107 are correctly classified, 11 misclassify as White females (correct by race, incorrect by sex), 6 misclassify as Black males (incorrect by race, correct by sex), and 1 misclassifies as Black females (incorrect for both race and sex). Note that at the bottom of the table, it is stated that the classifications were cross-validated. Cross-validation, sometimes called the hold-one-out method or jackknife method, means each individual is removed from the sample before being classified. This prevents an individual from contributing its own information to the function, resulting in an unbiased classification rate.
2. The second part of FD3 output is the most important because it contains the classification of the unknown skull. The multigroup classification table contains three kinds of information. The "Distance From" column is the Mahalanobis distance (D^2) of the unknown skull from each of the reference groups, presented in order of increasing distance. A skull is normally classified into the group to which it is most similar, that is, the group with the lowest distance, in this case Black males. Additional information in the table allows us to assess the reliability of the classification. The column labeled "posterior probability" gives the probability of the skull to each group, using the assumption that it must belong to one of the groups. The posterior probability will always be highest for the group to which the skull has the lowest distance. What is important in using the posterior probabilities is how they are distributed over the different groups. In this case, the posterior probability is 0.794 for Black males, which we can take to mean that the individual has an almost 80% chance of being a Black male, assuming it actually belongs to one of the four groups we have used.

Information in the remaining three columns contains various kinds of typicality probabilities. Unlike the posterior probability, typicality probabilities make no assumption that the skull must belong to one of the reference groups. The typicality probability addresses

Table 13.1 Basic FD3 Output for Cranial Analysis

Fordisc 3.1 Analysis of UT91-42

DF results using 17 variables:

AUB BBH BNL BPL DKB EKB FRC GOL NLB NLH OBB OBH OCC PAC UFHT XCB ZYB

From Group	Total Number	Into Group BF	BM	WF	WM	Percent Correct
BF	38	31	3	4	0	81.6
BM	41	3	31	4	3	75.6
WF	95	9	2	74	10	77.9
WM	125	1	6	11	107	85.6

Total correct: 243 out of 299 (81.3%) ***CROSS-VALIDATED***.

Multigroup Classification of UT91-42

Group	Classified into	Distance from	Posterior	Probabilities Typ F	Typ Chi	Typ R
BM	**BM**	26.8	0.794	0.559	0.061	0.143 (36/42)
WF		31.0	0.097	0.118	**0.020**	**0.031 (93/96)**
WM		31.1	0.092	0.081	**0.019**	**0.039 (121/126)**
BF		34.6	0.017	0.395	**0.007**	**0.026 (38/39)**

UT91-42 is closest to BMs.

	UT91-42	Chk	Group Means BF 38	BM 41	WF 95	WM 125
AUB	121		116.1	121.1	116.7	123.6
BBH	136		130.0	138.3	134.1	141.7
BNL	102		97.9	105.5	99.5	105.5
BPL	95		98.8	103.9	92.4	96.4
DKB	23		22.9	24.4	20.0	21.3
EKB	109	++	95.5	100.9	93.9	97.7
FRC	112		107.5	113.5	109.4	114.2
GOL	195	+	178.8	189.1	178.1	187.1
NLB	24		25.0	26.1	22.5	23.7
NLH	53	+	48.4	52.4	49.3	52.7
OBB	**46**	+++	38.3	40.4	39.2	40.6
OBH	35	+	34.7	34.9	33.2	33.7
OCC	106	+	96.7	99.7	97.6	100.5
PAC	123	+	112.3	117.0	112.8	117.9
UFHT	74	+	67.3	72.6	67.2	71.4
XCB	133	–	133.2	136.9	135.8	141.4
ZYB	130		122.0	130.9	120.3	130.1

Natural log of determinant = 38.9300.

the question of whether the skull could belong to one or more of the groups. Typ F converts the Mahalanobis distance to an F ratio, and typicality is the probability associated with that F ratio. Typ F is normally the most conservative. In the present example, we see that Typ F would say that it is typical of all groups (probability > 0.05). Note that White males have the lowest typicality because they have the largest sample size. Typ Chi is based on the chi square distribution of the Mahalanobis distance. It ignores sample size, effectively assuming it is very large. Typ Chi shows that the unknown skull is only typical of Black males, but just barely, and atypical of the remainder. Typ Chi will always vary directly with the Mahalanobis distance.

Typ R is arguably the most useful typicality probability because it is empirical and makes no assumptions about distributions. It is obtained by adding the unknown skull to each group in turn and calculating the Mahalanobis distance of each skull to its group centroid. The example in Table 13.1 will help clarify how this probability works and what it can tell us. The unknown skull ranks 36 out of 42 ($n+1$, where n refers to the reference sample size), meaning that 35 of the skulls that actually belong to the group are closer to the centroid than the unknown. The probability is obtained as $(42-36)/42=0.143$. That probability tells us that the unknown skull falls comfortably within the range of variation of black males. The unknown skull would be judged atypical of the other three samples. It does fall within their range of variation, but on the extreme margin.

Fordisc also lists the measurements for the unknown skull and the means for the reference samples chosen. The column labeled "chk" indicates how the individual deviates from the overall reference groups. A "+" means larger and a "–" means smaller, and the number of pluses or minuses indicates the magnitude of the deviation. In the present instance, OBB (orbit breadth) has three plus signs, meaning it deviates three to four standard deviations from the reference samples. Large deviations can occur because some dimensions may be larger or smaller, or they could indicate measurement error. In this case, it is the former, but large deviations should be checked to rule out error.

Sex and Ancestry from Postcranial Measurements

Fordisc offers the same analysis on postcranial measurements as that just presented using cranial measurements. Pushing the postcranial tab at the top of the screen puts up a postcranial screen like that shown in Figure 13.3. At present, the samples available for postcranial analysis are limited to Blacks and Whites, but Hispanics are coming soon. It often comes as a surprise, even to many experienced forensic anthropologists, that postcranial bones can discriminate ancestry as well as cranial bones. The reason postcranial remains are underappreciated in this respect is apparently because it is much easier to form visual assessments of skull morphology than it is for the postcranial skeleton, not that the skull is more differentiated.

Table 13.2 shows the FD3 output for the postcranial analysis from the options chosen in Figure 13.3. The overall classification rate is only about 2% lower than that seen for cranial classification. Table 13.2 shows that case UT91-42 is a Black male. That assessment agrees with the cranial classification, but the posterior probability is even higher, telling us that we have 94% chance of being correct, assuming the individual belongs to one of the groups we have selected. The typicality probabilities indicate that the skeleton falls comfortably within the range of variation of Black males and White males.

Table 13.2 Basic FD3 Output for Postcranial Analysis

Fordisc 3.1 Analysis of UT91-42

DF results using 13 variables:

FEMMAP	FEMMTV	FEMXLN	HUMXLN	ILIABR	RADXLN	SACABR
SACAHT	SCAPBR	SCAPHT	TIBDEB	TIBPEB	TIBXLN	

	Total	Into Group				
From Group	Number	BF	BM	WF	WM	Percent Correct
BF	25	20	0	5	0	80.0%
BM	55	1	46	1	7	83.6%
WF	73	14	0	56	3	76.7%
WM	154	6	24	3	121	78.6%

Total correct: 243 out of 307 (79.2 %) *** CROSS VALIDATED ***

Multigroup Classification of Current Case

	Classified	Distance		Probabilities		
Group	into	from	Posterior	Typ F	Typ Chi	Typ R
BM	**BM**	8.4	0.939	0.916	0.817	0.750 (14/56)
WM		13.9	0.061	0.477	0.383	0.355 (100/155)
BF		31.0	0.000	0.409	**0.003**	**0.038 (26/26)**
WF		40.8	0.000	**0.007**	**0.000**	**0.014 (72/74)**

Current case is closest to BMs.

			Group Means			
			BF	BM	WF	WM
Current	Case	Chk	25	55	73	154
FEMMAP	31		27.5	31.6	27.5	30.9
FEMMTV	28	+	23.8	27.8	24.3	27.9
FEMXLN	520	++	441.0	488.1	435.8	473.6
HUMXLN	370	++	308.8	340.7	305.1	334.6
ILIABR	154		144.3	153.4	155.2	160.9
RADXLN	278	+	235.3	267.7	227.6	253.3
SACABR	98	–	100.2	101.9	109.7	107.5
SACAHT	104		103.4	104.4	110.1	112.9
SCAPBR	117	++	94.2	109.5	94.8	108.2
SCAPHT	166	+	136.7	161.1	142.5	163.4
TIBDEB	48		45.3	51.3	46.5	52.0
TIBPEB	80	+	68.9	78.6	70.0	79.3
TIBXLN	429	+	366.4	409.2	357.8	392.9

Natural log of determinant = 47.2414.

Stature

Note a green button labeled "stature" at the bottom right of the postcranial screen in Figure 13.3. Pushing that button brings up the stature estimation screen, shown in Figure 13.4. The choices offered by this screen consist of different samples to be used to compute the regression and the kind of stature to be used. Groups available are Black or White males or females, Hispanic

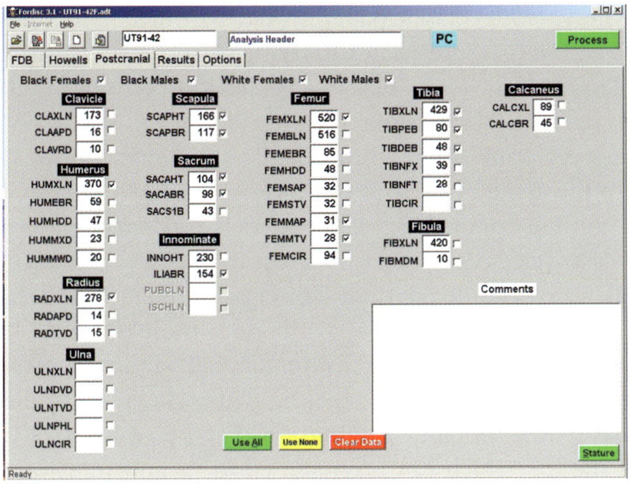

Figure 13.3 Basic Fordisc postcranial screen, which is parallel to the cranial screen as shown in Figure 13.2.

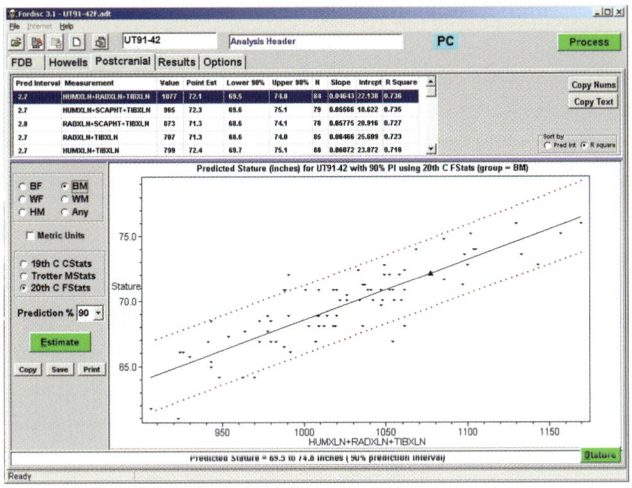

Figure 13.4 Stature screen showing choices of reference samples, kinds of statures available, and example results.

males, or any. The last should only be used if you have no idea of ancestry. Ancestry can make a substantial difference in the stature estimate because of different limb proportions.

It may be well to consider different types of stature. We often consider height to be a single number that describes an aspect of our body. It is normally included on documents such as driver's licenses, missing persons reports, descriptions of criminal suspects, or medical documents. In fact, it is a highly variable number, depending on its origin. Snow and Williams (1971) found variation as great as 5 in. in reported stature for a single individual from different sources. A person's height even varies throughout the course of a day. FD3 contains three types of stature:

1. *Nineteenth Century Cstats.* Cstats refers to cadaver statures. Choosing this option uses the cadaver statures from the Terry Anatomical Collection and included in

Trotter and Gleser (1952) classic paper on estimating height. There is little agreement on how cadaver stature relates to living stature, but it is usually considered to be larger. Trotter and Gleser (1952) suggested it exceeds living stature by 2.5 cm.

2. *Trotter Mstats* refers to the measured statures Trotter was able to obtain from World War II military personnel killed in the Pacific Theater. Height was measured upon induction into the armed forces, and Trotter was able to measure the long bones after death. Choosing this option uses the statures and long bone lengths from which Trotter and Gleser (1952) derived their stature regression equations. We should note that the sample sizes are different than Trotter and Gleser (1952) because we included some that Trotter did not use or those with one or more elements missing.
3. *Twentieth Century Fstats.* Fstats refer to forensic stature as defined by Ousley (1995). Forensic stature is a number that is written down somewhere, such as on a driver's license or other documents mentioned earlier. It has a lot in common with self-reported stature, which has been shown to be an overestimate of measured stature (Giles and Hutchinson 1991; Willey and Falsetti 1991). Forensic stature will normally result in a larger stature estimate and a larger prediction interval than measured stature, but this is acceptable because it is usually forensic stature to which our skeletal estimate will be compared.

After choosing the stature data, ancestry, and sex, and clicking on the "estimate" button, statistics pertaining to the stature estimate are displayed in the upper panel, and a plot of height on bone length appears in the lower panel, including the least squares regression line and the 90% prediction interval (Figure 13.4). The prediction interval can also be set to 95% or 99% by choosing the desired figure from the box just below the stature type. For purposes of this example, we chose Fstats for Black males. Note that the user can choose whether the results are expressed in inches or centimeters. We use inches in this example.

Results in the upper panel include all possible combinations of the sums of three bones, two bones, and individual bones, arranged in ascending order using R^2, or the prediction interval (the value in the left hand column of the upper panel). Normally, one would select the estimated stature in first row as the most accurate, in this case, 72.1 in. The upper and lower prediction intervals tell us that we can be 90% confident that the stature of the individual falls between 69.5 and 74.8 in. Upper and lower prediction intervals are obtained by adding and subtracting the prediction interval from the estimate.

What Fordisc has done is solve the least squares regression equation. The columns labeled slope and intercept are the two constants Fordisc uses to estimate the stature of the unknown case by solving for

Stature = 0.04643 * 1077 + 22.138, where 1077 is the sum of lengths of the humerus, radius, and tibia, given under the column heading "Value." Last, the column labeled R^2 gives the proportion of variation in height explained by the bone lengths. Subsequent rows present similar information for other combinations. Although the first row of the upper panel should normally be accepted as the most accurate because it has the lowest prediction interval, it may also be instructive to examine the other estimates. The different estimates are in good agreement, the highest (72.4 in.) and the lowest (71.3 in.) differing by just over an inch. Some variation is to be expected because different combinations of bones relate to stature in slightly different ways. In the present instance, those estimates lacking the humerus are lower than those which include it, suggesting the humerus is relatively longer in relation to stature than the scapula, tibia, and radius.

The graph in the lower panel gives the bivariate plot of stature on bone dimensions for the reference sample, along with the fitted regression line and 90% prediction intervals. Scrolling down brings up the graph for each combination in turn. The unknown's position is on the regression line and allows for a visual appreciation of where it falls in relation to the reference sample for bone dimensions and estimated stature. In the example given in Figure 13.4, it is apparent that the unknown is above average, but not extreme, for bone dimensions and therefore for estimated stature.

The forensic stature recorded for UT91-42 is 72 in. versus an estimated height of 72.1 in.; so, in this case, the estimate is very close to the recorded forensic stature.

Advanced Topics

What has been presented thus far is the basic procedure, but Fordisc has several important options that provide some additional analytical choices. We will describe these options, when to use them and how to use the results.

Howells' Data

The main Fordisc screen is designed to deal with the majority of the situations likely to be faced in the American context. The main screen contains samples drawn from the major populations in the United States. However, it can be the case that a cranium can come from anywhere in the world, for example, trophy skulls (Sledzik and Ousley 1991), archaeological specimens, or even immigrants from different parts of the world. Or questions sometimes arise concerning museum specimens and whether they are really what the museum records say they are and therefore may be subject to repatriation (Pickering and Jantz 1995). When context is lacking, Howells' worldwide data provide a larger framework against which to compare a specimen.

Howells' data also contain many more measurements than those on the basic forensic screen, 61 in total. Howells' measurements are carefully described (Howells 1973) and have become widely adopted as a measurement protocol. One important point to note is that those measurements on the FDB screen with three-letter codes (e.g., GOL) use Howells' definitions, while those with four-letter codes (e.g., UFBR) are either not defined by Howells or are defined differently (see Moore Jansen et al. 1994). Obtaining Howells' measurements requires either special instruments or a digitizer. If you have only taken the basic measurements required for the forensic screen, you can still compare your unknown skull to Howells' samples for those measurements. Using Howells' data is recommended when you suspect that the skull originates from outside the United States. In that case, Howells' data can provide some idea of skull's geographic origin.

Options

Clicking on the options tab on the right side of the tool bar brings up a screen with several analytical options. The screen with the default options checked is shown in Figure 13.5. On the left side of this is an option called "Transformations" with choices "None" (the default), "Log," and "Shape." Using the default is normally the best course of action. The "Log" option carries out the analysis after transforming the variables to natural logarithms, and the "Shape" option carries out the calculations after transforming the variables to Darroch

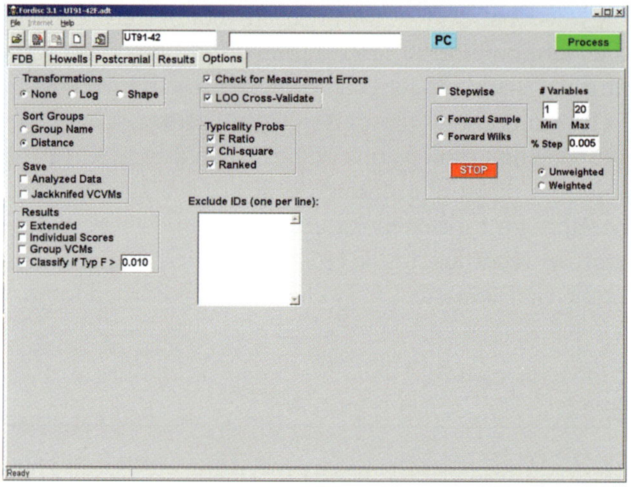

Figure 13.5 Options screen showing the various analytical options Fordisc offers. Defaults are checked.

and Mosimann (1985) shape variables. Logarithms may in some cases make the data more normally distributed, particularly if the original data have a positive skew.

Darroch and Mosimann's shape variables are obtained by dividing each variable by the geometric mean of all variables for each individual. The geometric mean serves as a measure of isometric size, and dividing each variable by it yields shape variables that are free of isometric size. Choosing the shape option may be desirable if a skull or postcranial skeleton is unusually large or small, and you wish to assess its relationships using shape alone. If the question you are asking Fordisc to answer pertains to ancestry, choosing shape may not make much difference, since ancestry variation is mostly shape-based. However, it makes a substantial difference for sex estimation because sex dimorphism has a substantial size component. For example, using 18 raw variables to classify the White male and female reference samples yields a correct classification of 90.5%. Using the same 18 shape variables reduces the classification to 78.2%. This illustrates the loss of discriminatory power resulting from removing size, but it also illustrates that considerable sex dimorphism remains in shape alone, since 78.2% correct classification is far above the chance expectation of 50%.

Check for Measurement Errors

To the right of "Transformations" is a check box that enables the user to turn off the measurement check option. The default is on, and there are not normally any reasons to turn it off. If you enter measurements that are outside the range of normal variation, Fordisc will tell you the measurement looks wrong and ask you if you want to change it.

LOO Cross-Validate

"LOO" means "leave-one-out," and it is the option discussed earlier in going over the classification of the reference samples. LOO turned on is the default. If it is turned off, the classification will be done without removing the classified individual, known as resubstitution, resulting in a biased classification rate of the reference samples. The only advantage of turning LOO off is that processing proceeds faster, which may be important when doing a large number of groups and variables.

Typicality Probs

This option presents check boxes that enable you turn the various typicality probabilities on or off. The default is on, and there is not normally a good reason to turn them off, since each presents some information about the skeleton being analyzed.

Stepwise

This option is an important one but also requires some care in implementing because it is a complex topic. Stepwise solutions in discriminant analysis are a well-known way of attempting to find a subset of variables that discriminates the reference samples as well as, or in some cases, better than the full set. It can be used to prevent something known as overfitting. Overfitting means that the sample sizes are insufficient to contain all the variability in the measurements; this can result in spuriously high correct classification rates, and the functions cannot be relied on to correctly classify the unknown. The most liberal rule concerning number of allowable variables is that the number of variables must be one less than the number of individuals in each group. The most conservative rule is that the number of individuals must be three times larger than the number of variables. When you are using the FDB screen, this will not normally be a problem, except possibly for Hispanic females. It is not advisable to use all of Howells' 61 variables because most samples have fewer than 61 individuals.

A disadvantage of stepwise procedures is that they capitalize on sampling error. Fortunately, most samples on the FDB screen are large enough so this may not be an important issue, but some combinations of variables (e.g., those in blue or red) and groups (e.g., Hispanic females) may create those problems and should best be avoided.

To use the stepwise option, you must check the "Stepwise" box to turn on the option. There is also a box where you can set the minimum and maximum number of variables you want stepwise to choose. You must then choose the kind of stepwise analysis you wish to use. The simplest and fastest is "Forward Wilks." It uses Wilks' lambda, a measure of variation among groups relative to the total. It starts with the variable with the lowest Wilks' lambda (lower values mean greater variation) and then finds the next variable that results in the greatest improvement, and so on until improvement is trivial.

Choosing the "forward sample" option bases variable selection on the percentage correct in the reference samples. You can choose the percent improvement required for the process to continue. The default is 0.005 or 0.5%. When the minimum number of variables is set to 1, stepwise chooses the best variable and then tries all others until adding an additional variable no longer exceeds 0.5%. If you set the minimum variables to 2, stepwise will try all possible combinations of two variables until it finds the best two and then adds others until the criterion is no longer met. The same is true of three variables and so on. For a minimum greater than three, the computation time rises rapidly because of the large number of permutations the program must try. If you start stepwise and it is taking longer than you want to wait, you can push the "stop" button and start over.

Criticisms, Limitations, and Opportunities

Criticisms

Fordisc was originally designed as a tool to be used by forensic anthropologists working in the United States. With the addition of Howells' data in Fordisc 2 and its expansion to all of Howells' variables in Fordisc 3, wider applications were inevitable and desirable. Also inevitable were tests of how well Fordisc performs in different circumstances. This is also desirable when the tests are honest attempts to define limits on Fordisc's applicability. For example, Ramsthaler et al. (2007) have asked whether Fordisc can be used to estimate sex from cranial measurements in European populations. They conclude that it presents biased results because of morphometric differences between American Whites and Europeans and that in order for Fordisc to be applied to recent Europeans reference samples from recent Europeans should be included. This is a conclusion with which we whole-heartedly agree, and we are working toward making Fordisc's database more representative of Europe and other parts of the world.

Other tests of Fordisc are seemingly designed to make it fail, suggesting that the desired outcome was decided in advance of the analysis. Elliott and Collard (2009) argue that Fordisc can only assess ancestry correctly 1% of the time. They reach this absurd conclusion by imposing unrealistic expectations and misusing Fordisc's statistics (Siegel and Ousley 2011). One can easily imagine that regular users of Fordisc would long ago have realized such a performance deficiency and ceased using it.

Other tests of Fordisc begin with the assumption that most of the variation is within races rather than among them, following Lewontin (1972), and therefore attempts at allocating crania to their correct groups are a futile endeavor. This is the view expressed in Williams et al. (2005), who, like Elliott and Collard, impose unrealistic expectations on Fordisc and refuse to be guided by the statistics it provides. Their conclusion is that skeletal remains cannot be sorted by geographic region except at the extremes, but forensic experience has shown that even populations in relatively circumscribed areas can be effectively allocated to the correct group, for example, North and South Japanese (Ousley et al. 2009).

Yet another direction from which criticism has come is the idea that in America, race is purely a social construct with no biological relevance (Goodman 1997; Albanese and Saunders 2006). Much has been made of the observation that sometimes forensic anthropologists make incorrect ancestry assessments. Goodman (1997) argues that the Giles and Elliot (1962) functions classify at a rate no better than by chance, again a predetermined outcome seeking support. The problems with Giles and Elliot have little to do with the nonexistence of race, but rather with the reference samples. A more realistic test of Giles and Elliot's discriminant functions revealed that it performed well except for Native Americans (Snow et al. 1979), which is a consequence of an inappropriate reference sample.

Is it necessary for race to exist as a valid biological taxon in order to justify using Fordisc in the way forensic anthropologists do? Not in our view. What we know exists are populations, and populations exist because humans develop a variety of mechanisms that structure mating. We accept that race in America is a social category, but it also plays a major role in mating. The very terms "African American" and "European American" imply origins from distinctive populations, which to a considerable degree have remained reproductively isolated. The U.S. Census and other federal documents require self-identification of a racial and ethnic category. Asking people to place themselves into racial categories such as White, Black, Native American, Asian, or Pacific Islander, or into ethnic categories such as Hispanic or non-Hispanic, is undoubtedly an oversimplification. Since the European colonization of America, these populations have evolved in various complex ways, giving rise to populations with various degrees of admixture (e.g., Parra et al. 1998). However, the U.S. Census data show that the majority of matings are within social race categories. It is a basic tenet of anthropological genetics that reproductive isolation maintains preexisting variation and allows new variation to emerge. We readily acknowledge that American populations are becoming more complex and that ancestry estimation is becoming more difficult. To those who argue that forensic anthropologists should not make ancestry assessments because they may be wrong, we would just say that practitioners should not make dogmatic statements and should be guided by probabilities in making their assessments. Of course we can be wrong, because the question asked pertains to social race, but the answer provided is based on biology. We would also say that it is rare that proper statistical evaluation of measurements cannot reveal useful information about the unidentified skeleton before you.

Limitations

Every method has limitations, and Fordisc is no exception. Allocating an unknown using group means as the criterion may not yield the optimal solution. Using K-nearest neighbor, where the criterion is the individual crania most similar to the unknown, to determine the classification may be more appropriate in some cases and is being considered as a future option for Fordisc.

The greatest limitation is lack of appropriate reference samples. American Whites, Blacks, and Hispanics of Mexican origin are now well represented, but Caribbean Hispanics are not. We have few American-born Asians, and the exceedingly variable Native American populations are underrepresented. The most recent U.S. Census shows that the American population is changing rapidly, and former barriers to intermarriage are breaking down. These new Americans will present increasingly complex challenges to forensic anthropology. It will not ever be possible to have adequate samples of every population in America, but the data bank (FDB) and forensic anthropology offer at least some hope of keeping up with its main components.

Another challenge is incorporating more of the world's populations. Fordisc is becoming more popular abroad, and in order to be useful, it must have samples from regions where it may be applied.

Opportunities

Some of the limitations mentioned earlier can be converted into opportunities, for example, improving the sample coverage or adding new procedures. However, for students and professionals alike, Fordisc provides some interesting opportunities beyond just evaluating forensic cases. It can be used to explore human cranial and postcranial variation. For example, it is often stated that the cranium is the second best area to use for sex estimation, after the pelvis, and should be used when the pelvis is unavailable (Byers 2008). It is easy to show using Fordisc that the cranium is inferior to most postcranial elements for metric sexing (Spradley and Jantz 2011). Or one can use the nineteenth and twentieth century Americans on the Howells' page to show that so much secular change has occurred in Americans over the past century that nineteenth and twentieth century American crania can be easily discriminated from one another (Jantz and Meadows Jantz 2000). Many other interesting questions can be formulated and addressed with Fordisc. Such questions will only increase as Fordisc's database and features continue to grow. We conclude with the recommendation that users of Fordisc update regularly. Updating can be accomplished using the "Internet" tab at the top of the opening screen. Updating will insure that you are using the most current version of Fordisc with the most up-to-date database. There is also a "Submit case to the FDB" option under the internet tab that enables you to submit a case to the FDB and participate in the effort to keep the database current.

References

Albanese J and Saunders SR. 2006. Is it possible to escape racial typology in forensic identification? In: Schmitt E, Cunha E, Pinheiro J (Eds.). *Forensic Anthropology and Medicine: Complementary Sciences from Recovery to Cause of Death*. Totowa, NJ: Humana Press, Inc., pp. 281–316.

Barnard MM. 1935. The secular variations of skull characters in four series of Egyptian skulls. *Annals of Eugenics* 6:352–371.

Byers SN. 2008. *Introduction to Forensic Anthropology*. Boston, MA: Pearson/Allyn and Bacon.

Darroch JN and Mosimann JE. 1985. Canonical and principal components of shape. *Biometrika* 72:241–252.

Elliott M and Collard M. 2009. Fordisc and the determination of ancestry from cranial measurements. *Biology Letters* 5:849–852.

Fisher RA. 1936. The use of multiple measurements in taxonomic problems. *Annals of Eugenics* 7:179–188.

Giles E and Elliot O. 1962. Race identification from cranial measurement. *Journal of Forensic Sciences* 7:147–151.

Giles E and Elliot O. 1963. Sex determination by discriminant function analysis of crania. *American Journal of Physical Anthropology* 21:53–68.

Giles E and Hutchinson DL. 1991. Stature-related and age-related bias in self reported stature. *Journal of Forensic Sciences* 36(3):765–780.

Goodman AH. 1997. Bred in the bone. *Sciences* 37:20–25.

Howells WW. 1973. *Cranial Variation in Man: A Study by Multivariate Analysis of Patterns of Difference among Recent Human Populations*. Papers of the Peabody Museum of Archaeology and Ethnology. Cambridge, MA: Harvard University.

Jantz RL and Meadows Jantz L. 2000. Secular change in craniofacial morphology. *American Journal of Human Biology* 12: 327–338.

Jantz RL and Moore-Jansen PH. 1988. A data base for forensic anthropology. Report of Investigations No. 47, Department of Anthropology, University of Tennessee, Knoxville, TN.

Lewontin RC. 1972. The apportionment of human diversity. *Evolutionary Biology* 6:381–398.

Mahalanobis PC. 1936. On the generalized distance in statistics. *Proceedings of the National Institute of Sciences of India* 2(1):49–55.

Moore-Jansen PH, Ousley SD, and Jantz RL. 1994. Data collection procedures for forensic skeletal material. Report of Investigation No. 48. Department of Anthropology, The University of Tennessee, Knoxville, TN.

Ousley SD. 1995. Should we estimate biological or forensic stature? *Journal of Forensic Sciences* 40:768–773.

Ousley SD, Jantz RL, and Freid D. 2009. Understanding race and human variation: Why forensic anthropologists are good at identifying race. *American Journal of Physical Anthropology* 139:68–76.

Parra EJ, Marcini A, Akey J, Martinson J, Batzer MA, Cooper R, Forrester T et al. 1998. Estimating African American admixture proportions by use of population-specific alleles. *American Journal of Human Genetics* 63(6):1839–1851.

Penrose LS. 1954. Distance, size and shape. *Annals of Eugenics* 18:337–343.

Pickering R and Jantz RL. 1995. Look again before repatriating. *Federal Archaeology* 7:44.

Ramsthaler F, Kreutz K, and Verhoff MA. 2007. Accuracy of metric sex analysis of skeletal remains using Fordisc based on a recent skull collection. *International Journal of Legal Medicine* 121(6):477–482.

Rao CR. 1952. *Advanced Statistical Methods in Biometrical Research*. New York: John Wiley & Sons.

Siegel ND and Ousley SD. 2011. The importance of testing and understanding statistical methods in the age of *Daubert*. Can Fordisc really classify individuals correctly only one percent of the time? *Proceedings of the American Academy of Forensic Sciences* 17:364–365.

Sledzik PS and Ousley S. 1991. Analysis of six Vietnamese trophy skulls. *Journal of Forensic Sciences* 36(2):520–530.

Smith CAB. 1980. Estimating genetic correlations. *Annals of Human Genetics*. 43:265–284.

Snow CC, Hartman S, Giles E, and Young FA. 1979. Sex and race determination of crania by calipers and computer: A test of the Giles and Elliot discriminant functions in 52 forensic cases. *Journal of Forensic Sciences* 24(2):448–460.

Snow C and Williams J. 1971. Variation in premortem statural measurements compared to statural estimates of skeletal remains. *Journal of Forensic Sciences* 16:455–464.

Spradley MK and Jantz RL. 2011. Sex estimation in forensic anthropology: Skull versus postcranial elements. *Journal of Forensic Sciences* 56:289–296.

Thieme FP. 1957. Sex in Negro skeletons. *Journal of Forensic Medicine* 4:72–81.

Thieme FP and Schull WJ. 1957. Sex determination from the skeleton. *Human Biology* 29:242–273.

Trotter M and Gleser GC. 1952. Estimation of stature from long bones of American Whites and Negroes. *American Journal of Physical Anthropology* 10:463–514.

Willey P and Falsetti T. 1991. Inaccuracy of height information on driver's licenses. *Journal of Forensic Sciences* 36(3):813–819.

Williams FE, Belcher RL, and Armelagos GJ. 2005. Forensic misclassification of ancient Nubian crania: Implications for assumptions about human variation. *Current Anthropology* 46:340–346.

Low-Velocity Trauma

14

HUGH E. BERRYMAN, NATALIE R. SHIRLEY, AND ALICJA K. LANFEAR

Contents

For the purpose of this chapter, low-velocity trauma refers to injuries caused by anything other than a fired bullet. Hammers, baseball bats, knives, and axes are examples of weapons commonly encountered in low-velocity trauma cases. Falls from heights, vehicle crashes, and pedestrian hits are also included in this category as well as fractures resulting from strangulation and fist fights. This chapter will present two distinct types of low-velocity trauma—blunt and sharp trauma—and briefly discuss the fracture mechanics and patterns associated with each of these broad categories.

Basic Bone Biomechanics

Forensic anthropologists use the principles of bone biomechanics to interpret skeletal trauma. The mechanical behavior of bone is determined by its material and structural properties (intrinsic variables), as well as the load properties (extrinsic variables) to which it is subjected. Intrinsic variables consist of material properties such as bone microstructure, cortical thickness, and trabecular thickness, while structural properties include bone morphology (i.e., size and shape). Extrinsic variables include the magnitude, direction, rate, area of application, and duration of the load applied to the bone. Put simply, intrinsic variables are those related to the bone, and extrinsic variables are those related to the weapon or object causing the injury.

Bone is *viscoelastic* and *anisotropic*. The viscoelastic nature of bone refers to the fact that it responds like a pliable material while having an elastic component that allows it to

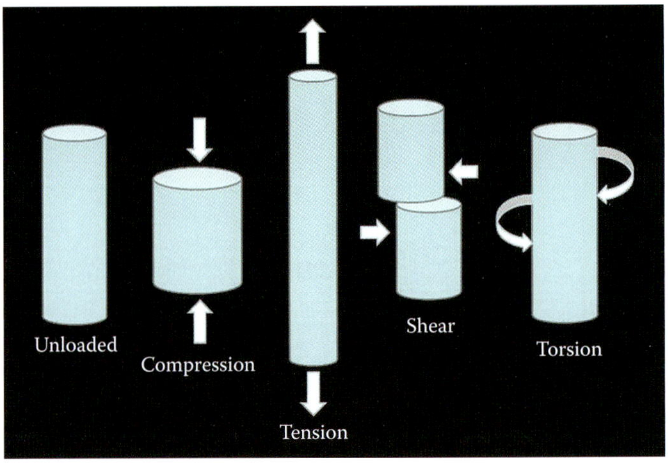

Figure 14.1 Several simple loading scenarios. The arrows indicate the direction of the force, and the cylinder illustrates the bony response to the loading. (Adapted from Nordin M and Frankel V. Basic Biomechanics of the Musculoskeletal system, Lea and Febiger, Philadelphia, PA, 1989.)

return to its original shape after deformation. However, with sufficient rate of loading, it can react as a brittle material. Anisotropy means that the mechanical properties of bone are directionally dependent, so bone strength varies with the direction of loading. As a rule, bone is strongest in the direction that it is normally loaded. For example, the femur normally experiences axial loading, making it stronger under compression than tension or shear. Figure 14.1 shows several simple loading scenarios, although in reality bones typically undergo combined loading.

A stress–strain or load–deformation curve is commonly used to illustrate a material's response to loading. In Figure 14.2, the portion of the curve from *x* to *y* denotes the *elastic region*. At any point along this portion of the curve, the material assumes its original size

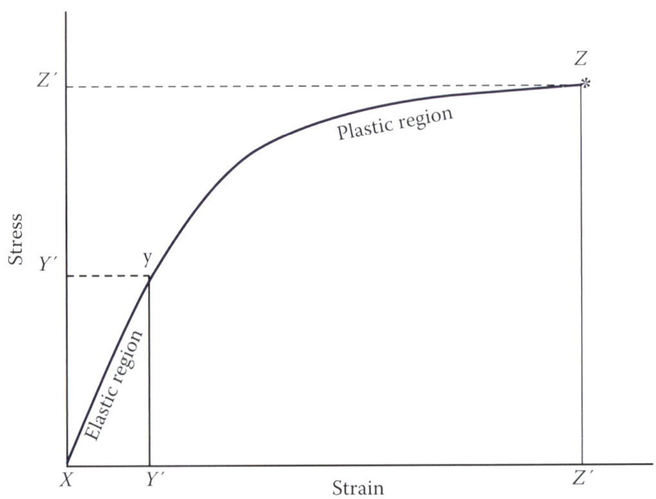

Figure 14.2 Hypothetical stress–strain curve. This curve is used to depict a material's response to loading. The area under the curve between *x* and *y* is the *elastic region*. The area under the curve between *y* and *z* is the *plastic region*. The asterisk marks the point of failure (fracture).

and shape if the load is removed. The portion of the curve between *y* and *z* represents the *plastic region*. At any point on this portion of the curve, the material deforms and will not assume its original form upon removal of the load. The asterisk denotes the point at which the material fails or fractures. Ductile materials have a larger plastic region, whereas brittle materials have a smaller plastic region and reach failure faster. Bone, as a viscoelastic material, tends to deform prior to fracture with low-velocity trauma, whereas it quickly reaches failure and experiences very little, if any deformation with high-velocity trauma. For a more in-depth review of bone biomechanics, refer to Currey (2002), McGowen (1999), and Vogel (2003).

With a sound knowledge of the intrinsic properties of bone, it is possible to interpret the result of extrinsic factors related to the weapon or object causing the injury. Different weapon types typically display distinguishing trauma or tool marks. Forensic anthropologists use these differences to classify bone trauma based on weapon type. For example, plastic deformation is a characteristic most frequently associated with blunt trauma. Sharp trauma usually manifests as incised wounds that may have characteristics indicative of the type of sharp instrument that produced it. Gunshot trauma produces entrance and exit wounds with beveling that indicates direction of fire. While these generalities often hold true, Kroman (2007) has proposed that bone trauma is too complex to neatly fit into discreet weapon-based categories. Instead, she offers a physics-based trauma continuum as a more meaningful way to conceptualize skeletal trauma. Seemingly discreet trauma categories actually overlap as exemplified by the fact that a 0.45 caliber round-nose bullet is similar in shape to a ball-peen hammer, yet it is the velocity that distinguishes the type of trauma produced.

Blunt Trauma

A major difference between blunt and sharp trauma is area of application, specifically the surface area of the body impacted by the injuring object. To illustrate this concept, Kroman (2007) gives the example of holding a 12 lb bowling ball in your palm. This force is not sufficient to cause injury because it is distributed over a large region. Stress is expressed in pounds per square inch (psi), and the stress of holding the 12 lb bowling ball is 1.33 psi. However, if a knife were inserted between the bowing ball and your palm with the tip of the knife in your palm, the stress rises to 120,000 psi because the surface area decreases significantly. If this principle is extended to skeletal trauma, it becomes obvious why these two low-velocity weapon categories (blunt and sharp) have distinctive trauma characteristics.

One signature of blunt trauma is plastic deformation, which presents when the rate of loading is sufficiently slow for the bone to permanently deform prior to failure. The extent of deformation depends on a number of variables, including the area of the body or type of bones experiencing the load. The extent of plastic deformation is frequently higher in cranial bones as compared to that exhibited in the long bones. Despite this, a common outcome of plastic deformation is the inability to perfectly reassemble bone fragments produced by low-velocity trauma. This is in contrast to fragmentation resulting from high-velocity trauma, during which bone behaves like a brittle material and shatters. Bone fragments produced by high-velocity trauma are usually undeformed and can be reassembled with near perfection.

When examining blunt trauma cases, forensic anthropologists are asked to assess the point of impact, the number of impacts, the sequence of the impacts, the amount of force, and possible weapon. The ability to sort each of these issues depends largely on the area of the body affected. What follows is a brief review of blunt trauma investigation in the skull, long bones, and axial skeletal elements. A detailed description of blunt trauma to each skeletal element can be found in Galloway (1999).

Cranium

Head injuries are common in homicides, motor vehicle collisions, and sports injuries. The 22 bones that comprise the skull encase and protect the brain. The bones of the neurocranium vary in thickness with an ectocranial cortical layer, a middle layer of spongy bone called diploë, and an endocranial cortical layer. The facial bones are much thinner and more fragile than the bones that comprise the vault. Consequently, although the cranium acts as a system, the morphological and microstructural properties of the craniofacial and neurocranial bones differ. An impact to the outer cortical surface of the neurocranium creates tension on the inner table. Hence, the bone fails first on the inner table producing fractures that propagate to the external table and radiate across the skull. Radiating fractures often define pie-shaped plates of bone. As the impacting object continues, it will displace these pie-shaped plates internally resulting in increased tension on the outer table and ultimately the formation of first-generation concentric fractures. Concentric fractures propagate perpendicular to the radiating fractures, and given sufficient force, second-generation concentric fractures will propagate (Figure 14.3; Berryman and Symes 1998). If the skull is positioned between an impacting object and another surface (e.g., a tire and the pavement), a contrecoup fracture can result from the "impact" against the opposing surface (Figure 14.4; Hein and Schulz 1990). These situations require careful scrutiny, as the two impact areas are a result of loading from two directions, but they are caused by a single traumatic episode.

Depending on the severity of the injury, facial fractures can be complicated. Rene Le Fort (1901a–c) devised a system of classifying facial fractures into three basic patterns (I, II, and III; Figure 14.5). A Le Fort I fracture separates the alveolar portion from the body of the maxilla and can be produced by a direct blow to the anterior portion of the alveolar

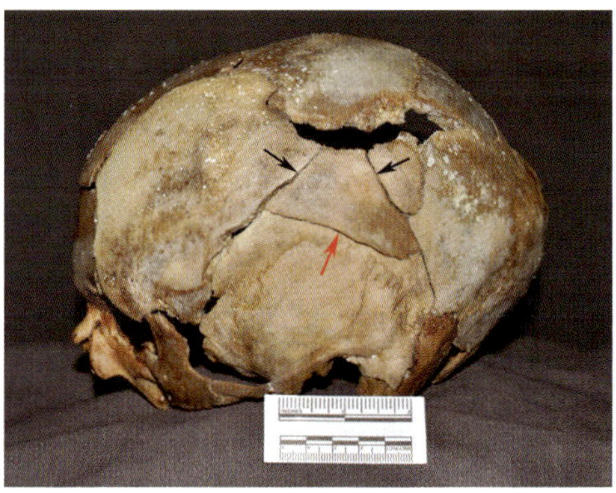

Figure 14.3 Lateral view of skull showing radiating (black arrows) and concentric fractures (red arrow). Point of impact/loading is the area of missing bone located superior to the radiating fractures. (Photograph courtesy of Forensic Anthropology Center.)

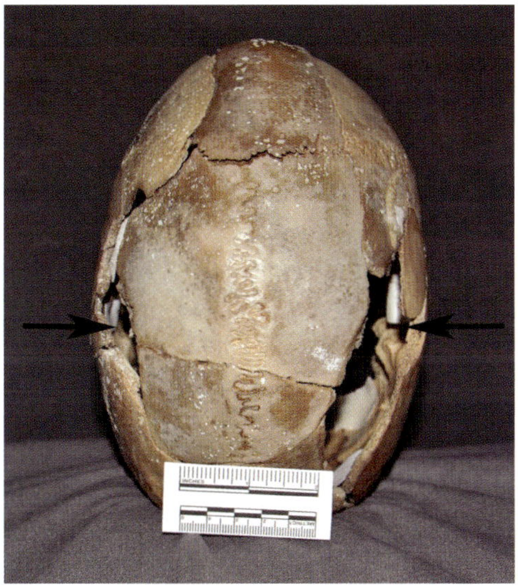

Figure 14.4 Two impact areas as a result of loading from two different directions (see arrows) from a single traumatic episode. One impact was from a tire, and the other was from the opposing surface—the pavement. (Photograph courtesy of Forensic Anthropology Center.)

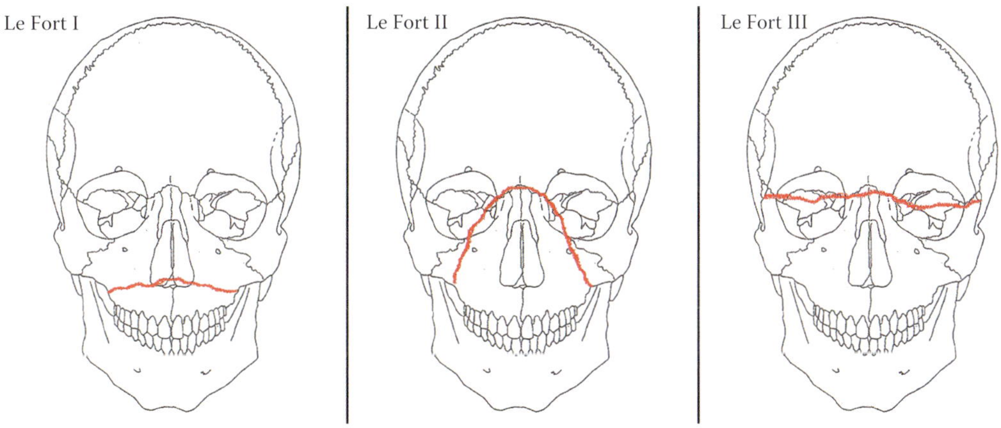

Figure 14.5 Le Fort I, II, and III fractures. Many times facial fractures represent a combination of these scenarios.

process. A Le Fort II fracture (also referred to as a *pyramidal* fracture) traverses the maxilla, lower orbital floor, and nasal bones and usually results from a more centrally directed blow. A Le Fort III fracture (transverse facial or cranial disjunction fracture) extends horizontally through the upper orbits and nasal bones separating the bones of the face from those of the vault. All three Le Fort fractures terminate after traversing the pterygoid process of the sphenoid bone. Although the Le Fort system is somewhat simplistic, it is a useful tool for diagnosing and describing facial fractures. In reality, many fractures are a combination or variation of these types. For example, Le Fort II and III are usually seen in combination (Galloway 1999). Furthermore, Le Fort fracture categories reference the lines of least resistance in the facial skeleton and are not confined to blunt force trauma. Gunshot wounds can produce fractures along these same lines.

Long Bones

Long bone fractures can take many forms, including transverse, oblique, spiral, butterfly, comminuted, depressed, avulsion, and buckle fractures (Figures 14.6 through 14.8). They may be complete or incomplete and may be located along the shaft of the bone and/or at the epiphyses. Motor vehicle crashes, falls from heights, pedestrian hits, and sports injuries are common causes of long bone fractures. In cases where a long bone is fragmented into a number of pieces, glue should be used to reconstruct the elements so that the fracture patterns are apparent. Reconstruction of blunt trauma cases involving long bones is less problematic than with cranial bones, in that they tend to show less plastic deformation. Proper interpretation of fracture patterns can provide clues about the direction of impact and the position of the body at the time of injury.

Recall that bones are strongest in the direction in which they are most frequently loaded. Many long bones, especially those in the lower limb, are weight bearing, so they are stronger in compression than in tension and shear. Applying this principle to fracture interpretation can help determine the direction of impact. The bone will fail at the site of

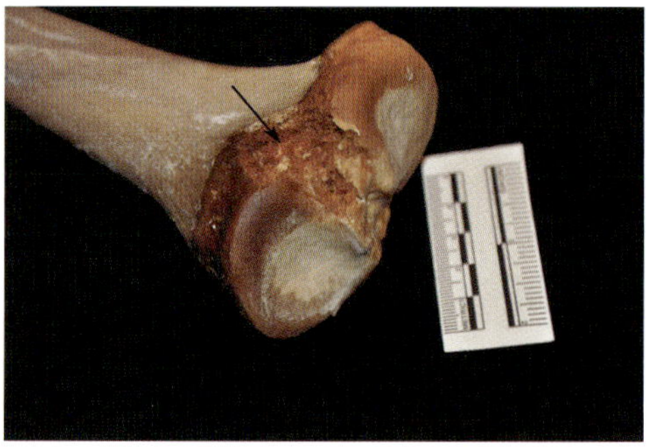

Figure 14.6 Avulsion fracture of the distal aspect of the proximal tibia (attachment site of the posterior cruciate ligament, or PCL). This avulsion fracture occurred as the knee was hyperextended; the PCL was stretched past its point of elasticity and tore, taking a portion of the adjacent bone with it. (Photograph courtesy of Forensic Anthropology Center.)

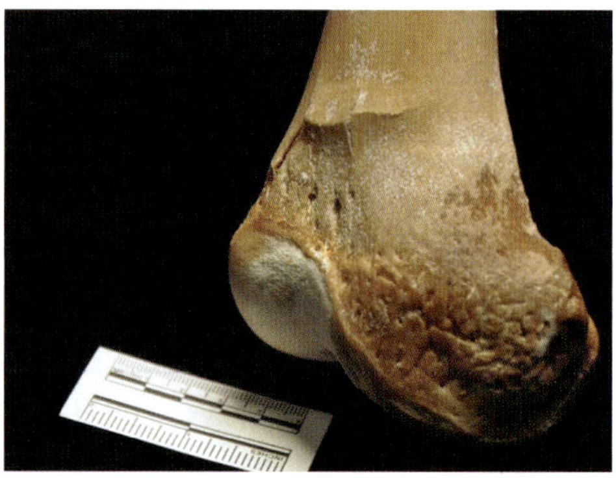

Figure 14.7 Buckle fracture of the distal femur in a 19-year-old male. Buckle fractures are more commonly seen in young individuals. As compression is applied to the bone from the superior–inferior direction, the cortex of the bone buckles under the load. The point of failure is the area where the cortex is undergoing maximum tensile stress. (Photograph courtesy of Forensic Anthropology Center.)

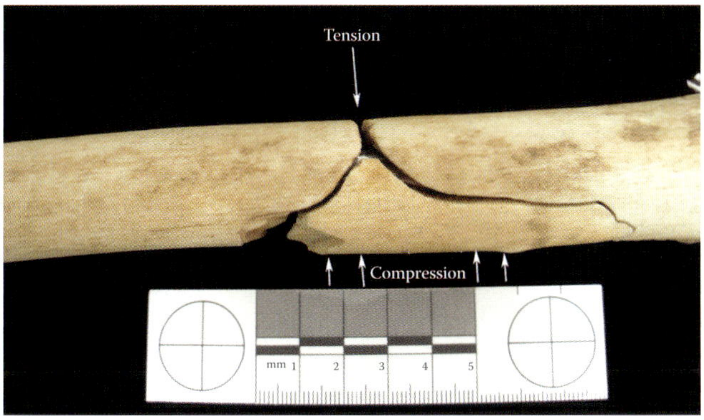

Figure 14.8 Typical butterfly fracture. (Photograph courtesy of Forensic Anthropology Center.)

greatest tension. Consider the act of breaking a pencil. You hold the pencil at both ends and apply pressure to the middle with both thumbs while bending the pencil toward you with your fingers. This type of loading is called three-point bending, and it creates maximum compression at the site of your thumbs and maximum tension directly opposite this site. The pencil will fail/break initially on the tension side opposite your thumbs. Applying these same forces to a long bone can create a *butterfly fracture* (Figure 14.8). The fixed ends of the joints generate the forces on either end of the bone, and the injuring mechanism generates the maximum stress in the shaft. The bone fails initially at the site of greatest tension, and the fractures travel back toward the site of compression. As it travels, it bifurcates to create a wedge. These fractures are commonly observed in pedestrian hits as the bumper comes in contact with the leg, but they can occur in non-weight-bearing elements as well. The exact mechanics involved in the production of a butterfly fracture is poorly understood.

A good approach to long bone fracture interpretation is to diagnose the type of fracture (spiral, butterfly, comminuted, etc.), consider the types of loads that produce that fracture etiology (bending, torsion, compression, etc.), and then relate those variables to the bony anatomy and common loading scenarios for that skeletal element. For example, a scaphoid waist fracture (a fracture at the narrowest portion, or waist, of the scaphoid) occurs when compressive loading of the dorsal surface creates tension on the palmar surface of the bone. The scaphoid is compressed between the distal end of the radius and the proximal side of the capitate. This type of loading is produced by falls onto an outstretched hand or blows to the palm of the hand (Galloway 1999). Many fracture classification systems are available, but it is more important for the forensic anthropologist to describe the location and nature of the fracture than to determine an exact category (Galloway 1999). Classification systems are primarily useful as tools for understanding the biomechanical loads that can generate various fracture patterns.

Axial Skeletal Elements

Unlike the long bones, the bones in the axial skeleton are lightweight and possess a morphology that can withstand multidirectional movements. They are comprised of a high percentage of trabecular bone that enables them to absorb a considerable amount of energy prior to failure. Impacts to the axial skeletal elements usually affect multiple bones both directly and indirectly (Galloway 1999). Axial elements resulting from direct trauma are common in falls from extreme heights. On the other hand, many vertebral injuries are secondary injuries. For example, fractures of the spinous and transverse processes result from the displacement of attached soft tissue that can occur from torsional forces in pedestrian hits where the victim is tossed over the car.

Direction of impact to the thorax is generally diagnosed by the location of the rib fractures. Loading distributed over a relatively broad surface area in an anterior-to-posterior direction produces fractures at the rib angles, whereas lateral loading tends to produce fractures at the sternal and vertebral ends of the ribs. However, a blow with a more focused area of impact can result in fractures at the impact site (e.g., ball bat to the ribs). Resuscitation efforts—especially with the elderly—with chest compressions can result in fractures to the sternal end of the ribs. In cases where the bone is more elastic than brittle, buckling may occur. In such cases, the adage that bone *always fails first under tension* seems inadequate. Buckling occurs on the compression side of the bone and appears as a crease aligned perpendicular to the long axis of the rib. Buckling results when the tension side of the bone possesses sufficient elastic component to allow bending without fracture. The bending action forces the cortical bone on the compression side to fold in an accordion fashion to compensate. Although the buckling fracture occurs on the compression side of the bone, it is still produced by the microstructure of each cortical fold failing first under tension (see Figure 14.7).

The bones of the shoulder and hip girdles are not part of the axial skeleton proper, but they are uniquely shaped bones that exhibit complex fracture patterns unlike those observed in other skeletal elements. High energy is required to produce pelvic and scapular fractures, so they are typically caused by falls from heights, automobile crashes, and pedestrian hits (Figures 14.9 through 14.11). Scapular and pelvic fractures can be caused by direct blows or indirectly by forces transmitted from the humerus and femur, respectively. As with fractures in other elements, the fracture patterns in these bones provide information about the nature of the force that caused the injury (i.e., direction and intensity).

When analyzing blunt trauma, the anthropologist should examine each fracture and skeletal element separately and then synthesize the information. This process helps to pinpoint any inconsistencies in the analysis and may facilitate interpretation. However, a case report should not suggest a specific scenario (i.e., *the victim was hit from behind and then flipped onto the hood of the car*), but instead should report on the nature of the forces that caused the fractures (i.e., *a butterfly fracture of the left tibia is consistent with a posterior impact to the leg*). Suggesting a specific scenario is not advisable; it galvanizes the expert's

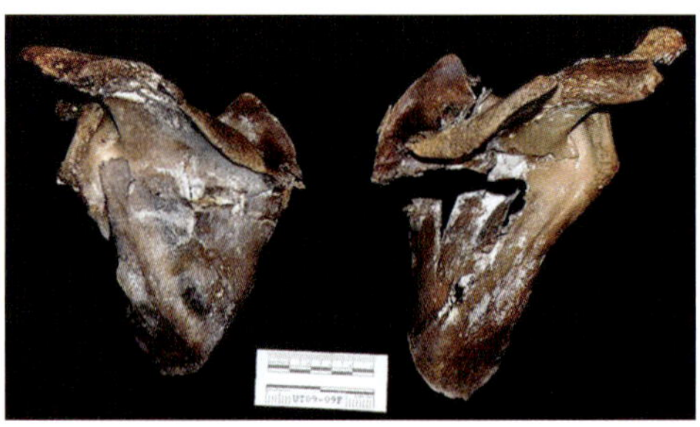

Figure 14.9 Scapular fractures resulting from a pedestrian hit. These fractures are indicative of broad impact trauma such as that experienced when the body impacts the hood of a vehicle or the road. (Photograph courtesy of Forensic Anthropology Center.)

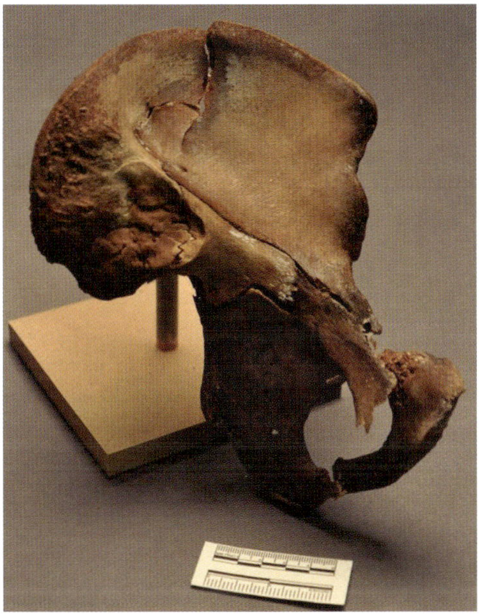

Figure 14.10 Pelvic fractures caused by a pedestrian hit. The entire pelvic ring is disrupted, as the ischiopubic ramus, pubic ramus, acetabulum, and ilium are fractured. Orthopedists refer to this as an unstable pelvic ring fracture. (Photograph courtesy of Forensic Anthropology Center.)

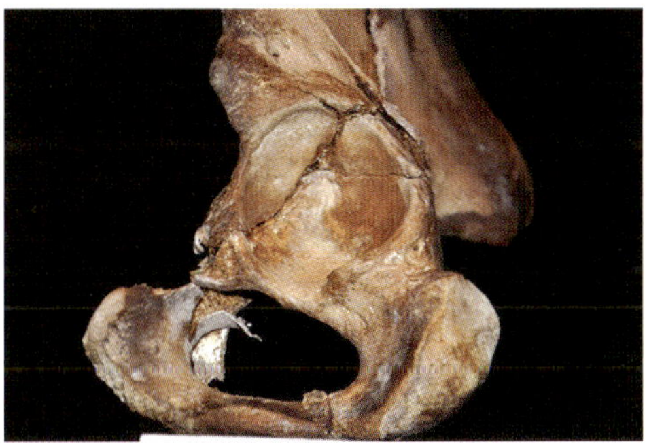

Figure 14.11 Close-up lateral view of fractured acetabulum of the os coxa in Figure 14.10. (Photograph courtesy of Forensic Anthropology Center.)

interpretation and could have detrimental effects in a court of law. As a rule, always describe trauma, but interpret *only* what is directly supported by the osseous evidence.

Sharp Trauma

Sharp trauma is low-velocity trauma produced by an edged object. Sharp instruments can be further divided into classes based upon their characteristics (i.e., short, long, light, heavy). Broadly speaking, sharp instruments that are easily wielded with one hand and are used primarily to cut or saw are termed *short-light* objects (Kimmerle and Baraybar 2008). Wound characteristics produced by an edged object vary according to the angle at which the edge strikes the bone, whether the edge is straight or serrated, the type of bone injured (cortical versus trabecular), and what portion of the edged object comes in contact with the bone. For instance, depending on where the body is struck, one knife used with the same amount of force can produce a variety of wounds. When directed to the sternum, the blade may easily penetrate the relatively thin overlying soft tissue to produce a large defect that resembles the cross-sectional shape of the blade. In the femur, however, the wound may resemble a shallow puncture since the thicker muscle mass would only allow the tip of the blade to contact the bone. A single stab to the rib cage may produce defects on two separate ribs that differ in appearance, especially if the blade edge contacts one rib while the back of the blade contacts the other. *Long-heavy* weapons such as machetes, swords, cleavers, hatchets, and axes produce highly destructive chop wounds (Spitz 1993). Chop wounds are rather large, gaping defects with a kerf indicative of sharp trauma and a distinctive angular margins often with associated crushing.

The *kerf* is the wall and floor of a cut mark (Figure 14.12). Microscopic examination of the kerf, especially with a scanning electron microscope, can yield highly diagnostic

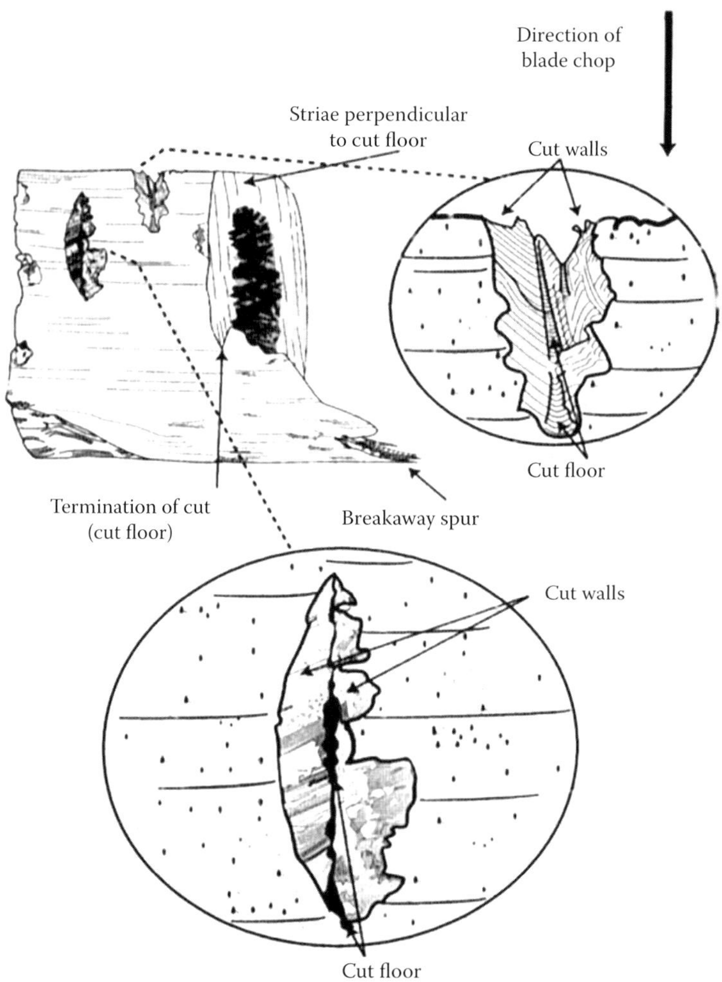

Figure 14.12 Sharp chop in a long bone illustrating v-shaped kerf floor. The walls and the floor comprise the entire kerf. (Illustration by David Alford; image provided by Steven A. Symes.)

information about the type of weapon. However, due to the significant overlap in cut mark width from different knife types, matching a specific knife to a wound is not recommended (Bartelink et al. 2001). The remainder of this section will discuss attributes of the various types of sharp trauma wounds and some of the features used to identify sharp injuries in bone.

Cut Marks

Cut marks are linear striations that generally have a V-shaped cross section (Kimmerle and Baraybar 2008; Figures 14.12 through 14.14). These wounds are typically made by short light instruments, and although wound appearance may seem to indicate blade design (i.e., single-edged, double-edged, or partially double-edged), caution must be exercised. A pointed oval perforation in bone that indicates two incised ends (i.e., mandorla-like shape) may suggest a double-edged or partially double-edged blade. A diamond-shaped perforation that indicates a single incised end may suggest a single-edged blade, but it may also be produced by a double-edged or partially double-edged blade inserted to a depth where the ricasso crushed one side of the perforation, mimicking the back of the blade. Much caution should be exercised in predicting blade design from the shape of the osseous defect. However, a defect produced by a serrated blade may be an exception. The points of each of the serrations may incise the bone providing the needed evidence. A blade may perforate the bone or it may simply penetrate the surface and leave a linear cut mark with a kerf. If the instrument strikes the bone at an

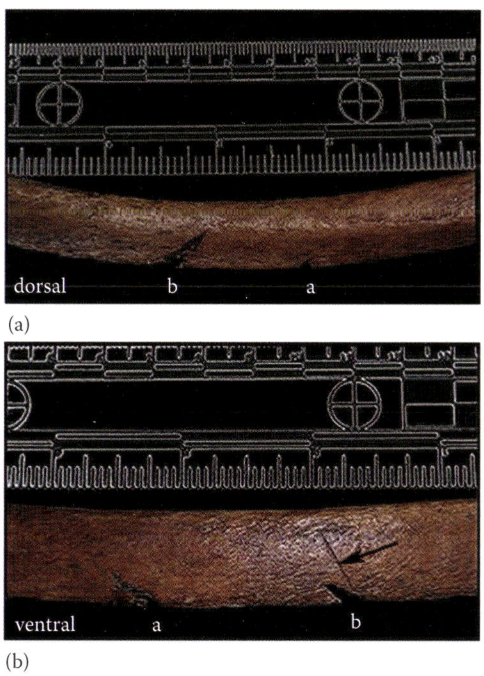

Figure 14.13 Two cut marks in a rib (a) and (b) viewed from the (a) dorsal and (b) ventral aspect of the rib. Arrow indicates a third incised wound. (Photograph by Natalie Shirley, courtesy of Forensic Anthropology Center.)

Figure 14.14 Two stab wounds to the scapula. (Photograph courtesy of Forensic Anthropology Center.)

angle, a fragment is lifted and peeled away from the bone; these defects are common in ribs when the knife enters at an angle nearly parallel to the rib surface (Kimmerle and Baraybar 2008).

Chop Wounds

Chop marks are caused by objects with either long or thick blades. The corresponding wounds are usually larger than cut marks and may have associated crushing and fractures with comminuted fragments. Kerley (1973) referred to this latter feature as *chattering*, and it occurs when bone fragments fracture at the lateral margins of the chop mark (Figure 14.15). Chop wounds may also exhibit *scoop marks* (Kimmerle and Baraybar 2008; Figure 14.16). The mechanism that results in a scoop mark is the same mechanism that produces peeled fragments. The incision penetrates sufficiently deep, and the fragment is completely separated from the bone shaft leaving a concave defect. Scoop marks are usually caused by swords, machetes, and other long-bladed instruments. Fractures may also be associated with chop marks. Kimmerle and Baraybar (2008) describe *slot fractures* in the skull caused by long-bladed weapons. Internal displacement of the cranial vault by the chopping action produces tension on the outer table that results in the secondary formation of a concentric fracture. Fractures that radiate from the edges of chop wounds can be used to determine the sequence of chops to a skull by examining intersecting fracture lines.

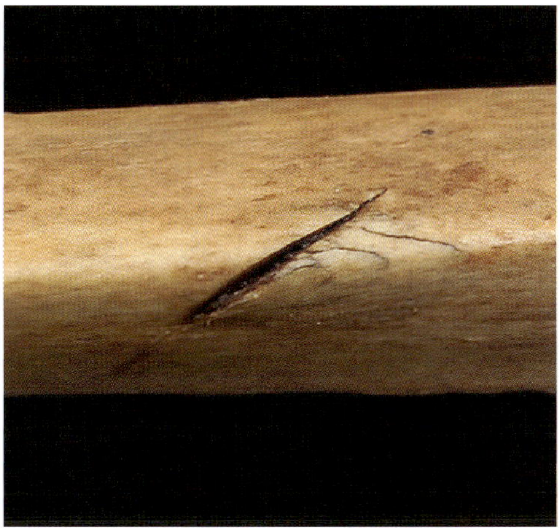

Figure 14.15 Chattering and linear fractures associated with an axe wound in the anterior tibia. (Photography courtesy of Georgia Bureau of Investigation Medical Examiner's Office.)

Figure 14.16 Scoop mark (arrow) on the cranial vault caused by an axe. (Photography courtesy of Georgia Bureau of Investigation Medical Examiner's Office.)

Saw Marks

Saws are a unique type of cutting implement in terms of the manner in which they are used. As opposed to a stabbing or chopping motion, saws are moved back and forth repeatedly, usually with the goal of dismemberment. Dismemberment is usually a post-mortem activity, but it has been reported as a cause of death in human rights violations (Campos Varela and Morcillo 2011), suicides (Asano et al. 2008; Gloulou et al. 2009; Grellner and Wilske, 2009; Tournel et al. 2008), and accidental deaths (Byard and Gilbert 2004; Haynes et al. 1980). The repetitive motion of the saw blade in the bone creates a number of diagnostic characteristics (e.g., number of teeth per inch, blade thickness, tooth design) that enable the trained expert to match the saw to the wound (Andahl 1978; Bonte 1975; Symes 1992; Symes et al. 1998).

As with cut marks, saws leave kerfs, but unlike cut marks, the kerf floors of saw marks have unique features, such as false starts and break-away spurs (Figure 14.17). False starts are simply aborted attempts to initiate a cut, and, depending on the sharpness of the saw

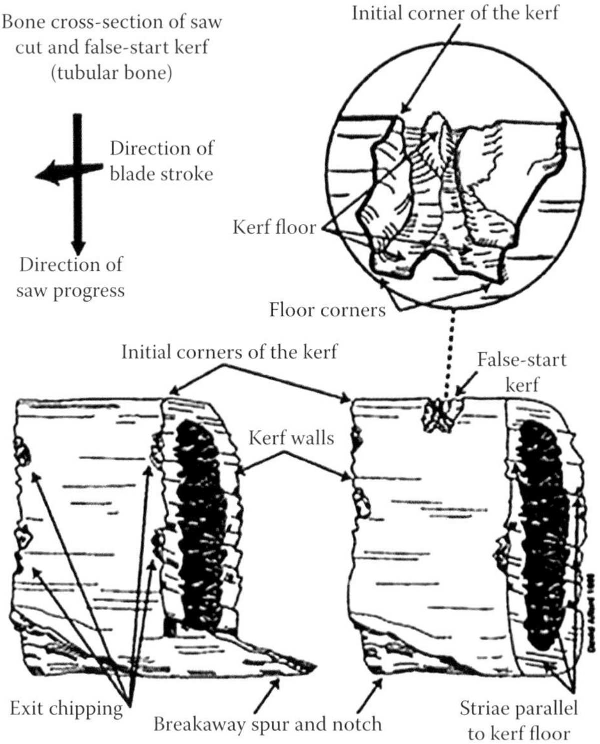

Figure 14.17 Saw cut in a long bone showing and false start kerf and breakaway spur. (Illustration by David Alford; image provided by Steven A. Symes.)

and difficulty of the sawing task, they may vary in number and in proximity to the completed cut. As a saw cut nears completion, applied pressure may result in a fracture that completes the cut. The fracture produces a breakaway spur at the bottom of the cut or kerf. The spur appears as a jagged piece of bone protruding from the terminal margin of the cut. In addition, the square kerf floor of a saw cut is easily distinguished from the V-shaped kerf floor produced by a knife (Symes et al. 2002).

The kerf floor contains information indicating saw class including set and number of teeth per inch (Symes et al. 2002, 1998). Kerf walls offer information about the points of the saw teeth, the tooth rows, teeth per inch, and the direction of the cut (Symes 1992). Kerf walls have striae that give clues about the sides of the teeth. The shape, depth, and frequency of the striae contain information about the blade shape, the amount of energy transferred to the bone, and the motion in which the blade moves to cut the bone (Symes 1992). A saw mark analysis should recognize kerf characteristics that reveal the dimensions and shape of the blade and teeth of a saw, and whether the saw was manually or mechanically powered—referred to by Symes (1992) as class characteristics—as well as how the saw was used to accomplish dismemberment or mutilation (see Box 14.1 for a discussion of class characteristics). For more information on and illustrations of these concepts, refer to Symes (1992), Symes et al. (1998, 2002), and http://www.symesforensics.com/documents/1SawMarkManual_Symes-web.pdf.

Whether cut, chopped, or sawed, sharp trauma leaves signatures on bone that enable experts to determine instrument class. Although weapon identification based solely on

BOX 14.1 SPECIAL FOCUS BOX

Five class characteristics are used to categorize saw types: saw size, saw set, saw shape, saw power, and direction of saw motion (Symes 1992). Documenting aspects of each of these class characteristics will help determine the type of saw. *Saw size* includes information about the blade width, teeth per inch, and tooth width. *Saw set* describes the lateral bend of the saw teeth. There are three major types of saw tooth set: alternating, raker, and wavy (Figure 14.18). In alternating sets, every other tooth is laterally bent to the opposite side in an alternating pattern, producing a kerf that is wider than the saw blade. Raker set teeth are like alternating set teeth except that a tooth with no lateral bend is added to the mix. Wavy set blades have groups of teeth that are laterally bent, but the number in the group varies; this pattern is common in fine-toothed hacksaws. *Saw shape* refers to the blade contour (flat or curved), the tooth as it is cut out of the blade (push saws versus pull saws), and whether or not the teeth are filed at an angle (rip saws versus crosscut saws). Blade contour is evident on the kerf floor, as flat blades leave flat kerf floors, and round blades produce curved kerf floors. *Saw power* is either manual or mechanical, and this characteristic affects parameters such as the consistency of the cut and the energy transferred to the bone (Figure 14.19). Furthermore, there may be more false starts with power saws than with manual saws as the user tends to start a new kerf when using a power saw instead of putting the blade back into the same kerf. Finally, the *direction of the saw motion* refers broadly to the blade progress through the cut (Figure 14.20). Blade stroke (i.e., the direction of the tooth movement as it cuts through the bone) is parallel to the tooth striae in the kerf walls. The plane formed between the false start and the breakaway spur indicates the direction of saw progress through the bone.

(a) (b) (c)

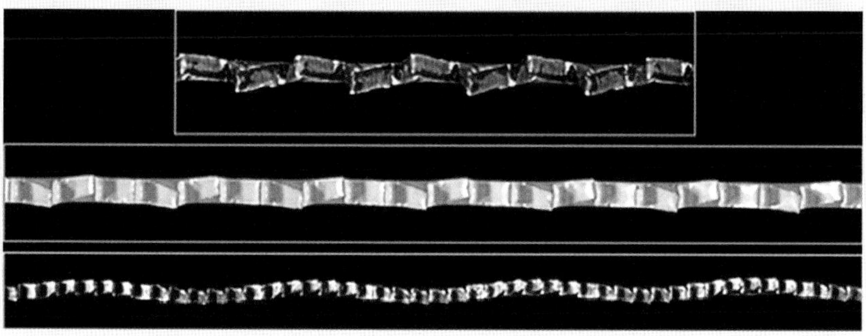

Figure 14.18 Saw tooth sets. (a) Alternating set. (b) Raker set. (c) Wavy set. (Image courtesy of Steven A. Symes.)

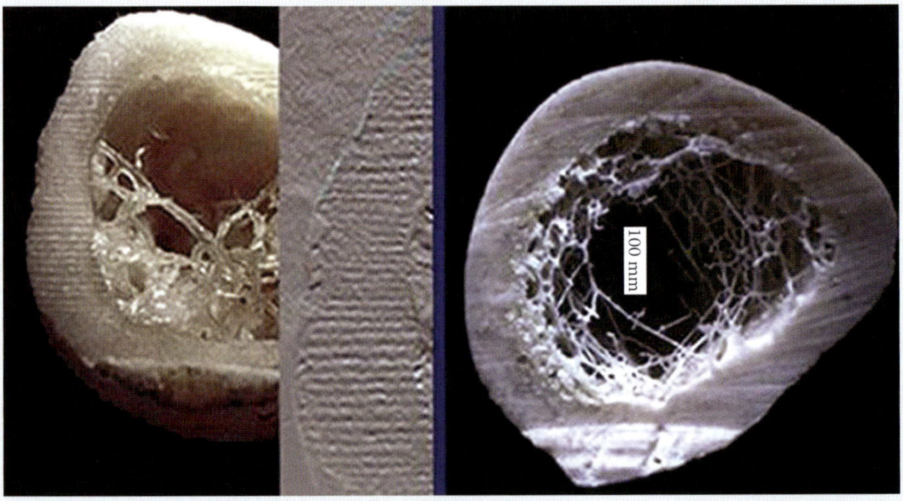

(a) (b)

Figure 14.19 Saw power. Cross-sectional views of saw cuts made with a mechanical saw (a) and manual saw (b). Note the regular striations produced by the mechanical saw (also shown in the embossed enlargement) versus the irregular striations produced by the manual saw. (Image courtesy of Steven A. Symes.)

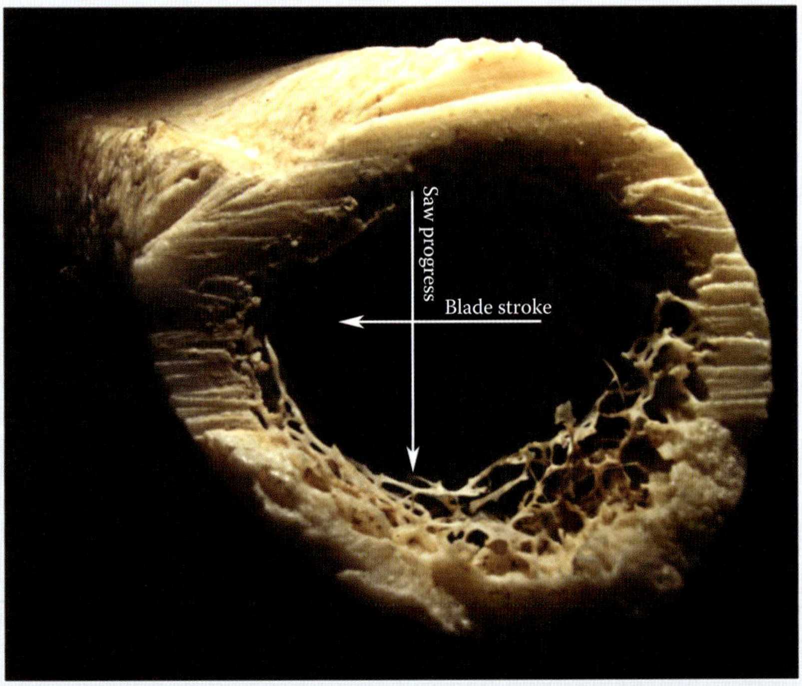

Figure 14.20 Direction of saw motion shown in a cross-sectional view of a long bone. The horizontal striations are produced by the blade stroke, and the vertical arrow shows the overall direction of saw progress through the bone. (Photograph courtesy of Steven A. Symes.)

class characteristics is usually not advisable, identifying a suspect weapon opens the possibility of finding additional and possibly incriminating physical evidence. The biomechanical principles are similar between sharp and blunt trauma in that these categories represent low-velocity trauma. The primary difference is the surface area interface between the bone and the weapon. Thus, sharp trauma wounds are distinct in appearance, but they can exhibit traits frequently associated with blunt trauma (i.e., concentric fractures on account of tensile strain on the outer table of the skull, associated fractures, crushing).

Research, Old and New: Cadaver Testing and Finite Element Analysis

Cadaver Testing

Much of this research has been done to test automobile safety equipment, military armor, and protective athletic gear; however, impact testing is beginning to surface in the forensic literature, as well. Kroman et al. (2011) used a drop tower to investigate a long-standing theory of fracture mechanics in the skull. Gurdjian's "stresscoat" experiments (Gurdjian et al. 1945, 1947, 1949, 1950a,b)—using heads coated with a brittle lacquer to visualize the stress in the bone—led him to suggest that blunt impacts to the skull result in an area of inbending at the site of impact and corresponding areas of outbending on other areas of the skull. Gurdjian surmised that the areas of outbending undergo maximum tensile stress. Fractures, then, initiate at a distance from the impact site and travel back toward the impact. Kroman et al.'s (2011) research using cadaveric heads with associated soft tissues found that radiating fractures initiated at the impact site not remotely as Gurdjian and his associates suggested. Maximum tensile stress occurs on the inner table of the skull at the impact site and propagated away from this site. Although the use of cadavers to explore biomechanical research questions is not novel, this type of research is beginning to resurface possibly due to access to cadavers for research in areas beyond that with safety implications (Yoganandan et al. 2011). One catalyst for this acceptance may be the use of human cadavers to study decomposition (discussed in Chapter 18; Shirley et al. 2011).

Finite Element Analysis

Recently, computer simulation has surfaced as an alternative to cadaveric testing. In particular, *finite element analysis (FEA)* involves the creation of a two- or three-dimensional model of a desired structure, subdividing the model into thousands or even millions of small *finite elements* and then simulating the stress and strain present in each element. Once established, macroscopic qualities, such as deformation and crack propagation, can be determined. FEA requires sophisticated and costly software; however, it offers promise in analyzing the response of body tissues to various loads without the need for a continual supply of cadavers. FEA models can be constructed from computed tomography or magnetic resonance imaging scans by using a software package to manipulate the scans and render the models. Once the model is imported into an FEA software package, the various parts of the model can be ascribed material properties of the corresponding biological structure(s). Finite element methods have the potential of being more representative of cadaveric specimens than artificial models such as crash test dummies. Much of the finite element model research has been done to simulate injuries resulting from automobile crashes and military protective equipment (blunt-ballistic impacts; Doorly and Gilchrist 2006; Horgan and Gilchrist 2003, 2004; Lee and Gong, 2010; Roberts et al. 2005, 2007; Shen et al. 2010). Berryman et al. (2003) presented the first forensic anthropology application of FEA in a study of fracture formation in tubular bone. Researchers are beginning to realize the potential of finite element models for understanding fracture biomechanics in forensic contexts (Motherway et al. 2009; Raul et al. 2006, 2008; Roth et al. 2007).

Summary

As presented in this chapter and proposed by Kroman (2007), the most meaningful way to conceptualize skeletal trauma is through a physics-based trauma continuum, rather than weapon-based categories. Although this is the best way to comprehend the mechanics behind fracture propagation, the forensic anthropologist must reference the specific weapon-based categories to be of value to the medicolegal end user. The forensic anthropologist's contribution to law enforcement can narrow the search for the suspect weapon or eliminate suspect weapons. More importantly, trauma investigation and accurate interpretation are the most significant contribution that a forensic anthropologist can provide the courts. Trauma interpretation will have a major effect on the lives of both the suspect and victim or victim's family. Although interpretation is a valuable benefaction, it is paramount that the anthropologist remain within his or her abilities and not extend the interpretation beyond what the evidence will support. It is acceptable to provide *only* a description of the trauma when certainty of interpretation is questionable. Inaccurate interpretation will likely result in an unjust judicial outcome.

With the return to cadaveric testing and the recent application of computer-simulated models, the future of low-velocity trauma interpretation appears promising. Experimental designs involving both of these models can provide a means of satisfying Daubert requirements for the acceptance of scientific evidence by the courts.

References

Andahl RO. 1978. The examination of saw marks. *J Forensic Sci Soc* 18:31–36.

Asano M, Nushida H, Nagasaki Y, and Ueno Y. 2008. Suicide by circular saw. *Forensic Sci Int* 182(1):e7–e9.

Bartelink EJ, Wiersema JM, and Demaree RS. 2001. Quantitative analysis of sharp-force trauma: An application of scanning electron microscopy in forensic anthropology. *J Forensic Sci* 46(6):1288–1293.

Berryman JF, Berryman HE, LeMaster RA, and Berryman CA. 2003. Numerical simulation of fracture propagation in a test of cantilevered tubular bone. *54th Annual Meeting of the American Academy of Forensic Sciences, Abstract in Proceedings of the American Academy of Forensic Sciences*, Chicago, IL, Vol. IX, p. 260.

Berryman H and Symes S. 1998. Recognizing gunshot and blunt cranial trauma through fracture interpretation. In K Reichs (ed.): *Forensic Osteology: Advances in the Identification of Human Remains*. Springfield, IL: Charles C. Thomas, pp. 333–352.

Bonte W. 1975. Tool marks in bones and cartilage. *J Forensic Sci* 20:315–325.

Byard RW and Gilbert JD. 2004. Characteristic features of deaths due to decapitation. *Am J Forensic Med Pathol* 25(2):129–130.

Campos Varela IY and Morcillo MD. 2011. Dismemberment: Cause of death in the Colombian armed conflict. *Proceedings of the 63rd Annual Meetings of the American Academy of Forensic Sciences*, Chicago, IL, Vol. 17, p. 356.

Cowin S. 1989. Mechanics of materials. In S Cowin (ed.): *Bone Mechanics*. Boca Raton, FL: CRC Press, pp. 15–42.

Currey JD. 2002. *Bones: Structure and Mechanics*. Princeton, NJ: Princeton University Press.

Doorly MC and Gilchrist MD. 2006. The analysis of traumatic brain injury due to head impacts arising from falls using accident reconstruction. *Comput Methods Biomech Biomed Engin* 9(6):371–377.

Galloway A. 1999. *Broken Bones: Anthropological Analysis of Blunt Force Trauma*. Springfield, IL: Charles C. Thomas.

Gloulou F, Allouche M, Khelil MB, Bekir O, Banasr A, Zhioua M, and Hamdoun M. 2009. Unusual suicides with band saws: Two case reports and a literature review. *Forensic Sci Int* 183(1):e7–e10.

Grellner W and Wilske J. 2009. Unusual suicides of young women with tentative cuts and fatal neck injuries by chain saw and circular saw. *Forensic Sci Int* 190(1–3):e9–e11.

Gurdjian E and Lissner H. 1945. Deformation of the skull in head injury: a study with the "stresscoat" technique. *Surg Gynecol Obstet* 81:679–687.

Gurdjian E, Lissner H, and Webster J. 1947. The mechanism of production of linear skull fractures. *Surg Gynecol Obstet* 85:195–210.

Gurdjian E, Webster J, and Lissner H. 1949. Studies on skull fracture with particular reference to engineering factors. *Am J Surg* 78:736–742.

Gurdjian E, Webster J, and Lissner H. 1950a. The mechanism of skull fracture. *J Neurosurg* 7:106–114.

Gurdjian E, Webster J, and Lissner H. 1950b. The mechanism of skull fracture. *Radiology* 54:313–338.

Haynes CD, Webb WA, and Fenno CR. 1980. Chain saw injuries: Review of 330 cases. *J Trauma* 20:772–776.

Hein P and Schulz E. 1990. Contrecoup fracture of the anterior cranial foss as a consequence of blunt force caused by a fall. *Acta Neurochir (Wein)* 105(1–2):24–29.

Horgan TJ and Gilchrist MD. 2003. The creation of three-dimensional finite element models for simulating head impact biomechanics. *Int J Crashworthiness* 8(4):353–366.

Horgan TJ and Gilchrist MD. 2004. Influence of FE model variability in predicting brain motion and intracranial pressure changes in head impact simulations. *Int J Crashworthiness* 9(4):401–418.

Kerley ER. 1973. Forensic anthropology. In CH Wecht (ed.): *Legal Medicine Annual*. New York: Appleton-Century-Crofts, pp. 163–198.

Kimmerle EH and Baraybar JP. 2008. Sharp force trauma. In EH Kimmerle and JP Baraybar (eds.): *Skeletal Trauma: Identification of Injuries Resulting from Human Rights Abuse and Armed Conflict*. Boca Raton, FL: CRC Press, pp. 263–299.

Kroman AM. 2007. Fracture biomechanics of the human skeleton. PhD Dissertation. University of Tennessee, Knoxville, TN.

Kroman A, Kress T, and Porta D. 2011. Fracture propagation in the human cranium: A re-testing of popular theories. *Clin Anat* 24:309–318.

Lee HP and Gong SW. 2010. Finite element analysis for the evaluation of protective functions of helmets against ballistic impact. *Comput Methods Biomech Biomed Engin* 13(5):537–550.

Le Fort R. 1901a. Fractures de la machoire superieure. *Revue de Chirurgie* 23:208–227.

Le Fort R. 1901b. Fractures de la machoire superieure. *Revue de Chirurgie* 23:360–379.

Le Fort R. 1901c. Fractures de la machoire superieure. *Revue de Chirurgie* 23:479–507.

McGowan C. 1999. *A Practical Guide to Vertebrate Mechanics*. Cambridge, UK: Cambridge University Press.

Motherway J, Doorly MC, Curtis M, and Gilchrist MD. 2009. Head impact biomechanics simulations: A forensic tool for reconstructing head injury. *Legal Med* 11:S220–S222.

Nordin M and Frankel V. (eds.) 1989. *Basic Biomechanics of the Musculoskeletal System*. Philadelphia, PA: Lea and Febiger.
Raul JS, Baumgartner D, Willinger R, and Ludes B. 2006. Finite element modeling of human head injuries caused by a fall. *Int J Legal Med* 120(4):212–218.
Raul JS, Deck C, Willinger R, and Ludes B. 2008. Finite-element models of the human head and their applications in forensic practice. *Int J Legal Med* 122(5):359–366.
Roberts JC, O'Connor JV, and Ward EE. 2005. Modeling the effect of non-penetrating ballistic impact as a means of detecting behind armor blunt trauma. *J Trauma* 58(6):1241–1251.
Roberts JC, Merkle AC, Biermann PJ, Ward EE, Carkhuff BG, Cain RP, and O'Connor JV. 2007. Computational and experimental models of the human torso for non-penetrating ballistic impact. *J Biomech* 40(4):125–136.
Roth S, Raul JS, Ludes B, and Willinger R. 2007. Finite element analysis of impact and shaking inflicted to a child. *Int J Legal Med* 121(3):223–228.
Shen W, Niu Y, Bykanova L, Laurence P, and Link N. 2010. Characterizing the interaction among bullet, body armor, and human surrogate targets. *J Biomech Eng* 132(12):121001.
Shirley NR, Wilson RJ, and Jantz LM. 2011. Cadaver use at the University of Tennessee's Anthropological Research Facility. *Clin Anat* 24:372–380.
Spitz WU. 1993. Sharp force injury. In WU Spitz (ed.): *Spitz and Fisher's Medicolegal Investigation of Death*. Springfield, IL: Charles C. Thomas. pp. 252–310.
Symes SA. 1992. Morphology of saw marks in human bone: Identification of class characteristics. PhD Dissertation, Department of Anthropology, University of Tennessee, Knoxville, TN.
Symes SA, Berryman HE, and Smith OC. 1998. Saw marks in bone: Introduction and examination of residual kerf contour. In KJ Reichs (ed.): *Forensic Osteology II, Advances in the Identification of Human Remains*. Springfield, IL: Charles C. Thomas. pp. 333–352.
Symes SA, Williams J, Murray E, Hoffman J, Holland T, Saul J, Saul F, and Pope E. 2002. Taphonomic context of sharp-force trauma in suspected cases of human mutilation and dismemberment. In W. Haglund and M. Sorg (eds.): *Advances in Forensic Taphonomy: Method, Theory, and Archaeological Perspectives*. Boca Raton, FL: CRC Press, pp. 403–434.
Tournel G, Dédouit F, Balgairies A, Houssaye C, De Angeli B, Bécart-Robert A, Pety N, Hédouin V, and Gosset D. 2008. Unusual suicide with a chainsaw. *J Forensic Sci* 53: 1174–1177.
Vogel S. 2003. *Comparative Biomechanics: Life's Physical World*. Princeton, NJ: Princeton University Press.
Yoganandan N, Stemper BD, Pintar FA, and Maiman DJ. 2011. Use of postmortem human subjects to describe injury responses and tolerances. *Clin Anat* 24: 282–293.

Basic Gunshot Trauma Interpretation in Forensic Anthropology

15

HUGH E. BERRYMAN, NATALIE R. SHIRLEY, AND ALICJA K. LANFEAR

Contents

The FBI's *Crime in the United States* reports that roughly two-thirds of homicides involve firearms, which includes the use of handguns, rifles, shotguns, other guns, or when firearm type was not stated in the report (Crime in the U.S., 2010). It is also important to note that the proportion of homicides that involve the use of firearms has remained consistent over the years that the FBI has published *Crime in the United States*, making gunshot injuries the most common type of violent trauma encountered in forensic casework. Forensic anthropologists are in a unique position as their typical casework lacks soft tissue and, consequently, the soft tissue clues associated with trauma identification. Forensic anthropologists must depend upon their familiarity of the biomechanical properties of bone for precise interpretation of trauma type. This chapter outlines the basic principles used to interpret medium-to-high-velocity penetrating injuries in bone.

Biomechanical Properties of Bone

Overall bone structure and composition determines its mechanical properties (Currey, 2002). The relative amounts of collagen and crystalline matrix in a given bone or area of bone, combined with the morphology or shape of the bone, influence how it will respond to various mechanical loads. Bone is microscopically and macroscopically organized to withstand loads imposed by various activities. For example, the femur is optimally designed to endure the daily stresses imposed by walking and standing; as such, the femur is stronger under compressive axial loading than under tensile loading (see Chapter 14 for more detailed discussion of bone biomechanics and an explanation of various load types).

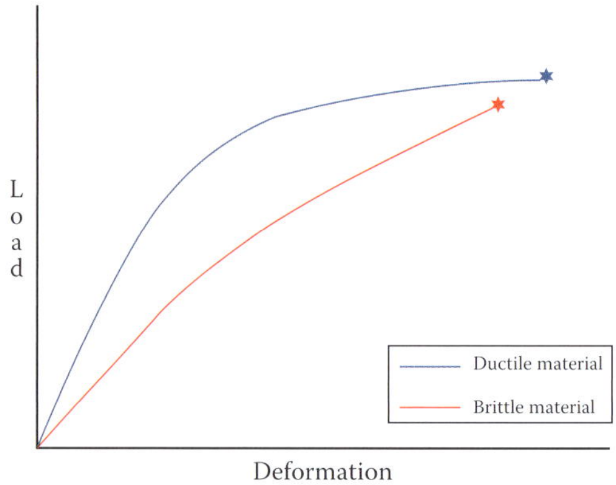

Figure 15.1 Stress–strain curve. The same load is applied to a ductile and a brittle material.

Bone is *viscoelastic*, meaning that it can behave as a ductile or brittle material depending on the velocity, rate, duration, and direction of the force(s) to which it is subjected. Ductile materials can absorb more energy prior to failure than brittle materials. Figure 15.1 contrasts the behavior of a ductile versus brittle material under similar loading. A ductile material undergoes a period of elastic deformation, during which the material will assume its original structure/shape if the load is removed. If the loading persists, the material undergoes plastic deformation. If the load is removed following plastic deformation, the material will not return to its original shape, but instead will remain permanently deformed. With continued loading, the material will fail. Brittle materials, on the other hand, undergo very little if any plastic deformation prior to failure. A mild steel provides an excellent example of a ductile material, and glass, a brittle material.

The viscoelastic nature of bone means that its behavior depends in large part on the characteristics of the load to which it is subjected. Bone's typical response to three rates of loading—static, slow, and rapid loading—is depicted in Figure 15.2. When subjected to a static load, bone is able to withstand the load without undergoing elastic deformation; its original size and shape properties are not altered. With slow loading, the bone deforms through its elastic phase and then its plastic phase before failing. When it fails, the fracture is relatively simple. Conversely, with rapid loading, especially high-velocity loading, the bone experiences catastrophic failure. It reacts as a brittle material and fails prior to

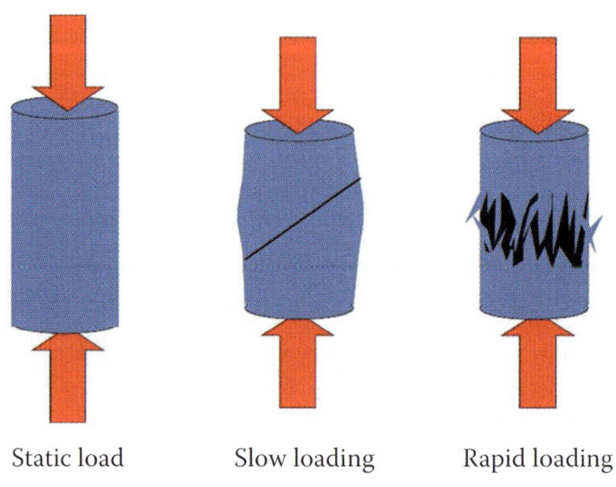

Figure 15.2 Illustration contrasting typical bony response to static, slow, and rapid loading. (Illustration by Hugh E. Berryman.)

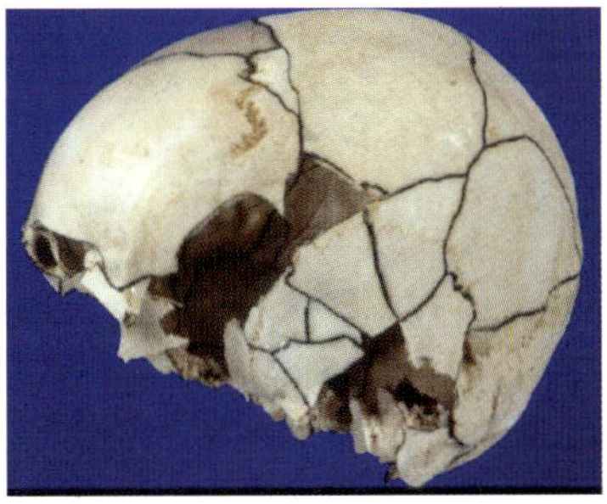

Figure 15.3 Cranial fracturing as a result of rapid loading. (Photograph by Hugh E. Berryman.)

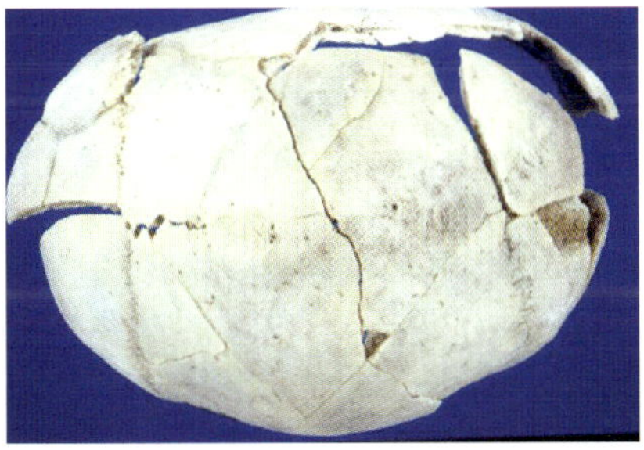

Figure 15.4 Cranial fracturing as a result of slow loading. (Photograph by Hugh E. Berryman.)

deformation. Thus, the resulting bone fragments can easily be reapproximated and reassembled (Figure 15.3). By contrast in slow loading, as commonly seen with blunt trauma, bone often fails after entering the plastic phase leaving the fragments warped and accurate reconstruction often impossible (Figure 15.4). In sum, bone acts like a brittle material when subjected to rapid loading, rendering undeformed fragments that can be reconstructed much like fitting the pieces of a puzzle together.

In terms of gunshot wound production, the examiner must be mindful of both the *intrinsic* and *extrinsic* factors that, in combination, dictate where and how a bone fractures. Intrinsic factors involve the material and structural properties of bone (e.g., mineral composition, which may be affected by age, nutrition, or disease; bone morphology), while extrinsic factors involve influences external to the bone (e.g., load mass, rate of application, area of application, and duration). With gunshot wound interpretation, considerations must be made for such extrinsic variables as bullet design, bullet composition, caliber, velocity, distance to target, intermediate targets, angle of impact, etc. Therefore, wound production is the result of the complex interplay of intrinsic and extrinsic variables with every fracture doggedly obeying the laws of physics. Fracture location, termination site, and pattern do not randomly occur. Understanding the contribution and interplay of intrinsic and extrinsic variables is essential for the accurate interpretation of skeletal trauma.

Gunshot Wound Appearance and Interpretation

The wounding capacity of a bullet is derived from the kinetic energy that it transfers to the body tissues. The formula for kinetic energy is $mv^2/2$, where m is the mass of the moving object and v is its velocity. The velocity component of the formula is squared, explaining why hunting and military rifles that fire bullets at 2000–4000 ft/s are more destructive than rifles and handguns with muzzle velocities of less than 1500 ft/s. In addition to this formula, bullet design affects how much kinetic energy is transferred to surrounding tissues. For example, those that are designed to remain in the body, such as hollow points, cause more damage to the tissues than round nose bullets of the same caliber and fired at the same velocity. The hollow point bullet deforms, causing it to slow and transfers more of its kinetic energy to surrounding tissues, whereas a bullet that exits transfers only a portion of this energy to the body. The fact that a bullet exits a body means that it takes some of its kinetic energy with it.

Cranial Gunshot Wounds

Fortunately, bullet wounds in bone leave signatures that indicate the direction of fire, sequence of fire, and, in some instances, the approximate angle of entry or exit. As a bullet penetrates a cranium, it produces an entry defect with well-defined edges on the outer table, and internal beveling resulting in a larger defect on the inner table. This inner table defect is sometimes characterized by irregularly shaped edges. The exit defect—the site where the bullet exits the cranium—is beveled externally and usually exhibits an irregular shape on the outer table, especially if the bullet deforms (Figure 15.5). This typical gunshot wound appearance is most apparent in the bones of the cranial vault (Figure 15.6a and b). However, paper-thin bones such as those of the orbit and maxilla do not clearly present bevel features because they are not structurally the same as vault bones. Unlike most of the bones of the vault, thin facial bones and the squamous portion of the temporal bones do not have a layer of diploë sandwiched between inner and outer cortical layers.

Occasionally a gunshot entrance wound will exhibit features that, with cursory examination, appear consistent with an exit wound defect (Figure 15.7). One type of wound that displays these characteristics is termed *keyhole defect*. A keyhole defect is caused by an impact from a bullet traveling at a tangential angle such that it leaves a well-defined circular outline on one side of the entrance defect and external beveling on the other (Dixon, 1982, Berryman and Symes, 2002). Figure 15.8a through c illustrates the wounding mechanics associated with the production of a keyhole defect. With these defects, bullet direction

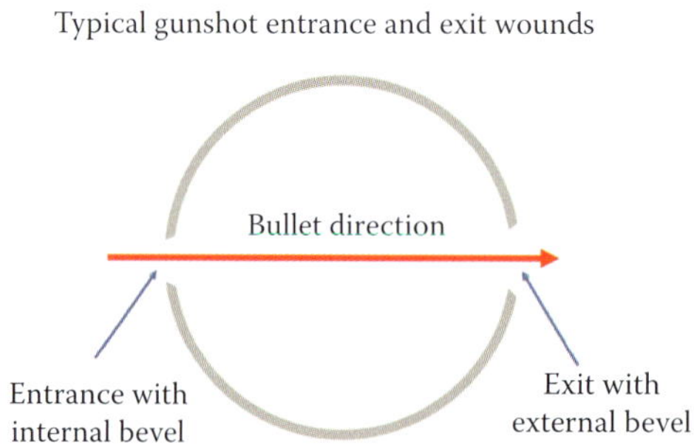

Figure 15.5 Illustration showing beveling in relation to entrance and exit sites. In "text book" gunshot wounds, internal beveling is associated with the entrance, whereas external beveling is associated with the exit. (Illustration by Hugh E. Berryman.)

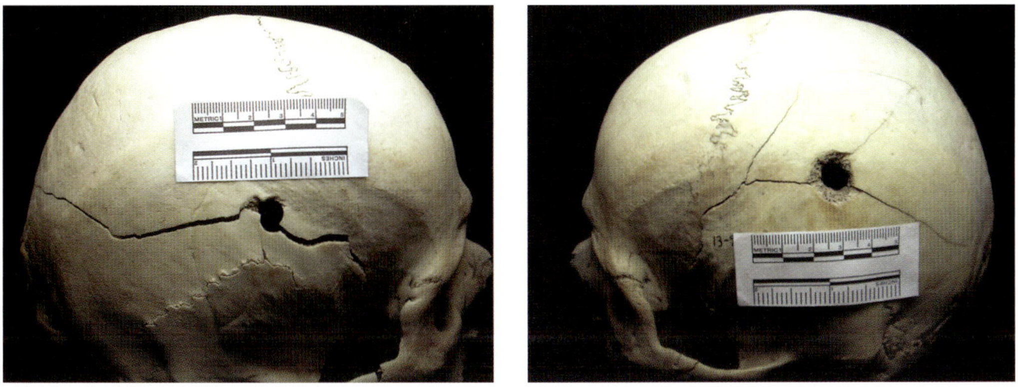

(a) (b)

Figure 15.6 (a) Entrance wound with radiating fractures. (b) Associated exit wound with external beveling and radiating and concentric fractures. (Photo by Natalie Shirley, courtesy of Forensic Anthropology Center, University of Tennessee, Knoxville, TN.)

Figure 15.7 Keyhole defect. The bullet traveled posterior to anterior (and slightly lateral), as indicated by the beveling on the anterior margin and the location of the radiating fractures. (Photo by Natalie Shirley, courtesy of Forensic Anthropology Center, University of Tennessee, Knoxville, TN.)

can be ascertained based on the location of the beveling relative to the nonbeveled edge. Additionally, two radiating fractures advance from the initial bullet impact site and diverge in the direction the bullet is going. Dixon (1984) has also reported keyhole defects associated with exiting bullets.

If sufficient energy is transferred to the skull, radiating fractures will travel from the site of entrance and/or exit (Figure 15.9a). Intracranial pressure, caused by the transfer of kinetic energy from the bullet to the brain tissue, can produce tensile strain on the inner table of the skull resulting in first-generation concentric fractures. With sufficient energy transfer, second-generation concentric fractures can form (Figure 15.9b and c). In 1903, a German forensic pathologist named Puppe recognized that intersecting fracture lines could be used to determine the sequence of blunt trauma impacts. Puppe noted that fractures caused by subsequent injury would terminate where the skull has already been compromised in preexisting fractures. Madea and Staak, (1988) summarize how Puppe's rule can also be applied to gunshot trauma to the skull. Entrance-related fractures of

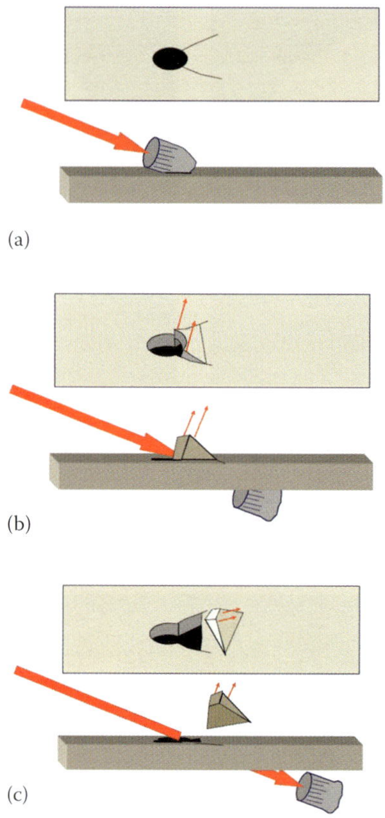

Figure 15.8 Mechanism of keyhole defect formation. (a) Entrance and radiating fractures. (b) Bone fragment fracturing off opposite of nonbeveled edge. (c) Removal of this fragment creates externally beveled edge. (Illustration by Hugh E. Berryman.)

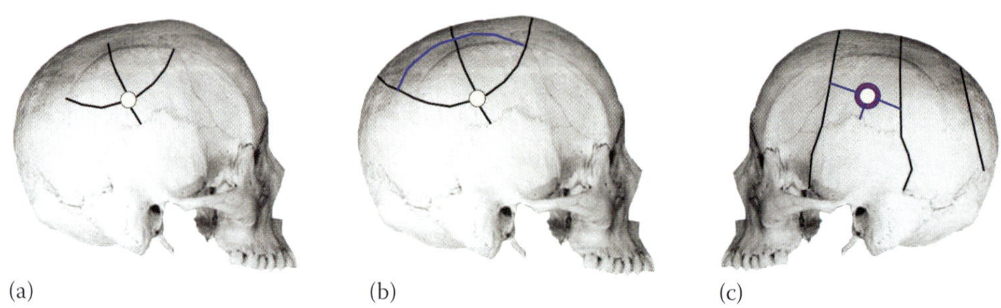

Figure 15.9 (a) Fracture lines radiating from entrance wound. (b) First-generation concentric fractures (blue). (c) Exit site: radiating fractures from the exit wound (blue) terminate into existing radiating fractures from the entrance site (black), as the latter were formed first. (Illustration by Hugh E. Berryman.)

subsequent bullet impacts will terminate into preexisting fractures associated with prior bullet wounds (Madea and Staak, 1988). As the cranial vault is a closed entity, it is possible to discern the sequence of gunshot wounds. Fracture lines at the entrance site can travel faster (approx. 450 m/s) than the bullet itself, so that radiating fractures from the exit site terminate into preexisting fractures from the entrance site.

Gunshot Wounds in the Thoracic Region

Gunshot wounds to the thorax are more common than gunshot wounds to the long bones, primarily due to the location of vital organs (e.g., heart, lungs, spinal cord), and the fact that shooters are often trained to place their shots "center mass." Nonetheless, little research has been conducted on the features and interpretation of gunshot wounds in bones of the thorax (e.g., ribs, sternum, clavicle, scapula, and vertebrae). Each of these skeletal elements has unique intrinsic properties from the high trabecular content of the sternum and vertebral bodies to the thin composition of the scapular body. These properties combined with the varied intrinsic characteristics of organs lend to the biomechanical complexity of the thorax. Furthermore, bullets can enter and/or exit intercostal spaces without leaving a mark on the bone, making it difficult to determine the exact number of gunshot wounds in the absence of soft tissue. As opposed to the cranial vault, the rib cage is *not* a closed environment through which fractures can travel and intersect; consequently, the sequence of gunshot wounds in the chest is not discernable from fracture patterns (Box 15.1).

Ubelaker (1996) presented a case analysis of multiple gunshot wounds to the thoracic region. He described several key features of these wounds and how these features could be used to ascertain the direction of fire. Ubelaker's (1996) analysis was done on the exhumed remains of Dr. Carl Austin Weiss, alleged assassin of Governor Huey P. Long of Louisiana in 1935. The remains were exhumed in 1991, and Ubelaker (1996) noted that at least 20 bullets penetrated Dr. Weiss' body, and the majority were in the chest. He documented features that indicated directionality such as displaced bone fragments, depressed fractures, beveling, and overall fracture patterns. Ubelaker (1996) was able to ascertain that most of the bullets that penetrated Dr. Weiss' body traveled from posterior to anterior, meaning that he was shot multiple times in the back.

Langley (2007), in a survey of 87 documented thoracic gunshot wounds, noted the same features that Ubelaker (1996) reported. The ribs were the most frequently injured bones in gunshots to the thoracic region, comprising 75% of the injuries in the study. Like the bones of the cranial vault, ribs are classified as flat bones. However, due to different intrinsic properties of ribs and the thoracic cavity in general, gunshot wounds in ribs appear different than that of cranial gunshot wounds. This is primarily due to the fact that the flat bones of the vault and the ribs have different trabecular bone densities, with this spongy bone layer being less dense in the ribs (Langley, 2007). Furthermore, the cortical layers are more compact in the vault than in the ribs (Langley, 2007). Structurally, the cranial vault is more rigid than the rib cage, which must allow for movements associated with breathing. Consequently, the kinetic energy released from a bullet as it passes through the chest cavity is absorbed by the larger volume of soft tissue and the more flexible characteristics of the bony structures of the chest wall. Contrasts between the intrinsic properties of the bony thorax and cranial vault result in different injury mechanics that may affect the appearance of gunshot wounds.

BOX 15.1 BONE DOES NOT ALWAYS PRODUCE TYPICAL FRACTURE PATTERNS, SO WHAT ARE WE TO DO?

The trauma chapters in this book have focused primarily on the typical fracture patterns in bone that are commonly associated with certain types of trauma. These chapters have also illustrated the complexities associated with interpretation of bone fracture patterns. Identifying atypical fracture patterns and determining the mechanism of trauma irrespective of fracture pattern are research areas that need further exploration. One study that addressed these concerns was based on an understanding of the shooting environment (Berryman et al., 2010). When a gun has been fired, the primer, propellant, lubricants, and metals that are found in the bullet, bullet jacket, cartridge casing vaporize. These vapors then coalesce and solidify, forming gunshot residues (GSR). Primer-derived GSR is of particular interest, as it has a unique elemental composition and appearance. It is the presence of primer-derived GSR particles on hand swabs that determines whether someone was in close proximity to a gun firing.

Berryman et al.'s (2010) research was sparked by a skeletal forensic case that presented a fractured rib with a missing segment. A gunshot wound was suspected, but the fracture lacked the typical bevel associated with a bullet. A forensic microanalyst from the Tennessee Bureau of Investigation used a scanning electron microscope (SEM) and energy dispersive x-ray (EDX) analysis to examine the bone in more detail for bullet wipe—specifically, lead, or other metals commonly associated with a bullet. Unfortunately, no evidence of bullet wipe could be found in this case.

Since no published literature existed that outlined what should be expected on a microscopic level when a bullet impacts bone, Berryman et al. (2010) devised a research study to determine whether bullet wipe could be detected on experimentally shot bone. Round nose lead and copper jacketed bullets were used, as the expectation was to see bullet wipe in the form of a metallic streak. Although bullet wipe could not be detected on the experimentally shot bone, high concentrations of certain particles were observed on the bone surface even at some distance away from the fracture site (Figure 15.10). Upon SEM–EDX analysis, trace amounts of lead, barium, and

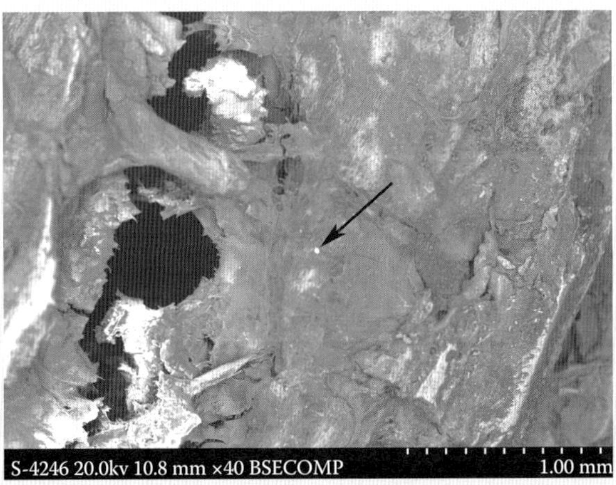

Figure 15.10 SEM micrograph of primer-derived gunshot residue particle on bone surface, indicated by arrow, on bone surface. (Micrograph by Alicja K. Lanfear, MTSU-MIMIC.)

antimony—components of bullet primer—were detected. Before this research, GSRs were only documented to the subcutaneous level (Brown et al., 1999a, b). Therefore, this research was the first to recognize the presence of primer-derived GSRs within the wound tract—a finding that is counter to the generally held belief that it is found only on clothing, skin, or at the subcutaneous level. As *primer-derived* GSR particles are unique in their elemental composition and appearance, their presence on bone using the method derived would confirm gunshot trauma when atypical fracture patterns are present (Berryman et al., 2010).

As a result, the shape of the externally beveled area in the ribs is irregular whereas it is typically more round in the vault (Figure 15.11). Another difference is the absence of concentric heaving fractures in ribs. This is due to the soft tissue structures of the chest, which accommodate temporary cavity formation (Coates and Beyer, 1962), and the rib cage, which lacks the structural integrity seen in the contiguous bones that make up the cranial vault. Additionally, depressed bone fragments around the entrance site and externally displaced bone splinters at the exit site occur more frequently in the ribs (Figure 15.12) than in the cranial vault. The intrinsic qualities of the ribs account for the prevalence of these features.

Langley (2007) reported that gunshot trauma to vertebrae typically resulted in massive comminution that was difficult to reconstruct due to the high percentage of trabecular bone present in vertebral bodies. Occasionally depressed fractures were present in vertebrae that could be used to support the interpretation of bullet direction. The sternum, however, exhibited the typical features that allow interpretation of bullet direction, particularly beveling, depressed fractures, and displaced bone fragments (Langley, 2007; Figure 15.13). Likewise, depressed fractures around the entrance site and displaced fragments surrounding the exit indicated bullet direction in the scapula (Figure 15.14). One clear picture that arises from Langley's (2007) study is that categorizing trauma according to bone type (i.e., flat bone versus long bone) is too simplistic. Instead, careful consideration of the complex interaction of intrinsic and extrinsic variables yields a more informed conclusion about gunshot trauma.

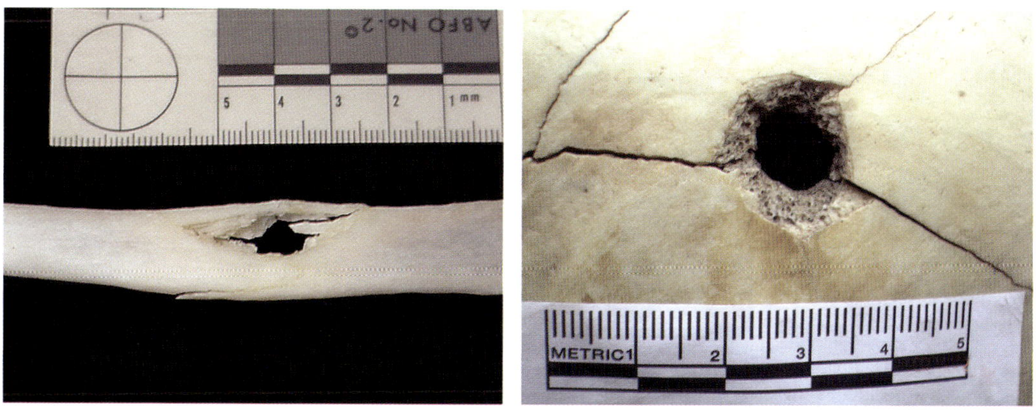

(a) (b)

Figure 15.11 (a) Irregular exit wound in a rib (note the external beveling). (b) More rounded exit wound in cranial vault. (Photographs by Natalie R. Shirley.)

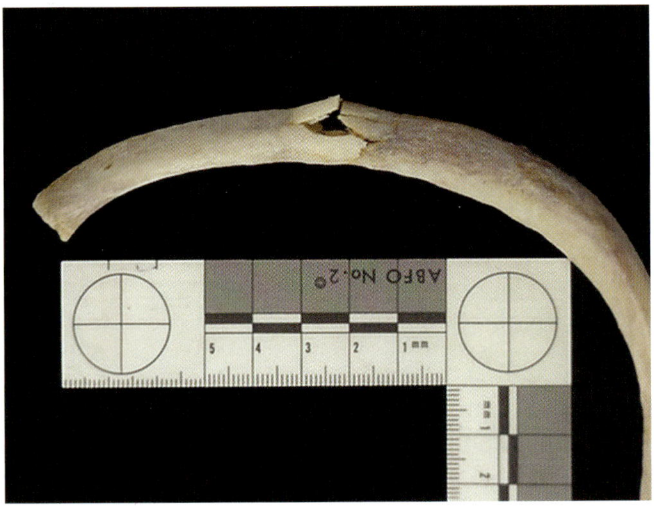

Figure 15.12 Displaced bone fragments at exit site on anterolateral aspect of rib. (Photograph by Natalie R. Shirley.)

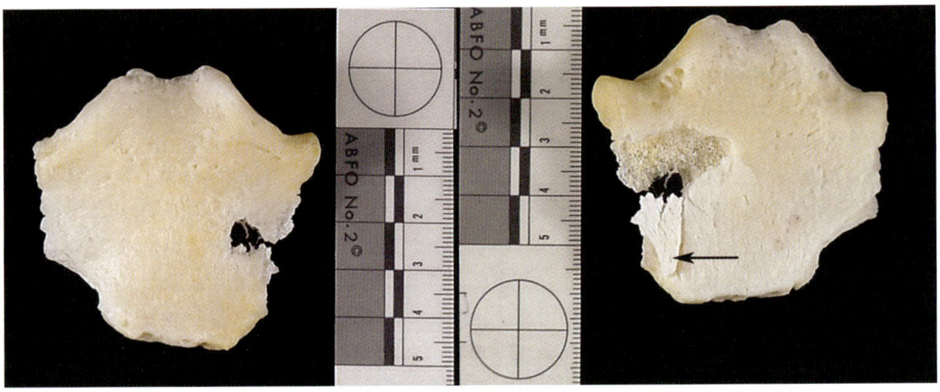

(a) (b)

Figure 15.13 (a) Entrance wound on manubrium of anterior sternum. (b) Corresponding exit wound on dorsal manubrium. Note beveling and displaced fragment (arrow). (Photograph by Natalie R. Shirley.)

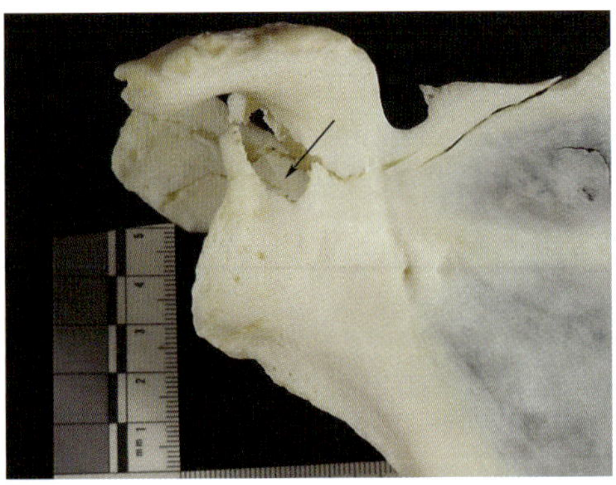

Figure 15.14 Anterior view of scapula. Depressed fracture surrounding entrance site inferior to coracoid process and medial to the glenoid cavity. (Photograph by Natalie R. Shirley.)

Gunshot Wounds in Long Bones

There has been little research on long bone ballistics. Beveling patterns that are present can allow for directional interpretation, but fracture lines may travel around the shaft so quickly that the bone is comminuted before a typical exit site can be produced. Langley (2007) noted that this was the case with most gunshot wounds in the clavicle. Smith and Wheatley (1984) investigated the biomechanics of femur fractures secondary to gunshot wounds. They state that the amount of fragmentation present at the exit site depends on the amount of energy transmitted to the bone. They also observed "impaction fractures," which are sites where the bullet did not penetrate the cortical surface completely, but instead fragmented or impacted the cortical surface superficially as a result of a glancing or grazing blows (Smith and Wheatley, 1984). The morphology of these impaction fractures is highly influenced by the angle of impact. The angle of bullet impact also affects the beveling characteristics. Smith and Wheatley (1984) also state that spiral fractures can form above or below the site of bullet impact. Spiral fractures, they argue, are a result of secondary stress risers some distance away from impact and have been attributed to falls reported by some individuals when taking steps after being wounded (Smith and Wheatley, 1984).

Berryman and Gunther (2000) have documented keyhole fractures in tubular bone resulting from gunshot wounds that are similar to those observed in the cranium. Their example of a keyhole defect in the humerus is not covered in the classification system of Smith and Wheatley (1984). Furthermore, the fracture pattern secondary to the bullet impact was much more complex than that depicted in Smith and Wheatley (1984). The complex fracture patterns documented by Berryman and Gunther (2000) are more representative of fracture patterns secondary to bullet impact, as intrinsic and extrinsic factors affecting fracture propagation vary from one site to another on a given bone. Reports such as Berryman and Gunther's (2000) demonstrate the need for further research in long bone ballistics.

Additional Factors to Consider

Ammunition for many handguns, rifles, and shotguns imparts a velocity to their projectiles that is substantial enough to cause bone to behave like a brittle material. Boney wound characteristics produced by shotguns are uniquely different from those produced by handguns and rifles. While the extrinsic variables discussed earlier (e.g., distance from target and intermediate targets) play a significant role in wound appearance, if all of these variables are held constant, certain key features become apparent in each weapon class. At close and intermediate gun to target distances, handguns are generally less destructive than hunting or military rifles and shotguns. An examination of the formula for wounding capacity ($KE = mv^2/2$) clearly shows that bullet velocity plays a greater role in bone and soft tissue damage than mass (i.e., bullet weight). Shotgun projectiles are propelled at relatively low velocities; however, the nature of the projectiles (i.e., masses of pellets or a single slug that is hollow and deforms drastically upon impact) radically damages bone or soft tissue in their direct path and slows within the body giving up more of the associated kinetic energy. At contact and close range, shotguns cause extensive fracturing often fragmenting a skull or other osseous structures in the path of the projectile.

At far distances, shotguns—firing pellets as opposed to slugs—are less destructive than handguns or rifles that fire solid, solitary bullets. Shotgun pellets lack the mass to be

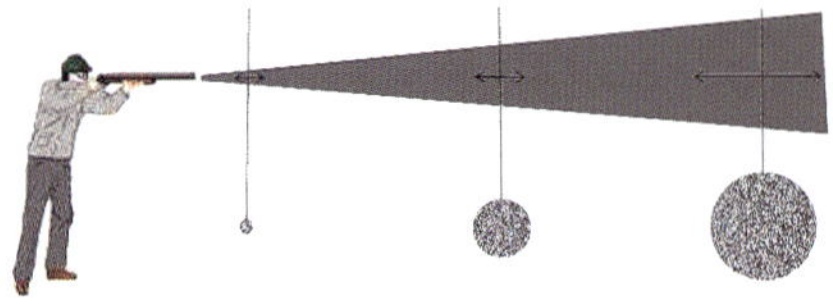

Figure 15.15 Shotgun pellet scatter with increasing distance from muzzle. (Illustration by Hugh E. Berryman.)

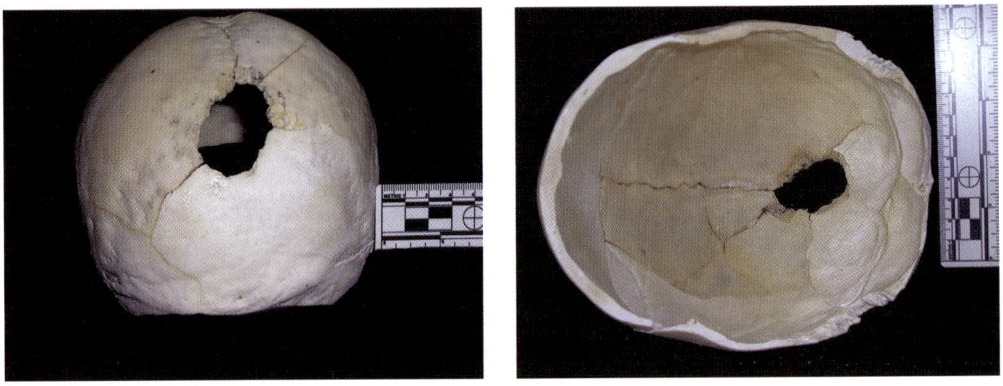

(a) (b)

Figure 15.16 (a) Shotgun entrance wound to occipital region. Note lead marks and depressions from pellet impacts. (b) Endocranial view of entrance wound showing internal beveling and lead fragments around the wound. (Photo by Natalie Shirley, courtesy of Forensic Anthropology Center, University of Tennessee, Knoxville, TN.)

projected a great distance and eventually begin to scatter and quickly lose velocity (Figure 15.15). At sufficient distances, shotgun pellets will lack the energy to penetrate the body, causing only minor injuries. Figure 15.16 shows a close range shotgun entrance wound. Note the lead marks and small depressions caused by individual pellet impact that surround the larger defect produced by the concentrated mass of pellets striking the bone (Figure 15.16a). Additionally, shotgun pellets are contained in a plastic shot cup within the shotgun shell casing. This cup holds the pellets in close proximity during the first few yards before it separates from the pellet mass. Contact or very close distances will reflect the effect of the shot cup, which allows the pellet mass to act more as a single entity until impact and initial entrance into the target.

Although shotgun wounds to bone can usually be distinguished from handgun and rifle wounds, estimation of gauge or caliber based on wound dimensions is discouraged. Ross (1996) has suggested that it is possible to distinguish between small and large caliber bullets in cranial gunshot wounds, but she reports an area of overlap and advises using caution in making these distinctions. Many extrinsic variables besides caliber can affect wound dimensions including firing distance, angle of entry, body position at the time of impact, surface treatment and strength characteristics of the bullet, and intermediate targets that may deform the bullet (Figure 15.17; DiMaio, 1993, Berryman et al., 1995). Although consistencies can exist under controlled conditions, clinical cases present many uncontrolled and unpredictable variables. For example, bullets can travel through a preexisting fracture and

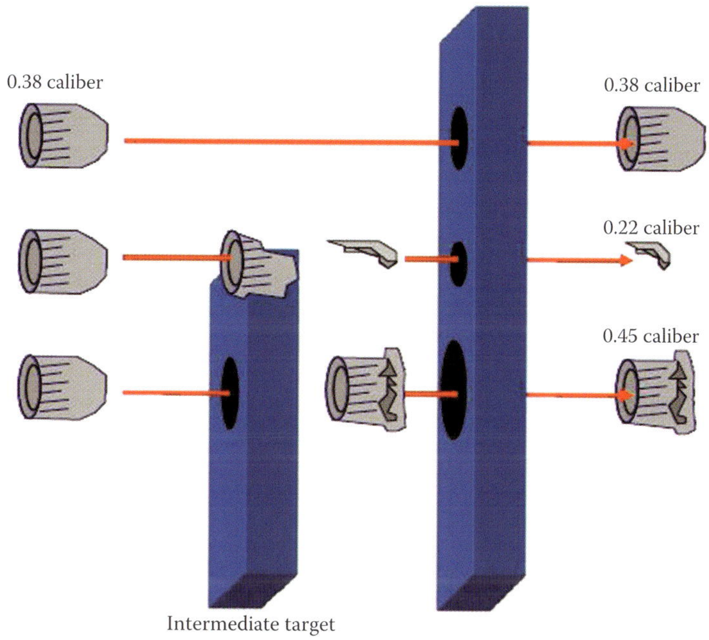

Figure 15.17 Various effects of intermediate targets on entrance wound dimensions. Top: No intermediate target; entrance wound is similar in size to bullet. Middle: Bullet is broken into fragments, and a small fragment enters the bone, resulting in a smaller entrance defect than would be expected. Bottom: Bullet flattens or mushrooms after hitting intermediate target, resulting in a larger defect than would be expected. (Modified from Figure 3 in Berryman, HE, et al., *J Forensic Sci* 40(5), 751, 1995.)

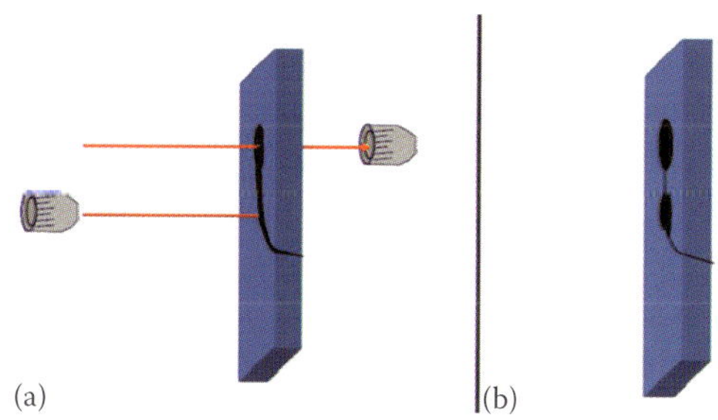

Figure 15.18 Scenario showing a bullet entering an existing fracture (a), causing a smaller wound (b) than it would in unaffected bone. (Illustration by Hugh E. Berryman.)

leave a hole much smaller than the bullet caliber (Figure 15.18). Moreover, as a bullet enters the body tissues, the kinetic energy produces a temporary cavity that undulates for 5–10 ms before settling into its final configuration (the permanent wound tract; Figure 15.19).

Regardless of the scenario, the case report should reflect only what the boney evidence supports. A good trauma analysis report should include detailed descriptions with photographs and/or diagrams, and if possible, a biomechanical explanation of what caused the trauma. The forensic anthropologist should avoid conjecture beyond what the evidence will

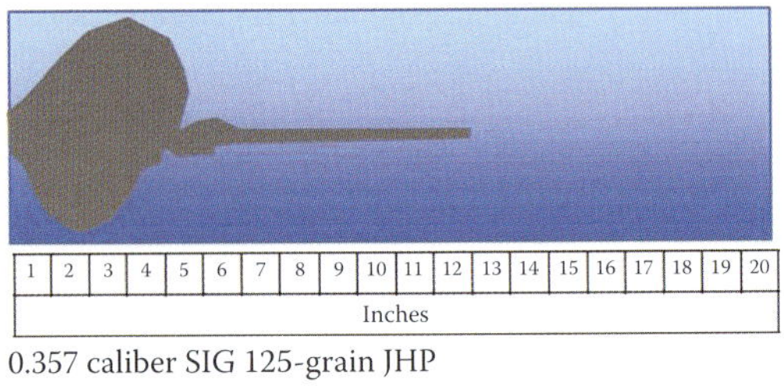

Figure 15.19 The depth of penetration and the temporary cavity for 0.357 caliber SIG 125-grain JHP. (Illustration by Hugh E. Berryman.)

support. In the presence of uncertainty, do not attempt an interpretation, simply describe, photograph, and diagram.

Recent Research

Technological advances have allowed the investigation of various biomechanical mechanisms of skeletal trauma. Two areas where significant improvements have been made are controlled experimental testing and finite element analysis. Traditionally, terminal ballistic testing is conducted using a substrate commonly referred to as *ballistic gelatin*. This substance allows for the visualization of the dimensions of temporary and permanent wound tracts. Although ballistic gelatin is engineered to represent muscle tissue, it falls short of replicating the complexities of the human body with its various tissue types. Experimental tests using human cadavers are not a novel idea. René LeFort (1901) used human cadavers to study facial trauma at the turn of the twentieth century. However, the majority of cadaveric research experiments have examined the body's response to low-velocity trauma. Outside of military research, high-velocity experimental cadaveric research is sparse, despite the high number of firearms homicides in the United States annually.

Virtual technology has begun to play a pivotal role in understanding the biomechanics of high-velocity injuries. Finite element analysis offers the ability to model anatomical regions. The structures within these regions are assigned physical properties (i.e., moment of inertia, stiffness, fatigue strength) that can then be subjected to various loads and forces. This mathematical approach allows for detailed visualization of how the material(s) behave under various forces. Although investigations of structures such as the maxillofacial region are still impractical, finite element analysis can still provide important information on the biomechanical mechanisms of wound ballistics. Finite element analysis has been used to model the wound ballistics of a pig mandibular angle (Chen et al., 2010) and of the human cranium (Mota et al., 2003). These preliminary studies demonstrate that it is possible to accurately model ballistic impact to bone. Important biomechanical information gathered from these preliminary studies indicate that trabecular bone has less stress concentration and a lower speed of stress propagation compared to cortical bone (Chen et al., 2010). More advanced finite element simulations have the potential to provide a unique tool to investigate the effect of caliber, trajectory (angle of impact), and velocity on the pattern and severity of the gunshot wounds (Mota et al., 2003). Reconstruction of bullet trajectory has already been achieved using three-dimensional multislice computed tomography (Puentes et al., 2009). For forensic anthropologists, advanced simulations such as these could allow fracture analysis to meet Daubert standards in expert testimony (Mota et al., 2003).

As with any area of scientific inquiry, more research is needed to understand the complexities of high-velocity injuries to various anatomical locations. Although finite element analyses offer promise, controlled experiments on human cadavers would yield the most accurate understanding of high-velocity trauma. Researchers should consider validating finite element models with cadaveric tests. These studies should not be limited to bone, but should include modeling of the surrounding soft tissues to determine the role these tissues play in bone fracture initiation, propagation, and severity. The more complete our understanding of the interplay of intrinsic and extrinsic factors in wound production, the more accurate our interpretation.

References

Berryman HE, Gunther WM. Keyhole defect production in tubular bone. *J Forensic Sci* 2000;45(2):483–487.

Berryman HE, Kutyla AK, Davis JR II. Detection of gunshot primer residue on bone in an experimental setting—An unexpected finding. *J Forensic Sci* 2010;55:488–491.

Berryman HE, Smith OC, Symes SA. Diameter of cranial gunshot wounds as a function of bullet caliber. *J Forensic Sci* 1995;40(5):751–754.

Berryman HE, Symes SA. Recognizing gunshot and blunt cranial trauma. In Kathleen J. Reichs (ed.), *Forensic Osteology: Advances in the Identification of Human Remains* (2nd edn), 2002. pp. 333–352.

Brown H, Cauchi DM, Holden JL, Allen FCL, Cordner S, Thatcher P. Image analysis of gunshot residue on entry wounds II—a statistical estimation of firing range. *Forensic Sci Int* 1999b;100:179–186.

Brown H, Cauchi DM, Holden JL, Wrobel H, Cordner S. Image analysis of gunshot residue on entry wounds I—the technique and preliminary study. *Forensic Sci Int* 1999a;100:163–177.

Chen Y, Miao Y, Xu C, Zhang G, Lei T, Tan L. Wound ballistics of the pig mandibular angle: A preliminary finite element analysis and experimental study. *J Biomechanics* 2010;43(6):1131–1137.

Coates J, Beyer J, (eds.). *Wound Ballistics*. Washington, DC: Office of the Surgeon General, Department of the Army, 1962.

Crime in the U.S. http://www.fbi.gov/about-us/cjis/ucr/crime-in the-u.s/2010/crime-in-the-u.s.-2010/tables/10shrtbl08.xls, accessed 12/19/2011.

Currey JD. *Bones: Structure and Mechanics*. Princeton, NJ: Princeton University Press, 2002.

DiMaio VJ. *Gunshot Wounds: Practical Aspects of Firearms, Ballistics, and Forensic Techniques* (2nd revised edn), New York: Elsevier Science Publishing Company, 1993.

Dixon DS. Keyhole lesions in gunshot wounds of the skull and direction of fire. *J Forensic Sci* 1982;27:555–566.

Dixon DS. Exit keyhole lesion and direction of fire in a gunshot wound of the skull. *J Forensic Sci* 1984;29:336–339.

Langley NR. An anthropological analysis of gunshot wounds to the chest. *J Forensic Sci* 2007;52(3):532–537.

Le Fort R. Etude experimentale sur les fractures de la machoire superieure. *Rev Chir Paris.* 1901;23:208, 360, 479.

Madea B, Staak M. Determination of sequence of gunshot wounds of the skull. *J Forensic Sci Soc* 1988;28(5–6):321–328.

Mota A, Klug S, Ortiz M, Pandolfi A. Finite-element simulation of firearm injury to the human Cranium. *Computational Mechanics* 2003;31:115–121.

Puentes K, Taveira F, Madureira AJ, Santos A, Magalhaes T. Three-dimensional reconstitution of bullet trajectory in gunshot wounds: A case report. *J Forensic and Legal Medicine* 2009;16:407–410.

Ross AH. Caliber estimation from cranial entrance defect measurements. *J Forensic Sci* 1996;41(4):629–633.

Smith HW, Wheatley KK. Biomechanics of femur fractures secondary to gunshot wounds. *J Trauma* 1984;24(11):970–977.

Ubelaker DH. The remains of Dr. Carl Austin Weiss: An anthropological analysis. *J Forensic Sci* 1996;41(1):60–79.

Taphonomy of Fire

16

JOANNE BENNETT DEVLIN AND
NICHOLAS P. HERRMANN

Contents

Introduction

Fire has long been utilized by humans for numerous activities ranging from food preparation and waste removal to body destruction. The latter has been employed throughout history in situations involving ceremonialism, suicide, and homicide. Undeniably, heat and flame can have a tremendous impact upon the soft and hard tissues of the human body resulting in substantial modification. Exposure to heat results in a progression of change from the loss of soft tissues to the alteration of hard tissues, culminating in change in the color, fragmentation, and shrinkage of the boney elements. These signatures are unique and serve as specific indicators of exposure to fire. The condition of the tissues results from the interplay of two important variables: (1) the heating temperature, and (2) the duration of exposure to heat (Bennett-Devlin et al., 2006). That said, fire is a dynamic entity and as such it is not possible to unequivocally dictate the specific impact it can have upon body tissues, though we can anticipate general patterns of destruction.

Although bodies react to heat in a generally predictable manner, there is not a specific pattern that can be used to characterize the condition of all victims in each fire event. It is, however, possible to recognize a general sequence of modification that results from heat and fire. The exposure of the body to fire results initially in the reduction of soft tissues as skin, muscle, and fat actually are sources of fuel that can sustain the fire; bone, too, is a fire-sustaining fuel. While fire can bring about the complete reduction of soft tissues, the properties of bone are such that it cannot be destroyed by heat or fire alone; it is not possible to completely destroy a body solely through heat. However, heat can severely affect bone tissue, making it highly fragile and, therefore, susceptible to further modification related to the fire or suppression efforts, in addition to discovery and recovery attempts.

Though modified, burned, and cremated remains are not beyond analysis, and, thus, a well-led investigation and subsequent analyses can potentially recognize the nature of the situation and ideally establish the biological profile of fire victims.

Undeniably, anthropologists can provide several specific and unique roles in investigations involving burned human remains. First, the anthropologist can aid in the discovery and recovery, which can be followed with analyses to create a biological profile. Furthermore, the anthropologist can assist in the establishment of identification. While the frequency of forensic cases that involve burned remains is likely lower than that of other traumas, the particulars of heat modification are so tremendous that it is imperative that practicing forensic anthropologists are aware of the general signatures of burning. To facilitate the development of information needed to function successfully in each of these stages of forensic work, the anthropologist must have an understanding of the mechanisms by which fire occurs and grows.

Fire Dynamics

To appreciate the impact fire can have on human remains, it is important to have an understanding of the dynamics of fire. While this is not the arena for a rich discussion of fire, it is important to have a basic sense of how fire spreads, grows, and the temperatures that it can reach. At the most basic level, fire is a chemical reaction and, as such, it is associated with the presence and interaction of several components: *heat*, *oxygen*, and *fuel*. The relationship between these entities is often represented and referred to as the fire triangle or fire tetrahedron. The latter more accurately reflects the complex reality of combustion and fire growth, and the reader is encouraged to supplement the present discussion with more detailed explanations (see DeHaan, 2002, 2008).

Heat involves raising the temperature of an object to its lowest temperature at which it will release vapors and, thus, sustain combustion. The amount of air or *oxygen* (identified as the oxidizing agent) must be of a certain level that can sustain combustion. Finally, the *fuel* refers to the combustible materials that are present and capable of being used to sustain the chemical reaction (fire). Obviously, an ignition source must also be present to initiate a burning event and to elevate the fuel to its ignition temperature. To appreciate the role of each of these components, consider the extinguishment that results if one or more of these is absent or removed. For example, reflect upon how the use of water can extinguish a fire; it reduces the temperature of combustible materials below the ignition point (removal of heat). Similarly removel of the fuel source will also bring about extinguishment. Also consider the practice of putting the lid on a pan in the event of a grease fire; extinguishment occurs because you have eliminated the oxygen source and altered the structure of the fire triangle. Importantly, the amount of each critical component (heat, oxygen, and fuel) that is present and available will dictate the duration and the intensity of the fire. While we recognize the products of fire as heat and light, the amount of both of these that is produced is directly dependent upon the interaction of the parts of the fire triangle. Simply then, it is these components that are responsible for the intensity (temperature) and duration of a fire.

Specific temperatures that are attained by fires are limited by the available fuel load (the nature of the material and how much is present). Simply, man-made products such as plastics will burn at higher temperatures than wood or natural materials. However, the duration of the fire is dictated by the amount that is present. While it is not possible to

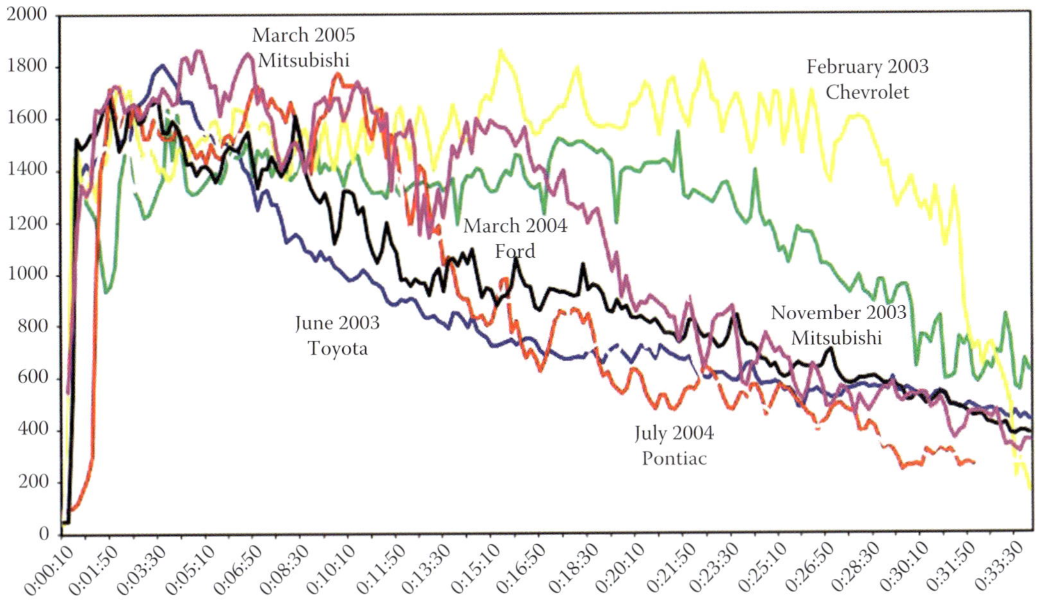

Figure 16.1 Interior temperatures attained during automobile training burns conducted between February 2003 and November 2005. Data, recorded in degrees Fahrenheit, were captured at 10 s intervals using a thermocouple wire mounted in the passenger compartment connected to DaqBook Data Acquisition System on a computer running DaqView 5.0. The presented data reflects only interior compartment temperatures collected during the first 35 min of each exercise.

isolate these influences, it is beneficial to have an awareness of the average temperatures that are reached in a variety of scenarios: residential fires, open fires, and automobile fires. The average residential fires attain temperatures of approximately 1200°F, while campfires have lower temperatures, rarely exceeding 600°F, though the type of wood used will influence the amount of heat that is generated. Data from experimentally burned automobile fires (conducted during the last decade) demonstrate that not only do cars generate temperatures in excess of 1800°F, they also reach maximum temperatures after a very short period of time (Devlin et al., 2004) (Figure 16.1).

Fire Statistics

The United States has one of the highest per capita fire death rates among industrialized nations with more than one million fires reported every year (Fire and Arson Scene Evidence, 2000; Karter, 2010). Of these, approximately half a million occur in structures, of which roughly 90% are classified as residential properties. Dating back to the 1974 formation of the United States Fire Administration (USFA), fire deaths were estimated at 12,000 annually, dropping to a low of 3,245 in 2006 (*US Fire Administration, 2009*). While recent decades have seen a dramatic decrease in the number of fatalities, the United States still ranks fifth worldwide in fire death rates; 2–2.5 times higher than many European Nations (Federal Emergency Management Agency, 2009). Among the highest recorded number of fire deaths in the world are those for the states of Alaska, Kansas, Mississippi, Tennessee, West Virginia, and the District of Columbia where rates exceed 25 per million residents

(Federal Emergency Management Agency, 2009). Statistics from the National Fire Protection Agency (NFPA) indicate that 76% of fires resulting in fatalities during 2007 occurred in residential properties, particularly in one- and two-family dwellings. The second largest losses occur in vehicles (281 fatalities) (Federal Emergency Management Agency, 2009).

Records of reported fires reflect several patterns with respect to the timing and causation of enclosure fires. The majority of fires (40%) are the result of failures or incidents involving cooking with heat ranked second at 14% (Federal Emergency Management Agency, 2009). These fires, however, are not associated with high rates of fatalities. Instead the majority of fatal fires are associated with smoking (18%). In the decades since the formation of the USFA, fire safety initiatives have resulted in a steady decline in the number of fires and fatalities. The increase in public education and awareness, and more consistent use of smoke detectors and sprinkler systems have likely contributed to the decrease in fires and fire fatalities over the last few decades. During this period, however, financial losses have grown steadily.

Victim Statistics

All demographic and socioeconomic groups are affected by fire, though more males than females die in fires (2377 and 1563, respectively, during 2006). Among those younger than 20, the rate is slightly higher for females. The majority of female deaths are among the elderly while male fatalities are highest among those aged 40–59. Overall fire deaths are high among older adults (32%) and, given the increasing proportion of senior citizens in the American population, the number of fatal fires may increase in coming years. Traditionally high fatality rates have been recorded among those younger than four, though the current trend is a decrease among this demographic group (Federal Emergency Management Agency, 2009). As noted, the majority of fire fatalities occurs in residential properties and is linked to smoking, though Shkrum and Johnston (1992) reported on rates of suicide by fire, finding that this accounts for approximately 1% of suicides.

Fire deaths disproportionately affect ancestral groups, with 22% of fire deaths during 2006 (848 fatalities) involved African-Americans who only comprise 13% of the population (Federal Emergency Management Agency, 2009). During this year, 44 fire deaths were reported among Native Americans, 2980 among European Americans, and 68 for Asian/pacific Islanders (Federal Emergency Management Agency, 2009).

These statistics focus solely upon injuries and deaths associated with thermal burns. This type of burn is associated with an increase in temperature from an external heat source that can result in cell death. Three other types of burns are recognized: radiation, chemical, and electrical burns. These also can lead to cell death through different mechanisms and will not be discussed here. Thermal burns are often described in two manners: the degree of burning and the level of body involvement. Several techniques are used by emergency responders and clinicians to enable appropriate communication about the severity of a situation. There are three commonly used tools for describing the total body surface area impacted by thermal burns. The most utilized is the *rule of nines* where the body is divided into 11 parts, each which represents 9% of the individual; the remaining 1% is the external genitalia. Another system is the *rule of palm* in which the surface area of the palm is considered to represent 1% of the total body surface area. The *Lund Browder chart* relies upon age grades such that reference tables incorporate the varied proportions that characterize individuals at different stages of development. All three of these systems provide a means to assess the total body surface area affected by heat, which is then commonly combined with an evaluation of the degree of destruction.

Clinicians utilize a five level system to describe and manage the degree of heat exposure. Burns labeled first degree or superficial commonly involve reddening of the epidermis without blistering. Continued exposure can lead to second degree or partial thickness burns that impact the epidermis and the upper dermal layer and are further characterized by blisters or sloughing of the epidermis. Third degree (full thickness) burns destroy the epidermis and dermis, further impacting vascular and nervous supply to the region. Assessment of the total body surface area that is involved is only conducted on cases involving second and third degree burns. Continued exposure leads to fourth degree characterized by charring (blackening) of tissues. Exposure of bone in regions where soft tissue layers are thin (e.g., shins and forehead) is common at this level as is the development of what is referred to as the pugilistic posture (boxers pose) which is recognized by flexion of major body joints due to the dehydration of muscle tissue (so named because of the characteristic flexion of the elbows and flexion of the hands which resemble the pose a boxer might take) (Figure 16.2). The legs flex at the knees, and often the head is bent backward and the tongue appears to slightly protrude. The pugilistic posture results from the natural fact that dominant muscle groups (flexor muscles) will contract leading to flexion (overpowering the extensor muscles) and produce this predictable pattern.

Continued exposure will lead to the loss of all soft tissues, or fifth degree burning, which is more commonly referred to as *cremation*; the resultant bone tissues are called *cremains*. Bone is the predominant product, and it will exhibit all the classic signatures of modification (i.e., grey and white in color, and highly fragmented and fragile). Similarly, teeth are impacted and, though roots and enamel may remain intact, they may separate from the tooth crypts and will be extremely fragile. The products used in dental restorations are able to withstand high temperatures: porcelain melts at 1232°C (~2250°F), while silver amalgam and gold last to 965°C (~1770°F), with the lowest burning temperatures for acrylic (i.e., dentures) 600°C (~1112°F) (see Norrlander, 1997 and Schmidt, 2008 for a review). Commercial cremations commonly consist of heating for periods of 2 h to 760°C–980°C (~1400°F–1800°F), though some may exceed 1000°C (~2000°F), generating bone fragments that are normally white to blue-gray in color (see Schultz et al., 2008 for a review). A comparable five level scheme of patterned destruction was presented by Glassman and Crow (1996). Designed to correlate the level of modification and destruction with the efforts

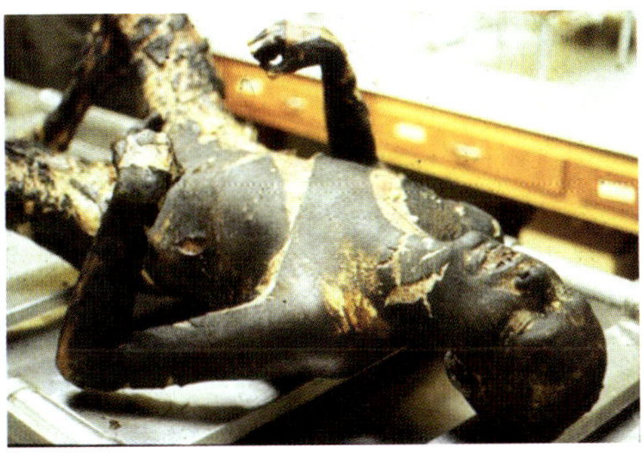

Figure 16.2 The pugilistic posture.

and resources of the forensic community, they developed the Crow–Glassman scale (CGS) (Glassman and Crow, 1996). The details of this scale are discussed later in this chapter.

Fire and Anthropology

Anthropological involvement in the examination of burned remains has a rich history. Beginning with macroscopic examinations of archaeologically recovered burned bone to experimental work and histological analyses, anthropologists are well versed in bone modification resulting from heat. Nonetheless, burned bone can present an interpretative challenge to forensic anthropologists given the color change, shrinkage, and fragmentation, in addition to fracturing and warping, that characterizes thermally altered remains. The level to which these signatures occur is due to the modification or destruction of organic and inorganic components of bone, which is dictated by the combination of heating temperature and duration of exposure. Our knowledge and understanding of the signatures of thermal alteration will be presented in the following literature review. In addition, experimental temperature data collected by the authors will be included.

Burned Bone Research

Burned bone is a unique artifact. When heated, it progresses through a sequence of changing colors from dark brown to black, then to gray, and finally to white (Figure 16.3). These colors are initially recognizable on the exposed surfaces, with internal surfaces lagging in color shifts. While a bone fragment can appear gray across much of its outer surface, the unexposed regions may still be black in color (Figure 16.4). Subtle variation in bone color is to be expected as heat and flame are not constant, but dramatic color variation can indicate differential heating which may be significant. Though surface color has long been considered a reliable indicator of the temperature of the fire, it is important to consider surface color as being additionally influenced by the length of exposure.

In addition to changes in color, bone material will distort and fragment. Variation in the degree of distortion can be observed in Figure 16.5, and it is likely that the level of modification is dually influenced by the preincineration condition of the material and the rate at which the maximum fire temperature was reached and subsided. Similarly, heat impacts the microscopic components of bone, and this is most recognizable as shrinkage. Here, too, the exact amount of size reduction cannot be predicted, though shrinkage is more apparent in bone that is white in color (also called *calcined* bone), demonstrating that this coloration is associated with higher temperature and greater duration of burning.

Figure 16.3 Burned bone fragments illustrating color changing sequence from unaltered (far right) to dark brown, black, gray, and then white (far left).

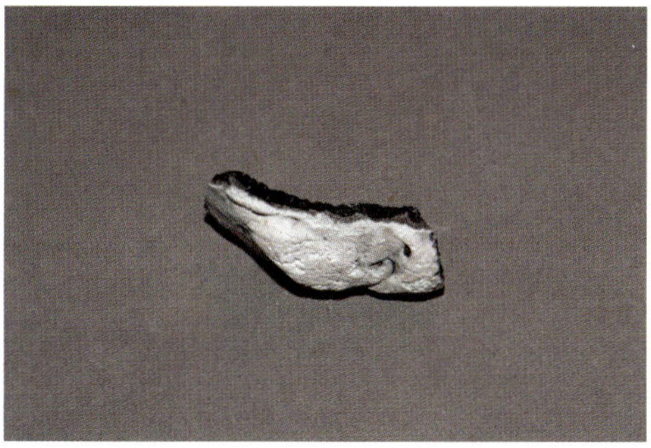

Figure 16.4 Color differences between the external (gray) and internal (black) bone surface on account of differential heat exposure. The external surface experienced more heat exposure than the internal surface of the bone.

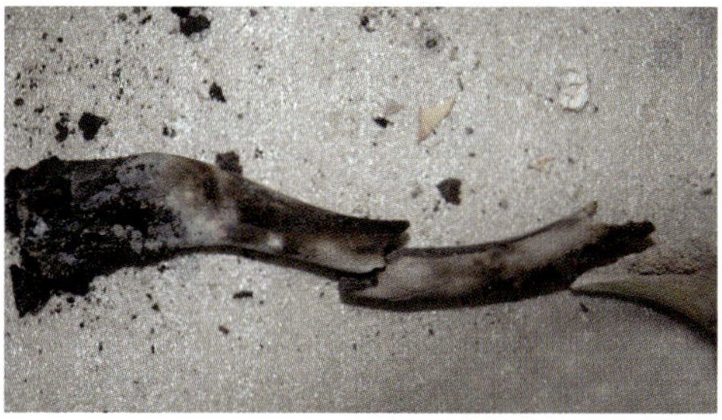

Figure 16.5 Burned clavicle exhibiting fragmentation and distortion.

Much of these observations are the result of a long history of examination and experimentation. Though not of a forensic nature, the earliest examinations of burned bone were motivated by attempts to interpret skeletal collections from archaeologically derived cremation sites (Webb and Snow, 1945; Baby, 1954; Wells, 1960; Binford, 1963). Baby (1954) promoted a three-way classification of burned bone that incorporates modification of element color and surface morphology by labeling bone as *completely incinerated*, *incompletely incinerated*, or *nonincinerated*. The observable variation was attributed to several factors, including duration of exposure and proximity of bone to the fire (Baby, 1954). Shortly thereafter, more formal examination of cremated remains was initiated by Wells (1960) who documented the effects of cremation and suggested that the degree of distortion was in part associated with firing temperature. Binford (1963) extended the study of cremations noting that particular patterns of warping and fracturing indicate the pre-incineration condition of the remains, suggesting that bone covered by soft tissue at the time of incineration will appear different from bone burned either devoid of soft tissues or lacking the grease and marrow of "fresh bone." Binford (1963) noted that the resultant condition and appearance of bone is attributable not only to the duration and intensity of the fire, but also to the condition of the material prior to heat exposure. In the decades since this early work, researchers have sought to establish a correlation between varied surface conditions as an indicator of the degree of heat exposure through both laboratory and natural context examinations (Thurman and Willmore, 1981; Shipman et al., 1984; Gilchrist and Mytum, 1986; Buikstra and Swegle, 1989; Spenneman and Colley, 1989; McCutcheon, 1992; Nicholson, 1993). Examinations have sought to investigate the impact of heat on bone by investigating the association between exposure temperature and surface color (e.g., Shipman et al., 1984) and the microscopic and structural impacts of heat upon skeletal material (e.g., Herrmann, 1977; Shipman et al., 1984; McCutcheon, 1992; Nicholson, 1993; Thompson, 2005).

Bone Color

The observable changes in surface color and element integrity are outward reflections of the modification of the chemical composition of bone in the presence of heat. Bone, as an organic material, evidences predictable changes when exposed to heat and displays a basic chronology of changes. Heating leads to the alteration of the chemical compounds and subsequent dehydration of the tissue, leading to an increase in the brittleness of the tissue. Heated bone is fragile and exhibits warping, shrinkage, fracturing, and color change. Researchers have reported identifiable stages in the process of cremation (Bonucci and Graziani, 1975; see Correia, 1997; and Thompson, 2005 for review). The first stage, *dehydration*, is characterized by the breaking of hydroxyl bonds, which causes water loss. As reviewed by Correia (1997), these events are associated with exposure to temperatures up to 600°C. Stage 2, *decomposition*, is characterized by the removal of the organic components and is associated with temperatures ranging from 500°C to 800°C. Exposure to temperatures ranging from 700°C to 1100°C causes the loss of carbonates that characterizes the third stage, referred to as *inversion*. The final stage, referred to as *fusion*, is associated with temperatures in excess of 1600°C and is characterized by melting of the crystals (Correia, 1997).

Dating back to the early reports of Baby (1954), anthropologists have incorporated the use of surface color descriptions of bone affected by heat. As described by Bonucci and Graziani (1975), the progression through heating stages (e.g., dehydration, decomposition, and inversion) is associated with outwardly apparent modification, including change in the surface color of bone. With increasing exposure to heat, bone progresses through a sequence of colors, from unburned tan to shades of dark brown to black, progressing to blue and gray, and finally to white. Bonucci and Graziani (1975:531) claim that "color itself can be used to some extent for deducing the approximate value of the temperature," correlating ochraceous to brownish colors with exposure to 200°C–300°C (392°F–572°F), black with temperatures of 300°C–350°C (572°F–662°F), grayish with temperatures of 550°C–600°C (1022°F–1112°F), and white for heating in excess of 650°C (1202°F). Black color and an increase in the fragility of bone involve combustion and progressive incineration of the organic materials of collagen and carbon. The gray and white colors (see Figure 16.3) result from continued combustion that impacts the crystalline structures.

The work of Shipman et al. (1984) systematically substantiated these color observations several decades later by using the Munsell (2000) soil color charts to code surface appearance. Shipman et al. (1984) standardized the description of surface colors on experimentally burned bone and recognized five distinct color stages associated with specific increases in temperature. Each stage is characterized by variation in hue, value, and chroma and is marked by dominant surface colors and multiple secondary colors. Shipman associated the dominant colors of pale yellow and very pale brown with exposure to temperatures less than 285°C (545°F). Temperatures from 285°C to 525°C (545°F–977°F) are associated with dominant colors of pink and black and secondary colors of very dark grayish brown and brown; "common colors are reddish brown, very dark gray-brown, neutral dark gray, and reddish yellow" (Shipman et al., 1984:313). Shipman and colleagues characterize stage three, delineated by temperatures up to 645°C (1193°F), by surface colors of "neutral black, with medium blue and some reddish-yellow appearing" (1984:313) and identify Munsell (2000) colors of light gray and secondary colors of brown and light brownish gray. Bone heated to 940°C (1724°F) exhibits neutral white and light blue gray colors. Elements heated to temperatures in excess of 940°C were found to exhibit neutral white and medium gray colors.

This association between heating temperature and surface color was echoed in later work by McCutcheon (1992) and Nicholson (1993). McCutcheon (1992) combined the assessment of surface color with microscopic criteria to recognize a three-level system for estimating exposure temperatures. He observed pale brown to black in specimens heated to 340°C (644°F), light brownish gray in elements heated to 600°C (1112°F), and white color dominating bone heated in excess of 650°C (1202°F) (McCutcheon, 1992). Bennett (1999) demonstrated that a change in the surface color could also occur through indirect exposure to heat. Black colors were observed on bone located beneath campfires maintained for 48 h. Recorded temperatures in these subsurface deposits were less than those normally equated with direct exposure (as promoted by others); however, the duration of the heating event was extended.

Recently, Beach et al. (2008) investigated heat-related color change of human teeth, concluding that color changes are similar to those reported for bone. Evaluating dentin and enamel colors using the Munsell (2000) charts, Beach et al. (2008:144) note "…that temperature is the most important variable when it comes to interpreting tooth color." Of interest is the overall pattern of dental modification that results from heat exposure such that the enamel tissue begins to flake at temperatures less than 600°C, dark grayish-brown enamel color characterized teeth heated to 700°C, and separation of the crown occurred at 800°C after only 30 min of exposure.

The assessment of surface color (traditionally employing Munsell (2000) soil color charts) has been part of the primary protocol in the examination and interpretation of burned bone assemblages. More recently Devlin and Herrmann (2008) presented the use of a photospectrometer as an objective approach for collecting bone color data (see also Herrmann et al., 2010). While the association between particular surface colors and exposure temperatures has become commonplace, Shipman et al. (1984:320) state that the reliance upon color as an indicator of exposure temperature is "an essentially imprecise criterion both because of individual differences in the ability to perceive fine color distinctions and because burnt bones may change color if they are buried." Nonetheless, they state that surface color can be informative as to the range of temperatures to which a bone has been exposed. As noted, the duration of exposure to a heat source is an additional force that can impact the condition and appearance of bone as addressed experimentally (see, e.g., Degraff, 1961; Bennett, 1999; Bennett Devlin et al., 2006; Pope, 2007; Walker et al., 2008). In their experimental work on the effects oxygen availability and environmental conditions have on burned bone, Walker et al. (2008:133) point out that the "…simplistic view of a one-to-one correlation between the color of cremated bones and the temperature to which they were exposed is erroneous." Instead, they promote that bone color is a reasonable indicator of the amount of collagen present and potentially a predictor of whether amplifiable is DNA present (Walker et al., 2008). It is appropriate, then, to regard the surface color as a basic indicator of thermal alteration and not explicitly as an indicator of heating temperature, and this is why the recent x-ray diffraction (XRD) research (Piga et al., 2009) on burned bone is so valuable.

Fractures and Distortion

Though several early studies were concerned with establishing criteria with which to permit demarcation between cremations of dry versus fleshed bone, a major component of such assessments involved a discussion of the fractures, cracks, or breaks. Symes and colleagues (2008) present a rich discussion of the biomechanics of burned bone and promote seven classes of fractures, including longitudinal, step, transverse, patina, splintering and delamination, burn lines, and curved transverse (Symes et al., 2008) (see Figures 16.6 through 16.9). This culminating work supplements and enhances the works promoted in earlier studies. Baby (1954) stated that superficial checking, longitudinal fractures, and transverse splitting characterize bone burned in a dry state. More recently, Buikstra and Swegle (1989:256) described transverse splitting as "shallow and infrequent" and suggest that assessment of such cannot be used to differentiate preincineration condition. They also noted the presence of deep curved fractures in bone burned in a recently defleshed state that Thurman and Willmore (1981) had earlier associated solely with fleshed cremations. Similarly, differences in soft tissue thickness and muscle attachment sites likely impact fracture and cracking patterns. Longitudinal and transverse fractures are commonly observed in burned bone. Unfortunately these so-labeled fractures can also result from blunt force trauma. The presence of curved transverse (thumbnail) fractures is solely associated with burned remains and, in particular, bone burned with soft tissues at the time of incineration (Figure 16.9). These fractures are most often observed on the diaphysis and, specifically, closer to the epiphyses, which are regions associated with soft tissue (ligamentous and tendonous attachments). The arrangement of thumbnail fractures is dictated by the patterned progression of the loss of soft tissue during heating (Symes et al., 2008).

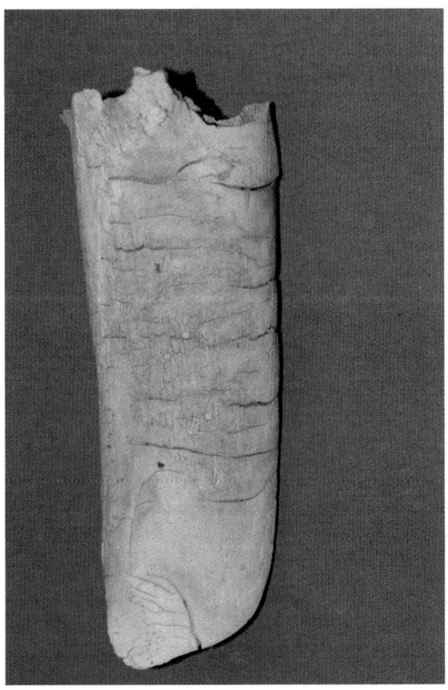

Figure 16.6 Transverse fractures.

Figure 16.7 Patina (note the crackled appearance of the cortical surface).

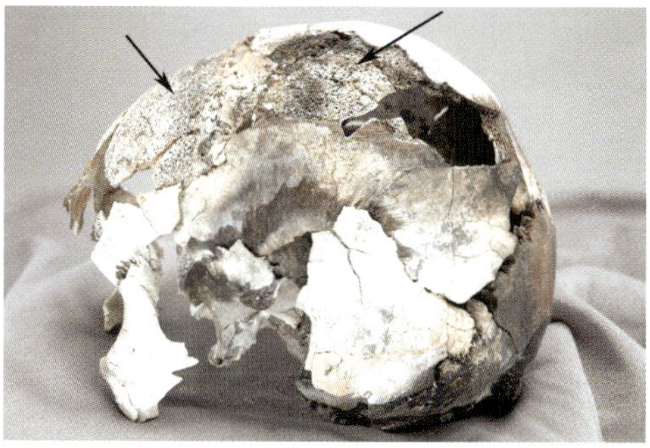

Figure 16.8 Delamination of the skull. Areas indicate areas of delamination where the outer table of the skull has separated from the underlying diploë.

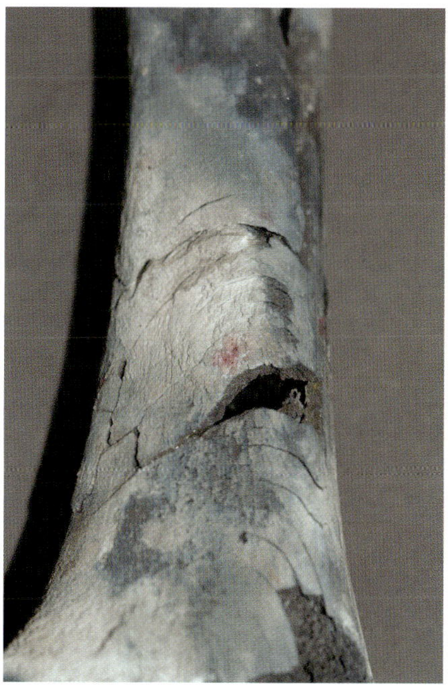

Figure 16.9 Curved transverse fractures on a long bone shaft.

Bone shrinkage of moderate proportion (in excess of 5%) has been associated with exposure to recorded temperatures greater than 650°C (Shipman et al., 1984). This degree of modification is recognized in calcined bone and is promoted by Shipman et al. (1984) as a function of heating temperature with increasing shrinkage directly proportional to increasing exposure temperatures. Buikstra and Swegle (1989) identify shrinkage of less than 3% in their sample of calcined bone. However, they noted average heating temperatures of less than 700°C. Although both research groups describe specimens as appearing calcined, dramatically different degrees of size reduction were noted, and different exposure temperatures were recorded. Thompson (2005) notes most shrinkage in epiphyses and further suggests that the degree of size reduction varies across different dimensions of bones. He points to the random arrangement of collagen fibers as a factor in the high degree of shrinkage associated with trabecular regions (Thompson, 2005). Further, he proposes that the degree of shrinkage is influenced by the interacting effects of the duration of exposure and the maximum temperatures attained. This proposal clearly accounts for the variations in shrinkage noted throughout the literature. Teeth, as well, are subject to shrinkage with reported size loss ranging from 10% to 15% (Shipman et al., 1984, Buikstra and Swegle, 1989).

Recently, Dehaan and Nurbakhsh (2001) suggested that the observable features of burned bone are not simply attributable to high exposure temperatures, but instead reflect a complex interaction of factors. In particular, they note the potential influence of blood, marrow, moisture, and fat in specimens on heating conditions. Obviously the preincineration condition of bone dictates the varying levels to which these components are present and subsequently influences the postincineration condition. Further, Dehann and Nurbakhsh (2001) note that the variation in flame temperatures that occurs naturally must be appreciated and suggest that such tremendous fluctuation would have a less destructive effect on dry bone. Recent work by Piga and colleagues (Piga et al., 2008, 2009) confirm the interaction between heating temperature and exposure duration in their observations of crystallite structure size. Further, using powder XRD on dry bones heated to varying temperatures for 18, 36, or 60 min, they detected microstructural hydroxyapatite mineral phase changes that correlate well with a specific heating temperature and exposure duration (Piga et al., 2009).

Fire Scenes

Fatal fire investigations must include an assessment of the fire scene in addition to an analysis of the human remains; the patterns documented in each of these steps must be consistent. As mentioned earlier, a useful tool was generated by Glassman and Crow (1996) with the formulation of the CGS. The CGS is a method that combines information about the level of body destruction, the appropriate field approach, and suggestions for establishing the system consists of five levels. The designation CGS1 implies a level of involvement similar to that noted with first degree burns. Glassman and Crow (1996) state that standard recovery techniques and traditional methods of identification are appropriate for use with this level of heat modification. An assessment of CGS2 indicates visible impact to lesser areas of the body (e.g., hands, genitalia); recovery may necessitate assistance, and identification may require specialists. More pronounced damage and major impacts to appendages characterize the CGS3 level, which will require the assistance of forensic anthropologists for recovery and identification using dental and or skeletal means. Damage to the axial regions is to be expected with the CGS4 designation. In addition, the skills of a forensic anthropologist are necessary for the detection and recovery of lesser elements of the appendages. The fifth level is associated with cremated remains that are highly fragmented, potentially scattered, and commingled, which undoubtedly requires an experienced anthropologist to locate, recover, and analyze the burned remains. The CGS can be a useful tool given that it incorporates the condition of the body to indicate the applicable and appropriate recovery and identification methods and the necessary resources. The NFPA 921, *Guide for Fire and Explosion Investigations*, 2001 ed., provides basic suggestions for how to conduct an investigation of a fatal fire. However, it is a guide and should be used only as that given that every fire is different and may involve circumstances that are not addressed in the guide.

Detection and Recovery

In situations that necessitate the search for burned human remains, it is imperative to have a team that is comprised of investigators who are aware of the signatures of heat alteration. As a burned property may easily retain heat for at least 48 h after extinguishment of the flames, the scene may need to be secured for a period of time until it is safe to investigate. Also, scenes that are still wet may be further complicated given that carbonized and/or cremated bone that is wet is more susceptible to postfire destruction.

Initial field work must include photography and documentation of the scene (see Dirkmaat, 2002). The discoloration of biological and structural materials resulting from the fire will require adjustments to standard camera settings. While the search for burned remains should be conducted like any other survey in that the scene must be fully assessed, all participants must be aware of the potential destruction associated with fire and the resulting highly fragile nature of burned bone. It is possible to obliterate a fragment of burned bone by merely exerting standard pressure between your fingers. As such, extreme care must be executed when dealing with burned bone. This is particularly important when attempting to locate heat-altered skeletal material. To do so effectively requires that the forensic anthropologist or archaeologist slightly modify standard search and recovery techniques. The search must be systematic and thorough, but will require slow progression through the fire residue.

Following initial documentation, illustrated, photographic, and written, the members of the search team should take positions next to one another and progress across the scene (Figure 16.10). This movement should consist of a methodical assessment of the residue. Consider that an entire house can be reduced to a layer of ash less than one foot deep which should be slowly cleared using hand tools. Align the team and have each individual gently scrape through the ash layer; depending on the depth, this can be a vertical or a horizontal approach. Work through the ash layer until undisturbed or uninvolved strata is visible. Small trowels, paint brushes, and other such instruments are useful tools in this phase of the investigation. In addition, mesh screens may be necessary if the scene requires sifting of debris (Figure 16.11). A mesh of less than 1/4 in. is preferred as bone may be highly fragmented. Also realize that screening can bring about further damage. Ideally, the discovery approach described here will enable anthropologists and investigators to locate skeletal remains which will then give rise to the recovery phase.

Figure 16.10 Teams preparing to search a house fire scene during a field exercise for a forensic anthropology center taphonomy short course.

Figure 16.11 Screening debris at a fire scene.

Once the site of burned remains has been identified, it is best to gently remove proximate residue to fully reveal the specific position and location of the material (Figure 16.12). This process need not initially involve the removal of all nonosseous material, but merely be sufficient to allow assessment of the position of the remains. Subsequent activity should focus on recording the location and distribution of remains using a standard technique for collecting such data points (see Chapter 6). An illustrated record should also be prepared at this time noting the appearance of the remains and serving also as a basic inventory.

Upon collection of all such information, the anthropologist can begin the recovery stage. Dry burned bone can be carefully extracted from the matrix and packaged for transport. Wrapping the bone and bone fragments in paper towels or similar products can provide a protective environment. These wrapped materials can then be placed in paper bags prior to transport. Avoid plastic bags or metal cans as they can cause further destruction with the former encouraging moisture and the latter contributing to further fragmentation. Consider the application of clear liquid glue (e.g., super glue) on the dentition prior to recovery of the skull for maintenance and preservation.

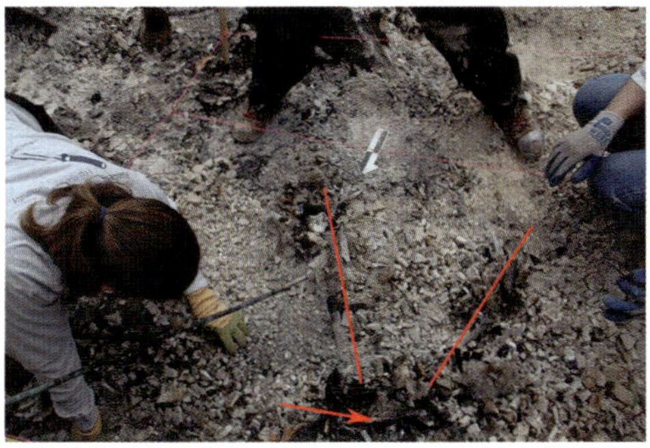

Figure 16.12 Fire scene with human remains. The debris was removed and remains were carefully cleaned to reveal the position of this fire victim. The location of the pelvis is indicated by the arrow; the lines show the position of the legs.

Analyses

Assessment should begin with a series of radiographs of all remains followed by (when possible) a pathological examination. If blood is available, it is desirable to arrange for a test of the level of Carboxyhemoglobin (COHb) present. With inhalation, any CO in the atmosphere will bind to the hemoglobin on the surface of red blood cells at the expense of the necessary oxygen. As cells need oxygen to survive, the presence of CO is not compatible and cell death will occur. The level of COHb can be regarded as an indicator of whether an individual was inhaling during a fire (as opposed to a subject being deceased prior to the fire). Arguably, levels above 40 are considered lethal though values as low as 30 may also suggest that death did not occur prior to the fire (Shkrum and Johnson, 1992; Wirthwein and Pless, 1996).

The anthropological analysis of burned remains and the construction of the biological profile are consistent with the standard approach described elsewhere in this volume. However, given the likelihood of shrinkage, the use of any metrics is inappropriate. While this disallows stature calculation, other analyses can be conducted, including the investigation of antemortem, perimortem (other than thermal trauma), and postmortem trauma. While the assessment of burned remains presents a complex

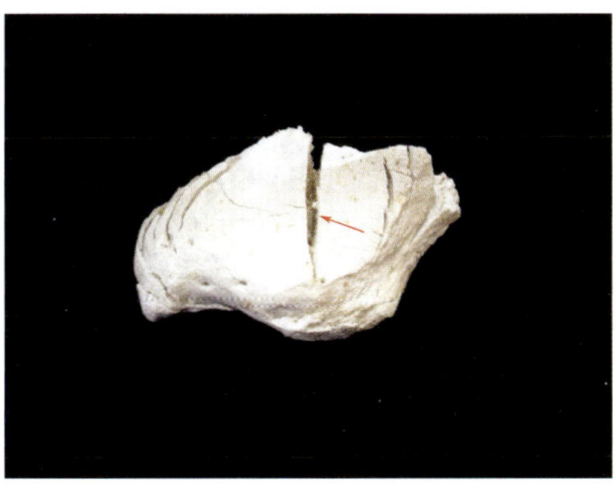

Figure 16.13 Sharp trauma evident on a pig (*Sus scrofa*) tibia. Note the straight margins of the cut mark (indicated by red arrow) compared to more irregular margins of the fire-induced fractures on the periphery of the bone.

situation for the forensic anthropologist, research has demonstrated that it is possible to identify the signatures of trauma on burned bone (Herrmann and Bennett, 1999) (Figure 16.13).

References

Baby, RS. 1954. Hopewell Cremation Practices. Ohio Historical Society Papers in Archaeology 1, 1–17.

Beach JJ, Passalacqua NV, and Chapman EN. 2008. Heat-related changes in tooth color: temperature versus duration of exposure. In: Schmidt, C, Symes, S, eds, *The Analysis of Burned Human Remains*. Elsevier Ltd., Burlington, MA. pp. 137–144.

Bennett, J. 1999. Thermal alteration of buried bone. *J Archaeological Sci* 26:1–8.

Bennett-Devlin, JL, Herrmann, NP, and Pollack, D. 2006. GIS analysis of cremated and commingled bone. Poster presented at *71st Annual Meeting of the Society for American Archaeology*, San Juan, PR.

Bennett-Devlin, JL, Kroman, A, Herrmann, NP, and Symes, S. 2006. Time temperature and color: Heat intensity versus exposure duration Part 1. Macroscopic influence on burned bone. *Proc Am Acad Forensic Sci* 12:311–312.

Binford, LR. 1963. An analysis of cremations from three Michigan sites. *Wisconsin Archaeologist* 44:98–110.

Bonucci, E and Graziani, G. 1975. Comparative thermogravimetric, x-ray diffraction and electron microscope investigations of burnt bones from recent, ancient and prehistoric age. Atti Memorie Accademia Nazionale die Lincei, Sci Fis Matem. *Nature* 59:517–534.

Buikstra, J and Swegle, M. 1989. Bone modification due to burning, experimental evidence. In: Bonnichsen, R, Sorg, M, eds. *Bone Modification*. University of Maine Press, Orono, ME. pp. 247–258.

Correia, PM. 1997. Fire modification of bone: A review of the literature. In: Haglund, W, Sorg, M, eds. *Forensic Taphonomy: The Postmortem Fate of Human Remains*. CRC Press, Boca Raton, FL. pp. 275–293.

De Graaf G. 1961. Gross effects of a primitive hearth. *S afrarchaeol Bull* 16:25–26.

DeHaan, J. 2002. *Kirk's Fire Investigation*, 5th edn. Prentice Hall, Upper Saddle River, NJ.

DeHaan, JD. 2008. Fire and bodies. In: Schmidt, C, Symes, S, eds. *The Analysis of Burned Human Remains*. Elsevier Ltd., Burlington, MA, pp. 1–13.

DeHaan, J and Nurbakhsh, S. 2001. Sustained combustion of an animal carcass and its implications for the consumption of human bodies in fires. *J Forensic Sci* 46:1076–1081.

Devlin, JL, Dalton, MW, and Kennamer, DC. 2004. Vehicle fires: actualistic investigations. *Proceedings of the American Academy of Forensic Sciences Annual Meetings*, Dallas, TX, Vol 10, p. 176.

Devlin, JB. and Herrmann, NP. 2008. Assessment of commingled human remains using a GIS based approach. In: Schmidt, C, Symes, S, eds. *The Analysis of Burned Human Remains*. Elsevier Ltd., Burlington, MA, pp. 109–128.

Dirkmaat, DC. 2002. Recovery and interpretation of the fatal fire victim: The role of forensic anthropology. In: Haglund, WD, Sorg MH, eds. *Advances in Forensic Taphonomy: Method, Theory, and Archaeological Perspectives*. CRC Press, Boca Raton, FL, pp. 451–472.

Federal Emergency Management Agency (FEMA). 2009. Fire in the United States 2003–2007, 15th edn. U.S. Fire Administration/National Fire Data Center, Report FA-325.

Fire and Arson Scene Evidence: A Guide for Public Safety Personnel. 2000. NIJ US Department of Justice Office of Justice Programs.

Gilchrist, M. and Mytum, H. 1986. Experimental archaeology and burnt animal bone from archaeological sites. *Circaea* 4:29–38.

Glassman, DM and Crow, RM. 1996. Standardization model for describing the extent of burn injury to human remains. *J Forensic Sci* 41(1):152–154.

Herrmann, B. 1977. On histological investigations of cremated human remains. *J Human Evolution*, 6:101–103.

Herrmann N and Bennett J. 1999. The differentiation of traumatic and heat-related fractures in burned bone. *J Forensic Sci* 44(3): 461–469.

Herrmann, NP, Stanton, J, and Devlin, J. 2010. Bioarchaeological Spatial Analysis of the Walker-Noe (15Gd56) Crematory. *Paper presented at the 67th annual meeting of the Southeastern Archaeological Conference*, Lexington, KY.

Karter, M. 2010. Fire Loss In The United States During 2009. National Fire Protection Association, Fire Analysis and Research Division. NFPA No. FLX09.

McCutcheon, P. 1992. Burned archaeological bone. In: Stein, JK, ed. *Deciphering a Shell Midden*, Academic Press, San Diego, CA. pp. 347–368.

Munsell Color Company. 2000. *Munsell Soil Color Charts*. Munsell Color Gretag Macbeth, New Windsor, New York.

National Fire Protection Agency (NFPA). 2001. Publication 921. Guide for Fire and Explosion Investigations. Fire and explosion Deaths and Injuries.

Nicholson, R. 1993. A morphological investigation of burnt animal bone and an evaluation of its utility in archaeology. *J Archaeological Science* 20:411–428.

Norrlander, AL. 1997. Burned and incinerated remains. In: Bowers, CM, ed. *Manual of Forensic Odontology*, American Society of Forensic Odontology, Colorado Springs, CO pp. 16–18.

Piga, G, Malgosa, A, Thompson, TJU, and Enzo, S. 2008. A new calibration of the XRD technique for the study of archaeological burnt remains. *J Archaeological Sci* 35:2171–2178.

Piga, G, Thompson, TJU, Malgosa, A, and Enzo, S. 2009. The potential of x-ray diffraction (XRD) in the analysis of burned remains from forensic contexts. *J Forensic Sci* 54(3):534–539.

Pope, E. 2007. Burned human remains: Myths in forensic sciences. *Proc Am Acad Forensic Sci* 13:379–380.

Schmidt, CW. 2008. The recovery and study of burned human teeth. In: Schmidt, C, Symes, S, eds. *The Analysis of Burned Human Remains*. Elsevier Ltd., Burlington, MA, pp. 55–74.

Schultz, JJ, Warren, MW, and Krigbaum, JS. 2008. Analysis of human cremains: Gross and chemical methods. In: Schmidt, C, Symes, S, eds. *The Analysis of Burned Human Remains*. Elsevier Ltd., Burlington, MA, pp. 75–94.

Shipman, P, Foster, G, and Schoeninger. M.1984. Burnt bone and teeth: an experimental study of color, morphology, crystal structure and shrinkage. *J Archaeological Science* 11:307–325.

Shkrum, M and Johnston, K. 1992. Fire and suicide: A three year study of self-immolation deaths. *J Forensic Sci* 37(1):208–221.

Spenneman, D and Colley, S. 1989. Fire in a pit: the effects of burning on faunal remains. *Archaeozoologia* 3:51–64.

Symes, S, Rainwater, C, Chapman, E, Gipson, R, and Piper, A. 2008. Patterned thermal destruction of human remains in a forensic setting. In: Schmidt, C, Symes, S, eds. *The Analysis of Burned Human Remains*. Elsevier Ltd., Burlington, MA, pp. 15–54.

Thompson, TJU. 2005. Heat-Induced dimensional changes in bone and their consequences for forensic anthropology. *J Forensic Sci* 50:1008–1015.

Thurman, M and Willmore, L. 1981. A replicative cremation experiment. *North American Archaeologist* 2:275–283.

US Fire Administration. 2009. Fire in the United States 2003–2007 15th edn. National Fire Data Center. FEMA.

Walker, PL, Miller KWP, and Richman, R. 2008. Time, temperature, and oxygen availability: An experimental study of the effects of environmental conditions on the color and organic content of cremated one. In: Schmidt, C, Symes, S, eds. *The Analysis of Burned Human Remains*. Elsevier Ltd., Burlington, MA, pp. 129–135.

Webb, WS and Snow, C. 1945. The Adena People No. 2. The University of Kentucky Reports in Anthropology and Archaeology 6. Lexington, KY.

Wells, C. 1960. A Study of cremation. *Antiquity* 34:29–37.

Wirthwein, DP and Pless, JE. 1996. Carboxyhemoglobin levels in a series of automobile fires. Death due to crash or fire? *Am J Forensic Med Pathol* 17:117–23.

Taphonomic Processes
Animal Scavenging

17

JAMES T. POKINES AND
MARIATERESA A. TERSIGNI-TARRANT

Contents

Introduction

Taphonomy was defined by Efremov (1940) as the "laws of burial." As such, taphonomy refers to the depositional history of a particular set of remains, explaining the natural and in some cases artificial processes that have acted upon the remains until the time of their discovery and removal from that depositional environment. Taphonomic research that is drawn from multiple academic disciplines, including ethology, botany, paleontology, archaeology, and physical anthropology, can illuminate the natural processes that have affected a particular crime scene or other forensic archaeological sites. Research focused on taphonomic processes in large part began as a method to interpret osseous data about past environments and ecological relationships in an effort to determine the causative agents of bone destruction and alterations that might bias these interpretations (Behrensmeyer 1991, Weigelt 1989). Taphonomic research is also rooted in differentiating between bone modification caused by hominids from bone modification caused by other animals (Binford 1981, Brain 1981, Kerbis Peterhans 1990, Payne 1983). Current taphonomic research covers a variety of topics ranging from weathering (i.e., the effects of exposure to sunlight, precipitation, etc.), damage from plant root growth, gnawing by scavengers, modifications made by fluvial transport or thermal damage, and the effects that burial in acidic soil will have on skeletal remains. See Chapters 16, 18, and 19 for a detailed discussion of various taphonomic processes.

Within forensic anthropology, taphonomic studies provide a wealth of information about the crime scene and the postmortem interval (Ubelaker 1997). If carefully analyzed, the taphonomic characteristics of a crime scene also can help to reconstruct events that occurred when it was created and the processes that have altered it since its creation, assist in interpreting the preservation of osseous and other types of evidence, identify the potential transport or dispersal of remains, and may elucidate confusing scene characteristics caused by the taphonomic processes themselves (Haglund and Sorg 1997b, Pokines 2009, Ubelaker 1997). The use of taphonomic research or methodology within forensic anthropology is often referred to as *forensic taphonomy*. In fact, Haglund and Sorg (1997a, p. 3) suggest that forensic taphonomy

> … refers to the use of taphonomic models, approaches, and analyses in forensic contexts to estimate the time since death, reconstruct the circumstances before and after depositions, and discriminate the products of human behavior from those created by earth's biological, physical, chemical and geological subsystems.

The following sections will discuss common types of osseous alteration encountered on the remains from forensic recovery scenes throughout the world: animal scavenging. These processes are largely destructive, removing entire bones or considerable portions of them, and they generally decrease the level of detail of the biological profile obtainable from the skeletal remains. Long bone epiphyses and weaker bones (especially ribs, vertebrae, innominates, and sterna) are especially vulnerable to these postdepositional forces. This information loss often prevents thorough metric assessment of human skeletal remains and removes other key pieces of information, such as the stage of epiphyseal fusion for age determination, fragile portions of the facial area useful for ancestry estimation, and evidence of perimortem trauma directly related to the cause of death. In turn, a thorough analysis of these processes yields other types of information, including estimates of postmortem interval and area of expected dispersal. In many ways, the forensic anthropologist must learn to read the postmortem history of bones from the alterations they have undergone in order to reveal the probable forces that caused these alterations, and the sequence in which these alterations occurred. Rarely has only one major taphonomic process affected a set of remains at a crime scene, and these overlapping signals can be decoded only through careful analysis.

Carnivore Damage to Skeletal Remains

The modification of vertebrate skeletons by other animals is a well-documented and routinely studied aspect of taphonomy. In archaeology, the characteristics of carnivore damage are studied to determine the effects that these species could have had on human and animal osseous assemblages, both through the complete removal/destruction of bone or through alterations made to surviving bone (Binford et al. 1988, Blumenschine and Marean 1993, Brain 1981, Haynes 1980). Within the subdiscipline of paleoanthropology, taphonomic studies have been used to determine whether early hominids or scavenging animals were responsible for the modification of remains (Binford et al. 1988, Blumenschine 1986, 1988, Brain 1981, Kerbis Peterhans 1990, Pobiner 2008, Stiner 1994). In forensic anthropology, the identification of characteristic carnivore damage to skeletal remains aids in the estimation of the postmortem interval and trauma analysis, as well as determining the method of remains dispersal over a large area. Characteristics of carnivore damage are also paramount in deciphering between postmortem and perimortem trauma. Dispersal of remains over a large area also may be the result of carnivore activity. Fortunately, disarticulation sequences of mammalian remains by carnivores has been studied in multiple environments and found to follow clear patterns (Blumenschine 1986, 1988, Hill and Behrensmeyer 1984).

Consumption of a large vertebrate carcass tends to proceed from the most easily accessible portions first and to the least desirable, lowest nutrient portions last

(Blumenschine 1986, 1988). The sequence often starts with the internal organs (heart, liver, and lungs), given their ease of access through the abdominal wall and high return of nutrients with little or no bone crushing necessary to consume them. Large muscle masses of the upper hind limbs often come next, leading to their disarticulation. Feeding can then proceed to the muscles of the thoracic cage or the upper front limbs. The ribs, sternum, and vertebrae pose little hindrance to large carnivores consuming a skeleton, and these are often fragmented as a part of overall feeding (Horwitz and Smith 1988, Kerbis Peterhans 1990, Pokines and Kerbis Peterhans 2007). By this time, most portions of the skeleton are disarticulated, allowing easier dispersal of remains over large distances. Movement of bone is a normal consequence of carnivore feeding, as it reduces competition while feeding and enables transportation to a den to feed cubs. Haglund et al. (1988, 1989) note an important difference in the aforementioned sequence of carcass consumption in their research on human remains scavenged by large canids in the Pacific Northwest, USA (dogs [*Canis familiaris*] and coyotes [*Canis latrans*]). They found that with human remains, the first portion of the body consumed often was the throat region. This different pattern may be due to the presence of clothing, restricting scavenger access to other portions of the body normally consumed earlier when other large vertebrates are scavenged.

Damage to the skeleton itself follows the same overall pattern of easiest portions first, with more gradual destruction of the better-protected portions later. The weaker elements of the thoracic cage often undergo some destruction during initial feeding and then undergo more as they are fragmented and consumed while their associated soft tissue is consumed. The smaller elements, including those of the hands and feet, can be consumed whole. Carnivore damage to the skeleton is most notable on the appendicular skeleton, in particular the long bones, since weaker elements are often completely destroyed by gnawing (Figure 17.1). The long bones pose the biggest obstacle to consumption, yet these hold an important food resource: the marrow cavity (in adult mammals) stores large supplies of fat, and the epiphyses also have high fat content. Carnivore gnawing normally starts on the epiphyses, as the thin layer of cortical bone covering the ends makes them easy to

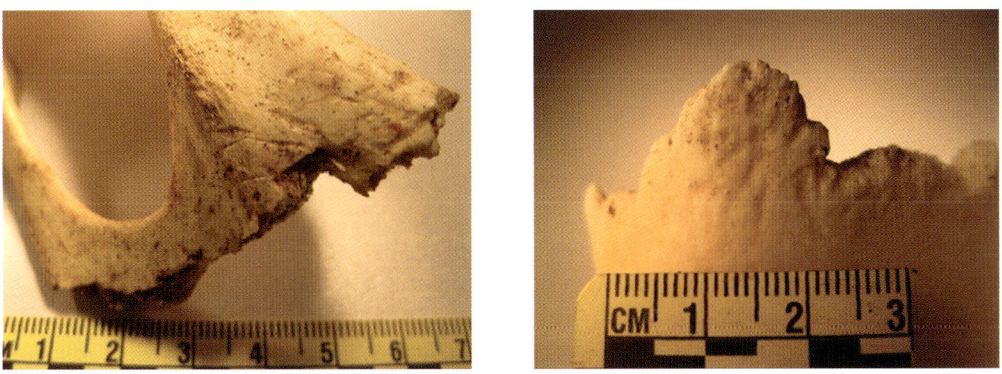

(a) (b)

Figure 17.1 Characteristic carnivore gnawing damage on human remains. (a) Left innominate of white-tailed deer (*Odocoileus virginianus*) gnawed on by a large carnivore. Note the ragged edge and multiple pits and striations. (b) Right proximal humerus shaft of cattle (*Bos taurus*) gnawed on by a large carnivore. Note the formation of edge polish on the exposed margin, the ragged edge, and the multiple shallow pits left in the cortical bone.

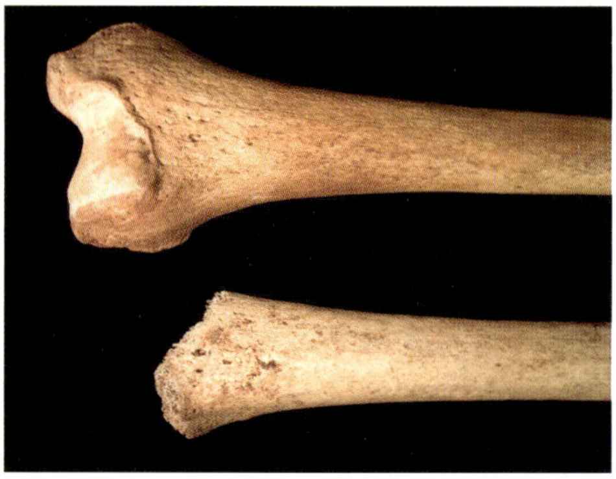

Figure 17.2 Carnivore damaged distal human femur (bottom) compared to undamaged femur (top). Note the complete absence of the distal epiphysis on the gnawed bone. (Courtesy of UT Forensic Anthropology Center, Knoxville, TN.)

access. In long bones, where one end tends to be more robust than the other (such as the distal humerus being much more robust than the proximal humerus in most mammals), scavengers often skip the more robust end entirely and focus their gnawing efforts on the easier portion (Pokines and Kerbis Peterhans 2007). Gnawing then proceeds by removal (and frequent consumption of) bone fragments, working inward toward the marrow cavity. This process often leaves a bone *cylinder* behind as the final result of carnivore gnawing of a long bone (Figure 17.2) (Kerbis Peterhans 1990). Gnawing of these more durable elements frequently takes place away from the kill site, where the carnivore can expend more time with less chance of food being stolen by a competitor.

The cranium often remains untouched by carnivores due to the difficulties of gnawing through such a large object, which is difficult to fit deep enough within a carnivore's jaws for consumption or to hold onto for transport away from the point of initial deposition for later gnawing. An exception to this pattern occurs when larger carnivores attack the crania of smaller species or the juveniles of larger species (Pokines and Kerbis Peterhans 2007). The brain tissue has a high fat content, so gnawing by carnivores is largely to access this food resource (Stiner 1994). Intact human crania can be transported several kilometers by scavengers for later consumption, even one as small as a striped hyena (*Hyaena hyaena*), a largely solitary species (Horwitz and Smith 1988).

Most gnawing is done by carnivores with their *carnassial* teeth, that is, those upper and lower teeth that have evolved to shear past each other (like scissors) for cutting meat and crushing bone. The specific teeth that evolved to fill this role are not the same from species to species. For example, in the genus *Canis* (which includes domestic dogs, wolves, and coyotes), the carnassial teeth are the maxillary fourth premolars and the mandibular first molars. Significant biting force can be applied at this point, because of the position of these teeth farther back in the mouth and the design of the mandibular lever system. The anterior teeth (i.e., the incisors and canines) have the least amount of biting force. The most common characteristics of carnivore damage to skeletal remains are multiple types of tooth marks; these have been defined in the taphonomic literature, primarily in the context of zooarchaeology (Binford 1981, Haglund 1997a, Haynes 1980, Lyman 1994, Pobiner 2008, Pokines and Kerbis Peterhans 2007). The various types of bite marks are (1) *pits*, which are small (usually oval or irregular) indentations in the bone that do not penetrate the cortical

Figure 17.3 Carnivore tooth punctures (likely raccoon—*Procyon lotor*) on a human ilium. (Courtesy of UT Forensic Anthropology Center, Knoxville, TN.)

layer and are typically found in areas with a thicker cortex; (2) *punctures*, which are similar in form to pits but are deeper indentations or perforations of the bone that do penetrate the cortical layer. Punctures can be caused by most teeth, and are typically found in thin cortical bone overlying cancellous bone (Figure 17.3); (3) *scores*, which are elongated marks that do not penetrate the cortical layer and are caused by carnivore teeth sliding across the outer surface of the bone; and (4) *furrows*, which are elongated like scores but do penetrate into the cancellous bone and are usually found in cancellous bone that has been previously exposed by gnawing.

In addition to these types of individual tooth marks, *edge polish* may be left behind on exposed cortical bone that has already been fractured, but worn down by repeated tooth wear from additional gnawing on the freshly exposed surface (see Figure 17.1) (Pokines and Kerbis Peterhans 2007). The more general term *gripping marks* refers to unpatterned pits and scores typically left on long bone shafts as a carnivore shifts the element within its mouth to reposition it for gnawing on the epiphyses or for transport. Continued gnawing of any bone tends to destroy earlier marks left behind in weaker areas of the bone. These areas are the most likely to exhibit more diagnostic tooth marks (punctures), yet they are also the areas most likely to be destroyed by subsequent gnawing. Similarly, it is rare to find furrows in long bones that have undergone significant gnawing, as continued gnawing will likely result in complete destruction of the cancellous portions of the epiphyses.

As mentioned earlier, tooth punctures offer the greatest potential to identify the taxon of predator that gnawed upon a bone, as these might conform to a tooth shape unique to that gnawing taxon (Murmann et al. 2006). These marks are most typically formed by the incisors, canines, or carnassial teeth. Canine teeth are not always useful in this regard, as they have a similar cone shape in most carnivores; as such a smaller canine puncture might be formed by a deeply penetrating smaller carnivore or by a shallowly penetrating larger carnivore.

While it is usually not difficult to determine if a skeleton has been altered by carnivores, it is often more difficult to identify the specific carnivore that caused the damage. Domínguez-Rodrigo and Piqueras (2003) attempted to develop techniques to determine carnivore taxa according to tooth mark location and size on the bones. They discovered that the tooth marks by themselves cannot be used to glean taxa information and can only distinguish between large carnivores (such as lions, bears, and large canids) and small carnivores (mustelids, small felids, and small canids). Other research into tooth impressions notes that while overall size classes of carnivore may be discernible, there is significant overlap between many common gnawing species (Delaney-Rivera et al. 2009, Murmann et al. 2006). Murmann et al. (2006) further note that the overall curvature of the anterior dental arcade, including the incisors and canines, varies by carnivore family, and the distance between pairs of upper or lower canine tooth impressions (in the rare cases where these are preserved in bone or other materials) may be useful in determining the size class (and hence taxonomic grouping) of the gnawing species.

Many obstacles make studies of this type difficult, including the difficulty in ascertaining that bones recovered from natural settings have been gnawed by only one species. For example, the difference between ursid (bear) and canid postmortem modification has been studied over the past decades. Haynes (1982) discusses the similarities of canids (specifically wolves) and ursids in their modification of 125+ carcasses and skeletons of bison (*Bison bison*), moose (*Alces alces*), and white-tailed deer (*Odocoileus virginianus*) in North America. He documented the dispersal of bones at kill sites and noted that characteristic gnawing damage occurs at kill sites, scavenge sites, and home sites. Haynes described the patterns of scatter and accumulation associated with both canids and ursids. Further, Haynes (1982) noted that if either canids or ursids encounter bones that have been exposed to the elements longer than 6 months, no gnawing generally took place on these "dry" bones. Carson et al. (2000) attempted to distinguish between canid and bear scavenging upon human remains based on the disarticulation pattern and specific elemental damage patterns. Bears removed the proximal and distal articular surfaces of limbs and also did significant damage to the iliac crest and ischial tuberosity. This pattern of damage, however, is also typical of large canid scavenging in multiple settings.

Haynes (1983) further explored the patterns of destructive damage to bones by large felids, bears, canids, and hyaenids. This research used captive animals in order to identify the sequence of damage, length of time it took for the damage to occur, types of damage created, and, finally, how long the bones were of interest to the scavengers. The study found that hyena and canid tooth marks were present on compact tissue. The research also suggested that bears grind with their molars, while the canids bit into or through the cortical bone. The characteristics of tooth impression shape were described as follows: bears had square-shaped tooth impressions (which is in keeping with their omnivorous dentition and its similarities to fellow omnivores, such as pigs and humans); hyenas and canids tended to leave cone-shaped impressions; and large cats left V shaped impressions on the bone. Again, subsequent gnawing of an already scavenged bone obscures existing marks that may have been more definitive as to a carnivore species, family, or size class. Forensic investigators may find it more rewarding to look for other field signs left behind by scavengers in order to identify them, including hair, footprints, and droppings (Einarsen 1956, Elbroch 2003).

Rodent Damage to Skeletal Remains

In contrast to the typical carnivore characteristics left on skeletal remains, rodent damage can be much more subtle. All rodent species (by definition) have paired maxillary

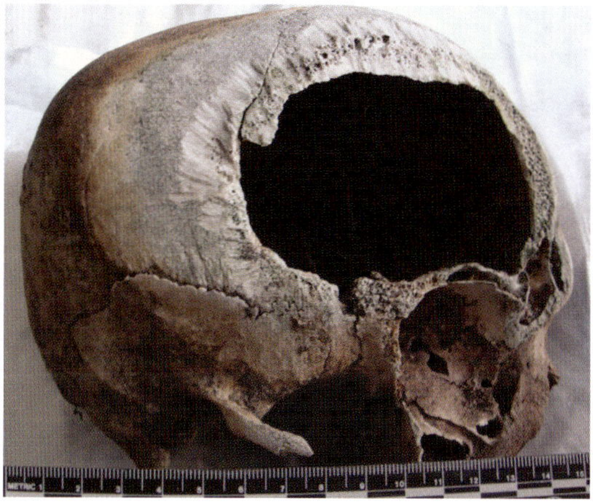

Figure 17.4 Characteristic rodent gnawing damage on a weathered cranium.

and mandibular incisors (for a total of four) that are continuously growing. These species need to gnaw on relatively hard items to keep these teeth at a usable length and to sharpen the cutting margins. Skeletal remains often are an ideal surface on which to wear down these teeth. The incisors, when scraped across a hard surface, produce parallel grooves that are unlike the characteristic pitting caused by carnivores (Figures 17.4 and 17.5). The parallel grooves may be found in a single layer or multiple overlying layers if further gnawing has obscured previous tooth striations. These grooves can be singular; that is, they have been produced by only one set of teeth being dragged across the bone surface, or they may converge to a point indicating that both the upper and lower incisors are used at the same time (Figure 17.6). Haglund (1997b) suggests that rodents prefer the epiphyseal cartilage and adjoining areas of long bones. Haglund (1997b) also notes that rodents tend to gnaw on the cranium where thin, exposed margins such as the eye orbits can fit within their jaw space.

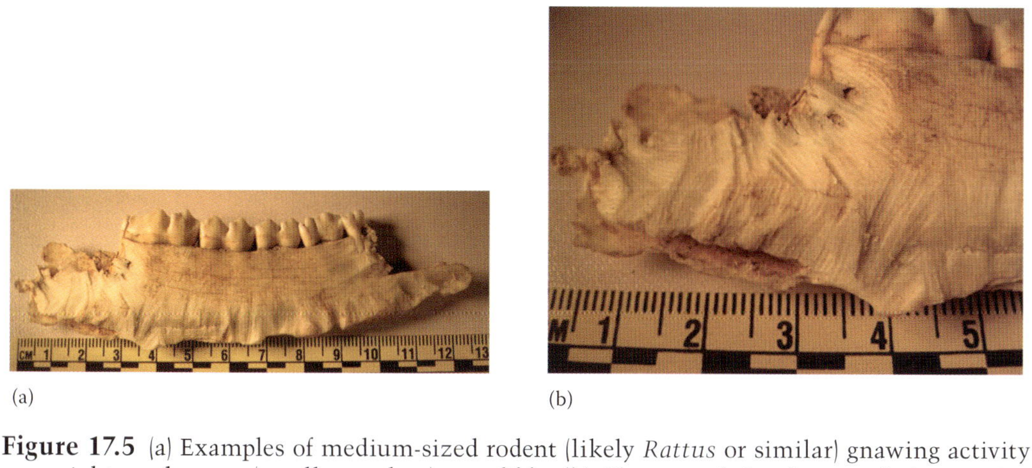

(a) (b)

Figure 17.5 (a) Examples of medium-sized rodent (likely *Rattus* or similar) gnawing activity on a right nonhuman (small ungulate) mandible. (b) Close-up of the characteristic gnawing pattern.

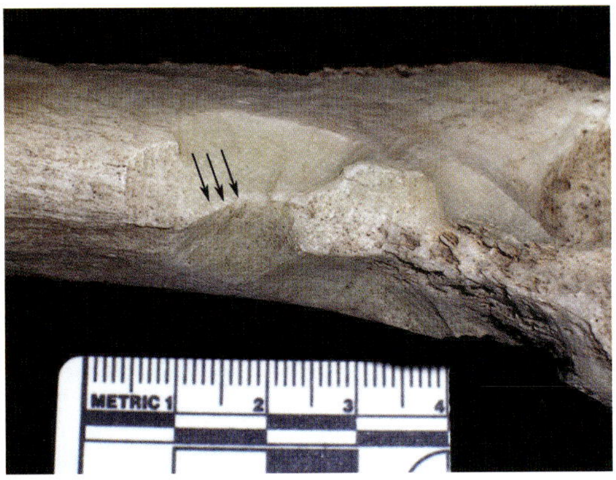

Figure 17.6 Rodent modification on distal humerus. Arrows showing convergence of rows to a point, indicating that both the upper and lower incisors were used at the same time. (Courtesy of UT Forensic Anthropology Center, Knoxville, TN.)

Several researchers determined that rodents also use skeletal remains to obtain nutrients from fat-filled trabecular bone or from the mineral component of the bone. An example of the former type of feeding is found among certain omnivorous rodents, including the widespread species black rat (*Rattus rattus*) and brown rat (*Rattus norvegicus*), which are attracted to skeletal remains during the early postmortem interval when fat remains in the trabeculae of the long bones. Brown rat consumption of the trabecular bone in the skeletal epiphyses produces a pedestal appearance, as these rodents gain access to these regions by targeting areas where the cortical bone is least dense such as along the epiphyseal lines. They proceed to hollow out the epiphyses, leaving behind the shaft and the articular portion of the epiphysis that is primarily cortical (Figure 17.7) (Klippel and Synstelien 2007). An example of the latter type of feeding (i.e., from the mineral content of bone) is found among some porcupine species that have been determined experimentally to consume dry bone material while gnawing (Duthie and Skinner 1986). This type of bone gnawing and consumption tends to occur later in the postmortem interval, where the rodents are attracted to bone only after the fat has leached from the bone. Multiple common rodent taxa have been noted to gnaw upon dry bone, including rats, house mice (*Mus musculus*), and squirrels (Sciuridae), although it is undetermined if the gnawing is confined to incisor-sharpening activity or if bone minerals are being consumed.

Larger rodents produce larger incisor marks. Throughout the United States and Canada, the North American porcupine (*Erethizon dorsatum*) is the most common large rodent known commonly to gnaw on bones (Roze 2009, Woods 1973). This species often consumes additional minerals to make up for deficiencies in its normal plant diet (Roze 2009). The individual marks that the porcupine leaves on bone are visibly larger and deeper than those left by rodents in the rat- to squirrel-size range (Figure 17.8).

Klippel and Synstelien (2007) attempted to clarify the characteristics of bone gnawing by rodents. They suggest that throughout the literature some researchers have described rodents as preferring dry bone, while others suggest that rodents seek fat-filled bone. Klippel and Synstelien found that brown rats preferred cancellous bone (normally full of fat), behavior

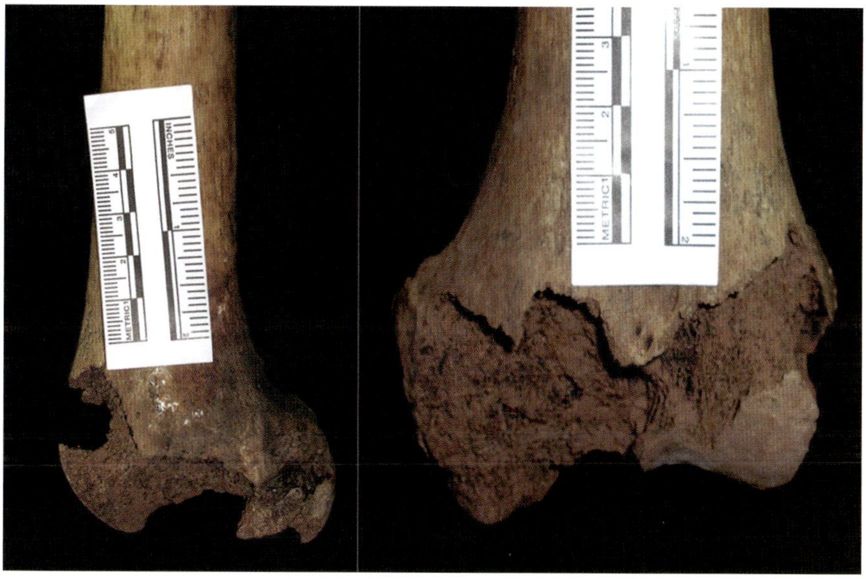

Figure 17.7 Rodent modification of distal femur to gain access to marrow in epiphysis (likely brown rat, *Rattus norvegicus*). Note the pedestal appearance created by the remaining cortical bone on the distal articular surface and the strut of bone connecting the shaft with the articular end. (Courtesy of UT Forensic Anthropology Center, Knoxville, TN.)

Figure 17.8 Extensive North American porcupine (*Erethizon dorsatum*) gnawing activity on a cattle (*Bos taurus*) femur that had been previously machine butchered (on the surface to the right).

associated with the acquisition of nutrients, whereas gray squirrels (*Sciurus carolinensis*) chose cortical bone where fat was no longer present, behavior associated with acquisition of the mineral component. They further suggest that given that gray squirrels do not show interest in gnawing bone prior to at least 30 months of exposure, the presence of gray squirrel gnaw marks on remains found in climates similar to that of East Tennessee could provide a minimum time since death estimate. Since rates of bone weathering (i.e., drying out) are variable based upon microenvironment, and the bone-gnawing behavior of so few rodent species (out of the over 2000 named species) has so far been studied, more research is needed in this area (Box 17.1).

BOX 17.1 CANID DIGESTION MODIFICATION OF SKELETAL REMAINS

Large-bodied carnivores consume large amounts of masticated bone fragments and small intact elements (including carpals, phalanges, etc.) during their normal feeding activities. Apart from the destructive effects of fragmentation, this ingested bone also undergoes significant modification from gastric acid and digestive enzymes as it passes through the alimentary canal and is deposited as feces or regurgitated. Carnivore taxa that have been researched in this regard include canids, felids, and hyaenids (Hill 1989, Payne and Munson 1989, Pokines and Kerbis Peterhans 2007, Shipman and Phillips-Conroy 1977, Stiner et al. 2012). This type of alteration is termed *gastric corrosion*. Gastric corrosion causes the formation of small holes in fragments/elements (referred to as *windowing*), the thinning of edges and a characteristic sculpted appearance to bone surfaces where the minerals have been dissolved (Brain 1981, Kerbis Peterhans 1990, Pokines and Kerbis Peterhans 2007). The size of the fragments is limited by the maximum size of bone that can be swallowed by the species of carnivore, so larger carnivore taxa tend to leave behind larger and potentially more identifiable digested bone fragments/elements. This differential modification is described by Payne and Munson (1989). They suggest that the corrosive digestive environment is very destructive to bone but qualify this by noting that acidity affects weaker parts of consumed bone (trabecular and thin cortical bone) more than the stronger parts (thick cortical bone). They also indicate that the effects of mastication and digestion tend to be more damaging to the skeletons of smaller vertebrates.

Andrews and Evans (1983) suggest that there are indeed differences between the modification caused by a canid gut and modification caused by the digestive enzymes of smaller animals (viverrids and mustelids). They suggest that canids are associated with more bone breakage than the other two groups. Their findings indicate that the digestive tracts of viverrids produce fragments that exhibit moderate rounding and little corrosion. The mustelids produce fragments that are moderately rounded with slight to moderate corrosion to bone and tooth dentine. The canids produce very rounded fragments that are severely corroded. This can occur to both bones and tooth enamel.

Even after exposure to the corrosive effects of the canid gut, cortical bone fragments can be identified as human or nonhuman, provided that the bone is not severely degraded as to damage the inner cortical structure (which is usually not the case). For example, in a case from Hamblen County, Tennessee, bone fragments retrieved from dog scat piles were sectioned and viewed under a microscope. Many of the fragments were trabecular bone, which could only be identified as large mammal in origin. Other fragments were cortical bone. Some of these fragments could indeed be ruled out as nonhuman due to their plexiform bone histological structure (Figure 17.9). Two fragments, each found in different scat piles, were examined and found to be consistent with human bone (Figure 17.10). Technically, these fragments could be aged using Samson and Branigan's (1987) method of age determination of fragmentary and weathered bone, although this would require that the fragment be identified as to its original element or at least whether the fragment came from the upper limb, lower limb, or axial skeleton. This method has a standard error of ±8 years for males and a standard error of ±16 years for females. If the sample is too degraded (i.e., cortical thickness reduced or Haversian structure eroded), all that can be determined is whether the individual is younger (has not undergone a great deal of remodeling) or older (extensive remodeling). Even this distinction can be problematic, since many metabolic and mechanical factors can affect secondary osteon population density (evidence of extensive remodeling). In the best case scenario, age can be determined on fragmentary remains that have passed through a canid gut, but many factors can affect that age estimate.

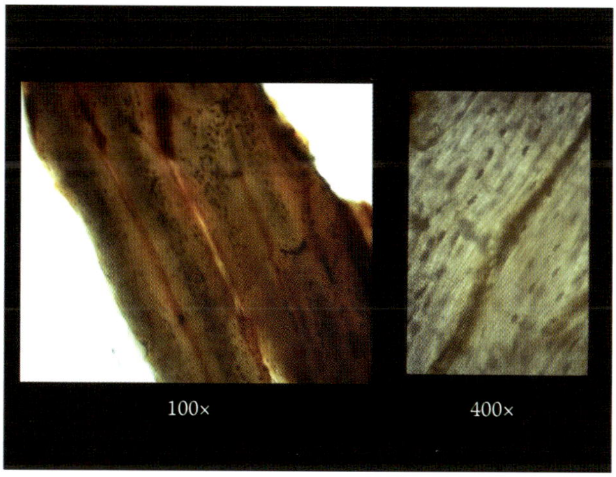

Figure 17.9 Microscopic analysis (100× and 400× magnification) of remains recovered from domestic dog (*Canis familiaris*) scat in Hamblen County, Tennessee: plexiform structure.

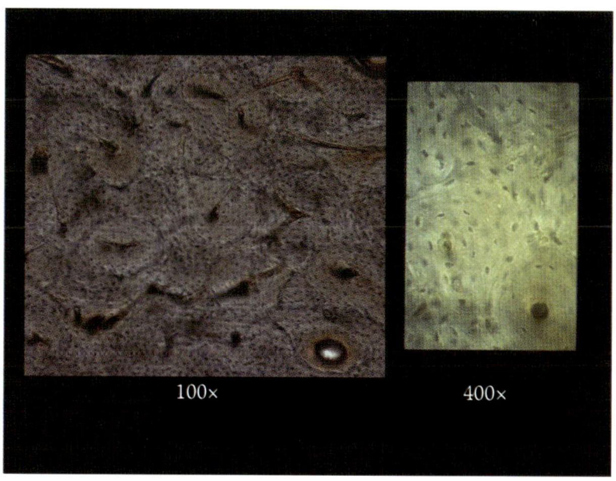

Figure 17.10 Microscopic analysis (100× and 400× magnification) of remains recovered from domestic dog (*Canis familiaris*) scat in Hamblen County, Tennessee: possible human osteonal structure.

References

Andrews P and Evans EN (1983) Small mammal bone accumulations produced by mammalian carnivores. *Paleobiology* 9:289–307.

Behrensmeyer AK (1991) Terrestrial vertebrate accumulations. In PA Allison and DEG Briggs (Eds.), *Taphonomy: Releasing the Data Locked in the Fossil Record.* Dordrecht, the Netherlands: Springer, pp. 291–335.

Binford LR (1981) *Bones: Ancient Men and Modern Myths.* New York: Academic Press.

Binford LR, Mills MGL, and Stone NM (1988) Hyena scavenging behavior and its implications for the interpretation of faunal assemblages from FLK 22 (the Zinj Floor) at Olduvai Gorge. *Journal of Anthropological Archaeology* 7:99–135.

Blumenschine RJ (1986) Carcass consumption sequences and the archaeological distinction of scavenging and hunting. *Journal of Human Evolution* 15:639–659.

Blumenschine RJ (1988) An experimental model of the timing of hominid and carnivore influence on archaeological bone assemblages. *Journal of Archaeological Science* 15:483–502.

Blumenschine RJ and Marean CW (1993) A carnivore's view of archaeological bone assemblage. In J Hudson (Ed.), *From Bones to Behavior.* Carbondale, IL: Center for Archaeological Investigations No. 21, pp. 273–299.

Brain CK (1981) *The Hunters or the Hunted? An Introduction to African Cave Taphonomy.* Chicago, IL: University of Chicago Press.

Carson EA, Stefan VH, and Powell JF (2000) Skeletal manifestations of bear scavenging. *Journal of Forensic Sciences* 45:515–526.

Delaney-Rivera C, Plummer TW, Hodgson JA, Forrest F, Hertel F, and Oliver JS (2009) Pits and pitfalls: Taxonomic variability and patterning in tooth mark dimensions. *Journal of Archaeological Science* 36:2597–2608.

Domínguez-Rodrigo M and Piqueras A (2003) The use of tooth pits to identify carnivore taxa in tooth-marked archaeofaunas and their relevance to reconstruct hominid carcass processing behaviors. *Journal of Archaeological Sciences* 30:1385–1391.

Duthie AG and Skinner JD (1986) Osteophagia in the Cape porcupine *Hystrix africaeaustralis. South African Journal of Zoology* 21:316–318.

Efremov IA (1940) Taphonomy, a new branch of paleontology. *Pan-American Geologist* 74:81–93.

Einarsen AS (1956) Determination of some predator species by field signs. *Oregon State Monographs Studies in Zoology* 10:1–34.

Elbroch M (2003) *Mammal Tracks & Sign: A Guide to North American Species.* Mechanicsburg, PA: Stackpole Books.

Haglund W (1997a) Dogs and coyotes: Postmortem involvement with human remains. In W Haglund and M Sorg (Eds.), *Forensic Taphonomy: The Postmortem Fate of Human Remains.* Boca Raton, FL: CRC Press, pp. 367–381.

Haglund W (1997b) Rodents and human remains. In W Haglund and M Sorg (Eds.), *Forensic Taphonomy: The Postmortem Fate of Human Remains.* Boca Raton, FL: CRC Press, pp. 405–414.

Haglund W, Reay DT, and Swindler DR (1988) Tooth mark artifacts and survival of bones in animal scavenged human skeletons. *Journal of Forensic Sciences* 33:985–997.

Haglund W, Reay DT, and Swindler DR (1989) Canid scavenging/disarticulation sequence of human remains in the Pacific Northwest. *Journal of Forensic Sciences* 34:587–606.

Haglund WD and Sorg MH (1997a) Introduction to forensic taphonomy research. In W Haglund and M Sorg (Eds.), *Forensic Taphonomy: The Postmortem Fate of Human Remains.* Boca Raton, FL: CRC Press, pp. 1–9.

Haglund WD and Sorg MH (1997b) Method and theory in forensic taphonomy research. In W Haglund and M Sorg (Eds.), *Forensic Taphonomy: The Postmortem Fate of Human Remains.* Boca Raton, FL: CRC Press, pp. 13–26.

Haynes G (1980) Evidence of carnivore gnawing on Pleistocene and recent mammal bones. *Paleobiology* 6:341–351.

Haynes G (1982) Utilization and skeletal disturbances of North American prey carcasses. *Arctic* 35:266–281.

Haynes G (1983) A guide for differentiating mammalian carnivore taxa responsible for gnaw damage to herbivore limb bones. *Paleobiology* 9:164–172.

Hill AP (1989) Bone modification by modern spotted hyenas. In R Bonnichsen and M Sorg (Eds.), *Bone Modification*. Orono, ME: Center for the Study of First Americans, pp. 169–178.

Hill AP and Behrensmeyer AK (1984) Disarticulation patterns of some modern East African mammals. *Paleobiology* 10:366–376.

Horwitz L and Smith P (1988) The effects of striped hyaena activity on human remains. *Journal of Archaeological Science* 15:471–481.

Kerbis Peterhans JC (1990) *The Roles of Porcupines, Leopards, and Hyenas in Ungulate Carcass Dispersal: Implications for Paleoanthropology*. PhD dissertation, Department of Anthropology, University of Chicago, Chicago, IL.

Klippel WE and Synstelien JA (2007) Rodents as taphonomic agents: Bone gnawing by brown rats and gray squirrels. *Journal of Forensic Sciences* 52:765–773.

Lyman RL (1994) *Vertebrate Taphonomy*. Cambridge, U.K.: Cambridge University Press.

Murmann DC, Brumit PC, Schrader NA, and Senn DR (2006) A comparison of animal jaws and bite mark patterns. *Journal of Forensic Sciences* 51:846–860.

Payne S (1983) Bones from cave sites: Who ate what? In J Clutton-Brock and C Grigson (Eds.)., *Animals and Archaeology: 1. Hunters and Their Prey*. Oxford, U.K.: BAR International Series 163, pp. 149–162.

Payne S and Munson P (1989) Ruby and how many squirrels? The destruction of bones by dogs. In NRJ Feller, DD Gilbertson and NGA Ralph (Eds.), *Paleobiological Investigations: Research Design, Methods, and Data Analysis*. BAR International Series 266, pp. 31–40.

Pobiner BL (2008) Paleoecological information from predator tooth marks. *Journal of Taphonomy* 6:373–397.

Pokines JT (2009) Forensic recoveries of U.S. war dead and the effects of taphonomy and other site-altering processes. In DW Steadman (Ed.), *Hard Evidence: Case Studies in Forensic Anthropology*, 2nd Edn. Upper Saddle River, NJ: Prentice Hall, pp. 141–154.

Pokines JT and Kerbis Peterhans JC (2007) Spotted hyena (*Crocuta crocuta*) den use and taphonomy in the Masai Mara National Reserve, Kenya. *Journal of Archaeological Science* 34:1914–1931.

Roze U (2009) *The North American Porcupine*, 2nd Edn. Ithaca, NY: Cornell University Press.

Samson C and Branigan K (1987) A new method of estimating age at death from fragmentary and weathered bone. In A Boddington, AN Garland, and RC Janaway (Eds.), *Death, Decay and Reconstruction: Approaches to Archaeology and Forensic Science*. Manchester, U.K.: Manchester University Press, pp. 109–126.

Shipman P and Phillips-Conroy JE (1977) Hominid tool-making versus carnivore scavenging. *American Journal of Physical Anthropology* 46:77–86.

Stiner MC (1994) *Honor Among Thieves*. Princeton, NJ: Princeton University Press.

Stiner MC, Munro ND, and Sanz M (2012) Carcass damage and digested bone from mountain lions (*Felis concolor*): Implications for carcass persistence on landscapes as a function of prey age. *Journal of Archaeological Science* 39:896–907.

Ubelaker D (1997) Taphonomic applications in forensic anthropology. In W Haglund and M Sorg (Eds.), *Forensic Taphonomy: The Postmortem Fate of Human Remains*. Boca Raton, FL: CRC Press, pp. 77–90

Weigelt J (1989) *Recent Vertebrate Carcasses and Their Paleobiological Implications*, Translation of 1927 Edn. Chicago, IL: University of Chicago Press.

Woods CA (1973) *Erethizon dorsatum*. *Mammalian Species* 29:1–6.

Further Reading

Buikstra JE and Ubelaker DH (1994) *Standards for Data Collection from Human Skeletal Remains*. Fayetteville, AR: Arkansas Archeological Survey Research Report No. 44.

Hart DL and Sussman RW (2005) *Man the Hunted: Primates, Predators, and Human Evolution*. Cambridge, MA: Westview.

Miller GJ (1969) A study of cuts, grooves, and other marks on recent and fossil bones. 1. Animal tooth marks. *Tebiwa* 12:9–19.

Morlan RE (1984) Toward the definition of criteria for the recognition of artificial bone alterations. *Quaternary Research* 22:160–171.

Time since Death Estimation and Bone Weathering

The Postmortem Interval

18

REBECCA J. WILSON-TAYLOR

Contents

Taphonomic research on human decomposition focuses on the stages through which a body progresses from "fresh" to the time a skeleton breaks down and involves a series of physiochemical changes that lead to the dissolution of soft tissue. As such, it involves evaluating all aspects of this process from the breakdown of the soft tissues, to arthropod infestation activities and animal scavenging, as well as subsequent effects on the contextual environment. The sequential nature of human decomposition makes it extremely important to the medicolegal investigation because the series can provide answers to essential questions.

When human remains are discovered, one of the first questions asked is how long the individual has been dead. In human decomposition the primary focus has been on determining time since death (TSD), or the postmortem interval (PMI). The PMI can provide investigators answers to some key questions: When did the individual die? Where did the individual die? What happened? Who is the individual? Many methods are available for determining PMI for early decomposition, or in the time period shortly after death. However, the longer the PMI, the harder it becomes to accurately and precisely estimate a PMI. Several precipitating factors arise as the PMI increases, such as animal scavenging, deposition environment, and the presence of coverings. The early stages of decomposition usually fall within the purview of forensic pathologists because the body tissues are still present and intact, but as the body deteriorates, a forensic anthropologist is typically employed in the determination of the PMI.

Decomposition

When the heart stops beating, cellular processes in the body do not cease immediately; these processes will continue until the oxygen supply is depleted. Once oxygen is depleted, carbon dioxide levels increase and poison the cells, thereby causing cell death as pH (parts of Hydrogen) levels within the cells decrease and the acidity within the body increases. The increase in acidity spurs enzymes in the cell organelles, particularly lysosomes, to digest the proteins that maintain the integrity of cellular structures. The resulting cellular breakdown causes a series of events, leading to the eventual disintegration of the soft tissues. Certain organs (e.g., the bowel) will breakdown faster than others because of their natural bacterial content, while others (e.g., skin) tend to mummify.

Two major processes dictate the timing and extent of human decomposition: autolysis and putrefaction. The combination of these two processes causes cells to die and tissues to break apart and leach enzymes, bacteria, and other microorganisms to feed on the now unprotected body compartments. Autolysis or "self digestion" involves a series of chemical reactions that break down cellular membranes and the junctions between cell membranes (Evans 1962, Gill-King 1997). The cell membrane is responsible for compartmentalizing the human body, so once these divisions are compromised chemicals, enzymes, and proteins within each cell are released into the body cavities. The chemicals released as a result of the disintegration of the cell membrane cause tissue breakdown from within the cells, typically beginning in enzyme-rich organs such as the pancreas, stomach area, and the liver (Gill-King 1997). An easily visible example of this process is "skin slippage." Skin slippage occurs when the epidermal and dermal layers of the skin start to separate causing the more superficial epidermal layer to become disconnected from the deeper dermal layer and slough off of the body. Skin slippage is first noticeable as blisters, or bullae (Figure 18.1) form in the skin and ultimately results in the "gloving" or "stocking" like removal of the epidermis (Clark et al. 1997; Figure 18.2). The same holds true for hair, because hair follicles, which are located in the dermis, are pulled out as the epidermis separates. The separation of the hair due to skin slippage produces a mass of hair or "hair mat" around the head, which highlights the early decomposition location of the head. This can be of great importance in contexts involving the movement of the body, because the hair mat indicates the primary decomposition area and is a great source to find missing teeth or other artifacts associated with the cranial region.

Putrefaction quickly follows autolysis in the decomposition of the human body and is highly correlated with ambient temperature and the health status of the individual.

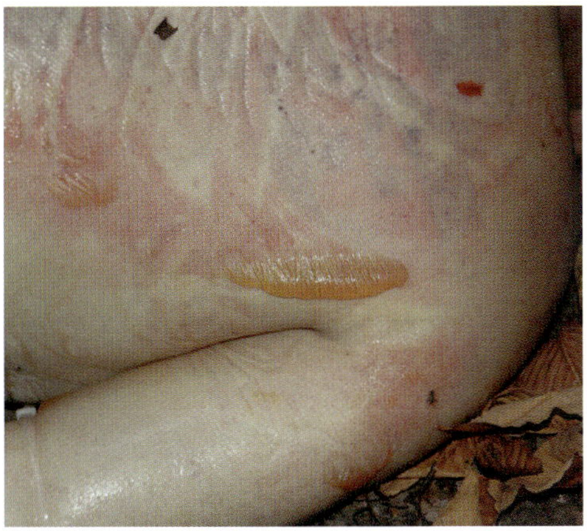

Figure 18.1 Bullae, separation of the dermal and epidermal layers of the skin, on the right posterior shoulder.

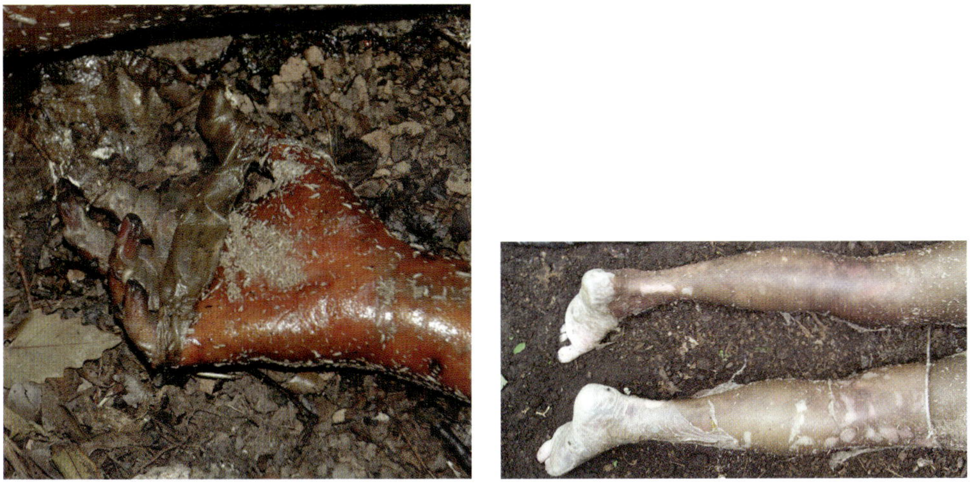

(a) (b)

Figure 18.2 (a) Gloving effect, skin slippage of the hand. (b) Stocking effect, skin slippage of the leg and foot.

The anaerobic environment produced through autolysis initiates putrefaction. This process is responsible for the typical sights and smells associated with human decomposition. Putrefaction is the breakdown of tissues as the result of microorganisms. Enteric and transient microorganisms, specifically bacteria, are released from cells within the body or enter through portals of entry, such as the respiratory and genital tracts, and feed on the nutrients that have been released through autolysis. For example, once cells in the digestive tract break down the bacteria that assist in extracting nutrients from food in living individuals, they start to feed on body tissues upon death. Since bacteria do not need oxygen to survive, it can thrive in the anaerobic environment of a deceased body. Putrefaction is initially expressed as discoloration in the lower right quadrant of the abdomen, where the greatest amounts of enteric bacteria reside within the body. As the bacteria feed, they produce gaseous byproducts, including carbon dioxide, nitrogen, and methane, that give off

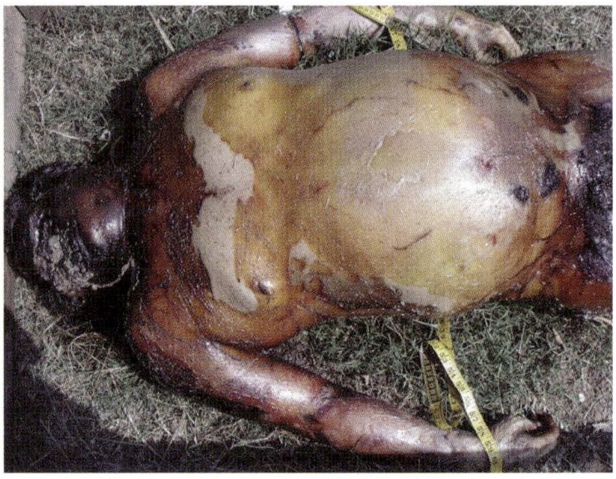

Figure 18.3 Bloating, gaseous by-products of microorganisms cause swelling of associated tissue.

distinct odors (Clark et al. 1997) and cause distention of the soft tissues in the immediate locale of bacteria, otherwise known as "bloating" (Clark et al. 1997). "Bloating" can occur in all locations of the body, including the extremities, but is more prominent in the abdomen and face (Figure 18.3). The abdomen has the highest accumulation of gases because of the uncontrolled enteric bacterial growth and the fact that it contains the most blood. Typically, areas with more blood will be more distended because of these gasses (Clark et al. 1997). For example, an autopsied body placed at the Anthropological Research Facility at the University of Tennessee, Knoxville, will display a higher degree of bloating in the extremities because of the lack of blood in the torso region. The odorous by products can be linked to the state of putrefaction and also aid in the estimation of the PMI (Vass et al. 2008). Furthermore, the height of arthropod activity, specifically larval activity, is associated with putrefaction (Haskell et al. 1997, Hart and Whitaker 2006), and this process is also the most attractive for animal scavengers, which can cause extreme fragmentation and/or scattering of the remains (Haglund 1997 a,b, Klippel et al. 2005, Reeves 2009, Synstelien 2009).

The order in which tissues decompose differs between autolysis and putrefaction. In autolysis, organs that have the highest rate of ATP (adenosine triphosphate) production break down first. These organs include those of the digestive and circulatory systems, and their breakdown produces much of the characteristic color changes in the human body. The respiratory organs are next, followed by the kidneys and bladder of the urinary system. The brain, the skeletal muscles, and connective tissue are the last to decompose. See Tables 18.1 and 18.2 for the order of tissue decomposition due to autolysis and putrefaction, respectively.

After the anaerobic fermentation of putrefaction, remnants of decomposition in the form of adipocere are commonly found. Adipocere, or "grave wax," is the grayish-white substance that develops from hydrolysis or hydrogenation of lipids or through what is known as "saponification" (Mant and Furbank 1957; Figure 18.4). Two major forms of adipocere are known to exist: a hard, crumbly variety that is produced quickly through sodium's reaction with interstitial fluid and a soft paste-like variety that is slowly produced through potassium's interaction with the cell membranes of adipose tissue cells (i.e., adipocytes; Vass et al. 2002). Because adipocere is developed from the body's own substances, human adipocere has a unique volatile fatty acid (VFA) composition compared to other

Table 18.1 Order of Tissue Decomposition from Autolysis

Order	Tissue
1	Digestive organs, blood, circulatory system
2	Air passages and lungs
3	Kidneys and bladder
4	Brain and nervous tissue
5	Skeletal muscle
6	Connective tissue

Table 18.2 Order of Tissue Decomposition from Putrefaction

Order	Tissue
1	Air passages and lungs
2	Digestive organs, heart, blood
3	Brain and nervous tissue
4	Kidneys and bladder
5	Skeletal muscle
6	Connective tissue

(a)

(b)

Figure 18.4 Adipocere, a decomposition by-product often seen in association with advanced decomposition, mummified, or mostly skeletal remains.

animals (Vass et al. 2002). Adipocere formation is prevalent in warm, moist, and alkaline conditions, be it natural or man-made (Forbes et al. 2005a). For example, to conditions that promote saponification are high humidity (natural) and a burial environment (typically man-made; Mant and Furbank 1957, Mann et al. 1990, Forbes et al. 2005b,c). Also, adipocere formation can occur rapidly in submerged bodies, especially if the water is warm (O'Brien 1997). Obese individuals, females, and infants are more likely to experience saponification because of the increased levels of adipose tissue in their bodies (Evans 1962, Gill-King 1997).

When the environmental conditions are suitable, mummification can also occur. Mummification results from the drying out of the body tissues. Most mummification in a decomposing corpse is partial mummification of the connective tissues, such as ligaments and tendons, and of the overlying skin. Conditions where there is high heat, low humidity, and good air flow around the body are ideal for mummification. For example, a hanging context encourages mummification because there is airflow 360° around the body. Typically, mummification begins with the drying of the face, hands, and feet, but can include the whole body. A brown to golden-brown discoloration and shriveling or wrinkling of the skin are associated with the drying process. Mummification is more common during the cooler months, even in the Southeastern United States, as well as in more arid climatic zones of the American Southwest. In the dry southwestern regions of the United States, the internal organs undergo rapid putrefaction, but the more superficial connective tissue mummifies. It is not uncommon to retrieve small pieces of mummified tissue with a skeleton in most temperate climates.

Variables Affecting Decomposition

Taphonomic processes that can affect the decomposition rate of a cadaver can be classified into environmental/meteorological, individual, and cultural/case-specific factors. See Table 18.3. Environmental factors can be further divided into those caused by living organisms (biotic) and those not (abiotic). Root etchings on bone, maggot holes in skin, and carnivore gnawing are all biotic alterations to remains. Abiotic environmental factors are created by the nonliving forces in the environment such as the effects of temperature,

Table 18.3 Factors Affecting Decomposition Rates (from Greatest Effect to Lowest)

Factor	Types of Factor
Temperature	Environmental factors
Access by insects	Depositional factors
Burial depth	Depositional factors
Scavenging	Depositional factors
Trauma	Culturally mediated case-specific factors
Humidity level	Environmental factors
Body Size	Culturally mediated case-specific factors
Embalming—chemical treatment of remains	Culturally mediated case-specific factors
Clothing	Culturally mediated case-specific factors
Deposition substrate	Environmental factors

water, and soil composition. Individual taphonomic factors are the effects that the remains bring to the decomposition process, such as health and body size. Cultural factors are those that another person induces to a cadaver, such as embalming, burial, coverings, and trauma (Rodriguez and Bass 1985, Calce and Rogers 2007, Dautartas 2009). These factors all play a role in developing the context in which a cadaver is found and the rate at which the body will decompose in this context. There is much debate about the role many of these factors play in the decomposition process, because even though a plethora of factors affect decomposition, the significance of each varies depending on the case under investigation (Adlam and Simmons 2007, Simmons et al. 2010). For example, a decedent's metabolic state can affect the starting temperature for the decomposition process (Spitz 2006). However, regardless of the debate, several key parameters will affect the rate of decomposition: temperature, humidity, animal scavenging, and trauma (Mann et al. 1990).

The single most important criterion for decomposition, regardless of the scenario, is temperature (Mann et al. 1990, Megyesi et al. 2005, Simmons et al. 2010). The ambient temperature around a corpse depends on the altitude, the burial depth, the presence of water, air movement around the body, and surrounding foliage, to name a few variables. In general, temperature dictates the speed at which chemical reactions occur. Van't Hoff's rule, "the rule of ten," states that the rate of chemical reactions increases two or more times with each 10°C increase in temperature (Gill-King 1997). When applied to decomposition rates, this suggests that the enzymes involved in decomposition work more quickly to break down tissues at higher temperatures as opposed to lower temperatures. The amount of arthropod activity associated with a decomposing corpse is directly proportional to the temperature: the warmer the climate, the greater the insect activity (Haskell et al. 1997). The opposite can be said for cooler climates. Because flies tend to be inactive below 50°F, oviposition, or egg laying, is decreased in these conditions and bacterial activity ceases at 4°C (Micozzi 1991). Figure 18.5 shows winter versus summer with 14 days exposure.

Other environmental factors that affect the decomposition process include humidity, amount of rainfall, and available water, all of which affect the decomposition rate of soft tissue as well as the subsequent diagenesis of the skeleton and adipocere formation. (Ubelaker 1997, Behrensmeyer 1978). Humidity is a significant factor in that it produces a moist environment that is ideal for soft tissue decomposition and prolongs favorable conditions for insects because it slows the drying of skin and connective tissues. This is the main reason why corpses decomposing in arid climates undergo mummification and have

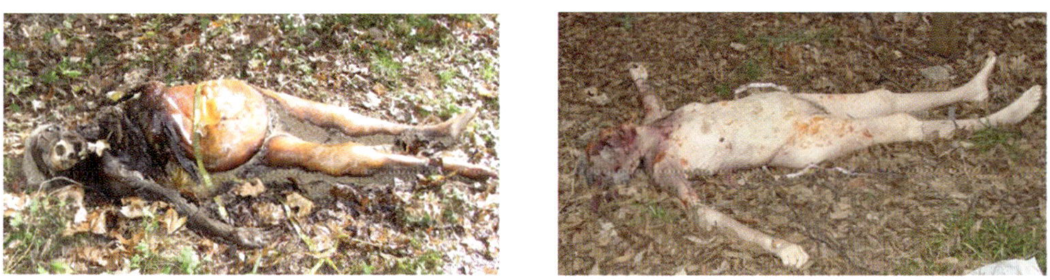

(a) (b)

Figure 18.5 (a) Temperature is one of the most important variables affecting the rate of decomposition. A cadaver with fourteen days exposure in the summer/warm months. (b) A cadaver with fourteen days exposure in the winter/colder months.

less associated arthropod activity (Galloway et al. 1989). Rainfall can also contribute significantly to biomass reduction. An increase in larval activity is common in light rain or just after a rainfall because rain rehydrates dried tissues. At the University of Tennessee outdoor research facility in Knoxville, Tennessee, rapid decomposition changes have been observed due to a rain after a prolonged dry period. However, little fly activity is noted in periods of heavy rain, such that these conditions can result in a reduction of larval activity as the flies do not have the ability to lay eggs.

The amount of water near and around the body plays an important role in decomposition, as well. Water contributes to relative humidity, corpses contain a certain amount of water, and water can act as a locale for the deposition of a body. Water is an excellent solvent and heat regulator. Water plays a role in diluting concentrations of chemicals, which moderates the pH in soil environments and on body surfaces (Gill-King 1997). Also, water has a high specific heat which helps stabilize temperatures. For example, if a warm body is submerged in water, decomposition will be slower than if the same body were placed on the ground surface because the surrounding water will absorb the heat. Seet (2005) evaluated submerged bodies through a review of 69 cases from Eastern Tennessee highlighting that the water temperature, depth of water, water chemistry, salinity, and available aquatic life all play significant roles in the decomposition of a body. Micozzi (1991) found that the partial or total submergence of a body can slow or speed decomposition depending on the chemical composition (pH) of the water, whether the water was salty or fresh, and whether a current was present. Also, the presence of water may increase saponification.

Depositional factors include the pH of the surrounding soil, which is of great importance to a burial environment. However, the acidity of the surrounding soil also dictates the maintenance of plant life and microbial activity in the soil. The body monitors and controls internal pH levels with buffering systems. A significant change in pH outside the "normal" range affects the ability of enzymes to act as buffers and results in a decrease in effectiveness of chemical reactions. However, the release of organic acids during the initial stages of decomposition cause a rapid drop in pH, which in turn creates a suitable environment for bacterial fermentation. Soil pH can greatly affect the rate of decomposition and the decomposer communities found in soils (Neher et al. 2003, Tibbett et al. 2004). Typically, acidic soils (pH 3.0–5.5) are dominated by fungal communities, whereas neutral soils (pH 5.5–7.5) provide conditions in which bacteria have a competitive advantage. In the case of alkaline soils (pH 7.5–9.0), fungi may dominate again, especially in the conditions created by the putrefaction process (Carter and Tibbett 2003, 2006, Carter et al. 2007, Sagara et al. 2008). The decomposition process proceeds up to three times faster in acidic soil compared to alkaline soil if the rate of soft tissue loss is correlated with the measured microbial respiration in the soil (Haslam and Tibbett 2009). The surrounding environment (soil) is typically more alkaline than a body, so fluids leaching from the body tend to shift the soil pH, which then causes plant death and a shift in soil microbes' effectiveness. This leaching of fluids from the body produces the decomposition stain, which is an indicator of the primary deposition and decomposition location. In cases of long-term exposure or burial, the soil pH also plays a role in the demineralization of bone. Acidic soils attack the inorganic mineral components of bone that help maintain bone integrity; thus, an acidic environment deteriorates bone quality.

Depositional factors also include the presence of structures limiting exposure to the meteorological elements or physical barriers that protect the body, such as clothing

(Shean et al. 1993, Ubelaker 1997, Srnka 2003, Ritchie 2005). Placement of the corpse can affect exposure to environmental factors, access to the oxygen needed to drive chemical reactions, and accessibility to scavengers (Mann et al. 1990, Shattuck 2009). The local differences between sunlight and shade can shift temperature and suitability for arthropods (Srnka 2003). Hence, proximity to the sun or other heating elements can affect bodies in the same environment significantly. A corpse located within a climate-controlled structure, like a house, will exhibit a more gradual systematic progression of decomposition stages because of stable temperatures and environmental conditions (Ritchie 2005). Burial depth can also play a major role in limiting arthropod activity and lowering temperatures (Rodriquez and Bass 1985) or the oxygen needed to drive the chemical reactions that break down tissues (Mann et al. 1990). When the burial depth is more than 2 ft, temperature, arthropod activity, and oxygen levels decrease, and decomposition rates are slower (Rodriquez and Bass 1985). The slower rate of decomposition is a direct result of anaerobic degradation, which is slower than degradation in an aerobic environment. Also, when a physical barrier prevents scavenger access to a corpse, biomass reduction from animal feeding is inhibited, and any decrease in biomass is directly related to the actual breakdown of tissues. A rule of thumb in the pathological literature is that 1 week on the surface equals 2 weeks in water, and 8 weeks in a burial environment (Spitz 2006).

Case-specific variables include the presence of trauma or bonding agents (rope or tape) (Haskell et al. 1997). Haskell et al. (1997) indicate that any artificial opening (surgery, trauma, or autopsy) in the body enhances insect activity in the region affected and speeds up the reduction of biomass in that area. This can cause differential decomposition in which one area of the body shows an unusual rate of decomposition. For example, raccoons have been observed creating artificial openings in the extremities of bodies and then feed on the larvae that enter this area, which in turn causes these areas to become skeletal more quickly than would be expected for the actual PMI (Synstelien 2009). Some suggest the size of an individual can affect the decomposition process, because more material available for larval feeding increases their presence at the corpse, while others maintain that body size is not a major contributing factor to the decomposition process (Vass et al. 2008, Parmenter and MacMahon 2009, Simmons et al. 2010). However, based on personal observations at the University of Tennessee research facility in Knoxville, TN, body size of human being does not cause significant differences in the rate a corpse decomposes, but it plays a larger role in the actual amount of biomass reduced and in the amount of adipocere produced, as larger individuals tend to have more adipose tissue. In warm, humid conditions, adipose tissue is converted to adipocere through the process of saponification, so higher amounts of adipose tissue result in more adipocere formation. Also, the bruising and rupturing of tissues (Mann et al. 1990, Calce and Roger 2007) caused by trauma provides additional openings for arthropod colonization (Haskell et al. 1997); thus accelerating decomposition.

Postmortem Changes in the Body

The macroscopic postmortem changes (i.e., those visible to the investigator) follow a fairly regular pattern regardless of the contextual environment. However, the *rate* at which these changes occur varies with the context. Postmortem changes to the body are often grouped according to when they appear, which allows researchers to organize events into specific

Table 18.4 Stages of Decomposition Following Reed (1958) and Marks et al. (2009) and Intervals Following Clark et al. (1997)

Decomposition Stage	Characteristics	Time Interval
Fresh	Algor mortis, livor mortis, rigor mortis	1 day to approx. 1 week
Discoloration	Marbling, abdomen slight green, skin slippage	Day 1 to weeks
Bloat (active decomposition)	Distention of tissues, overall color changes, leaching of VFAs	Starts within 48 h
Advanced decomposition (initial skeletonization)	Purging of body fluids, exposure of skeletal elements	Starts at least 1 week after death
Skeletonization	Exposure and drying of the entire skeleton	Several weeks to months after death

decomposition stages. Anthropologists have generally agreed on 4–5 surface decomposition stages, with a few researchers having more elaborate schemes (Payne 1965, Galloway et al. 1989, Bass 1997, Marks et al. 2000, 2009, Clark et al. 1997). These stages all focus on decomposition being a fairly linear progression of events driven by autolysis and putrefaction.

A five stage sequence using gross anatomical changes is the most comprehensive but parsimonious (following Marks et al. 2009 and Reed 1958 and outlined in Table 18.4). Other systems have been developed based on the biochemical and entomological changes associated with a human body (Payne 1965, Vass et al. 1992, Tibbett and Carter 2008). Additionally, stage sequences have been developed for buried human remains (Payne et al. 1968, Tibbett and Carter 2008). Nevertheless, surface decomposition stages include the fresh stage, the discoloration stage, the bloat or active decomposition stage, advanced decomposition or initial skeletonization, and skeletonization. All bodies generally move through these five stages, but the rate at which they move from one stage to the next may vary. The temperature of a specific environment largely determines the duration of a particular stage. To determine the PMI, forensic anthropologists categorize the amount of decomposition observed on a cadaver into one or more of the decomposition stages.

The fresh stage is typically associated with algor mortis, livor mortis, and rigor mortis. It is during the fresh stage that techniques established by pathologists are the most reliable for determining the PMI (i.e., body temperature). Initial oviposition by flies in the Calliphoridae family also occurs during the fresh stage (Bass 1997). There are minimal biochemical changes to the environment surrounding the corpse, and a full standard autopsy and identification via photos is still feasible during this stage (Figure 18.6).

The discoloration stage is a highly variable stage. In warmer climates and conditions it can be quite rapid in appearance and progression, while in cooler conditions it is prolonged and associated with microbial growth (mold and/or fungi) on the skin of a corpse (Bass 1997, Tibbet and Carter 2008). Discoloration is predominantly a side effect of the decomposition of the blood and associated tissues, which allows hemoglobin to interact with sulfide. This interaction causes the formation of sulfhemoglobin in the cutaneous vessels, producing a greenish color in the outer layers of skin, especially in the abdominal region (Gill-King 1997). In dry conditions, cold or warm, the face, hands, and feet exhibit a yellow-maize color. Also there is a receding of the lips and eyelids, which turn a golden

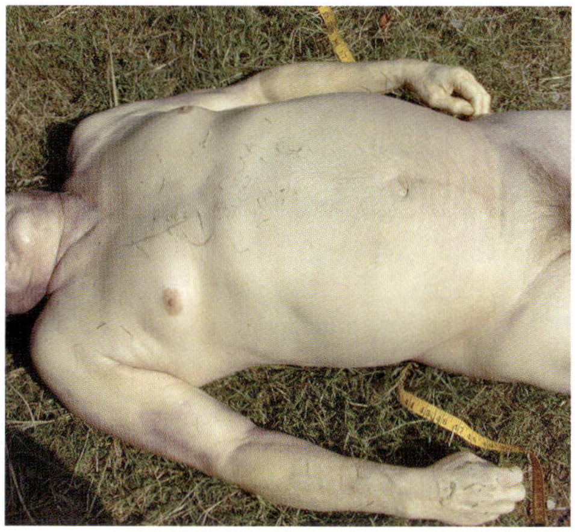

Figure 18.6 Fresh decomposition stage characterized by general loss of color of the entire body.

brown color. It is common to see the yellow-maize discoloration in conjunction with some drying out of the skin in situations where an individual is found within a couple of days of death in a home in which the heat is turned up and the temperature is quite warm. A more expected phenomenon during the discoloration phase is "marbling," although this can begin as early as the fresh stage. "Marbling" is a product of the breakdown of tissue and the contamination of blood within the circulatory system (Figure 18.7). Marbling is the "state of being veined like a marble" (Agnew et al. 1965: 874). Marbling will be more apparent in individuals with less subcutaneous fat content because the circulatory vessels are more visible. The various colors observed in marbling correspond to different chemical reactions occurring between hemoglobin and the now free chemicals. For example, most people understand that deoxygenated hemoglobin produces a purplish color that looks blue when viewed through the skin. When hemoglobin interacts with sulfur a green color is produced. Most marbling is a direct result of the degradation of hemoglobin and the conversion of heme to a series of bile pigments, which account for the various colors seen in a decomposing body. The actual color expressed depends on the oxidative state of the bile (Gill-King 1997). Biliverdin will appear as a green precipitate in the skin, bilirubin will be red, and urobilin will appear brown and is associated with an increased acidic environment, so it is commonly produced later in decomposition (Gill-King 1997).

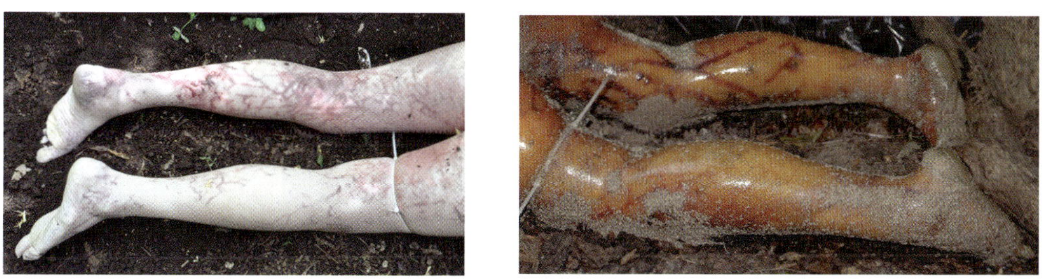

(a) (b)

Figure 18.7 (a) Early appearance of marbling, streaking effect caused by breakdown of the circulatory system. (b) Marbling can occur and be visible throughout active decomposition.

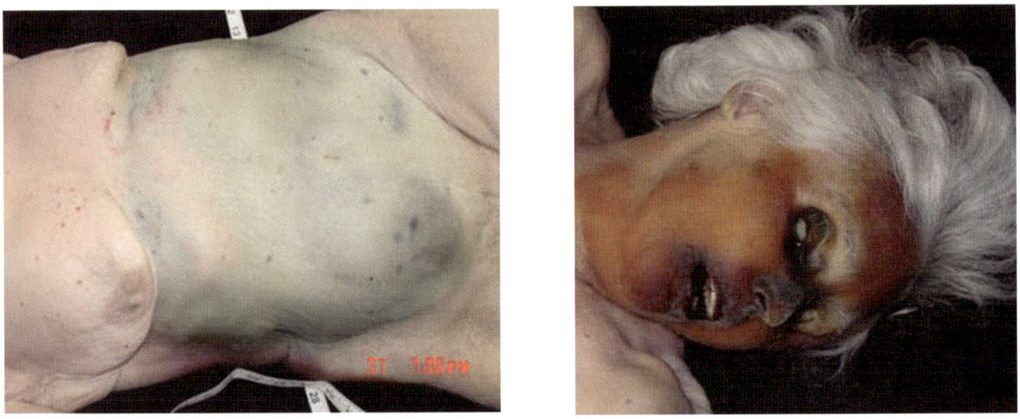

(a) (b)

Figure 18.8 (a) Initial discoloration of the body occurs in abdomen and is usually a green-blue color. (b) Discoloration can also be seen in the hands and face in which there is an orange to golden brown appearance due the drying of tissue.

The onset of marbling is determined by the temperature and the body composition. The appearance of marbling is brief at warmer temperatures, in which it is more common to get overall body color changes (Figure 18.8a and b). Colder temperatures, on the other hand, prolong the appearance of marbling and highlight its appearance. A body that has been frozen and is thawing will also demonstrate extensive brilliant marbling across the skin. During the discoloration stage, VFAs, or decomposition fluid, begin to leach from the body, usually through the mouth and facial area. The first signs of skin slippage are frequently observed as well. Pruning or wrinkling of the hands and/or feet and bullae formation on larger areas of the body are diagnostic features of autolysis, which drives the skin slippage (Figure 18.9).

Active decomposition and bloating is a direct result of autolysis and putrefaction. The body will appear swollen with a distended abdomen, owing to the gaseous by-products of putrefaction (hydrogen sulfide, methane, etc.) (Figure 18.10a and b) This stage also marks the height of blowfly larval activity, the early signs of beetle activity,

Figure 18.9 Autolysis, the breakdown of cells, causes the layers of the skin to separate and appears as "dishpan hands" where there is a wrinkling of the epidermal layer of the skin.

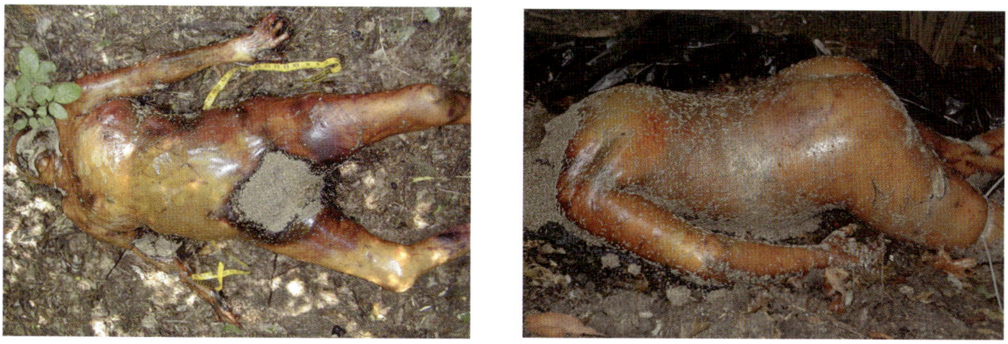

(a) (b)

Figure 18.10 Active decomposition is associated with an overall color change that is golden to dark brown, bloating, and an abundance of larvae.

and an increase in animal scavenging. Also associated with active decomposition is the increased release of decomposition fluid (VFAs) from the body, causing discoloration of the surrounding vegetation, a change in the soil pH, and an increase in nutrients available for environmental microbes (Vass et al. 1992). Decomposition fluid, primarily composed of VFAs, is the direct product of both autolysis and putrefaction breaking down the body tissues. It is specifically formed from the decomposition of fat and muscle and is extremely important in active decomposition until the point at which skeletonization is achieved. The purging and leaching of decomposition fluids from the body produces the diagnostic soil stain associated with a corpse as the pH of the fluid interacts with the pH of the surrounding soil. The change in pH in the soil causes a darkening, or burnt look, to surrounding vegetation and leads to the eventual death of the vegetation as the optimal soil pH necessary to support certain plants is compromised. The soil stain can remain for the better part of 1 year or a full cycle of seasons before renewed plant growth ensues and the stain dissipates. Skin slippage, discoloration, and bacterial growth continue throughout active decomposition, causing a major reduction in the cadaver's biomass.

Advanced decomposition, initial skeletonization, involves the purging of most decomposition fluid through the natural body orifices (mouth, nose, rectum, and genital areas) causing a deflation of the body and wrinkling/crevice formation in the remaining skin, as well as vegetation death around the body (Figure 18.11). Additionally, this stage indicates the most significant biochemical changes in the surrounding environment because of the large amount of VFAs now entering the soil (Tibbett and Carter 2008). Initial exposure of the skeleton, especially the areas of the body with the least amount of soft tissue like the cranium, will be seen. There will be a major reduction in the amount of blowfly larvae activity, as well as migration of blowfly larvae away from the body. The later aspects of this stage will produce an almost completely exposed skeleton with some dried tissue remaining (Figure 18.12).

The last phase of decomposition is the skeletal phase. This phase is marked by a nearly complete to complete skeletonization and the subsequent breakdown of the skeletal elements. Even though soft tissue decomposition ceases, digenesis of the bone occurs over a long period of time. Bone weathering involves the drying out of the bone, bleaching from the sun, exfoliation and removal of the cortical surface, and demineralization (Behrensmeyer 1978). When these features are present, they most often indicate long-term exposure to the

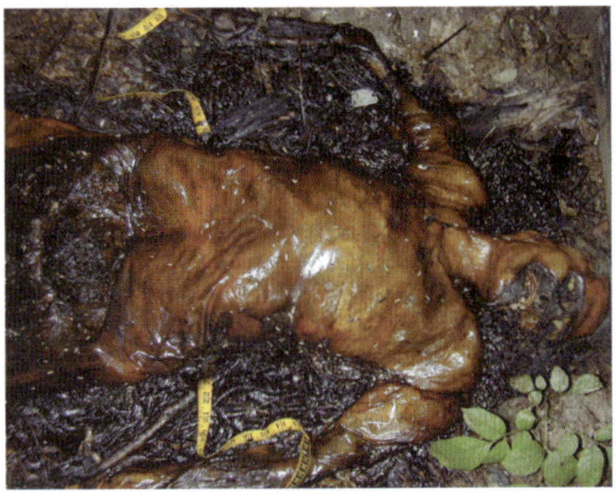
(a)

(b)

Figure 18.11 The cadaver fluids produced by the decomposition process will leach into the surrounding substrate changing the chemical composition of the soil causing the characteristic decomposition stain.

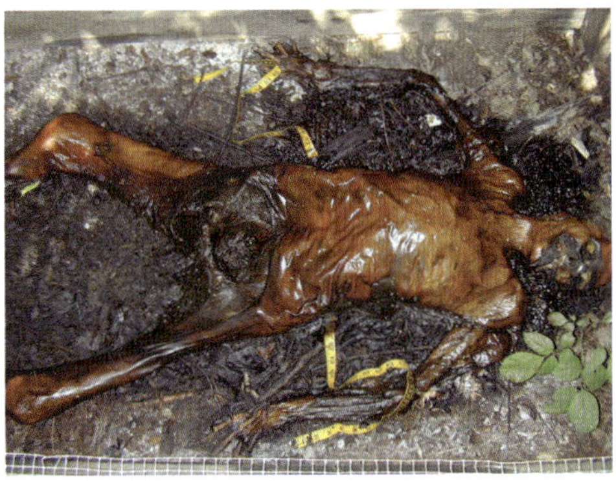

Figure 18.12 Advanced decomposition is marked by a deflation of the body, a darkening and drying of the outside tissue, and a purging of the cadaver fluids into the surrounding substrate.

physical environment. Other factors that come into play include additional scattering from animal activity and bone loss from scavengers (Haglund 1993, Klippel and Synstelien 2007, Reeves 2009, Synstelien 2009). Small rodents, specifically the gray squirrel, show a preference for dry bone that has been exposed to the environment for at least 9 months to 1 year; this rodent is one of the most significant contributors to long-term bone loss in forensic contexts (Klippel and Synstelien 2007). Soil staining of the bone is also associated with the skeletonization stage. Staining of the bone can be partially attributed to decomposition fluids, but most staining is a result of the substrate surrounding bone. Bone is porous and will absorb materials from the environment. When exposed for one or more years, this causes color changes that are similar to those of the surrounding soil matrix. Other discolorations have been noted, such as green staining from certain metals (i.e., copper) and algae growth if the bone was located in a wet environment. As the skeletonization stage proceeds, the biochemical nutrients that were leached from the corpse in preceding stages diminish (Tibbett and Carter 2008) and plant growth is renewed after extended periods of time. Roots and other vegetation may grow within and around the bone, causing damage to the bone. However, vegetation growth can assist in determining the PMI (Willey and Heilman 1987, Hall 1997, Figures 18.13 and 18.14).

(a) (b)

Figure 18.13 (a) Skeletonized remains will typically reflect the surrounding substrate by being stained a similar color and also show signs of wear and tear from the environment. (b) Long term exposure of the skeleton will cause a bleaching/whitening of the bone, a cracking of cortical bone, and renewing vegetation growth in and around the elements.

Figure 18.14 The multi-year exposure of elements allows vegetation to growth through the bone in addition to the bleaching and wearing away of the bone surfaces.

Determination of the Postmortem Interval

Various methods are available to the forensic community for estimating a PMI for a deceased individual. All methods are not equally reliable, and some methods have been outdated and replaced by more recent and reliable techniques (Box 18.1). Several methods that have been used to determine a PMI include forensic entomology (Rodriguez and Bass 1983, Higley and Haskell 2001, Anderson 2001, Schoenly et al. 2007), biochemical fluid and tissue analyses (Vass et al. 1992, 2002), aroma (Vass et al. 2008), biochemical analyses of soil and decomposition substrates (Vass et al. 1992, Tibbett and Carter 2008), botanical studies (Willey and Heilman 1987), and body appearance (Bass 1997). Significant advancements have been made in TSD estimation using biochemistry, forensic entomology, and, more recently, soil chemistry (Vass et al. 2002, Schoenly et al. 2007, Tibbet and Carter 2008). However, there has been little advancement in statistical applications pertaining to

BOX 18.1 THE CASE OF COLONEL SHY

In 1977, Dr. William M. Bass was requested to assist in the recovery and analysis of a disturbed burial in Franklin, Tennessee. The burial was located in a family cemetery on the Shy property. Dr. Bass meticulously recovered all the skeletal elements from the burial, noting a strong odor. Decomposing remains typically have a pungent, acridic odor that is quite discernable. The body itself had decayed to the point that it was no longer articulated in anatomical order. The lower and upper extremities were not attached to the torso, and the skull was not present, but pink tissue was still present on the femora. Initial inspection of the remains suggested an intrusive burial in which a secondary burial was placed above a cast iron coffin dating to the Civil War era, and eventual collapse of the coffin had apparently caused intermingling of the remains. A biological profile and a tentative PMI were assessed at the scene; indicating 6–12 months based on the odor and pink tissue. Dr. Bass based the PMI on that fact that prior burial recoveries in Tennessee from the Civil War period were poorly preserved or had a very dark soil staining. Neither of these characteristics was exhibited by the well-preserved remains from the cast iron coffin.

The remains were brought to Knoxville, Tennessee, for further analysis, and Dr. Bass realized the remains had been treated with embalming fluid. This led to further inspection of the coffin and the recovery of the fragmentary skull consisting of 17 separate bone fragments. The combination of the fragmentary skull, the State Crime Laboratory's assessment that all of the clothing was cotton, and the presence of embalmed tissue led Dr. Bass to conclude that "though my determination of age at death was entirely accurate, my estimate of length of time since death had been off by 112 years."

William Shy was a colonel in the Confederate military until his death on December 16, 1864. He was killed by a Rebel attack during the battle of Compton's Hill at Nashville, Tennessee. He was killed by a Minnie ball to the head at the age of 26 and returned to his family for burial. The presence of pink tissue in the casket after so many years is a result of the unique environment that is created by cast iron coffins. These coffins created an oxygen-deprived environment, which significantly retards the decomposition process. These conditions, combined with the embalming of Colonel Shy's body, preserved the remains more than Dr. Bass had initially expected.

As a result of this case, Dr. Bass has sought to address the lack of understanding of human decomposition and the general dearth of literature available for forensic anthropologists to consult. It also led to the founding the Anthropological Research Facility at the University of Tennessee in Knoxville, Tennessee (Figure 18.15).

Figure 18.15 Colonel Shy.

estimating a PMI from the gross morphological changes of the human body, which is the method commonly employed by anthropologists. Early postmortem changes in a corpse represent the first 2 h after death and are associated with the loss of color, the relaxation of sphincters and associated fecal soiling, and the purging of fluids from the stomach and/or respiratory tract (Clark et al. 1997). Several methods are used to determine the PMI during this early postmortem period where the body is still in a flaccid or limp state (Swift 2010). These methods range from measuring directly observable physiochemical changes (i.e., taking rectal or core temperatures and determining lividity status; Kaliszan et al. 2009), to evaluating the chemical composition of the body fluids (such as the change in potassium in the vitreous fluid in the eye; Spitz 2006), to studying the residual reactivity of muscles to electrical stimuli (Henssge et al. 1995). A series of subsequent postmortem changes occurs within the first 48 h after death. Traditionally, pathologists ascertain the PMI using three soft tissue indicators: algor mortis, livor mortis, and rigor mortis (DiMaio and Dana 2006).

Algor mortis is the cooling of the body to the ambient/atmospheric temperature, typically a 1.5°F reduction in body temperature every hour in temperate climates, while in tropical climates the temperature change is only 0.75°F (Spitz 2006). However, research has indicated that the decrease in body temperature is more of a sigmoid curve in which there are stepped plateaus (Henssge et al. 1995). Body temperature decreases initially by 2.0°F–2.5°F and then slows to 1.5°F. A higher temperature can remain for 3–4 h postmortem as a result of residual metabolic activity in the body (Hutchins 1985), possibly the result of illness. The most common method of determining body temperature is to take an inner core temperature rather than a surface temperature (Kaliszan et al. 2009).

The visceral organs will have a slower, more regular decline in temperature, whereas the decline in skin temperature is quite variable. Typically, the skin cools faster because it is one of the main pathways of heat loss for the human body. Core temperatures can be taken in the brain, liver, or the preferred rectal areas. Knight (1988) provides a thorough review of postmortem cooling in which he acknowledges that the overall accuracy of methods used to determine the PMI from body temperature is questionable, despite the extensive research that has been conducted on the topic. Quite simply, numerous variables influence the process by which a body cools.

Livor mortis, or lividity, is the pooling or settling of liquid blood in the body to the lowest available parts of the body. Lividity is linked with the positioning of the body at death, which can provide important clues during an investigation. For example, hanging victims typically have increased lividity in forearms and lower legs compared to the rest of the body. Also, when an individual has been pressed against an object (such as a floor or bed), a pale area will be present on the body in the compressed area. Livor mortis is visible in the form of a red-purple color within 2 h postmortem as the quantity of deoxyhemoglobin increases in the body. Within 5 h postmortem, there is a combination of fixed and unfixed lividity, where the body presents a mixture of areas that are permanently red-purple in color and areas that blanch if pressure is applied. Lividity is usually fixed within 8–12 h after death. In later stages of lividity, there can be splattering or splotching of the lividity, known as Tardieu spots (Spitz 2006). Once lividity is completely fixed, its usefulness in PMI estimation decreases (Figure 18.16).

Rigor mortis is the stiffening of the muscles that occurs after the initial period of flaccidity. The increase in muscle rigidity can start 1 h postmortem in moderate temperatures and peak after about 12 h, or it can last for another 10–12 h. The smaller muscles with the highest metabolic activity will fix prior to larger muscles. This phenomenon explains why the eyelids may remain open, whereas the gluteal muscles are still flaccid/soft. Rigor mortis occurs because the metabolic process of muscle contraction continues

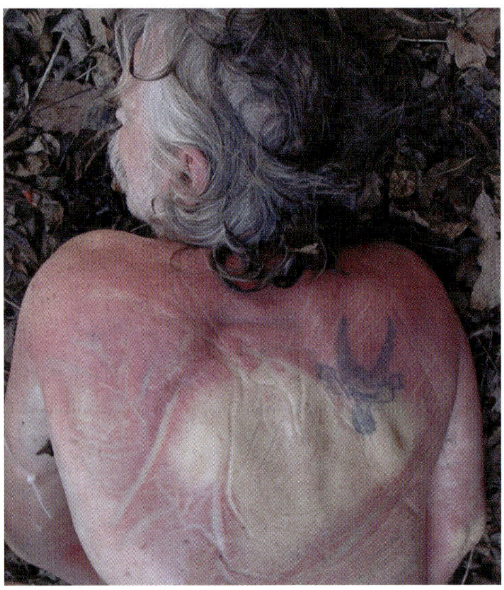

Figure 18.16 Lividity, caused by a settling of the blood within the body, causes a pink discoloration of the surface and is used as an early indicator in estimating the time since death.

but there is no ATP available to reverse the process and relax the muscles. In life, muscle contractions are initiated by the targeted release of calcium ions (Ca^+) from reservoirs. Ca^+ initiates muscle contraction by freeing the proteins, actin and myosin, in muscle filaments to allow them to bind, which in turn causes the muscle fibers to shorten and thus contract. As the cell membrane of muscle cells breaks down after death, Ca^+ is released from the cells, thereby causing muscle contraction. Because of the lack of oxygen in a deceased individual, this process cannot be reversed, so actin and myosin remain joined. Oxygen is necessary in cellular respiration to form ATP, and ATP is necessary to break the bond between actin and myosin and to recapture the Ca^+ into reservoirs. Therefore, the lack of oxygen, and thus ATP, causes the muscles to remain in the contracted state until further breakdown of the proteins involved in this process (Gill-King 1997). Consequently, higher ambient temperatures shorten the time a body spends in rigor mortis.

Although a number of methods are available for determining TSD in recently deceased, once a body moves beyond the late postmortem stage as defined by Clark et al. (1997), other approaches should be utilized and investigated. Traditionally, these methods have been based on the sequential nature of observed gross anatomical changes (Reed 1957, Payne 1965, Bass 1984, 1997, Galloway et al. 1989). Unfortunately, observation-based techniques are highly qualitative and subjective because they rely on the anthropologists' background and experience. There is a need in the anthropological community to devise a more scientifically rigorous approach to PMI estimation. A few mathematical models have been employed for PMI estimation that include variables, such as health, cause of death, temperature, level of ventilation and air humidity, presence of clothing, and access of the body by insects (Campobasso et al. 2001). Other authors suggest temperature-based methods (Megyesi et al. 2005, Simmons et al. 2010) or body fluid chemistry changes, which can provide a statistical confidence interval of 95% depending on the PMI, availability of equipment, circumstances of the death, and environment (Clark et al. 1997, Campobasso et al. 2001, Vass et al. 2002).

Forensic Entomology

The forensic entomological community has developed useful ways to estimate PMI based on the developmental sequence of forensically significant arthropods commonly associated with a decomposing corpse (Payne et al. 1968, Goff 1993, Tabor Kreitlow 2010). Insects and other invertebrates feeding on and around a cadaver form a distinct faunal succession associated with the various stages of decay and fall into several distinct groups: necrophagous species, predators and parasites of the necrophagous species, omnivorous species, adventive species, and accidental species (Smith 1986, Byrd and Castner 2010).

Flies are most often the first insects observed on carrion and are predominantly used in PMI estimations (Rodriguez and Bass 1983, Kulshrestha and Chandra 1987, Shean et al. 1993, Haskell et al. 1997). More specifically, flies from the family Calliphoridae, otherwise known as the blowflies, have an inherent ability to detect and colonize a cadaver soon after death, which makes them extremely useful in PMI estimations. In warm temperatures, Diptera will be on the body within minutes of deposition and begin oviposition. Areas of the body that are first colonized by insects include the eyes, mouth, nasal cavity, anus, vagina, and areas of trauma (Sledzik 1998). Several other flies are also typically associated with decaying remains: Sarcophagidae (flesh flies), Phoridae (humpbacked fly), Sepsidae (black scavenger flies), Sphaeroceridae (small dung flies), and Stratiomyidae (soldier flies) depending on the time of year and region of the world (Haskell et al. 1997). The family Piophilidae, Piophila casei (cheese skipper), is found in advanced decomposition stages when the connective tissue is drying (Goff 2010). Beetles are also extremely important to PMI estimations, especially in latter stages of decomposition. The beetle orders more relevant to TSD estimation include Coleoptera, silphids (carrion beetles), dermestids (hide beetles), nitidulids (sap beetles), and clerids (checker beetles), which feed on the body; and the families of the Staphylinidae (rove beetles), Silphidae (carrion beetles), Histeridae (hister beetles), and Hydrophilidae (hydrophilid beetles), which are found on or around the body (Goff 2010).

There are two main approaches to the forensic entomological PMI estimations: analysis of the pattern of successive colonization of different arthropods or the determination of the life stage of the specific insects, which are usually blowflies. The timing of specific arthropod species in relation to the decomposing cadaver provides a basis for estimating the PMI. For example, adult blowflies lay eggs and colonize a cadaver within the first 24 h of death, but within just a few days beetles will be present that feed on both the body and the larvae. The presence of both species on the same cadaver indicates a slightly longer PMI. More precise methods to estimate PMI typically use the life cycle of specific insect species. Many species of insects, like the blowfly, have well-documented developmental rates. Thus, recognition of the different immature stages of arthropod species involved, together with the knowledge of their rates of development, can give an indication of the PMI (Smith 1986). Use of developmental stage is most useful for early decomposition, that which is under 15–20 days, because this is the average life cycle for most blowflies (Haskell et al. 1997). The application of developmental stages is based on the fact that insect growth is directly correlated to the ambient temperature. Thus, one would need to identify the species collected from a cadaver, note the developmental stage, obtain weather data for the deposition location, and then calculate the amount of time that would be required to reach the developmental stage observed for that species.

Most forensic entomology techniques focus on the determination of the accumulated degree days (ADD) or accumulated degree hours (ADH) needed for specific larvae to reach a certain growth stage. ADD and ADH are heat unit values calculated from ambient air temperatures that represent the heat energy needed for larvae to reach a specific growth stage in a particular environment (Haskell et al. 1997). Although forensic entomology is arguably the most successful way to estimate PMI after the first 72 h (Anderson and Van Laerhoven 1996), the blow fly larvae typically associated with a decomposing body are most valuable in the early stages of decomposition or until the time of pupation, so other methods must be employed for longer time intervals (Payne 1965). Another potential ecological-based research area is evaluating post-putrefaction fungi, which have been shown to have successive fruiting phases associated with the cadaver breakdown (Sagara 1995).

Forensic Botany

Forensic botany is the application of botanical studies to the medicolegal context. It can provide significant contributions to depositional contexts involving the movement of a body from one location to another. Moreover, forensic botany can be used to estimate a

PMI. Botanical analyses relating to the depositional environment is a relatively underutilized avenue for PMI estimations. Botanical-based estimates rely on the recognition of flora associated with a cadaver, documentation of location, systematic collection and preservation, and determination of growth rate for each species (Coyle et al. 2005). One of the major issues with botanical-based methods is the lack of good preservation of evidence, so estimates are often based on missing information. However, if quality documentation and preservation techniques are employed, these data can provide PMI estimations for the longer time intervals. The flora surrounding a body can give an indication of the time interval that a body was at that location. Plants can be annual and/or seasonal in nature, so they can suggest time of year of deposition or suggest particular weather conditions when a body was deposited. This includes aspects of a plant life cycle such as number of leaf falls or presence of specific pollens (Hall 1997). Also, the amount of growth that has occurred in a plant can indicate exposure length in years, especially if plant roots are growing through naturally existing foramina of the skeleton (Box 18.2; Willey and Heilman 1987).

Soil Chemistry

Recent research in soil chemistry has demonstrated that depositional environment holds promise in the development of rapid and reliable techniques to estimate PMI. The basis for soil analyses is acknowledging that soil, a complex, ever-changing combination of biological, chemical, and physical properties, is significantly changed when a cadaver comes into contact with it. Soil chemistry is of specific importance to the burial context, because it can dictate how well skeletal remains are preserved. The color, consistency, and texture of soil all play a significant role in the appearance of remains, because of the exchange that can occur between them. However, chemical-based methods are also relevant to surface decomposition environments. When a body decomposes, it creates an influx of organic material into the surrounding soil, which creates a "cadaver decomposition island (CDI)" (Carter et al. 2007). For example, the CDI will initially have a negative effect on the surrounding vegetation, but as the characteristics of the CDI change itself there is a renewed vegetation growth. Pioneering research by Vass et al. (1992) demonstrated that ADD correlates with actual biochemical decomposition of body tissues. VFAs from the breakdown of tissues leach into the surrounding soil and change the soil chemistry. A soil sample from where the corpse decomposed can be compared to a sterile sample from the same general locality. The ratio of the VFAs in the soil where decomposition occurred correlates with a particular ADD and is considered the maximum TSD (Vass et al. 2002). This research has even proven effective in situations in which there is advanced decomposition with skeletonization. Also, Spicka et al. (2008) indicate that the concentration of ninhydrin-reactive nitrogen in grave soil associated with juvenile- to adult-sized cadavers (20–50 kg) remains at similar levels to the predepositional levels until 2 days postmortem. See Table 18.5 for outline of the effects of the decomposition on soil.

The biochemical methods eliminate the subjectivity inherent in observation-based data and have the potential to control for the increasing time error that accompanies extended decomposition stages (Tibbet and Carter 2008). Consequently, soil chemistry is a growing area of research for statistically valid PMI estimations. However, because many of these biochemical techniques require special laboratories to conduct the analysis, ongoing

BOX 18.2 LONG-TERM DECOMPOSITION AND THE ROLE OF BOTANY

In 1995, remains were discovered in a secluded area of West Knoxville, TN. The remains were discovered by several boys playing in the area and resulted in the cranium being taken from the scene. Examination of the scene indicated well-scattered remains with leaf litter covering much of the skeleton. The mandible was firmly secured to the ground by a root mass (Figure 18.17a). A shirt made of synthetic material was found adjacent to the mandible. The shirt had vertebrae and ribs associated with it and was also penetrated with roots. Several ribs and vertebrae were found downslope of the shirt. The innominate was secured to the ground by a root that had grown through the obturator foramen (Figure 18.17b). Bones of the lower limbs were discovered in close proximity to each other in the center of the scatter. Both femora and cranium were recovered from separate locations of the scatter.

Analysis of the remains indicated that rodent and carnivore gnawing were present throughout the skeleton. The cranium had rodent gnawing on the supra-orbital margins, zygomatic bone, and maxillae. The postcrania exhibited carnivore punctures and gnawing on the ribs, vertebrae, and epiphyseal areas of the long bones. Also, the remains had a dark staining due to the depositional environment, the soil and leaf litter. This was particularly evident on the right side of the cranium. However, the occipital bone exhibited a green coloration from algae growth, and moss had grown on several of the vertebral elements. Desiccated tissue, (dried soft tissue) adhered to the toe phalanges. No other soft tissue was present on the remains.

Based on the extensive root growth, degree of skeletonization, and organic staining of the bones, it was clear that the remains had been exposed for an extended period of time. The rodent gnawing, which is consistent with gray squirrel activity, supported the assessment and suggested a PMI of greater than 1 year. A root sample, which had grown through several layers of the shirt fabric, was examined by a Dr. Heilman at the University of Tennessee. He found that the root was in its fourth year of growth, thus indicating that the shirt associated with the remains had to have been at the location for no less than 4 years.

(a) (b)

Figure 18.17 (a) Mandible that is embedded within a root mass. (b) Root that had grown through the obturator foramen of the oscoxa.

Table 18.5 Decomposition Effects on Soil with Associated Time Intervals

Decomposition Stage	Soil Changes	Time
Fresh	Little to no	<48 h
Bloat	Increase in pH, initial influx of nutrient sources into soil such as, ammonia, calcium, magnesium, ninhydrin-reactive nitrogen, potassium, sodium, sulfate, and VFAs	24 h to 1 week
Active decomposition	Increased levels of all of the above	48 h to 2 weeks
Advanced decomposition	Peak concentrations of VFAs, chemicals, and microorganisms	1 week to several months
Dry remains	Decrease in concentrations over time to eventually reestablishing "virgin" soil levels	2 weeks to 2 years

Sources: Adapted from Tibbett, M. and Carter, D.O., Research in forensic taphonomy: A soil-based perspective, in Ritz, K., Dawson, L., and Miller, D. (eds.) *Criminal and Environmental Soil Forensics*, Springer, New York, 2009; Payne, J.A., *Ecology*, 46(5), 592, 1965; Vass, A.A. et al., *J Forensic Sci*, 37, 1236, 1992; Spicka, A. et al., Cadaver mass and decomposition: How long does it take for a cadaver to increase the concentration of ninhydrin-reactive nitrogen in soil?, in *Proceedings of the American Academy of Forensic Sciences*, vol. 14, p. 178, 2008.

research is focusing on ways to convert observation-based methods and the accompanying categorical data into statistically significant TSD estimations.

Morphoscopic Techniques

Megyesi et al. (2005) proposed one of the first methods to incorporate gross observations of the cadaver with ADD. This research developed a scoring system for decomposition on different body areas/regions, in which the regional scores are summed to produce a total body score (TBS). This TBS is independent of the depositional environment because it focuses strictly on the condition of the body (Box 18.3). The TBS is correlated with a calculated ADD to produce the estimate for time since death, which could be statistically validated and thus upheld in court. However, several caveats must be considered when applying the Megyesi et al. (2005) technique: the technique was developed using without an exact known TSD (estimates were obtained using forensic entomological techniques), the body was evaluated and scored using pictures, and the scoring criteria produced were based on a combination of reviewing the literature for known stages of decomposition and adjusting the criteria based on photographs of actual forensic cases. Nonetheless, it demonstrates potential for combining multiple lines of evidence and highlights the importance of temperature as a major variable affecting the decomposition rate. Simmons et al. (2010) further suggest the validity of using ADD as a standard in PMI situations. This review of research conducted at the University of Central Lancashire combined with previously unreported research indicates that ADD can be used as a means to compare decomposition experiments conducted under vastly different conditions. However, rabbits are the primary carrion used in the University of Central Lancashire studies. Payne et al. (1968) and subsequently Schoenly et al. (2007) have demonstrated the usefulness of pigs as a proxy for human decomposition, but they note that pigs should not be considered a replacement for human-based experiments. Vass et al. (2008) detected significant biochemical differences between the bones of humans and those of other mammalian species. Further, Parmenter and MacMahon (2009) and Simmons et al. (2010) found that carcass size plays a significant role in the decomposition process in that smaller carcasses decompose faster than larger carcasses. Thus, some nonhuman animals may not be an appropriate proxy for humans.

More recently, Vass (2011) has demonstrated the effectiveness of ADD by combining ADD data with the percentage of body decomposition and incorporating the role of humidity in the decomposition process. This research is the culmination of observations from numerous cadavers at the Anthropological Research Facility in Knoxville, TN, over the last 20 years. The research integrates earlier work where Vass et al. (2002) determined the time decomposition ceases in ADD units, and provides estimation equations for both surface and burial contexts (see Box 18.4). This method provides a "rule of thumb" approach for estimation of the PMI for decomposition events greater than 2 days. His formulae rely on the fact that temperature, moisture, and partial pressure of oxygen have the

BOX 18.3 CASE-SPECIFIC VARIABLES: HANGING IN THE OUTDOOR CONTEXT

Most suicidal hangings occur indoors, but outdoor hangings often result in more questions than answers after the investigation. A common issue with outdoor hangings is the long time delay before remains are found, often resulting in the recovery of decayed or skeletonized remains. Skeletonized remains alone make it very difficult to recreate the deposition scenario and to determine the PMI. There is very little published research on how hanging affects the rate of decomposition, despite detailed literature documenting the stages of decomposition related to surface scenarios. Understanding factors that could affect the decomposition process (e.g., distance from the ground, positioning of the body in relation to the asphyxiation device, and the type of noose used) may allow for more accurate evaluations of outdoor hanging scenarios.

In 2009, the Anthropological Research Facility in Knoxville, Tennessee initiated a long-term project to address outdoor hanging scenarios. A 10 ft high wooden device was built to bear a maximum load of over 600 lb with a pulley/crank system to ease the force required to lift individuals into the hanging position (20 cm above the ground). The number of variables were limited so that seasonal differences can be appreciated (clothes were eliminated, the knot type standardized, and the same type of rope was used in all trials). A cadaver was also placed on the ground near the hanging individuals to serve as the control for each trial. Observations were recorded twice daily using video and still photography, written annotations, and data loggers. A time lapse camera was also utilized to capture hourly photos throughout the decomposition process. Samples for entomological examination were collected and included eggs, larvae, pupae, and adults that are present on and around the body.

Similar decomposition events for the control and hanging cadavers are apparent, specifically features such as skin slippage, marbling, and bloating, but there are a few key differences. These differences include the entomological colonization (both species present and oviposition pattern), the amount of biomass reduction prior to mummification, and the overall rate of decay. This study confirms earlier work of Goff (1991) using a carrion model for hanging, suggesting that a hanging cadaver will have a reduced if not complete elimination of ground dwelling taxa feeding on the soft tissue. Additionally, few fly larvae could be found in the latter instar stages of development on the body surfaces of the hanging cadaver. The larvae are not able to mass, which is vital for them to maintain their body temperatures. We observed that once the maggots started to clump they fell off of the body and onto the ground below the body, creating a "drip zone" area that encircled the base of the body in which they massed and fed on the falling soft tissue. The ideal environment for feeding by blowfly larvae was also diminished due to a rapid rate of mummification of tissue. Hide beetles and cheese skippers were prevalent fairly early on, within a few weeks postmortem, and remained well into the second year of the study.

Initial observations indicated similar oviposition patterns between the control and the hanging cadaver. The most significant difference between the control and the hanging individuals was temperature. The hanging cadaver maintained ambient temperature because of the 360° air circulation around the body; and thus exhibited putrefaction and advanced decomposition much later in the study. This corresponds with previous surveys indicating that decomposition rates are significantly slower in hangings at higher heights as opposed to individuals partially on the ground (Komar et al. 1999). A clear difference was noted in the summer versus the winter trials. The cadavers placed in the summer had rapid decomposition events associated with the higher temperatures, but did not exhibit the skin removal typically seen in summer decomposition. The outer tissues of the body mummified, but internal decomposition still occurred, resulting in the settling of the organs in the lower abdomen and the eventual disintegration of the perineum, causing the internal organs to fall into the "drip zone" below the body. This accelerated the mummification process by providing additionally air circulation around the body surfaces. The loss of internal organs significantly reduced the biomass of the cadaver, thus lightening it and prolonging the ability of the cadaver to remain hanging. The winter trials displayed similar early decomposition events, but much of the putrefaction needed for internal organ decomposition was slowed. This caused the retention of the internal organs and perineum, even though the organs settled into the lower abdomen. The greater biomass retention in the winter produced a heavier cadaver that reached the ground and fell after the first year of the study.

Even though this research was a pilot project, it demonstrates the continued need for observation-based studies that are actualistic in nature. Actualistic studies look at the process as it occurs in order to better understand what is happening. Observing the hanging cadavers makes us rethink blindly applying surface deposition ranges for the PMI to a unique context. The depositional scenario significantly affected the rate of decomposition and encouraged preservation of tissue. When a cadaver is found hanging, demonstrating significant mummification and mold growth, a prolonged time interval should be suggested (Figure 18.18).

(a) (b)

Figure 18.18 (a) Experimental, Hanging cadaver after 20 months exposure. (b) Control, surface cadaver after 20 months exposure.

greatest influence on decomposition, and that soft tissue decomposition ceased at 1285 ± 110 ADDs. However, much of his work is based on personal observations and has not been validated by other researchers as of yet. Also, more research on the reliability of the percentage scoring system versus a TBS system needs to be completed, so that definitions can be clearly written for practitioners. Nonetheless, Vass (2011) demonstrates the advances in decomposition research and the need for statistically derived PMI estimations.

BOX 18.4 "RULE OF THUMB" CALCULATION OF THE PMI

Dr. Arpad Vass, a researcher at the Oak Ridge National Laboratory in Oak Ridge, Tennessee, has conducted biochemical research on human decomposition at the Anthropology Research Facility in Knoxville, Tennessee, since the early 1990s. He has published several landmark papers relating to chemicals given off by a decomposing cadaver. In 2011, he published a culminating paper representing his many years of research and observations (*The Elusive Universal Post-mortem Interval Formula*) to establish methods of making PMI estimations for empirical versus more subjective approaches.

According to Vass (2011) PMI estimations can be calculated for surface decomposition and burial decomposition contexts. The following formula outlines the calculation for surface contexts in which there is access to oxygen. This would not be relevant for confined spaces above the ground; rather, the burial formula should be implemented. This formula is designed for scenarios for which soft tissue is still present (pre-skeletonized stages), there is little to no adipocere development, and limited scavenging has occurred as this is known to affect rate of decay. However, it is still important to note the macroscopic changes of the body in addition to the overall percentage of decay, because of the many context-specific variables that cannot be accounted for in the formula.

$$\text{PMI (aerobic)} = [1285 \times (\text{decomposition}/100)]/[0.0103 \times \text{temperature} \times \text{humidity}],$$

Where

1285 = a constant that represents the ADD (accumulated degree day) value for which VFAs cease to be released from soft tissue. It is considered the end of soft tissue decomposition and typically is associated with skeletonization of a cadaver (Vass et al. 1992).

decomposition = a value from 1 to 100 that represents the percentage of total soft tissue decomposition. This requires an understanding of the decomposition process and of the appearance of specific features during the process. Unless one is confident in their estimations, a range of percentages should be used in the calculation.

0.0103 = constant that represents the effect of moisture on the decomposition rate. Prior unpublished work by Vass indicates that the humidity and moisture content released from a decomposing corpse follows a generalized linear curve. Further research is needed in other climatic zones to determine if this trend holds.

temperature = average ambient temperature (°C) for the depositional location (can be for the day of discovery or for a period of time). It is better to use a range of days and not the average for the day of discovery since temperatures can fluctuate considerably within and between days.

Humidity = a value from 1% to 100% represents the average humidity at the depositional location (can be for the day of discovery or for a period of time).

Future Directions

The accumulative degree day approach for estimating PMI has shown great success in entomology and has a strong foundation for use from biology and engineering (Vass et al. 1992, Haskell et al. 1997). However, this approach assumes regularity to the decomposition process when applied to soft tissue changes. Most PMI estimation methods focus on decomposition as a series of sequential events in which TSD is the "calculation of a measurable date along a time-dependent curve back to the start point" (Henssge and Madea 2007: 182). This model simplifies the relationship between the various factors that influence decomposition to fit into a linear, sequential model. Hypothesis testing using a linear regression approach is complicated by the fact that the variables affecting the decomposition process are continually changing. Therefore, PMI estimation may be more statistically rigorous if evaluated using models that viewed decomposition as process that goes through several transitions; the TSD estimate could then be based on the probability of reaching a particular transition at a given time.

Decomposition Research

Longitudinal studies of human decomposition in the literature have been limited by access to the appropriate number of human models to make studies statistically relevant (Mant 1953, Rodriguez and Bass 1983, 1985, Mann et al. 1990), locations to conduct this research, and graduate students willing to dedicate years to developing and conducting these experiments. The University of Tennessee, Knoxville, has been essential in developing a location in which these types of experiments can be conducted on human cadavers in a natural setting. The advent of other outdoor research facilities, such as those at Sam Houston University, Western Carolina University, and Texas State University-San Marcos, combined with the 30 year research tradition of the Anthropological Research Facility in Knoxville, are needed to continue to broaden the knowledge base necessary to fully understand human decomposition.

Based on actualistic studies and personal experience, Bass (1997) established the progression of decomposition events in warm moist climates found in the southeastern United States. He outlined the basic features of human decomposition in the greater East Tennessee area, a climate in which it is possible to get a complete skeleton in as little as 2 weeks in the summer months (Bass 1997). This speed requires the ideal complement of temperature, humidity, and arthropod activity (Mann et al. 1990). Regardless of the rate, a decomposing corpse undergoes a specific series of documented stages: fresh, fresh-bloat, bloat-decay, dry, and bone breakdown (Figure 18.19a and b; Table 18.6).

Arid environments cause rapid desiccation of soft tissues that often results in mummification. Galloway et al. (1989) and Rhine and Dawson (1998) have established criteria and trait lists for decomposition in hot, arid conditions. Galloway et al. (1989) examined 189 cases found in southern Arizona and found that early decomposition and bloating occurred rapidly, but the outer tissues became dehydrated quickly and formed a hard, mummified shell. Correspondingly, larval activity quickly declined because dried tissue is not a variable environment for oviposition or feeding. Rhine and Dawson (1998) surveyed 270 decomposition-based cases from the New Mexico Office of the Medical Examiner to sequence the changes leading to skeletonization and indicated similar processes as

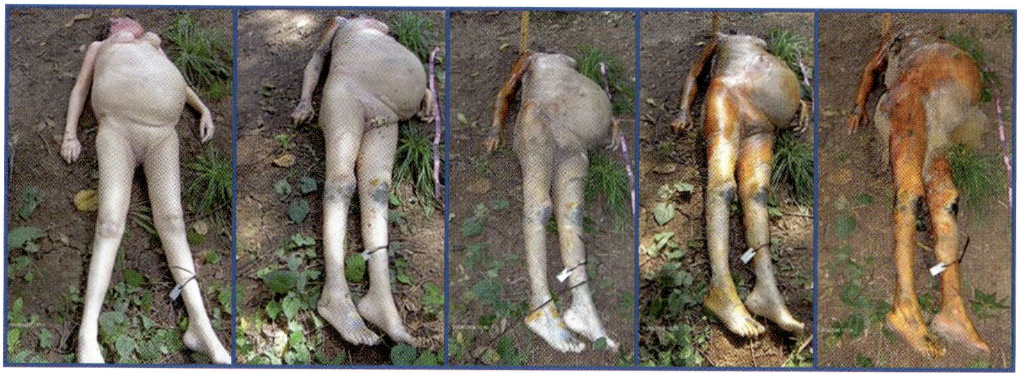

(a)

(b)

Figure 18.19 (a) Fresh to active decomposition stages. (b) Active decomposition to skeletonization stages. (Photos courtesy of Dr. Andrew Hart.)

Galloway et al. (1989). However, they highlight the fact that the rate, and not the sequence, of events is the primary difference in decomposition in various climatic zones (Table 18.7).

Little research has been conducted on decomposition in cold weather climates, and much of the existing research utilized carrion models. Komar 1998 provides a review of forensic cases from the Edomonton area of Canada, while Micozzi (1986, 1991) focused on actualistic studies using carrion models to evaluate cold weather. Both studies suggest that temperature is the key factor in altering the rate of decomposition, which is further highlighted by Stokes et al. (2009). An examination of 20 cases from the Medical Examiner's office in Edmonton, Alberta, Canada, suggested that skeletonization can occur within 4 months even in freezing temperatures (Komar 1998). Remains that experience decomposition in regions where winters are cold and harsh can undergo a putrefactive stasis during subfreezing temperatures. The stasis can result in an inaccurate assessment of decomposition and result in an imprecise estimation of the PMI (Dudzik et al. 2011). Micozzi (1991) found that frozen environments alter the environmental context greatly, in which a thawed body may in fact decompose at a faster rate than a fresh body. This was further supported by Dudzik et al. (2011), who demonstrated the rate at which a body becomes frozen (delayed versus rapid) during the freeze–thaw cycle of a Montana winter and spring alters the expected decomposition pattern. Thawing causes decomposition from the "outside-in"

Table 18.6 Decay Rates for Warm/Moist Climates

Time	Expectations
Day 1	Oviposition, egg masses, slight marbling, release of body fluid from mouth and genital area (from sphincter relaxation)
Week 1	Larval activity (especially in facial area) and a presence of beetles, beginning of skin slippage and hair mass production, pronounced marbling, distinct odors associated with decomposition, bloating of abdomen and extremities, mold growth, initial decomposition stain production from VFAs release and associated vegetation death, animal scavenging
Month 1 (2nd to 4th week)	Reduction in larval activity and increased beetle activity, body appears to be deflating (skin is wrinkling and fluid is being purged), skin will have a leathery appearance and will be drying, variety of molds will cover remaining skin, dark, distinctive stain will be present around the body, adipocere may form (especially if moisture content is high), initial skeletonization (head, neck, genital areas initially)
Year 1 (after first month)	Complete exposure of the skeleton, exposed elements will begin drying and the cortex will become bleached, algae or moss growth if shaded and in a moist area, rodent gnawing in the latter months, rodent and wasp nest production
Decade 1	Deterioration of the skeleton itself, continued bleaching with exfoliation of cortex (this is enhanced by periods of high moisture followed by drying periods), cracking of the cortical bone (typically seen in the long bones, scapulae, and os coxae initially), root growth in and out of bones, staining of skeletal elements from substrate (especially from leaf falls and darker soil types), extensive rodent gnawing causing severe bone destruction

Sources: Based on Bass, W.M., Time interval since death: A difficult decision, in Rathbun, T.A. and Buikstra, J.E. (eds.) *Human Identification: Case Studies in Forensic Anthropology*, CC Thomas, Springfield, IL, pp. 136–147, 1984; Bass, W.M., Outdoor decomposition rates in Tennessee, in Haglund W.D. and Sorg M.H. (eds.) *Forensic Taphonomy: The Postmortem Fate of Human Remains*, CRC Press, Boca Raton, FL, pp. 181–186, 1997.

Table 18.7 Decay Rates for Dry Climates

Time	Stage of Decomposition	Expectations
Day 1–7	Fresh	Lividity, egg deposition, little to no animal scavenging
Day 1–5 to day 3–8 Larvae present by day 2 Bloat present by day 2, but typically lost by day 7	Early decomposition	Skin slippage. Gray to green discoloration of overall body. Distal extremities have a brownish discoloration, bloating and post bloating. Purple to black discoloration of appendages
Day 4–8 to 2 months Mummification 2 months to 6–9 months	Advanced decomposition	Deflated, concave abdomen, bone exposure with moist decomposition. Mummification with or without internal organ retention. Adipocere development
2 months to 1 year	Skeletonization	Greasy bones with some body fluids or desiccated tissue, but less than half the skeleton. Mostly dry bone
6 months + Exfoliation 12–18 months	Extreme decomposition	Bleaching and exfoliation of cortex of bone. Bone degradation with metaphyseal loss and cancellous bone exposure

Sources: Galloway, A. The process of decomposition. A model from the Arizona-Sonoran Desert, in Haglund, W.D. and Sorg, M.H. (eds.) *Forensic Taphonomy: The Postmortem Fate of Human Remains*, CRC Press, Boca Raton, FL, pp. 139–149, 1997; Galloway, A. et al., *J Forensic Sci* 34(3), 607, 1989.

as opposed to the decomposition from the "inside-out" that is typically seen in an exposed surface deposition without freezing (Micozzi 1991, Parsons 2009). Micozzi (1986) concludes that decomposition in remains that have been frozen proceeds from the "outside-in" by aerobic decay, disarticulation, and foreign organisms. Decomposition of remains that have not been frozen proceeds from the "inside-out" due to putrefaction and autolysis. Importantly, Micozzi (1991) did not observe putrefaction in temperatures colder than 4°C, which is why refrigeration slows the decomposition process and why "bloating" is much less pronounced in the winter months. However, others have indicated that decomposition still occurs at 0°C due to the elevated salt content in the human body (Vass et al. 2002) and that heavy snowfall may act as an insulator, thus creating a situation in which the temperature near the carrion is higher than the ambient temperature (Parsons 2009). Also, the process of freezing and thawing of tissues results in rapid disarticulation of remains as it weakens skin, connective tissues, and joints (Micozzi 1986, 1991). Carnivore activity is an important factor in the decomposition and disarticulation of remains in cold climates, as well (McKeown et al. 2011). Regardless of the reason for a cold climate (i.e., confined area, altitude, or latitude), the lower temperatures slow decomposition rates, resulting in a longer time interval to skeletonization (Galloway et al. 1989, Bass 1997; Komar 1998, see Table 18.8).

The pattern of decomposition in water is different from decomposition observed in terrestrial environments (Haglund 1993, Boyle et al. 1997). Research on soft tissue decomposition in aqueous environments indicates that water slows the decomposition process overall, but temperature, bacterial content, and water movement all affect the rate of decomposition (Simpson and Knight 1985, Haglund 1993, MacDonnell and Anderson 1997, Seet 2005). Early work in this area focused primarily on arthropod activity in relation to the cadaver, noting that the succession of specific arthropods that colonize a submerged body can be used to estimate TSD (Payne and King 1972, Haskell et al. 1989). A few key points are notable: water encourages adipocere development; autolysis and putrefaction continue with submerged remains, but the rate of these processes depends directly on the water temperature; and salt water slows the rate of putrefaction because salinity retards bacterial growth (Evans 1962, Cotton et al. 1987). Flies are attracted to exposed areas of the body, and fish and other aquatic animals often feed on the remains below the water line. Also, remains will sink initially if not prevented by clothing or other devices, but as remains become bloated the body will resurface. Disarticulation usually follows a sequence of hands first followed by feet, head and lower jaw, lower legs, forearms, and, finally, the

Table 18.8 Rates of Decomposition in Cold Climates

Time	Stage	Expectations
—	Fresh	*Was not included in study*
Day 1 to 3½; months	Moderate	Partial exposure of bone, loss of some bone elements from scavenging, and slight adipocere formation
3½; to 32 months	Advanced	Mummification with or without internal organs, extensive adipocere formation, moderate bony exposure
4–42 months	Skeletal	Little wet soft tissue or desiccated tissue with most of skeleton exposed
2 months to 8 years	Completely Skeletal	Fully exposed, dry skeleton with no associated tissue

Source: Adapted from Komar, D.A., *J Forensic Sci*, 43, 57, 1998; p. 58, Table 18.2.

pectoral girdle, leaving the torso and pelvis (Haglund 1993). As the remains disarticulate, gasses created during putrefaction escape, and the remains sink again. However, other factors are involved when considering salt water, such as salinity, tides, currents, depth in the water column, substrate type, season, and the species and numbers of colonizing animals (Sorg et al. 1997, Hobischak and Anderson 2002, Anderson 2010). Sorg et al. (1997) describe four roles of the carcass in an ocean environment: the remains may become food for many vertebrate and invertebrate scavengers, may provide shelter for other species, may attract secondary scavengers, and the bones may eventually provide a source of minerals and act as a substrate for bacterial grazers. Anderson (2010) summarizes research that has been conducted over the last decade comparing shallow and deep saltwater environments. In both contexts, the amount of biomass lost was not solely the result of decomposition. Opportunistic scavenging and body movement expedited skeletonization, and more rapid skeletonization occurred in the deeper waters because of scavenging.

Another important body of research focuses on the burial context (Payne 1968, Rodriguez and Bass 1985, Turner and Wiltshire 1999, Wilson et al. 2007, Carter and Tibbett 2008, Sagara et al. 2008, Vass et al. 2008). TSD is more difficult to predict with buried bodies because of the many variables at play. Factors that will affect the rate of decomposition include the nature of the soil, water content, redox potential, pH, and the nature of the body itself (cause of death, clothing, wrapping/coverings, and the depth of the burial; Janaway 1996). The depth of the burial is directly proportional to the decomposition rate; the deeper the burial, the slower the rate of decomposition. The slower rate is a factor of the reduction in free oxygen available for biochemical reactions and the decreased presence of arthropods. However, the naturally occurring microbial community within the soil environment also plays an important role in the decomposition of a buried body (Parkinson et al. 2008). The soil type (e.g., sand versus clay) will directly impact the microbes, which play a vital role in maintaining ecological homeostasis within a particular location. Long-term preservation of the buried skeleton and associated artifacts is related directly to the soil chemistry; more acidic soils (low pH) are less suitable for preservation than soils with a higher pH (Janaway 1996, Carter and Tibbett 2008, Vass et al. 2008, Haslam and Tibbett 2009). See Table 18.9: Associated artifacts and materials preservation to the burial context.

Chapter Summary

- Decomposition of the human body follows a series of events that can be used to determine the postmortem interval (PMI) of a deceased individual.
- The physical breakdown of soft tissues relies on the processes of autolysis and putrefaction.
- Autolysis and putrefaction are responsible for the gross anatomical changes observed during the decomposition process.
- The anatomical changes in a body have been categorized into stages of decomposition: fresh, discoloration, active decomposition, advanced decomposition, and skeletonization.
- Adipocere formation and mummification can result as byproducts of the decomposition process.
- Several categories of factors dictate the rate at which a body will decompose: environmental, individual, and cultural factors.

Table 18.9 Degradation of Textile Fibers

Textile		Susceptibility	Time (Depending on pH)
Wool		Alkaline condition, temperature increase Fungi and bacteria More resistant to moisture	Longer than cotton, <24 months. 5–15 months
Paper		Extremely susceptible	1–5 months
Silk		More resistant to moisture than other natural fibers. Will preserve in anaerobic conditions	Slightly less resistant to decay than wool. <24 months 7–15 months
Cotton		Acids, microorganisms, fungi, and bacteria	Natural cotton will show active decay 60 days in "biologically" active soil and almost complete degradation by 2 years Typical, treated cotton 7–10 months
Linen		More resistant than cotton, affected greatly by microorganisms	<1 year. Not a good fabric for forensic investigations due to instability in preservation
Leather		Modern leather—fairly resistant compared to vegetable-based tanned leathers	Years
Cotton-polyester blends		Vulnerable to decay, but degradation is based on mix	~25 months material displays clear signs of degradation
Synthetic materials		Very resistant to environmental conditions (see Rowe 1997)	Rayon after 4 months shows signs of decay
Nylon	Rayon	Rayon is affected greatly from moisture and acids	Acetate after 3 months shows signs of decay
Polyester	Cellulose acetates	Nylon is very resistant to the effects of water	Nylon—2+ years. Polyester—2+ years
Acrylics		Acrylics resistant to water and chemical decay, but when mixed with other materials resistance is compromised	Acrylics—2+ years

Sources: Janaway, R.C., The decay of buried human remains and their associated materials, in Hunter, J., Roberts, C., and Martin, A. (eds.) *Studies in Crime: An Introduction to Forensic Archaeology*, Batesford, London, U.K., pp. 58–85, 1996; Janaway, R.C., Degradation of clothing and other dress materials associated with buried bodies of both archaeological and forensic interest, in Haglund, W.D. and Sorg, M.H. (eds.) *Advances in Forensic Taphonomy: Method, Theory, and Archaeological Perspectives*, CRC Press, Boca Raton, FL, pp. 279–402, 2002; Janaway, R.C., Decomposition of materials associated with buried cadavers, in Tibbett, M. and Carter, D.O. (eds.) *Soil Analysis in Forensic Taphonomy: Chemical and Biological Effects of Buried Human Remains*, CRC Press, Boca Raton, FL, pp. 153–202, 2008.

- Environmental factors are the most influential factors on the decomposition process, with temperature being the most significant variable.
- Standards have been proposed for decomposition in warm-moist environments, cold climates, and dry-arid environments. Currently, the only data based on actualistic research comes from studies done in warm-moist environments.
- Several methods have been developed to estimate the PMI: entomology, botany, associated materials, biochemistry of tissues, soil chemistry, and observational changes.

- Forensic entomology techniques are based on the life cycle and succession of arthropods attracted to the human body. These methods are most reliable in the early stages of decomposition.
- Botany focuses on the adaption of plant life to the presence of a cadaver in order to determine the PMI.
- Biochemical changes within the body tissues and the leaching of these chemicals into the soil have shown success and demonstrated the potential to enhance PMI estimation accuracy beyond the early stages of decomposition.
- Observational changes in body appearance have been used traditionally by forensic anthropologists for PMI estimation.
- Recent research has statistically linked the observation of a body's appearance with environmental variables to improve the accuracy and reliability of PMI estimates.

Review Questions

1. What are the primary stages of decomposition and how does temperature affect them?
2. Compare and contrast autolysis and putrefaction.
3. Describe the major features associated with soft tissue changes during decomposition.
4. What are the major environmental factors that affect decomposition and explain how each could change the rate of decomposition?
5. What types of cultural factors could potentially alter the decomposition rate of a body?
6. Explain the basis of forensic entomological PMI estimates.
7. Why is it important for continued research investigating statistical techniques for determining the PMI?
8. What PMI estimation methods are available for long-term decomposition events?
9. How is a surface context different than a burial context in relation to decomposition rates?
10. What is adipocere? How is it formed?

Exercises

1. The police provide you with a photo of a decomposing body with little bony exposure in a lightly wooded area in Montana with moderate animal scavenging present on the remains. Can you provide a PMI estimate? Why or why not? If yes, what is the stage of decomposition and the time range associated with this estimate?
2. Human remains were found in southern Virginia in March. The remains were mostly dry, have desiccated soft tissue adhering to the skeleton, and have no associated odor. The police believe these are the remains of an individual that went missing 6 months ago. Can the remains be the missing person based on the condition of the remains? Why or why not?
3. A skull was found within the high grass on the sunny side of a hill in East Tennessee. There was a violet growing through the superior orbital fissure and a small root around the zygomatic arch, which has two rings. Did these remains originate on the sunny hillside? What lines of evidence can be used to estimate the PMI? What would be your PMI estimate?

4. A body was found in a shallow grave in Chattanooga, Tennessee. There was heavy plant growth and root infiltration around the remains. The bones showed evidence of wear with epiphyseal damage, softening of the ribs, and dark staining consistent with the grave soil. The associated clothing was all but destroyed except for nylon shorts. How long could the body have been there?
5. Remains were found in New Mexico with most of the soft tissue present, but mummified. The police believe that the remains are those of a person that went missing three years ago. Is the state of preservation consistent with the time interval? Why or why not?

Suggested Readings and Additional Resources

Warm, Humid Environments

Bass WM. 1984. Time interval since death: A difficult decision. In: Rathbun TA and Buikstra JE, eds. *Human Identification: Case Studies in Forensic Anthropology*. Springfield, IL: CC Thomas, pp. 136–147.

Bass WM. 1997. Outdoor decomposition rates in Tennessee. In: Haglund WD and Sorg MH, eds. *Forensic Taphonomy: The Postmortem Fate of Human Remains*. Boca Raton, FL: CRC Press, pp. 181–186.

Love JC. 2001. Evaluation of decay odor as a time since death indicator. Thesis presented for the Doctorate of Philosophy. The University of Tennessee, Knoxville, TN.

Love JC, Marks MK. 2003. Taphonomy and time: Estimating the postmortem interval. In: Steadman DW, ed. *Hard Evidence: Case Studies in Forensic Anthropology*. Upper Saddle River, NJL: Pearson Education, Inc., pp. 160–175.

Marks MK, Love JC, Dadour IR. 2009. Taphonomy and time: Estimating the postmortem interval. In: Steadman DW, ed. *Hard Evidence: Case Studies in Forensic Anthropology*, 2nd edn. Upper Saddle River, NJ: Prentice Hall, pp. 165–178.

Reed HB. 1958. A study of dog carcass communities in Tennessee, with special references to the insects. *Am Midland Naturalist* 59:213–245.

Srnka CF. 2003. The effects of sun and shade on the early stages of human decomposition Thesis Presented for the Master of Arts Degree. University of Tennessee, Knoxville, TN.

Cold Weather

Bunch AW. 2009. The impact of cold climate on the decomposition process. *J Forensic Identification* 59(1):26–44.

Decker P. 1978. Postmortem bacteriology. *Bull Ayer Clin Lab New Ser* 4(2):2–5.

Dillon LC. 1997. Insect succession on carrion in three biogeoclimatic zones of British Columbia. Master's Thesis. Department of Biological Sciences, Simon Fraser University, Burnaby, British Columbia, Canada.

Komar KA. 1998. Decay rates in a cold climate region: A review of cases involving advanced decomposition from the medical examiner's office in Edmonton, Alberta. *J Forensic Sci* 43:57–61.

Micozzi MS. 1986. Experimental study of postmortem change under field conditions: Effects of freezing, thawing and mechanical injury. *J Forensic Sci* 31:953–961.

Micozzi MS. 1997. Frozen environments and soft tissue preservation. In: Haglund WD and Sorg MH, eds. *Forensic Taphonomy: The Postmortem Fate of Human Remains*. Boca Raton, FL: CRC Press, pp. 171–180.

Terneny TT. 1997. Estimation of time since death in humans using mature pigs. Masters' Thesis. Department of Anthropology, University of Montana, Missoula, MT.

Aqueous Environments

Anderson GS, Hobischak NR. 2004. Decomposition of carrion in the marine environment in British Columbia, Canada. *Int J Legal Med* 118(4):206–209.

Boyle S, Galloway A, Mason RT. 1997. Human aquatic taphonomy in the Monterey Bay area. In: Haglund WD, Sorg MH, eds. *Forensic Taphonomy: The Postmortem Fate of Human Remains.* Boca Raton, FL: CRC Press, pp. 605–613.

Davis JB, Goff ML. 2000. Decomposition patterns in terrestrial and intertidal habitats on Oahu Island and Coconut Island, Hawaii. *J Forensic Sci* 45(4):836–842.

Dix JD. 1987. Missouri's lakes and the disposal of homicide victims. *J Forensic Sci* 32(3):806–809.

Dumser TK, Turkay M. 2008. Postmortem changes of human bodies on the Bathyal Sea floor—Two cases of aircraft accidents above the open sea. *J Forensic Sci* 53(5):1049–1052.

Ebbesmeyer CC, Haglund WD. 1994. Drift trajectories of a floating human body simulated in a hydraulic model of Puget Sound. *J Forensic Sci* 39(1):231–240.

Haglund WD. 1993. Disappearance of soft tissue and the disarticulation of human remains from aqueous environments. *J Forensic Sci* 38:806–815.

Haglund WD, Sorg MH. 2002. Human remains in water environments. In: Haglund WD and Sorg MH, eds. *Advances in Forensic Taphonomy: Method, Theory and Archeological Perspectives.* Boca Raton, FL: CRC Press, pp. 201–218.

O'Brien TG. 1997. Movement of bodies in Lake Ontario. In: Haglund WD, Sorg MH, eds. *Forensic Taphonomy: The Postmortem Fate of Human Remains.* Boca Raton, FL: CRC Press, pp. 559–565.

Payne JA, King EW. 1972. Insect succession and decomposition of pig carcasses in water. *J Georgia Entomol Soc* 73:153–162.

Dry Environments

Galloway A. 1997. The Process of decomposition. A model from the Arizona-Sonoran Desert. In: Haglund WD and Sorg MH, eds. *Forensic Taphonomy: The Postmortem Fate of Human Remains*, Boca Raton, FL: CRC Press, pp. 139–149.

Galloway A, Birkby WH, Jones AM, Henry TE, Parks BO. 1989. Decay rates of human remains in an arid environment. *J Forensic Sci* 34(3):607–616.

Rhine S, Dawson JE. 1998. Estimation of time since death in the southwestern United States. In: Reichs KJ, ed. *Forensic Osteology: Advances in the Identification of Human Remains*, 2nd edn. Springfield, IL: Charles C. Thomas, pp. 145–159.

Biochemistry

Hopkins DW, Wiltshire PEJ, Turner BD. 2000. Microbial characteristics of soils from graves: an investigation at the interface of soil and microbiology and forensic science. *Appl Soil Ecol* 14: 283–288.

Jaggers KA and Rogers TL. 2009. The effects of soil environment on postmortem interval. A macroscopic analysis. *J Forensic Sci* 54(6):1217–1222.

Tibbett M, Carter DO. 2008. *Soil Analysis in Forensic Taphonomy: Chemical and Biological Effects of Buried Human Remains.* Boca Raton, FL: CRC Press.

Tibbett M, Carter DO. 2009. Research in forensic taphonomy: A soil-based perspective. In Ritz K, Dawson L, and Miller D, eds. *Criminal and Environmental Soil Forensics.* New York: Springer.

Vass A, Barshick SA, Sega G, Caton J, Skeen JT, Love JC et al. 2002. Decomposition chemistry of human remains: A new methodology for determining the postmortem interval. *J Forensic Sci* 47(3):542–553.

Adipocere

Kahana T, Almog J, Levy J, Shmeltzer E, Spier Y, Hiss J. 1999. Marine taphonomy: Adipocere formation in a series of bodies recovered from a single shipwreck. *J Forensic Sci* 44(5):897–901.

Lo SJ. 2007. Factors influencing adipocere formation. BA Hons Thesis. Simon Fraser University, Burnaby, British Columbia, Canada.

Mant AK. 1960. *Forensic Medicine: Observation and Interpretation*. Chicago, IL: The Year Book Publishers Inc.

Mellen PFM, Lowry MA, Micozzi MS. 1993. Experimental observations on adipocere formation. *J Forensic Sci* 38:91–93.

O'Brien TG. 1994. Human soft-tissue decomposition in an aquatic environment and its transformation into adipocere. University of Tennessee, Knoxville, TN.

O'Brien TG, Kuehner AC. 2007. Waxing grave about adipocere: Soft tissue change in an aquatic context. *J Forensic Sci* 52(2):294–301.

Recent Research

Damann FE. 2010. Human decomposition ecology at the University of Tennessee Anthropology Research Facility [PhD Dissertation]. University of Tennessee, Knoxville, TN.

Dautartas AM. 2009. The effect of various coverings on the rate of human decomposition. Thesis Presented for the Master of Arts Degree, University of Tennessee, Knoxville, TN.

Ritchie G. 2005. A comparison of human decomposition in an indoor and an outdoor environment. Thesis Presented for the Master of Arts Degree, University of Tennessee, Knoxville, TN.

Sauerwein K. 2012. Estimating the postmortem interval from the pattern of staining on skeletal remains. *Proceedings of the American Academy of Forensic Sciences*, Atlanta, GA, p. 384.

Suckling JK. 2011. A longitudinal study on the outdoor decomposition sequence in Central Texas. American Academy of Forensic Sciences. Chicago, IL, p. 376.

Vass AA, Smith RR, Thompson CV, Burnett MN, Dulgerian N, Eckenrode BA. 2008. Odor analysis of decomposing buried human remains. *J Forensic Sci* 53(2):384–391.

Forensic Entomology

Byrd JH, Castner JL. 2010. *Forensic Entomology: The Utility of Arthropods in Legal Investigations*, 2nd edn. Boca Raton, FL: CRC Press, pp. 251–269.

Goff ML. 1993. Estimation of postmortem interval using arthropod development and successional patterns. *Forensic Sci Rev* 5:81–94.

Rodriguez WC, Bass WM. 1983. Insect activity and its relationship to decay rates of human cadavers in east Tennessee. *J Forensic Sci* 28:423–432.

Schoenly KG, Haskell NH, Hall RD, Gbur JR. 2007. Comparative performance and complementarity of four sampling methods and arthropod preference tests from human and porcine remains at the Forensic Anthropology Center in Knoxville, Tennessee. *J Med Entomol* 44(5):881–894.

Williams RE, Haskell NH. 2009. *Collection of Entomological Evidence at the Death Scene. Entomology and Death: A Procedural Guide*. Clemson, SC: Forensic Entomology Partners, pp. 85–101.

Forensic Botany

Coyle MH. 2005. *Forensic Botany: Principles and Applications to Criminal Casework*. Boca Raton, FL: CRC Press.

Hall DW. 1997. Forensic botany. In: Haglund WD, Sorg MH, eds. *Forensic Taphonomy: The Postmortem Fate of Human Remains*. Boca Raton, FL: CRC Press, pp. 353–362.

Morse D, Duncan J, and Stoutamire J. 1983. *Handbook of Forensic Archaeology and Anthropology*. Tallahassee, FL: Rose Printing.

Rowe WF. 1997. Biodegradation of hairs and fibers. In: Haglund WD and Sorg MH, eds. *Forensic Taphonomy: The Postmortem Fate of Human Remains*. Boca Raton, FL: CRC Press, pp. 337–352.

References

Adlam RE, Simmons T. 2007. The effect of repeated physical disturbance on soft tissue decomposition—Are taphonomic studies an accurate reflection of decomposition? *J Forensic Sci* 52(5):1007–1014.

Agnew LCR, Aviado DM, Brody JI. 1965. *Dorland's Medical Dictionary*, 24th edn. Philadelphia, PA: WB Saunders Co.

Anderson GS. 2001. Insect succession on carrion and its relationship to determining time since death. In: Bryd JH and Castner JL, eds. *Forensic Entomology: The Utility of Arthropods in Legal Investigations*. Boca Raton, FL: CRC Press, pp. 143–175.

Anderson GS. 2010. Decomposition and invertebrate colonization of cadavers in coastal marine environments. In: Amendt J, Goff ML, Campobasso CP, and Grassberger M, eds. *Current Concepts in Forensic Entomology*. London, UK: Springer Press, pp. 223–272.

Anderson GS, VanLaerhoven SL. 1996. Initial studies on insect succession on carrion in southwestern British Columbia. *J Forensic Sci* 41(4):617–625.

Bass WM. 1984. Time interval since death: A difficult decision. In: Rathbun TA and Buikstra JE, eds. *Human Identification: Case Studies in Forensic Anthropology*. Springfield, IL: CC Thomas, pp. 136–147.

Bass WM. 1997. Outdoor decomposition rates in Tennessee. In: Haglund WD and Sorg MH, eds. *Forensic Taphonomy: The Postmortem Fate of Human Remains*, Boca Raton, FL: CRC Press, pp. 181–186.

Boyle S, Galloway A, Mason RT. 1997. Human aquatic taphonomy in the Monterey Bay area. In: Haglund WD and Sorg MH, eds. *Forensic Taphonomy: The Postmortem Fate of Human Remains*, Boca Raton, FL: CRC Press, pp. 605–614.

Behrensmeyer, AK 1978. Taphonomic and ecologic information from bone weathering. *Paleobiology* 4(2):150–162.

Calce SE, Rogers TL. 2007. Taphonomic changes to blunt force trauma: A preliminary study. *J Forensic Sci* 53 (3): 519–527.

Campobasso C, Di Vella G, Introna F. 2001. Factors affecting decomposition and diptera colonization. *Forensic Sci Int* 120:18–27.

Carter DO, Tibbett M. 2003.Taphonomic mycota: Fungi with forensic potential. *J Forensic Sci* 48:1–4.

Carter DO, Tibbett M. 2006. Microbial decomposition of skeletal muscle tissue (*Ovis aries*) in a sandy loam soil at different temperatures. *Soil Biol Biochem* 38:1139–1145.

Carter DO, Tibbett M. 2008. Cadaver decomposition and soil: Processes. In: Tibbett M and Carter DO, eds. *Soil Analysis in Forensic Taphonomy: Chemical and Biological Effects of Buried Human Remains*. Boca Raton, FL: CRC Press, pp. 29–52.

Carter DO, Yellowlees D, Tibbett M. 2007. Cadaver decomposition in terrestrial ecosystems. *Naturwissenschaften* 94:12–24.

Carter DO, Yellowlees D, Tibbett M. 2008a. Temperature affects microbial decomposition of cadavers (*Rattus rattus*) in contrasting soils. *Appl Soil Ecol* 40:129–137.

Carter DO, Yellowlees D, Tibbett M. 2008b. Using ninhydrin to detect grave soil. *J Forensic Sci* 53(2):397–400.

Clark MA, Worrell MB, Pless JE. 1997. Post-mortem changes in soft tissue. In: Haglund WD and Sorg MH, eds. *Forensic Taphonomy: The Postmortem Fate of Human Remains*, Boca Raton, FL: CRC Press, pp. 151–164.

Cotton GE, Aufderheide AC, Goldschmidt VG. 1987. Preservation of human tissue immersed for five years in fresh water of known temperature. *J Forensic Sci* 32(4):1125–1130.

Coyle HM, Lee C, Lin W, Lee HC, Palmbach TM. 2005. Forensic botany: Using plant evidence to aid in forensic death investigation. *Croat Med J* 46(4):606–612.

Dautartas AM. 2009. The effect of various coverings on the rate of human decomposition. M.A. Thesis, University of Tennessee, Knoxville, TN.

DiMaio VJM, Dana SE. 2006. *Handbook of Forensic Pathology*. Boca Raton, FL: CRC Press.

Dudzik B, Parsons HR, McKeown AH. 2011. Using the freeze-thaw cycle to determine the postmortem interval: An assessment of pig decomposition in west central Montana. In: *Proceedings from the American Academy of Forensic Sciences Meeting*, Chicago, IL, p. 375.

Evans WE. 1962 Adipocere formation in a relatively dry environment. *J Med Sci Law* 3:145–153.

Forbes SL, Dent BB, Stuart BH. 2005a. The effect of soil type on adipocere formation. *Forensic Sci Int* 154:35–43.

Forbes SL, Stuart BH, Dent BB. 2005b. The effect of burial environment of adipocere formation. *Forensic Sci Int* 154:24–34.

Forbes SL, Stuart BH, Dent BB. 2005c. The effect of the burial method on adipocere formation. *Forensic Sci Int* 154:44–52.

Galloway A. 1997. The process of decomposition. A model from the Arizona-Sonoran Desert. In: Haglund WD and Sorg MH, eds. *Forensic Taphonomy: The Postmortem Fate of Human Remains*. Boca Raton, FL: CRC Press, pp. 139–149.

Galloway A, Birkby WH, Jones AM, Henry TE, Parks BO. 1989. Decay rates of human remains in an arid environment. *J Forensic Sci* 34(3): 607–616.

Gill-King H. 1997. Chemical and ultrastructural aspects of decomposition. In: Haglund WD and Sorg MH, eds. *Forensic Taphonomy: The Postmortem Fate of Human Remains*, Boca Raton, FL: CRC Press, pp. 93–108.

Goff ML. 1993. Estimation of postmortem interval using arthropod development and successional patterns. *Forensic Sci Rev* 5: 81–94.

Goff ML. 2010. Early postmortem changes and stages of decomposition. In: Amendt J, Goff ML, Campobasso CP, and Grassberger M, eds. *Current Concepts in Forensic Entomology*. London, UK: Springer Press, pp. 1–24.

Haglund WD. 1993. Disappearance of soft tissue and disarticulation of human remains of aqueous environments. *J Forensic Sci* 38(4):806–815.

Haglund WD. 1997a. Dogs and coyotes: Postmortem involvement with human remains. In: Haglund WD and Sorg MH, eds. *Forensic Taphonomy: The Postmortem Fate of Human Remains*, Boca Raton, FL: CRC Press, pp. 367–382.

Haglung WD. 1997b. Rodents and human remains. In: Haglund WD and Sorg MH, eds. *Forensic Taphonomy: The Postmortem Fate of Human Remains*, Boca Raton, FL: CRC Press, pp. 405–414.

Hall DW. 1997. Forensic botany. In: Haglund WD and Sorg MH, eds. *Forensic Taphonomy: The Postmortem Fate of Human Remains*, Boca Raton, FL: CRC Press, pp. 353–363.

Hart AJ, Whittaker AP. 2006. Forensic entomology: Insect activity and its roles in the decomposition of human cadavers. *Antenna* 30(4):159–164.

Haskell NH, Hall RD, Cervenka VJ, Clark MA. 1997. On the body: Insects' life stage presence, their postmortem artifacts. In: Haglund WD and Sorg MH, eds. *Forensic Taphonomy: The Postmortem Fate of Human Remains*, Boca Raton, FL: CRC Press, pp. 353–363.

Haskell NH, McShaffrey DG, Hawley DA, Williams RE, Pless JE. 1989. Use of aquatic insects in determining submersion interval. *J Forensic Sci* 34(3):622–632.

Haslam TCF, Tibbett M. 2009. Soils of contrasting pH affect the decomposition of buried mammalian (*Ovis aries*) skeletal muscle tissue. *J Forensic Sci* 54(4):900–904.

Henssge C, Knight B, Krompecher T, Madea B, Nokes L. 1995. *The Estimation of Time since Death in Early Postmortem Period*. Boston, MA: Arnold.

Henssge C, Madea B. 2007. Estimation of the time since death. *Forensic SciInt* 165(2–3): 182–184.

Higley LG, Haskell NH. 2001. Insect development and forensic entomology. In: Bryd JJ and Castner JL, eds. *Forensic Entomology: The Utility of Arthropods in Legal Investigations*. Boca Raton, FL: CRC Press, pp. 287–302.

Hobischak NR, Anderson GS. 2002. Time of submergence using aquatic invertebrate succession and decompositional changes. *J Forensic Sci* 47(1):142–151.

Hutchins GM. 1985. Body temperature is elevated in the early postmortem period. *Hum Pathol* 16(6):560–561.

Janaway RC. 1996. The decay of buried human remains and their associated materials. In: Hunter J, Roberts C, and Martin A, eds. *Studies in Crime: An Introduction to Forensic Archaeology*. London, UK: Batesford, pp. 58–85.

Janaway RC. 2002. Degradation of clothing and other dress materials associated with buried bodies of both archaeological and forensic interest. In: Haglund WD and Sorg MH, eds. *Advances in Forensic Taphonomy: Method, Theory, and Archaeological Perspectives*. Boca Raton, FL: CRC Press, pp. 279–402.

Janaway RC. 2008. Decomposition of materials associated with buried cadavers. In: Tibbett M and Carter DO, eds. *Soil Analysis in Forensic Taphonomy: Chemical and Biological Effects of Buried Human Remains*. Boca Raton, FL: CRC Press, pp. 153–202.

Kaliszan M, Hauser R, Kernbach-Wighton G. 2009. Estimation of the time of death based on the assessment of postmortem processes with emphasis on body cooling. *Leg Med (Tokyo)* 11(3):111–117.

Klippel WE, Hamilton MD, Synstelien JA. 2005. Raccoon (*Procyon lotor*) foraging as a taphonomic agent of soft tissue modification and scene alteration. In: *Proceedings of the American Academy of Forensic Sciences*, New Orleans, LA, vol. 11, p. 333.

Klippel WE, Synstelien JA. 2007. Rodents as taphonomic agents: Bone gnawing by brown rats and gray squirrels. *J Forensic Sci* 52(4):765–773.

Knight, B. 1988. The evolution of methods for estimating the time of death from body temperature. *Forensic Sci Int* 36:47.

Komar DA. 1998. Decay rates in a cold climate region: A review of cases involving advanced decomposition from the medical examiner's office in Edmonton, Alberta. *J Forensic Sci* 43:57–61.

Kulshrestha P, Chandra H. 1987. Time since death: An entomological study on corpses. *Am J Forensic Med Pathol*, 8(3): 233–238.

MacDonnel N, Anderson G. 1997. Aquatic forensics: Determination of the time since submergence using aquatic invertebrates. Technical Report: Canadian Police Research Center, Ottawa, Ontario, Canada.

Mann RW, Bass WM, Meadows L. 1990. Time since death and decomposition of the human body: Variables and observations in cause and experimental field studies. *J Forensic Sci* 35(1):103–111.

Mant AK. 1953. Recent work on post-mortem changes and timing death. In: Simpson K, ed. *Modern Trends in Forensic Medicine*. London, UK: Butterworth and Co., pp. 147–162.

Mant KA, Furbank R. 1957. Adipocere—A review. *J Forensic Med* 4:18–35.

Marks MK, Love JC, Dadour IR. 2009. Taphonomy and time: Estimating the postmortem interval. In: Steadman DW, ed. *Hard Evidence: Case Studies in Forensic Anthropology*, 2nd edn. Upper Saddle River, NJ: Prentice Hall, pp. 165–178.

Marks MK, Love JC, Elkins SK. 2000. Time since death: A practical guide to physical postmortem events. In: *Proceedings of the American Academy of Forensic Sciences*, Reno, NV, pp. 181–182.

McKeown AH, Kemp WL, Dudzik B, Parsons HR. 2011. Scavenging and its relationship to decomposition in the Northern Rockies. In: *Proceedings from the American Academy of Forensic Sciences*, Chicago, IL, p. 387.

Megyesi MS, Nawrocki SP, Haskell NH. 2005. Using accumulated degree days to estimate the postmortem interval from decomposed human remains. *J Forensic Sci* 50(3):618–626.

Micozzi MS. 1986. Experimental study of postmortem change under field conditions: Effects of freezing, thawing, and mechanical injury. *J Forensic Sci* 31(3):953–961.

Micozzi MS. 1991. *Postmortem Change in Human and Animal Remains: A Systematic Approach.* Springfield, IL: Charles C. Thomas.

Micozzi MS. 1997. Frozen environments and soft tissue preservation. In: Haglund WD and Sorg MH, eds. *Forensic Taphonomy: The Postmortem Fate of Human Remains*, Boca Raton, FL: CRC Press, pp. 171–180.

Neher DA, Barbercheck ME, El-Allaf SM, Anas O. 2003. Effects of disturbance and ecosystem on decomposition. *Appl Soil Ecol* 23:165–179.

O'Brien TG. 1997. Movement of bodies in Lake Ontario. In: Haglund WD and Sorg MH, eds. *Forensic Taphonomy: The Postmortem Fate of Human Remains.* Boca Raton, FL: CRC Press, pp. 559–566.

Parkinson RA, Dias KA, Horswell J, Greenwood P, Banning N, Tibbett M, Vass AA. 2009. Microbial Community Analysis of Human Decomposition in Soil. In: Ritz K, Dawson L, Miller D, eds. *Criminal and Environmental Soil Forensics.* New York: Springer. pp. 379–394.

Parmenter RR, MacMahon JA. 2009. Carrion decomposition and nutrient cycling in a semiarid shrub–steppe ecosystem. *Ecol Monogr* 79(4):637–661.

Parsons HR. 2009. The postmortem interval: A systematic study of pig decomposition in west central Montana. MA Thesis. The University of Montana, Missoula, MT.

Payne JA. 1965. A summer carrion study of the body pig *Sus scrofa* Linnaeus. *Ecology* 46(5):592–602.

Payne JA, King EW. 1972. Insect succession and decomposition of pig carcasses in water. *J Georgia Entomol Soc* 7(3):153–162.

Payne JA, King EW, Beinhart G. 1968. Arthropod succession and decomposition of buried pigs. *Nature* 219:1180–1181.

Reed HB. 1958. A study of dog carcass communities in Tennessee with special reference to the insects. *Am Midl Nat* 34(3): 213–245.

Reeves N. 2009. Taphonomic effects of vulture scavenging. *J Forensic Sci* 54(3):523–528.

Rhine S, Dawson JE. 1998. Estimation of time since death in the southwestern United States. In: Reichs KJ, ed. *Forensic Osteology: Advances in the Identification of Human Remains*, 2nd edn. Springfield, IL: Charles C. Thomas, pp. 145–159.

Ritchie GT. 2005. A comparison of human decomposition in an indoor and an outdoor environment. MA Thesis. The University of Tennessee, Knoxville, TN.

Rodriguez WC, Bass WM. 1983. Insect activity and its relationship to decay rates of human cadavers in east Tennessee. *J Forensic Sci* 28(2):423–432.

Rodriguez WC, Bass WM. 1985. Decomposition of buried bodies and methods that may aid in their location. *J Forensic Sci* 30(3):836–852.

Sagara N. 1995. Association of ectomycorrhizal fungi with decomposed animal wastes in forest habitats: A cleaning symbiosis? *Can J Bot* 73(Suppl. 1):S1423–S1433.

Sagara N, Yamanaka T, Tibbett M. 2008. Soil fungi associated with graves and latrines: Towards a forensic mycology. In: Tibbett M and Carter DO, eds. *Soil Analysis in Forensic Taphonomy: Chemical and Biological Effects of Buried Human Remains.* Boca Raton, FL: CRC Press, pp. 67–108.

Schoenly KG, Haskell NH, Hall RD, Gbur JR. 2007. Comparative performance and complementarity of four sampling methods and arthropod preference tests from human and porcine remains at the Forensic Anthropology Center in Knoxville, Tennessee. *J Med Entomol* 44(5):881–894.

Seet BL. 2005. Estimating the postmortem interval in freshwater environments. MA Thesis. The University of Tennessee, Knoxville, TN.

Shattuck JK. 2009. An analysis of decomposition rates on outdoor surface variations in central Texas. MA Thesis. Texas State University, San Marcos, TX.

Shean BS, Messinger L, Papworth M. 1993. Observations of differential decomposition on sun exposed v. shaded pig carrion in coastal Washington State. *J Forensic Sci* 38(4):938–949.

Simmons T, Adlam RE, Moffatt C. 2010. Debugging decomposition data-comparative taphonomy studies and the influence of insects and carcass size on decomposition rate. *J Forensic Sci* 55(1):8–13.

Simpson K, Knight B. 1985. *Forensic Medicine*, 9th edn. London, UK: Edward Arnold.

Sledzik PS. 1998. Forensic Taphonomy: Postmortem decomposition and decay. In Reichs KJ, ed. *Forensic Osteology: Advances in the Identification of Human Remains*, 2nd ed, Springfield, IL: Charles C. Thomas. pp. 109–119.

Smith KGV.1986. A manual of forensic entomology. British Museum, London.

Sorg MH, Dearborn JH, Monahan, EI, Ryan HF, Sweeney KG, David E. 1997. Forensic taphonomy in marine contexts. In: Haglund WD and Sorg MH, eds. *Forensic Taphonomy: The Postmortem Fate of Human Remains*, Boca Raton, FL: CRC Press, pp. 567–604.

Spicka A, Bushing J, Johnson R, Higley LG, and Carter DO. 2008. Cadaver mass and decomposition: How long does it take for a cadaver to increase the concentration of ninhydrin-reactive nitrogen in soil? In: *Proceedings of the American Academy of Forensic Sciences*, vol. 14, p. 178.

Spitz WU. 2006. *Spitz and Fisher's Medicolegal Investigation of Death: Guidelines for the Application of Pathology to Crime Investigation*, 4th edn. Springfield, IL: Charles C. Thomas Press.

Srnka CF. 2003. The effects of sun and shade on the early stages of decomposition. MA Thesis. The University of Tennessee, Knoxville, TN.

Stokes KL, Forbes SL, Tibbett M. 2009. Does freezing skeletal muscle tissue affect its decomposition in soil? *Forensic Sci Int* 183:6–13.

Swift B. 2010. Methods of time since death estimation within the early post-mortem interval. *J Homicide Major Incident Invest*, National Policing Improvement Agency 6(1):97–112.

Synstelien JA. 2009. Raccoon (*Procyon lotor*) soft tissue modification of human remains. In: *Proceedings of the American Academy of Forensic Sciences*, vol. 15, p. 359.

Tabor Kreitlow KL. 2010. Insect succession in a natural environment. In: Bryd JH and Castner JL, eds. *Forensic Entomology: The Utility of Arthropods in Legal Investigations*, 2nd edn. Boca Raton, FL: CRC Press, pp. 251–269.

Tibbett M, Carter DO. 2008. *Soil Analysis in Forensic Taphonomy: Chemical and Biological Effects of Buried Human Remains*. Boca Raton, FL: CRC Press.

Tibbett M, Carter DO, Haslam T, Major R, Haslam R. 2004. A laboratory incubation method for determining the rate of microbiological degradation of skeletal muscle tissue in soil. *J Forensic Sci* 49:560–565.

Turner B, Wiltshire P. 1999. Experimental validation of forensic evidence: A study of the decomposition of buried pigs in a heavy clay soil. *Forensic Sci Int* 101:113–122.

Ubelaker D. 1997. Taphonomic applications in forensic anthropology. In: Haglund WD and Sorg MH, eds. *Forensic Taphonomy: The Postmortem Fate of Human Remains*, Boca Raton, FL: CRC Press, pp. 77–92.

Vass AA. 2011. The elusive universal postmortem interval formulae. *Forensic Sci Int* 204(1):34–40.

Vass A, Barshick SA, Sega G, Caton J, Skeen JT, Love JC. 2002. Decomposition chemistry of human remains: A new methodology for determining the postmortem interval. *J Forensic Sci* 47(3):542–553.

Vass AA, Bass WM, Wolt JD, Foss JE, and Ammons JT. 1992. Time since death determinations of human cadavers using soil solution. *J Forensic Sci* 37:1236–1253.

Vass AA, Smith RR, Thompson CV, Burnett MN, Dulgerian N, Eckenrode BA. 2008. Odor analysis of decomposing buried human remains. *J Forensic Sci* 53(2):384–391.

Willey P, Heilman A. 1987. Estimating the time since death using plant roots and stems. *J Forensic Sci* 32:1264–1270.

Wilson AS, Janaway RC, Holland AD, Dodson ID, Baran E, Pollard AM et al. 2007. Modeling the buried human body environment in upland climes using three contrasting field sites. *Forensic Sci Int* 169:6–18.

Taphonomic Processes
Analysis of Fragmentary Skeletal Remains

19

MARIATERESA A. TERSIGNI-TARRANT

Contents

The frequency of fragmentary human skeletal casework in forensic medicine has increased in recent years. Depending upon fragment size and location within the skeleton, bone fragmentation challenges the quintessential task of discerning the elements of the biological profile (age, sex, ancestry, and stature), as the morphological traits routinely examined to make these estimations are often missing or not discernible. Most of the techniques that help to estimate the biological profile require nearly complete if not entire bones of the skeleton. Thus, fragmentary remains prove difficult to identify as human, let alone to discern biological age, sex, ancestry, and stature from those fragments. This chapter reviews information regarding how the microstructural morphology (the signatures of the bone growth and development processes discussed in detail in Chapter 4) can aid in distinguishing human from nonhuman, as well as provide further information about the remains in question.

Bone Modeling and Remodeling

Before we can identify how bone microstructure is used to make a determination regarding whether material is osseous in nature or if it is human in origin, it is important that we review a few of the key processes of human bone formation and maintenance in more detail. Formation and maintenance of bone occurs by the processes of modeling and remodeling during growth and development. Modeling is the term used to describe the shaping of bones by osteoblasts and osteoclasts working on different areas of the bone. In modeling, osteoblasts and osteoclasts work independently to change bone size and shape (for a detailed discussion of bone cells and the processes of endochondral and intramembranous bone formation, refer to Chapter 4). This process occurs at a fairly rapid rate until skeletal maturity, when the rate decreases significantly. Modeling is necessary because longitudinal growth alone will not produce a bone of the correct size and shape. Modeling can be either resorptive or formative, that is, it can remove bone in a particular area or add bone to a particular region. For example, modeling at the metaphyses reduces the bone diameter in order to create a diaphysis. This occurs when osteoclasts work on the periosteal surface of the metaphysis to trim the shaft down to the appropriate size. Modeling can also occur at the diaphysis to increase diameter of the bone or change the curvature of the bone. Long bone shafts increase in diameter by osteoblasts slowly adding bone to the periosteal surface while osteoclasts remove bone on the endosteal surface.

Modeling also occurs on the flat bones of the skeleton, though modeling in flat bones is a much more detailed process. For example, to increase the size of the cranial vault, as occurs during the subadult stages of cranial vault growth, bone cannot just be laid down at the area of the sutures as this does not allow alteration of the shape of the vault bones to accommodate the growing brain. Instead, the inner surface of the vault bones must first be resorbed by osteoclasts while on the outer surface, osteoblastic activity builds bone in the appropriate manner to account for change in size and shape.

The remodeling process can occur in both long bones and flat bones in response to stressors such as tension, applied load, hormonal changes, and the amount of activity or inactivity that a bone undergoes (Bergman et al., 1996; Eroschenko, 1993). Remodeling occurs throughout life, although the rate is significantly reduced after growth ceases. In remodeling, there is no change in size or shape of the bone, as remodeling involves simply maintenance of the current structure. Remodeling systematically removes older bone and replaces it with newly formed bone. This eliminates damage to old bone and prevents fatigue fractures that can occur in old bone as a result of mechanical stress. Remodeling is not a continuous process, instead it is episodic, with each episode having a definite beginning and ending. Remodeling determines the structure of most of the skeletal tissues, as well as their mechanical properties and resistance to fatigue or failure. Remodeling is the process during which bone repair occurs at a particular site via BMUs (basic multicellular unit). BMUs are comprised of both osteoblasts and osteoclasts working together.

Harold Frost (1969) first coined the term BMU and was one of the first to describe the work of osteoclasts and osteoblasts as a combined effort, rather than independently resorbing and laying down bone as seen in the modeling process. The BMU consists of about 10 osteocytes and several hundred osteoblasts. Frost (1969) indicates that the BMUs operate on multiple bone surfaces including the periosteal, endosteal and trabecular surfaces, as well as within the cortical bone itself. Each BMU has three stages of activity: activation, resorption, and formation. During activation, chemical and/or mechanical signals cause the fusion of monocytes to form osteoclasts. The resorption process is the stage during which osteoclasts resorb (i.e., remove) particular areas of bone. Once osteoclasts have removed a certain amount of bone, the formation stage begins with the differentiation of mesenchymal cells into osteoblasts over the next few days. The newly formed osteoblasts begin replacing the resorbed bone. The process of formation is much slower than resorption. An osteoclast can resorb tens of micrometers per day, while an osteoblast can only form 1 μm of bone per day. As a result, the resorption process takes about 3 weeks, while the formation process in the same area takes about 3 months. The BMUs tunnel longitudinally through compact bone, creating a secondary osteon. The tunnel cannot be completely filled in by osteoblasts because the blood supply needs to be maintained throughout the bone; thus, the osteoblasts leave a new Haversian canal that houses both a return vessel and a supply vessel. On average, BMUs replace 5% of bone per year in adults. Trabecular bone is remodeled in the same way as cortical bone, but the BMUs work on each of the trabeculae by scooping bone out and then refilling it, much like the digging of a trench.

The deposition and resorption of bone is a constant process regulated by a number of systems within the body revolving around the level of calcium in the blood. Since the majority of the body's calcium is stored within the skeleton, there is very little free calcium in the blood itself. The calcium in the blood aids in intercellular communication, muscle contraction, and nerve cell activity. Even slight changes in blood calcium levels of the body could cause a disruption in any or all of these functions. Therefore, if blood calcium levels are high, hormones are released that stimulate osteoblasts to lay down bone and inhibit osteoclast activity. When the blood calcium levels are low, osteoclast activity is stimulated and osteoblast activity is inhibited (Schinke and Karsenty, 2002).

This constant resorption and laying down of bone leads to a distinct microscopic signature (see Table 19.1 for an overview of the typical osteon life cycle). When looking at a section of dry human bone, one can recognize Haversian systems (osteons) as concentric circles surrounding an inner Haversian canal which would have held a blood vessel or neurovascular bundle during life. Within some sections, especially those from older individuals, it is quite common to see a newer (younger) Haversian system on top of an older Haversian system. The newer Haversian system is termed a *secondary osteon.* A clear reversal (cement) line distinguishes where the bone resorption ended and the bone building began (Figure 19.1). As the process of remodeling occurs throughout life, the number of secondary osteons tends to increase with age. As secondary osteons are laid down over older primary osteons, the number of fragmentary primary osteons also increases (Figure 19.2) (Bergman et al., 1996; Stout, 1992).

Table 19.1 Six Stages of an Osteon's Life Cycle

1. Activation

   Differentiated cells are collected from a precursor cell population and are moved to the area in which the new osteon is to be formed.

2. Resorption

   Osteoclasts resorb bone by moving longitudinally through the bone at a rate of 40 μm/day. The BMU has a diameter of 200 μm and a resorption area of a few hundred micrometers long.

3. Reversal

   Transition from osteoclast activity to osteoblast activity takes several days, and the reversal area is the lag space between the resorptive and refilling regions. The reversal line will eventually form the cement line. This process takes about 30 days.

4. Formation

   Osteoblasts appear at the periphery of the newly formed tunnel. They close approximately 1–2 μm per day. They leave a central passage (Haversian canal) for blood vessels to maintain the BMU, bone matrix, and to carry calcium and phosphorus back and forth. This phase takes 3 months.

5. Mineralization

   In this phase the osteoid is mineralized. There is a lag time of 10 days between the deposition of osteoid and the mineralization. Thus, there is an osteoid front between the osteoblasts and the mineralized bone. Primary mineralization occurs within the first few days after mineralization starts. Secondary mineralization occurs as more minerals are added over the next several months.

6. Quiescence

   After the BMUs have completed their process of remodeling, the osteoclasts disappear and the osteoblasts become osteocytes and maintain the bone.

Source: After Springer Science+Business Media: *Skeletal Tissue Mechanics*, 1998, Martin, R.B., Burr, D.B., and Sharkey, N.A., London, U.K.

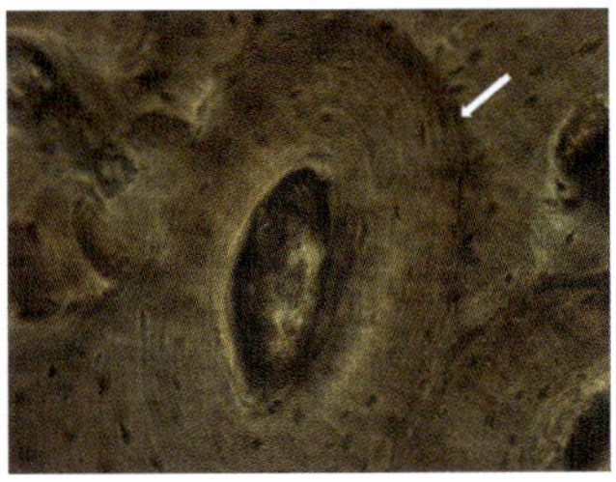

Figure 19.1 Cement (reversal) line. Digital image (200×) of a cement line around an osteon (arrow) in the femur midshaft demarcating the area in which the osteoclasts completed breaking down the bone and where osteoblasts began rebuilding the bone.

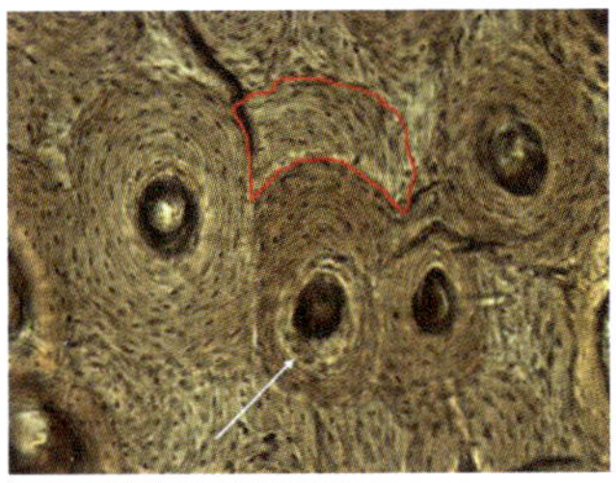

Figure 19.2 Fragmentary osteon associated with secondary osteons. A digital image (200×) of an osteon fragment (outlined) associated with an intact secondary osteon (arrow).

Determination of Human or Nonhuman Using Histomorphology

The increased need for species identification of fragmentary remains, as well as recent improvements in microscopic techniques, has led to advances in the forensic application of bone histological research. Using thin sections of cortical bone, the histological structure of bone can aid in the determination of whether fragments are *human* or *nonhuman*. In 1956, researchers were diagnosing bone at the genus and species level based upon bone histomorphology, that is, differentiation between reptile, mammal, and fish (see Enlow et al., 1956a–c). Within the class Mammalia, the histomorphological structure, or microscopic signature, can be quite similar among genera. For example, sheep and goats have similar plexiform or parallel layered bone. However, some mammals do have distinct histomorphology; humans, for example, are one of the only species within Mammalia to have full Haversian (osteonal) bone from the periosteal (outer) to the endosteal (inner) surface, that is, the full thickness of the cortical layer. Many dogs can have osteonal bone in the center of the cortical layer while still maintaining plexiform bone near the endosteal and periosteal regions. Chimpanzees also have full Haversian bone, although the osteon size and arrangement is quite distinct from human.

When examining fragmentary remains, it can be relatively simple to recognize nonhuman from human if the section contains plexiform organization (Figure 19.3). This morphology directly contrasts with the circular Haversian systems that are the hallmark of human histological pattern. Plexiform bone is not found in developing or mature human bone. Although plexiform is diagnostic of nonhuman bone, the presence of Haversian bone does not necessarily indicate that the bone is of human origin (Figure 19.4). Canines, mature bovids, *Pan* (chimpanzee and bonobos), and several

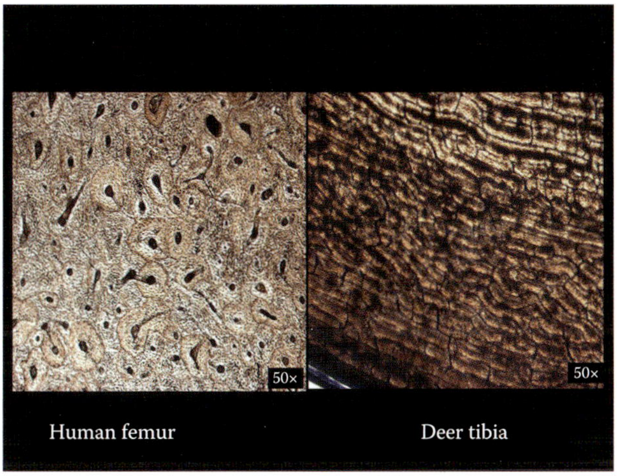

Figure 19.3 Human Haversian bone compared to deer plexiform bone.

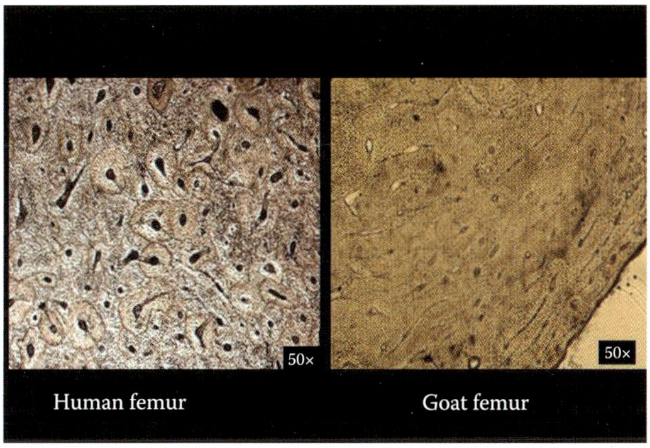

Figure 19.4 Human Haversian bone compared to nonhuman Haversian bone.

other larger mammals develop some cortical Haversian bone, although the osteonal arrangement differs from the arrangement in humans when viewed at 100× magnification. In nonhuman mammals that possess Haversian bone, osteons tend to be arranged in bands with four to six osteons arranged linearly (Mulhern and Ubelaker, 2001). As this phenomenon does not occur in human Haversian bone, it can often allow for species identification. Although several methods suggest that species differentiation can be achieved in cases of full osteonal bone based upon osteon diameter, osteon area, Haversian canal diameter, or Haversian canal area (see Cattaneo et al., 2009; Hillier and Bell, 2007; Martiniaková et al., 2006; Tersigni-Tarrant et al., 2011), much large sample sizes and more validation studies need to be undertaken before these can be incorporated into the tested methodology category. Based on current best practice methodology, if osteonal bone is present, we can go no further than to say this bone is consistent with human bone, as it has circular osteons; however, we cannot rule out nonhuman remains. (see Box 19.1 for a discussion of suggested best practices for the determination of human or nonhuman remains using microscopic analysis.)

BOX 19.1 SWGANTH GUIDELINES FOR THE DETERMINATION OF HUMAN OR NONHUMAN REMAINS

The process of fragmentary remains identification has become such a concern in recent years that the SWGANTH has dedicated a portion of their "Guidelines for the Determination of Medicolegal Significance" to this topic (www.swganth.org, 2010). The purpose of this document is to provide guidance as to the best practices for distinguishing bone from nonbone, human bone from nonhuman bone, and, finally, the determination of whether remains are of medicolegal significance. These guidelines for best practices include suggestions as to when it is appropriate to use microscopic techniques for the analysis of human remains and provide a framework for the discussion of the results of such analyses in terms that can be universally understood.

Bone versus Nonbone

According to the SWGANTH guidelines, microscopic analysis is warranted in the process of determining whether material is bone or not bone. In such cases, the analyses would attempt to identify cellular structures consistent with bone. The terminology used to report the findings of such an analysis are stated as "Consistent with Osseous/Dental Material," "Inconsistent with Osseous/Dental Material," or "Inconclusive." This codified terminology aids the analyst by providing universal terminology by which to account for the microscopic findings for a bone or nonbone analysis.

Human versus Nonhuman

The SWGANTH guidelines suggest that in the cases of fragmentary remains, microscopic analysis is an appropriate analytic tool for the determination of human or nonhuman osseous remains. The guidelines suggest looking for micromorphological patterns of plexiform bone or patterned osteons within the microscopic slides to aid in this determination, though they advise extreme caution, as the micromorphology that is consistent with human remains can also be found in some large animals. The terminology they have chosen for this type of analysis reflects this conservative approach by using "diagnostic of human," "diagnostic of nonhuman," and "inconclusive."

Unacceptable Practices

The SWGANTH guidelines are resolute in their discussion of histological techniques and other specialized techniques as being an important part of the practice of forensic anthropology. However, they strongly caution against the use of these techniques without the proper specialized training. It is imperative, then, that practitioners familiarize themselves with these techniques, through one-on-one tutorial with an expert in the method or through continuing education courses and practice performing them prior to implementing them in medicolegal casework. Alternatively, practitioners who do not feel comfortable with these techniques are encouraged to seek the aid of those who are well-versed in each method.

Demographic Uses of Bone Histology

Once the determination is made that a fragment is of human origin, additional information can be gleaned from the histomorphology that can aid in the development of the biological profile, specifically age and other demographic information. Historically, there have been numerous attempts to use bone microstructure to age individuals (see Robling and Stout, 2000). While it is by no means a highly accurate technique, histological aging methods provide a way to age individuals when no other macroscopic means to estimate age at death are feasible. These methods can also serve as an additional way to corroborate macroscopic age estimations developed from other bones of the skeleton.

There are many techniques to estimate age based upon the bone microstructure, and each is not without its problems or critics. It is difficult to learn to age remains in this fashion and is even more difficult to master any one technique. In fact, many of the techniques use specific terminology or quantification methods that may or may not be used by other histological aging techniques, often making the methodology confusing. Following is a discussion of a few key aging techniques in the literature with a critique of the usefulness and practicality of each.

In 1965, Ellis Kerley pioneered the use of histomorphometry as an age at death estimator. Using transverse sections from the midshaft of the femur, tibia, and fibula, Kerley quantified the number of osteons, number of fragmented old osteons, percent of circumferential lamellar bone (primary bone), and number of non-Haversian canals within each section at four fields situated at the anterior, posterior, medial, and lateral portions of the section. For each thin section, the quantities identified in each of the regions were summed across the four regions. Kerley's results indicate that 87.3% were within 5 years of their actual chronological age and that all of his specimens were within 10 years of their actual age. There are problems with this technique, including the fact that this method cannot be used if there are no pelvic limb bones or if the remains are fragmentary, as a complete transverse section from the midshaft is necessary to use the method. Additionally, the definitions of the microstructures are imperative since Kerley defines intact osteons as being be 80% complete without remodeling evidence. This is different than the definition later suggested by Stout (1992). Another methodological issue is that the original article did not address field size, which is important because structures are counted even if they are only partially present in the field. Kerley and Ubelaker (1978) tried to standardize this shortcoming of Kerley (1965) with an estimation of the original field size as 2.06 mm^2 and added a correction factor for field size in case the field size differed from this value. Stout and Gehlert (1982) suggest that in using this method one should use field size as close to 2.06 mm^2 since the structures are not randomly distributed throughout the section and may skew results.

In 1969, Ahlqvist and Damsten published a modification to the Kerley method to simplify the method, as well as avoid the linea aspera. The linea aspera may skew results given the bony variation due to muscle attachment sites and mechanical stress at this site. To avoid the linea aspera, these researchers used quadrants equidistant between the Kerley quadrants. They also employed a counting reticle at the level of the section that consisted of a 100 square grid to more precisely estimate the percentage of the grid that was covered by Haversian bone, and then they averaged counts across the four fields or quadrants. The problems with this technique include the fact that their study only looked at the femur and, as with the original Kerley method, requires a complete transverse section. Furthermore,

Stout and Stanley (1992) suggested that the percentage of Haversian bone has a nonsignificant relationship with age but that osteon counts have a significant relationship with age. This would indicate that this characteristic should not be used, or at least not alone as it is in this study. Stout and Gehlert (1982) compared the two methods and determined that Kerley's original method was better at age determination than the Ahlqvist and Damsten (1969) method.

In 1992, Stout and Paine published a method of age determination based on the middle third of the sixth rib and the clavicle midshaft. These bones were used for a number of reasons, including the fact that anthropologists do not generally like to section long bones, but ribs are not needed intact for any osteological measurements and other long-bone measurements tend to be favored over clavicle measurements. Additionally, the sternal rib end aging technique is not affected since the section is taken within the rib shaft. Furthermore, ribs and clavicles are easy to extract at autopsy for the purpose of study. This technique can also be used on a fragmentary skeleton. From the two sections, the number of intact and fragmentary osteons per unit area was identified using a counting reticle. They define intact osteons as 90% complete while everything else is considered a fragment. Stout and Paine (1992) suggest that at least two sections of each bone should be used in order to minimize sampling error that can exist even in serial sections (Frost, 1969). The total osteon density is then determined by summing the number intact and fragmentary osteons and then putting the figures into a regression equation. This technique seems to have minimal methodological and practical problems other than the fact that it only works on clavicle and rib and requires a complete cross section.

There are a few methods that do not require a complete transverse section of bone. One example is Singh and Gunberg's (1970) method which uses small sections taken from the anterior femur and tibia and the posterior mandible. They look at two fields at the periosteal portion of the bone looking for three variables. Their study claims to give age estimation in males within 6 years of the actual age. The study does not examine females and suggests that there are no sex differences in females according to a small comparative study. Besides the lack of females in this sample, the male sample is skewed to the older age ranges with a mean age of approximately 64 years old.

Thompson (1979) describes a method of age assessment that uses tiny cores of bone taken from the femur, tibia, humerus, and ulna. This study looked at over 100 individuals, including females. It uses 19 different variables, including macroscopic (cortical thickness) and microscopic (secondary osteon populations) details. Thompson tested the method on eight forensic cases and suggested that an age range as low as ±3 years from the known age is possible. In another article, Thompson et al. (1981) test the method against 28 forensic cases and came up with a mean age range of ±7.6 years; however, they refer to an equation that is not in the 1979 article. Stout (1992) indicates that the equation used to derive these ranges is unknown.

Ericksen (1991) used a sample of over 300 individuals with a broad age range to examine her method of histological aging. She used a wedge of bone from anterior femur at midshaft. Using pictures and the microscope simultaneously, she counted the secondary osteons, osteon fragments, non-Haversian canals, and percentage of unremodeled bone. Once again, the limitation of this technique is that it has only been used for the femur, and the anterior midshaft of the femur must be intact.

Samson and Branigan (1987) developed a method of histological age estimation for highly fragmentary or weathered bone using the femur. They examined characteristics such as mean cortical thickness and number of Haversian canals. This method gives an age range for males of ±8 years, though its utilization in the forensic setting may be limited as there is an error rate of ±16 years for females. However, the drawback to this method is that one must first determine sex, which is difficult in instances in which the bone is fragmentary. An initial attempt by Benedix (2004) to rectify these shortcomings in sorting fragmentary remains explored the differentiation between the human and nonhuman species at the microscopic level. Benedix focused primarily on animal species found in Southeast Asia where fragmentary animal remains are often commingled with or mistaken for those of missing servicemen from past military conflicts. Benedix discovered that while some animal bones can be distinguished from human at the microscopic level, it may be difficult to distinguish between some fragmentary animal remains and the remains of humans when there are no macroscopic morphological features available to make the distinction, as their histological structure is often quite similar.

According to Robling and Stout (2000) there are many problems with microstructural bone aging of human remains. They specifically note the various publications that indicate whether certain microstructural characteristics increase, decrease, or stay the same with age. They examined some of the most commonly measured microstructure characteristics, such as osteon size and Haversian canal size. Using Haversian canal size as an example, they point out that some publications say that Haversian canal size increases with age, others say that it decreases with age, and still others maintain that there is no change in the size associated with age. This discrepancy in different bones of the skeleton and by different researchers could create a significant issue when trying to discern methodological problems with existing techniques or identify new techniques for microscopic age estimation.

Another key issue with histological aging of human bone is that most methods utilize only the midshaft. In a cursory look at the numerous methods, the following elements of the human skeleton are represented in the histological aging literature: *femur* (Ahlqvist and Damsten, 1969; Branigan, 1987; Drusini, 1987; Eriksen, 1991; Kerley, 1965; Kerley and Ubelaker, 1978; Samson and Narasaki, 1990; Singh and Gunberg, 1970; Thompson, 1979), *tibia* (Kerley, 1965; Kerely and Ubelaker, 1978; Singh and Gunberg, 1970; Thompson and Galvin, 1983), fibula (Kerley, 1965; Kerely and Ubelaker, 1978), *ulna* (Thompson, 1979), clavicle (Stout et al., 1996), *fourth rib* (Stout et al., 1994) and *sixth rib* (Stout and Paine, 1992), *second metacarpal* (Kimura, 1992), *occipital* (Cool et al., 1995), *mandible* (Singh and Gunberg, 1970), and *humerus* (Thompson, 1979; Yoshino et al., 1994).

The majority of the long bone methods for histological aging require sectioning at midshaft regardless of whether the technique requires transverse sections or cores. However, when analyzing fragmentary remains, it is not always possible to identify whether the remains are derived from the midshaft. This begs the following question: Is it possible to use the methods created for use at the midshaft to analyze any part of the long bone? That is, is the osteon population static through the length of the shaft, or do osteon populations differ depending upon muscle attachment sites or proximity to articular surfaces and, therefore, trabecular bone?

It makes intuitive sense that the areas of bone that are subjected to more mechanical stress throughout life would show more osteonal turnover than other areas. That is to say, that the pulling of muscles directly on the bone at muscle attachment sites must cause more bone remodeling than occurs at nonattachments sites simply due to the strain placed on the bone at that site. Moreover, areas of the shaft where the cortical bone surrounds trabecular bone, such as those near proximal and distal articulating surfaces, may have a lower osteon population simply due to the thin the cortical bone in these areas. Tersigni (2005) showed there was a great deal of differentiation throughout the shaft of long bones in terms of osteon population and showed that these changes can sometimes alter the age estimate significantly. Due to these differential populations of osteons, Tersigni reiterates Kerley's (1965) suggestion that techniques derived from the midshaft of the bone should not be used on areas of the shaft that fall outside of a 3 in. distance from midshaft.

A number of metabolic and mechanical processes can affect osteonal remodeling and, thus, affect the accuracy of histological aging techniques. Some of these have been enumerated by Frost (1985), including hormonal response, regional trauma, usage or nonusage (disuse atrophy), paralysis, and metabolic diseases. As discussed in the next section, other metabolic and systemic disorders can affect the bone microstructure and thus affect the ability to accurately age using bone histology.

Bioarchaeological and Paleopathological Uses of Bone Histology

The use of bone histology has tremendously affected paleopathology and, for that matter, bioarchaeology as a whole. The microscopic analysis of human bone has allowed for a more complete analysis of skeletal remains. That is, the use of bone histology has facilitated the identification of diseases on an individual basis, the identification of disease distribution within and among populations, and the history of disease within a population (Schultz, 2001). Bone histology can also help to identify disease loads, living conditions, and general life ways of ancient populations. According to Larsen (1997), histological morphology can indicate stress within a population since remodeling rates of human bone are affected by disease and nutrition. Stout (1989) suggested that, based on the differing histological signatures, maize agriculturalists have greater remodeling rates than hunters and gatherers. He suggests that this reflects effects of over-productivity of parathyroid hormone resulting in low calcium and high phosphorous concentrations; thus, as described earlier, osteoclasts are overstimulated to break down bone, thereby increasing remodeling. Larsen (1997) even discusses that the mineralization period (Stage 5 of the osteon life cycle) can be influenced by stress. He provides an example of using bone histology as a means of determining modes of subsistence by comparing the osteon structures of Eskimos (primarily meat eaters), Arikara (foraging and farming), and Pueblo (primarily maize-based subsistence). This research suggests that Eskimos have a higher rate of type II osteons (secondary, or smaller, remodeling sequences) than the other two groups because of their increased calcium intake from meat consumption.

Schultz (2001, 2003) has furthered the study of bone histology in paleopathology with diagnoses of skeletal diseases using histology. This prolific writer has pushed the differential diagnoses of pathological conditions to new heights through his use of microstructure analysis of ancient populations. In fact, his contributions are so important to paleopathology that Ortner (2003) devotes an entire chapter to the differential diagnoses of bone disease by histological analysis in his landmark textbook on the identification of pathological diseases. In addition to the normal uses of bone histology, including the identification of fragmentary remains as human or nonhuman and microscopic aging techniques, Schultz's research in bone histology has identified the bony signatures of metabolic diseases as well as physical/mechanical infirmities (such as atrophy) that cannot necessarily be identified macroscopically. Schultz (2003) nearly mandates the use of microscopic techniques for differential diagnosis of disease by paleopathologists. He suggests that the histological signature could identify bone tumors, lesions, specific and nonspecific bone inflammations, metabolic disorders, age associated changes, and early stages of bone disease that are not macroscopically identifiable. This is evidenced by his discussion of a population that was examined twice, first macroscopically then microscopically. The initial diagnosis concluded that there was high prevalence of osteomyelitis and anemia and low incidence of meningeal irritation within this population. The microscopic analysis revealed that the anemia and osteomyelitis frequency were actually significantly less than originally thought and that the meningeal irritation frequency increased. Additionally, microscopic analysis identified rickets in bones that were macroscopically identified as osteomyelitis.

Schultz (2001) argues that the microscopic determination of bone disease is more reliable than any macroscopic evaluation. In short, any disorder that can cause a bony response can be identified with the use of histology. He indicates that treponemal diseases, rickets, scurvy, meningitis, and leprosy can usually only be diagnosed with histology, as well as the microscopic changes and stages of bony destruction cause by venereal syphilis and yaws. According to Schultz (2001, 2003), the value of bone histology in bioarchaeology and paleopathology is used as an epidemiological tool to assess disease effects on ancient populations. In many ways, his research may well help to alleviate one of the major theoretical problems in bioarchaeology today: the osteological paradox as described in Wood et al. (1992). This theory describes the hidden heterogeneity within populations. The individuals in an archaeological population are an unknown mixture of people who each had differing frailty or susceptibility to disease. Wood et al. (1992) give an example of this paradox using a fictitious population with three subgroups. They describe a major stressor (disease) that differentially affects these three subgroups. The first subgroup does not encounter the stressor. The second subgroup is moderately affected by the stressor, which produces bony lesions within the population. The third subgroup is affected significantly by the stressor, to an end that most of its members die quickly even before lesions can form. Wood et al. (1992) conclude that by just looking at the gross morphology of the skeletons, one could probably only identify two groups of skeletons macroscopically: those with lesions and those with no lesions. From two groups, one could not glean the fact that there were three groups experiencing varying risks of disease and death. It is possible, however, that with the use of histological analysis, early bony changes (i.e., those changes experienced prior to death) could be identified, thus splitting the population into the three actual groups.

Further information can be identified by simply looking at the actual metric size of each osteon. The exploration of osteon area measurements may inform about differential biomechanical loading, population health (Pfeiffer, 1998), age-related bone change (Stout and Teitlebaum, 1976), relationships between disparate samples, and species identification. Osteon area, in general, is expected to remain unchanged between Neanderthals, prehistoric peoples, and modern populations (Sawada et al., 2004), though the driving factors that guide osteon area are presently unknown (Pfeiffer, 1998, 2000). Using modern populations, Cho et al. (2002) performed a histological examination of European-American and African-American remains and found that osteon area was also influenced by ancestry. It may also be necessary to consider the warning in Kim et al. (2007) of potential analysis errors due to osteon drift in the assessment of total osteon area. This problem is exacerbated by the scarcity of information on the measurement and impact of osteon drift.

Bone Histomorphology Used to Identify Postmortem Taphonomy

Bone histomorphology is often used to determine if postmortem taphonomic damage due to biological and nonbiological degradation has occurred to the bone or bone fragment in question. Schultz (2001, 2003) indicates that bone histology can also be used for the identification of preservation state of remains. This can be helpful in determining whether or not further chemical/genetic analysis of skeletal remains could be successfully undertaken, which, in turn, can save the needless waste of time and money on the analysis of poorly preserved bone.

Schultz (1997) discusses a case in which differential decomposition of remains was noted only after histological analysis. One burial had a skeleton that was missing a portion of the lower limb and it was presumed amputated. Upon further analysis of fragments of trabecular bone within the soil, it was determined that the lower limb was present at the time of burial, but had subsequently decomposed in a differential manner than the rest of the body.

There are numerous taphonomic processes that can be identified using thin sections of bone and either light microscopy or scanning electron microscopy. These include root infiltration, fungus or bacterial growth, insect infestation, and fire modification (Schultz, 1997).

Fungus, bacteria, and even algae infiltration can seriously degrade the internal and external structures of bone (Schultz, 1997). There are differential signatures within the bone microstructure that would suggest the presence of algae, fungus, or bacteria. Schultz suggests large tubular spaces in the microstructure are indicative of fungus infiltration, while bacteria can cause channels to form within the bone (1997). These channels are usually filled by fungus, algae, and other bacteria that colonize the bone after the initial damage. All of these organisms will continue to reproduce and damage the bones they invade for years until the bone is completely degraded, preventing any sort of isotopic or microstructural analysis.

Bones that have been modified by heat or fire could also be precluded from isotopic or microscopic analysis. This is directly dependent on the duration of the heat/fire as well as the temperature to which the bones were heated. Differential temperature can lead to diverse morphological changes within the bone microstructure (Schultz, 1997). In some cases, the bone is minimally altered at the microscopic level, and, in other cases, the bone is maximally altered, losing its entire organic component, thus making it extremely friable and an unlikely candidate for isotopic or microstructural analysis.

At the microscopic level, if the bone section is very fragmentary, or is missing large portions of the osteons (especially concentrated around the Haversian canal), it is possible to exclude these samples from further analysis citing heavy taphonomic damage as the basis for exclusion. Additionally, if the section is completely devoid characteristic microstructure (Haversian systems, osteons plexiform bone, etc.), it may be prudent to rule these sections inadequate for further analysis.

Future of Bone Histology within Physical Anthropology

Despite the numerous sanctions preventing the wholesale and systematic destruction of bone from paleontological, bioarchaeological, and historical sites for histological assessment, there is much to be learned about the microscopic variables that vary with age, sex, and within and between bones of the same individual. Continued research in these areas will provide the necessary data that will enable us to accurately diagnose disease using clinical exemplars. It is clear that the future of histological research within forensic anthropology will also allow for the further analysis of highly fragmentary remains. As evidenced by the increasing number of publications relating to histological analysis of osseous remains, as well as the inclusion of methods within the best practices suggested by the Scientific Working Group for Anthropology (SWGANTH), histological analysis of osseous remains has a distinct place within the modern medicolegal system and can undoubtedly aid in the identification of highly fragmented human remains.

References

Ahlqvist J and Damsten O (1969) A modification of Kerley's method for the microscopic determination of age in bone. *J Forensic Sci* 14:205–212.

Benedix DC (2004) Differentiation of fragmented bone from South East Asia: The histological evidence. Dissertation. University of Tennessee Electronic Library, Knoxville, TN.

Bergman RA, Afifi AK, and Heidger Jr. PM (1996) *Histology*. Philadelphia, PA: W.B. Saunders Company, pp.64–75.

Cattaneo C, Porta D, Gibelli D, and Gamba C (2009) Histological determination of the human origin of bone fragments. *J Forensic Sci* 54(3):531–533.

Cho H, Stout SD, Madsen RW, and Streeter MA (2002) Population-specific histological age-estimating method: A model for known African-American and European-American skeletal remains. *J Forensic Sci* 47(1):12–18.

Cool SM, Hendrikz JK, and Wood WB (1995) Microscopic age changes in the human occipital bone. *J Forensic Sci* 40:789–796.

Drusini A (1987) Refinements of two methods for the histomorphometric determination of age in human bone. *Z Morphol Anthropol* 77:167–176.

Enlow DH and Brown SO (1956a) A comparative histological study of fossil and recent bone tissue. Part I. *Texas J Sci* 8:405–443.

Enlow DH and Brown SO (1956b) A comparative histological study of fossil and recent bone tissue. Part II. *Texas J Sci* 9:186–214.

Enlow DH and Brown SO (1956c) A comparative histological study of fossil and recent bone tissue. Part III. *Texas J Sci* 10:187–230.

Ericksen MF (1991) Histological estimation of age at death using the anterior cortex of the femur. *Am J Phys Anthropol* 84:171–179.

Eroschenko VP (1993) *di Fiore's Atlas of Histology with Functional Correlations*. Philadelphia, PA: Lea and Febinger, pp.37–49.

Frost HM (1969) Tetracycline based histological analysis of bone remodeling. *Calcif Tissue Res* 3:211–237.

Frost HM (1985) The "new bone": Some anthropological potentials. *Yearb Phys Anthropol* 28:211–226.

Hillier ML and Bell LS (2007) Differentiating human bone from animal bone: A review of histological methods. *J Forensic Sci* 52(2):249–263.

Kerley ER (1965) The microscopic determination of age in human bone. *Am J Phys Anthropol* 23:149–164.

Kerley ER and Ubelaker DH (1978) Revisions in the microscopic method of estimating age at death in human cortical bone. *Am J Phys Anthropol* 49:545–546.

Kim YS, Kim DI, Park DK, Lee JH, Chung NE, Lee WT et al. (2007) Assessment of histomorphological features of the sternal end of the fourth rib for age estimation in Koreans. *J Forensic Sci* 52(6):1237–1242.

Kimura K (1992) Estimation of age at death from second metacarpals. *Z Morph Anthropol* 79:169–181.

Larsen CS (1997) *Bioarchaeology: Interpreting Behavior from the Human Skeleton*. Cambridge, U.K.: Cambridge University Press, pp. 6–63.

Martin RB, Burr DB, and Sharkey NA (1998) *Skeletal Tissue Mechanics*. London, U.K.: Springer-Verlag London Limited.

Martiniaková M, Grosskopf B, Omelka R, Vondrá ková M, and Bauerová M. (2006) Differences among species in compact bone tissue microstructure of mammalian skeleton: Use of a discriminant function analysis for species identification. *J Forensic Sci* 51(6):1235–1239.

Mulhern DM and Ubelaker DH (2001) Differences in osteon banding between human and non-human bone. *J Forensic Sci* 46:220–222.

Narasaki S (1990) Estimation of age at death by femoral osteon remodeling: Application of Thompson's core technique to modern Japanese. *J Anthropol Soc Nippon* 98:29–38.

Ortner DJ (2003) *Identification of Pathological Conditions in Human Skeletal Remains*, 2nd Edn. New York: Academic Press.

Pfeiffer S. (1998) Variability in osteon size in recent human populations. *Am J Phys Anthropol* 106(2):219–227.

Pfeiffer S. (2000) Palaeohistology: Health and disease. In: Katzenberg M and Saunders S (Eds.), *Biological Anthropology of the Human Skeleton*. New York: Wiley-Liss, pp. 287–302.

Robling AG and Stout SD (2000) Histomorphometry of human cortical bone: Applications to age estimation. In: Katzenberg MA and Saunders SR (Eds.), *Biological Anthropology of the Human Skeleton*. New York: Wiley-Liss, Inc., pp. 187–213.

Samson C and Branigan K (1987) A new method of estimating age at death from fragmentary and weathered bone. In Boodington A, Garland AN, and Janaway RC (Eds.), *Death, Decay and Reconstruction: Approaches to Archaeology and Forensic Science*. Manchester, U.K.: Manchester University Press, pp. 109–126.

Sawada J, Kondo O, Nara T, Dodo Y, and Akazawa T (2004). Bone histomorphometry of the Dederiyeh Neanderthal child. *Anthropological Science* 112:247–256.

Schinke T and Karsenty G (2002) Transcriptional control of osteoblast differentiation and function. In: Bilezikian JP, Raisz LG, and Rodan GA (Eds.), *Principles of Bone Biology: Volume 1*, 2nd Edn. New York: Academic Press. pp. 83–92.

Schultz M (1997) Microscopic investigation of excavated skeletal remains: A contribution to paleopathology and forensic medicine. In Haglund W and Sorg M (Eds.), *Forensic Taphonomy: The Postmortem Fate of Human Remains*. Boca Raton, FL: CRC Press, pp. 201–222.

Schultz M (2001) Paleohistopathology of bone: A new approach to the study of ancient diseases. *Yearb Phys Anthropol* 44:106–147.

Schultz M (2003) Light microscopic analysis in skeletal paleopathology. In: Ortner DJ (Ed.), *Identification of Pathological Conditions in Human Skeletal Remains*. New York: Elsevier Science, pp. 73–109.

Singh IJ and Gunberg DL (1970) Estimation of age at death in human males from quantitative histology of bone fragments. *Am J Phys Anthropol* 33:375–382.

Stout SD (1989) Histomorphometric analysis of human skeletal remains. In İşcan MY and Kennedy KAR (Eds.), *Reconstruction of Life from the Skeleton*. New York: Wiley-Liss, pp. 41–52.

Stout SD (1992) Methods of determining age at death using bone microstructure. In Saunders SR and Katzenberg MA (Eds.) *Skeletal Biology of Past Peoples: Research Methods*. New York: Wiley-Liss, pp. 21–25.

Stout SD, Dietze WH, İşcan MY, and Loth SR (1994) Estimation of age at death using cortical histomorphometry of the sternal end of the fourth rib. *J Forensic Sci* 39:778–784.

Stout SD and Gehlert SJ (1982) Effects of field size when using Kerley's histological method for determining age at death. *Am J Phys Anthropol* 58:123–125.

Stout SD and Paine RR (1992) Brief communication: Histological age estimation using rib and clavicle. *Am J Phys Anthropol* 87:111–115.

Stout SD, Porro MA, and Perotti B (1996) Brief communication: A test and correction of the clavicle method of Stout and Paine for histological age estimation of skeletal remains. *Am J Phys Anthropol* 100:139–142.

Stout SD and Stanley SC (1992) Percent osteonal bone vs osteon counts: The variable of choice for estimating age at death. *Am J Phys Anthropol* 86:515–519.

Stout SD and Teitelbaum SL (1976). Histomorphometric determination of formation rates of archaeological bone. *Calcif Tissue Res* 21(3):163–169.

Tersigni MA (2005) Serial long bone histology: Inter- and intra- bone age estimation. Dissertation. University of Tennessee Electronic Library, Knoxville, TN.

Tersigni-Tarrant MA, Byrd JE, and Manabe J (2011) Test of osteon circularity as a method of human/non-human identification. *Proceedings of the American Academy of Forensic Sciences Annual Scientific Meeting*, Chicago, IL, February 21–26 p. 381.

Thompson DD (1979) The core technique in the determination of age at death in skeletons. *J Forensic Sci* 24:902–915.

Thompson DD and Galvin CA (1983) Estimation of age at death by tibial osteon remodeling in an autopsy series. *Forensic Sci Int* 22:203–211.

Thompson DD, Salter EM, and Laughlin WS (1981) Bone core analysis of Baffin Island skeletons. *Arctic Anthropol* 17:87–96.

Wood J, Milner G, Harpending H, and Weiss K (1992) The osteological paradox. *Current Anthropology* 33:343–370.

Yoshino M, Imaizumi K, Miyasaka S, and Seta S (1994) Histological estimation of age at death using microradiographs of humeral compact bone. *Forensic Sci Int* 64:191–198.

www.swganth.org (2010) Determination of medicolegal significance from suspected osseous and dental remains. Online document.

Methods of Personal Identification*

20

ANGI M. CHRISTENSEN AND BRUCE E. ANDERSON

Contents

Introduction

The identification of unknown individuals is an integral aspect of the medicolegal death investigation and is important in our society for both legal and humanitarian reasons. Legally, many issues depend on the ability to establish identity, including inheritance and succession to property, collection of insurance policies and pensions, detection of fraudulent deaths, accident reconstruction, remarriage, issuance of a death certificate, and other matters concerning property and business interactions. Morally, identification is often critical in closure and resolution for surviving relatives and friends as well as being important in matters of international concern such as conflict and human rights investigations.

Confirmation of personal identification is usually the responsibility of the medicolegal authority (usually a forensic pathologist or coroner) or law enforcement officer. While other law enforcement officials, professionals, and scientists may assist in the investigative process, it is ultimately their responsibility to determine identification and issue a death certificate. Frequently, however, the actual task of identification falls upon a forensic scientist (forensic anthropologist, forensic odontologist, fingerprint examiner, etc.). Valid methods of personal identification (also called *individuation*) are based on two established and previously known facts—the identity of that individual, and a record of his or her own

* Names of commercial manufacturers are provided for identification purposes only, and inclusion does not imply endorsement of the manufacturer, or its products or services by the FBI. The views expressed are those of the authors and do not necessarily reflect the official policy or position of the FBI or the U.S. Government.

particular uniqueness(es). Identification is then the process of verifying that the individual concerned is the same as the one that is known. A personal identification can be made on the basis of a single unique identifier and/or the presence of multiple consistent features. Forensic experts in identification often use a variety of methods and lines of evidence in order to assess identity as accurately as possible. Because all identification methods require the comparison of antemortem and postmortem data, the identification method(s) used is dictated by the postmortem condition of the body as well as the availability, quantity, and quality of antemortem information about the deceased. The reliability of individual methods varies, but corroboration of several methods can increase the probability of a correct identification.

Personal identification is usually categorized as being tentative, circumstantial, or positive, although currently no consensus exists amongst forensic scientists as to the usage of these terms (Anderson 2007). A tentative identification is one in which the identity of the decedent is suspected. This may be based on associated items such as a driver's license. Circumstantial identification, also known as presumptive, possible, probable, or putative identification, is based on strong consistencies between the remains and the missing person. It meets a higher standard than tentative identification, but a lower standard than positive identification (although in some cases a circumstantial identification can be as certain as a positive identification if based upon adequate contextual and situational information). A personal identification may also be made by a preponderance of evidence, also known as identification by multiple corresponding factors, or multiple points of similarity. This level of identification is based on a number of uncorrelated pieces of evidence including, for example, body location, biological profile, tattoos, scars, personal effects, skeletal anomalies, and mitochondrial DNA. Identification by exclusion may be used in mass fatality situations with a "closed" population, defined by having a list of occupants, when all other individuals have been identified. Examples of such closed systems include car crashes with multiple individuals, most aircraft accidents, and other mass-fatality accidents. Positive identification is also known as personal, biological, or scientific identification, and is made through the use of information that is exclusive or unique to one individual.

Identification is often a straightforward process, particularly when death was recent, remains are fresh, and many clues are readily available. In these cases, soft tissues can often provide individualizing information. Visual examination of soft tissue features is the most frequently used method of personal identification (Sopher 1972). It usually involves recent deaths with well-preserved bodies whose facial and other physical features or markings are not distorted by decomposition or injury and can be readily identified by relatives or friends, or hospital or home deaths in which identity is not in question. This means of identification can be termed *positive-by-laypersons*. Although common, this method of identification is not considered scientific and is subject to considerable error. A more reliable soft tissue identification method is the comparison of friction ridges or fingerprints. Fingerprint comparison provides perhaps the most widely used scientific means of identification in the presence of soft tissues (Sopher 1972) and is based on the belief that the probability of two individuals having identical fingerprints is extremely remote. Little research on friction ridge analysis, however, has been directed toward developing population statistics (Committee on Identifying the Needs of the Forensic Sciences Community 2009).

One challenge in identification is that of establishing the identity of bodies that are skeletal, decomposed, dismembered, or badly burned. Visual recognition in these cases is obviously out of the question, and fingerprint evidence is often unobtainable. In cases where visual or fingerprint identification is not possible, anthropological methods of identification can be of great utility because the skeleton, including teeth, will usually survive longer than other identifiable features and, hence, are almost always available for examination. In these cases, forensic anthropologists are often asked to assist in the identification process due to their expertise in human osteology and their ability to glean biological information from the skeleton and detect subtle differences between individuals and other anomalies or features that may distinguish that person's skeleton.

A personal identification utilizing forensic anthropological evidence is based on agreement between the unidentified skeleton and facts known about a putative deceased's body who has been selected for comparison on the basis of being missing and possibly deceased (Kerley 1977). Any distinguishing features such as prosthetics or evidence of previous medical care, fractures, congenital or traumatic deformities, unusual allometric relations, epigenetic traits, morphological peculiarities, and abnormalities may be particularly convincing evidence and can often provide the basis for a highly probable identification. The greater the number of skeletal features that match those of a sought-for individual and the more unusual the features, the greater the probability that the identification is correct. (Dutra 1944). In most cases, it is even possible to quantify the strength of an osteological identification using statistical methods (Steadman et al. 2006).

While anthropological evidence for identification can be straightforward in many cases, it is important that the skeletal information be evaluated by a qualified forensic anthropologist who is equipped with a knowledge and appreciation for how, why, and where a structure may vary, and what constitutes "normal" and "nonnormal" variation. Such an appreciation can be gained only through a comprehensive understanding of skeletal biology including a working knowledge of growth and development, sources of variation, and the purpose and function of the structure(s). This knowledge may be particularly useful in cases where explainable differences occur. Differences observed between antemortem and postmortem information can be evaluated to determine whether they represent real structural differences that may be the basis for exclusion, issues with methodology, or whether they can be explained by chronological (age/time-related) factors. Explainable differences may result from trauma or surgical intervention, or simply growth and degenerative changes that accumulate slowly over time (Komar and Buikstra 2008).

Although forensic anthropologists can take measures to produce, collect, or document high quality postmortem data, the availability, quantity, or quality of antemortem data may limit the ability to make meaningful identification comparisons. It is important that anthropologists do not overemphasize the probability of correct identification based on skeletal evidence and recognize and articulate limitations of the data or identification method. The confidence placed in a correct identification is dependent not only on the quality of the data for comparison, but also on the known frequency of the shared trait or characteristic (such as a fracture, pathological condition, skeletal anomaly, or surgical hardware). These frequencies are rarely known, nor may it be known how these features vary between sex and age or by geographic location or socioeconomic status (Komar and Lathrop 2006). Furthermore, training and expertise in various identification methods may not be equivalent among practitioners. Therefore, the ethical and professional responsibility of the forensic anthropologist is to recognize the extent of their expertise and not to participate in identification procedures beyond their expertise and/or for which they lack adequate training.

Depending on the postmortem condition of the remains and the antemortem data available for comparison, several methods may be used to compare antemortem and postmortem skeletal information, including comparative radiography and photography, nonimaged records comparison, and photographic superimposition. The following section describes these techniques in more detail. More information about current standards and practices can also be found through the Scientific Working Group for Forensic Anthropology (or SWGANTH) whose purpose is to identify and publish "best practices" for methods, techniques, and approaches used in forensic anthropology (www.swganth.org).

Current Techniques and Practices

Comparative Radiography

Comparative radiography in the personal identification process involves the direct visual comparison of antemortem and postmortem radiographs and matching specific visual findings or features on the antemortem and postmortem radiographs of that person (Brogdon 1998). Radiographic identification is routinely used following mass disasters and in the identification of burned, mutilated, decomposed, fragmented, skeletonized, and otherwise unrecognizable human remains. Especially in these latter cases, radiography is sometimes the only means by which an individual's identity can be established. Fortunately, the potential for available antemortem images is great because radiographs have become a common diagnostic tool for various medical investigations, thus increasing the availability of antemortem radiographs for comparison. Indeed, radiographic comparison has become a regular procedure in the identification of unknown remains in most forensic facilities throughout the world (DiMaio and DiMaio 1989) and is probably the most commonly used method of personal identification from skeletal remains. The method is also not limited to conventional radiography; computed tomography (CT), multislice computed tomography (MSCT), and magnetic resonance imaging (MRI) are also becoming increasingly common procedures and may be used in radiographic comparisons (Dedouit et al. 2007, Haglund and Fligner 1993, Pfaeffli et al. 2007, Sidler et al. 2007).

Radiographic investigation of human remains began soon after the discovery of x-rays in 1895 as investigators came to realize that x-rays provided a nondestructive means of examining human remains. The method was first applied to ancient rather than forensic specimens, with several radiographs being made of Peruvian and Egyptian mummies by the end of the nineteenth century (Petrie 1897, Rowe 1953). Other early applications of radiography in anthropology included the study of bone pathologies (Hooton 1930) and bone growth and development (Greulich and Pyle 1959). Early radiographic investigations, however, typically considered only general anthropological and pathological findings with little or no emphasis on skeletal variability (Brothwell et al. 1968).

The earliest suggestion of the use of radiography in the identification of unknown human bodies was by Schuller (1921) who called attention to the potential use of frontal sinus variability in this context (see Figure 20.1). Radiography soon found applications in many medicolegal and forensic anthropological investigations, including age estimation; sex assessment; ancestry estimation; stature estimation; determining whether or not remains were human; locating and recovering bullets and other foreign bodies and

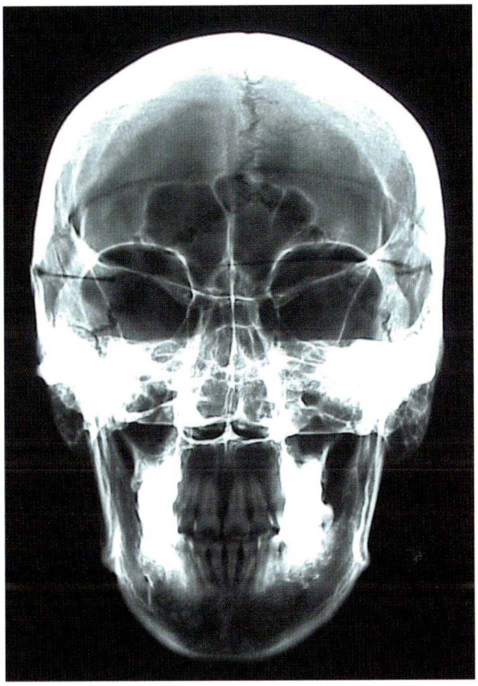

Figure 20.1 Radiograph depicting cranial features, including frontal sinuses.

determining the direction, angle, and location of wounds; detecting air-embolisms; detecting and aging fractures and other trauma; diagnosing tuberculosis; examining hyoid or cartilage fractures in hanging or strangulation victims; examining past medical history; illustrating dental morphologies and anomalies; separating skeletal remains from wood charcoal and other charred material; diagnosing premortem skeletal health; studying the relationship between bone and soft tissue; detecting metallic poisons such as arsenic, lead, and mercury in suspected poisoning cases; and examining burned, skeletonized, or decomposed individuals for the purpose of identification (Camps 1969, Eckert and Garland 1984, Fatteh and Mann 1969, Greuilch and Pyle 1959, Krogman and Iscan 1986, McCormick et al. 1985, Messmer 1986, Morgan and Harris 1953, Murphy and Gantner 1982, Rowe 1953, Schmidt and Kallieris 1982, Stewart 1979). As a result, the value of radiography has become well established in the criminal and medicolegal communities. Comparative radiography for the purpose of identification has become a commonly used technique in forensic anthropology, and it has been said to compare favorably with fingerprint identification (Murphy et al. 1980).

The typical method of comparison generally follows these steps: (1) A suitable antemortem radiograph of the putative decedent is obtained from an appropriate source. Typically, this is accomplished with the assistance of law enforcement officials who search for medical facilities possibly visited by the putative deceased and request available radiographs. (2) A radiograph of the unidentified remains is taken with a similar scope, orientation, and magnification as the antemortem image. As discussed earlier, not all forensic anthropologists have commensurate training; thus, anthropologists who do not have sufficient experience taking radiographs should solicit the assistance of a radiologist. (3) The two radiographs are compared either by direct visual inspection of side-by-side films or by superimposing

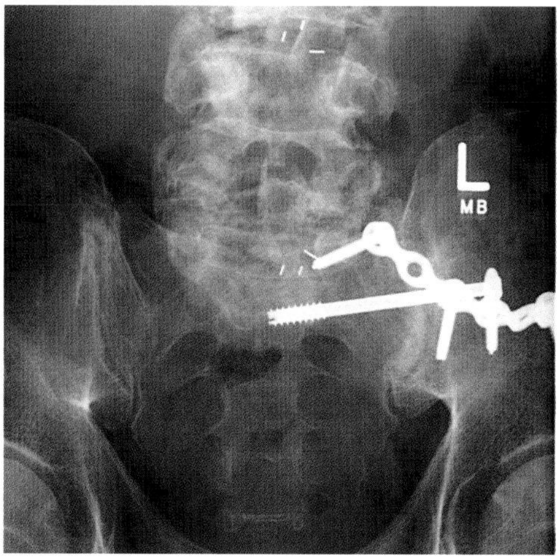

Figure 20.2 Radiograph depicting spinal and pelvic features and surgical hardware.

the images, looking for consistencies and inconsistencies in, for example, bone morphology, trabecular patterns, orientation, and placement of foreign materials such as surgical implements, enteric accretions, skull features (paranasal sinuses, sella turcica, and cranial sutures), and dental features (morphology, restorations, pathologies, and missing teeth).

Abnormal features such as anomalous or unusual development, healed fractures, deformities, degenerations, pathologies, abnormal calcifications, tumors, trauma, and prosthetic devices can be important for radiographic identification purposes (Brogdon 1998, Murphy et al. 1980), as they often contribute to a radiographic image that is unique to that individual (see Figure 20.2). Moreover, in the event of some injury or abnormality, the chance that the individual will have an antemortem radiograph for comparison is greater. This technique has been applied in various published case studies in identification involving, for example, anomalies of the feet and legs (Owsley and Mann 1989, Sudimack et al. 2002), postsurgical defects and devices (Hogge et al. 1995, Penalver et al. 1997, Sivaloganathan and Butt 1988), pelvic deformities and peculiarities (Angual and Derczy 1998, Brogdon 1998, Murphy and Gantner 1982, Rogue et al. 1993, Varga and Takacs 1991), wrist fractures (Atkins and Potsaid 1978), and a patellar defect (Riddick et al. 1983).

Although some abnormalities may indeed be unique to an individual, the richness of normal anatomical detail revealed in radiographs may be equally, if not more, important. The widespread occurrence of nonpathological anatomical features available for comparison in most radiographs may obviate the need to use pathological or abnormal features and significantly increase the potential number of corresponding features for identification (Joblanski and Shum 1989). Numerous reported cases illustrate the use of radiography to establish individuality using nonpathological variation of elements of the skeleton, including parts of the skull (Christensen 2005a, b, Culbert and Law 1927, Fatteh and Mann 1969, Joblanski and Shum 1989, Kirk et al. 2002, Murphy et al. 1980, Rhine and Sperry 1991, Sassouni 1959, Singleton 1951, Thorne and Thyberg 1953), the chest (Martel et al. 1977, Murphy et al. 1980, Singleton 1951), the sternum (Rouge et al. 1993), the abdomen (Angyal and Derczy 1998, Joblanski and Shum 1989, Murphy et al. 1980), costal cartilage (Marek et al. 1983), the spine (Brogdon 1998, Fatteh and Mann 1969, Jensen 1991, Kahana et al. 1998, 2002, Murphy et al. 1980, Owsley et al. 1993, Singleton 1951, Stevens 1966,

Valenzuela 1997), the clavicle (Adams and Maves 2002, Marek et al. 1983, Sanders et al. 1972), the scapula (Ubelaker 1990), the hand and wrist (Greulich 1960, Koot 2003), the pelvis (Singleton 1951), the femur (Dutra 1944), and the ankle and foot (Kade et al. 1967, Singleton 1951).

Identity can be established in these cases by comparison of the size, location, and external cortical contours and bone surfaces including spines, processes, exostoses, tubercles, sutures, foramina, and medullary cavities (Kerley 1977); metric analysis (Sassouni 1959, Thorne and Thyberg 1953); and internal architecture of the bones such as trabecular lattice pattern (Joblanski and Shum 1989, Kahana et al. 1998, Kahana and Hiss 1997, Mann 1998), vascular grooves (Brogdon 1998), unique areas of lucency, bone density, and cranial sinus shapes and patterns. Many, if not all, parts of the skeleton are useful for identification, and while those that tend to be more variable may be more reliable, nearly every bone in the body could be used for personal identification (Hogge et al. 1993).

Comparison of antemortem and postmortem dental radiographs is a well-documented, accepted, and widely used procedure and is considered one of the most effective means of identification of unknown bodies (Sainio et al. 1990). Because teeth and dental restorations are more resistant to destruction than osseous elements, they are more likely to be available for comparison. The method's reliability is a product of the numerous combinations of restorations, prosthetics, diastemata, and carious lesions that an individual may possess that can be highly visible in radiographic images. Nondental elements, such as the morphology of the maxillary sinus inferior margin (floor) and the mandibular canal, are also frequently imaged in radiographic films made by dentists and can be utilized in the antemortem–postmortem radiograph comparison. There is some debate as to whether it is appropriate for a forensic anthropologist to compare antemortem dental radiographs with skeletal remains. While it is almost certainly the case that specific statements regarding dental therapeutic procedures and treatments are best left to dentists, teeth and surrounding structures are part of the skeleton, and thus comparisons of bone and tooth structure and morphology are well within the expertise of the forensic anthropologist. As is true with forensic anthropology's overlap with radiology, the scientific community should acknowledge the overlap between forensic anthropology and forensic odontology and concede that forensic anthropologists with sufficient training and experience can competently perform personal identification based upon the dentition. Those forensic anthropologists who practice in jurisdictions where forensic odontologists also practice are fortunate, but not all medicolegal jurisdictions utilize both disciplines.

There is no recognized number of "points of concordance" that must be demonstrated to support a personal identification, but the antemortem and postmortem radiographs should match in sufficient detail to conclude that they are from the same individual *and with no unexplainable differences*. When making statements regarding identity (or probability of correct identification) based on comparative radiography, consideration should be given to the uniqueness or population frequencies of particular skeletal features, if known. Figure 20.3 illustrates an example of a comparison of antemortem and postmortem radiographs.

An important concern regarding radiographic comparison is that the morphology of adult bone is not stable, but continually remodeled and restructured in response to changes in function. The stability of bone is related to the stability of the loading regimes to which it is subjected as well as age, which is associated with a loss of cortical bone. These factors may lead to time and age-related changes in bone structure and, therefore, in radiograph

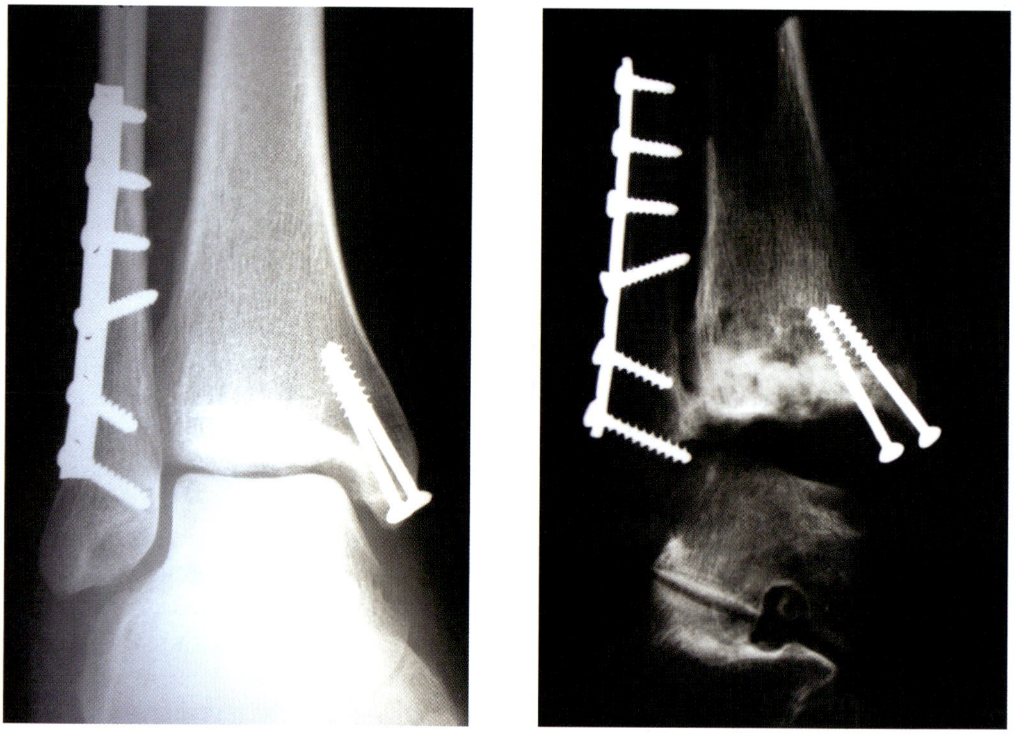

(a) (b)

Figure 20.3 Comparison of antemortem (a) and postmortem (b) radiographs of an ankle.

images. However, osseous remodeling generally follows the existing architecture within the skeleton, and as the bone cells are replaced (approximately 7 years for complete osseous turnover), the morphological intricacies are usually maintained. One study (Sauer et al. 1988) demonstrated that aspects of the postcranial skeleton generally chosen to compare for identification are quite stable, and the ability to make a positive identification from postcranial axial material may not diminish, even after two-and-a-half decades.

Another difficulty with this comparative method is that it involves a visual comparison with the consequence that the final identification decision may be somewhat subjective. As a recent study demonstrated, however, even very small frontal sinus radiograph pairs can be matched with a high rate of success, even by those will little or no experience (Smith et al. 2011). Nonetheless, other studies as well as professional standards support the need for trained interpreters (SWGANTH) (Hogge et al. 1993). However, it must again be emphasized that when performing these comparisons in the medicolegal world, experience is monumental. No errors are allowable because mistakes can mean that families of a decedent are provided with a misidentification. While an inexperienced examiner may be able to correctly match 19 out of 20 radiographs for a "high rate of success" on an exercise, that single misidentification cannot be tolerated in the medicolegal arena and would not be expected if the comparison were performed by a more experienced examiner.

Historically, research in comparative radiography involved the publication of successful case reports (some examples of which are listed earlier). More recently, efforts have included the investigation of validity, individuality, reliability, and error estimation

(Christensen 2004, 2005a,b, Koot et al. 2005), as well as attempts to facilitate and standardize the comparison process (Cox et al. 2009, Ribeiro 2000, Yoshino et al. 1987).

Nonimaged Records Comparison

Nonimaged records comparison is a personal identification method involving the comparison of antemortem records such as notes, charts, or other recorded information to features or characteristics of skeletal remains. When antemortem radiographs or other medical images are not available, other information contained in medical and/or dental records may include documented features or patterns of the skeleton that may be individuating and, therefore, useful for identification (see Figure 20.4). Such information may include records of surgical procedures (including implanted devices), dental patterns (including supernumerary and occult teeth), injury treatments, and pathologies and anomalies. Examples of these nonimaged record comparisons include a history of a broken bone that required medical attention, a surgical procedure such as a ventriculostomy (Anderson and Gilson 2005) or orthopedic hardware, orthodontic braces worn as a child that resulted in a recognizable pattern of caries beneath the bracket or band, the retention of an orthodontic appliance after the therapy is complete, and an unusually rare pattern of missing teeth. For each of these examples, it is preferred to have antemortem records from a dental office or medical facility for comparison with the postmortem findings, but sometimes family recollection must suffice.

The procedure for identification by written records comparison typically involves (1) identification of the pattern, injury, pathology, or anomaly that the practitioner believes may be useful for identification; (2) obtaining antemortem medical or dental charts and/or notes on the suspected deceased (similar to the method of locating imaged records following a presumptive identification); and (3) comparing the record to features of the skeletal remains, looking for consistencies and inconsistencies. As with other comparative methods, some inconsistencies may be explainable, while those that are not must be the basis for exclusion.

Surgical implants (e.g., surgical implements, artifacts, and appliances) often have serial numbers and stamps of the manufacturer and may be linked with an individual or associated with a particular shipment of surgical implements that can be tracked to a specific area during a certain time period (see Figure 20.5). Once the manufacturer's symbol and lot and/or serial number from the device have been located, local or national registries or the manufacturer may be contacted for information associated with that number. It may

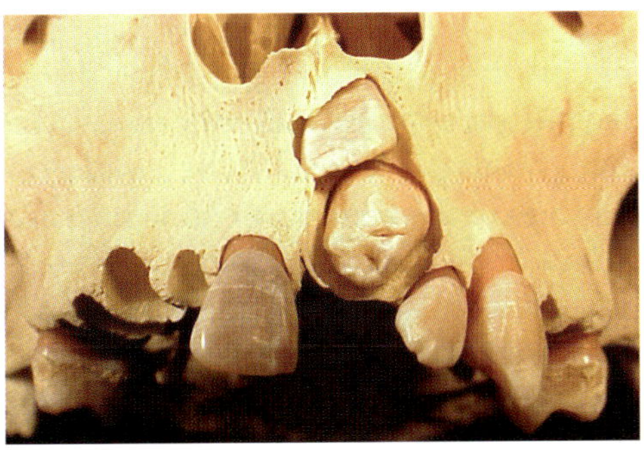

Figure 20.4 Unusual dental pattern that may be useful for personal identification.

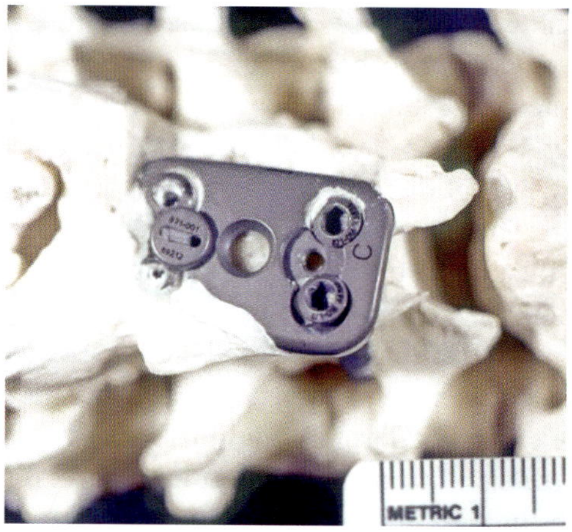

Figure 20.5 Surgical implant with visible manufacturer information.

be possible to link the device to an individual if there is a written or otherwise documented record of the device information in the patient's record (Mackinnon and Mundorff 2006). In other cases, however, it may only be possible to narrow the search, since registries may not necessarily provide adequate information to associate the surgical implement with a particular individual. It is also common to contact sales representatives of the manufacturer of the appliance (e.g., Zimmer, Synthes, and Astromedica) directly for information on the geographical regions that a particular surgical implant may have been marketed. It is our experience that someone in these offices is always eager to perform some "detective work" and thus possibly aid in locating the appropriate medical records.

Adams (2003b) reported that reference data sets show a high diversity present in dental patterns, and found that even a small number of common (charted, nonradiographic) dental characteristics may produce a rare dental pattern that is useful for identification. Indeed, the diversity of dental patterns has been said to be comparable to the diversity found in mitochondrial DNA (Adams 2003a). A computer program has even been developed (OdontoSearch—available at www.cilhi.army.mil) that uses reference databases and allows practitioners to calculate frequency information regarding the incidence of specific dental traits in the general population (Adams 2003b).

Records of pathologies, anomalies, and injuries may also be very useful for identification, even in the absence of an imaged record. Identification proceeds by describing and differentially diagnosing the lesion, defect, wound, or anomaly on the skeleton and conducting appropriate comparisons to the antemortem record. Examples of pathological conditions include chronic infectious disease, metabolic disorders, neoplastic diseases, developmental defects, degenerative joint conditions, ossified arterial plaque, cartilage, or other soft tissue, and autoimmune diseases. The antemortem record may be compared to observations of gross findings in the skeleton or bone microscopy (London et al. 1994). Examples of anomalies include accessory bones; bipartite bones; sternal, septal, and other apertures; bifid and/or supernumerary ribs; vertebral shifts and other axial anomalies; prominent features (e.g., everted gonia, bilobed chin, unusually large or small facial features); cranial asymmetry or modification; premature closure of cranial sutures; premature ossification of cartilage; supernumerary teeth, extra dental roots; fused teeth; dental agenesis; and polydactly. In the case of injuries, descriptions of the injury type, location, and severity in the medical record may be examined for consistency or inconsistency with the presence of fracture calluses or other injury-related lesions on the skeletal evidence. Once recognized, two criteria must be met in order for a pathological condition, anomaly or injury to be potentially useful for identification purposes (www.swganth.org). The trait must have been recognized and documented *in vivo*, and the relative frequency of the condition must be known. The more uncommon the condition, the more potential it may have in contributing to identification. Unfortunately, the frequency of different pathological conditions or anomalies is typically not documented adequately in the clinical literature. Again, experience comes into play, as the more seasoned forensic scientist may have a better understanding of the relative occurrence of some of these discriminators.

Examiners should be cautious in excluding individuals due to the absence of a condition in the medical record. Conditions identified on the skeletal evidence may have been subclinical and therefore undocumented at the time of death or at the time the medical record was prepared. Also, if the medical records indicate a condition in the skeleton (such as an osseous fracture), and no corresponding condition can be found on the skeletal evidence, this inconsistency should not necessarily be the basis for exclusion. In some osseous fractures the healing process completely, or nearly completely, remodels the bone to the point where it may not be possible to correctly determine that a fracture was once present. Thus, exclusions based upon the lack of evidence typically are not recommended. However, if the antemortem injury was exceptionally severe, some indication of the healing process in the affected bone would be expected, and thus the lack of any indication of a remodeled callus could be the basis for an exclusion.

Practitioners should also take caution that medical and dental charts and notes may not necessarily be accurate representations of an individual's medical or dental record. Every effort should be made to verify the medical record, especially if there is conflicting information. Problems may arise due to insufficient recording, recording mistakes, or insurance fraud. In addition, differences may exist in the recording systems used. Moreover, although there are usually written or typed summaries of medical problems and treatments, these summaries tend to be generalized and lack extensive detail (e.g., fracture to distal right fibula). Consequently, the nature of these records may mean that consistencies provide circumstantial evidence only.

In some cases, there is no basis for assumption of identification and no circumstantial clues to suggest identity and even a tentative identification cannot be made. In these cases, an anthropological analysis may be used to estimate biological information about the individual including the ancestral affinity, sex, age, dental characteristics, and living stature of an individual. The estimation of a postmortem interval (PMI), or time-since-death, can also be a useful descriptor in evaluating whether an unidentified person might match a description of a missing person, if the length of disappearance is known. Estimating these biological and taphonomic characteristics was the topic of previous chapters in this volume and will not be described further here. This assessment, though useful in narrowing the pool of potential candidates in the search for identity, is never a positive identification, although concordance between these antemortem and postmortem data many times directs the obtainment of the types of antemortem records than can affect such an identification. To wit, the biological information is compared to documented information or databases of missing persons (e.g., www.NamUs.gov), and individuals may be included or excluded from further consideration based on the fit with the biological profile. In the absence of other antemortem information on a presumptive deceased, a biological profile consistent with documented information about the presumed victim can provide corroborative evidence of identification.

As with radiographic comparisons, much of the early research involved case reporting. More recent research has involved the investigation of diversity and populational frequencies of specific dental patterns and skeletal conditions (Adams 2003a, Komar and Lathrop 2006, Nozawa et al. 2002).

Craniofacial Superimposition

Craniofacial superimposition (also known as *photographic superimposition* or *video superimposition*) is an identification method applied when an investigation has suggested that a set of remains relates to a particular missing person for whom photographs, videos, or other images (and no other antemortem data) are available (Ubelaker 2000). This method involves the superimposition of an image of a known individual (the suspected decedent) over a radiograph, photograph, negative, or drawing of the skull and/or the comparison of the photograph and skull through the use of digitized images (Ubelaker et al. 1992).

One of the earliest uses of craniofacial superimposition was a study of the remains of Johann Sebastian Bach (His 1895). The method was first applied in forensic context in the 1930s. Although the details of exactly how the comparison was conducted are not available, it involved the comparison of photographs viewed through a stereoscope to the three-dimensional head shape of the submitted skull (Glaister and Brash 1937, Ubelaker 2000). By the 1980s, the technique of craniofacial superimposition was somewhat standardized by using a skull, mirrors, metrical scales, and a camera. During this time, this identification technique was routinely utilized by the U.S. Army's Central Identification Laboratory (CILHI) in Hawaii and by the Human Identification Laboratory at the University of Arizona (Anderson, personal communication). Also by the 1980s, video cameras were being utilized instead of still cameras at the Human Identification Laboratory at the University of Florida (Austin-Smith 1999). Craniofacial superimposition has been applied in numerous documented cases using various images and comparison methodologies (Banjeree 1964, Basauri 1967, Delfino et al. 1983, Dorion 1983, Engel 1954, Koelmeyer 1982, Sen 1962, Verma 1981, Webster 1955).

The ideal image for this method is a close-up facial view with the individual directly facing the camera and the teeth revealed. The skull is then imaged using, where possible, comparable scaling, positioning, lighting, perspective, and angle as the original portrait. The two images are then superimposed, usually by selecting some facial anthropometric landmark in the subject photograph and cranial anthropometric landmark on the skull (see Figure 20.6). The practitioner then examines the superimposed images, looking for

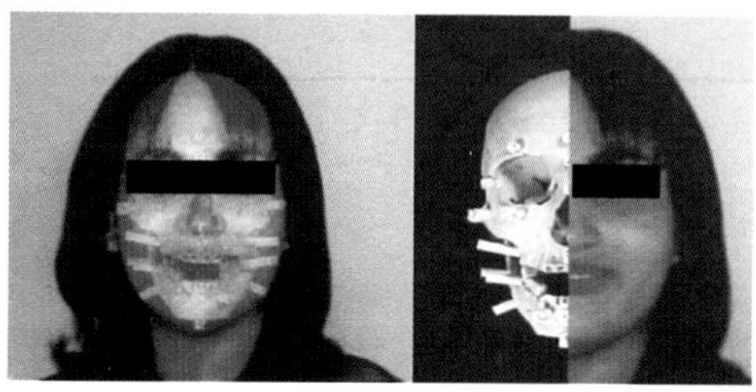

Figure 20.6 Craniofacial superimposition.

congruence of the lines and curves of the face and dental structures (Webster et al. 1986), or any other consistencies and inconsistencies in structures that are visible in both the antemortem and postmortem materials. An individual can be included if there is concordance between bony and/or dental landmarks, while exclusion results when there are irreconcilable disagreements between them. It will often be the case that some of the landmarks will perfectly match, some will partially do so, and others will not, and the practitioner will then make a decision about whether the skull corresponds to the photograph or not.

This approach is most often used to corroborate other identification methods or as a tool to include or exclude a possible identification (Kerley 1977), but positive identification is possible depending on the uniqueness of the features observed (Austin-Smith and Maples 1994, Ubelaker 2000). Craniofacial superimposition should be conducted by experts with thorough knowledge of human cranial anatomy and variation (www.swganth.org) and possibly computer science. Empirical testing of the method has demonstrated that the probability of misidentification is relatively low (Austin-Smith and Maples 1994). One of the difficulties of this method is trying to find a good fit between a two-dimensional representation of the face with a three-dimensional skull. While early attempts often involved laborious and time-consuming manual superimposition methods that may incorporate significant error, researchers are now developing computer-assisted methods (Ricci et al. 2006, Ubelaker et al. 1992) as well as designing automated superimposition methods (Ibanez et al. 2009).

DNA and Forensic Anthropology

Scientists have realized since the 1950s that an individual's DNA (located in the cellular nuclei and cytoplasm of all living organisms) encodes information about the individual's inherited characteristics, and, moreover, that the nuclear code is unique to each individual. Nuclear DNA analysis allows identification by reference to the alleles and nucleotide sequences of heritable traits and markers contained in any human nucleated cell, while the cytoplasmic mitochondrial DNA (mtDNA) allows for the determination of maternal relatives. Skeletal analyses by the forensic anthropologist may guide the molecular investigation by utilizing the biological profile to narrow potential comparisons, by determining sample selection from a single skeleton, and by choosing samples from comingled cases. Utilizing the forensic anthropologist in these ways saves the families of the unidentified time and saves the particular medicolegal jurisdiction money.

Obtaining DNA for identification purposes is not generally the responsibility of a forensic anthropologist, although a growing number of these "molecular anthropologists" are applying their expertise to medicolegal matters. The great advantage to having anthropologists perform both the skeletal and molecular analyses, even if not by the same anthropologist, is that the close proximity of skeletal and molecular analyses (especially within the same or adjacent laboratories) can save a great amount of time because of more immediate lines of communication. Typically, however, the forensic anthropologist is simply asked to collect samples or identify potentially useful skeletal material. Forensic anthropologists are frequently in the best position to decide on how DNA may be utilized to resolve issues of identity involving skeletonized remains. Many forensic anthropologists routinely make decisions regarding which skeletal elements should be sampled when dealing with commingled remains. Selecting duplicated elements, such as sampling three right femora, will undoubtedly yield three unique genomic profiles, but using the skills of a competent skeletal biologist, the selection of other skeletal elements can be included or excluded based upon skeletal morphology. For instance, if three adults were commingled and one was deemed morphologically to be significantly more robust than the other two, fewer samples from the robust individual might be needed because of morphological similarity, and more samples from the two more gracile individuals could be sampled to resolve the commingling between these two.

When skeletal remains of the same individual are recovered across time and/or space, DNA analysis can aid the forensic anthropologist while at the same time being aided by the forensic anthropologist. A thorough examination of a partial skeleton by the forensic anthropologist reveals those portions that are missing. In the event that those skeletal elements are subsequently recovered, they can be tentatively associated with the principal remains on morphological bases. However, DNA testing can be utilized to confirm the tentative placement of the additional remains. This feedback loop of using DNA to confirm morphological suspicions and using morphological suspicions to select those skeletal elements to undergo molecular testing is healthy for the field of forensic anthropology. Simply put, DNA analysis may support forensic anthropological investigations not only in the confirmation of identity, but also in the efforts to separate commingled remains, or reassociate remains (Mundorf et al. 2008). Contrary to those who see DNA as a threat to the field of forensic anthropology, there are many good reasons to argue that DNA analyses and results will serve to enrich the field by confirming (or refuting) associations based on morphological grounds by identifying compromised remains that could not be identified in any other matter, thus confirming (or refuting) the various assessments associated with the biological profile. This issue of compromised remains is also important in understanding which tissue types will and will not produce a full DNA profile.

While the cost of testing for nuclear DNA can be prohibitive, recent developments surrounding the President's Initiative for DNA has provided free DNA analyses for any unidentified remains. However, with the tremendous backlog of casework yet to be completed by the DNA labs performing this U.S. government–sponsored molecular testing, the time necessary to complete a case has become time prohibitive for families and the medicolegal community. Suffice it to say that DNA analyses, whether genomic or mitochondrial, are more costly than other methods of identification such as fingerprints, dental, radiological, or anthropological. Blind hits in large DNA databases (e.g., CODIS) have the potential to match an unidentified sample to an antemortem sample of that person or to a family reference sample (single or multiple family members), although the usual scenario that utilizes DNA in the identification process involves a presumptive, or tentative, identification with comparative samples from the individual or family reference samples.

Additional Considerations

Admissibility of Evidence

Forensic experts including anthropologists, radiologists, and pathologists are expected to meet structured standards regarding the validity, reliability, and application of their methods (Committee on Identifying the Needs of the Forensic Sciences Community 2009, Saks and Koehler 2005), including personal identification methods based on comparisons of skeletal evidence. The pursuits of forensic scientists and practitioners differ from those of purely academic physical anthropologists who are largely research-driven and not concerned with medicolegal issues. In addition to performing research and acquiring knowledge as an end unto itself, forensic practitioners must also consider the applications and implications of their findings in relation to legal matters. Several landmark rulings in U.S. courts have shaped how forensic scientists conduct research, evaluate methods, and present results in a court of law (Christensen 2004, Christensen and Crowder 2009, Steadman et al. 2006).

The first such ruling was issued in *Frye v. United States* (1923). The case involved the attempted admission of systolic blood pressure deception testing ("lie detector"), which was a new technique at the time, thereby leaving the court unsure as to how to assess its validity. The court offered the following opinion on the standard for admissibility of scientific expert witness testimony: "Just when a scientific principle or discovery crosses the line between the experimental and demonstrable stages is difficult to define. Somewhere in this twilight zone the evidential forces of the principle must be recognized, and while courts will go a long way in admitting expert testimony deduced from a well-recognized scientific principle or discovery, the thing from which the deduction is made must be sufficiently established to have gained general acceptance in the particular field in which it belongs" (*Frye v. United States* 1923). The court concluded that the lie detector had not yet gained the required standing and scientific recognition among authorities in the fields of physiology and psychology to be considered scientific (McCormick 1972). This "general acceptance test" for admissibility of scientific evidence became known as the "*Frye* Standard" and was the dominant standard in the majority of courts, facilitated in large part by the fact that the rule was easy to apply and required little scientific sophistication on the part of the judges.

Over time and with advancements in science, many courts and legal commentators began to modify or ignore the Frye standard. One of the key concerns was that new scientific evidence, though sound, often failed the Frye test. Critics argued that "general acceptance" should not be the criterion for the admissibility of scientific evidence, and that any relevant conclusions supported by a qualified expert witness should be admissible unless there are other reasons for exclusion (McCormick 1972).

In 1975, Congress enacted the *Federal Rules of Evidence* (1975) which was the first modern and uniform set of evidentiary rules for the trial of civil and criminal cases in federal courts. *Rule 702* specifically addressed expert witness testimony, stating that "If scientific, technical or other specialized knowledge will assist the trier of fact to understand the evidence or to determine a fact in issue, a witness qualified as an expert by knowledge, skill, experience, training or education may testify thereto in the form of an opinion or otherwise." The enactment of the *Federal Rules of Evidence*, however, did not eliminate the uncertainty in the courts, but rather led to a mixed use of *Frye*, the *Federal Rules of Evidence*, or some hybrid of the two. The confusion continued until the U.S. Supreme Court decided *Daubert v. Merrell-Dow Pharmaceuticals, Inc.* (1993).

The parents of Jason Daubert and Eric Schuller filed suit against the pharmaceutical company Merrell-Dow claiming that their children's birth defects were the result of the mothers' prenatal ingestion of the prescription drug Bendectin, which is designed to alleviate morning sickness. Crucial scientific evidence showing a causal relationship between the use of the drug during pregnancy and birth defects was deemed inadmissible because it did not meet the *Frye* standard. The supreme court ruled that *Federal Rules of Evidence Rule*

702 superseded the *Frye* test, thus determining the standard for relevance and reliability of expert testimony. Furthermore, the court ruled that it is the trial judge who must ensure that all scientific testimony is relevant and reliable. To assist the trial judges, the court provided the following general guidelines for assessing the admissibility of scientific testimony, which have collectively become known as the "*Daubert* criteria" or "*Daubert* standard":

1. Has the theory or technique been tested?
2. What is the known or potential rate of error?
3. Do standards exist for the control of the technique's operation?
4. Has the theory or technique been subjected to peer review and publication?
5. Has the theory or technique been generally accepted within the relevant scientific community?

Two other U.S. Supreme Court cases have supplemented and clarified the *Daubert* decision. Confronted with some of the more difficult issues regarding expert testimony, the Supreme Court's decisions in *General Electric Co v. Joiner* (1997) and *Kumho Tire Co v. Carmichael* (1999) were explanatory of *Daubert*. In *General Electric Co v. Joiner*, the Supreme Court explained that methodology and conclusions are not completely distinct from each other, but are linked together, and that an expert's conclusion should be excluded in the event that valid reasoning does not support it. Overall, the *Joiner* decision questioned and clarified the language in *Daubert* and solidified the burden of admissibility for the trial courts. In *Kumho Tire Co v. Carmichael*, the court reaffirmed the gatekeeper role of the judge and held that both scientific and nonscientific expert witness testimony must be reliable and relevant to be admissible, and noted that there must be a flexible approach for assessing expert testimony because types of evidence may vary across disciplines.

These landmark cases form the "trilogy" of Supreme Court decisions that set the legal standard for evaluating the admissibility of expert testimony. In 2000, *Federal Rule 702* was amended to include "...if (1) the testimony is based upon sufficient facts or data, (2) the test is the product of reliable principles and methods, and (3) the witness has applied the principles and methods reliably to the facts of the case." The implication for forensic anthropology and for evidence pertaining to personal identification is that anthropologists should employ methods of data collection, comparison, and interpretation that are considered valid and reliable. The strength of conclusions should not be overstated, and limitations of the selected technique(s) should be considered and presented appropriately.

Facial Approximation

Facial approximation (also known as craniofacial reconstruction, facial reconstruction, forensic reconstruction, and facial reproduction) is an artistic reproduction of the soft tissue features of an individual (Komar and Buikstra 2008) and involves the estimation or artistic reproduction of possible facial features based on the underlying skeletal structures. The practice of facial approximation is intended to capture public attention in regards to an unidentified person when all scientific leads have been exhausted, but is never a means of personal identification.

Facial approximation was first attempted in Europe in the late nineteenth century and was a combined effort of anatomists and a sculptor using facial tissue depth measurements taken from cadavers (Hiss 1895, Kollman and Buchly 1898). The technique was made famous by the reconstruction of Johann Sebastian Bach (His 1895), and was first applied in a forensic case in 1913 (Wilder and Wentworth 1918). The tissue depth method, which involves the building up of soft tissues upon the skull (including muscle, fatty and connective tissue, glandular, and skin) to depths at specific osseous landmarks determined by needle probe or ultrasound, was further developed by Rhine and Campbell (1980). Another method, the anatomical method, uses muscle origins and insertions to rebuild each muscle, and was introduced in the 1920s by Russian anthropologist M.M. Gerasimov (1971). The tissue depth method is more widely used today in attempts to identify the deceased, perhaps because the anatomical method requires more expertise in anatomy and biomechanics and is rather time consuming, whereas the tissue depth method is quicker and requires less anatomical training.

Knowledge of human cranial anatomy and variation as well as artistic ability is essential for the production of useful facial images. The production of facial approximations should, therefore, be a joint effort between anthropologists, anatomists, and artists. Anthropological analysis is critical in providing the demographic information such as age, sex, and ancestry. Because of their familiarity with skeletal landmarks, anthropologists are often responsible for the placement of appropriate tissue depth markers on the skull. Anthropological collaboration is also helpful in calling attention to details that may be useful to incorporate into the approximation such as size and shape of supraorbital ridges, shape characteristics of the nasal area, evidence of healed trauma, and unusual dental features (Ubleaker 2000).

The work then shifts to an artist who marries the skull image and all other information in an appropriate manner (Ubelaker 2000). This step requires advanced artistic abilities and training and may not be practical or even possible for most forensic anthropologists to perform. Indeed, many practitioners of facial approximation including Frank Bender (frankbender.us) are trained in fine art rather than forensics and regard the practice as more artistic than scientific (Bender 2009). Artistic approximations may include two- or three-dimensional drawings done over frontal and lateral photographs of the skull, or clay reconstructions applied directly to the skull or to a replica of the skull. Although reproductions were traditionally manual, computer-assisted approaches are becoming more prevalent (Shahrom et al. 1996, Turner et al. 2005, Ubelaker and O'Donnell 1992). The selection of which method to use may be up to the artist, but each method has advantages. Two-dimensional approximations are generally easier to change and are cheaper, while three-dimensional approximations are more time consuming but generally appear more lifelike (Caldwell 1986). The availability of images on a computer provides an advantage in facilitating the final comparison (Ubelaker and O'Donnell 1992). Although the skull itself is the basic reference for all techniques, quality photography and evidence collection are important to the accuracy of the approximation (Powers 2005).

One of the greatest limitations of the technique is that there are no credible ways to estimate many of the most distinctive and individuating structures of the face including eye color, ears, lips, parts of the nose, and head and facial hair color/length/form because they do not have an underlying bony structure from which to glean reliable information. These facial details are often considered crucial in the recognition of a human face by other individuals, but they must be interpreted from parts of the skull and other anthropological data available, or may often be simply an artistic rendition or guess.

After an approximation is complete and publicized, a visual recognition by a relative, friend, or acquaintance may be made. This tentative identification is not a final identification and must be verified subsequently through scientific means. Although popular in the media and impressive to the public (probably because of the attention received by successful attempts while the unsuccessful ones get little attention), the method lacks scientific rigor, is associated with a high degree of error, and should be used for investigative purposes only. Suffice it to say that the results of any facial approximation are simply a lead that may be followed, and nothing more. Many anthropologists are critical of the approach (Stephan 2003), and emphasize that statements regarding the power or value of facial imagery methods should be presented carefully. Recent research in this area has been aimed at assessing the accuracy of approximations and evaluating craniofacial tissue depth measurements (Quatrehomme et al. 2007, Stephan and Simpson 2008a,b).

Summary

- Personal identification is important in our society for both legal and humanitarian reasons.
- Personal identification should involve a multidisciplinary approach and strive for as many lines of evidence as possible.
- Anthropologists are often asked to assist in the personal identification process because the skeleton usually survives longer than other identifiable features and because forensic anthropologists can glean biological information from the skeleton and detect subtle differences among individuals.
- Anthropological methods of investigating personal identification include radiographic comparison, nonimaged records comparison, and craniofacial superimposition.
- Several U.S. Supreme Court rulings have shaped how anthropologists conduct research, evaluate methods, and present results in a court of law.
- Personal identification should employ methods of data collection, comparison, and interpretation that are considered valid and reliable.
- Facial approximation is not a means of personal identification; this methodology is merely an investigative lead.
- DNA analyses can be aided by forensic anthropologists through the proper selection of samples.
- Forensic anthropology can be aided by DNA analyses by confirming associations and tentative identifications based upon morphological analyses.

Questions

20.1 Why is personal identification important?

20.2 Who is responsible for determining a personal identification?

20.3 What determines the method of personal identification used?

20.4 What is the most frequently used method of personal identification? When is it typically used, and what are some of the problems associated with it?

20.5 What are the different "levels" of identification, and what types of evidence do they typically involve?
20.6 Why is it important for forensic anthropologists to have a comprehensive understanding of skeletal biology?
20.7 What is the Scientific Working Group for Forensic Anthropology (SWGANTH)?
20.8 Do all forensic anthropologists have equivalent training in personal identification methods?
20.9 What are some examples of features that can be used for identification by comparative radiography?
20.10 Why is normal anatomical variation seen in radiographs important to the personal identification process, and what are some examples of normally varying features that are often used for personal identification?
20.11 Why is it not always possible to make a personal identification from a surgical implant?
20.12 What criteria must be met in order for a pathological condition, anomaly or injury to be potentially useful for identification purposes?
20.13 What identification methods can be used when there is no antemortem medical or dental information available?
20.14 How do age- or time-related changes in the skeleton affect anthropological methods of personal identification?
20.15 When would craniofacial superimposition be used as a means of personal identification?
20.16 What are the *Daubert* criteria and how do they affect personal identification?
20.17 What is the purpose of facial approximation, and why can it not be used as a means of personal identification?
20.18 What should be the strategy when selecting samples for DNA analyses when dealing with skeletal elements that may represent multiple individuals?
20.19 How might the results of DNA analyses improve the field of skeletal analyses by forensic anthropologists and forensic odontologists?
20.20 What can forensic scientists do to minimize the possibility of contamination when resecting skeletal samples to be used in DNA analyses?
20.21 What is NamUs?

References

Adams B.J. 2003a. The diversity of adult dental patterns in the United States and the implications for personal identification. *Journal of Forensic Sciences* 48(3):497–503.

Adams B.J. 2003b. Establishing personal identification based on specific patterns of missing, filled, and unrestored teeth. *Journal of Forensic Sciences* 48(3):487–496.

Adams B.J. and R.C. Maves. 2002. Radiographic identification using the clavicle of an individual missing from the Vietnam conflict. *Journal of Forensic Sciences* 48(2):369–373.

Anderson B.E. 2007. Comment on statistical basis for positive identification in forensic anthropology. *American Journal of Physical Anthropology* 133(1):741–742.

Anderson B.E. and T.E. Gilson. 2005. Modern day trepanation: The ventriculostomy utilizing an intracranial pressure bolt. *Proceedings of the 57th Annual Meeting of the American Academy of Forensic Sciences*, New Orleans, LA.

Angyal M. and K. Derczy. 1998. Personal identification on the basis of antemortem and postmortem radiographs. *Journal of Forensic Sciences* 43:1089–1093.

Atkins L. and M.S. Potsaid. 1978. Roentgenographic identification of human remains. *Journal of the American Medical Association* 240:2307–2308.

Austin-Smith D. 1999. Video superimposition at the C.A. Pound laboratory 1987 to 1992. *Journal of Forensic Sciences* 44(4):695–699.

Austin-Smith D. and W.R. Maples. 1994. The reliability of skull/photograph superimposition in individual identification. *Journal of Forensic Sciences* 39(2):446–455.

Banjeree A. 1964. Camera identifies human skull. *Indian Police Journal* 2:42.

Basauri C. 1967. A body identified by forensic odontology and superimposed photographs. *International Criminal Police Review* 204:37.

Bender F. 2009. https://www.frankbender.us.

Brogdon B.G. 1998. Radiological identification of individual remains. In: *Forensic Radiology*, ed. B.G. Brogdon, pp. 149–187. Boca Raton, FL: CRC Press.

Brothwell E.F., T. Molleson, and C. Metreweli. 1968. Radiological aspects of normal variation in earlier skeletons: An exploration study. In: *The Skeletal Biology of Earlier Human Populations*, ed. D.R. Brothwell, pp. 149–172. New York: Pergamon Press.

Caldwell P.C. 1986. New Questions (and some answers) on the facial reproduction techniques. In: *Forensic Osteology: Advances in the Identification of Human Remains*, ed. K.J. Reichs, pp. 229–255. Springfield, MA: Charles C Thomas.

Camps F.E. 1969. Radiology and its forensic application. In: *Recent Advances in Forensic Pathology*, ed. F.E. Camps, pp. 149–160. London, U.K.: J. & A. Churchill.

Christensen A.M. 2004. The impact of *Daubert*: Implications for testimony and research in forensic anthropology (and the use of frontal sinuses in personal identification). *Journal of Forensic Sciences* 49(3):427–430.

Christensen A.M. 2005a. Assessing the variation in individual frontal sinus outlines. *American Journal of Physical Anthropology* 127(3):291–295.

Christensen A.M. 2005b. Testing the reliability of frontal sinus outlines in personal identification. *Journal of Forensic Sciences* 50(1):18–22.

Christensen A.M. and C.M. Crowder. 2009. Evidentiary standards for forensic anthropology. *Journal of Forensic Sciences* 54(6):1211–1216.

Committee on Identifying the Needs of the Forensic Sciences Community, National Research Council. 2009. *Strengthening Forensic Science in the United States: A Path Forward*. Washington, DC: National Academies Press.

Cox M., M. Malcolm, and S.I. Fairgrieve. 2009. A new digital method for the objective comparison of frontal sinuses for identification. *Journal of Forensic Sciences* 54(4):761–772.

Culbert W.L. and F.L. Law. 1927. Identification by comparison of roentgenograms of nasal accessory sinuses and mastoid processes. *Journal of the American Medical Association* 88:1634–1636.

Daubert v. Merrell Dow Pharmaceuticals, Inc., 509 U.S. 579 (1993).

Dedouit R., N. Telmon, R. Costagliola, P. Otal, L.L. Florence, F. Joffre, and D. Rouge. 2007. New identification possibilities with postmortem multislice computed tomography. *International Journal of Legal Medicine*121:507–510.

Delfino Y.P., M. Colonna, F. Introna, M. Potente, and E. Vacca. 1983. Identification by computer aided skull-face superimposition. Paper presented in the *Forensic Anthropology Symposium (MY Iscan, Organizer) 11th International Congress of Anthropological and Ethnological Sciences*, August 20–25, Vancouver, British Columbia, Canada.

DiMaio D.J. and V.J. DiMaio. 1989. *Forensic Pathology*. New York: Elsevier Saina Publishing Co.

Dorion R.B.J. 1983. Photographic superimposition. *Journal of Forensic Sciences* 28(3):724–734.

Dutra F.T. 1944. Identification of person and determination of cause of death from skeletal remains. *Archives of Pathology* 38:339–349.

Eckert W.B. and N. Garland. 1984. The history of the forensic applications in radiology. *American Journal of Forensic Medicine and Pathology* 5:53–56.

Engel C.E. 1954. Superimposition. *Medical Radiography and Photography* 30:20–23.

Fatteh A.V. and G.T. Mann. 1969. The role of radiology in forensic pathology. *Medicine, Science and the Law* 9:27–30.

Federal Rules of Evidence. 1975, 2000.

Frye v. United States, 293 F. 1013 (C.A.D.C 1923).

General Electric Co v Joiner, 522 US 136 (1997).

Gerasimov M.M. 1971. *The Face Finder*. Philadelphia, PA: JB Lippincot.

Glaister J. and J.C. Brash. 1937. *Medico-Legal Aspects of the Ruxton Case*. Baltimore, MD: William Wood and Co.

Greulich W.W. 1960. Skeletal features visible in the roentgenograms of hand and wrist which can be used for establishing individual identification. *American Journal of Roentgenology Radium Therapy and Nuclear Medicine* 83(4):756–764.

Greulich W.W. and S.I. Pyle. 1959. *Radiographic Atlas of Skeletal Development of the Hand and Wrist*. Palo Alto, CA: Stanford University Press.

Haglund W.D. and C.L. Fligner. 1993. Confirmation of human identification using computerized tomography (CT). *Journal of Forensic Sciences* 38(3):708–712.

His W. 1895. Anatomische Forschungen uber Johann Sebastian Bach's Gebeine und Antlitz nebst Bemerkungen uber dessen Bilder. *Abhandlungen der mathematisch-physikalischen Klasse der Koniglichen Sachsischen Gesellschaft der Wissenschaften* 22:379–420.

Hooton E.A. 1930. *Indians of the Pecos Pueblo: A Study of Their Skeletal Remains*. Andover, U.K.: Yale University Press.

Hogge J.P., J.M. Messmer, and Q.N. Doan. 1993. Radiographic identification of unknown human remains and interpreter experience level. *Journal of Forensic Sciences* 39:373–377.

Hogge J.P., J.M. Messmer, and M.F. Fierro. 1995. Positive identification by post-surgical defects from unilateral lamdoid synostectomy: A case report. *Journal of Forensic Sciences* 40(4):688–691.

Ibanez O., L. Ballerini, O. Cordon, S. Damas, and J. Santamaria. 2009. An experimental study on the applicability of evolutionary algorithms to craniofacial superimposition in forensic identification. *Information Sciences* 179:3998–4028.

Jensen S. 1991. Identification of human remains lacking skull and teeth. A case report with some methodological considerations. *American Journal of Forensic Medicine and Pathology* 12(2):93–97.

Joblanski N.G. and B.S. Shum. 1989. Identification of unknown human remains by comparison of antemortem and postmortem radiographs. *Forensic Science International* 42:221–230.

Kade H., H. Meyers, and J.E. Wahlke. 1967. Identification of skeletonized remains by x-ray comparison. *The Journal of Criminal Law* 58:261–264.

Kahana T., L. Goldin, and J. Hiss. 2002. Personal identification based on radiographic vertebral fractures. *American Journal of Forensic Medicine and Pathology* 23(1):36–41.

Kahana T. and J. Hiss. 1997. Identification of human remains: Forensic radiology. *Journal of Clinical Forensic Medicine* 4:7–15.

Kahana R., J. Hiss, and P. Smith. 1998. Quantitative assessment of trabecular bone pattern identification. *Journal of Forensic Sciences* 43(6):1144–1147.

Kerley E.R. 1977. Forensic anthropology. In: *Forensic Medicine,* Vol. 2, eds. C.G. Tedeschi, W.G. Eckert, and L.G. Tedeschi. Philadelphia, PA: W.B. Saunders Company.

Kirk N.J., R.E. Wood, and M. Goldstein. 2002. Skeletal identification using the frontal sinus region: A retrospective study of 39 cases. *Journal of Forensic Sciences* 47(2):318–323.

Koelmeyer T.D. 1982. Videocamera superimposition and facial reconstruction as an aid to identification. *American Journal of Forensic Medicine and Pathology* 3(1):45–47.

Kollman J. and W. Buchly. 1898. Die Persistenz der Rassen und die Reconstruction der Physiognomie prahistorischer Schadel. *Archiv fur Anthropologie* 25:329–359.

Komar D.A. and J.E. Buikstra. 2008. *Forensic Anthropology: Contemporary Theory and Practice*. New York: Oxford University Press.

Komar D. and S. Lathrop. 2006. Frequencies of morphological characteristics in two contemporary forensic collections: Implications for identification. *Journal of Forensic Sciences* 51(5):974–978.

Koot M.G. 2003. Radiographic human identification using bones of the hand: A validation study. *Proceedings of the 55th Annual Meeting of the American Academy of Forensic Sciences*, February 17–22, Chicago, IL.

Koot M.G., N.J. Sauer, and T.W. Fenton. 2005. Radiographic human identification using bones of the hand: A validation study. *Journal of Forensic Sciences* 50(2):263–268.

Krogman W.M. and M.Y. Iscan. 1986. *The Human Skeleton in Forensic Medicine*, 2nd edn. Springfield, MA: CC Thomas.

Kumho Tire Co. v. Carmichael, 526 U.S. 137 (1999).

London M.R., N.P. Libbey, D.G. Shemin, and J.A. Chazan. 1994. Renal osteodystrophy and dialysis artifacts as indicators of identification. *Forensic Science International* 65:81–96.

MacKinnon G.E. and A.Z. Mundorff. 2006. The world trade center—September 11, 2001. In *Forensic Human Identification: An Introduction*, eds. T. Thompson and S.M. Black, pp. 485–499. Boca Raton, FL: CRC Press.

Mann R.W. 1998. Use of bone trabeculae to establish positive identification. *Forensic Science International* 98(1–2):91–99.

Marek Z., J. Kusmiderski, and Z. Lisowski. 1983. Radiograms of the paranasal sinuses as a principle of identifying catastrophe victims and unknown skeletons. *Arch Kriminol* 172(1–2):1–6.

Martel W., J.D. Wicks, and R.C. Hendrix. 1997. The accuracy of radiological identification of humans using skeletal landmarks: A contribution to forensic pathology. *Radiology* 124:681–684.

McCormick C.T. 1972. *McCormick's Handbook of the Law of Evidence*, 2nd edn., ed. E.W. Cleary. St. Paul, MN: West Publishing Company.

McCormick W.M., J.H. Stewart, and L.A. Langford. 1985. Sex determination from chest plate roentgenograms. *American Journal of Physical Anthropology* 68:173–195.

Messmer J.M. 1986. Radiographic identification. In: *CAP Handbook for Postmortem Examination of Unidentified Remains*, ed. M.F. Fierro, pp. 68–75. Skokie, IL: College of American Pathologists.

Morgan T.A. and M.C. Harris. 1953. The use of x-rays as an aid to medicolegal investigations. *Journal of Forensic Medicine* 1:28–38.

Mundorff A.Z., R. Shaler, E. Beischke, and E. Mar-Cash. 2008. Marrying Anthropology and DNA: ssential for Solving Complex Commingling Problems in Cases of Extreme Fragmentation. In: Recovery, Analysis and Identification of Commingled Human Remains, ed. B. Adams and J. Byrd, pp. 285–299. Totowa, New Jersey: Humana Press.

Murphy W.A. and G.E. Gantner. 1982. Radiologic examination of anatomic parts and skeletonized remains. *Journal of Forensic Sciences* 27:9–18.

Murphy W.A., F.G. Spruill, and G.E. Gantner. 1980. Radiologic Identification of unknown human remains. *Journal of Forensic Sciences* 25:727–735.

Nozawa H., K. Watanabe-Suzuki, H. Seno, A. Ishii, and O. Suzuki. 2002. An autopsy case of human skeletal remains with a numerical variation in the thoraco-lumbar vertebrae. *Legal Medicine* 4:123–126.

Owsley D.W. and R.W. Mann. 1989. Positive identification based on radiographic examination of the leg and foot. *Journal of the American Podiatric Medical Association* 79(10):511–513.

Owsley D.W., R.W. Mann, R.E. Chapman, E. Moore, and W.A. Cox. 1993. Positive identification in a case of intentional extreme fragmentation. *Journal of Forensic Sciences* 38(4):985–996.

Penalver J.J., T. Kahana, and J. Hiss. 1997. Prosthetic devices in positive identification of human remains. *Journal of Forensic Sciences* 47:400–405.

Petrie W.M.F. 1989. *Deshasheh 1897. Mem 15.* London, U.K.: Egyptian Exploration Fund.

Pfaeffli M., P. Vock, R. Dirnhofer, M. Braun, S.A. Bollinger, and M.J. Thali. 2007. Post-mortem radiological CT identification based on classical ante-mortem x-ray examinations. *Forensic Science International* 171:111–117.

Powers R. 2005. Remains to be seen! *Journal of Forensic Identification* 55(6):687–696.

Quatrehomme G., T. Balaguer, P. Staccini, and V. Alunni-Perret. 2007. Assessment of the accuracy of three-dimensional manual craniofacial reconstructions: A series of 25 controlled cases. *International Journal of Legal Medicine* 121:469–475.

Rhine J.S. and H. R. Campbell. 1980. Thickness of facial tissues in American Blacks. *Journal of Forensic Sciences* 25:847–858.
Rhine S. and K. Sperry. 1991. Radiographic identification by mastoid sinus and arterial pattern. *Journal of Forensic Sciences* 36:272–279.
Ribeiro F.A. 2000. Standardized measurements of radiographic films of the frontal sinuses: An aid to identifying unknown persons. *Ear, Nose and Throat Journal* 79(1):26–33.
Ricci A., G.L. Marella, and M.A. Apostol. 2006. A new experimental approach to computer-aided face/skull identification in forensic anthropology. *American Journal of Forensic Medicine and Pathology* 27(1):46–49.
Riddick L., B.G. Brogdon, J. Laswell-Hoff, and B. Delmas. 1983. The accuracy of radiologic identification of charred human remains through use of the dorsal defect of the patella. *Journal of Forensic Sciences* 28(1):263–267.
Rouge D., N. Telmon, P. Arrue, G. Larrouy, and L. Arbus. 1993. Radiographic identification of human remains through deformities and anomalies of post-cranial bones: A report of two cases. *Journal of Forensic Sciences* 38(4):997–1007.
Rowe J.H. 1953. Technical aids in anthropology: A historical survey. In: *Anthropology Today: An Encyclopedic Inventory*, ed. A.L. Krober, pp. 895–940. Chicago, IL: University of Chicago Press.
Sainio P., S.M. Syrjanen, and S. Komakow. 1990. Positive identification of victims by comparison of ante-mortem and post-mortem dental radiographs. *The Journal of Forensic Odonto-Somatology* 8:11–16
Saks M.J. and J.J. Koehler. 2005. The coming paradigm shift in forensic identification science. *Science* 309:892–895.
Sanders I., M.E. Woesner, R.A. Ferguson, and T.T. Noguchi. 1972. A new application of forensic radiology: Identification of deceased from a single clavicle. *American Journal of Roentgenology, Radium Therapy and Nuclear Medicine* 115(3):619–622.
Sassouni V. 1959. Cephalometric identification: A proposed method of identification of war dead by means of radiographic cephalometry. *Journal of Forensic Sciences* 4:1–10.
Sauer N.J., R.E. Brantely, and D.A. Barondess. 1988. The effects of aging on the comparability of antemortem and postmortem radiographs. *Journal of Forensic Sciences* 33(5):1223–1230.
Scheuller A. 1921. Das Rontgenogram der Stirnhohle: ein Hilfsmitten fur die Identitasbestimmung von Schadeln. *Monatsschrift feur Ohrenheilkunde und Laryngo-Rhinologie* 5:1617–1620.
Schmidt G. and D. Kallieris. 1982. Use of radiographs in the forensic autopsy. *Forensic Science International* 19:263–270.
Scientific Working Group for Forensic Anthropology (SWGANTH). https://www.swganth.org.
Sen N.K. 1962. Identification by superimposed photographs. *International Criminal Police Review* 162:284.
Shahrom A.W., P. Vanezis, R.C. Chapman, A. Gonzales, C. Blenkinsop, and M.L. Rossi. 1996. Techniques in facial identification: Computer-aided facial reconstruction using a laser scanner and video superimposition. *International Journal of Legal Medicine* 108(4):194–200.
Sidler M., C. Jackowski, R. Dirnhofer, P. Vock, and M. Thali. 2007. Use of multislice computed tomography in disaster victim identification—Advantages and limitations. *Forensic Science International* 169:188–128.
Singleton A.C. 1951. The roentgenologial identification of victims of the "Noronic" disaster. *American Journal of Roentgenology* 66:375–384.
Sivaloganathan S. and W.P. Butt. 1988. A foot in the yard. *Medicine, Science and the Law* 28(2):150–156.
Smith V.A., A.M. Christensen, and S.W. Myers. 2011. The reliability of visually comparing small frontal sinuses. *Journal of Forensic Sciences* 55(6):1413–1415.
Sopher I.M. 1972. The dentist, the forensic pathologist, and the identification of human remains. *Journal of the American Dental Association* 85(6):1324–1329.
Steadman D.W., B.J. Adams, and L.W. Konigsberg. 2006. Statistical basis for positive identification in forensic anthropology. *American Journal of Physical Anthropology* 131(1):15–26.

Stephan C.N. 2003. Anthropological facial reconstruction—Recognizing the fallacies, "unembracing" the errors and realizing method limits. *Science and Justice* 43(4):193–200.
Stephan C.N. and E.K. Simpson. 2008a. Facial soft tissue depths in craniofacial identification (Part 1): An analytical review of published adult data. *Journal of Forensic Sciences* 53(6):1257–1272.
Stephan C.N. and E.K. Simpson. 2008b. Facial soft tissue depths in craniofacial identification (Part 1): An analytical review of published sub-adult data. *Journal of Forensic Sciences* 53(6):1273–1279.
Stevens P.J. 1966. Identification of a body by unusual means. *Medicine, Science and the Law* 6:160–161.
Stewart T.D. 1979. *Essentials of Forensic Anthropology*. Springfield, MA: Thomas.
Sudimak J.R., B.J. Lewis, J. Rich, D.E. Dean, and P.M. Fardal. 2002. Identification of decomposed human remains from radiographic comparisons of an unusual foot deformity. *Journal of Forensic Sciences* 47(1):218–220.
Thorne H. and H. Thyberg. 1953. Identification of children (or adults) by mass miniature radiography of the cranium. *Acta Odontologica Scandinavica* 11(2):129–140.
Turner W.D., R.E.B. Brown, T.P. Kelliher, P.H. Tu, M.A. Taister, and K.W.P. Miller. 2005. A novel method of automated skull registration for forensic facial approximation. *Forensic Science International* 154:149–158.
Ubelaker D.H. 1990. Positive identification of American Indian skeletal remains from radiographic comparison. *Journal of Forensic Sciences* 35(2):466–472.
Ubelaker D.H. 2000. A history of Smithsonian-FBI collaboration in forensic anthropology, especially in regard to facial imagery. *Forensic Science Communications* 2(4).
Ubelaker D.H., E. Bubniak, and G.E. O'Donnell. 1992. Computer-assisted photographic superimposition. *Journal of Forensic Sciences* 37:750–762.
Ubelaker D.H. and G.E. O'Donnell. 1992. Computer-assisted facial reproduction. *Journal of Forensic Sciences* 37:155–162.
Valenzuela A. 1997. Radiographic comparison of the lumbar spine for positive identification of human remains. A case report. *American Journal of Forensic Medicine and Pathology* 18(2):215–217.
Varga M. and P. Takacs. 1991. Radiographic personal identification with characteristic feature in the hip joint. *American Journal of Forensic Medicine and Pathology* 12:328–331.
Verma M.S. 1981. Skull-photograph superimposition: A case study. Paper presented at the *35th Annual Meeting of the American Academy of Forensic Sciences*, February 17–20, Los Angeles, CA.
Webster G. 1955. Photography as an aid to identification: The Plumbago Pit case. *Police Journal* 28:185.
Webster W.P., W.K. Murray, W. Brinkous, and P. Hudson. 1986. Identification of human remains using photographic reconstruction. In: *Forensic Osteology—Advances in the Identification of Human Remains*, ed. K.J. Reichs, pp. 256–289. Springfield, MA: Charles C Thomas.
Wilder H.H. and B. Wentworth. 1918. *Personal Identification: Methods for the Identification of Individuals, Living or Dead*. Boston, MA: Gorham Press.
Yoshino M., S. Miyasaka, H. Sato, and S. Seta. 1987. Classification system of frontal sinus patterns by radiography. Its application to identification of unknown skeletal remains. *Forensic Science International* 34(4):289–299.

Suggested Readings

Holland T.D., R.W. Mann, and D.H. Ubelaker. 1999. *Advances in Personal Identification in Mass Disasters*. U.S. Army Central Identification Laboratory, Hawaii.
Stewart T.D. 1971. *Personal Identification in Mass Disasters*. Washington, DC: Smithsonian Institution.
Thompson T. and S.M. Black. 2006. *Forensic Human Identification: An Introduction*. Boca Raton, FL: CRC Press.

Forensic Anthropology
A Human Rights Approach

21

ERIN H. KIMMERLE

Contents

Holocaust survivor Elie Wiesel wrote, "This is the duty of our generation as we enter the twenty-first century—solidarity with the weak, the persecuted, the lonely, the sick, and those in despair. It is expressed by the desire to give a noble and humanizing meaning to a community in which all members will define themselves not by their own identity but by that of others." International forensic investigations into human rights abuses, torture, war crimes, and genocide enforce human rights through judicial accountability. For example, the identification of victims of mass atrocities is a process that gives families and survivors *access to justice* and is defined as a human rights issue. Human identification has always been at the center of medicolegal death investigations, whether the ultimate purpose is to seek criminal prosecution or to achieve other humanitarian goals for surviving family members such as reparations and the repatriation of human remains. The challenges involved with investigations into missing persons and unidentified human remains pose problems in every nation, though individuals may go missing for a variety of reasons ranging from homicide to genocide. In areas of conflict the problem is exacerbated as hundreds, thousands, or millions of people go missing due to war, enforced disappearances, forced relocations, internal displacements, and mass killings. Forensic investigations in the human rights (HHRR) arena often fall within the framework of *transitional justice*, which is a concept that broadly encompasses judicial reform that takes place as nations transition to peace. Through transitional justice initiatives, efforts to locate missing persons, identify civilian victims, repatriate human remains, account for human rights violations, and professionalize medicolegal death investigations are taking center stage.

The purpose of this chapter is to discuss the role of forensic anthropology in human rights investigations and the range of duties forensic anthropologists perform internationally. Investigations into genocide and war crimes over the past 20 years have led to significant changes in the ways in which we think about war, define human rights, and hold men accountable for their actions. For example, the *Mothers of the Plaza de Mayo*, comprised of Argentine women, are human rights activists who fought for the right to reunite with their abducted children and grandchildren. Argentina is one of the first examples of the combined use of anthropology and forensics as legal tools to *enforce* human rights through judicial accountability. The pioneering work of Clyde Snow and his team that began in 1982 in Argentina (Stover and Eisner 1982, Snow et al. 1984, Fondebrider 2002) has been modeled around the world as a standard for the exhumation of mass graves for victim identification, skeletal analysis for the prosecution of crimes, the repatriation of human remains for funerary rites, and reconciliation for transitioning communities.

Morris Tidball-Binz (2006), Director for *The Missing Project* at the International Committee for the Red Cross (ICRC), wrote that "Forensic sciences are recognized as indispensable for the proper recovery, handling and identification of dead people reported missing, as well as for identifying the living." Increasingly, International Human Rights Laws (IHRL) and International Humanitarian Laws (IHL) are redefining the ways in which missing persons and human identity are valued and treated. The *International Convention for the Protection of All Persons from Enforced Disappearance* (United Nations General Assembly, December 2006) affirms the right of victims to know the truth about the circumstances of an enforced disappearance and the fate of the disappeared person. It also clearly outlines the rights of family members to seek, receive, and impart information toward this end and is generally thought of simply as "The Right to Know …" The additional protocols to the Geneva Conventions of 1949 relating to the Protection of Victims of International Armed Conflicts (Protocol I, June 8, 1977) and the fourth Convention (IV) relative to the Protection of Civilian Persons in Time of War (Geneva, August 12, 1949) state that:

> Families have the right to be informed of the fate of missing relatives (API Art. 32). The parties to a conflict must search for persons reported missing by an adverse party API Art. 33 and facilitate enquiries made by members of families dispersed as a result of the conflict so as to help them restore contact with one another and try to bring them together again. A further responsibility incumbent upon the parties to a conflict concerns deceased persons: lists showing the exact location and markings of the graves, together with particulars of the dead interred therein, must be exchanged API Art. 34. Similar treaty-based and customary rules apply in non-international armed conflicts.

The ways in which human rights are protected are based increasingly on medicolegal and criminal investigations, including the application of forensic science to missing person and unidentified person cases. Although criminal prosecution is one form of accountability, it may or may not occur in association with the process to exhume graves, identify the dead, or create memorials and historical records of the events that occurred.

Call (2003) argued that forensic science is "tremendously important for the survivability of an everyday relevance of democracy, given that crime is the chief threat to support for democracy." The ability for families of the decedent to play an active role in this process is an exercise of their rights (i.e., access to knowledge or due process). Exercising these rights may take many years and vary at different times based on security and the formation or changing structure of judicial systems. As a result, investigations into extrajudicial executions often occur many years after the fact when leadership changes. The timing of such investigations further place forensic anthropology at the center of these investigations as there is a need to excavate remains from clandestine graves or sometimes exhume victims that may have been buried following the initial investigation. Additionally, medicolegal death investigations provide a platform for education, fair elections, and sustainable peace-building programs following conflicts (UN, ICTR Tribunal at a Glance). The missions of the International Criminal Tribunals established by the United Nations Security Council for Rwanda (ICTR) in 1994 and the Former Yugoslavia (ICTY) in 1993 have enabled public discourse and reconciliation while prosecuting offenders for violations

Table 21.1 Summary Information about the ICC and the United Nations ICTY and ICTR

ICC

- International Criminal Court
- ICC is governed by the Rome Statute, entered into force July 2002 after ratification by 60 countries
- Located in the Hague, the Netherlands
- *What they investigate*: genocide, war crimes, and crimes against humanity
- *Scope of authority*: This is the first permanent, treaty-based, ICC established to investigate serious crimes for the international community
- *Scope of investigations*: The ICC investigates cases that occurred after 2002 and are initiated by a state party, the Prosecutor or the United Nations Security Council

ICTY

- International Criminal Tribunal for the Former Yugoslavia
- Established May 1993, through UN Security Council Resolution 827
- Located in the Hague, the Netherlands
- *What they investigate*: grave breaches of the 1949 Geneva conventions, violations of the laws or customs of war, genocide, and crimes against humanity
- *Scope of authority*: crimes committed in the territory of the former Yugoslavia from 1991, including the six republics of The Socialist Federal Republic of Yugoslavia (SFRY): Bosnia and Herzegovina, Croatia, Macedonia, Montenegro, Serbia (including the regions of Kosovo and Vojvodina), and Slovenia
- *Scope of investigations*: crimes committed by individuals in the territory of the Former Yugoslavia

ICTR

- International Criminal Tribunal for Rwanda
- Established February 1995, through UN Security Council Resolution 955
- Located in Arusha, United Republic of Tanzania
- *What they investigate*: genocide, crimes against humanity, and violations of Article 3 common to the Geneva Conventions and of Additional Protocol II
- *Scope of authority*: crimes committed between January 1 and December 31, 1994
- *Scope of investigations*: crimes committed by Rwandans in the territory of Rwanda and in the territory of neighboring States, as well as non-Rwandan citizens for crimes committed in Rwanda

to IHL and IHRL (Table 21.1). For example, in the course of prosecution, the ICTY took the testimony of more than 4500 witnesses who were able to give their name, document their story, and testify in court, thereby creating an historical account of what they experienced (UN, ICTY Tribunal at a Glance).

Human rights investigations, particularly those involving mass killings or war crimes, tend to share a number of characteristics (Table 21.2). Patterns among these types of investigations pose unique challenges and often require a wider range of skills and solutions than the "typical" case (Skinner 1987, Haglund 2001). For example, in human rights cases, there tend to be a high number of victims and an even higher number of missing persons due to internal displacement and refugees who flee a conflict area. However, many missing persons are not reported as missing, and antemortem records such as medical or dental records may not exist or may have been destroyed through the course of war. Therefore, significant challenges arise when attempting to orchestrate human identification on a massive scale. Second, abuses may occur over many years but may not be investigated until years after the fact, which means critical evidence may be lost. In these cases, the investigation typically focuses on humanitarian efforts such as identification and reburial, rather than criminal prosecution.

Table 21.2 Patterns among Human Rights Investigations

- Human rights violations tend to occur on a massive scale, over a wide geographical area, or over long periods of time
- In many critical incidents, such as explosions or warfare, there may be more injured persons than fatalities. There may also be high numbers of fatalities and refugees or internally displaced persons, which challenges antemortem data collection for missing persons
- Continued conflict may result in prolonged humanitarian crises and basic human security threats that further delay judicial processes
- Individual skeletal remains often exhibit multiple injuries possibly even resulting from multiple mechanisms of injury (i.e., gunfire and explosions). This also results in commingling of remains and may impede the identification process
- Criminal acts tend to be investigated years after the incident or not at all
- Evidence may be altered or destroyed to hide crimes

Physical Evidence: Corroborating the Story

The fundamental purpose of forensic science and crime scene processing is to identify, collect, and preserve physical evidence (Figure 21.1). This tangible, physical evidence is used to understand the circumstances surrounding the death event in order to reconstruct that event. Physical evidence is critical for corroborating the statements obtained from survivors or witnesses and establishes certain facts, with varying levels of certainty.

The ICTY and ICTR relied heavily on "large-scale forensic evidence for the prosecution of war crimes" according to Baraybar and Gasior (2006). For example, forensic investigations were organized and carried out by the Office of the Prosecutor in Kosovo in 2000. During that time more than 1500 bodies were exhumed for autopsy. In many of those cases the identity of the decedents was presumed to be known and families gave permission for the exhumation/autopsy. Through the course of the investigation, the identifications were confirmed and the cause and manner of death was determined for each case. The cause and manner of death became critical evidence in showing what crimes had been committed and provided physical evidence of the circumstances surrounding the murder of thousands of individuals. Witnesses provided testimony that could be substantiated through the postmortem record. The power of autopsy is a postmortem record that provides physical evidence of the circumstances surrounding a death (Figures 21.2 through 21.4).

Figure 21.1 Example of surface remains. Forensic anthropologists work at the crime scene with detectives, medical examiners, and crime scene technicians to document and excavate the site.

Figure 21.2 Mass grave excavation. Forensic anthropologists prepare the site for excavation. The topsoil was removed using heavy equipment. Differences in the color of soil indicate disturbed and sterile soils. The disturbed area represents a long trench indicating a mass grave.

Figure 21.3 Forensic anthropologists begin to excavate the mass grave depicted in Figure 21.2 using shovels, picks, and trowels. Each layer of soil is removed and carefully sifted. Any artifacts, bones, or evidence is documented, mapped, and photographed *in situ*.

Figure 21.4 The first layer of bodies is exposed. Note the remains are piled on top of one another. Careful excavation means that the context is preserved and associated remains and evidence will be excavated together.

In a landmark case, two indictments against former Kosovo Liberation Army commanders resulted in successful prosecutions (*The Prosecutor v Limaj et al.* IT-03-66) based in part on skeletal evidence of torture (Kimmerle and Baraybar 2008). The skeletonized remains of 11 adult males exhibited blunt force trauma applied to the chest cavity, sternum, tibia, and teeth. Specifically, fractures to the ribs, sternum, and tibia showed evidence of reactive bone formation and areas of resorption around or adjacent to the fracture edges, thereby indicating short-term survival following the initial injuries. Overall, this provided evidence of repeated physical abuse while the men were detained. Documentation of the skeletal fractures corresponded to injuries described by witnesses (*The Prosecutor v Limaj* et al. IT-03-66, June 1, 2005, T 1341–1342):

> Q: I know it's unpleasant, but I'm going to ask you to describe that occasion for the Trial Chamber. First, do you remember how many men were there being beaten?
> A: They brought four or five of them. I don't know the exact number, but it wasn't more than five. They lined them up and started beating them. They would beat everyone one of them for five or ten minutes, slapping them, kicking them, hitting them on their legs. One of them was unable to stand at all. At any rate, they were beaten up.

The skeletal analysis of the 11 victims revealed that 7 individuals had been fatally shot to death and that 10 of the victims had antemortem fractures resulting from blunt trauma in the form of beatings. As this example demonstrates, skeletal fracture patterns and defects provide critical evidence for determining the circumstances, cause, and manner of death (Table 21.3). The morphology of skeletal trauma is shaped by internal factors (i.e., the particular bone affected), extrinsic factors (i.e., the type of weapon), and contextual factors (i.e., whether or not it resulted from act of volition). Critical information is obtained about the type of weapon, the number of injuries, and the sequence of injuries through the careful diagnosis of skeletal trauma (Figures 21.5 through 21.7).

The presence of other forms of evidence associated with a body such as ligatures may also indicate murder. Physical evidence retrieved from mass graves in Bosnia included folded clothing, stretchers, ligatures, and blindfolds. For example, investigators recovered 448 blindfolds on or with bodies at 10 separate sites (Krstić Trial Chamber Judgment, par. 75). At least 423 ligatures made of cloth, string, and wire were used to bind victims' wrists together and were found at 13 separate sites (Krstić Trial Chamber Judgment, par. 75). Such physical evidence demonstrates the circumstances around the deaths and that crimes occurred.

Table 21.3 Epidemiological Framework for Trauma Analysis

- Demography
- Context
- Fatal environment
- Intent
- Scientific protocols
- Methods for differential diagnosis
- Weaponry and ballistics science
- Estimation of cause of death
- Manner of death
- Intrinsic biological factors (i.e., the bone impacted)
- Extrinsic factors (i.e., type of weapon or caliber of bullet)

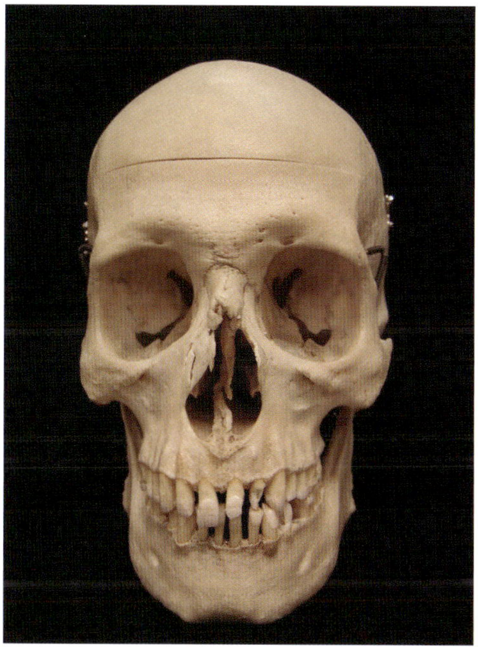

Figure 21.5 Male skull frontal view. Note the morphological traits of the face are indicative of a male, including a large glabella region and supraorbital ridge.

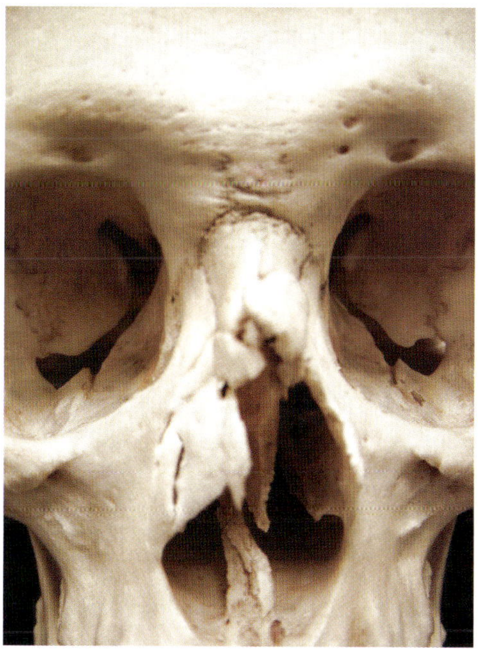

Figure 21.6 Male skull close-up view of nasal region showing multiple healed fractures. Antemortem fractures may be useful parameters through the identification process. When they occur on the face, they are also important for creating accurate facial approximations.

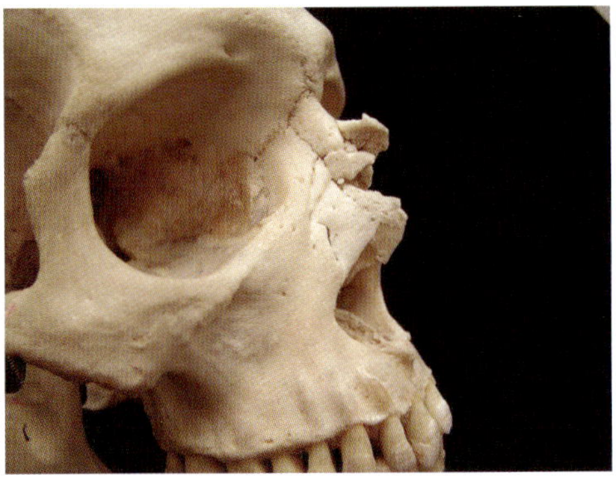

Figure 21.7 Right lateral view of nasal area, depicting antemortem fractures.

Likewise, moving human remains from *primary* interments, or graves, to new locations in an attempt to hide their existence shows intent to conceal evidence. In the 2001 verdict against General Radislav *Krstić* (*The Prosecutor v. Krstić*, IT-98-33: 596, p. 212), evidence of *secondary* burials was accepted by the trial judges as

> … a strong indication of the intent to destroy the group as such in the concealment of the bodies in mass graves, which were later dug up, the bodies mutilated and reburied in other mass graves located in even more remote areas, thereby preventing any decent burial in accord with religious and ethnic customs and causing terrible distress to the mourning survivors, many of whom have been unable to come to a closure until the death of their men is finally verified.

In addition to witness statements about moving graves, several forms of physical evidence were present in the mass graves excavated by the ICTY that helped lead to this ruling, including (1) the presence of human remains, artifacts, and trace evidence from a single source scattered among more than one site, and (2) commingled and disarticulated skeletal materials showing the bodies were decomposed at the time of burial. Building materials and body parts were reassociated from multiple scenes. In some instances, the building materials recovered from graves could be further linked to the primary locations in which the murders occurred.

Global Examples: Past and Present

In the course of human rights investigations, forensic anthropologists contribute through casework, research, and training. Specifically, they assist with witness interviews, the collection of antemortem data about missing persons, the creation of biological profiles from skeletal analysis to establish the initial parameters of identification at autopsy, grave search and recovery, exhumations, trauma analysis, and expert testimony. As with any domestic case, the methods anthropologists use must be legally defensible. Appling protocols and methods to a variety of cultures, populations, judicial systems, and political contexts can be challenging. Ultimately, as with any forensic specialist or investigator, everything the anthropologist does through the course of the investigation has to follow the rules of evidence, maintain chain of custody, and ensure the admissibility of evidence into court should prosecution be sought.

A variety of organizations employ forensic anthropologists to monitor, collect, document, and analyze evidence for international investigations into human rights violations. These groups work for family associations, prosecutorial offices or courts, truth commissions, governments, nonprofit organizations, and universities such as the United Nations, the American Association for the Advancement of Science (AAAS), Physicians for Human Rights (PHR), Amnesty International, and various regional forensic teams (i.e., the Argentine Forensic Anthropology Team, EAAF; the Guatemalan Forensic Anthropology Foundation, FAFG; the Peruvian Forensic Anthropology Team, EPAF; and the Colombian interdisciplinary team on forensic work and psychosocial assistance, EQUITAS). These types of investigations are ongoing today in countries throughout Asia, Europe, Africa, and the Americas in a variety of different contexts.

The United Nations Office of the High Commissioner for Human Rights has the responsibility to protect human rights. Regional human rights courts and commissions also exist under the auspice of regional human rights treaties throughout the Americas, Europe, and Africa. International judicial bodies include the International Court of Justice, the International Criminal Tribunals for the Former Yugoslavia and Rwanda (ICTY and ICTR), and the International Criminal Court (ICC). Further judicial bodies, such as the European Court of Human Rights, the Inter-American Court on Human Rights, and the African Court on Human and People's Rights, also have jurisdiction over aspects of IHRL (Romano et al. 2004). Therefore, the types of cases in which anthropologists consult are diverse and, accordingly, the duties and roles of the anthropologist in these investigations are highly varied. Anthropologists assist in the field with searches, excavations, and the recovery of human remains. They also assist investigators by collecting antemortem data about missing persons and work directly with families to collect witness statements. Once human remains are excavated and brought to the morgue, anthropologists inventory the remains, collect associated physical evidence from the remains such as bullets or shrapnel fragments, create biological profiles, and determine the presence of perimortem trauma. Skeletal analysis provides the initial parameters for identification (i.e., sex, age, ancestry, stature, unique identification markers, and skeletal pathology), as well as evidence of trauma or possible causes of death, and the time since death or postmortem interval (PMI).

More frequently, anthropologists work directly with prosecutors and testify in court. Forensic anthropologists qualify as expert scientific witnesses based upon their training, case experience, active research agenda and publishing record, and ability to teach professional level courses. Each of these areas is important for building credibility in court both in the United States and internationally, although the actual process of becoming recognized as an expert by a court varies by jurisdiction. Forensic anthropologists routinely testify in the international ICTY and ICTR courts, as well as for truth commissions and domestic courts.

Most often, human remains that are skeletonized or decomposing are found in public spaces. The medical examiner, coroner, prosecutor, or law enforcement may call a forensic anthropologist to assist in the field with recovery, in the morgue at autopsy, or to review prior cases based on reports and photographs. In the context of human rights investigations and extrajudicial killings, it is common that two or three autopsies will be preformed, and experts may be asked to review these cases years following the event. In such cases, each autopsy may result in a different cause and manner of death, hence complicating the investigative process. If the anthropologist had the advantage of assisting in the field, then the inventory, of skeletal elements and documentation of the context of remains can be done more easily and accurately. This process is critical when multiple victims are present, remains are scattered or incomplete, or the remains are commingled. Another advantage that anthropologists bring in the field is that they employ archaeological excavation techniques to systematically recover all evidence, even material as small as hair and fibers. Additionally, anthropologists collect soil, insects, and botany samples that can be used in combination to provide a strong PMI estimate or used to link multiple crime scenes together.

Though most casework follows a similar protocol, forensic anthropologists may be called on to provide an opinion on a wide range of topics. For example, they may be asked to provide an age estimate for a living individual from radiographs when a person's identity is in question, to create a facial approximation (Figure 21.8) for decomposing or skeletonized remains, or to review radiographs for trauma diagnosis (Figures 21.9 through 21.14). The skeletal data about age, sex, stature, ancestry, pathology, and unique individual traits are used to estimate the initial parameters of identity (Table 21.4). When it comes to human identification, there are different categories of identification that provide varying measures of group or individual identity (Table 21.5). *Presumptive* and *positive* identification establish individuality, whereas *collective* or *contextual* identification either places

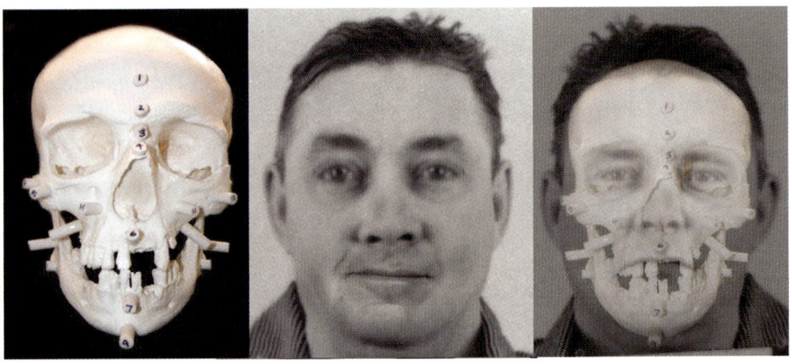

Figure 21.8 Example of facial reproduction using 2D composite method. Tissue depth markers are placed on the skull based on the demographic profile estimated from the remains. The underlying skeletal anatomy is used to build a face.

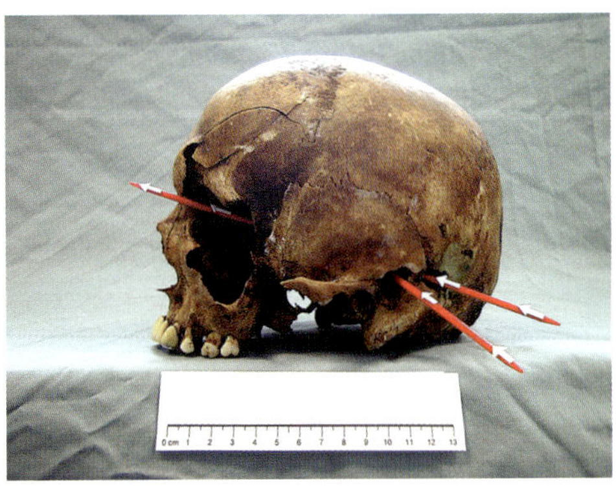

Figure 21.9 Left cranium showing two gunshot entry wounds. Both shots exited through the facial region of the skull. (Reproduced from Kimmerle EH and Baraybar JP. *Skeletal Trauma: Identification of Injuries Resulting from Human Rights Abuse and Armed Conflict*, CRC Press, Boca Raton, FL, p. 493, 2008.)

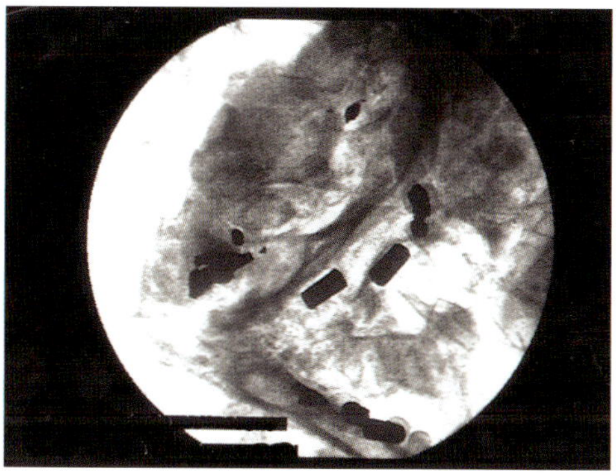

Figure 21.10 Shrapnel from blast injury depicted in fluoroscope image alongside skeletal remains. (Reproduced from Kimmerle EH and Baraybar JP. *Skeletal Trauma: Identification of Injuries Resulting from Human Rights Abuse and Armed Conflict*, CRC Press, Boca Raton, FL, p. 493, 2008.)

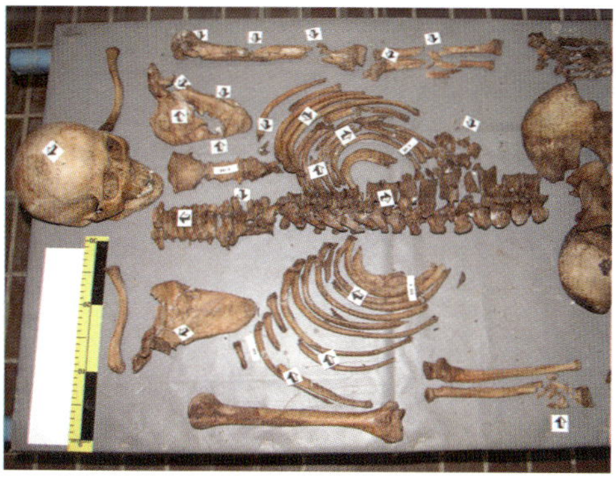

Figure 21.11 Skeleton showing multiple perimortem fractures due to blunt impact and gunfire injuries. (Reproduced from Kimmerle EH and Baraybar JP. *Skeletal Trauma: Identification of Injuries Resulting from Human Rights Abuse and Armed Conflict*, CRC Press, Boca Raton, FL, p. 493, 2008.)

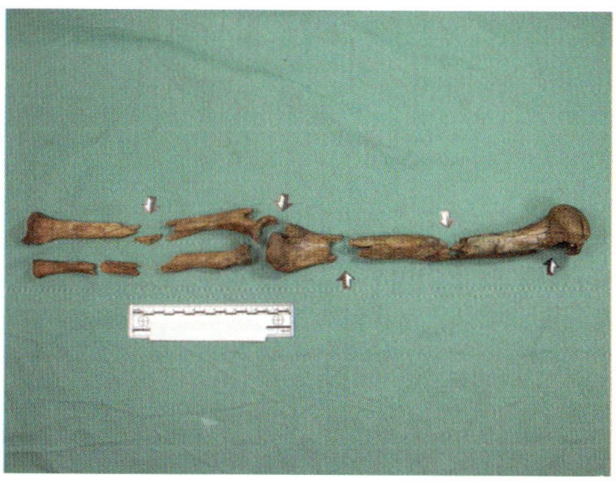

Figure 21.12 Left-arm bones showing multiple gunfire injuries. (Reproduced from Kimmerle EH and Baraybar JP. *Skeletal Trauma: Identification of Injuries Resulting from Human Rights Abuse and Armed Conflict*, CRC Press, Boca Raton, FL, p. 493, 2008.)

Figure 21.13 Left skull showing multiple blunt impact injuries. (Reproduced from Kimmerle EH and Baraybar JP. *Skeletal Trauma: Identification of Injuries Resulting from Human Rights Abuse and Armed Conflict*, CRC Press, Boca Raton, FL, p. 493, 2008.)

Figure 21.14 Knee region showing cut marks and blunt trauma due to machete. (Reproduced from Kimmerle EH and Baraybar JP. *Skeletal Trauma: Identification of Injuries Resulting from Human Rights Abuse and Armed Conflict*, CRC Press, Boca Raton, FL, p. 493, 2008.)

Table 21.4 Primary Components in Human Identification

Profile Component	Methods
Sex estimation	Pelvic morphology Pelvic metric analysis Cranial metric analysis Cranial morphology Long bone metric analysis
Age estimation	Pubic symphysis morphology Auricular surface morphology Sternal rib morphology Dental metrics Osteoarthritis and degenerative joint changes Dental wear Cranial sutures
Stature estimation	Long bone metric analysis
Ancestry or ethnicity estimation	Cranial metric analysis Cranial morphology Postcranial metric analysis Postcranial morphology
Pathology/unique markers	Documented prior skeletal disease, trauma, or medical intervention/modification Congenital abnormalities
Human identification	Facial approximations/superimpositions/photo ID DNA Fingerprints Clothing identification Artifact/jewelry identification Circumstantial evidence, i.e., witness accounts or geographical locations Dental records Radiographic imaging of skeletal or dental anatomy

an individual into a group or establishes a set of factors about an individual (Kimmerle et al. 2009). Identification categories have different meanings and are used for different purposes depending on the case. In terms of human repatriation, a positive or presumptive identification is necessary so that the individual is known. Collective or contextual identifications are increasingly useful as evidence in criminal cases into IHL or ILHR. The role of demography in prosecuting war crimes is expanding and has become its own area of research and study. Coupland (2001, p. 33) wrote:

> … weapons differ considerably both in the way they are used to execute violence and in their potential to do so; and the type and number of weapons available influence not only how, when, and why the violent act is committed, but also who the victims are and how they are affected.

Therefore, the age and sex distribution of victims, as well as the ratio of wounded to killed, can provide evidence as to whether a crime was committed in some cases (Salama et al. 1999, Reza et al. 2001).

The process of human rights work in the area of forensic anthropology involves working with communities and providing education and research, as well as casework. A number of

Table 21.5 Categories of Human Identification

Identification	Description
Presumptive identification	The possible identity of an individual based on information that is consistent with individuality but that is not mutually exclusive to only one person. Presumptive identifications may be based on recognized facial composites, clothing, or identification papers in a wallet. Characteristics listed on a missing persons report may also match the general descriptive characteristics found during the postmortem investigation, including biological factors or material items associated with the decedent
Positive identification	The identity of an individual established through information that is exclusive to only that individual (i.e., DNA, fingerprints, unique skeletal or dental morphology, or sinus patterns). Positive identifications are derived by comparisons of ante- and postmortem information that are unique to a particular individual
Collective identification	The identification of an individual into a particular cultural, demographic, religious, or ethnic group. General descriptive characteristics about the individual place him/her within a particular group. For example, the age, sex, or ethnicity of the individual may demonstrate group membership based on biological factors. This form of identification has been particularly useful in war crime and genocide investigations (i.e., group membership may be ethnic or demographic, such as "Men of Fighting Age"). Further, associated material artifacts may demonstrate group affiliations (i.e., religious items indicating a "Muslim" or "Catholic" affiliation)
Contextual identification	For an individual or group of individuals, contextual identification is a similar to collective identity but can be applied at the individual or group level. This form of identification serves to inform about the status and context of the individual, such as "foreign-born individuals" or "homeless." In this context, the characteristics about an individual are consistent with certain population characteristics, but limited to strict "group" membership

excellent sources discuss the roles of anthropology in human rights types of investigations (i.e., Kirschner and Hannibal 1994, Burns 1998, Ferllini 1999, 2007, Cordner and McKelvie 2002, Okoye et al. 2006). For example, education and research in the areas of forensic science and pathology is emerging in Lagos, Nigeria, through the work of Dr. John Obafunwa at the Lagos State University, College of Medicine (LASUCOM). In November 2008, a forensic anthropology team from the University of South Florida (USF) began working with LASUCOM to research population variation in aging and its effects on human identification methods. This research collaboration, funded through the National Institute of Justice, created a large international database for human identification that records known skeletal and demographic factors about individuals, as well as medical histories and specific information about nutritional and metabolic disease as it may contribute to skeletal variation (Figure 21.15). Large international databases with data from contemporary populations is important for identification in the United States as many decedents are foreign born. Likewise, Americans die in foreign countries and must be identified as American in order to be repatriated to families in the United States. For more information refer to www.icfahr.usf.

In October 2009, the USF Departments of Anthrpology, History, and the Libraries Holocaust and Genocide Studies Center invited some of the witnesses and survivors from Asaba, Nigeria, to attend a two-day symposium on memory and memorials. During the symposium, witnesses and survivors were interviewed in closed, taped conference rooms and were also asked to provide a public speech about their experience. All of these interviews were

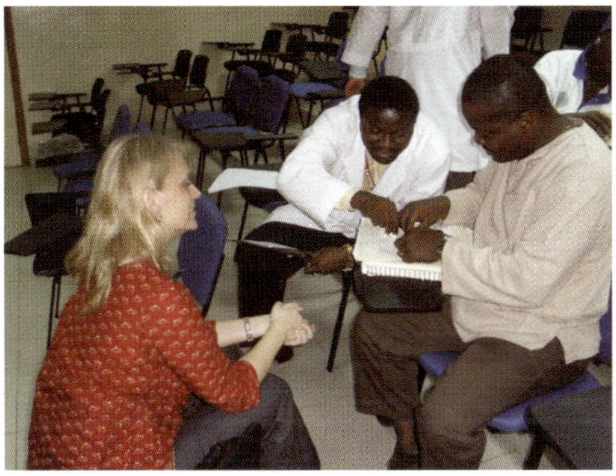

Figure 21.15 Training researchers and medical examiners are a critical part of applied research and foreign service, where forensic anthropology methods are being incorporated into emerging forensic science protocols. Here, Kimmerle and medical residents collect data on aging methods in Lagos, Nigeria.

recorded to create an archive of the event, and, during that initial symposium, more than 30 h of witness testimony through formal interviews were conducted. The investigative team is a multidisciplinary team, including forensic anthropologists, cultural anthropologists, historians, and homicide detectives. The goal of this project was to document a massacre of Igbo civilians that took place in Asaba, Nigeria, in October 1967 and to provide a foundation for research into human identification and missing persons in an international context.

Generally, the events unfolded in October 1967 when Federal troops entered Asaba, Nigeria. People were killed over a several day period, but some of the largest atrocities occurred when the men and women were separated in the center of town. An estimated 500 people were buried by survivors in mass graves according to numerous witnesses. By burying victims in mass graves without regard to their age, sex, or social status, important ceremonial practices for funerals were not possible. Survivors testified at the 2001 Nigerian Human Rights Violations Investigation Commission (HRVIC), also called the Oputa Panel. General Yakubu Gowon, who had been the Nigerian Head of State during the war, made a public apology to the people of Asaba in September 2001. An excerpt from a speech "Ogbeosowa: The Rise from the Dead" by Dr. Ify Uraih at the Asaba Memorial Symposium Lecture Sequence, October 10, 2009, stated as follows:

> I was standing with my elder brother Emma at the edge of the crowd. He was holding my hand... He let go my hand and pushed me further into the crowd. I saw Emma struggling with one of the soldiers and another one shot him from behind at point blank range. Emma fell to the ground with blood gushing out from his back like from a pool. And his shattered vertebrae exposed in the afternoon gloom, the first victim of the massacre that followed.

Accounting past events is not only important for creating a record of what events occurred, but also plays a role in the reconciliation process (Figures 21.16 and 21.17). This point is exemplified by some of the responses by audience members who attended the symposium and who heard others share their stories for the first time. For example, one response stated,

> Just to say that I was there and it was the first time...I have heard a story from an eye witness and survivor!!! ... I was really moved to tears...somebody whose defenseless brother was shot...and rose from amongst dead bodies ....

Figure 21.16 International forensic anthropology and pathology team members, Tony Falsetti, Greg Burg, Casey Anderson, and Erin Kimmerle meet with community leaders in Asaba, Nigeria, to discuss mass atrocities that occurred in the region and the application of forensic anthropology methods for human identification.

Figure 21.17 Community members in Asaba, Nigeria, retell their experiences during the civil war and how mass graves were created to bury the dead.

HHRR Model for Cases in the United States

Applying a human rights approach to the problem of missing persons and unidentified human remains in the United States is also improving domestic investigations. The estimated number of forensic cases that remain unidentified in the United States, approximately an estimated 15,000 persons, is due to a number of factors including funding, access to the latest tools and technologies, limited antemortem data for comparisons, and high mobility patterns among individuals in our society (Kimmerle et al. 2009). Additionally, persons who are likely to go missing and subsequently become part of the unidentified population when remains are found tend to come from at-risk groups that present unique obstacles to case solvability. This population tends to consist primarily of adults, males, and foreign-born individuals. The number of cases that remain unidentified is due in part to a historical trend to give "cold cases" lower priority. However, this is changing, and significant efforts are being made to identify America's unknown decedents through cold case initiatives. Efforts in the United States mirror international reforms, which have redefined the problem of missing persons and unidentified remains. From a human rights model, the families of victims have the right to due process, repatriation of the remains, reparations, information, and access to justice. Therefore, an HHRR model for forensic anthropology and medicolegal death investigations is as relevant in the United States as it is internationally.

References

Baraybar JP, Gasior M. 2006. Forensic anthropology and the most probable cause of death in cases of violations against international humanitarian law: An example from Bosnia and Herzegovina. *Journal of Forensic Sciences*. 51(1):103–108.

Burns K. 1998. Forensic anthropology and human rights issues. In: *Forensic Osteology: Advances in the Identification of Human Remains*. Reichs K. (Ed.), 2nd edn. Springfield, IL: Charles C. Thomas, pp. 63–85.

Call CT. 2003. Democratization, war and state-building: Constructing the rule of law in El Salvador. *Journal of Latin American Studies*. 35(4):827–862.

Cordner S, McKelvie H. 2002. Developing standards in international forensic work to identify missing persons. *International Review of the Red Cross*. 848(84):867–884.

Coupland RM. 2001. Armed violence. *Medicine and Global Survival*. 7:33–37.

Ferllini R. 1999. The role of forensic anthropology in human rights issues. In: *Forensic Osteological Analysis: A Book of Case Studies*. Fairgrieve S. (Ed.), Springfield, IL: Charles C. Thomas, pp. 287–301.

Ferllini R. 2007. *Forensic Archaeology and Human Rights Violations*. CC Thomas Publisher, p. 304.

Fondebrider L. 2002. Reflections on the scientific documentation of human rights violations. *International Review of the Red Cross*. 84:885–891.

Haglund WD. 2001. Recent mass graves, an introduction. In: *Advances in Forensic Taphonomy: Method, Theory and Archaeological Perspectives*. Haglund WD, Sorg MH. (Eds.), Boca Raton, FL: CRC Press, pp. 234–262.

International Committee of the Red Cross (ICRC) website: http://www.icrc.org/eng/index.jsp

Kimmerle EH, Baraybar JP. 2008. *Skeletal Trauma: Identification of Injuries Resulting from Human Rights Abuse and Armed Conflict*. Boca Raton, FL: CRC Press, p. 493.

Kimmerle EH, Falsetti T, Ross AH. November 2009. Immigrants, undocumented workers, runaways, transients and the homeless: Towards contextual identification among unidentified decedents. *Forensic Science Policy & Management: An International Journal*. 1(4):178–186.

Kirschner RH, Hannibal KE. 1994. The application of the forensic sciences to human rights investigations. *Medicine and Law*. 13(5–6):451–460.

Okoye, MI, Kimmerle EH, Baraybar JP. 2006. Forensic investigations of human rights violations, abuse, mass graves, and war crimes. In: *Forensic Sciences*. Wecht C. (Ed.), Vol. 2. LexisNexis Matthew Bender.

Reza A, Mercy JA, Krug E. 2001. Epidemiology of violent deaths in the word. *Injury Prevention*. 7:104–111.

Romano CPR, Nollkaemper A, Kleffner JK (Eds.). 2004. *Internationalized Criminal Courts: Sierra Leone, East Timor, Kosovo, and Cambodia*. Oxford, U.K.: Oxford University Press, 552pp.

Salama P, Laurence B, Nolan ML. 1999. Health and human rights in contemporary humanitarian crises: Is Kosovo more important than Sierra Leone? *British Medical Journal*. 319:1569–1571.

Skinner MF. 1987. Planning the archaeological recovery of evidence from recent mass graves. *Forensic Science International*. 34:267–287.

Snow CC, Levine L, Lukash L, Tedeschi LG, Orrego C, Stover E. 1984. The investigation of human remains of the "Disappeared" in Argentina. *American Journal of Physical Anthropology*. 5(4):297–299.

Stover E, Eisner T. 1982. Commentary: Human rights abuses and the role of scientists. *Bio Science*. 32(11):871–875.

The Prosecutor v. Fatmir Limaj, Haradin Bala and Isak Musliu, Case No. IT-03-66-PT; Decision on Prosecution's Motion to Amend the Amended Indictment ("Second Amended Indictment" attached to the "Prosecution's Motion to Amend the Amended Indictment" filed on November 6, 2003). 2004. International Criminal Tribunal for the former Yugoslavia. In: http://www.un.org/icty/limaj/trialc/decision-e/040212.pdf

The Prosecutor v. Radislav Krstic, Case No. IT-98-33-T; Judgment. 2001. International Criminal Tribunal for the former Yugoslavia. In: http://www.un.org/icty/krstic/TrialC1/judgement/krs-tj010802e.pdf, Appeals Chamber judgment of April 19, 2004, www.un.org/icty/Supplement/supp49-e/krstic.htm, Trial transcript, www.un.org/icty/transe33/000530it.htm, Trial Chamber judgment, www.un.org/icty/krstic/TrialC1/judgement/index.htm

Tidball-Binz M. 2006. Forensic investigations into the missing: Recommendations and operational best practices. In: *Forensic Anthropology and Medicine*. Schmitt A, Cunha E, Pinheiro J. (Eds.), Totowa, NJ: Humana Press, pp. 383–408.

UN, ICTR Tribunal at a glance: http://www.unictr.org/

UN, ICTY Tribunal at a glance: http://www.icty.org/

Forensic Anthropology in Mass Disasters

22

PAUL S. SLEDZIK

Contents

Disasters, by their nature, cause chaos. In response, societies strive to bring normalcy to the affected community. When a disaster kills a large number of people, the response often poses unique challenges for disaster responders, the community, and particularly the families and friends of those killed. The return to normalcy becomes more complex as the cultural response to mass death intersects with the requirements of the forensic response to recover and identify the dead.

Regardless of the cause of the disaster, those killed in mass fatality events must be searched for, recovered, identified, and provided with final disposition in accordance with society's religious and cultural beliefs. In addition, because the response to mass death can affect societies in complex ways, care must be taken to properly address the concerns and expectations of the next of kin and the community. Cultures have practices for handling a normal death: private and public rituals involving the body, the grief and mourning process for family members, and customs to respect and honor the deceased that bring the death into the cultural order. Funerals, public mourning periods, viewing of the body, and appropriate final disposition following cultural beliefs allow for acceptance of the normal death by family members and the community (Morgan et al. 2006).

Mass fatality events result in deaths which fall outside the normal death process, and, thus, disrupt these rituals and beliefs. Bodies may not be recovered or identified; many may not be viewable or even complete. The culturally required time period for receiving and handling remains for the postdeath rituals may not be met. This disruption of expected cultural responses to death, sometimes referred to as unresolved grief, stresses societies recovering from a mass fatality event. This stress can be compounded if the response is not managed properly. For example, the use of mass graves and cremations to deal with human remains from disasters has been shown to have adverse long-term mental health, economic, political, and religious implications for the affected families and society. Unresolved grief can be mitigated through events of public mourning that allow families and communities to console one another and express sympathy through collective commemoration (Pan American Health Organization 2004).

Even with the complex nature of the cultural response to mass fatality events, forensic science plays an integral role in the response. Although the forensic work is done for legal reasons, it ultimately helps family members and society. The role of forensic scientists in an effective mass fatality response is to search for, recover, and identify the dead in a timely and efficient manner and to keep family members informed about the process. Forensic pathologists, forensic anthropologists, forensic dentists, DNA analysts, medicolegal investigators, and evidence managers each have significant responsibilities in the response.

Forensic anthropologists bring knowledge, training, and experience to the mass fatality response in several key areas: population-based training, knowledge of human identification modalities, understanding of taphonomic factors and their impact on recovery and identification, abilities in archaeological recovery, and a working appreciation for the cultural and religious sensitivities surrounding death, mourning, and the handling of human remains and working with next of kin, as listed in Table 22.1 (Sledzik 2009). Anthropologists also bring their skills from unidentified/missing persons cases and mass grave work to the collection and interpretation of antemortem information. Beyond their forensic training, however, forensic anthropologists have also served in essential management roles in mass fatality responses and as liaisons between family members and the forensic operation. This chapter explores the role of the forensic anthropologist in mass fatality incidents and examines some broader forensic considerations of such events.

Table 22.1 Forensic Anthropological Skills in Mass Fatality Incidents

Disaster scene
Devise, implement, and manage effective evidence search and recovery protocols based on size and scope of event
Locate, recognize, and recover human remains and other evidence, especially those impacted by disaster forces (e.g., burned and fragmented remains)
Incident morgue
Participate in triage of remains and devise probative value for identification potential
Separate and document commingled remains
Describe human remains (particularly when fragmented, burned, and decomposed)
Determine biological profile and distinguishing characteristics of remains
Assess radiographs for age estimation and unique skeletal features
Determine minimum number of individuals based on remains recovered
Conduct identifications using anthropological features
Assess skeletal trauma evidence and incident-related injuries
Mass fatality management
Manage of overall victim identification efforts
Manage morgue to ensure efficient and effective remains management
Establish quality control and assurance programs for morgue operation
Serve as forensic science liaison with family members concerning methods of identification and other medicolegal concerns
Assess and solve problems in management of antemortem and postmortem data
Examine antemortem data collection issues, including availability and accuracy

History of Forensic Anthropology in Mass Fatality Response in the United States

In the United States, the role of the anthropologist in mass fatality response in the past 70 years has evolved from supplying technical expertise for the processing of victim's remains to serving as operational and organizational subject matter experts in the overall management of the mass fatality process (Dirkmaat et al. 2008; Sledzik 2009). Forensic anthropology's involvement in mass fatality response began during the U.S. military war dead identification efforts during World War II, the Korean War, and the Vietnam War. For anthropologists, these efforts typically focused on identifying individual servicemen killed in battle, but these skills were applied specifically in situations where large numbers of troops were killed in accidents (Sledge 2005). During World War II, anthropologists Harry Shapiro, Mildred Trotter, and T. Dale Stewart provided their skills in the identification of war dead, and during the Korean and Vietnam wars anthropologists Charles Warren, Ellis Kerley, and Thomas McKern conducted similar work and assisted in disaster situations (Wood and Stanley 1989; Ubelaker 2000). This period culminated in Stewart (1970) edited a volume "Personal Identification in Mass Disasters," the first significant publication combining new technical aspects of identification and their role in disaster victim identification (Box 15.1).

In the 1980s and 1990s, anthropologists joined with other forensic scientists as integral interdisciplinary team partners in mass fatality response. Following her response to the 1986 crash of a military aircraft accident in Gander, Newfoundland, Madeleine Hinkes (1989) detailed how victim identification efforts benefited from the inclusion of anthropologists in all stages of the response from recovery through final evaluation. After the burning of the Branch Davidian compound in Waco, Texas, in 1993, an anthropological team conducted scene documentation, search and recovery, trauma analysis, and victim identification (Owsley et al. 1995; Ubelaker et al. 1995; Houck et al. 1996). That same year, another team of anthropologists were essential to the identification efforts following the flooding of several hundred graves from a rural Midwestern cemetery (Sledzik and Hunt 1997). A few years later, the fragmentation of remains following the 1996 crash of Valujet 592 required anthropologists to assess the age of the juvenile victims using radiographs of the wrist and hands (Warren et al. 2000).

With the establishment of the Disaster Mortuary Operational Response Team (DMORT) in the 1990s, American anthropologists began to serve as key personnel in national-level mass fatality response (Sledzik and Willcox 2003). DMORT anthropologists have responded to numerous mass fatality events including aviation accidents (e.g., Korean Air 801, Alaska Air 261, EgyptAir 990, and Continental Connection 3407), the Murrah Building bombing, Hurricane Katrina, cemetery floods in North Carolina and Georgia, and the Tri-State Crematory in Noble, Georgia (Steadman et al. 2006). Following the September 11, 2001, terrorist attacks, anthropologists served as DMORT team commanders, disaster morgue managers, and coordinators for the long-term identification efforts (London et al. 2003; Rodriguez 2003; Sledzik et al. 2003; Warren et al. 2003; Mundorff 2008) (See Box 22.1). Following the Asian tsunami in December 2004, Hurricane Katrina in 2005, and the Haitian earthquake of 2010, anthropologists served again the dual roles of technical experts to assess biological features useful for identification and as coordinators of the identification efforts (Fulginiti et al. 2006; Tyrrell et al. 2006).

BOX 22.1 CASE STUDY: FORENSIC ANTHROPOLOGY AT THE WORLD TRADE CENTER DISASTER

The mass fatality events of September 11, 2001, presented forensic anthropologists with a unique opportunity to take on important responsibilities in the management of these complex human identification efforts. The characteristics of the three disaster sites revealed complex levels of fragmentation and commingling, posing challenges for victim recovery and analysis. Anthropologists working in New York; Washington, DC; and Pennsylvania served as managers of victim identification teams, quality control teams, and morgue operations, and as coordinators of long-term identification efforts (Mundorff and Steadman 2003; Sledzik et al. 2003; London et al. 2003; Rodriguez 2003; Warren et al. 2003). Their efforts highlight the capabilities of forensic anthropologists as broadly trained experts in human identification who can manage complex human identification events.

As an example, anthropologists working at the World Trade Center (WTC) disaster developed and employed two important quality assurance/control procedures that reduced errors and resolved issues of commingling and contamination before remains were released to next of kin. The thousands of remains being examined and the related data from each proved highly complex. "Anthropological verification" was devised by Amy Mundorff (the chief forensic anthropologist for the WTC response) to resolve errors (e.g., misnumbering, siding errors) by physically reexamining over 16,000 specimens. Her team's work revealed new identifications and associations between remains that had been previously unassociated. (Wiersema et al. 2003; Budimlija et al. 2003; Mundorff et al. 2008). "Final anthropological review" took place once an identification had been made and ensured the certainty of the identification and reduced the possibility of misidentification. In the words of the anthropologists who devised the system, the review was critical in resolving "any final and outstanding issues of commingling and contamination, and ultimately provided the opportunity to reconfirm the correlation between the case files, the identification modality/ies, and the physical remains, before final repatriation of the victim occurred" (MacKinnon and Mundorff 2006).

Anthropological perspectives, both forensic and cultural, are included in recent important mass fatality publications. "Mass Fatality Incidents: A Guide for Human Identification" (United States Department of Justice 2005) was produced by experienced mass fatality forensic responders, including several anthropologists, and includes a section on anthropological work at disaster sites. The Pan American Health Organization's "Management of Dead Bodies in Disaster Situations" (2004) examines preparedness for mass death response, medicolegal examinations, health considerations, sociocultural issues, psychological concerns, legal concepts, and several case studies from recent South and Central American disasters. Concepts from this document are promoted by a variety of nongovernmental organizations, including the Pan American Health Organization, the World Health Organization, the International Committee of the Red Cross, and the International Federation of Red Cross and Red Crescent Societies.

With their backgrounds in cultural understanding and broad-based human identification knowledge, anthropologists have also proven effective in working with family members of disaster victims in the efforts of family assistance programs (Mundorff and Steadman 2003; Sledzik et al. 2006). Family assistance programs address the unique needs of family members of those killed in disasters by providing access to information and support services such crisis grief counseling. Although family members of the deceased may also need traditional disaster services (e.g., food, water, shelter, and medical care), they often have questions about the search, recovery, and identification process; the condition of remains; and the return of personal effects (Blakeney 2002; Eyre 2002). The family assistance model establishes a structure whereby family members receive accurate and timely information and answers to their questions. Forensic anthropologists have served as scientific specialists interacting with family members to address their questions in a factual, compassionate manner. Because of their understanding of science and culture, forensic anthropologists can balance the complex issues related to victim identification, the questions of family members, and the technical limitations of the human identification sciences (Sledzik 2009).

Current Standards of Practice: Forensic Anthropology at the Mass Fatality Event

Forensic anthropologists involved in mass fatality response are part of an interdisciplinary team of forensic scientists and support personnel. Typically, these teams conduct their work at the disaster scene and in a temporary morgue created for the forensic response. The work at the scene can be complex and difficult depending on the conditions of the disaster. For example, an aircraft accident scene is small and often more easily managed compared to a large city devastated by an earthquake. Work at the disaster morgue can range from field conditions (working in tents) to modern medicolegal facilities. In both cases, the process of managing the dead involves applying standardized procedures for documentation both at the scene and in the disaster morgue.

The size and scope of the disaster scene dictates the procedures used, although a systematic approach to search, documentation, and recovery is consistently applied. These techniques are taken from burial and fire scene applications of forensic archeology and require a thorough search and recovery of human remains in various conditions (Dirkmaat et al. 2008). Global positioning systems and total station surveying equipment gives the anthropologist tools to produce three-dimensional maps of the scene which show the location of the various classes of evidence: human remains, personal effects, wreckage, etc. Human remains impacted by the forces of the disaster can become fragmented, burned, commingled, decomposed, and skeletonized and are often unrecognizable to untrained recovery personnel (Sledzik and Rodriguez 2002). However, since forensic anthropologists work with remains in these conditions on a regular basis, they are often the single specialists that can distinguish them at the scene. In addition, human remains may be intermixed with personal effects, plane wreckage, organic items (such as sticks, leaves, and dirt), nonorganic items, and remnants of homes and buildings. Discerning and understanding the importance of these classes of evidence requires the same anthropological skills applied at buried body or fire scenes. When left to inexperienced personnel, mistakes can occur during recovery: body parts can be inaccurately reassociated based on proximity to one another at the scene, and nonbiological material is sometimes placed in the body bag. These mistakes are rectified in the morgue operation. The recovery process ends with the removal of all remains and associated evidence from the scene and transfer of these items to the disaster morgue.

The staff working in the disaster morgue has several responsibilities: documentation and processing of remains, identification of the victim, examination of remains for medicolegal interpretations (e.g., cause of death), and documentation of the overall process. This work has little room for error, and quality control procedures and standard operating procedures are the keys to a successful disaster morgue operation. The forensic specialists in the morgue—forensic pathologists, forensic odontologists, forensic anthropologists, fingerprint specialists, DNA analysts, and medicolegal investigators—are supported by mortuary personnel and technicians. The amount of information generated in a morgue operation is immense, and proper attention must be paid to accurate collection and storage of this information.

Before the victim recovery and identification efforts begin, the medicolegal authority must answer several essential questions regarding the forensic characteristics of the disaster. The answers to these questions provides focus for the disaster victim identification teams, determines how long the identification process may take, exposes potential limits to the process, and establishes the roles of the various forensic science disciplines in the overall identification efforts (United States Department of Justice 2005; United States Department of Justice 2006; Sledzik and Bryson 2009). These questions are as follows:

- What caused the event (i.e., natural event, technological error, criminal intent)?
- What is the number of fatalities?
- What challenges exist in searching for and recovering the victims (i.e., small area or large area, whole bodies or fragmented remains)?
- Is the victim population open or closed (i.e., number of names of the dead unknown or known)?
- What is the condition of the remains (complete, fragmented, burned, dismembered, etc.)?
- What antemortem information is available? How accurate is the information?
- Will the forensic efforts be focused on identifying all victims or all remains?
- What will be the role (and the limits) of DNA identification efforts?
- What are the concerns and expectations of the next of kin, the community, and the government about the identification efforts? Can they be appropriately and effectively addressed?

The intertwined factors of the number of disaster dead, the victim population type, and condition of remains are often most important in planning for the forensic response. For example, in large-scale natural disasters such as hurricanes and earthquakes, accurate counts of fatalities are often difficult to obtain soon after the event because of limited access to the affected areas. Antemortem records may also be destroyed or damaged in the event. Often, in open population disasters, the number of people reported missing is much greater than those actually missing, and this discrepancy must be reconciled before identification begins. In small-scale technological disasters, such as an aviation accident, the disaster site is limited in size and the number of fatalities known. Aviation accidents also present a closed population where the number of fatalities and the victims' names are known through the flight manifest and associated ticketing procedures.

The condition of remains determines the methods used in morgue processing and identification. Because complete bodies contain all the unique physical features needed to identify the victim, they are often simpler to identify when antemortem records are available. In the case of fragmented remains, body parts may contain these unique identifiers (e.g., dental work or medical implants), and these parts can be identified. Although identification of a body part signifies both proof of death and identification of the victim, the remaining fragments of that victim must also be identified. Remains with no unique physical identifiers may be identified using DNA. However, not all DNA analyses result in a profile usable for identification.

The decision to identify all victims or all remains is often driven by the victim population. In a closed population, high-fragmentation accident, forensic investigators work to identify all the victims, with an understanding that not all remains will be identified because of technological limitations of DNA or because family members wish for those remains that can be identified quickly to be returned. In an open population, high-fragmentation event, the focus is to identify all remains because the number and names of decedents are unknown. Unidentifiable remains are referred to as "group remains" and they must be managed carefully. Family members must be informed of the presence of group remains and involved with its final disposition.

Remains coming to the disaster morgue from the scene are typically stored in refrigerator trucks or a similar holding location. These holding locations are often designated as "unprocessed" (awaiting morgue processing) and "processed" (completed with morgue processing) to keep remains organized. Controlling the flow of remains entering the morgue allows for efficient processing and prevents the morgue team from making mistakes and feeling overwhelmed. For example, in an event with one hundred complete bodies, the morgue manager may decide to examine 10 bodies at a time depending on the space within the morgue and the forensic personnel available. Remains entering the morgue are first radiographed in their container (e.g., body bag, pouch, transfer case) to reveal potential important evidence, such as unexploded ordnance and personal effects. With fragmented remains, the radiograph can reveal potentially identifiable body portions such as implants and dental evidence, as well as the extent of commingling.

In order to focus the initial forensic efforts on the remains with the greatest potential for identification, a process called triage is the next step in the morgue flow (Kontanis and Sledzik 2005; Mundorff 2008) (Figure 22.1). Triage is most often used in cases involving fragmented remains. The triage process involves a team composed of a forensic anthropologist, a forensic pathologist, a forensic dentist, and a DNA analyst. Using the radiograph taken at the previous step, the triage team separates commingled human remains, personal effects, wreckage or other types of nonbiological evidence, and nonhuman biological material (e.g., animal bone and sticks). No assumption is made that commingled remains placed together at the disaster scene are related; only remains connected by anatomical tissues are considered a single specimen. The team then focuses on the human remains, sorting remains which have a potential for identification from those with little or no potential. Remains with potential for identification would be those with dental remains, implants, fingers, unique biological features, and remains with potential for DNA results. Small pieces of tissue or bone are set aside for later analysis, if needed. Depending on the decisions

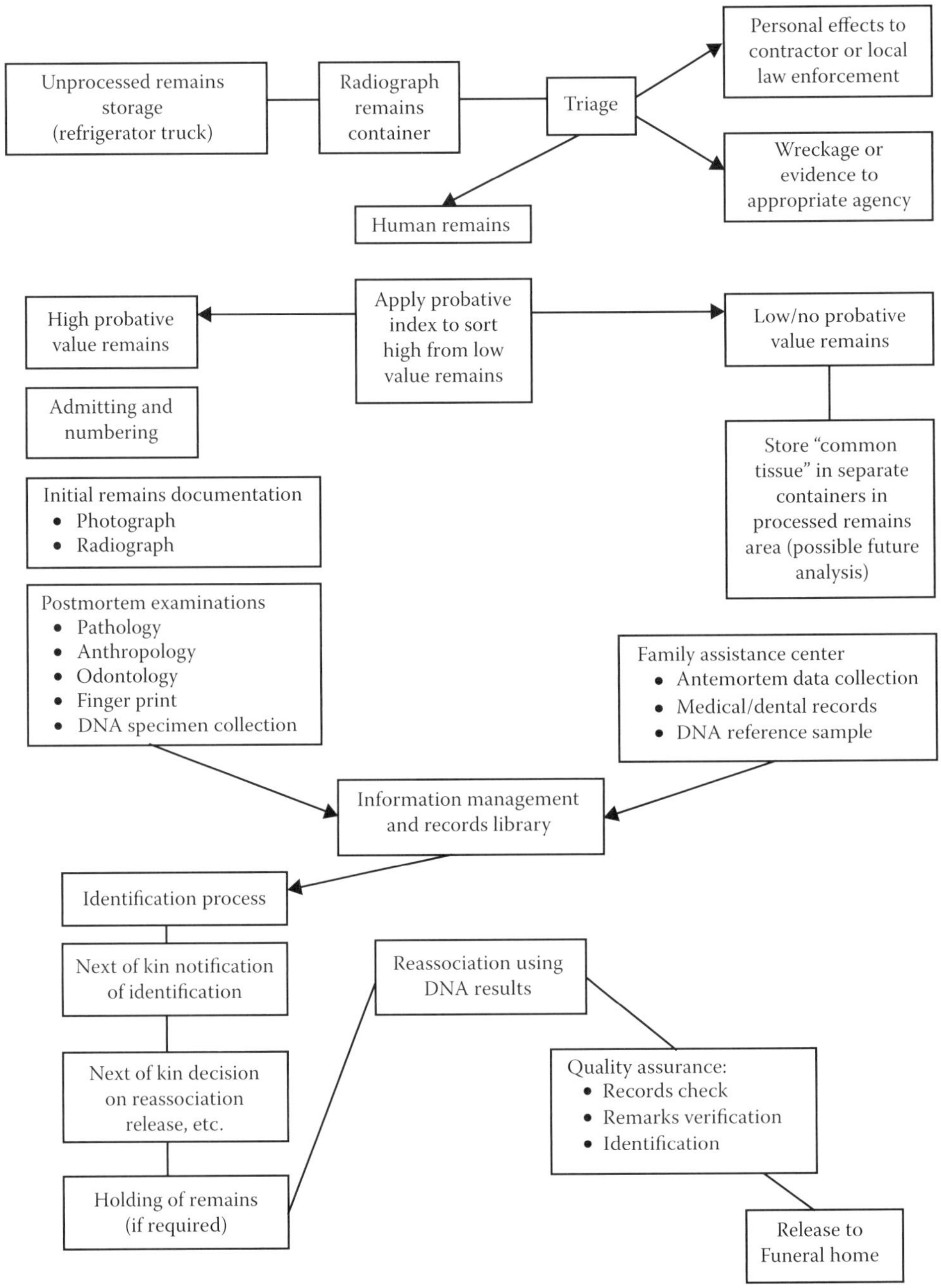

Figure 22.1 Morgue flow diagram: fragmentary remains.

made about the focus of the identification efforts, these remains may be considered group remains or may need to be further analyzed to account for all victims.

After triage, remains are formally accessioned into the morgue flow. A case file is created for each specimen and the remains are assigned a number. In the case of whole bodies, numbers are often assigned at the scene. Simple numbering systems reduce administrative errors and confusion. Once admitted, remains are individually radiographed, photographed, and then move to each postmortem examination station for analysis. Forensic specialists staff these examination stations—often designated as dental, pathology, anthropology, fingerprint, and DNA. At each station, information is collected according to standard protocols pertinent to that discipline. These analyses provide the data that will be used for identification. If additional remains are found commingled during the course of these analyses (e.g., the remains were not separated at triage), then the new remains reenter the morgue through the admitting station.

While the morgue personnel are conducting their work, antemortem information about the victims is being collected from family members, medical and dental offices, and other potential sources. The antemortem data collection process often occurs at a family assistance center where funeral service and forensic identification specialists interview the family members using standard interview forms. Using the information acquired, the antemortem team contacts dentists and doctors to obtain records, searches databases for fingerprints, examines evidence of the unique biological aspects of the deceased, and collects information about personal effects belonging to the deceased.

Since identification requires comparing the postmortem data with antemortem information, factors influencing the availability and accuracy of antemortem records impact the identification process. Locating, obtaining, and evaluating antemortem data is often more time consuming and complex than the postmortem examinations in the morgue (De Valck 2006). Socioeconomic status, cultural practices, and religious beliefs of victims and their next of kin impact antemortem record availability. Not all records obtained for comparison are accurate or useful. Forensic odontologists have reported the concerns of accuracy, completeness, and legibility of dental records (Brannon and Kessler 1999). If a victim never visited a dentist or doctor, no records will be available. Likewise, if family members do not know the victim's dentist or doctor, records will not be obtained. Many people have never been fingerprinted, or if they were, the prints may not be stored where they can be easily located and retrieved. In some instances, family members may not wish to provide DNA family reference samples for religious or other reasons. Each of these scenarios complicates the positive identification process and presents unique challenges to be handled by the trained personnel.

Forensic specialists begin the process of identification by comparing the data collected in the morgue with the information obtained during the antemortem collection process. Identifications in disaster events are typically based on unique biological attributes (Fierro 1993). These methods include DNA analysis, odontology, prints (fingerprints, handprints, and footprints), radiology, and implanted medical devices with serial numbers. Distinctive physical characteristics (e.g., scars, moles, and tattoos) with appropriate antemortem photographic documentation can be used to make an identification if the context of such evidence allows. Identification by distinctive physical characteristics is best applied in closed population events. Identifications are not made using personal effects and clothing—these are used as a preliminary step, pointing toward a particular victim, and the scientific procedures mentioned earlier are then used to complete the identification.

The identification process is completed during regular meetings held between the medicolegal authority and the forensic specialists who present the details for the authority's agreement and authorization. All specialists must agree on the identification. If there is disagreement, all evidence is reexamined until agreement is reached. When finalized, the next of kin is notified of the identification via the local jurisdiction's process for death notification.

Future Areas of Research

The potential for research within the forensic aspects of mass fatality response focus on increasing efficiency and accuracy of the recovery and identification processes. Devising and testing protocols for thorough search and recovery in various mass fatality scenarios would help responders implement effective procedures without having to create the process *ad hoc*. A comprehensive examination of the availability and accuracy of antemortem data would improve mass fatality planning and response efforts. For example, knowing the percentage of a population with dental radiographs or chest radiographs and how and where these records are stored would allow forensic responders to plan the resources needed to collect such records.

Chapter Summary

- Mass fatality events are complex human identification efforts.
- Responders must consider both scientific and cultural aspects of mass fatality events.
- Forensic anthropologists provide a variety of expertise in mass fatality response.
- Many factors influence the complexities of the mass fatality identification efforts.

Disclaimer

The author is an employee of the National Transportation Safety Board. The views expressed are the personal views of the individual and do not necessarily represent the views of the National Transportation Safety Board or the United States Government.

References

Blakeney, R.L. 2002. Providing relief to families after a mass fatality: Roles of the medical examiner's office and the family assistance center. Department of Justice, Office for Victims of Crime Bulletin, November 2002. http://ojp.usdoj.gov/ovc/publications/bulletins/prfmf_11_2001/welcome.html (accessed June 29, 2010).

Brannon, R.B. and H.P. Kessler. 1999. Problems in mass disaster dental identification: A retrospective review. *J Forensic Sci* 44:123–127.

Budimlija, Z.M., M.K. Prinz, A. Zelson-Mundorff et al. 2003. World Trade Center Human Identification Project: Experiences with individual body identification cases. *Croat Med J* 44:259–263.

De Valck, E. 2006. Major incident response: Collecting antemortem data. *Forensic Sci Int* 159:S15–S19.

Dirkmaat, D.C., L.L. Cabo, S.D. Ousley et al. 2008. New perspectives in forensic anthropology. *Yearb Phys Anthropol* 51:33–52.

Eyre, A. 2002. Improving procedures and minimizing stress: Issues in the identification of victims following disasters. *Aust J Emerg Manag* 17:9–14.

Fierro, M.F. 1993. Identification of human remains. In *Spitz and Fisher's Medico-legal Investigation of Death: Guidelines for the Application of Pathology to Crime Investigation*, ed. W.U Spitz, pp. 71–117. Springfield, IL: Charles C. Thomas.

Fulginiti, L.C., M.W. Warren, J.T. Hefner, L.R. Bedore, J.H. Byrd, V. Stefan, and D.C. Dirkmaat. 2006. Anthropology responds to Hurricane Katrina. *Proc Am Acad Forensic Sci* 12:305.

Hinkes, M.J. 1989. The role of forensic anthropology in mass disaster resolution. *Aviat Space Environ Med* 60:A18–A25.

Houck, M.A., D. Ubelaker, D. Owsley et al. 1996. The role of forensic anthropology in the recovery and analysis of Branch Davidian Compound victims: Assessing the accuracy of age estimations. *J Forensic Sci* 41: 796–801.

Kontanis, E.J. and P.S. Sledzik. 2006. Resolving commingling issues during the medicolegal investigation of mass fatality incidents. In *Recovery, Analysis, and Identification of Commingled Human Remains*, eds. B.J. Adams and J.S. Byrd, pp. 317–337. Totowa, NJ: Humana Press.

London, M.R., D.M. Mulhern, L.T. Barbian et al. 2003. Roles of the biological anthropologist in the response to the crash of United Airlines Flight 93. *Proc Am Acad Forensic Sci* 9:279.

Mackinnon, G. and A.Z. Mundorff. 2006. The World Trade Center—September 11th, 2001. In *Forensic Human Identification: An Introduction*, eds. T. Thompson and S.M. Black, pp. 485–499. Boca Raton, FL: CRC Press.

Morgan, O., M. Tidball-Binz, and D. Van Alphen. 2006. *Management of Dead Bodies after Disasters: A Field Manual for First Responders*. Washington, DC: Pan American Health Organization.

Mundorff A.Z. 2008. Anthropologist-directed triage: Three distinct mass fatality events involving fragmentation of human remains. In *Recovery, Analysis, and Identification of Commingled Human Remains*, eds. B.J. Adams and J.S. Byrd, pp. 123–144. Totowa, NJ: Humana Press.

Mundorff, A.Z., R. Shaler, E.T. Bieschke, and E. Mar-Cash. 2008. Marrying of anthropology and DNA: Essential for solving complex commingling problems in cases of extreme fragmentation. In *Recovery, Analysis, and Identification of Commingled Human Remains*, eds. B.J. Adams and J.S. Byrd, pp. 285–300. Totowa, NJ: Humana Press.

Mundorff, A.Z. and D.W. Steadman. 2003. Anthropological perspectives on the forensic response at the World Trade Center Disaster. *Gen Anthropol* 10:2–5.

Owsley D.W., D.H. Ubelaker, M.M. Houck et al. 1995. The role of forensic anthropology in the recovery and analysis of Branch Davidian Compound victims: Techniques of analysis. *J Forensic Sci* 40:341–348.

Pan American Health Organization. 2004. *Management of Dead Bodies in Disaster Situations*. Disaster Manuals and Guidelines Series, No. 5. Washington, DC: Pan American Health Organization.

Rodriguez, W.C. 2003. Attack on the Pentagon: The role of forensic anthropology in the examination and identification of victims and remains of the 9/11 terrorist attack. *Proc Am Acad Forensic Sci* 9:280.

Sledge, M. 2005. *Soldier Dead: How We Recovery, Identify, Bury and Honor Our Military Fallen*. New York, NY: Columbia University Press.

Sledzik, P.S. 2009. Forensic anthropology in disaster response. In *Handbook of Forensic Anthropology and Archaeology*, eds. S. Blau and D.H. Ubelaker, pp. 374–387. Walnut Creek, CA: Left Coast Press.

Sledzik P.S. and S.W. Bryson. 2009. Mass fatality management. In *Koenig and Schultz's Disaster Medicine: Comprehensive Principles and Practices*, eds. K.L. Koenig and C.H. Schultz, pp. 312–325. New York: Cambridge University Press.

Sledzik, P.S. and D.R. Hunt. 1997. Disaster and relief efforts at the Hardin cemetery, In *In Remembrance: Archaeology and Death*, eds. D.A. Poirier and N.B. Bellantoni, pp. 185–198. Westport, CT: Bergin and Garvey.

Sledzik P.S., L.M. Jantz, A.Z. Mundorff et al. 2006. Working with family members of decedents: A discussion of techniques for forensic scientists. *Proc Am Acad Forensic Sci* 12:301–302.

Sledzik, P.S., W. Miller, D.C. Dirkmaat et al. 2003. Victim identification following the crash of United Airlines flight 93. *Proc Am Acad Forensic Sci* 9:195–196.

Sledzik, P.S. and W.C. Rodriguez. 2002. Damnum fatale: The taphonomic fate of human remains in mass disasters, In *Advances in Forensic Taphonomy: Methods, Theories and Archaeological Perspectives*, eds. W.D. Haglund and M.H. Sorg, pp. 321–330. Boca Raton, FL: CRC Press.

Sledzik, P.S. and A.W. Willcox. 2003. Corpi Aquaticus: The Hardin cemetery flood of 1993, In *Hard Evidence: Case Studies in Forensic Anthropology*, ed. D.W. Steadman, pp. 256–265. Upper Saddle River, NJ: Prentice-Hall.

Steadman, D.W., K. Sperry, F. Snow, L. Fulginiti, and E. Craig. 2006. Anthropological investigations of the Tri-State Crematorium incident. In *Recovery, Analysis, and Identification of Commingled Human Remains*, eds. B.J. Adams and J.S. Byrd, pp. 81–96. Totowa, NJ: Humana Press.
Stewart, T.D. (ed.) 1970. *Personal Identification in Mass Disasters*. Washington, DC: Smithsonian Institution.
Tyrrell, A.J., E.J. Kontanis, T.L.V. Simmons, and P.S. Sledzik. 2006. Restructuring data collection strategies in investigation priorities in the resolution of mass fatality incidents. *Proc Am Acad Forensic Sci* 12:165.
Ubelaker, D.H. 2000. The forensic anthropology legacy of T. Dale Stewart (1901–1997). *J Forensic Sci* 45:245–252.
Ubelaker, D.H., D.W. Owsley, M.M. Houck et al. 1995. The role of forensic anthropology in the recovery and analysis of Branch Davidian Compound victims: Recovery procedures and characteristics of victims. *J Forensic Sci* 40:335–340.
United States Department of Justice, Office of Justice Programs. 2005. Mass fatality incidents: A guide for human forensic identification. Washington, DC. http://www.ojp.usdoj.gov/nij/pubs-sum/199758.htm (accessed June 29, 2010).
United States Department of Justice, Office of Justice Programs. 2006. Lessons learned from 9/11: DNA identifications in mass fatality incidents. Washington, DC. http://massfatality.dna.gov/ (accessed June 29, 2010).
Warren, M.W., L.E. Eisenberg, H.A. Walsh-Haney, and J.M. Saul. 2003. Anthropology at fresh kills: Recovery and identification of the World Trade Center victims. *Proc Am Acad Forensic Sci* 55:278.
Warren, M.W., K.R. Smith, P.R. Stubblefield, S.S. Martin, and H.A. Walsh-Haney. 2000. Use of radiographic atlases in a mass fatality. *J Forensic Sci* 45:467–470.
Wiersema, J.M., E. Bartelink, Z. Budimlija et al. 2003. The importance of an interdisciplinary review process in the World Trade Center mass disasters investigation. *Proc Am Acad Forensic Sci* 55:194.
Wood, W.R. and L.A. Stanley. 1989. Recovery and identification of World War II dead: American Graves Registration activities in Europe. *J Forensic Sci* 34:1365–1373.

Suggested Readings

Disaster Myths that Just Won't Die, http://www.paho.org/English/DD/PIN/Number21_article01.htm
Forensic Processing of the Terrestrial Mass Fatality Scene: Testing New Search, Documentation and Recovery Methodologies, http://mai.mercyhurst.edu/files/mai-research/dirkmaat-2008_nij_1793-narrative-short.pdf
Lessons Learned from 9/11: DNA Identification in Mass Fatality Incidents, http://massfatality.dna.gov/
Management of Dead Bodies in Disaster Situations, http://www.crid.or.cr/digitalizacion/pdf/eng/doc15631/doc15631.pdf
Mass Fatality Incidents: A Guide for Human Identification, http://www.ojp.usdoj.gov/nij/pubs-sum/199758.htm
Providing Relief to Families After a Mass Fatality: Roles of the Medical Examiner's Office and the Family Assistance Center, http://www.ojp.usdoj.gov/ovc/publications/bulletins/prfmf_11_2001/welcome.html

Index

B

C

G

U